MW00985242

KŪ KANAKA—STAND TALL

KŪ KANAKA STAND TALL

A SEARCH FOR HAWAIIAN VALUES

George Hu'eu Sanford Kanahele

A Kolowalu Book
UNIVERSITY OF HAWAII PRESS

© 1986 UNIVERSITY OF HAWAII PRESS
ALL RIGHTS RESERVED
PRINTED IN THE UNITED STATES OF AMERICA
PAPERBACK EDITION 1992

06 07 08 09 10 11   9 8 7 6 5

Library of Congress Cataloging-in-Publication Data

Kanahele, George S.
  Kū kanaka, stand tall.

  (A Kolowalu book)
  Bibliography: p.
  Includes index.
  1. Hawaii—Civilization. 2. Ethnopsychology.
3. National characteristics, Hawaiian. I. Title.
DU624.5.K33   1986   996.9   86-1374
ISBN: 0–8248–1008–2

ISBN-13: 978-0-8248-1500-4 (pbk)
ISBN-10: 0-8248-1500-9 (pbk)

Originally published with support from
the Waiaha Foundation

University of Hawaiʻi Press books are printed on
acid-free paper and meet the guidelines for permanence
and durability of the Council on Library Resources.

www.uhpress.hawaii.edu

METHOD OF
CITING REFERENCES

To help readers who may want to explore further some of the ideas and issues advanced in this book, names of authors of works cited in the text are indicated in parentheses. In cases involving two or more works by the same author, the year of publication is given also. A bibliography is provided to assist the interested reader in tracing sources.

CONTENTS

FOREWORD

As its very name indicates, the state of Hawai'i preserves a large legacy from the primal people who first inhabited our islands. About two hundred thousand of us who live here now carry some of the genes inherited from those primal people. Nearly a million of us love the music, the dances, the surfing, canoeing, fishing, and swimming that our kūpuna loved. Many of us depend for our living on the millions of visitors who come here, lured by our expressions of aloha. The Hawaiian ethos endures still in our land. And it is deeply ingrained in the way we Hawaiians approach the many problems with which we have to cope today.

Yes, the primal Hawaiians, their ethos and their values, are integral parts of our society. Yet the true definition of this Hawaiian presence seems to elude us. We talk about it, invoke it, profess to live by it, but disagree interminably about its essentials.

Students of other cultures have filled vast libraries with documentation. China, India, ancient Rome and Greece, and many other societies have been studied, recorded, analyzed, and evaluated. But there has been relatively little such treatment of the native Hawaiian civilization. In this book George Kanahele seeks to correct this situation. He presents a careful, detailed exposition of the essential primal Hawaiian culture, from a Hawaiian point of view. Because of the very lack of documentation, he has had to use the deductive method to create much of his model. Like a Sherlock Holmes, he has sifted through all the available evidence of every type to deduce some ideas about the ethos of our ancestors who lived in these islands before Captain Cook's expedition arrived in 1778. He has looked into other, similarly beset primal cultures for possible insights. He has searched non-Western, non-Aristotelian belief systems. And as he looked at the accounts left by early West-

ern visitors to Hawai'i, he has had to be fully aware of the biases
that those early observers necessarily carried.

This is an ambitious work, and a vitally needed work. It is presented as an answer to the perennial question, "What is a Hawaiian?" The complexities and subtleties involved in answering that
question can be appreciated when we realize that the primal
Hawaiian would never have asked it. To him, the universe he
knew was coherent and harmonious. The asking of such a question is for people of our era, to whom the cosmos has become an
incomprehensible puzzle. For the further our science takes us up
into cosmic space, and down into microphysics, the less it serves
us as an acceptable discipline for living. In the studies reported in
this book we will find what George Kanahele found: that the civilization of the ancient Hawaiians was based on a belief system that
presupposed an orderly cosmos. In their cosmos a question such as
ours had no meaning, and therefore was never asked.

George Kanahele has analyzed the ancient Hawaiian civilization as though it still exists today, and he uses contemporary disciplines to lay out for us, in modern terms and ways of thinking, the
essence of that culture. He does not approach it as something
exotic, or trivial, or inferior, but rather as a creation that is vital,
alive, and practical. Thus we can perceive it more clearly as a living and dynamic society, and we can extract from that perception
the central values and beliefs upon which the Hawaiian culture
was based.

Then he traces the passage through history of those values and
beliefs down to the present time. And he sets out an agenda for us
to follow which will enable us to benefit today from the truths
which our Hawaiian ancestors lived by yesterday.

So in answering the question "What is a Hawaiian?" he offers us
not only knowledge about the kind of people our ancestors were,
but, even more important, the discovery that their ways and
beliefs and values still carry the power, the mana, to serve us well
today. Although the innocence of believing in a harmonious, purposeful cosmos has been taken from us by our modern science,
many of the ways that the old Hawaiians generated out of that
innocence can serve us very well today. And this book presents us
with a modern synthesis through which we may live richer, more
satisfying lives, by drawing upon the deep and abiding strengths in
the ways of our ancestors

Finally, for me personally, the thoughts presented in this book represent a great advance in a journey of discovery that started many years ago. As a part-Hawaiian, I had long been troubled by seeming conflicts between the values emphasized by my different heritages. My haole heritage has been available to me from the beginning in rich, almost endless diversity, while, according to the prejudices in my youth, my Hawaiian heritage was all but neglected. And yet I felt that strength, richness, and beauty ennobled that Hawaiianness. I saw that fact and felt its strength in the Old Ones I knew. And perhaps my Hawaiian genes even whispered of it to me. But I had no source to whom I could go in order to immerse myself in that rich culture. So, all alone at first, I began the journey. And soon I learned that many others were embarked on the same quest. Through the "Maori Connection," and a series of fortuitous events which George Kanahele records at the start of this book, many of us were helped immeasurably along our way. This book's message takes us another great distance toward our goal.

And, wondrous to say, for me the journey turns out to be one not only of discovery, but also of reconciliation. It not only proves the validity of my intuitive respect for my Hawaiian heritage, but at the same time it tells me that, rather than conflicting with my haole culture and heritage, Hawaiianness offers resolution, harmony, richness, and enhancement to it, and to life.

KENNETH F. BROWN

PREFACE

On a chilly winter Sunday in June 1981, we huddled at the entrance to the John Waititi Marae in Auckland, New Zealand. We were a group of five Hawaiian businessmen and with our spouses, newly arrived that morning, beginning a seven-day, first-of-its-kind goodwill mission to establish links with Maori business persons. With the exception of myself, none of our party had been ceremonially welcomed to a marae before and therefore did not know what to expect. Nothing in Hawaiian culture, at least in modern times, can compare with the Maori marae, a sort of communal center dedicated to special occasions such as funerals, hui or gatherings, the welcoming and entertaining of guests. In the communal complex, the marae itself is the sacred ground in front of the whare hui, or meeting house, that is reserved for the formal welcoming. Thus, what was about to happen was an entirely new and intensely moving spiritual experience.

While we waited at the main gateway, the afternoon sky had turned black and ominous. Obeying the kawa, or protocol of the marae, as the manuhiri, or visitors, we were waiting to be called in by our hosts, who were already positioned inside the marae proper. Then a light rain began to fall, an omen that we of Hawai'i recognized. Kenneth Brown, the leader of our party, noticed soaring above us a few white sea gulls, in which, I later learned, he found another auspicious sign. Finally we heard the high-pitched voice of an old woman, inviting us to "come up" rather than to "come in": *"Piki mai, kake mai, eke mai,"* symbolizing the movement from the profane world outside to the tapu realm within the marae. And, as we slowly walked toward the sacred ground, a distance of several hundred feet, the heavens thundered and for a few moments heavy rain poured down. Just as we stopped at the border of the most tapu space in the marae, where we would be received, the rain halted, the rumbling ceased, and sunlight broke through the thick clouds. It was a very profound moment, only the first of many to follow.

The greeting ceremony, or mihi, began when our first host speaker, a Maori elder bearing a finely carved staff, shouted, *"Tihei mauri-ora!"* meaning literally "Sneeze and life!" (which, except for the differences in spelling, has exactly the same significance in Hawaiian). While we did not understand Maori, we were thoroughly impressed by his manner of speaking, his gestures, posture, voice, and facial expressions—we were listening not to a mere speech but to a genuine oration. We could feel the power, the mana, emanating from his whole being. Our ears caught the sound of a familiar word, "Hawaiki"—the original homeland of the Polynesians—and we knew that he was talking about us. As is customary, the speaker's purpose is not only to greet but also to establish the identity of the visitor and, if possible, to point out any ancestral linkages. We understood that he had accepted us as blood kinsmen or, as he put it humorously, "younger cousins."

His was a hard act to follow, but custom required a reply from the oldest member of our group. Kenneth Brown was ready, for in a real sense he had been waiting for seventeen years, since his first and last trip to Aotearoa, for some such kind of personal reunion with his Polynesian past. Thoughts of his great-grandfather, John Papa 'I'i, and of his grandmother, Irene Kahalelaukoa 'I'i, ran through his mind as he stepped forward to speak. After paying respects to our hosts and the spirits of the dead, to whom every marae is dedicated in part, he spoke about "coming home," not in any geographical sense, but rather about being carried back in time to when Hawaiians and Maoris shared a common homeland, the same cultural roots. He mentioned the natural omens, including the thunder, or what he called the "celestial nudging," that accompanied us to the tapu ground, as a kind of cosmic approval of our coming together, although at the time he did not know for what exact purpose we had been gathered. Neither did anyone else for that matter.

By the end of the ceremony, we understood the purpose of the mihi: to cause hosts and strangers to feel good about each other by establishing genealogical or social and emotional ties in a spiritual setting. The ceremony ended with both hosts and guests lining up and hongi, or nose kissing, each other. We did not doubt that the mihi had achieved its purpose. The "vibes" were great, and we all felt like members of one big family. While the mihi was very solemn, it was also moving and meaningful, and as good a way as a cocktail party, if not a better one, of bringing us together. Strangely enough, at about the moment we entered the covered porch of the meeting house, the rain and thunder began again.

The tone for the entire day and, in retrospect, for our mission, was set by our initiation into the life of the marae because it is the very heart of Maori society. We spent the rest of the afternoon joined in a meeting in the whare hui, where guests and hosts sat on the floor opposite each other, exchanging views, and ended the day with a hangi, the Maori version of a Hawaiian lūʻau. During the next six days, as we visited other marae, including Turangawaewae, the "Maori Queen's" marae, and as we met and talked with Maoris from all walks of life, the feelings and impressions we had gained from our initial experience were only reinforced. And by the time we returned to Auckland for our flight back to Honolulu, not only Kenneth Brown knew, in part at least, the reason for our mission.

Ostensibly, we had come as businessmen to talk about business with our Maori counterparts and to explore opportunities for financial profit. But, in addition, we talked a lot about Maori cultural beliefs and values, like the tapu and the ritual of the marae, the role of the modern day tohunga, or kahuna, the great respect and reverence paid to their dead, the relevance of the Maori language to their everyday lives, the vitality of their mythology and enduring gods. To be sure, we held several meetings with Maoris in business and discussed a wide range of problems and opportunities, yet, ironically, these discussions seemed to be of secondary importance to us. One evening, for example, we invited John Rangihau, a lecturer in Maori studies at the University of Waikato and one of the most respected authorities on the traditional culture —who just happened to be traveling with us—to talk to us about Maori thought and customs. One of the first things he did was to diagram a series of Maori values and beliefs centered around aroha, explaining how each related to the other in order to form a well-integrated value system. It was beautiful! I was stunned by the neatness and the symmetry of the model, by the systematic and logical way through which modern Maoris have been able to construct a traditional philosophy of life for use in the twentieth century. At that moment all the feelings and images that I had been collecting about the Maoris merged in one clear message: they have got their act together. They know who and what they are.

On our last day in New Zealand Kenneth Brown and I spent several hours with John Rangihau, reviewing some of our experiences and perceptions and explaining what we had resolved to do. Our visit had begun as a business mission, but ended by being one of spiritual and cultural rediscovery. In the course of finding out about Maoris, we discovered ourselves—and saw what we as Hawaiians could be culturally. The Maoris gave us reasons for hope that, despite the shocks and changes of the past two hundred years of westernization, Hawaiians could recover and rebuild a strong culture anchored in its ancient traditions yet capable of withstanding the worst hazards of the postindustrial age.

As we Hawaiians grew rhapsodic about the Maoris, John Rangihau remained almost silent. I suspect he knew that we were romanticizing and idealizing them, for not all Maoris have got it all together, especially among the urban youth of New Zealand. Indeed, many of them have troubles with their cultural identity as well as with social, economic, and political status in a pakeha-dominated society. Probably he did not say anything in order to avoid dampening our enthusiasm. That was a case in which preserving the illusion was more important than revealing the truth, because in our idealization of the Maoris we were conjuring up a picture all our own of what we as Hawaiians could become. While it may not have been perfectly clear, what we saw or hoped for in our mind's eye was a people who would be secure in their self-esteem as a result of a better understanding of their essential selves, and who therefore would be better able because better motivated to achieve their fullest potentials both as individuals and as a people.

What our exposure to the Maoris had done was to sharpen our awareness of that elusive hope and vision, but at the same time goad us to act. When we asked ourselves what and how we should act, the first step toward an answer came to us in the form of the familiar and troubling question: "Who and what is a Hawaiian?" Since the question demanded an answer, our task was laid out for us. It all seemed so simple, but little did we know at the time how difficult and complex the job would be. As happens so often in life, had we known, we might not have begun. But, apart from this "ignorance is bliss" kind of start, many good reasons encouraged us to persevere.

In any event, that is how Project Waiaha and this book were born on a Sunday afternoon in June of 1981, in Aotearoa, the "Land of the Long White Cloud."

ACKNOWLEDGMENTS

Since this book would never have been written without his inspiration and perseverance, I must express my deepest gratitude to Kenneth F. Brown. That he obtained the resources to develop and complete this effort deserves every bit of our gratitude, but he is owed even more for his philosophical insights and understanding of the major life themes that we have examined in this book. His insights are found throughout. So is his mana.

Also with heartfelt thanks I acknowledge Amfac Corporation and its chairman, Henry Walker, for funding this project. Business corporations have made numerous contributions to the community of Hawai'i, but no precedent is known for this singular demonstration of sensitivity and support by a major corporation in Hawai'i for a project of this kind.

I must thank, too, the members of the advisory council of Project Waiaha, who encouraged and helped in every activity connected with the preparation of this work. They are: Robert Lokomaika'iokalani Snakenberg, Violet Ku'ulei Ihara, Marjorie Barrett, William Kea, Dr. Donald Kilolani Mitchell, and Harry Matte. Kenneth Brown serves as chairman of the council.

Special thanks go to the following, who consented to be contributing writers before plans were changed: John R. K. Clark, Pierre Bowman, Malcolm N. Chun, Neil Hannahs, Abraham and 'Ilima Piianaia, Cecilia Kapua Lindo, Bill Tagupa, Amy Stillman, Ho'oulu Cambra, H. Rodger Betts, Dr. Richard Kekuni Blaisdell, Dr. Rubellite K. Johnson, John Dominis Holt, and Lokomaika'iokalani Snakenberg.

I want to recognize our Maori "cousins" who provided, however unwittingly, hope and a challenge. Thanks especially to Kara Puketapu, former secretary of Maori Affairs, John Rangihau, and

Dr. Tamati Reedy, currently secretary of Maori Affairs, George and Maori Marsden, Hamuera Mitchell, Mike Barns, Reitu Robson, Dennis Hansen, Albe Williams, Professors Hugh Kawharu, and Ralph N. Love of Massey University.

To many persons whose brains I picked either by interview or by letter, I convey my mahalo for their kōkua. They include the Reverends Ed Kealanahele, Darrow 'Aiona, David Ka'upu, and Bill Kaina; Hīnano Paleka, Edith McKenzie, Lydia Taylor Maioho, Noelani Māhoe, Māhealani Pescaia, Mālie Mossman; Charles Heen; State Representatives Clayton Hee, Whitney Anderson, and Henry Peters; William Richardson; "Sis" Wiedermann, Monsignor Charles Kekumano, Watters Martin, Steve Cunha, Bill Tagupa, Julieann Cachola, Professor Ishmael Stagner, Sarah Quick, Sarah Nākoa, Māpuana DeSilva, Larry Kimura, R. Kawika Makanani, Cy Bridges, Fred Cachola, VerlieAnne Malina-Wright, Gladys Brandt, Winona Rubin, Clorinda Lucas, Nāinoa Thompson, and Leimomi Mo'okini Lum.

I thank the librarians at the main branch of the State of Hawai'i Library, the Hamilton Graduate Library at the University of Hawai'i, and the Mission Houses Museum, particularly the Hawaiian specialists of these treasure troves of knowledge. And I add a special note of thanks to Kenneth Brown, whose private collection of books on philosophy and mythology proved invaluable.

Another group deserving of gratitude are the hundred or so participants in the Ho'okanaka Training Workshops, whose collective insights and opinions were of immeasurable importance to some of our findings on values. Also, thanks go to the fifty especially invited participants in the first Waiaha Seminar held on October 24, 1981, who got us off to a running start.

Also, I owe a debt of thanks to the people who took the trouble to read parts of the draft manuscript: Dr. Richard Kekuni Blaisdell, Momi Cazimero, Bill Quinn, Dewey Caldwell, John Charlot, Reuel Denney, Andrew Lind, Rubellite Johnson, Will Kyselka, James Reeder, Carl Lindquist, Kioni Dudley, Nathan Nāpōkā, Marjorie Barrett, Albert Kanahele, George Kanahele, Jr., Kanta Devi, Ku'ulei Ihara, George Marsden, Dr. Tamati Reedy, Dr. Donald Kilolani Mitchell, and R. Lokomaika'iokalani Snakenberg. Again, to Kenneth Brown, who read *all* the drafts and revisions, and Dr. Niklaus Schweizer and Mona Nakayama, who kindly toiled through the final draft, go my special thanks.

I need to say mahalo to Hawaiian linguists Robert Lokomai-ka'iokalani Snakenberg and Larry Kimura, who rescued me from committing errors in the Hawaiian language.

I am also thankful for the research assistance rendered by Carol Silva, Bernice Brown, Kauana Kanahele, and the special help of Dr. Frances Brown.

Needless to say, I alone am responsible for any errors of fact or of interpretation that may have slipped my attention, despite our best efforts to prevent them.

Finally, I wish to give personal thanks to Dr. Gene Ward, my business partner, for allowing me the time away from the office, and to my wife Jeanne and daughter Joanna Leiko for putting up with months of neglect and occasional outbursts they generously attributed to the trials of creativity.

Introduction

IN SEARCH OF
HAWAIIAN VALUES

Who and What Is a Hawaiian?

Anyone familiar with recent developments among Hawaiians knows that this is not a new query: it has been asked many times by many people, both Hawaiians and non-Hawaiians. In 1964, for example, John Dominis Holt, the respected Hawaiian writer and publisher, began his short and popular essay "On Being Hawaiian" with the question: "What is a Hawaiian? Who is a Hawaiian in the modern State of Hawai'i?" Samuel Crowningburg Amalu, Hawaiian iconoclast, raised the question in one form or another in many of his weekly columns for the *Honolulu Advertiser*. In 1979 the Hawai'i Foundation for History and the Humanities sponsored a series of public discussions entitled "What Makes a Hawaiian a Hawaiian?" It featured Hawaiians such as Homer Hayes, Professor Pauline King Joerger, and Lynette Paglinawan, as well as a few non-Hawaiians, who together offered a wide assortment of opinions but in the end reached no consensus. It is no wonder that a reporter for the *Honolulu Star-Bulletin* was moved to ask, in large bold type, "Exactly What is a Hawaiian?"

That's a good question, because it continues to challenge the best of us. We can empathize with John Holt, who, worrying over the conditions of today's Hawaiians, asks, "Do we really know ourselves as Hawaiians, enjoy being Hawaiians, and strive to find places in which we can use our talents in all areas of present-day life as active, participating, productive, first-class citizens of the United States?"

Samuel Amalu says the Hawaiian "lost his own soul" when he surrendered to Western culture. "So now when people ask me what a Hawaiian is," he writes, "I can only reply that I do not know. I have never seen one. The last Hawaiian died many years ago." And as for himself, apparently speaking for a lot of marginal Hawaiians, he confesses, "I am not quite certain what I am."

Understandably, the question elicits many different answers, probably as many as there are Hawaiians. A haole reporter asked a young Hawaiian doctor, "What's a Hawaiian?" and he replied, "On the island of Moloka'i, local people say a Hawaiian is someone who eats palu (a relish made out of the head or stomach of a fish, mixed with kukui nut, garlic, and chili peppers)." An elderly Hawaiian matriarch and community leader on the Big Island of Hawai'i says, "Being Hawaiian today is finally feeling at home after nearly a century of trying to live like foreigners told us we should live in our own land." A young Hawaiian wahine professional expressed her irritation with the question by stating, "I had the feeling that this question was completely passé. I thought we had gotten to the point that if you felt Hawaiian, you were Hawaiian." Many a Hawaiian has pointed to a Japanese or a haole who, without an ounce of Hawaiian blood, has mastered the language or the culture for one or another reason, and said, "That's a Hawaiian." The author suggested several years ago that "These days any resident of this State who considers Hawai'i his home and who has a (true) understanding of the values of Hawaiian culture ought to consider himself or herself a Hawaiian."

The question, in fact, raises more questions than it provides answers. Is being Hawaiian dependent upon having some Hawaiian blood? If so, how much Hawaiian blood? Does it mean looking like a Hawaiian? What physical features, then, are acceptable as being Hawaiian? Is the ability to speak the language important? Does one have to believe in the old gods and myths to be truly Hawaiian? Is it also a matter of eating palu—or poi, kālua pig, laulau, and other traditional foods? Does it mean displaying such skills as dancing the hula, lei making, lau hala weaving, canoe paddling, and so on? Can one be a real Hawaiian and yet be part-Japanese, or Filipino, German, Portuguese, or Korean? Is not a modern Hawaiian a different kind of creature from the Hawaiian of old? The responses seem to go on and on, without end.

The fact that our simple question generates as much wide and deep interest as it does among Hawaiians today should not come as a surprise, for what we are dealing with here is something very basic in human psychology: one's feeling of identification with a distinctive group of people. Whether one is a black, or a Pole, Indian, Chicano, Jew, or Maori, this feeling for identity is deep-seated. Like religion and patriotism, it is a powerful source of motivation, for which people are willing to live or die. University of Chicago professor Edward Shils has called this force "primordial," one that is rooted in a sense of "blood and land," and so much so that when this sense is threatened by an invader from outside, a man, his wife, and children are quite ready to fight to defend it. Thus, even when the odds are stacked against them, when preserving one's ethnic identity seems irrational or hopeless, some "ethnics" persist, hanging on determinedly to the cultural image that they think distinguishes them. In a real sense, they consider such a struggle as being one of survival against the threat of personal or collective extinction.

In academic terms of today, this awareness of identity is called "ethnicity." Professor George De Vos defines it as "a subjective sense of continuity in belonging." In other words, it is our "historical memory"—not so much of a set of events, artifacts, or things, but, rather, it is a set of feelings, expectations, patterns of emotion and behavior, symbols, and values, that separates us from other groups. It is our psychocultural identity that is determined not only by what we do or say, but by how we feel and think about ourselves. The urge to preserve all this is at the bottom of knowing who and what we are.

The most striking evidence of the modern Hawaiians' interest in ethnicity is the unprecedented revival of activity in things Hawaiian by Hawaiians (and by some non-Hawaiians as well), beginning in the late 1960s and early 1970s. These activities range from featherwork and dancing the hula kahiko, or ancient hulas, to speaking the Hawaiian language and reviving the old religion. All this renewed interest has been called, not inappropriately, the "Hawaiian Renaissance." While periods of cultural revival have happened in the past—as in the reign of King Kalākaua during the 1880s, and as in the 1920s, centered on personalities such as John Wise and Prince Kūhiō Kalanianaʻole—the current range of activities is unmatched in the number of people involved and in the intensity and variety of their levels of interest. Although it is very much a cultural or arts-related manifestation, the renaissance has spilled over into economic and political fields also, as is evidenced in the creation of the Office of Hawaiian Affairs in 1978 in response to action by the Hawai'i State Constitutional Convention, and in the increasing range of Hawaiian economic and business activities. Significantly, the renaissance has been a "young movement," since its leadership and supporters have tended to be younger activist Hawaiians—bright, well educated, articulate, and confident, and not members of the "shadowed margins" of society, as John Holt puts it. Consequently, while some people may be tempted to see revivals of any sort as trendy or faddish, the involvement of the younger generation, infused with purpose and even with a sense of manifest destiny, gives the movement a degree of commitment and permanency that goes beyond being a "momentary flirtation with one's exotic past." In our judgment, this renaissance is perhaps the most significant chapter in modern Hawaiian cultural history—which, if it proves to be right, underscores again the importance of our question, "Who and what is a Hawaiian?"

Lest we seem to be too ethnocentric and provincial, we need to be aware of the fact that the recent Hawaiian enthusiasm for reaffirming ethnic identity did not emerge wholly or spontaneously out of the Hawaiian community. Rather, it arose as part of national and worldwide movements, by which racial or ethnic minorities sought to rediscover and revitalize their ties to their cultural past. In the United States, this "ethnic fever" started with the blacks, when they launched their civil rights movement in the 1950s, and then spread to other racial groups, such as the Chicanos, Puerto Ricans, American Indians, Japanese- and other Asian-Americans, who formed a loosely organized coalition under the banner of the Third World. Although most people think of this movement as involving only the "colored" minorities, it also included the "white ethnics"—Jews, Italians, Poles, and others of European ancestry, such as the Cajuns of Louisiana. By the late 1960s "ethnic fever" had also hit local ethnic groups in Hawai'i, including the Hawaiians. Whereas for decades America's racial groups were encouraged to move toward integration or assimilation into the American "melting pot," after 1960 the pendulum swung the other way, as these groups rejected the process of being lumped into one undifferentiated mass. Through the revival of their identifying art, literature, religion, games, music, and dance, they sought to promote ethnic pride and solidarity, and to affirm their right to enjoy a separate identity. Nonetheless, the fact that, among Hawaiians, the renaissance is a by-product of a universal movement begun elsewhere should not detract from its intrinsic strength and significance as Hawaiians' response to a felt need.

A great deal of interest exists among Hawaiians wanting to know more about who and what we are and some of the reasons why. That is the first point to remember.

The second point is that we already know a lot about ourselves. One need only visit the Hawaiian collections in our libraries to appreciate this fact. We are far from being ignorant about either our past or our present. We have a good understanding of our traditional arts and crafts, that is, music, dance, sculpture, weaving, tapa and lei making, featherwork, and canoe building. We have a fairly good knowledge of our habits, both old and new, with regard to play, work, leisure, eating, sleeping, and other day-to-day activities. Thanks to the efforts of scholars and practitioners, in recent years we have come to know a lot more about Polynesian long-distance voyaging, navigation, knowledge of stars, and many other ocean-related accomplishments. We also know about our old myths, rituals, symbols, and religious beliefs and practices. Although we bemoan the seemingly inevitable loss of our language, we now know more about it today than at any other time in recent memory.

This knowledge of ourselves is not limited to the past, although apparently those who have studied and written about Hawaiians have devoted more of their attention to history. We know a good deal regarding contemporary Hawaiian social and educational practices and beliefs, due in part to the work of Hawaiian agencies such as the Queen Lili'uokalani Trust's Children's Center and the Kamehameha Schools. We are finding out more about Hawaiian economic and business behavior. And to this we might add Hawaiian political and leadership behavior as well.

In short, we already have an extensive knowledge about ourselves, and, no doubt, we will continue to accumulate more and more knowledge, partly because curiosity is never satisfied and partly because Hawaiians will demand to know more. Hence, when we ask the question "Who and what is a Hawaiian?" it is not an admission of complete ignorance.

Still, there is much that we do not know about ourselves and do not understand very clearly. The more we discover about ourselves, the deeper we probe into our feelings and motives and primordial instincts, the more we need to discover and understand. One of the subjects we do not know enough about lies at the very center of our psychocultural universe. The reason why we have neglected to probe it fully for all these years is not very clear, because it is central to our understanding of who and what we are. The subject is our values—our Hawaiian values.

The standards of worth and behavior which are prized by the members of a society are known as values. They determine and reflect what the members of a society are, essentially, both as individual human beings and as parts of an ethnic group. They are both cause and effect of what we are, for without them we can do, say, or think nothing that is rational. They shape, influence, guide, and temper our feelings, ideas, expectations, goals, hopes, and dreams. They are a significant part, if not the essence, of our self-identity.

Formulating the Search

When the state of Hawai'i decided to celebrate the bicentennial of the arrival of Captain Cook's expedition in 1778, not all Hawaiians were enthusiastic about commemorating an event which brought so much trauma and upheaval in its wake. Some even suggested that the occasion should be one of mourning rather than of celebration. But by far the majority of Hawai'i's citizens deemed Cook's arrival as worthy of some kind of official remembrance.

Governor George A. Ariyoshi appointed Kenneth Brown to coordinate the program for the state. Brown was fully aware of the many cross-currents as he pondered what to do. Exactly when, how, and where it happened he does not recall, but the solution came to him in a flash of insight. Instead of celebrating Cook's coming, he thought, why not celebrate the culture and the people who discovered him? Brown recognized that, like many other people, including Hawaiians, he learned about Hawai'i from a foreign vantage point, as if he were a passenger on board the *Resolution* or the *Discovery*. What he proposed for the bicentennial was a reversal of roles, viewing Cook's arrival from the perspective of the insiders, the Hawaiians onshore.

Brown's idea was sympathetically received by many people, especially Hawaiians. Indeed, probably Cook himself would have gone along with his idea, for Hawai'i had made a great impression on him. A summary statement in the official narrative of this voyage showed his awareness of Hawai'i's importance: "Few . . . now lamented our having failed in our endeavors to find a Northern Passage homeward, last summer. To this disappointment we owed our having it in our power to revisit the Sandwich Islands, and to enrich our voyage with a discovery which, though the last, seemed, in many respects, to be the most important that had hitherto been made by Europeans, throughout the extent of the Pacific Ocean."

In order to bring a focus to the celebration of the Hawaiian culture, Brown considered what were the most essential parts of any culture. Having already been, in his opinion, a "dilettante" in cultural philosophy for many years and an avid student of the writings of Mircea Eliade, the Romanian-born authority on comparative mythology, he had long since concluded that "the essence of any society is its system of values." Knowing also that the mood of the ongoing Hawaiian renaissance was favorable to an exploration of traditional values, he decided that the focus of the celebration should be upon values. In a long proposal, called *Nānā I Ke Kumu,* "Look to the source," which he wrote himself, and based on several discussions with other Hawaiians and non-Hawaiians, he proposed a number of activities centered around a Bicentennial Conference on Hawaiian Values. The goal of the conference lay in "rediscovering the essence that was here upon the arrival of Cook. Our purpose will be to understand ourselves better by tracing the values of Hawai'i from the beginnings of western influence."

He defined the task of the conference in three simple questions: (1) What were the values of Hawai'i's people before Cook? (2) How have those values changed since? (3) What is their present-day validity? Because the simplicity of the questions may have covered up the complexity of the task, Brown issued a fair warning. "This is a large order. A voyage of rediscovery back into the past can be a hazardous undertaking. It could flounder. The essence of that long ago society may elude us or its values prove forever lost." Yet, the risks were very much worth the taking. For, as he put it, "The rewards of success hold such promise for us that the journey is compelling. We [Americans] are a people of vaunted technological prowess [who are] only now becoming aware of our peril for having lost our harmony with nature and ourselves. The values we seek, then, could have meaning for our survival—for this harmony

was so evident in Hawaiian society." It was, in his words, "an integrated society in the full sense of the word," in which Hawaiians
"had it all together."

So far as we know, it was the first time that such a proposal had
been advanced in the field of values. Unhappily, for a variety of
logistical reasons, the conference was not held. But in our little
story about the unfolding of the study of Hawaiian values, the
proposal did lead to several important conclusions: it reempha-
sized the need for a native perspective of modern Hawaiian history; it spotlighted the need to examine Hawaiian values as a distinct object of study; and it outlined very clearly the three-pronged
approach to the task—which we have followed in the organization
of this book. Furthermore, the proposal continues to remind us of
the benefits we can derive today from the ancient value system in
resolving modern-day problems and in leading what for us may be
called "the Good Life."

After the bicentennial ended, Brown was called upon once more
for help, this time to serve as chairman of the Hawai'i Foundation
for History and the Humanities, established in 1969 by the state
legislature. In this new capacity (and remembering his proposal
for the bicentennial celebrations) he started the first Hawaiian
Values Project. Its goal was the same: to establish the nature of
Hawaiians' social values in the pre-Cook era, and to trace their
survival down to our own times. The project did a number of
things, including sponsoring the public discussions referred to earlier on the topic "What makes a Hawaiian a Hawaiian?" One of
the notable investigations supported by the project was videotap-
ing interviews with fifty-one kūpuna, whose personal histories
were to be used in illustrating the evolution of Hawaiian values
from at least "neo-traditional" to modern times. (Some of that
material has been used in the writing of this book.) Unfortunately,
the project's efforts were cut short by lack of funding, when the
legislature dissolved the foundation in 1980.

Despite the fits and starts, the work on values by Brown and his
colleagues was having some effect on others in the community.
One of those was Rubellite Kawena Johnson, a noted Hawaiian
scholar and professor of Hawaiian literature and language at the
University of Hawai'i. At a humanities conference held in Honolulu in 1979, two years after Brown's entry into the field, she
raised a series of provocative questions concerning the ability of

humanities scholars to come to terms with the study of Hawaiian traditional values. Some of the questions she raised then are worth repeating here: Can traditional Hawaiian values be known? Are we able to discover them? Do we know what values motivated the ancient Hawaiian society and to what extent are they present now in Hawaiian society? Moreover, do we know what values are proper for present-day Hawaiians in a multiethnic society? If such values are worth recovering, should they be applied to present-day social aims to promote interethnic understanding? Or should they be applied strictly toward Hawaiians participating in the "Hawaiian Renaissance"? If so, how should they be applied and who should determine the effective means of implementation? Does all this concern imply that Hawaiians today genuinely feel that something of tremendous value has been lost to all of our modern society that was formerly unique to the aboriginal group? What, then, do we wish to recover for the sake of all and also what, specifically, for the sake of Hawaiians?

While she was content to ask questions, which sometimes is as important a contribution to thought as giving answers, she made a strong plea for the need to study traditional Hawaiian values. Not only can such values be uncovered, she said, but they must be. She emphasized that humanities scholars, particularly philosophers, have a responsibility to do so. Though we know much of our cultural heritage through the work of archaeologists, historians, anthropologists, and ethnologists, she stated that "the question of values, however, has not been specifically addressed . . . except in a peripheral sense." She attributed this partly to the lack of interest by professional philosophers who have been "more oriented toward societies with a highly-developed literature of critical examination of belief and value." And she concluded that because now enough material about Hawai'i's old culture is available, the time for humanities scholars to really get involved "has arrived."

We readily concur with Professor Johnson's views. As previously pointed out, little work has been done on Hawaiian values. A quick survey of the current Hawaiian bibliographies shows this lack, especially in the field of philosophy. It is quite proper to single out philosophy because the study of values is a branch of the philosophical discipline. As a matter of fact, philosophers have paid relatively little attention to Polynesian society as a whole. While scholars have a right to study what they wish, the lack of any serious philosophical studies of Polynesian cultures has prompted many people to jump to the conclusion that Polynesians, including Hawaiians, had no philosophical inclinations to speak of. Such reasoning is absurd, of course, because it would be the same as saying that anything scholars have not studied must not be very important or must not exist. The lack of scholarly involvement may well betray professional prejudices or other inabilities rather than a people's intellectual shortcomings. But, the fact is, as serious students will attest, Polynesians, judged by material available so far, reveal profound and complex philosophical insights in their cosmological and mythological thinking. In any event, one of the things this book will demonstrate is that philosophical thought was almost as much a part of Hawaiian traditional concerns as religious thought, and that, along with values, it deserves much more serious scholarly attention than it has received.

Each of Professor Johnson's questions will be taken up at one point or another in this book. Moreover, she has hit upon a paramount theme, namely, the relevance of Hawaiian values not only to blood Hawaiians but to non-Hawaiians as well. As we shall show, the relevance is due partly to the universality of certain values, and partly to the deep understanding of the environment that Hawaiians have developed over the course of many centuries.

Perhaps not enough time has elapsed since 1778 to enable humanities scholars and others, especially sociologists and psychologists, to respond to the challenges put forth by Brown and Johnson. But until now we have neither seen nor heard of any major attempt to examine the nature, origins, and evolution of Hawaiian values from the past to the present. To be sure, the subject is touched upon directly and indirectly in many contemporary articles, monographs, and books dealing with Hawaiian society; after all, values are manifest in all human events. Excellent sources are the works by Kawena Pūku'i, particularly the two-volume study *Nānā I Ke Kumu*, compiled in collaboration with Dr. W. E. Haertig and Catherine A. Lee, and her latest book, *'Ōlelo No'eau, Hawaiian Proverbs and Poetic Sayings* (1983), from which we draw throughout this study. Nonetheless, at present Project Waiaha and this book remain the only major contributions devoted entirely to the study of Hawaiian values and related concepts.

Defining Values

Clearly, if our search is to continue, we need to define our most basic term—values. Nowadays we hear politicians, preachers, coaches, managers, judges, and many others talking (or writing) about "values," but not very often are we told what values really are. The word or its synonyms fly out of mouths (or word processors) easily, quickly, and continuously—and they go right over our heads. Quite possibly, for example, up to this point no two readers of the pages we have written so far are certain about our intended meaning or the way in which we have used the term "values." Unconsciously, if not deliberately, most people take for granted that nice-sounding, well-used words such as "values" should be understood immediately, when in fact they tend to be least understood either because they are overused or too often are used indiscriminately. We intend to be not guilty of this uncertainty.

Alas, defining "values" is not a simple process, because even the experts have differing points of view. But let us start from the beginning and see where the idea of values originates. As human beings we value or prize things or ideas because they represent needs we want to fulfill in order to maintain our physical, psychological, or spiritual well-being. Each of us has biological, sensual, sexual, emotional, intellectual, artistic, spiritual, aesthetic needs, and a lot of others besides. We need to be loved, to be respected, to be understood, or to belong to a family, a group, or an association, to achieve something memorable, to own a parcel of land, or to get rich. Such needs are the causes or sources of our values, because we require and demand that those needs be satisfied in one way or another. And the values we attach to those needs help us to recognize their relative importance and thereby help us to fulfill them.

Simply put, a value indicates a need to be fulfilled or a desire that is based upon a need. In a word, a value is related to a satisfaction, which is always an intangible—a thought or desire—not a thing or object as such. Not the bread, but the satisfying of hunger is a value; not the sculpture, but the satisfying of our sense of beauty in the sculpture is a value. That is to say, things may be valuable, but they are not values. We project value onto things in the external world, attributing it to the things that serve desire, but the value resides in our minds. For convenience we speak of things or objects as having value (as occasionally we lapse into doing in this book); indeed, when you think about it, rarely do we talk about values without referring them to some corresponding valuable objects. But we must not forget that things do not really have value unless we give them attributes of desire.

Sometimes a distinction is made between values as ends and values as means, which are called "terminal" and "instrumental" values respectively. Efficiency, for example, is a means value, since it leads to the sense of achievement; honesty and humility are instrumental in attaining inner peace; and courage is the necessary means to overcoming trial and tribulation in seeking salvation, and so on. Often, however, an instrumental value can become a terminal value, as in the case of aloha, or love. That is, you can be in love as an end condition, or you can love someone in order to attain some other end. The values we talk about in the forthcoming chapters are of both types, depending on the situations.

Still another dimension of values is important to keep in mind, namely, values as standards that define for a person how he or she should behave in life, what actions or events merit approval or disapproval, what patterns of relations should prevail among people, groups, or institutions. In this sense, values tell a person what kind of human being he or she wants to be, or what kind of world he or she wants to live in, or how he or she wishes to judge or evaluate him- or herself and the world. We all set for ourselves some guidelines of behavior, and when we do so we are establishing values as standards.

A Values Theory

Just as a search party looking for a lost hiker has a much better chance of finding him by using a good map, so do we have a better chance of identifying and understanding Hawaiian values by using a good theory. The function of a map is to locate specific points in a given area by providing you with the proper orientation. Similarly, the function of a good theory is to identify specific concepts and relationships by giving you a coherent framework. A theory consists of assumptions, hypotheses, or generalizations that explain in the abstract how some real-life situation is or behaves. You may think of these assumptions, hypotheses, and so on, as lines or coordinates on a map. Both serve as reference points to help you find your way through unknown realms, whether the territory is conceptual or physical. In short, a good values theory will help us to know where we are going and what we are talking about.

One of our basic assumptions is that every society has a concept of the Good Life, a desirable and ideal way of living that produces happiness or some highly acceptable state of well-being. The members of a society who share certain common beliefs, practices, and aspirations strive to attain that Good Life. It is their reason for being, because the more values they accept and respond to, the more needs they fulfill and, therefore, the greater is their happiness. Hence, the Good Life may be defined as the constant and rewarding pursuit of all these "life-serving" values.

As students we learn about the concept of the Good Life in Greek philosophy (for example, in Plato's or Aristotle's ideas of the Highest Good), or in Christian and Buddhist thought. But seldom, if at all, do we learn about the Good Life as it is defined in Hawaiian philosophy. So unaccustomed are we to making such a connection that to talk about it requires considerable intellectual effort on our part. Nonetheless, if our assumption is true—that every society does have a concept of the Good Life—then the Good Life is as valid a notion for Hawaiian thinkers as it is for Greek, French, or Chinese philosophers and, beneath them, their people.

What was the Good Life for Hawaiians of old? If for us the Good Life is the sum total of what we think and feel to be satisfying, virtuous, worthy, uplifting—that is to say, good—then the answer to that fundamental question must lie in our values. Therefore, as we identify and clarify traditional Hawaiian values, so will we uncover the essence of the Hawaiians' reason for living. As we shall see, spiritual attunement with the gods, harmony with the cosmos and nature, loyalty to leaders, unity with companions, physical and mental health, personal achievement, hospitality and generosity, and aloha are some of the values that characterize the Good Life of ka po'e kahiko, the people of old.

Another of our basic assumptions is that values may vary from society to society, and from individual to individual in any given community. This is understandable, because values are essentially based upon needs, which in turn are determined by a variety of factors and conditions, ranging from climate, genetic makeup, and diet to economics, politics, religion, technology, and natural resources. The values of an Indian tribe who hunt game are different from those of a tribe who grow crops, because the two lifestyles are so very different. The values of the Watusi who live in the highlands of Eastern Africa are distinct from the values of the Pygmy living in the tropical forests of equatorial Africa. Such examples are too numerous to dwell upon. Similarly, the values of individuals may vary within the same community or association or even family. How many families do you know whose sons or daughters, raised in the same house by the same parents with virtually the same opportunities, grow up to be such different persons in attitude, outlook, and goals? This and similar experiences underscore the truth about the uniqueness of each human being.

If we accept this assumption of value differentials among societies and individuals, it should also hold true for people living in any group, place, or time. When we look more closely at the people in ancient Hawai'i, for instance, we should expect to see variations in values among individual members of families as well as those of clans or communities dwelling in separate islands or districts. Just as we should not be surprised to see modern Hawaiians developing their own personal value systems, so should we not be surprised to see ancient Hawaiians doing the same.

One clear implication of this principle is that we should not look back and regard all ka po'e kahiko, people of olden times, as having been the same. Time and distance tend to distort our perceptions of reality, as, all too often, we ignore natural discrepancies and obvious contradictions, to end up with a pleasant but bland uniformity. Hawaiians were not then—as they are not now—one absolutely identical and homogeneous people. We can appreciate, then, how hazardous it is for anyone, including us today, to make or accept any generalizations about Hawaiians without appropriate disclaimers or qualifications.

Closely linked to this idea is the relativity of human values. We use the term in two senses: the first maintains that the concept of value involves a relationship—the relation of some aspect of reality to man. In other words, what we prize is always related to something else that we may prize more or less. The second, and more common, sense maintains that values are better understood when we relate them to a specific cultural or historical situation, rather than to one single all-encompassing universal tradition.

We might ask, if this is so, if any such thing exists as a universal or absolute value. Aren't some norms or standards prized by all people, regardless of place, creed, or genetic makeup? When we say "people are all the same," don't we mean that we, in spite of our differences, share some of the basic values? Cultural historians and others tell us, for example, that every society places a value on sustaining human life, on beauty, or on the sacred, that is, the "mysterious." Furthermore, we take a lot of values to be absolute, such as "You must not kill," or "You must not lie." Can we find a place in our values theory for these universals?

A place does exist in our values theory for the *ideas* about them, but they must be qualified, for always we can discover the exception to the rule. So we say that "beauty lies in the eye of the beholder," that the "mysterious" is "only a figment of one's imagination," that our morality permits a soldier on a battlefield to kill his enemy, or that sometimes "white lies" are justified. In other words, a universal truth is universal only until or unless it meets an accommodation or a compromise.

What this means in practice is that values can be contradictory. That is to say, one value might apply to one situation but not to another, as in the commandment against killing. In order to protect ourselves from the inner turmoil that would result from trying to deal endlessly with value-conflicts—a condition no human being could tolerate for long without going mad—we are forced to rank our values according to certain personal criteria. In other words, we assign priorities to our values. What this means in practice is that in any given community the people as a group may acknowledge the same system of values but will develop different sets of personal values because of the way each gives priorities to them.

Perhaps this hypothesis might offer a way out of our dilemma about universal versus relative values. That is, while a group of like-minded members of a society may accept all its values as being universal, they can still regard many of those values as being relative to their individual circumstances through the device of assigning priorities.

Our values theory also poses the idea that values, or at least the priorities attached to them, can change from one historical period to another. The values we accept as children, for example, are not the same as those we adopt as adults, although nowadays psychologists and educators tell us that most of the values we acquire as children stay with us throughout our lives. The values of a society or nation also may change, as it reaches certain levels of economic and political development or passes through certain historical periods. The America of the 1980s in many respects is different from the America of the 1920s or of the 1880s. Postwar Japanese society entertains a greater number of different values than it did before the 1940s. And, clearly, contemporary Hawai'i has a different system of values from those of Hawai'i before Captain Cook arrived in 1778, just as Hawai'i in the year 2050 undoubtedly will respond to another set of values.

Implicit in our values theory is the axiom that human beings choose their values. Our very nature makes us want to make choices. We are constantly being confronted with many possible courses of action, and, even if we wanted to, we could not escape the need to choose one out of those many. Unlike lower animals, we are not biologically programmed to make choices dictated by some predetermining genetic instruction. In short, we are free agents, with freedom of choice.

Later we shall test this hypothesis about the "nature of man" in regard to the degrees of freedom that the maka'āinana, the commoners in ancient Hawai'i, had in choosing their personal values. Some people maintain, for example, that the political system under the sacred ali'i nui of ancient Hawai'i was so repressive that commoners exercised almost no freedom in choosing their values, but that, rather, those were dictated to them by the chiefs and priests in power. We shall see that the whole edifice of values theory would collapse in the absence of freedom of choice.

The point bears restating: the perceptions of ourselves that we recognize will play a critical role in determining how we choose our values. If, for example, a person should regard his brown skin, childhood in a poor neighborhood, lack of education, or short height as real handicaps in life, he would select quite a different set of values from those of someone who may regard the same characteristics much more positively, if not exactly as advantages. The degree of one's self-confidence and self-esteem, or the lack of them, will necessarily affect the goals one sets. The extent to which one views the world or society as being open or closed to one's understanding and action will also influence the range of one's ambitions or choice of friends, and so on. Thus, while we may exercise our freedom of choice in the selection of our values, that exercise is limited by the quality of our self-image and self-esteem. All these points of view will influence the way we describe and assess Hawaiian values of the past and the present.

At this point we need to clarify the differences between values and beliefs, or concepts, for they are easy to confuse. A teacher of Hawaiian culture in a local high school, for example, tells his students that the values and the religious beliefs of the ancient Hawaiian were one and the same. But they could not have been the same. While the distinction may be subtle, it is important. Beliefs are simply conceptual statements describing a particular phenomenon. They may shape or influence the choosing of a value, but they are not values in and of themselves. A belief becomes a value only when someone attaches a worth to it. Ancestral gods, sacred time, mana, and other such concepts stand alone as intellectual constructs, as ideas. But they are transformed into values the instant one acts in accordance with them. This differentiation of meanings should not be dismissed as "hairsplitting," because the distinction is going to be important in our analysis. Especially is this true of ancient Hawaiian values, where we shall have to deduce a great deal of what we say about those values from mythological beliefs and religious customs.

Finally, every good theory must be able to answer the question "So what?" What is the ultimate benefit or purpose of values? The answer is simple: they are necessary to the perfection of one's ideal nature. This is what the famous psychologist Nathaniel Branden calls the "essential self." Our theory presupposes that we cherish an ideal or essential self, as opposed to our existing real self, or the "existential" self. The difference is this: the latter encompasses everything a person is, the good and the bad, the virtuous and the evil, the beauty and the beast in all of us, while the former is everything that is life affirming, that is symbolized in the Good Life. But only because we are able to recognize this difference between the two selves, the ideal and the real, can we recognize that it is possible and necessary for us to aspire to the Good Life. In other words, the function of values, or the process of "valuing," is to help us to eliminate the deficiencies in our "existential" self so that we can realize our fullest potential—which resides in our essential or ideal self. The essence of life is in choosing and achieving values—*higher* values—with each new choosing.

Our purpose is not to elaborate a comprehensive values theory as much as to clarify some principles and provide a frame of reference. We have borrowed and adapted ideas and insights from some major figures in the field of "axiology," as the study of values is called, but even they must come up with a comprehensive and universally acceptable theory of their own. As Dale Simmons, in his book *Personal Valuing*, describes the situation: "Each of us faces the possibility that our world does not know how to prove beyond a doubt what are the truly good values. We must also deal with the further realization that even scholars who study personal valuing cannot agree upon its exact nature. . . . No agreed upon criteria have been established for what constitutes a complete set of human values, nor are there criteria for determining the complete set of human values, nor are there criteria for determining the completeness of any theory or model of valuing."

Hoʻokanaka Training Workshops

A theory is good only if it can survive being tested and applied to real life. Part of what we have said about values theory was tested in a series of four Hoʻokanaka Training Workshops. These were held at monthly intervals during the latter half of 1982 and involved small groups of participants, mostly Hawaiians. The main purpose of the workshops was to help Hawaiians to realize their "Hawaiianness" mainly by clarifying their values and goals. In the process, we were able to clarify some of our own assumptions and findings about Hawaiian values, both traditional and neotraditional. The term hoʻokanaka means to be courageous or to be manly, but it was intended to convey the meaning of the Maori concept of tu tangata, referring to the idea of standing tall. It could also mean one's stance, or where, when, and how one stands with respect to one's convictions and values. Hoʻokanaka training, then, was aimed at helping workshop participants "to stand tall" as Hawaiians. Parenthetically, anyone familiar with early modern Hawaiian history would appreciate the use of the word because, in earlier days, kanaka was the usual way in which foreigners referred to Hawaiians, often derisively.

About one hundred people, so selected as to represent a cross section of the Hawaiian community, participated in groups averaging twenty per workshop. Although the vast majority (about 90 percent) were Hawaiians, several nonethnic Hawaiians, including local haole, Japanese, and Maori residents, were invited to attend. Thus, one group included an attorney, an MTL bus driver, a hotel manager, a number of university students, several entertainers, a kumu hula, a school principal, and a kupuna. The youngest person was eighteen and the oldest more than sixty, with the average age ranging between the late twenties and the early thirties. The sexes were about equally divided, with a few more women than men. And although most were residents of Oʻahu, a handful of participants came from Hawaiʻi, Maui, and Kauaʻi. Finally, also in attendance were parents-children, wife-husband, and girlfriend-boyfriend combinations. In short, a serious attempt was made to involve a broad and diverse group, in order to represent the widest array of experiences and ideas.

We asked the participants to identify what they thought were important Hawaiian values. This was done first with individuals, later with members of small discussion groups. Then all the suggestions were compiled, compared, and analyzed in a general discussion. This process was planned and carried out in a systematic step-by-step manner, with each participant working out of his or her own manual containing specific instructions and exercises. Out of the scores of values mentioned, we assembled a list of twenty-five. These are not in any order of importance.

1. Aloha
2. Humility (haʻahaʻa)
3. Generosity (lokomaikaʻi)
4. Hospitality (hoʻokipa)
5. Spirituality (haipule or hoʻomana)
6. Obedience (wiwo)
7. Cooperativeness (laulima)
8. Cleanliness (maʻemaʻe)
9. Graciousness, pleasantness, manners (ʻoluʻolu)
10. Industry, diligence (paʻahana)
11. Patience (hoʻomanawanui)
12. Playfulness (leʻaleʻa)
13. Competitiveness (hoʻokūkū)
14. Keeping promises (hoʻohiki)
15. Forgiveness (huikala)
16. Intelligence (naʻauao)

17. Self-reliance (kūha‘o)
18. Excellence (kela)
19. Courage (koa)
20. Helpfulness (kōkua)
21. Balance, harmony, unity (lōkahi)
22. Dignity (hanohano)
23. Leadership (alaka‘i)
24. Achievement (kū i ka nu‘u)
25. Honesty (kūpono)

At the end of the workshop series we asked the participants, by means of a mail survey, to rank the first twenty of the listed values according to their own personal priorities. As one would expect, there was no consistent pattern in the ranking. Aloha, for example, which we expected would be ranked first in *all* responses, was found scattered among many places on the scale. However, in our tabulation of the weighted results overall, aloha did rank at the top, followed by humility, spirituality, generosity, graciousness, keeping promises, intelligence, cleanliness, and helpfulness among the first ten. The second ten began with forgiveness, followed by hospitality, self-reliance, industry, cooperativeness, excellence, courage, obedience, playfulness, and ended with competitiveness. We had asked participants to select their choices according to their perceptions for today; but had we also asked them to choose them on the basis of a traditional Hawaiian's views, that listing might well have been different. Indeed, as we shall see in later chapters of this book, Hawaiians before 1778 would have placed such values as hospitality, courage, and excellence high on the list. Obviously, vastly different historical conditions account for such differences.

What we learned from the responses of workshop participants, and from others in the community with whom we talked about Hawaiian values, gave us a framework of reference points for our analysis of traditional and modern values. In a way, it tended to bias our search for traditional values because we looked for those values first and may have closed our eyes to others that may have been more important. As a matter of fact, in one glaring instance, as we attempt to show in the chapter on "The Dynamics of Aloha," aloha probably is of far more importance to modern Hawaiians than it ever was to ancient Hawaiians.

It is one thing to draw up a list of Hawaiian values, but quite another thing to explain why and how those values functioned historically and culturally in Hawaiian society. While some of the participants were very knowledgeable, others did not know much about Hawaiian history or culture, and, hence, drew up their lists based on the smattering of knowledge that they had picked up over the years and on their own important but limited intuitive understanding of their cultural past. This was brought home very clearly by the difficulty that some participants had in understanding a list of 141 Hawaiian customs and concepts when they were asked whether or not they accepted them. There is a clear correlation between one's understanding of one's culture and history and the understanding of one's values. While reasonable minds will accept this self-evident proposition, many people in fact can never really make the connection. In a real sense, our search for values is finding that connection. Hence, much of this book is devoted to recounting and reconstructing bits and pieces of knowledge about ancient Hawaiian society, in order to understand why our kūpuna accepted certain standards while rejecting others.

Ho'okanaka was a relatively brief part of our preparations for writing this book, but a most important one. Frankly, if we had any doubts about the need for this book, or something like it, the enthusiastic reactions of the participants to the workshops removed those doubts. In postworkshop evaluations, the cumulative tabulations of the responses showed that nearly 95 percent of the participants thought the workshops were beneficial, even beyond their expectations. The MTL bus driver from Wai'anae said, "I have a pretty routine job, but this workshop has really opened my eyes to raising my goals and looking at my potentials." Another participant said, "It only deepened my yearning for my Hawaiianness." Six months, even a year, after the workshops, several individuals said that the workshop experience had been a turning point in their lives. One of the mothers who attended the workshop with her young daughter reported more than a year later that it had been a decisive juncture in the life of her daughter. As one teacher put it, "What a marvelous discovery of self this has been."

The Ghost of Inferiority

"Every Hawaiian has a built-in inferiority complex," a well-educated, well-paid Hawaiian professional has said. "You can't help but have it, because you come from a culture that's 'no good,' and nothing in it is good. You have no solid foundation. So you flounder around and you can't find a place for yourself. Everywhere you go, you get reminded of the fact that you are Hawaiian . . . that you're lazy, that you don't have a brain. . . . There is this emptiness that exists for a Hawaiian."

That was a sentiment reported in 1970, but one can hear the same thing today from many Hawaiians, both old and young. The feeling of inferiority is often concealed by self-deprecating jokes or swipes at other "ethnics." But everyone knows that such humor is a defense mechanism which may defend one's perimeter, perhaps, but does not prevent the hurt to one's inner self. Only the dullest can fail to detect the emotional jarring a Hawaiian suffers when he or she is the target of a negative stereotype. True, some Hawaiians, especially those of the "renaissance generation," do not feel inferior at all, but for almost all their parents the ghost of racial inferiority still lurks in the recesses of their minds.

Our search for values is also a search for renewed pride in our traditions, but this is unlikely to be realized unless the ghost of inferiority is fully exorcised. Part of this task involves careful uncovering of the traditions of the past and reevaluating their meaning and efficacy on the basis of their own merits and by comparisons with other primal cultures. But the task also requires explaining the origins of the ghost and understanding how and why it has succeeded in haunting us for so long. After all, we must assume that Hawaiians before 1778 did not believe that they were an inferior people. That alien notion came from the outside.

Indeed, it came in the Pandora's box of the Westerners who followed in Captain Cook's wake. Perhaps the beginnings lay not so much in the fact that Hawai'i's natives were inferior, but that the whites brought things that made them seem superior. In either event, the germ of the idea—more deadly to the soul of Hawaiians than any disease germ—was racism. We must understand that racism, whether mild or virulent, was part and parcel of the prevailing attitudes of those representatives from "the civilized world." Those attitudes were based on social, political, and biological theories about race that were held widely in eighteenth- and nineteenth-century Europe and America. David Hume, the arrogant and misinformed Scots philosopher in the late 1700s, spoke for his generation when he said that there had never been "a civilized nation of any other complexion than white, nor even any individual eminent either in action or speculation. No ingenious manufacturers amongst them, no arts, no sciences. Such a uniform and constant difference could not happen, in so many countries and ages, if nature had not made an original distinction betwixt these breeds of men." Whiteness was perceived as perfection and the white man as "a little more like God's own image." Indeed, Christianity for centuries had painted God and his angels white and Satan and his devils black, proof positive of the superiority of the white race and of the inferiority of the black.

Stephen J. Gould, in his prize-winning book *The Mismeasure of Man*, gave us an important insight into this lordly mind-set by examining some of the biological theories of "scientific racism" from earlier centuries. A widely accepted concept was "racial ranking" with the whites on top, blacks at the bottom, and the "coloreds" in between. All of America's great cultural heroes, from Benjamin Franklin and Thomas Jefferson to Abraham Lincoln, did not question the acceptability of racial ranking. The pseudoscience of craniometry was one of several techniques developed by biological determinists to demonstrate the validity of a racial pecking order. Samuel G. Morton, for example, an authority on the technique and one of the most respected scientists in America in the mid-1800s, measured the skulls of American Indians in North and South America, compared them with white skulls, and concluded that American Indians were "savages" who were "not only averse to the restraints of education, but for the most part incapable of a continued process of reasoning on abstract subjects." Since American policy was to liquidate the native American Indians, at least in some areas, it is not at all surprising that Morton's "scientific" views were used to buttress political rhetoric. He of course was lending support to notions that even the early New England colonists, including the Pilgrims, shared about the "barbarous" Indians.

"Monogenism," another notion which was based on scriptures, upheld the unity of all peoples descended from Adam and Eve. It postulated that all the human races had degenerated from the perfection of those first parents in the Garden of Eden, but that they had declined in different degrees, whites the least, blacks the most, and colored peoples presumably somewhere in between. A related theory, known as "polygenism," asserted that each race was a sepa-

rate biological species, the descendents of different Adams and
Eves. Given that premise, blacks or American Indians obviously
were separate species, and definitely inferior to whites. Polygeny,
in fact, became so identified with American scientific thought in
the second half of the nineteenth century that Europeans considered it the "American school" of anthropology. But it was used
also as one of the principal arguments in favor of racial segregation, justifying the "innate" differences in abilities among the races
—blacks, for example, were good at hand work, whites, at mind
work.

Even after the opinions of biological determinism had been
overtaken by those of Darwinian evolution, many other theories
were spawned to fortify racist assumptions. One of these, "recapitulation," ranks among the most influential in late nineteenth-
century science. Briefly, the idea was that an individual, in its
growth, passes through a series of stages representing adult ancestral forms in their correct order. Thus, in human evolution, the
"gill slits of an early human embryo represented an ancestral adult
fish; at a later stage, the temporary tail revealed a reptilian or
mammalian ancestor." One of the consequences of recapitulation
was the idea that "adults of *inferior* groups must be like *children* of
superior groups, for the child represents a primitive adult ancestor." While it was common for "learned people" to compare savages and other despised groups with children, now the popular
metaphor had scientific backing. G. Stanley Hall, then America's
leading psychologist, stated the widely accepted argument in
1904: "Most savages in most respects are children."

There was also the old chestnut that climate is a primary cause
for racial differences. Buffon, the great naturalist of eighteenth-
century France, believed that people who live in the colder temper-
ate climates between the fortieth and fiftieth degrees of latitude are
"the most handsome and beautiful men." Although he supported
the abolition of slavery, he, like so many other intellectuals and
scientists of his time, never doubted the "inherent validity of a
white standard."

Incomplete as this appraisal may be, it presents the major ideas
of the intellectual world out of which came Hawai'i's first Westerners—the navigators, traders, sailors, teachers, missionaries, ad-
venturers, and other wanderers. Naturally, they brought with
them sets of beliefs, perceptions, words, images, and metaphors

about race that were not very different from those afloat in the
mainstream of European or American thinking. Thus, we can
understand how those new arrivals thought of Hawaiians and
their culture in none other than the terms, such as "primitive" and
"savage," that they had been accustomed to using in their "superior" homelands. Even for Captain Cook, who was quite favorably impressed with the Hawaiians, they were still savages,
although not the "Noble Savages" that some Europeans romanti-
cized. There was no question in his mind, or in those of his fellow
officers, about who was superior and who was inferior. They
called Hawaiians "Indians," as most Europeans of the time commonly referred to Polynesians—and "Indians," wherever they
might be found, were painted with the same brush. So, from the
very start of their acquaintance with the reincarnated deity Lono,
the idea of brown inferiority was planted in the Hawaiian consciousness. That impression could only have grown as it was reinforced with the arrival of every new "civilized" European, if not
through words, spoken and unspoken, then by the cumulative
impact of new and powerful ideas, technologies, and the awesome
force of cannons and muskets.

An altogether new dimension to brown inferiority was added
when the missionaries arrived in 1820: the charge of heathenism.
Hiram Bingham made no bones about calling the natives of
Hawaii "those stupid, unlettered, unsanctified heathen tribes."
Naturally, equating racial ranking with religious ranking came as
easily: "The heathen system tends to immeasureable evil, but the
Christian system to immeasureable good." So also did comparing
the "barbarous" kanaka to children, according to the concept of
the "recapitulated" savage. He wondered, too, "By what means
shall the knowledge of arts and science be acquired by a nation so
stupid and ignorant, whose destitution seemed almost to forbid
their progress?" To his credit, he never conceded that Hawaiians
were ever so perverse as to be beyond the missionaries' ability to
convert to Christianity.

Sixty years after Captain Cook's visits, white men's perceptions
of Hawaiians were still the same. James Jackson Jarves, who
arrived in Hawai'i in 1837, wrote about "the barrenness of the
savage intellect" but hoped "contact of a better race must necessarily cause some improvement" in the natives. He observed, "Like all
branches of the Malay family, their perceptive and imitative facul-

ties are more developed than their reflective, which however cannot be said to be very deficient, though talent in the European sense is very rare." Sheldon Dibble, a contemporary of Jarves, complained in his own *History of the Sandwich Islands* about the lack of reasoning ability of a "heathen's mind." "It is an almost entire destitution of the power of reflection—of originating thought, or of carrying on a continuous chain of reasoning. Among the uneducated heathen (I speak not of those trained in schools), instances are very rare of those who have strength and discipline of mind enough to connect three links of a chain together, and come to a satisfactory conclusion. There are instances of native shrewdness that may surprise and startle you, but very little of the power of reasoning. They are just the opposite of what we call a thinking people."

But the historical record of the first hundred years of Western contact with Hawaiians is far more loaded with examples of an undisguised sense of white superiority, on the one hand, and of native inferiority, on the other. However well-meaning and sincere the early newcomers may have been, they could not have thought otherwise: they were "programmed" by at least two hundred years of racist reasoning, supported by divine and scientific authorities, to think of nonwhite primitives as savages or heathens.

Imagine, if you will, the effect these prejudices must have had on Hawaiians—as they met, year after year, those superlative specimens from the Western world, to be told in the most unqualified terms that they were inferior, stupid, unreasoning, and depraved and debauched to boot. How would you feel if, after having gone to bed one night, confident of your self-identity and assured in your self-esteem, you were to wake up the next morning with both body and spirit wracked by a bad dream of self-rejection, if not of self-destruction. To be sure, Hawaiians who were rooted in centuries of pride and confidence in their achievements did not simply fall over at the first sneer that they were "savage" or "heathen." Such words meant nothing to them—at first. But, as the accusations mounted, Hawaiians, who may have become victims of their own immemorial belief in the mana of the spoken word, eventually came to understand those hurtful epithets. When repeated often and long enough, even the most insidious and distorted ideas, provided they are accepted, can become part of one's perception of self. Thus, in time, many Hawaiians began to believe the unthinkable. The haoles, right in everything else, must have been right when they said that Hawaiians were inferior, stupid, irrational—indeed, heathen and savage. This response assuredly differed from individual to individual, but we are talking here about the collective consciousness of the Hawaiian people. This process of betrayal was abetted by the gradual alienation from their myths, rituals, priests, and gods, and by their own demoralization as a result of the relentless diminution of their numbers and their economic and political power. In chronological terms, all of this required decades to accomplish, but, in the broad sweep of human history, it might just as well have happened during one dark, hellish night.

Once they'd been firmly implanted in our consciousness as a people, these feelings have been transmitted among us from one generation to the next. It's been a vicious cycle, because subsequent perceptions of Hawaiian inferiority, such as the stereotyping of Hawaiians as "dumb" and "lazy," have only replaced the "savage" and "heathen" labels of the past. While many modern Hawaiians have broken out of this cycle, still too many others have not done so—too many, in fact, for even the most successful ones to feel secure about their collective identity as Hawaiians. In a sense, just as we relive so often the nightmares of our childhood, so do all modern Hawaiians, consciously or subconsciously, to one degree or another, continue to feel and fear those burdens of inferiority, negation, and rejection that oppressed our forefathers.

We can hope that this account of how the ghost was let loose among us will help us get rid of it, once and for all. What we must carefully guard against, however, is resorting to methods that in the end are self-defeating, such as the reverse racism which some young Hawaiians manifest today. In their excessive enthusiasm for the "renaissance" they flaunt their Hawaiianness. Almost as bad is the form of racism practiced among and between some Hawaiians, in which one calls another a "coconut," meaning brown on the outside and white on the inside, the local variant of Uncle Tomism. Above all, we must avoid unloading our resentment for the insults suffered during our race's history on those living today, whatever their race. To do so is to hold children guilty for the sins and mistakes of their parents, and that would be compounding one injustice with another even greater injustice. If we must vent our emotions, let them be in expressions of pity and regret for the stupidity and bigotry of racists and racism in whatever form, at any time, and anywhere, from whatever source.

One of the greater tragedies in our history lies in the fact that many postcontact Hawaiians believed in their racial and personal inferiority and therefore were ashamed of their ancestors' practices and ideas. We can understand now the psychological reasons for that shame, although we cannot accept their judgments about the quality of Hawaiian civilization in the days of old. Today we can demonstrate through a broad sweep of activities in the traditional Hawaiian culture—from religion and mythology, cosmology, time and space, philosophy, natural science, technology (from mechanics to mathematics), economics, management, to politics and leadership—that ka po'e kahiko, considering their historical period, location, population, and available natural resources, managed to achieve levels of development equal to and in many cases greater than those reached by comparable societies. In the light of those achievements, no Hawaiian today should feel or believe that the builders of ancient Hawai'i were inferior in any way to any other primal peoples.

This book is concerned indeed with a search for values. But it is also meant to be an awakening of awareness and a recapturing of pride in a noble heritage.

PART ONE

RELIGION, MYTHOLOGY, AND RITUAL

1

THE WORLD OF THE SACRED

The Time Machine

Suppose we are passengers in a time machine that is taking us back to Hawai'i in the year 1750. As we hover above the islands and peer out of our windows, the first man-made objects we see, because of their size, are the fish ponds and the heiau, or temples. Of the two, we are most impressed with the heiau because of their great bulk, diversity in shape, and number. Literally hundreds of them, in all sizes and shapes, rise from the land. Passing over the Ahupua'a Pu'uepa in Kokoiki, North Kohala, on the island of Hawai'i, we gaze down at one of the largest of all heiau, the Mo'okini Luakini, with its huge stone walls, 30 feet high, 15 feet wide at the base and 13 feet wide at the top, built in the shape of an irregular parallelogram, about 250 by 125 feet along the sides. Including the sacred spaces outside the walls, the total area exceeds 10 acres. We marvel not only at the engineering skills that went into erecting such a massive structure, but even more at the power of the motivation that commanded the energies of the populace. More than fifteen thousand men, we are told, built the temple between sunset and sunrise of a single night centuries ago. Even if legend has exaggerated the capacities of our ancestors, we should ask what kind of conviction would impel them to raise such a testimony to faith.

We move on, across the island, to inspect other temple sites and see, ranged around them, carved wooden images standing upright, like sentinels. In fact, they are so numerous that we cannot count them. We wonder how many master carvers spent how many hours, days, months, and years of labor in making the likenesses of the great gods Kū and Lono, and of lesser deities. We observe the priests, clad in robes of white kapa, conducting the sacred

ceremonies, some for commoners and others for chiefs. These rites
are well attended by males, since the penalty for not being present
is severe. We are fascinated by the mōhai rituals, or the sacrificing
of living things as offerings to the gods. We wonder again at the
large amount of resources—in manpower, animals, plants, time,
and thought—that are required to sustain these temples, the
priests, the whole "sacred technology."

We visit the kauhale, or residences of the people, and see the
family altars, smaller carved images, the offerings—as if all these
are miniature replicas of the greater heiau. We hear the prayers,
long, fervent pule, being intoned by the family elder to Lono and
Kāne and to the family 'aumākua. We witness the domestic kapu
in action—the men eating the offerings placed for the god Lono in
the ipu o Lono, which is suspended in a net in the hale mua, the
house that women never enter. We observe the women eating sepa-
rately, partaking of only certain foods, and see the coming together at night of men and women in the hale noa, which are free from
the kapu.

We are astonished by the elaborate, complex system of rules
that prescribes how men and women, chiefs and commoners, warriors and craftsmen, priests and worshipers, and all other folk
should behave at any given time and place. Yet we cannot help but
admire the discipline, orderliness, efficiency, and rhythm by which
each community seems to conduct its manifold affairs. We wonder
once more at the source of the power and genius that makes the
society work . . .

What our make-believe flight into the past should confirm is the
very important fact that the source of this power and genius is religion. Religion was the central authority of early Hawaiian society.
Apart from it, Hawai'i could not exist at all. Religion influenced,
if it did not control directly or indirectly, every phase of each person's individual and communal life, from birth to puberty, adulthood, marriage, death, and, at last, immortality. No activity of
any consequence lay outside the influence of the kāhuna, the kapu
they pronounced, the rituals, symbols, and myths of religion. It
dictated the content, tempo, direction, and destiny of the life of
every man, woman, and child. Religion enveloped nearly everything—the hula and mele, wars and games, planting and harvesting, healing and dying, dreaming and prophesying, and procreat-
ing. Life and religion were inseparably one.

The Secular Present

Two hundred years later, Hawai'i can hardly be called a theocracy. Religion and its supporting institutions have long since been pushed aside by business, labor, science, education, technology—even by television and a lot of other profane things. We live in the United States, a nation which is founded on a constitutional separation of church and state, wherein court decisions over the years (such as banning prayer from public schools) have made that division much wider. In a secular state, religious authorities wield little influence outside the walls of their churches. Among our major political and government leaders none are also "high priests" of religion. Many religious leaders, in fact, might share comedian Rodney Dangerfield's lament, "I don't get no respect." Furthermore, whether in the name of science or of technology, many of the basic religious beliefs—the ultimate whys of life—are more often than not being challenged, undermined, denied, and rejected. Ideologies from communism to capitalism offer new modes of salvation. Some people might say we live now in a society in which religion has been reduced to a Sunday charade or to a token ceremony at Christmastime or at Easter. Religion has become a sideshow rather than a drama occupying the center stage of our lives.

On the other hand, people in the United States are undergoing a revival in religious thinking and behavior. Thousands of new sects, independent of the major Catholic and Protestant denominations, such as the Rev. Robert Schuller's Chrystal Cathedral in Garden Grove, California, have mushroomed in the last few years. Across the country communities devoted to Eastern religions have sprung up, such as those of Hare Krishna and Nichiren, both fast gaining in members. In addition, "electronic religion" has grown enormously, with more than thirteen hundred stations and dozens of television channels devoting all or most of their air time to religion. Another indicator of the popularity of religion is that evangelical publishers now account for a third of the total domestic commercial book sales. And finally, probably no better proof of success can be found than the fact that this revival is being supported by billions of dollars drawn from the seemingly bottomless pockets of countless "born-again" people.

The state of Hawai'i is a microcosm of the United States and the general picture of religion throughout the nation no doubt exists here as well. The estimated 181,000 Hawaiians and part-Hawaiians who live in the islands today are probably as much a part of this picture as are any other ethnic group, for few of us are unaffected by the social, economic, and political currents of American life.

Yet, as heirs to a culture that once was so rich in religious values, we Hawaiians must ask ourselves whether we have retained any of those old concepts and values. We can hardly claim any meaningful identity with our native past if we recognize no religious legacy from that past. So the question is: are we still a religious people?

We received part of an answer from a kahu, or "Pastor," as he likes to be called, a modern kahuna, who wears the cloth of a Christian minister and who preaches Christ, yet still invokes the help of his 'aumakua, his ancestral guardian spirit or god. He speaks as casually about his "astral traveling" and annual conventions with long dead kāhuna from around Polynesia as he talks about computers and word processors. He serves a small congregation, but he also ministers to the sick, inmates in prison, students, and "the poor and the rich." Not all of his "flock" are Hawaiians; he finds himself increasingly drawn to people of other ethnic backgrounds as they are to him. He is a fascinating blend of the old Hawaiian and the new universal values.

A man with definite opinions on a seemingly limitless number of subjects, he was asked what he thought of the religious position of Hawaiians today. Drawing from his personal experience of working for many years with Hawaiians as individuals, groups, and congregations, he concluded that they are not as religious now as their kūpuna had been, but that in many ways they still are a religious or spiritual people. He pointed to his success in developing his own ministry (not to mention the evidences of success in that ministry, such as a business office), the upsurge in interest among Hawaiians in traditional religious ideas and practices (although he was quick to warn of persons who "did not know anything," in other words, charlatans), and the general air of revivalism.

We probed the same topic in our Ho'okanaka workshops and the solid consensus from all the groups was that Hawaiians still tend to be religiously or spiritually "oriented," and that one of the more important Hawaiian values was and is ho'omana, or "spirituality." But when we got down to specific beliefs and practices, there was not much consensus. The kumu hula who talked about communing with spirits in the forest elicited less than enthusiastic reaction from some people who hold no truck with "animism." The tūtū who told stories about kahuna ʻanāʻanā and flying fireballs got signs of disbelief from younger participants. In fact, none of the workshop participants preferred the term "religious" over "spirituality," yet none would dispute the fact that we were dealing with a religious culture.

If one detects notes of dissonance in these discussions, it's because that's the way the music is being played these days. In other words, our situation of finding links between the past and present is like playing an arrangement in counterpoint, with two or more independent melodies that are supposed to end up sounding like one harmonized piece—except that it doesn't always sound right. After two hundred years and more of cultural change and exchange, we can expect a lot of counterpoint—and some dissonance. There are many reasons for this, but one pivotal factor is that we can find relatively little agreement about what our major terms mean, beginning with religion.

The Essence of Religion

Religion is a troublesome word to define, for there are probably as many attempts at definition as there are religions in the world. At last count, there were twenty-two thousand! Finding features common to all is nearly impossible, inasmuch as what is "good" for one, may well be anathema to another. Some religions, for example, reject supernatural beings, sacraments, priests, prophets, revelations, miracles, temples, icons, angels, and so on, just as others could not exist without them. Yet, since religion is so integral a part of human history and culture, something about it must be shared in common by most human beings. It must appeal to some fundamental, deep-seated need or feeling in human beings, whatever their circumstances. And what is that something?

It is the sense of the sacred, our feeling for the extraordinary, the mysterious, the supernatural, the numenous. The essence of religion is the fundamental capacity of human beings for experiencing this feeling of holiness, just as, in other responses, they have the capacity for experiencing love or hate, sympathy or terror. Strip away all the accouterments—the robes, altars, chapels, scriptures, ministers, music, and evangelical preachings—and what remains as the irreducible component of all religion is this sense of the sacred.

Rudolph Otto, the Protestant theologian, who is credited with having done the major study on this aspect in his book *The Idea of the Holy*, said:

> It first begins to stir in the feeling of "something uncanny," "eerie," or "weird." It is this feeling which, emerging in the mind of primitive man, forms the starting-point for the entire development of religion in history. "Daemons" and "Gods" alike spring from this root, and all the products of "mythological fantasy" are nothing but different modes in which it has been objectified, and all ostensible explanations of the origin of religion in terms of animism or magic or folk psychology are doomed from the outset to wander astray and miss the real goal of their inquiry, unless they recognize this fact of our nature—primary, unique, underivable from anything else—to be the basic factor and the basic impulse underlying the entire process of religious evolution.

It is difficult to make the point any stronger and more uncompromising than that.

The same point is made by a scientist, Julian Huxley, the famed English biologist and philosopher, who was thought by some people to be against religion and an atheist. He defined religion as "a way of life which follows necessarily from a man's holding certain things in reverence, from his feeling and believing them to be sacred. And those things which are held sacred by religion primarily concern human destiny and the forces with which it comes into contact." From his biopsychological point of view, he said this feeling for the sacred is innate, part of our genetic stock as human beings. Thus, a person's feeling for the sacred is just as natural as is his or her feeling for colors, heat or cold, and similar responses to physical phenomena.

Instead of the term "sacred," others have used the term "supernatural." For example, Professor Wilson D. Wallis in his book *Religion in Primitive Society* wrote, "The supernatural is a primary and fundamental element in religion, for men spontaneously react to phenomena which they deem supernatural. Religious attitude, that is, emotional, ritualized, or rationalized response to the supernatural, characterizes *all cultures and every stage of history* [italics added]." Some modern Hawaiians reject the term when discussing Hawaiian religion because, to them, all phenomena in nature are "natural." But, in our view, the term supernatural refers not to the unnaturalness of sacred phenomena but to the hiddenness of their naturalness from our common sense perspective. It may also refer to the power that is the ultimate source of things, before they become apparent as natural phenomena.

Interestingly, in 1909 an English anthropologist, Robert R. Marett, chose the term mana to describe the sacred or holy. He argued that the Polynesian "meaning of *mana* justifies its use as a term of wide application, covering all manifestations of mysterious, or supernatural, power in magic and religion alike. Science, then, may adopt *mana* as a general category to designate the positive aspect of the supernatural, or sacred, or whatever we are to call that order of miraculous happenings which . . . is marked off perceptibly from the order of ordinary happenings."

Paradoxically, premodern Hawaiians did not have a word for religion as such, but when they decided to make one up—or, more likely, to apply an existing word to the newly introduced Western concept—the word they chose was "ho'omana." Unknown to Dr. Marett, of course, Hawaiians agreed that religion could best be described as the awareness of mana—the supernatural, divine power.

In sum, when we speak of religion, we begin, at the very least, with acknowledging the human capacity for feeling dimensions of the sacred however it is manifested or perceived: whether in the technicolor beauty of a sunset, the cosmic grandeur of the galaxies, the miraculous healing of the sick, the perfected grace of a dance, the awesome force of a volcano's eruption, the delicate structure of a butterfly's wings, the mystery of life at the birth of a child, or the revelation of divinity itself. We all have this capacity, and to that extent we are all religious.

Thus, to understand Hawaiian religion, we must somehow come to an understanding of the Hawaiian world of the sacred. Reading words printed on paper is undoubtedly the poorest way for considering the apprehending of the mysterious, but, under the circumstances, it is the only feasible way.

The World of the Sacred

We must recognize a vital difference between what we today mean as sacred as compared with what Hawaiians of old meant as sacred. We can clarify this difference by considering the psychology involved. When we call something sacred, we do so with a mixture of awe, wonder, admiration, or fear. When Hawaiians of old thought of the sacred their responses involved those same emotions but also included potency, danger, prohibition as well. The difference is what constitutes the meaning of kapu, probably the most powerful regulator of human thought and behavior in ancient Hawaiian society.

We today would consider only a few things sacred, but in old Hawai'i, a bewildering number of things could be held as kapu: stones, ancestors' bones, trees, animals, images, altars, chants, names, places, canoes, priests, chiefs and their belongings, and so on. Also, the degree of kapu could differ from object to object; indeed, the kapu, or sanctity of an object, could be ended, at which it became noa, or free of kapu. Fortunately, by far the greatest number of things were noa, or, in Western terms, "profane."

Everything that related to the gods and the spirit world or the hereafter was kapu. For example, the great chiefs with the purest bloodlines, who could trace their lineage back to Wākea and Papa, the Father God and the Mother God, "with no small names" among more recent ancestors, were regarded as living akua, deities invested with the greatest amount of mana. So kapu were they that any lesser person whose shadow fell upon them or upon anything that belonged to them—a house, a piece of clothing, or even a spitoon—was put to death, no questions asked. Malo wrote that "when a tabu chief ate, the people in his presence must kneel, and if any one raised his knee from the ground, he was put to death. If any man put forth in a *kioloa* (a long, swift racing canoe) at the same time as the tabu chief, the penalty was death."

In our democratic age, we may think this rather harsh, if not abominable and inhuman treatment. But, then, let us get back in our time machine. For the Hawaiian, "divine" power, or mana, was the greatest reality, the most potent force and the most dangerous. Touching a chief, eating his food, or anything similarly intrusive, could make the offender sick, possibly unto death, because he became contaminated with supernatural power. The effect was not unlike Paul's encounter on the way to Damascus with the light of God, which was so powerful that it blinded him. Exposure to radioactive fall-out may be a more modern metaphor.

From the chief's point of view, he had to protect his sanctity from being defiled by a noa person, because that could cause him to lose his mana. The supernatural force in him would be drained away, at least in part, by such contact. Thus, the kapu was designed to protect not only the chief but the innocent retainer as well.

Being one of these highest chiefs was not easy. They led restricted lives, "entirely exclusive, being hedged about with many tabus" of their own. As a rule, for instance, they went about only at night and so were called "nocturnal chiefs" (ke ali'i o pō). A few, trying to escape the constraints of rank, went into the countryside in disguise, and sometimes had to endure very ungodly experiences. Not recognizing such pretenses, the country folk would order them to fetch water or do other odd jobs, and even called them by "country names." As a matter of fact, so restricted were their movements, according to Malo, that many commoners never even saw any of those highest chiefs.

Many lesser pedigreed chiefs had no important kapu. Such were the ali'i lalolalo, a man enriched by a chief with a gift of land, or an ali'i lepo pōpolo, literally a "black dirt chief," one of lowborn status. An ali'i kauholopapa, a clothes-rack-chief, knew that he had some small amount of ali'i blood and on that account could not allow his clothing to be put on the same frame or rack as that of a lower person.

The priests, especially when carrying out their formal duties, were very kapu. Any person in the prayer circle at any of the special rituals for the opening of a luakini heiau who moved from the prescribed position during the priest's intoning could be put to death. As we shall see later, a good reason required this strict obedience, because the ritual was supposed to reenact what the gods had done in an earlier time, and was performed in the potent presence of the gods. Any mistake not only displeased the gods but endangered the lives of everyone participating in the ceremony.

The sanctity or kapu of a person or object was not permanent. A chief who was defeated in battle and taken captive (although most were killed either in combat or in sacrifice) would lose his mana and kapu. A kapu on a hālau or a canoe could be removed, that is, it was made noa, by a special ceremony. A priest could weaken and lose his kapu if he did not avoid certain foods or sexual activity before performing certain significant rituals.

Some animals, such as important birds and fishes, could be regarded as kapu not for any specific god-related reason but for practical economic reasons. ʻŌpelu and aku, for example, were protected by kapu during the spawning season, and only priests were allowed to open the fishing season. Clearly, this kapu was a conservation measure. The ʻelepaio bird (a flycatcher) was sacred, revered by canoe makers, because it pecked at tree trunks in search of insects and thereby indicated whether a tree was sound enough to make a good canoe. A popular saying was *"Ua ʻelepaio ʻia ka waʻa,"* or "The canoe is marked by the ʻelepaio."

Hawaiians are not unusual for revering birds. Navahos and other American Indian tribes still revere the eagle and hawk, and will not kill them. If its feathers are needed, an eagle may be trapped and its feathers are plucked, but the bird will be released. The feathers in turn are used for ornaments, headdresses, and other objects that are sacred. Waterfowl, shore birds, hummingbirds, bats, crows, and buzzards are other flying creatures that different Indian tribes deem sacred. Aztecs venerated the eagle and Egyptians and Ethiopians the ibis. Maoris employed several species of birds in rites conducted at a village shrine, a burial cave, and at the opening and naming of a new fort. The miromiro was used as a messenger in certain love charms. In short, almost every religious culture has made certain birds sacred.

Plants, as might be expected in an agricultural society, commanded a great deal of attention. The more useful the plant, the more attention it got. The hala, or pandanus, breadfruit, coconut, sweet potato, and taro were personified as kino lau, or body forms, of provident gods, and were featured in many myths and legends.

Martha Beckwith's observation is noteworthy: "Vegetable growth is regarded by Hawaiians with more religious awe than animal life." She explained that animal life is less "intimately" related to people than plants, a recognition which is especially true of an agricultural economy. Besides, Hawaiʻi had few domesticated animals—only the pig, dog, chicken, and rat, all introduced by the first Polynesian immigrants. Had Hawaiians been a hunting society, dependent on animals for food and other necessities, animals would have been given more attention. This is precisely what happened among such hunting peoples as the Eskimo, Apache, and Cree of North America, and the Ainu of Japan (who may have regarded some animals as superior even to man).

Individual trees, and whole forests, too, could be considered kapu. The ʻōhiʻa lehua tree was revered by canoe builders, because it was the manifestation of the god Kūkaʻōhiʻalaka, but also because it happened to be an excellent hardwood for making canoes. Entering a forest too early was kapu, because doing so might disturb the resident spirits who protected the trees.

Special objects were very sacred; such were the "mythological heirlooms," which belong to the gods rather than to people. A good example of this is the sacred pū (conch trumpet) named Kihapū. It was given into the care of the father of Liloa, the fifteenth-century progenitor of the dynasty of great chiefs on the Big Island of Hawaiʻi.

Certain stones were held as sacred partly because of their connection with god forms. One such stone was Kānepōhakukaʻa. Sometimes they were set up as gods for presiding over certain types of games.

Stories of sacred stones abound in other primal cultures too. The Jibaros, a South American tribe, believe that certain small brown stones of peculiar shape promote the growth of plants. The stones contain portions of the soul of Earth-mother, and hence some of her power. Other Indians worship so-called lightning-stones, meteorites, stone axes, and other stone implements, all of which have some supernatural force. Bantu tribes and Hottentots of South Africa thought that stones, because of their hardness, possessed supernatural power and could be used to drive away evil spirits. The Maori believe that stones, being endowed with sex, can mate and produce children. This belief is familiar to Hawaiians, who gathered ʻiliʻili hānau, reproducing stones, at the seashore near Punaluʻu in Kaʻū, Hawaiʻi.

Many places were kapu, such as a spot in a forest, a promontory, a rocky seashore, or a mountain associated with a mythical event or an akua. Kaʻena Point, on Oʻahu, was kapu because it is supposed to be one of the places where spirits departed this earth for the underworld. "Storied places," or wahi pana, were regarded as holy because of some association with a family ʻaumakua, or guardian spirit. Of course heiau, household temples, shrines, burial sites, places of refuge, and chiefs' residences also were sacred.

Of all the sacred places, none evoked the kind of awe as did planet earth and the cosmos beyond. We may gaze at the heavens with "cosmic awe," but for many people today the awe is reserved for our scientific and technological abilities. In contrast, when the Hawaiians of old gazed up at the heavens, they felt the true awe for the sacred, for they worshiped the distant heavenly bodies as the veritable bodies of their gods. Not only was the cosmos an object of supreme reverence, but it was also regarded as the Mysterious Mover of human events, capable of revealing the destinies of chiefs and commoners alike. Thus, in many ways, cosmic awe transcended the feelings for the sacred that might have been held for other lesser things.

To recapitulate, we all see the world through our "mind's eye," the set of ideas and conceptions that is the gift of our society. What the Hawaiians saw through their mind's eye was divided into two realms: the sacred—the extraordinary, supernatural, all-powerful, the kapu—and the profane—the ordinary, natural, common, the noa. While much of the world is noa, the sacred is the realm that defines its inner and outer boundaries. Although potent and dangerous, and therefore unapproachable by the ordinary person, paradoxically, the sacred is the most real, because it is the most powerful.

Nonetheless, ancient Hawaiians constructed their sacred world in such a manner that they were not overwhelmed and rendered numb and ineffective by their own creation. On the contrary, it was by and large a very well-ordered, practical, and efficient world: well-ordered because of their imperative need to impose some control over the unpredictable and uncontrollable forces of nature, and practical because their survival depended on the best and most efficient way of using the available resources. This may not be the way we normally think of things that are sacred or mysterious, but one of the marks of Hawaiian thought is the success with which they equated the sacred with the organized ideal. This adaptation is shown in the very word kapu, with its double meanings, referring to both the sacred property in a thing and to the law or prohibition that guards it.

Take, for example, the kapu regulating fishing seasons, or planting methods, or the disposing of human wastes. All of these rules were practical ways of respecting the sacred while still adapting it to serve utilitarian purposes. Indeed, the kapu system was a simple but ingenious approach to elicit respect and compliance from people. After all, what higher authority could be invoked in gaining public respect and obedience than the supernatural power incarnate in the very gods? As it became ultimately a matter of conscience, the kapu was a self-regulating system in which "the idea of the holy" acted as the policing and enforcement arms of society. In effect, the whole kapu system, with its rules and penalties, was an elaborate codification of laws governing interpersonal relationships as well as those between gods and human beings. Not much was left to chance or whim in matters of religious import.

Even the remote gods and the living akua were not above the law of order implicit in the construction of this world of the sacred. As we shall see, gods could be done away with if they failed to fulfill their promises. Chiefs who were defeated in battle or who flagrantly violated the principles of pono, right conduct, could lose their mana and position. Priests, too, could lose their holiness by disobeying the rules of the ritual or of pono.

Thus, an unmistakable and ruthless efficiency entered into the way Hawaiians of old dealt with the world of the sacred. We note this, for example, in the close correspondence between the usefulness of an object and the degree of its sanctity. The plants, trees, animals, fishes, and other natural resources that were used the most were treated with the greatest amount of reverence. On the other hand, those that were less beneficial, were treated more casually. This also had economic implications, because the "price" of an object was based partly on its sacred value. Thus, the feather capes, the most precious material objects in old Hawai'i, were regarded as extremely kapu, and therefore only the highest members of the nobility could wear them. We shall explore this interesting relationship between sacred value and economic value in a later chapter.

The respectful mind, perforce a religious mind, developed important attitudes and values regarding orderliness, neatness, preciseness, even a sense of perfection. In contrast, to the modern and westernized Hawaiian mind such values are more likely to be commonly associated with the secular world of industry, government, business, science, and the military. We think of these values,

for example, when we are balancing budgets, achieving organizational objectives, getting optimal performances from men and
women or machines, keeping the staff productive, and so forth,
but not when we are involved in some religious pursuit, whether it
be in private prayer or at a baptism. Religion was certainly not the
only source of these values for Hawaiians of old, but it was an
important source.

If a lesson is to be learned from these contrasting views, perhaps
it is that whereas we tend to distance ourselves from the world of
the sacred as being something "eerie" and "uncanny," and therefore
irrelevant and impractical, the traditional Hawaiian embraced his
kapu world and, in doing so, was able to make it much more
meaningful and beneficial to his life. We moderns, it seems, are too
uneasy, too uncomfortable, with the sacred. What we need to do,
for our sanity's sake, is to relearn and rediscover that healing
capacity and sensitivity possessed by ka poʻe kahiko, the people
of old.

Symbols: The Language of the Sacred

Unless one understands and speaks the language of the sacred,
however, the world it tries to report remains forever in the eerie
distance. Thus, for Hawaiians of old, religious or sacred symbolism served a far more vital function than it does for the secularized
people of today. We take for granted that we live in a world of
symbols which are necessary but generally inadequate in conveying the meanings of the objects or the phemonema they represent.
We recognize that words, whether spoken or written, are symbols
of things or ideas, that the shapes and figures we use in mathematics, buildings, dance, or graphic art are symbolic, and that even
the most concrete objects, whether a phallic rock or a constellation of stars, can assume symbolic significance. But for the most
part we look upon the world of sacred symbolism today with an
odd or casual interest at best. In contrast, the traditional Hawaiian took the offerings of sacred symbolism—the poetic imagery,
the allusions, metaphors, double meanings or kaona—much more
seriously and much more accurately. In primal cultures in which
rationalism yields to spiritual forces, meaningful symbolism is
characteristic of their art and religion.

For primal peoples, symbol is the raw material, what Walter

Brenneman calls the "first form," out of which they build their religion. That is to say, the mind of man cannot construct a sacred world unless or until he has conceived a form to put it in. Thus, the gods he creates are created not in his human image, but, more precisely, in the form of the symbols that man produces to represent them. When form and god come together, the symbolic embodiment of divine power is achieved. In this sense, symbol is creative when power takes on form.

The idea that symbols are the stuff out of which religion is made coincides with the Hawaiian's belief in the power in words. Like all Polynesians and all primal peoples the world around, he believed that certain words when spoken have a power of their own. The conventional explanation is that its force comes from the sound that is "breathed" into the word, thereby giving it life. The idea is that when we speak words, we use our breath in making the sounds, and breath is life-giving. Through the hā, or breath, we infuse mana into the sound, hence, the meaning or intent of the word. But quite apart from the sound, the thought represented in the word has symbolic significance as well. The notion that the word-thought has a power of its own suggests that it also has an existence of its own, which is not unlike Plato's concept of the existence of ideas as independent objective realities.

For the Hawaiian believer, all religious symbols point to things that are sacred, and at the same time participate in what they symbolize. For example, iwi, or human bones, were sacred because they symbolized immortality, for, unlike ephemeral flesh, they remain intact for a very long time. The bones of the dead were "guarded, respected, treasured, venerated, loved or even deified by relatives"—or seized and despoiled by enemies of the dead man or of his family. Like the tooth of the Buddha, or the relics of Catholic saints, bones were believed (at least among the laity) to have sacred power. Examples of such venerated relics abound in Hawaiian traditional religion, and some are still respected today.

An important aspect of Hawaiian belief in symbolism maintains that, whatever power such objects might possess, that power is not released until one's psyche engages it. In other words, the efficacy of symbolic power is a function of belief or faith in the symbol. This relationship parallels the relationship between man as creator and the products of his creation—gods, myths, and rituals —which live and die according to the will of man. Consider

Pūku'i's comment (Pūku'i, Haertig, and Lee) on how people treated supposedly sacred stones: "Sometimes people have these stones that help them, but when a stone becomes troublesome, they take it out to sea, drop it, then turn right around and never look back."

The pervasive influence of symbolism is easily shown in the way Hawaiians viewed dreams. Today some people may regard dreams as "wish fulfillments" (Freud), or as "those flimsy, evasive, unreliable, vague and uncertain fantasies" (Jung). Still others think dreams are simply neurobiological phenomena without any meaning. For Hawaiians of old, dreams were visions of another reality, parallel to those seen in the waking world. That is, the mind in dream produces symbols which have causal or purposive meanings, with some definite relationship to reality. Like other Polynesians, Hawaiians believed that dreams were caused usually by the movements of one's 'uhane, or spirit, or by the 'aumākua. But some dreams might be caused by physiological reactions, for example to eating a particular food, or by deep subconscious desires, as in wishing for some object or outcome. Whatever the cause, dreams with all their symbolism greatly affected the everyday life of Hawaiians. They revealed the future, solutions to problems, hidden places and lost persons, past events, warnings of disaster, and a host of other things. Revelatory dreams, or hō'ike na ka pō (literally, "exhibits of the night"), usually involved messages from ancestral gods who "spoke clearly or in allusion . . . appeared visually in any of their mystical plant, animal, or mineral forms [or] hid their appearance in symbol and allegory" (Pūku'i, Haertig, and Lee). Anyone who ignored their messages did so at some peril to himself, inasmuch as dreams were regarded as valid forms of communication between men and gods. All this, of course, strikes a familiar chord with biblical students, recalling the prophetic dreams of characters in the Old and New Testaments.

If dreams are made out of the stuff of symbols, then the key to understanding and interpreting those dreams is knowing what the symbols mean. Hence, among Hawaiian occupational specialists were the trained kāhuna who understood the process of dreams and who knew and could interpret the symbols revealed in dream language. Dr. John F. McDermott, Jr., of the department of psychiatry at the University of Hawai'i's John A. Burns School of Medicine, stated: "Hawaiians had a remarkable understanding of the nature of dreams, and to an extent, the very process of dreaming" (Pūku'i, Haertig, and Lee). They recognized various levels of dreamlike states, that eating a certain fish might trigger nightmares (the fish is weke pahulu, or goatfish, which contains certain special amino acids), that dreams are caused by behavior during the previous day (or what is called in modern psychiatry "day residue"), and so on.

With dream symbolism being so much a part of daily life, probably every Hawaiian had to understand it to some degree or other. A Hawaiian, then, had to be bilingual: he had to speak his native tongue, of course, but he also had to "speak" the language of symbols as well. It was essential in order to function not only socially or psychologically, but also religiously as well.

We know little about this "second" Hawaiian language, because much information about it has been lost or garbled, but some of the vocabulary is familiar to us. Wai, or fresh water, for example, represents purification, and was used in ritual cleansing baths. If sea water was used, the ritual was called kapu kai. Sometimes simple sprinkling rites were followed, using fresh water or salt water and a frond of the pala fern. Salt and, to a lesser extent, fire were also symbolic of purification. Expressions of height, or any of its extensions, such as lofty, sublime, heaven, firmament, and so on, all symbolized superiority, hence, royalty, the gods, or the sacred. Deities, for instance, dwelled in lewa lani, the highest stratum of space, and 'io, the hawk, is symbolic of royalty because of the altitudes to which it can soar. Height is almost a universal symbol not only as it applies to deity, but also to the value or worth of something, as in the expression for achievement, kūlia i ka nu'u, meaning literally, "climb to the top." Related to the world above is light, or ao, which stood for awareness, knowledge, or enlightenment, as in the term na'auao, which also can mean intelligence or wisdom. Light probably is as widely distributed a symbol among cultures as height is. Less universal or more localized symbols include the gourd, which in dreams symbolized man: the filled gourd is the living man, and the broken or empty gourd is the dead. In rituals, the gourd represented the body of Lono. Another was the color black, hiwa (also hiwahiwa), which is identified with Lono, the god of rain and hence of the black rain clouds laden with moisture. Thus, the pig used in offerings and sacrifices to Lono was always black. The symbolism goes further, however, for one of

Lono's body forms, or kino lau, is Kamapua'a, the pig god. The black pig was the choicest food of the mythic gods and of the nobility. Hawaiian symbolism takes off in many directions when one dwells on linkages among kino lau. To illustrate: Kamapua'a has both plant and sea forms, such as hinupua'a (a variety of banana), 'ama'ama (mullet), kūmū (a reddish fish), and limu līpu'upu'u (a green seaweed). While much of this symbolic variety may mean little to us today, it clearly had enormous spiritual and practical relevance for Hawaiians of old. Knowing the kino lau symbolism for Lono, for instance, enabled one to make the right substitutions for the pua'a hiwa, black pig, in offerings meant for Lono. Similarly, knowing the kino lau symbols for one's 'aumakua meant that you could avoid risking the displeasure of your ancestral god by mistakenly eating one of his forms. Being aware of the meaning of dream symbols could save a lot of psychological pilikia, or anxiety, not to mention punishments of other kinds, both spiritual and physical.

In sum, myth communicates with us through the medium of language, but what it communicates—messages about things sacred—often defies the power of ordinary language to convey. Therefore the language of myth is wrapped in metaphors, poetic images, similies, allegories, word play, or kaona—symbolism that can convey the mystical experience through what we might call its "subliminal reach," that is, its ability to tap the subconscious faculty of understanding. While the language of myth has a consistency and logic of its own, it transcends rules of logic; while it has common sense, it makes uncommon sense; while it has a technique, it is never technically exact; while it must be definable, it deals with the undefinable—with what "surpasseth all human understanding"—with the world of the sacred that binds and connects all things to its center.

2

THE REALITY
OF MYTHOLOGY

Myth Is Not Myth

Mythology tells about the world of the sacred, the supernatural, about the gods and their deeds. To Hawaiians of old, their mythology was the most important of their creations—and the most real. So it was and is with all peoples and cultures. Joseph Campbell, one of the world's leading authorities on myth, wrote in his brilliant book *The Hero with a Thousand Faces*:

> Throughout the inhabited world, in all times and under every circumstance, the myths of man have flourished; and they have been the living inspiration of whatever else may have appeared out of the activities of the human body and mind. It would not be too much to say that myth is the secret opening through which the inexhaustible energies of the cosmos pour into human cultural manifestations. Religions, philosophies, arts, the social forms of primitive and historic man, prime discoveries in science and technology, the very dreams that blister sleep, boil up from the basic, magic ring of myth.

In spite of the achievements coming forth from this old "science," many people today still regard myth as something false or fabricated. To speak of myth to the average person is to evoke images in him of monsters or superheroes performing fantastic and unbelievable feats in the cosmos, and other such visions of superhuman power. In short, myth is usually taken to mean the "unreal," "fantasy," and the "make-believe"—it has nothing to do with the real, concrete, practical, empirical world we know.

But if we are to understand the concepts, practices, and related values of traditional and modern Hawaiians, we must expunge from our minds the notion of myth as falsehood. If we do not do this, we cannot be honest and effective in our search for Hawaiian values, because in myth we find the primeval source and rationale of Hawaiian religion, the fountainhead of our ideals.

For some if not most modern Hawaiians, however, particularly among the older generation, this process of liberating themselves from the idea of myth as falsehood may not be easy. The difficulty does not lie in semantics, the meanings of words, but in emotions —in being psychologically comfortable with a subject that can generate all kinds of mixed feelings. Many adult Hawaiians, for instance, grew up in an atmosphere both at home and beyond it that generally scorned the old mythology. Parents and grandparents who were or are Christians know little or nothing about Hawaiian mythological traditions, and either say nothing about them or dismiss them as "silly," "old-fashioned," "foolish" ideas or, more often than not, as "superstitions." When pressed by an eager inquirer, the kūpuna refuse to talk about the subject either out of fear or antipathy toward what they now believe to be things inspired by the Devil or bad kāhuna. (I can remember my Mormon father behaving precisely in this way when asked a question about traditional Hawaiian religious beliefs.)

Furthermore, ministers and teachers in churches, including some Hawaiian churches, praise the tenets and practices of Christianity, but often condemn the "heathen" rituals of the past with the kind of virulence and fanaticism typical of the convert. Moreover, teachers and others in schools invariably impress upon young minds the fairy-tale aspects of Hawaiian mythology. Whether dealing with the menehune, the Shark God, Pele, Kamapua'a, and other legendary figures, they stress the make-believe and fanciful aspects of the "stories," not the deep and sacred symbolism underlying them.

The minds of many adult Hawaiians are encrusted with layers of decidedly ambivalent feelings toward the myths of the past. Overcoming such feelings in order to gain a positive and sympathetic approach to reevaluating the ancient mythology may involve some emotionally wrenching experiences; indeed, for a few, the ambivalence (like the "ghost of inferiority") may have to be submitted to treatment resembling exorcism.

Of course, the experience of alienation from and rejection of the primal myths is hardly peculiar to Hawaiians. In the history of religion, almost all peoples at one time or another reject an old belief to accept a new gospel. Many people do not realize that conversion does not necessarily mean a rejection of mythology as such, but only the substitution of one for another.

But as we examine now in retrospect the values of our past, we need to understand why the old mythology played such a dynamic role in the past, and how it has influenced and continues to influence the thoughts and values of modern Hawaiians. The persistence of feelings of ambivalence, skepticism, guilt, or shame should not prevent anyone from examining again the sacred mythology of the 'āina o nā akua, the land of the gods.

The Sacred Reality

What is myth? What did it mean to ka po'e kahiko?

The Trobrianders are a small group of Melanesians who live in the Trobriand Islands in the Solomon Sea. They are the subject of one of the landmark books on Pacific anthropology, written by Bronislaw Malinowski. In 1948 he described how the natives thought about myth. "[It is] a special class of story regarded as sacred, embodied in ritual, morals, and social organization, and constituting an integral and effective part of religion and magic. These stories do not live by idle interest; they are not narrated as historical accountants of ordinary facts. They are to the natives a statement of a higher and more important truth, of a primeval reality." Studies of other Pacific island cultures bear out this view of native islanders that myth is real.

The Hungarian-born scholar, Mircea Eliade, who has spent a lifetime studying the mythology of cultures all over the world, gave us a comprehensive look at myth as it is experienced by traditional or "archaic" societies. In 1963 he wrote that: (1) generally myths constitute the history of the acts of gods or "supernaturals"; (2) this history is regarded as being absolutely *true* and *sacred* because it is concerned with the actions of the gods which are both realities and supernatural; (3) this history is always related to a "creation" of something by telling how that something came into existence, or how a pattern of behavior, an institution, a manner of working were established; (4) by knowing the myth one knows the "origin" of things and hence can control and manipulate them at will; and (5) in one way or another a person "lives" the myth, in the sense that he or she is seized by the sacred, the holy, the exalting power of the events recollected or reenacted.

"Living a myth" implies a genuinely "religious" experience, since it differs from the ordinary experience of everyday life. This religious experience is due to the fact that a person reenacts "exalted" events or witnesses enactments of the creative deeds of the gods, and in so doing ceases to exist in the everyday world and enters a "transfigured" world permeated with the presence of the "supernaturals." Eliade concluded, "In short, myths reveal that the World, man, and life have a supernatural origin and history, and that this history is significant, precious, and exemplary."

In sum, a myth is a sacred narrative that above all things tells us about the gods and their deeds, because they represent reality. That is, nothing is more real than what the gods say or do. Myth, therefore, deals only with what really *is* or what has already happened. It is concerned with the beginnings of the world, the primal past, and sometimes with the "dramatic breakthroughs of the sacred" or what might be called the "miraculous." Myth focuses on ritual and symbols because they breathe life into the abstract retelling. It deals with the whole of the cosmos, nature, or just a fragment of reality—an island, a species of plant or animal, a particular kind of human behavior, an institution, or an event. Myth is also about power, or mana, and the laws that determine human destiny.

Sometimes, however, myth is confused with some rationalized explanation about natural phenomena. It should not be taken as a "primitive science" that seeks to explain the facts and mysteries of the universe. Malinowski observed that primal peoples had their science and their religion, which were of course two different things, since myth does not explain nature but rather only regulates human actions.

Mo'olelo

The Hawaiian term for myth is mo'olelo, consisting of two root terms. Mo'o means a series or succession, especially of a genealogical line, and 'ōlelo means tongue or language. Traditionally, mo'olelo referred to a true narrative either about historical figures or about the gods, or both. Insofar as it tells of the akua, it is a sacred story—a true myth. However, the word was also used to refer to secular narratives dealing with folklore, such as legends and family stories. Although they were often based on historical and factual accounts, they were not holy or sacred. This dual use of the word suggests that perhaps the line between the secular story and the sacred story was not always clearly drawn.

A superb example of a Hawaiian myth is *The Kumulipo*, as recorded by King Kalākaua, which, interestingly enough, is not called a mo'olelo but a pule ho'ola'a, or "sacred prayer." If we compare its basic elements with Eliade's formula, we find a very good fit. *The Kumulipo* tells of: (1) the deeds of the akua, or "supernaturals"; (2) the creation and hence the beginnings of primordial time; (3) the origins of things in nature; (4) historical personages of chiefly rank; (5) their genealogical links with the gods; and (6) some of the values that supported the existing socioreligious order.

We include under this general classification of mo'olelo the mele, or chant, although nowadays the mele is often thought of as being part of Hawaiian music rather than of mythology. The repertoire of the mele includes three types of sacred chant: (1) mele ko'ihonua, or genealogy chant, such as *The Kumulipo*; (2) mele kānaenae, or a prayer of supplication and praise to a god; and (3) mele pule, or prayer chant. The last kind is most numerous and includes mele pule kala, a prayer for protection from evil; mele pule ho'oulu, an appeal for divine inspiration; mele pule kāhea, an invocation of family gods; and mele pule ho'omaika'i, a prayer of thanks.

Not all chants were sacred, for, like secular mo'olelo, many deal with popular themes such as amusements, games, sports, and so on. In Martha Beckwith's book *Hawaiian Mythology* (1970), for example, many, if not most, of the stories are secular tales, some of which teem with monsters, ghosts, animals endowed with human powers, weird and magical adventures. Some of these stories, like the Trickster tales about Māui, and those that deal with mo'o (lizard) or manō (shark) themes, are known far and wide throughout Polynesia, while others were recited only in Hawai'i or were limited to one island or place in Hawai'i.

The Process of Mythmaking

While it may sound romantic and mysterious to say that the origins of our myths are enshrouded in the beginnings of our primeval past, or something to that effect, they probably had far more prosaic beginnings. Possibly certain events or concepts refer back to some unknown source, but the actual making of the story or narrative could have been initiated in several simple w.ays. A high chief, eager to have his genealogy validated by the gods, might have composed a mythic chant or have outlined his ideas to a professional composer, a haku mele, to put it all together. Or a highly regarded kahuna haku mele, on his own accord and with the approval of his fellow priests, might have taken the initiative to compose a story. Possibly, too, a council of people from the court, or priests, prophets, and other prominent specialists might have convened a meeting to decide what traditions, stories, concepts, and so on that may have been subjects of conversation should be formalized in chants. Or a solitary prophet, after years of living like a "hermit" (as Malo described one such man) might have come out with a "revelation" of his own. Other possibilities for creation exist. But regardless of authorship, none of these myths would have included anything not composed or produced by one or more human beings. In other words, mythology is created by people, not by gods.

The Kumulipo probably was composed when the ruling chief commanded that it be done. The court composer would have been the natural person to undertake the task. As Martha Beckwith (1951) observed: "Since writing was unknown in Polynesia before contact with foreign culture, a master of song (haku mele) usually gathered together two or more of his fellows to edit and memorize the lines or themselves to contribute passages." The composition may have been entirely original, emerging as an embryonic idea out of the composer's mind, or it may have been built upon or woven around an older existing incident or part of a moʻolelo. This is likely to have been the case with The Kumulipo. The process probably would have included consultations with the ruling chief and his counselors, followed by preliminary refining, further discussions and reediting, until finally the narrative was completed and accepted by the chief.

The next step might have been its promulgation by the chief as a part of the mythological record. Presumably, the chief would have consulted first with his priests in order to gain their support, since in the end they would have had the major responsibility for "preaching" its message or passing it on to others.

But usually, in the history of sacred literature, texts or books are not accepted as sacred immediately after they are composed. In the case of Christian scripture, for example, many books of the Bible were not formally approved until the Church fathers met at the Council of Nicaea convened by Emperor Constantine in A.D. 325. Among the Maori, a whare wananga hui, or conference of the house of learning, was convened in the late 1800s by a group of Maori elders in order to preserve their historical and mythological accounts then being threatened by the invading European religion.

In any event, in ancient Hawai'i, kāhuna nui, or high priests, and other religious notables quite possibly summoned conferences or meetings from time to time, in order to review the body of sacred narratives, or to promulgate new myths or interpretations of existing narratives. An additional aim may well have been to challenge the claims made by other chiefs and priests to the legitimacy of their versions of mythical events.

However those myths were formally approved or certified, the only meaningful kind of approval came when the people in general believed and lived the myths in their daily life. To put it another way, until such time that a myth was "internalized" as part of the people's value system, no amount of promotion in the highest councils could legitimize it if the people refused to believe them.

Given the thousands of narratives that have been collected from old Hawai'i and other Polynesian groups, we can safely assume that mythmaking went on continuously, involving many mythmakers and resulting in many competing products. The several great chiefly families, priesthoods, and cult groups on different islands or in districts would have wanted to advance their own views and chant their own praises. Personal rivalries would have intensified the process leading to alterations in texts, in order to suit the whims or claims of the moment. Beckwith (1951) referred to Kupihea as saying that "King Kalākaua changed and adapted the original source material (of *The Kumulipo*) in order to jeer at rival factions among the chiefs of his day and laud his own family rank."

One of the inevitable consequences of such a situation is not only the proliferation of narratives but also the inconsistencies among different versions of the same myth. Modern anthologies of Hawaiian myths are full of versions differing from one island or district to another. As Malo stated, "It is very surprising to hear how contradictory are the accounts given by the ancients of the origin of the land here in Hawai'i." He illustrated the point by citing the discrepancies in the genealogies of the families concerned.

Perhaps we should not be surprised that such variations in the myths do exist. They were created by different persons at different times, in different places and for different reasons. Each composer or group of composers perceived the realm of the sacred from their own private perspectives. Indeed, the wonder is not that the myths are different and inconsistent but that they are so similar and close in spirit and theme. The abundance and richness of Hawaiian myths underscore as forcefully as does any other fact the powerful appeal that mythology has to the human mind.

We need to keep in mind that mythmaking was an important part of the long evolution of Hawaiian society. Our words on paper tend to freeze events as if no variables affect them, only constants. Yet we know that Hawaiian culture and society were not static, but dynamic. Changes occurred, however imperceptibly and slowly, as the fortunes of ruling families and burgeoning kingdoms were affected by natural and socioeconomic forces. New knowledge—that is, new perceptions, attitudes, ideas, opinions, standards, values, facts, and theories—no doubt influenced change—and the mythmaking process. For example, as people's knowledge of botany, astronomy, navigation, forestry, and other natural sciences grew during many generations of experience, rational knowledge and understanding replaced uninformed assumptions and premature judgments. Since those who composed mythology were the society's most learned and informed people, we must assume that their creative narratives did reflect their understanding of the "facts" at any particular time. In short, mythology does not ignore the shifting scenes of the real world.

As we can see, many important factors affected the process of mythmaking, but undoubtedly the central actors in the development were those who communicated ideas about the supernatural to mortal beings. Those actors were the mythmakers.

The Mythmakers

Someone has said that in the mythological realm the ultimate reality is ourselves. That is to say, the sacred narratives that tell about the gods are composed by people, for just as people create their own gods, so do they create their own myths. The mythmakers, like the godmakers, were real people. Indeed, they may well have been the same people in ancient Hawai'i.

Who were the mythmakers? Why did they do what they did? And how did they function? These and similar questions are important, for if the mythmakers are responsible for explaining and validating the gods and their deeds—which are the greatest realities to a people—they certainly must have ranked among the most valuable figures in Hawaiian society. Yet, by and large, historians and scholars have paid relatively little attention to them. The time has come to rescue them from obscurity.

Mythmakers belong to a class of society that might be called, to use a phrase of David Malo, "the thinking people" or "ka po'e no'ono'o." As in most archaic societies, these "mind-workers" are mostly the "clerics" or priests (as in Europe's Middle Ages) or the artists attached to the courts (as in imperial China or Russia). Similarly, in old Hawai'i they were the poets, prophets, genealogists, teachers, kāhuna, and haku mele, or composers of chants. Those gifted men and women, either by temperament or because of their positions, whether inherited or gained by personal achievement and influence, spent much of their time doing mental rather than physical labor. They dealt with abstract, philosophical, and cosmological matters and other intellectual issues that required analyzing, speculating, contemplating, and conceptualizing. "Thinking people," especially mythmakers—the Homers, Isaiahs, Pauls, Mohammeds, and others like them—are found in all societies, but always are relatively few in number at any one time.

In old Hawai'i the mythmakers would have included the haku mele, or composers of chants, especially those in the employ of a high chief. The author (or authors) of *The Kumulipo* certainly would have been one of those, as described by Beckwith (1951): "The work of weaving genealogies into a hymnlike chant commemorating the family antecedents was the work of a *Haku-mele* or 'Master-of-song,' attached to the court of a chief, one who occupied also the special post of a *Kū'auhau* or genealogist. He held an honored place in the household. It was his duty to compose name chants glorifying the family exploits and to preserve those handed down by tradition, but especially to memorize the genealogical line through all its branches." Queen Lili'uokalani, in her introduction to her translation of *The Kumulipo*, even identified the haku mele Keāulumoku as the composer of the chant.

As mythmaker, the haku mele's role was to compose, to memorize, and to recite the sacred stories. Each of those tasks required different skills and a vast amount of training and experience. Composing demanded not only creativity but a masterful command of the language in its most difficult and complex form—poetic imagery and metaphorical symbolism, loaded with kaona, or hidden meanings, in which usually the chant is composed. Those composers did not have the convenience of working with pen and paper. All composing was done mentally, line by line. Hence, they were required to commit their works to memory, because they had no other way of preserving them. The haku mele were, in effect, the living and walking libraries of traditional times, in whose minds the myths and other bits of sacred knowledge were catalogued, stored, and kept available for retrieval upon request. Memory was more important than composing, because composed knowledge would vanish without memory's aid. Recitation involved another set of skills, such as diction, projection, rhythm and pace, and other vocal techniques, supported by devices of acting and staging. All these were indispensable in conducting the sacred rituals. Because the premium placed on delivering a perfect performance was so high—a wrong intonation or emphasis on a phrase, a lapse of memory, might lead to the chanter's death—we need not wonder that the haku mele's position in court was so honored (if also somewhat precarious).

Like the bards of medieval England and Ireland, a haku mele served a king or chief by whom he was maintained and protected. As an employed mythmaker, his obligation was to compose, among other things, chants that would preserve and strengthen the prestige and power of his patron. Because every chief wished to enhance his prestige and position, the content of all sacred chants or stories affecting his rule or family would have to be acceptable to him. Thus, *The Kumulipo*, no matter how sacred it was considered to be, is still a calculated endorsement of its owner, Chief Kaʻīʻimamao, who lived around the turn of the eighteenth century. To put it in the vernacular of today, the job of a mythmaker was to make the chief look good, so as to ensure popular support among his court and people. We may state as a general proposition that all myth involving genealogical or other themes relating to the standing of a ruling chief were shaped not only by the subject matter of the myth, but by the social, economic, and political ties of the mythmaker and his patron.

While the haku mele probably felt keenly his dependency on the chief, he must also have had a certain professional pride or integrity in his calling. He was, after all, not simply a composer but undoubtedly a kahuna as well, which made him a representative or agent of the gods whose acts and wills he was responsible for transmitting to people. Most likely this was a responsibility he had inherited, it having been handed down through several generations in his family and, therefore, a calling for which he must have undergone long and arduous training. He may also have been gifted with the intellectual and mystical powers that enable great mythmakers to attain remarkable insights into the world of the sacred. In short, he had standards and resources of his own, independent of his immediate patron.

Like professionals today who work for somebody else, the haku mele served more than one master: his employer-patron and his values, standards, and traditions. He had "divided loyalties," and his ever-present dilemma was how to achieve the appropriate balance between the gods on earth and those dwelling in his own mind.

Whatever his motivations, ultimately the mythmaker's task was to ascertain and explain reality as he perceived it in the varied manifestations of the supernatural force, or mana. This is an intellectual process and Malo's description of the "thinking people" is a perfect label for this job. But, we might ask, how did ka poʻe noʻonoʻo think? Did pre-Cook, premodern, and prescientific Hawaiians think as we do—logically, rationally, intuitively, empirically? If we knew the nature of their minds, perhaps we might better understand and evaluate their myths.

Let us say at the outset that human beings seek knowledge about reality in three ways: (1) observation and refinement of observation through experimentation and measurement; (2) reason or logic; and (3) intuition and inspiration. The first is commonly thought of as the method of science, the second as speculative thought or philosophy, and the third as the poetic or mystical vision. People have used these methods in apprehending two kinds of realities: the secular, that is, that which exists already in our experience; and the sacred, that which is not yet known, and therefore is "new truth." As members of the class of "thinking people," the mythmakers were familiar with all of these methods of thought.

That Hawaiians were close observers of nature requires no elaboration for anyone familiar with the ancient culture. How else could they have developed a sophisticated agricultural society, or mastered navigation to and from Central Polynesia, or achieved such high skills in so many natural sciences of their time and environment? Planters regularly experimented, as is evidenced in the hundreds of varieties of taro that they developed. Astronomers, engineers, and navigators, among others, took measurements based on their mathematical system. Every society, no matter how primitive and "underdeveloped," has its own methods for observing natural phenomena, however rudimentary those methods may be. And the Hawaiian methods were far from rudimentary.

Did Hawaiians think logically? Many people in the modern world have wondered if primal peoples whose lives are supposedly so pervaded by beliefs in spirits, demons, omens, "superstitions," and the like, "really think like we do." Half a century ago the French psychologist Lucien Levy-Bruhl wrote *Primitive Mentality*, the famous book in which he depicted the "primitive" mentality as being always "prelogical," that is, nonlogical, because primal people supposedly never do reach the stage of logical thinking. He probably would have said the same about the ancient Hawaiians, at least in their early development. Levy-Bruhl's theory, however, has been abandoned by most scholars.

To argue whether the Hawaiians of old thought logically is really pointless. If they had developed powers of observation, measurement taking, and experimentation on the scale that they did, then the presumption we have to make is that they must have been able to think logically. Logical thinking, after all, is nothing more than the process of taking data, or evidence, and arriving at a sustainable conclusion by comparing it with perceived reality and then making some meaningful relationships. Had Hawaiians not been able to function logically, they could not possibly have attained their relatively advanced stage of cultural development. They could not even have found Hawai'i!

The ability of the Hawaiian mythmakers to think logically is amply illustrated in the structure and content of their myths. Thus, the belief in mana, the creation of the gods and their intricate relationships, the formulation of kino lau, incarnation and transfiguration (as in the kākū'ai ritual), immortality, the eternal 'ohana, and a number of other religious concepts—and their implied values—all are products of a process of reasoning and systematic thought. Consider the opening lines of *The Kumulipo*, from Rubellite Johnson's translation (1981):

> When space turned around, the earth heated
> When space turned over, the sky reversed
> When the sun appeared standing in shadows
> To cause the light to make bright the moon,
> When the Pleiades are small eyes in the night,
> From the source in the slime was the earth formed
> From the source in the dark was darkness formed
> From the source in the night was night formed
> From the depths of the darkness, darkness so deep
> Darkness of day, darkness of night
> Of night alone.

When the entire chant of more than two thousand lines is examined in terms of its content, structure, syntax, or science, little room for doubt remains about the logical capacity of the Hawaiian mythmaker who composed that great work.

If the mythmaker can think logically, then he can think analytically, synthetically, and systematically. All these categories of thought are interrelated, and all enter interdependently and simultaneously into the mental process. *The Kumulipo* and other Polynesian myths, particularly those about creation and cosmology, long esteemed by scholars as being "unusually elaborate," attest to these intellectual skills. One must be doubly impressed with: (1) what is on the surface, the superbly economical use of descriptive language and factual observation; and (2) what is below the surface, in terms of the multiple levels of meanings embedded in the kaona of the sacred poetry. Only a high order of skills in creative thought, synthesis, and integration, all based on logical thinking as well as on intuition, could create this Hymn to Life.

The Kumulipo reveals another characteristic thought process of the mythmakers: a proceeding from the simple to the complex in a gradual progression. Note, for example, the earth's transformation, beginning with the "slime" (walewale), the primordial matter, into living things, starting with the simplest organisms, then evolving into the invertebrates, the more complex insects, then birds, reptiles, and ultimately to the warm-blooded mammals.

This is an instance of inductive thinking, beginning with concrete particulars, in order to arrive at the universal, or the broadest generalizations. A good deal of Hawaiian thinking, by the way, is inductive, but this does not mean that Hawaiians were not equally adept at the reverse, at deductive reasoning. Many examples of both may be found in the moʻolelo (and, of course, in all branches of their secular knowledge, as we shall see in later chapters). In either case, whether thinking inductively or deductively, the mind of the Hawaiian of old worked logically.

We do not intend to make the Hawaiian thinker into a "rational animal," or into a carbon copy of the so-called Western mind. Rather, we want to show only that ka poʻe noʻonoʻo could and did think logically, analytically, synthetically, abstractly, and systematically. The myths they composed are creations of these intellectual processes at work in the minds of haku mele.

Now we must consider the third and last method of thinking that characterized the Hawaiian mythmaker, namely, intuitive thinking. While some modern Hawaiians may have trouble in fully accepting the claim that their kūpuna thought logically, none would have any hesitation at all about accepting the idea that they thought intuitively. Indeed, nowadays the tendency is to overstate Hawaiian reliance on intuition. But for the mythmakers, prophets, seers, and priests, intuitive thinking was completely compatible with their approach to apprehending supernatural or sacred realities. This is not much different from that of the mythmakers, prophets, mystics, and gurus representing both Western and Eastern religions, who have long preferred the more direct intuitive ways of seeking the ultimate reality.

By intuition we mean the immediate and direct apprehension of an idea, feeling, or essence of a thing, without the intermediate service of words or data. Unlike logical thinking, intuition is non-inferential—as, for example, when you have a sudden insight or a hunch about the truth of something for which there is no observable evidence. It is like the "Aha!" moment when, in a flash, you understand the meaning of something, or "see" the solution to a problem. On a higher plane, intuition usually is referred to as the "poetic vision" or the "mystical experience." We know that some of our best answers to the mysteries of life have come from poets or prophets in moments of mystic awareness. While they may observe reality just as others do and can reason or think logically, they have the extraordinary ability to perceive certain dimensions of reality that ordinary human beings do not experience. We say they have powers of perception that seem to come from a superhuman source—or, indeed, that God speaks to them.

In other words, intuition is a psychological/spiritual rather than an intellectual approach to discerning reality. No conceptualizing, no synthesizing, no rationalizing, no inductive or deductive reasoning, are involved, no tedious hypothesizing and testing and gathering of data. This is not to say that those thought processes may not precede or prepare the way for the flash of insight to occur, for this is how even some scientists make their discoveries. In short, "to intuit" something is to effect the most direct and immediate connection possible between the subject and its object.

If we have difficulty in communicating the process that is because its final object—ultimate reality—lies beyond the realm of the senses and of the conscious intellect from which our words and concepts are derived. The Hindu Upanishad describes this realm as follows:

There the eye goes not;
Speech goes not, nor the mind.
We know not, we understand not
How one would teach it.

Yet this is the realm that the mythmakers seek to penetrate, whether they are called St. Paul, St. Augustine, Mohammed, the Buddha, Lao Tzu, the Yaqui "sorcerer" Don Juan, or Keāulumoku.

The Hawaiian mythmakers, prophets, mystics, or even sorcerers who sought this realm no doubt had a great store of mana, but they also enjoyed the special gift of 'ike pāpālua, which is, as Pūku'i (Pūku'i, Haertig, and Lee) described it, "intuitive communication with the gods." Literally, the phrase means "double knowledge" or "twice seeing." Pūku'i stated that "People with 'ike pāpālua would know what was going to happen. And they could know what was happening right then to somebody at some other place. They could *see two ways* [italics added].' " Only a few possessed this gift, we are told. In modern terms, 'ike pāpālua refers to the several categories of extrasensory perception, such as clairvoyance, clairaudience, and telepathy.

The mythmaker may have used specific techniques to achieve the states of consciousness necessary to enter the realm of the supernatural. These would include pule (prayer), no'ono'o (meditation), akakū (trance), noho (possession), and hō'ike na ka pō (revelatory dream). Prayer, of course, was common to all Hawaiians, but the kind of prayer needed by the haku mele was of a different order, one that would lead to "revelation." Interestingly, when Pūku'i (Pūku'i, Haertig, and Lee) was asked whether fervent prayer ever culminated in "that overwhelming feeling of one-ness with a supreme deity that is termed the 'great transcendental experience,' " she believed that in old Hawai'i it did not, *except* among the "prophets *(kāula)* who lived as hermits."

The literature is sparse on meditation and trance practices in old Hawai'i, but they are so prevalent in Asian and American Indian cultures that we can assume that the deeply mystical priest of Hawai'i, the haku mele, too, would have resorted to them. Noho, taking possession, we know, was widely practiced among the kāhuna in Hawai'i and throughout Polynesia. Akua noho, for example, meant that a god could enter or take possession of a human medium in order to express him or herself directly, and in such a state a mythmaker or prophet might have uttered "new truths."

Hawaiian mythology is full of the products of intuitive thinking, from the idea of pō, or darkness, as the primordial beginning and the formation of life out of a watery "slime," to the transfiguration of 'aumākua and the existence of the gods—as well as a number of other insights about the nature of the cosmos and humankind. In the last analysis, much of Hawaiian mythology is the expression and affirmation of intuitive thought.

In summing up this discussion on the traditional mythmakers, we have tried to demonstrate that Hawaiian mythology is the product of ka po'e no'ono'o, "thinking people," who represented the elite of Hawaiian society, who, because well endowed, well born, well trained, enjoyed priestly authority and the protection of the nobility, and who, therefore, occupied privileged positions. We have also tried to show that the thought processes that they used in composing the myths were the same that human beings in many other societies have used at different stages of development in order to understand and apprehend the realm of the ultimate reality. If we measure the quality of a piece of art or of a product by the quality of the artisan who made it, then we can measure the quality of our myths, too, by the quality of our mythmakers. While we have been able to offer mainly circumstantial evidence, can we not conclude that only the best of minds were likely to have produced the great myths? And if so, that those myths represent some of the best thinking of the people who in themselves summed up the cumulative experience of Hawaiian religious intellectuals? However quick some Hawaiians today may be to dismiss the old myths, we should remember that those myths reflect the best creations that came out of Hawaiian culture. Now, as then, they are still the best.

Myth and Values

Religion, as we have said, deals with the supernatural, the sacred world of the gods; it represents whatever is of transcendent worth. Hence, the thoughts, words, and achievements of the god world form the primal source of our values. Because they are sacred values, they are absolute standards applicable to all human behavior and activities. As models these values are described, preserved, and validated in myths. Myths are the most potent transmitters of values.

Joseph Campbell wrote that because no human society has yet been found in which "mythological motifs have not been rehearsed in liturgies; interpreted by seers, poets, theologians, or philosophers; presented in art; magnified in song; and ecstatically experienced in life-empowering visions," myths have been the most universal and effective means of conveying to the human consciousness the existence of a divine and sacred order. The human encounter with the sacred, that is, the experience with the superhuman reality, is the agency which awakens in the mind the possibility that something *really exists*, that *absolute realities* are embodied in the gods—and hence that absolute values, in turn, not only exist but are capable of guiding human beings and of giving meaning to their existence.

Myth is the vehicle which religion uses to transport people to a comprehension of the world, the cosmos, the sacred, the mysterious, the multi-universe. Through myth the ultimate source of our values can be apprehended, and these values serve to reaffirm, enlarge, and revitalize each new generation of humankind. The function of myth is to reveal models as values and, by so doing, to give significance and purpose to human life. This is why myth has played and continues to play an incomparable role in the history of the world—including those Hawaiian people who are in search of meaning.

All other functions of myth are subordinate to its value-making and value-transmitting roles, but they are all interlocked. Myths can serve as instructions for adjusting an individual to his or her group, and for shaping, in turn, the group to society and society to its elite leaders or rulers. Provided, of course, that values implicit in the instructions are acceptable both vertically and horizontally throughout the levels of society, then myths perform an integrating function that no other agency can do as well. We have already suggested this role in our previous discussion of kapu as a regulator of behavior for members of Hawaiian society. As we have indicated, we can take a more conspiratorial view for the mythmaker, or haku mele, who served the socioeconomic or political interests of his patron, and point to priests and chiefs, either alone or jointly, devising or perpetrating certain mo'olelo, or convenient versions of them, in order to expand and consolidate their own rule and influence, whether for good or for bad. Hence, we should remember that a myth is not necessarily a guarantee of pono, or goodness.

Myth, of course, serves an important philosophical role in that it deals with the ultimate whys of human existence, the underlying causes and principles of reality, the ideals and standards—in other words, the values of humankind. While mythology and philosophy may serve common ends, they are not the same. Philosophy seeks to apprehend reality primarily through speculative and logical thought, whereas mythology approaches reality directly and frontally through an intuitive leap. While philosophy tends to be hypothetical, tentative, and conditional, mythology is absolute, final, and imperative. A wise man doesn't fool around with myths, as other men might do with philosophical musings.

Of all its functions, whether ideological, intellectual, explanatory, or axiological, the value-making and value-transmitting functions of myth remain foremost.

New Myths

When Hawaiians abandoned the old religion and accepted Christianity, they did not abandon mythology. They merely replaced one form with another. In converting to the new Gospel, they did not recant their old need for believing in an ultimate reality, in supernatural or divine power, immortality, faith, prophecy, miraculous healing, ritual, worship, values, or a vehicle for transmitting values. In a sense, they simply converted the packaging, without ever disavowing the need for the gifts within. This is certainly one of the reasons for the success of the Christian missionaries: Hawaiians never denied the need for religion and mythology. They were always receptive to the "ideal of the holy."

We do not know how difficult Hawaiians found the process of converting from one mythology to another, but we can conclude that they must have understood the purpose and function of a vital mythology. They must have recognized the symbolism in the Bible when it describes, for example, the three angels visiting Abraham, Moses receiving the tablets of the law, Isaiah seeing in his vision not God himself but only a manifestation of himself, God addressing one man in thunder and another in a gentle breeze, Balaam's she-ass possessed of better vision than her rider, the Resurrected Christ saying "Touch me not," his Ascension, the Descent of the Holy Ghost. The wonder and mystery of these happenings were, perhaps, no more marvelous than the accounts of Māui, Lono, Kū, and other Hawaiian gods in the old myths. In either case, the issue ultimately was not whether one accepted the literalness of the mo'olelo instead of the Paipala, but whether one could participate in its inner meanings, whether the images of the myth pointed beyond themselves to something no image can express: to ultimate realities.

No doubt, a struggle ensues when one myth confronts another, but it does not take place at a rational level, for it is a spiritual struggle fought with mythical images—with ambiguities, metaphors, symbolism, hidden realities. It is also a struggle not between armies but between modes of thinking in individuals. The outcome is decided only when the individual accepts or rejects the myth, on the basis of how it affects his personal actions and conduct. The efficacy of myth is ultimately—and always—a matter of individual struggle. Hence, in the final analysis, the conversion of Hawaiians to Christianity was a yielding of individuals who struggled not physically but spiritually, who contested not in rational but in mythical terms.

This is not to ignore the realities of political, technological,

social, and economic forces that impinged on the struggle. That
history has been well recited. But what has not been told, so far as
we know, is the history of the spiritual struggles within individual
Hawaiians when the old and new mythologies confronted each
other. When that story is brought to light, we shall know much
more about how the new mythology affected the mythic values of
the postcontact Hawaiian.

Nonetheless, in the overall scheme of things, Hawaiian mythology did not put up much of a struggle after 1820. The record
shows that the old myths were tampered with in order to make
them conform to Christian teachings. The deliberate adaptation of
The Kumuhonua (the Maui-island version of *The Kumulipo*) to
Christian ideas, and Kepelino's reinterpretations of the Hawaiian
hierarchy of gods to erect the Trinity are but two examples of this
tampering. Ironically, Kepelino, Kamakau, and other early Hawaiian converts who tried to retell the moʻolelo in the new Christian style did not realize that they were carrying on the mythmaking function of the haku mele of earlier times. On the other hand,
we know of no attempt by Christian missionaries to rewrite biblical accounts to fit Hawaiian myths, although in due course some
compromises were made with certain nondoctrinal procedures,
adapting them to indigenous circumstances.

Apparently, only after the Christian conquest was finished and
the dust of combat had settled, did a few Hawaiians seriously
return to their ancient myths, wanting to revive and preserve
them. King Kalākaua has been credited with leading this effort
during the "renaissance" of the 1870s and 1880s. The movement
succeeded in restoring *The Kumulipo* and in publishing, under the
king's name, *The Legends and Myths of Hawaiʻi*.

One of the more remarkable later incidents of this kind concerned the efforts of Mrs. Emma Ahuʻena Taylor to reestablish the
cult of Io in the 1920s and 1930s. She claimed that Io was the
supreme creator, "the Holy Spirit of the Ancient Maolis of
Hawaiʻi," who was worshiped by her precontact kūpuna. When
asked why the cult had not been heard of before then, she replied
that it had been forgotten partly because the name was considered
"too sacred or too fearsome to utter in the open." She also contended that "some of the older generation have a tradition that *Io*
left Hawaiʻi when the chieftain *Hema* departed for New Zealand
to live after his feudal warfare with his brother *Puha. Hema* did

not worship as his gods the guardians of the sea, fresh water, or the mountains; so *Io* loved him and went away with him."

Taylor's claims, however, were challenged by anthropologist Kenneth Emory (1941), who argued that in Hawai'i "all cults were esoteric" and that no cult of importance would have survived for so many years in silence and then suddenly reappear for the first time. He stated that "the cult of *Io*" was an attempt to show that the Hawaiians had a cult equivalent to the Maori cult of Io. His suspicion, in fact, was that Taylor had become acquainted with the Maori Io in 1920, when a group of Maori Mormons first came to the Mormon temple at Lā'ie, O'ahu, because before then no record was known of a god with such attributes.

While Taylor did not succeed in reviving the cult, it is an interesting and singular attempt to rework Hawaiian mythology in reverse, that is, by claiming that a monotheistic tradition existed before the arrival of Christianity. It is interesting, too, because, despite earlier references to the absence of monotheism among "primitive" religions, Mircea Eliade (1957) suggested that a single supreme being may have been the protodeity at the beginning of creation, only to be gradually forgotten as the creation was finished and actually replaced by the more concrete and more dynamic great or major gods. In other words, monotheism preceded polytheism.

More generally, in the past few years, more or less coinciding with the resurgence in Hawaiian culture, frequent attempts have been made to rework the old myths, using them to legitimize or promote this or that Hawaiian cause or organization. The efforts of the Protect Kaho'olawe 'Ohana to justify the sacred importance of that island by invoking its ancient name and other related traditions associated with it are good examples. One might even say that parts of this book represent an attempt to use the myths of the past to rationalize the myths of the present. Be that as it may, as we search for Hawaiian values, we cannot help rediscovering part of our mythological past and in the process give our myths new life and value.

3

THE GODS

The 40,000, 400,000 and 4,000 Gods

When Hawaiians of old prayed, in order not to omit or offend any of the akua they added to the prayer the words, "Invoke we now the 40,000 gods, the 400,000 gods, the 4,000 gods—*E hoʻoulu ana i kini o ke akua, ka lehu o ke akua, ka mano o ke akua*." This is only a figurative expression, because no one really knows how many gods dwelled in the Hawaiian pantheon. Kepelino, a Hawaiian historian, said there were "millions upon millions" of gods. And Martha Beckwith (1970) added, "Nothing is more characteristic of Hawaiian religion than the constantly increasing multiplicity of gods and the diversity of forms which their worship took."

How was that possible? Why so many gods? This is a question that rushes into the mind of almost any Hawaiian today who has been raised in the Christian precept of one god or a single godhead. But before we attempt to answer this question, let us seek a better view of that godly population.

Hawaiians honored a kind of diffused hierarchy of gods, headed by Kāne, Kū, Lono, and Kanaloa. Kanaloa was often left out, leaving a trinity at the top. While Kāne even today is sometimes referred to as the "leading god" among the akua, each has his areas of responsibility or "departments." (Interestingly, some Maoris refer to them as "departmental gods.") Kāne, for example, heads the departments of procreation, water, forests, certain plants and animals. Kū oversees wars, certain fishes and shrubs and trees. Lono is in charge of the weather—clouds, thunder, lightning, earthquakes, the rainbow, rain, winds, and several important plants. Kanaloa's specific responsibilities are not clear, in sharp contrast to his functions in other Polynesian island groups, where he is given very important roles as god of the oceans and of fishes, for example

In addition to these great patron gods, many lesser deities were recognized who had their own responsibilities. Thus, a class of akua watched over certain professions and occupational groups. Bird snarers and featherworkers prayed to Kūhuluhulumanu, fishermen to Kūʻula, healers to Maʻiola, hula dancers to Laka, makers of canoes and gourd bailers to Hina i ke kā, tapa makers to Haʻina kolo, sorcerers to Kūkuaʻe and Uli, warriors to Lonomakaihe, fish pond guards to Haumakapau, soothsayers and astrologers or astronomers to Kuhimana. Even thieves had their own god, called Makuaʻaihue (literally, "thieving elder").

Some gods took care of women's special needs. Such was Laʻahana, the patron goddess of tapa makers. Gods for male and female chiefs were separate from those serving the commoners and from gods for places. David Malo wrote that the number of gods who were supposed to preside over districts, islands, specific localities, paths, trails, mountains, and so on, were "countless." People honored even gods for the doorway (Kānehohoio), the fireplace (Kānemoelehu), precipices or pali (Kāneholopali), and the direction points east, west, south, and north.

Also, there were ʻohana, or family, gods, as well as gods for individuals. (In other parts of Polynesia, as in New Zealand, there were tribal, or iwi, gods and subtribal, or hapu, gods as well.) These were ʻaumākua, ancestral guardians or spirit gods, as distinguished from akua, a distinction which we shall make clearer later.

Finally, there were the vast number of demigods, or kupua, the so-called upstart gods who were identified with definite localities. They were considered to be relatively benign deities unless mistreated, and then woe to the offender.

To return to our question of why this rampant polytheism. While some of us may regard the question with complete objectivity, others might have a hard time concealing a sense of disbelief, or even of shame, as if to say, "How could our ancestors have been so superstitious?" This kind of attitude is natural when we don't understand the subject. But it also betrays the usual arrogance of persons who think, whether consciously or unconsciously, that somehow they are superior to polytheists. Yet when we examine closely the reasons for having so many gods, we cannot help but admire the rational and intelligent way in which our kūpuna arranged their relationships with the divine forces about them.

We should first realize that historically, and throughout the world, polytheism has been the norm among almost all peoples. Monotheism, strictly speaking, has been extremely rare. In fact, Paul Radin (1924) has said that among archaic people it was never found. In other words, at their stage of historical development, Hawaiians were not much different from everybody else. Even today, many millions of Hindus, Buddhists, Shintoists, and members of other religions still accept polytheism. If we think that the Hawaiians had many gods, consider the Hindus of today who count their deities in many crores, where one crore equals 10 million. At last count, Hindus allow for thirty-three crores, or 330 million gods. If for no other reason, one must respect the mathematical genius and the capabilities for storing and retrieving information of Hindus and Hawaiians for accommodating so many gods. Nonetheless, whether millions or even billions of deities are accepted is immaterial, because what really matters is not the numbers of them but the rationale that endorses their existence.

It makes perfect common sense to honor many gods who will take care of the countless, constant, and varied demands rising up from so many people in so many places. The old Hawaiians must have reasoned that no single god could be so omniscient, immanent, and ubiquitous as to be able to do everything everywhere and at the same time. How could one deity attend to the pleas for help from so many people, when they must often be contradictory —one supplicant asking for this, and another for that which is completely opposed to the first, both at the same time and place? The task of handling this unimaginable torrent of requests alone, they reasoned, would have overwhelmed even the greatest deity. But even more important, the idea of many gods being available for consulting should have assured mortals that no one personal god would ever be so busy as not to hear his petitions. This trust must have been a source of enormous comfort to the believing Hawaiian.

This pragmatism is illustrated in a wonderful incident that Peter Buck (1970) related about a Polynesian elder who told an early Christian missionary that he could not understand how one god could possibly attend to all the different requests made upon him. In his religion, he observed, a person consulted the god of his particular choice and, therefore, had a better chance of receiving prompt attention. Hence the elder considered his polytheistic religion superior to Christianity. Plainly, with so many gods to share their responsibilities, no Polynesian or Hawaiian felt that he or she was ever abandoned and helpless, whatever the need.

Since human beings perceive and interpret things in the light of their own experiences, we can reasonably assume that our kūpuna perceived the gods operating in a world not unlike their own. The division of labor attributed to the god hierarchy, for example, is clearly patterned after the arrangements by which their own society was organized on earth. The occupational gods are aligned perfectly with the known professions and guilds, even to such highly specialized tasks as bailing of canoes. If specialization is an efficient way of producing goods and utilizing skills and resources among mortals, why shouldn't it be the same for the akua?

Furthermore, the hierarchy of the gods, with its varied levels of rank arranged according to the deities' powers and responsibilities, genealogy, and, presumably, a kind of godly track record of accomplishments, seemed to be modeled upon the highly stratified, rank-conscious Hawaiian society. Certainly, for the chiefs for whom the exercise and retention of power was all-important, their vested interests as children of the gods motivated them to perpetuate a system in the hereafter that would preserve or enhance the status they'd achieved in this life.

But the most significant explanation for polytheism has to do with the way gods are created.

Created in the Image of Man

The book of Genesis says that God created man in his own image but Hawaiians say that man created the gods in his own image. This challenge to biblical doctrine probably will upset some Hawaiian Christians and amaze others. In either case, this notion of man-made gods is undoubtedly the key to a greater understanding of how the Hawaiians viewed not only the nature of the gods but their own human nature as well.

When we say "man-made gods" we do not mean that the Hawaiians really believed that they actually created objective, independent, living beings possessing divine powers. Rather, our hypothesis maintains that they created, in their own minds, entities or beings formed out of the "divine stuff," or mana, they assumed to exist in the universe, and then called these conceptualizations akua, gods. To put the process in another way, Hawaiians did not make any supernatural organisms which then grew into gods, but merely projected qualities and shapes onto superhuman forces, so that men could understand or relate to them in a meaningful way, that is, in a human way.

We know that Hawaiians, like all Polynesians, believed in the existence of a superhuman force they named mana. While there are many interpretations of what mana means, basically it represents the most primordial force in the universe that animates or gives life or power to all things. It is *the* creative source, as when Samuel Kamakau (1976) wrote of Kānenuiākea. "His was the *mana* that made the earth and the things that fill it." In other words, just as the earth was created out of mana, so was Kānenuiākea created as an akua. We shall discuss mana at length later, but we mention it here to emphasize that the idea of "man-made gods" does not mean that gods are conceived out of nothing. Hawaiians took the preexistent mana and gave it feelings and forms resembling those of human beings.

The Greek philosopher Epictetus, in the sixth century B.C., observed that "men imagine gods to be born, and to have raiment and voice and body like themselves" (cited in W. Wallis). He illustrated his point by describing the Ethiopian gods, who had dusky cheeks, thick lips, and woolly hair, and the Grecian gods, who were tall, bright eyed, and fair. Epictetus meant, wherever we go, gods tend to look like those who revere them.

How do we know for sure that this is the way that Hawaiians made their gods? Frankly, we don't know this for sure. No kahuna theologian or philosopher from the time before 1778 has left us any clear exposition, except for this singular passage from the "Creation Song" of the Kamehamehas: "*Mai ke kanaka mai ke akua, mai ke akua mai no ke kanaka.* Man creates the god, the god creates man." If its source (Samuel Crowningburg-Amalu, "The Creation of the Hawaiian Gods," in *The Sunday Star-Bulletin & Advertiser,* August 30, 1981) can be accepted, this passage confirms our hypothesis.

In any case, the idea of man-made gods helps to explain certain concepts in Hawaiian religion that might otherwise be difficult to rationalize. Among these concepts are the origin of 'aumākua, the deification of ancestors, the mortality of the gods or the notion that gods can die or can be eliminated, the personification of natural phenomena as gods, and polytheism.

Let us illustrate what we mean, first, by returning to our explanation of polytheism. While a staunch monotheist may be unable to believe that there are as many gods in the universe as grains of sand on an island beach, if Hawaiians of old believed that they made their own gods, why couldn't they have created as many gods as they wished? There seemed to be no limit to either their creativity or to the raw material out of which gods could be made. Nor was there any limit on the demand by the people for divine kōkua, or aid. Nothing in their logic or theology seemed to prohibit them from doing so. We have already mentioned the other practical reasons why they made so many gods. Therefore, what more reasonable way to explain the proliferation of gods can be found than to accept the premise that Hawaiians believed they could "manufacture" them? Clearly, "the more gods we have, the better for us" seemed to be the Hawaiian way of thinking.

But what has polytheism to do with values? For one important thing, a common trait of polytheistic religions is the capacity of its members for tolerance toward other religions, other ways. The adherents of certain sects of Mahayana Buddhism, for example, are notable for their ability to take new strains of religious thought from other sources and blend them with their own. Hinduism also has been noted for its "catholicity," its ability to absorb the doctrines as well as the gods of other systems. In Japan's Shintoism this tolerance is revealed in the familiar aphorism: Just as there are many paths that lead to the top of Mount Fuji, so are there many gods or religions that can lead man to heaven. Vedanta's summary is even shorter: There are many paths to God.

Similarly, we suggest that Hawaiians' polytheistic religion made them more tolerant of the gods introduced by other people. This is not to say that families, chiefs, or cults and groups of different kinds did not champion their own gods, indeed, wage wars over them. But the very fact that their worldview was based in part on the acceptance of a multiplicity of gods means that they had come to terms with polytheism. And one of those terms, our logic would insist, was a mutual tolerance of each others' gods. "You let us have our gods," said the people of old, "we'll let you have yours." Without that concession, how could the system have survived as long as it did?

Perhaps more to the point was the peaceful encounter between Hawaiians and the Christians' Jehovah after 1820. Many factors

assisted the newly arrived rival god—the timely overthrow of the
kapu system, the destruction of the heiau and their wooden
images, the impact of Western ideas and technology upon the
native ways, followed by the loss of cultural pride and self-esteem,
were only the most obvious—and all help to explain the relatively
easy and rapid conversion of Hawaiians to Christianity. One factor that has been overlooked was this willingness of Hawaiians
to accommodate many gods, particularly any new gods that appeared to possess more mana than did the old ones. Granted that
in this sense Hawaiian tolerance may have been based on a keen
appreciation of practical self-interest, nonetheless, Hawaiians
were predisposed toward tolerance by their religious beliefs.

Implicit in the idea of tolerance is the willingness to allow others
"to do their thing," as we say today, to be free. Freedom, at least a
certain amount of intellectual freedom, seems to be very much a
part of the logic of polytheism. If a person can create his or her
own gods, then he or she is free to do so. Since the act is a matter
of private conscience, that person necessarily exercises freedom of
choice. We can only conclude that because they recognized so
many gods, many such choices were made by many Hawaiians,
among both commoners and chiefs, continuously throughout Hawaiian history before 1778. If this is so, tolerance and freedom, in
the sense of spiritual freedom, are two important values that we
can trace to Hawaiian religion. We shall say more about this soon.

Gods Can Die

A few years ago *Time* magazine announced on its cover "God Is
Dead," thereby shocking many a true believer in the country. After
all, God cannot possibly die; he is the immortal and eternal Creator. The editors of *Time*, of course, knew that and were not
really writing God's obituary. But they were reporting the widespread lack of interest in God—and in his churches—on the part
of many Americans during the 1960s. Some priests and ministers
feared that so many people had just forgotten about God—and
that for all practical purposes he was dead.

We suspect that if a similar announcement had been made in old
Hawai'i, the public's reaction would have been not so much one of
shock as of curiosity. They might well have asked "Which god?"
rather than question the statement, for to Hawaiians of old the

gods were mortal. Hawaiians believed that if they could make gods, they could also get rid of them. And that is what they did, well into the 1800s.

Evidence for this practice includes several reliable statements and some fascinating incidents. R. M. Dagget, for example, writing in his introduction to King Kalākaua's *The Legends and Myths of Hawai'i*, stated, "The people made their own household gods, and destroyed them when they failed to contribute to their success." We should take note of two features in that comment: (1) the fact that commoners as well as priests and chiefs were godmakers, and also that they possessed sufficient freedom and mana to kill off their gods; and (2) the very pragmatic motive for such action, underscoring a typical attitude of Hawaiians' religious behavior.

War gods were particularly susceptible to being done away with. Beckwith (1970) wrote: "Impotent gods who remained obstinately passive were rejected by war leaders or the battle was called off. Kawelo, the story says, smashed the god Kūlanilehu with a club and called it a coward because it showed not even a flutter of feathers when consulted about the success of his expedition to Kaua'i." We do not know to what extent military leaders and their warriors were held responsible for mistakes in battle, but apparently the gods had to shoulder a good deal of the responsibility for the outcome. Again, as in our previous example, the same pragmatic test of success-or-else was applied.

The most vivid and dramatic episode occurred in 1819, when King Liholiho ordered destruction of all heiau and burning of the carved images on all the islands, following his public eating with Ka'ahumanu and other women—an act of daring symbolizing the overthrow of the kapu decreed by the ancient religion. The scale of that massive killing of the gods, in what we might call a "mass theocide," was unprecedented. Among the factors that should be included in any analysis is the pragmatic view that Hawaiians had taken toward their deities. By the time Liholiho made his fateful decision, many others, including the high priest Hewahewa, whose position in the religious hierarchy could be compared to that of a pope, evidently had concluded that the old gods were not competent to meet the challenges that were being hurled at them by the cannons, gadgets, and ideas of the modern world. The gods had become useless, so their creators got rid of them. We should add that not all Hawaiians were so willing; a few valiantly

defended the old gods at the Battle of Kuamoʻo. But they lost, and
went down to defeat with the gods.

Three years after the coming of the Congregational missionaries
from America in 1820, William Ellis, who toured the islands with
his Tahitian assistants, recorded the manner in which Chief Kamakau had discarded a useless idol. "As they went from his house
[Chief Kamakau's] to the beach, they passed by a large idol, that
Kamakau had formerly worshipped, lying prostrate and mutilated
on the rocks, and washed by the waves of the sea as they rolled on
the shore. . . . On his being asked why he had worshipped that
log of wood? he answered,—because he was afraid he would
destroy his cocoa-nuts. But were you not afraid to destroy it? 'No,
I found he did me neither good nor harm. I thought he was no
god, and threw him away.' "

The practice of disposing of gods was not peculiar to Hawaiians, being shared by other Polynesians as well. In Tahiti, for
example, the story is told about the priest of a family that had suffered defeat in war. He went to the temple and chanted: "There is
a casting off, I am casting thee off. Do not come in to possess me
again; let me not be a seat for thee again! Let me not know thee
again; do thou not know me again. Go and seek some other
medium for thyself in another home. Let it not be me, not at all! I
am wearied of thee—I am terrified with thee! I am expelling thee."

A milder and even more poignant example is illustrated in
another incident from Tahiti, which tells how a bereaved father
bitterly berates Turanga, the god of his dead child's mother, the
god whom he blames for the death of his favorite son. He chants
as if speaking to the child:

> Ah, that god—that bad god!
> Inexpressibly bad, my child!
> I am disgusted with thy mother's god.
> Oh, for some other Helper!
> Some new divinity to listen to the sad story of thy wasting
>   disease . . .
>
> (Cited in Luomala 1956)

Although in this tale the offending god is being simply disowned
and displaced, that, for deity, probably is as bad a fate as being
killed off

Casting off, smashing, burning, disowning—whatever the method used to get rid of gods—may strike the Christian mind as incredible, if not a bit frivolous, but obviously it was neither unbelievable nor capricious to our kūpuna. In the first place, getting rid of gods is a logical extension of the idea that they are "man-made." What man gives, he can also take away, because not the gods but men are the form-givers. Granted that we are only talking about gods as conceptualizations. But that is precisely the reason why it is possible for us to dispose of them. Our original hypothesis makes sense because it is the only one that can logically explain an otherwise "incredible" notion. In the second place, notwithstanding the mechanisms by which Hawaiians of old might have disposed of their gods, such acts could not have been taken lightly. Hawaiians were far too serious about mana and the sanctity of their gods to be frivolous about terminating them. Only in moments of great despair, utter defeat, or profound disillusionment could they have resorted to such action. We can guess that it would have been a wrenching psychological experience, with effects akin to a breakup in a long and dependent relationship.

We must look at another side of the problem, too. If people can get rid of gods, they can also keep them alive. An apt illustration of this is provided by a Maori witness who appeared before a judge in a native land court in New Zealand (this separate court handles and adjudicates only land-related matters affecting Maoris) and said, "The god of whom I speak is dead." When the judge replied, "Gods do not die," the witness said, "You are mistaken. Gods do die unless there are tohungas (priests) to keep them alive" (Buck 1982).

And how are the gods to be sustained and maintained? By the tohunga, the kāhuna, who are set apart from all other men to perform the sacred rituals and sacrifices, to conduct the special prayers of gratitude or repentance, to make offerings, to build temples, to create new myths and preserve old ones—to do all the duties needed for supporting the religious structure. Of course the people, too, had to present prayers, songs of praise, offerings, in addition to sustaining the priesthood. Interestingly, the supporting of gods is not simply a process of providing spiritual or ritual sustenance, but demands also the offering of actual foods. As Kawena Pūku'i (Pūku'i, Haertig, and Lee) wrote: "'*Awa* was considered food for the gods. It was essential for the nourishment and growth

of the spirit beings, just as *poi* and fish were essential to man."
According to Pūku'i, "Cut off the flowers of speech as well as the
offerings of its worshippers, and a *kupua* (demi-god) would soon
dwindle into nothingness."

In the end, what the gods seem to want most can be summed up
in the statement found in a Maori myth, in which a deity is
addressing another deity and says, "When men no longer believe
in us, we are dead." (*Time* was scooped a long time ago, by a
Maori myth!) If we can take the word of Maori deities—and in
this instance there is no reason why we cannot—the implication is
clear: only people can keep their gods alive.

What all this leads up to is the way in which Hawaiians of old
defined their relationship with their gods. Simply put, gods and
people are interdependent: for better or for worse, they need each
other. It is not a relationship in which one functions as the slave of
the other, or lives at the expense of the other, or takes from the
other without returning benefit or hurt. Rather, it is the perfect
symbiotic relationship, in which both parties mutually benefit
from living and working together.

Underlying this relationship are two principles that are at the
heart of the Hawaiian values system: reciprocity and the mastery
of one's destiny. Reciprocity may be compared with a gigantic spi-
der web, whose threads represent the mutual obligations that each
member of society bears toward others. As long as each person
fulfills his or her responsibilities, the web holds together in beautiful symmetry; when individuals fail to live up to those responsibilities, the threads are broken, the web weakens and eventually falls
apart. As with all Polynesian societies, traditional Hawaiian society was very much like this web, because it operated on the principle of reciprocity. The moral explaining how a human society
should function was declared in the way Hawaiians defined their
symbiotic relationship with the gods: it was a mutual giving and
taking, with benefits accruing to both, allowing both to achieve
their respective functions and aspirations.

The give-and-take of reciprocity means that neither party in a
relationship dominates the other, because both must enjoy a fair
share in self-determination. Thus, in any transaction between
Hawaiians and their akua, people would never be put at the mercy
of the unilateral power of the gods. Although Hawaiians of old no
doubt stood in awe and in trembling fear before some of their

great gods, this did not numb them into surrendering entirely their sense of spiritual independence and integrity. While the fact that the gods were creatures of their own making may not always have registered on an individual's consciousness as sharply as it has been presented in these pages, still he realized that no matter how tremendous may have been the power of the gods, he too had some control over his own destiny—or at the least over his spiritual well-being.

The ʻAumākua Affinity

Probably many more ʻaumākua than akua survived the overthrow of the great gods in 1819. We do not have hard evidence for this, but we do have many good reasons to believe this happened. Being beloved family guardians, bonds with ʻaumākua and mortals were much more intimate, therefore stronger. Since the family was the dominant social unit, important values were associated with ʻaumākua. Furthermore, because Hawaiians viewed "salvation" to be more a family than an individual affair, ʻaumākua played a critical part in determining the nature of a man's sojourn in the hereafter. And, in the deification of the ʻaumākua, we have the plainest evidence of the possibility that some people might become gods.

In the simplest definition of the concept, ʻaumākua are selected spirits from among the dead who, because of their achievements or special qualities during life, are deified after death and transfigured into gods. Exactly how the Hawaiians of old explained the process of transformation is not at all clear, but what is significant for our purposes is the fact that the living played an essential part in that process. David Malo, for example, explains how on the death of a chief the body was taken to a heiau and laid before the multitude so "that it might be deified and transformed into an *ʻaumakua.*" The solemn ritual was called kākūʻai and involved a series of elaborate ceremonies extending over a period of at least ten days. In one of the last stages, according to Malo, the kahuna, through special incantations, imparts "godlike power" to the bones that have been previously stripped of flesh. And then, Malo concluded, "with the apotheosis of the dead king being accomplished, he was worshipped as a real god *(akua maoli).*" Pūkuʻi (Handy and Pūkuʻi) also described a similar ritual that her family performed for deceased members. "They would take the bones after the flesh was all gone, wrap the bones in red and black tapa, and take them to the volcano. Then the *kahuna* would prepare the *'awa*. . . . After the *'awa* had been poured into the crater, the bones were thrown down there. For generations, some of our folks were taken there. . . . The last time my people conducted *kākū'ai* rituals was when my grandmother was taken to the volcano."

The dead do not deify themselves, but the living—the families, friends, and supporters of the dead, and, most of all, the kāhuna. The prayers, incantations, sacrifices, symbols, everything else that is ritually required, are prepared and performed by priests. And, if Malo is right, the priests are the ones who ultimately empower and legitimize the dead as 'aumākua. Presumably the departed spirit, too, has some role to play in his or her apotheosis, but as far as we know today, only the living can make gods of ancestors.

In 1931 Peter Buck (1970) startled not a few people at a series of lectures he presented at Yale University when he spoke of "manufactured" Polynesian gods. He explained his theory about how the gods were created, beginning with the deification of ancestral spirits. In effect, he likened deification to the modern manufacturing process of mass production. Since each family would want to honor its own 'aumākua, the total number of families, over a long period of time, would deify, that is, "manufacture," large numbers of 'aumākua. Thus, mathematically speaking, Kepelino's reference to "millions and millions" of gods may not have been too farfetched. We have pinpointed the cause for "rampant polytheism" here, in the deification of countless beloved ancestral spirits.

Significantly, death was not an automatic ticket to godhood. While apparently everyone was granted immortality, only a selected number was eligible for 'aumākua status. Clearly, that was regarded as both a prize and a responsibility which was not accorded automatically to just anyone. If that were so, being an 'aumakua would have been pointless. It was not an honor received as a matter of course, but one achieved in consequence of service, character, and potent mana exhibited during life.

Who were eligible? What qualities did candidates for elevation to 'aumakua have to possess? We have no revealed information on this subject, but can glean much from the roles that were conceived for them by living people. These roles included: (1) man-

ager of the spiritual affairs of the temporal family; (2) comforter
and counselor; (3) disciplinarian; (4) advocate of causes for both
individuals and 'ohana; (5) avenger of wrongs done to family
members; (6) guide in the afterlife; (7) protector and savior in time
of peril; and (8) patron. Pūku'i (Handy and Pūku'i) summed up
what 'aumākua do in these words: "As gods and relatives in one,
they give us strength when we are weak, warning when danger
threatens, guidance in our bewilderment, inspiration in our arts.
They are equally our judges, hearing our words and watching our
actions, reprimanding us for error, and punishing us for blatant
offense."

From these expectations we may infer some of the qualifications
and experiences required of an ancestor for becoming a god: (1)
knowledge and understanding of the personalities, desires, aspirations, and problems of members of an 'ohana; (2) the ability to
relate well to the family; (3) leadership in 'ohana activities; (4)
mediating experience in family disputes; (5) seniority in the 'ohana
hierarchy; (6) recognition and acceptance by the family; and (7)
possession of a high level of mana, with the ability to use it wisely.
Implicit in all this are such qualities as fairness, intelligence, maturity, leadership, aloha, empathy, toughness, and perhaps even a
sense of humor. We are told that 'aumākua were known for playing jokes on people and provoking mischief in general.

A typical candidate for 'aumakua status might have been the
haku, or master of the 'ohana, usually the oldest male in the senior
branch of the whole extended family. In life he presided over family councils, supervised family work within and outside the household, took care of family worship, divided the harvests or catches
of fish, oversaw the composing of eulogistic chants, and in general
exercised authority over the communal activities of the family.
E. S. Craighill Handy and his collaborator, Kawena Pūku'i
(1972), described the family haku. "Someone must speak for the
families and households, and the senior male member most competent to do so became the *haku*. Respect and affection vested him
with such authority as he had." He was the "revered" leader but
not a "dictator." The older folk of the 'ohana were "strong of character" and "extremely independent," so that the haku received the
advice and opinions of all family members.

Whatever the qualities were of a potential 'aumakua, whether a
haku or simply an elder, the presumption is that if he or she was

good enough to be honored in this life, he or she would be good enough to be revered in the next life. Therefore, the transition between being a mortal model of excellence and an immortal 'aumakua essentially involved a consensus of confidence (as opposed to a vote of confidence) by the 'ohana, whereupon this consensus was ritualized in the form of the kākū'ai, or deification ceremony.

In this process the central step is the approval and support of the 'ohana members, because not only is that necessary for the ritual to take place, but, perhaps even more imperative, that support must continue in the hereafter, in order to maintain an effective relationship between 'aumakua and 'ohana. If the akua, as recounted earlier, needed to be "believed in," that is, supported, it was even more necessary for the 'aumākua to be believed in. We stress this point to remind us of the margin of self-determination and freedom that Hawaiians seemed to reserve for themselves with respect to their gods.

Perhaps the best single word to describe the relationship between 'aumakua and 'ohana is partnership, not necessarily one of equals, but nonetheless a close-working family alliance. On the one hand, the 'aumākua protect, warn, counsel, heal, forgive, avenge, discipline, and administer, while on the other hand, the 'ohana members do good deeds, propitiate the 'aumākua, heed their warnings, offer nourishment, and pay homage to them. Both parties to the compact have joint as well as separate responsibilities and, as in any partnership, it is only as viable and as strong as the ability of the partners to carry out their duties makes it.

The underlying value at work here is reciprocity. In fact, nothing seems to have been so characteristic of the Hawaiian relationship between the temporal and spiritual world as the notion of reciprocal obligations. During the centuries, Hawaiians must have developed very sensitive antennae that allowed them to receive and interpret signals originating in the realm of the 'aumākua. Hawaiians of old, then, may have needed to make only half a step to transfer this sensitivity to ordinary social behavior in the form of empathy (another value we shall discuss later).

Essential to the concept of reciprocity is the principle of accountability, in the strictest sense of the word. That is, both parties must not only be willing to accept responsibility for their acts, but also must take account of each act as it might affect the 'aumakua, or vice versa. In other words, a monitoring or periodic evaluation of activities must go on all the time, for in such an important relationship nothing can go unnoticed. This is done not so much to check on the other party as to be able to measure and determine what, when, why, and how something should be represented and repaid. Keep in mind that this accounting becomes indispensable when and if there is a falling-out between 'ohana members and their 'aumākua.

Not bringing shame on one's family was one of the most important injunctions of old Hawai'i. Since one's education, status in the community, and all of one's life necessities, mutual support, and aloha, among other things, depended on the family, it is easy to understand the importance placed on the admonition. But its importance takes on much greater meaning when the consequences from a shameful act committed by one or several family members will affect the honor of generation upon generation of the "eternal" family. One of the functions of the 'aumakua was to ensure the preservation of the honor and dignity of the family by preventing such acts or, at the least, by minimizing their effects.

To the Hawaiian who believes in the concept of the "eternal" family in partnership with 'aumākua, death loses its sting. He has no fear of a hereafter in which his soul will be warmly received and safely guided by his 'aumakua. Hence, he has no fear of death. Many are the observations or stories of how Hawaiians of old faced death calmly, with remarkable composure, of how, while dying, they coolly and clearly expressed their last wishes, almost controlling the time of death. Since death is not the ultimate farewell, grief of parting is only for a momentary separation. It never becomes pathological. At the appointed time, death is a welcome passage to the "mystic sea of Pō," where guardian and kindred spirits dwell.

Today a remarkable affinity still endures among Hawaiians for their 'aumākua. Take any random group of Hawaiians and ask them about their thoughts or sentiments regarding 'aumākua, and more likely than not the majority will have "good vibes" to the idea. In our Ho'okanaka workshops, almost all of our participants had positive feelings about 'aumākua. In a casual survey of Hawaiian clergy or lay ministers, including a Mormon, Episcopalian, Congregationalist, Catholic, and a "neotraditional" religious kahuna, none felt negative about 'aumākua as such, although as individuals they had reservations about many related concepts. Young people in particular, once they get into the study of Hawaiian religion or culture, are fascinated by the concept of their 'aumākua. Even the more skeptical Hawaiian is more for it than against it, if only "to hedge my bets," as one person (an attorney) put it.

Several reasons explain this lingering affinity. As a general comment applicable to other cases in which traditional concepts and values still persist, one of the reasons is the possibility that ethnic groups have a "genetic memory," upon which are imprinted our past experiences. The residual imprint for 'aumakua-related ideas and feelings apparently is still active. More specifically, strong sentiment continues for keeping the 'aumakua system because "family" and family-associated values still rank very high among contemporary Hawaiians. When these are coupled with our instinctual hope for being together with loved ones in the hereafter, 'aumakua-like concepts have a great appeal. Having an 'aumakua is also compatible with popular Christian religious notions, such as ministering angels or guardian angels, widely taught in both Catholic and Protestant sects. And, of course, Japanese recognize in their ujigami the same kind of deified guardian ancestors that Hawaiians call 'aumākua.

The traditional values demonstrated in the Hawaiian concept of the 'aumakua system—the dignity of the family, avoiding acts that bring shame on the family, family solidarity, "salvation" as a group, perhaps even, ultimately, achieving godliness as an 'aumakua, maintaining open relations between the temporal and spiritual worlds, reciprocity, and others—are appealing to many if not most modern Hawaiians, partly because these ideas keep a timeless relevance, that is, they are good for any generation. Indeed, they speak to many of the hopes and desires of people trapped in the toils of our modern society. If they are worth preserving and strengthening, the pertinent question follows: How much of the old ways can we realistically preserve or strengthen, without accepting all the concepts and practices from which those values are derived? Is it possible (or necessary) to revive kākū'ai and its related priesthood in order to sustain a modern 'aumakua system? Or have we become so democratic and egalitarian as to make impossible the deifying of any great person? How much can we adapt and compromise without violating the integrity of the system and thereby lose its intrinsic values? If we cannot possibly duplicate the past, should we not create a new set of beliefs in order to ensure the same values? We introduce the problem here because we shall have to grapple with it throughout this book.

Perhaps most people who think of ancestral gods and ancestor worship accept them naturally as being two sides of the same coin, just as the Greek philosopher Euhemerus said a long time ago. Interestingly enough, however, modern Hawaiians who identify with their 'aumākua resist the notion of ancestor worship, mostly because it does not take into account the "partnership" in the relationship between 'aumākua and family members, which stresses two-way cooperation rather than one-way veneration. Nonetheless, a great deal of reverence is shown 'aumākua, although this is not done ritualistically. (Incidentally, it is not difficult for Hawaiian believers in 'aumākua to identify with the followers of certain Buddhist sects whose homes often feature a family altar, or butsudan, used in part to venerate the memory of departed family members.)

Finally, an intriguing aspect of modern Hawaiians' feelings about their 'aumākua is their belief in kino lau, that is, in the multiple manifestations of gods in such forms as sharks, owls, mudhens, caterpillars, lizards, eels, and even rocks and plants. It is not unusual to meet Hawaiians today, some strongly Christian, who talk sincerely, although often guardedly, about their manō (shark) or mo'o (lizard) 'aumākua. Even some with "scientific" or skeptical mind-sets see no intellectual conflict between their scientific view of natural phenomena and a spiritual view of their shark god. Very few Hawaiians, however, are as aware of a related 'aumakua concept, namely, the 'unihipili, the spirit of a dead person, who "was sometimes held and converted into a controlled spirit living in the unseen but tied to a place or object and to a keeper *(kahu)*." Often 'unihipili were associated with trouble, and most Hawaiians preferred to leave such spirits alone. But the modern Hawaiian's lack of awareness of 'unihipili is more a matter of ignorance than of fear.

Attributes of the Gods

One of the paradoxes of Hawaiian religion is that we know so much about the gods yet know so little. We have a rich oral literature with numerous epic stories relating countless incidents and events about so many gods that we should not want for answers. But when, for example, we ask the question about what the specific attributes of the gods are, we must study long and hard. In truth, we seem to know what the gods *do*, but not what they *are*.

We might illustrate this by comparing the ease with which a Christian Hawaiian would answer the same question about Jehovah or Jesus Christ. If he or she has had any exposure to Sunday school or the Bible, probably the response would include such statements as: "God is Love," or "God is Truth," or "God is a Jealous God," or "God is Good," and so on. The ordinary believer may have trouble with defining these several attributes, but not much difficulty in listing them.

On deeper reflection, however, our paradox is quite understandable. Actually, we asked the wrong question at the start, one that a monotheistic Christian would ask. Had we asked the right question, one a polytheist would ask, our paradox immediately disappears. Because there are so many gods in polytheism, we must direct the query to a specific god. To wit, what are the attributes of Kū? Of Lono? Kāne? Kanaloa? Laka? Pele? Of Kū'ulakai, the god of fishermen? And so on. Now we have a manageable question, because each god is different from all the others.

So, if we have some difficulty in identifying general attributes of Hawaiian gods, that is because the sheer number of deities makes it impossible to specify a list applicable to akua, 'aumākua, 'unihipili, kupua, and all the lesser gods as well. The diversity of Hawaiian gods simply precludes making any broad yet meaningful generalizations.

What has all this to do with values? Everything. We must identify these traits because believers hold their gods up as models to imitate and their attributes as ideals to achieve. Just as the Hawaiian Christian who really believes that "God is Love" will try to practice love, so the Hawaiian of old who believed that Lono stood for ho'okipa, or hospitality, would try to act hospitably. In short, since godly attributes are "divine" and therefore of supreme worth, they become some of the more important standards that believers try to live by.

While it is not exactly like trying "to find a needle in a haystack," identifying the godly traits and their implied values requires a good bit of intellectual detective work. For unlike the Gospel "myths" of Matthew, Mark, Luke, and John, which clearly spell out Christ-like attributes, Hawaiian myths do not. Instead, they concentrate on relating the deeds and functions of the gods. What we must do, then, is to deduce from the sacred accounts, using inferential or circumstantial evidence contained in them, the attributes and values we are looking for. We do not get much help in this from modern commentaries by Malo, Kamakau, Kepelino, and Pūkuʻi, who have chosen to emphasize matters other than values as such.

One of our best leads is to examine the functions of the principal gods and their many alternate titles and forms. Let us begin with Lono, who was regarded as the god of clouds, winds, rain, sea, agriculture, and fertility. But he appeared in some fifty forms, such as Lonoikamakahiki, patron god of the annual harvest festival, or Makahiki; Lonomakaihe, god of spear throwers; Lono-pūhā, god of healing; Lonoikeaweawealoha, god of lovemaking and mercy; and so on. Certain attributes or values follow from certain functions or actions represented by a god. Lono, for example, exemplified peace because as god of the Makahiki he, in effect, outlawed war and closed the temples of Kū for the four-month festival. In a society where fighting was not uncommon, Lono demonstrated not only his influence over the people but also their desire for peace. So we may conclude that attaining peace, however unrealistic and idealistic it may have appeared at times, was an important value to Hawaiians.

The Makahiki celebrated Lono as provider of the rains that water the crops which in turn ensured food and nourishment for the people. Inadequate rains meant drought and poor harvests, which led to famine, one of the more dreaded calamities in old Hawaiʻi. For an agriculture-based economy, the generous provision of rains by Lono was of supreme importance. Thus, in making the land fertile and productive, one of the values symbolized by Lono was that of giving, and of giving generously. Because generosity ranked near the top of the scale of Hawaiian values, it seems reasonable to conclude that one of the main purposes of the festival was to reinforce this important value.

An allied value celebrated by the Makahiki, and therefore associated with Lono, is one we have stressed before, namely, reciprocity. It is symbolized in the important ceremonies surrounding the presentations of hoʻokupu, or contributions by the common peo-

ple to the ali'i who represent Lono. The ritualization of the act of
returning something to Lono is the best evidence of the god's
acceptance of its symbolic value since, as we shall see later, religious ritual is the reenactment of a divine deed or the confirmation
of a divine principle. As a matter of fact, most offerings and sacrifices to the gods are but ritual endorsements of the value of reciprocity.

As patron of the Makahiki, Lono was also the sponsor and
booster of the Hawaiian version of the Greek games at Olympia.
In Hawai'i, too, these contests of the Makahiki presented the
greatest athletes and sporting events of the year. Lono himself was
particularly skilled at spear throwing. Other gods not only patron-
ized sports but also engaged in contests either between themselves
or with men, but Lono of all the gods exemplified the worth of
both recreational and competitive physical activity. Since such
activity filled an important part of Hawaiian life, placing it under
the patronage of the gods was only natural. It must have been both
a source of inspiration and motivation for athletes of old Hawai'i
to be able to look up to a god who provided divine support and
who was a sportsman himself. This is a point that should not be
lost by those who are attempting to revive Makahiki-type sports
festivals today.

Lono, too, was regarded as a god of healing and also an important patron of kahuna lā'au lapa'au, or herbal doctors. Therefore,
he would have stood for maintaining good health and, because of
his strong connection with sports, for physical fitness in particular.
This is all consistent with Hawaiians' appreciation of an appealing
and handsome body as expressed in the phrase "pali ke kua," literally "the back is a cliff," said of strong and attractive persons.
Needless to say, these values have a contemporary ring because of
the importance, sometimes exaggerated and distorted, our society
today places on fitness, health, and handsomeness.

Let us turn to Kū, the object of much misunderstanding among
Hawaiians and non-Hawaiians since the missionaries came in
1820. Anyone who has stood before the most famous image of
Kūkā'ilimoku, now at the Bishop Museum, probably backs away
from it with an unforgettable impression and perhaps surge of
fear. Standing about four feet high and covered with red feathers,
the idol—its mouth armed with triple rows of dog's teeth, the eyes
represented by shells glaring with mother of pearl and black nuts

for pupils, and with long tufts of black human hair flowing from its head—is a figure calculated to arouse dread in the beholder. Fierce, defiant, frightening, merciless, bloody, cruelly chilling—these are only some of the feelings that the image conjures up.

But Kū, as a deity, is intended to arouse more than fear and battle rage. He represents many diverse functions and forms, ranging from defense in war to blackest sorcery, fishing, planting, feather-work, and other occupations. Thus he is the source of a complex set of traits. To be sure, he was the god of war, Kā'ilimoku, the divider of lands. But there are two sides to war: the offensive and the defensive. The offensive aspect has been emphasized and popularized, in part by Kamehameha the Great for the battles of conquest that culminated in his rule over all the islands of Hawai'i. Yet Kū's original role, if not one of his most important functions, was to serve as the protector and defender of the territorial integrity of individual chiefdoms. When we manage to see Kū in this dual stance, both defensive and offensive, for his peoples' sake, we can no longer regard him as merely an aggressive, bloodthirsty conqueror-brute, eager for war and slaughter.

The key attribute or value that Kū personified is revealed in his name, which means "upright"—standing tall, as in *"Kū kanaka!"* A warrior who is standing tall on the battlefield clearly is being brave in the face of the enemy. Kūkā'ilimoku's presence not only put fear in the hearts of the opposing forces, but also inspired the "good guys" with a fighting "go for broke" spirit that would lead them to victory. He gave them not only physical courage but also, more important, moral courage—the feeling of confidence and pride—that is the source of all acts of bravery and valor.

This is the kind of courage that Kū glorifies, not the violences of war. The failure to appreciate this distinction has led some people to argue that the Hawaiians of old were basically a fierce and warlike race. Such accusers point not only to Kūkā'ilimoku but also to luakini heiau, the war temples where human sacrifices were dedicated to Kū and, of course, to the high incidence of warfare, especially in the eighteenth century. A war temple, or heiau waikaua, according to David Malo, was built by a king "when he was about to make war upon another" or "when he heard that some other king was about to make war against him." In the temple he prayed to his gods "to look with favor upon him," to obtain "assurances of victory over his enemies," or to receive "warnings of defeat at their hands." In other words, a luakini was built for a specific purpose associated with warfare—to accomplish victory or to forestall defeat. Hence, there were many luakini. But no one permanent war temple as such was built and dedicated solely to glorify all wars and for all times. Furthermore, as Malo said, luakini could be built also for a very unmartial purpose: "to make the crops flourish."

In terms of Hawaiian values and practices connected with the gods, we have yet to find in Hawaiian religion any that clearly praise and dignify war as such. On the other hand, compelling evidence is plentiful for ceremonies and rituals that promoted peace. Thus, no festivals were held that honored war; the one major festival of ancient Hawai'i honored peace and Lono; the most important rite in boyhood, when a boy was removed from the company of women to the company of men, was a dedication to Lono; and the operation of subincision, with its ritual, consecrated the boy as a potential procreator to Kāne, the Creator God (Handy and Pūku'i).

From a technological and economic point of view, Kū's responsibilities for planting, fishing, featherworking, canoe and adze making, far overshadow in importance his function in warfare. As Kūka'ō'ō, Kū the digging stick, he represented the most important agricultural tool in old Hawai'i. It was used for cultivating the soil, hence, in the labors of planting and harvesting, the beginning of the food cycle. In presiding over these functions in the food production cycle, Kū was far more important on a farm than on a battlefield, at least among the maka'āinana who tilled the land. As Kū'ulakai, red Kū of the sea, he protected fishermen. Because the ocean was the second most important source of foods, the economic importance of fishing requires no elaboration. As Kūpā'ai-ke'e, Kūpā who eats defects, he had invented the adze which, as an all-around tool, was second to none among Hawaiian implements. As Kū'ālanawao, he was god not only of canoe makers but also of the forest, or wao, from which the great logs were gathered. The worth that Hawaiians placed on canoes as means of fishing and transportation cannot be doubted. Since all these activities deal with the basic physical needs for human survival, they show Kū to us in proper perspective.

Kū personified many of the technological and economic values that enabled Hawaiian society to achieve one of the highest levels of development among Pacific island cultures. These values would include industriousness, thrift, efficiency, productivity, quality, precision, utility, innovativeness, adaptability, competitiveness, achievement, excellence, organization, cooperativeness, awareness, and knowledge. As we shall see in later chapters about their science, technology, and economics, there is no lack of evidence to show how Hawaiians demonstrated these values in their accomplishments in botany, medicine, navigation, engineering, construction, toolmaking, canoe building, "capital improvement" projects, and arts and crafts, among other fields. Kū, then, is really the god of Hawaiian technology.

If you have ever wondered why so many Hawaiian surnames are derived from Kāne (for example, the Oʻahu telephone directory lists many more for Kāne than for Lono or Kū), one reason lies in the lasting impact he has had on the Hawaiian consciousness because of his primeval role as the Giver of Life, Creator of Man, progenitor of Papa and Wākea, patron deity of fresh water, taro, ʻawa, sunlight, precipices, rainbows, and winds, among other natural phenomena. Kāne has countless forms, and many of these overlap some of the functions of other deities, especially Lono and Kanaloa, but he is probably more ancient and exalted than any of the akua. As a god, then, he is one of the primordial models of Hawaiian values.

Since life is more important than anything else, the life-giving power of Kāne transcended in meaning any other single divine deed. Does that necessarily mean, however, that Hawaiians placed supreme value on human life? Practices such as human sacrifice and infanticide, by today's standards, tend to suggest otherwise, but reasonable explanations can be made for such practices when viewed in the Hawaiian context. For example, infanticide was done mainly to prevent "adulteration of the purity of *aliʻi* blood lines," as in the case of a woman of low rank bearing a child fathered by an aliʻi, or vice versa (Handy and Pūkuʻi). Infanticide was never done simply because a child was unwanted for economic or social reasons. And human sacrifice, practiced by many peoples such as the Egyptians, Arabs, American Indians, the Aztecs, Vikings, Romans, and the Jews of Old Testament times, was more concerned with the ritualistic acquisition of mana, or godliness, than with the mindless killing of another human being. (We shall discuss this at length in the chapter on rituals.) And, rather than Kāne, Kū, as Kūwahailo, Kū maggot mouth, or the sorcery god, through the agency of his priesthood is supposed to have introduced the rites of human sacrifice and maintained them in his heiau.

As god of procreation, Kāne exemplified those values relating to the perpetuation of the human species. The reproductive power of man or woman was celebrated in the great importance placed on the sexual organs, which were honored in the hula and laudatory chants. Many a Hawaiian chief had his own special mele ma'i, or genital chant, with appropriate descriptions for the genitalia. Such a chief was King Kalākaua, whose chant credited him with hālala, or very big sexual equipment. The primary purpose of breeding, of course, is the bearing and raising of children, whom Hawaiians cherished with enormous care and affection. The value placed on children, as is clearly evidenced in the hānai system of adopting or fostering children, far outweighs the seeming lack of concern in the rare case of infanticide. Breeding, in the final analysis, is charged with the continuation of the family line. In this sense, Kāne could be regarded as the supreme father of the 'ohana system, although, as we have previously discussed, within an individual family its 'aumākua took charge of its interests.

Just as Kāne gives life to man and to woman, so does he give life to earth through his procreative energy in the bounties of water and sunshine. For Hawai'i's agricultural economy of old, as of today, the worth of these two elements, particularly water, is obvious. So highly prized was water that the Hawaiian word for wealth is waiwai, water-water. As Kāneikawai, or Kāne in the water, he could be regarded as the god of wealth. In fact, as with Kāne, so with the other major gods: each personifies important economic as well as spiritual values.

Kāne's many natural forms reveal one of the great truths of Hawaiian religion: "the omnipresence of the divine in nature." As we shall discuss this in detail in the next section, we need only say here that Kāne and the other gods exemplify such values as reverence for nature, the interrelatedness of man and nature, the mauli ola, or life principle, of nature, seeking harmony with one's environment rather than domination over it, and the precept that we have only been entrusted with care of the 'āina, the land, and not given ownership of it. Other ideals and standards may be mentioned that define the spiritual as well as temporal relationship between man and nature in Hawaiian religion, but all have their origin in the gods.

Hina, Papa, Haumea, Nuʻakea, Pele, Kapo, Laka, Alalalahe, and Kihawahine all have a singular attribute in common: each is a goddess. Hina, the most widely known goddess in Polynesia, appears in many forms: as the mother of Kamapuaʻa and Māui; as the wife of Wākea (after he "divorced" Papa); as the mother of the island of Molokaʻi; as goddess of the moon, corals, and spiny sea creatures; and as patroness of fishermen. Haumea is the patroness of childbirth, "the great source of female fertility," the mother of Pele. Nuʻakea is the goddess of lactation, helping mothers to nurse and wean their babies. Kapo, the sister of Pele, is a goddess of the hula and also a fierce goddess of sorcery. Laka is the most famous goddess of the hula, and of maile, ʻieʻie, and other forest plants. Alalalahe is the goddess of love, Kihawahine is one of the best known lizard, or moʻo, goddesses. Papa is Mother Earth and the first wife of Wākea (Father Sky). And Pele, of course, is the volcano goddess, the deity of fire.

Even the world of the gods appears to be a "man's world," inasmuch as all these goddesses are classed as "lesser" gods, but their powers and deeds are hardly less imposing than are those of some of their male counterparts. Nothing in Hawaiʻi shows the awesome power of nature as often or as dramatically as do its volcanoes, yet this power is personified by a supposedly "lesser" deity. Hina displays many powers comparable to those of Kū, with whom she collaborated in many ventures, including the gods' "first" landing in Hawaiʻi. Depending on the mythological data source, Haumea may have made the first man, or may have been the "destroyer and guardian of wild growth" and the inventor of the first mat sail.

While we must be able to distinguish between what is truly mythical (that is, ultimately real) and what is only fanciful in understanding the myths, we cannot help but be impressed with the overlapping and interlocking functions shared among gods and goddesses. At times the gender of the god is not important, as long as the job is done or the supplicant's prayer is answered. Whether male or female, the gods seem to be equal in their ability to use their mana. Perhaps the best term for describing the male-female relationship among the gods is complementarity, as opposed to equality.

Some very important Hawaiian values were expressed in the functions and attributes of the goddesses. We are all deeply indebted to Laka for the hula, because in dance we understand the power of the body to communicate. Hawaiians of old considered the hula sacred because it was a means of communication between people and their gods. Laka's identification with the hula imprints on our consciousness the recognition that dance is the essence of sacred ritual. As an art form, hula exemplifies many important aesthetic and associated values, ranging from harmony, balance, and symmetry, to spiritual communion with the gods and the natural phenomena that the dance imitates. That some, although certainly not all, of these values are recognized to this day is evidenced in the popularity of the hula, both modern and ancient, among both men and women. (See chapter 4 for a more extensive discussion on hula as ritual.)

In Papa we find those significant values that primal peoples almost everywhere associated with "Mother Earth." Their regard is summarized in the familiar expression among Hawaiians: "Treat her with respect." As we shall see later, this attitude toward the earth may have influenced even the way old Hawaiian toolmakers fashioned the ʻōʻō. It certainly affects the way some modern Hawaiians consider the steel blade of a bulldozer as a machine of desecration.

Nature and the Gods

One of the great truths about Hawaiian gods is their omnipresence. Indeed, that presence is so intertwined and inescapable that gods and the manifestations of nature become embodiments of each other. This integrated view of the divine in nature has had such a profound influence on Hawaiian thinking that we need to examine it in more detail.

Hawaiians believed that all things—"animate and inanimate, objects and creatures"—are interrelated by the all-pervading creative force: mana, the divine power of the gods. That universal energy activates all things. No matter how infinite the variety of forms of nature or of the gods, all are expressions of the fundamental force: mana. We see, however faintly, the principle at work in kino lau, and in the transmutation of multiple forms; the shapes may change, but the essential elements in them do not. Precisely how this happens is unknown to us, but no doubt Hawaiian mystics of old had an intuitive if not an intellectual explanation for the mystery.

Some modern physicists offer an explanation for a somewhat analogous view of nature. Fritjof Capra, in *The Tao of Physics*, wrote that "the basic oneness of the universe . . . is one of the most important revelations of modern physics." According to quantum theory, now widely accepted as a consistent and accurate description of all atomic phenomena, the universe is not a collection of unrelated physical objects, but rather "a complicated web of relations between the various parts of a unified whole." Capra stressed the point that "the most important characteristic of the Eastern world view—one could almost say the essence of it—is the awareness of the unity and mutual interrelation of all things and events, the experience of all phenomena in the world as manifestations of a basic oneness." This ultimate reality in Hinduism is called Brahman, in Buddhism Dharmakaya, and in Taoism Tao. In Hawaiian religious thought it is mana.

We get a similar view of nature from an entirely different side of science, biology. Lewis Thomas, in *The Lives of a Cell*, said: "We are told that the trouble with Modern Man is that he has been trying to detach himself from nature. . . . Man is embedded in nature. The biological science of recent years has been making this a more urgent fact of life. The new, hard problem will be to cope with the dawning, intensifying realization of how interlocked we are." He declared that "the whole earth must be taken as a single organic unity" for "it is *most* like a single cell."

Finally, another modern scientist, Errol Harris (cited in McLean), summed up current scientific thinking as follows: "The outcome is a conception of nature as a single, individual totality, organismic throughout, in which distinctions are always relative; partial elements are always determined in their individual form, and dovetailed behaviour by the over-arching pattern of the totality."

One of the moral imperatives that emanates from the view of the omnipresence of the divine in nature is respect for nature. The object of respect is the divinity and therefore the sacredness of nature, not its mere outward physical manifestations. Mana, the ultimate reality, articulated by thunder, radiated by the sun, blown by the winds, erupted by volcanoes—that is the reason for reverence from comprehending men. Not all things in nature are simply respected; some things are venerated or worshiped. In other words, although nature as a totality or in its designated god forms may be held sacred, this sacredness does not hold true for every thing around us. We still observe the dichotomy of kapu versus noa, the sacred versus the profane, in nature near us and in the vast universe beyond as well. Also, reverence for nature in the Hawaiian mind does not equate with "reverence for life" of the late Albert Schweitzer's school of thought, or the more extreme Hindu and Buddhist sects that try to avoid killing any form of life. While one may not reverence or venerate all things in nature, the minimum expected of one is respect.

Echoes of the same moral imperative are heard today from naturalists, environmentalists, and poets, among others. W. H. Auden, the noted poet, said, "The great vice of Americans is not materialism but a lack of respect for matter" (i.e., nature). Christopher Derrick, in *The Delicate Creation*, wrote:

> A society in which Nature was deeply and genuinely respected . . . would hardly desire to indulge in the activities that now cause such varied and frightening kinds of trouble. . . . The kind of society that is likely to survive and prosper is the kind of society in which men would never dream—individually or collectively—of treating Nature in the disrespectfully manipulative fashion, the essentially hostile fashion that we now take for granted. . . . Where we continue to fight nature . . . humanity will continue to foul its own nest most suicidally, to saw away at the slender ecological branch upon which it perches. *We are part of Nature* [italics added].

While Hawaiians of old may not have thought of respect for nature in such global terms, they did show respect in many ways: by not intruding noisily in a forest in the morning, or by carelessly trampling upon ferns and shrubs, or by polluting a fishing area, or by thoughtlessly discarding their noisome wastes. Whether on a global or a local scale, the principle of respect is the same: it is essentially an attitude of mālama and aloha, as Hawaiians say, that is, of caring with love. René Dubos, in *So Human an Animal*, wrote exactly this: "Technicized societies thus far have exploited the earth: we must reverse this trend and learn to take care of it with love."

Another moral imperative is encapsulated in the Hawaiian concept of lōkahi, harmony in unity. Since man is a part of nature, it necessarily follows that he should strive to be in balance with his surroundings. By balance is meant, to use a popular in-word, being "in sync." When a man is not synchronized with a place and the things in it, he cannot avoid the inevitable disharmony which brings pain and unhappiness. The very essence of our humanity causes us to strive for that ideal natural equilibrium. Yet this involves knowing what the measure against which the balance is determined should be for any given situation. If one is walking along a high wire, he can easily determine what is necessary to maintain his balance. But while many situations in life, figuratively speaking, may be likened to walking a high wire, still with them the problem of balancing is far more complex. Knowing the moral imperative is one thing, but knowing all the nuances for applying it is quite another matter. Any sinner can testify to that.

Here, then, we need to introduce the Hawaiian concept of dualism, because it bears closely on understanding the workings of lōkahi. Dualism refers to the idea that all phenomena in our universe are organized in pairs of opposites: night and day, light and darkness, water and land, large and small, left and right, male and female, good and bad, and so on and on. We recognize that between the paired opposites a dynamic relationship is always at work, ranging from completest repulsion to completest attraction, from thesis, or affirmation, to antithesis, or denial. The ideal condition occurs when the two poles, or extremes, come together, however briefly, in a state of rest, or synthesis, blending their opposite elements in a new relationship. This is what happens when balance or harmony is achieved. The "grand motif" of Chinese art and science, the Yin-Yang principle, is the perfect symbol for this duality.

Lōkahi really deals with the human dialectic—the reconciling of contradictions in life—and as such is both intellectually and philosophically a challenge. We can be sure that the learned kāhuna of old appreciated the depth of that challenge. But we are less certain about some modern Hawaiians who frequently use the term, sometimes as a political shibboleth, without any reference to its traditional religious or spiritual import.

A corollary to the principle of man's lōkahi with nature is the idea that nature, too, has its limits—and that we must abide by those limits or suffer the consequences. This belief is certainly part of the basis for the Hawaiian practice of conservation by imposing kapu on harvesting of fish or crops at certain times or places. They recognized all too clearly the fact that, while they were blessed with many gifts of nature, their resources were not infinite. Man lives in what is essentially a dependent's changing relationship with nature. We today perhaps understand the bounds of that shifting relationship much better than our ancestors did, and therefore should appreciate the dangers in environmental exploitation. But if ever we do give those dangers a thought, we do so less for religious than for economic and political reasons. The words of Stephen Schneider and Lynne Morton are pertinent. "The power that Nature wields over man, in terms of both the limitations imposed and the opportunities offered, has shaped a bond that has held man to Nature for as long as we can determine. This primordial bond remains today, despite the struggles of many to break it." If we here, in this book's analysis, are dealing with primordial conditions, we are also dealing with primordial values.

In a sense, the gods of old still try to speak to us, for we inhabit the same universe under essentially the same cosmic conditions that impose upon us the same limitations and their corresponding obligations. The chief difference between us now and the people of old is that the new "gods" of modern science have added their voices to the chorus of confirmation for many of the old Hawaiian truths.

4

RITUAL AND SACRIFICE

Ritualmania?

Johannes C. Andersen may have been right when he stated in his *Myths and Legends of the Polynesians* that nowhere in Polynesia was so much "ceremony observed as in Hawaii." Ceremonies or rituals ranged from healing of the sick and gift exchanges to rain-making and exorcising of evil spirits. If it were possible to record all the rites that Hawaiians ever used, along with their prescribed rules, sanctions, times and places for their enactment, accompanying incantations, and so on, the material would fill a whole big volume.

Hawaiian civilization probably resembled the American Indian Zuni culture. As W. Wallis has said, if Zuni culture had a style, that style was one of ritual. Their daily life was ritualized from morning until night; almost nothing was done without a rite; and immense amounts of time, effort, and resources were used on such activities. If most people in the world of everyday are creatures of habit, the Zuni were creatures of habitual ritual.

People today who live in a highly rationalized and technological society would have difficulty in visualizing and empathizing with a ritualistic culture. Modern rationalist ideology that worships reason is anti-myth and therefore anti-ritual. Religious sacraments, processions, holy days, and other rites, along with incense, icons, bells, vestments, and so on, are noticed with amusement or are dismissed as "ritual hype" designed to appeal to emotions and not the intellect. All those activities are nothing more than playacting, the scoffers say, outward show without much substance within. This prejudice is manifest in some puritanical sects that make a virtue out of banning all ritual, although part of the reason for this attitude may lie in the fact that most of them are too new to have recognized a need for ritual. The older the religious organization is, the more tradition it has to sustain it and the greater is the reliance upon ritual.

But when we examine ritual in its broadest secular sense, including everything from the military salute to courtroom decorum and presidential pomp, we see that our modern society is just as much bound by it as was any primal culture. Like mushrooms that appear overnight on a lawn, new rituals appear with nearly every new fad, invention, musical pop group, spiritual movement, and threat from the unknown. Educators, psychologists, politicians, generals, actors, and many others have long recognized and even exploited the rewards of ritual. In fact, in recent years social scientists have turned their critical attention upon ritual in business and industry, and have concluded, among other things, that it is important in achieving social cohesion and realizing life values (Bocock). Perhaps no one has yet counted the number and variety of rites and ceremonies that modern societies observe, on both religious and secular occasions, but when anyone does take that census, we should not be surprised if "ritualmania" becomes a term more appropriately applied to the modern rather than to the so-called primitive world.

Nonetheless, we are concerned mainly with ritual based on religion. In this regard, present-day Hawaiians, as a group, may be a little more tolerant of ritual than are the general run of Americans. A lot of it is still practiced in the hālau hula, either in initiation or ʻūniki graduation ceremonies; indeed, some people believe that the hālau hula may be the last stronghold of the oldest sacred rites. Hawaiian ministers of the several Christian sects conduct rites that are based on many traditional concepts, and even employ materials used by priests of old, such as tī leaves, ʻōlena, or turmeric, salt, and sacrosanct stones. Some of the ceremonies of our fraternal societies are also tradition based, although often they show the influence of Masonic rites, once very popular with nineteenth century leaders, such as King Kalākaua. Nostalgic ceremony is still reenacted in the pageantry of neotraditional events, such as Aloha Week with its "royal court" and colorful parades. Those Hawaiians who still harbor monarchical sentiments place great importance on protocol, as in determining the proper order for front-row seating or for leading their groups in parades and processions. Interestingly, among other Polynesian peoples today, such as

Samoans, Tongans, and Maoris, ritual and protocol based on strict rules and procedures still play a far more important and visible role, with very clear implications for the maintenance of their personal and communal value systems.

The Myth and Ritual Connection

The relationship between myth and ritual was explained by Walter Brenneman in these terms:

> Ritual plays the role of an instinctual action and myth of the psychic image which apprehends that action. Myth, then, could be understood as archetypal image expressed in word, and ritual, as archetypal image expressed in gesture. . . . Mythic motifs, therefore, imply and impel corresponding ritualistic gestures. Contained latently within each mythic image is an impulse to corresponding action and vice-versa. Each action or image, as the case may be, extends the meaning of the other through its complementary medium. Action materializes the image through gesture and myth clarifies the gesture through image. . . . Thus neither myth nor ritual precedes the other in terms of importance or meaning.

In sum, myth and ritual—and, we should add, the gods too—are inseparable.

Myth and ritual forge the links that bind the traditional Hawaiian to his religion and society: through myth he defines his ultimate values in the realm of the sacred, and through ritual he affirms and reenacts those values. In essence, ritual means the acting out of mythic values based on the deeds of the gods as they are recounted in the moʻolelo. Or, in other words, ritual is the reenactment of supernatural actions or events applied to human endeavors. Of course, not all ritual is myth related, but in Hawaiʻi of old, for all intents and purposes, it was.

Let us illustrate this connection between myth and ritual with the Hawaiian festival best known today, the Makahiki. In modern Hawaiʻi most people think that the event is a sports or arts celebration that is held for a single day. Few people realize anymore that, for the Hawaiians of old, the Makahiki was a time of instructive ritual, marking the year's most important season. During those four months of plenty and peace, the whole populace, through a succession of ceremonies directed by chiefs and priests, gave thanks to the gods for the blessings they had bestowed. And with those many rituals, ranging from the most awesome to the happily festive, all the people were reminded anew of the laws by which they lived here on earth below, according to the mandates of the great gods in the realm above. In other words, the festival was a great ritual consisting of many individual rites exemplifying the deeds of Lono as the god of rains, harvests, peace, and physical fitness.

The Makahiki enacted only those parts of the Lono myth that were connected with his life on the island of Hawai'i. According to the ancient story, Lono had come from Kahiki to Hawai'i and lived with his wife at Kealakekua. He killed her in a fit of jealousy, instituted the Makahiki in her honor, went around the island challenging likely opponents to wrestle with him. Finally, he built a canoe, the people filled it with provisions, forty men carried it to a launching place, and from there Lono alone sailed forth to Tahiti. But he promised the people that someday he would return, not by canoe but on an "island shaded by trees, covered over by coconuts, swarming with fowl and swine" (Beckwith 1970).

The Makahiki festival served five purposes for the people of old: (1) it ushered in the new year; (2) it marked the beginning of the annual harvest season, with the arrival of the winter rains; (3) it facilitated the collection of taxes for the ali'i nui, or paramount chief; (4) it gave reason to hold the competitive games; and (5) it provided a time of peace. The Makahiki season began with the appearance in the month now known as November of the Pleiades, which Hawaiians called Makali'i. (Some people believed that a man named Makali'i served as the navigator for Hawai'i Loa, the legendary discoverer of Hawai'i.) At that time of year the winter rains usually set in. They come from the south, where lies Kahiki, from whence Lono promised to return. During the initial period of the festival, the luakini or other heiau dedicated to Kū, along with their rituals and sacrifices, were suspended, hence the interval of peace. The first ritual performed, "ka niu a ke ali'i nui," "the coconut of the high chief," involved breaking open a carved coconut receptacle which contained miniature symbols of objects important in the material culture, signifying that during the months of winter a kapu had been placed on the occupation represented by each object. An image of Lono, called akua loa—a long pole with a cross arm at the top, from which hung a large piece of white tapa—was borne, along with images representing other gods, in a ceremonial procession around the island. The procession, which lasted twenty-three days, went in clockwise fashion, with the right hand of the god pointing inland toward the center of the island, signifying Lono's retention or appropriation of the land. At the same time, a counterclockwise procession walked around the island, carrying the akua poko, or short god, as opposed to the akua loa, long god. This short god toured the ruling chief's own lands, signifying the loss of his power over them during the annual ascendancy of Lono as the reigning lord. This also meant that the ruling chief and the high priest must be secluded and kept from public view for the while, and the priest was blindfolded so as not to see the people's celebrations. During the procession Lono was ritually fed by the king and the high chiefs at their local shrines, and received their homage and offerings in the rites of hānaipū. The ranking wives of the high chiefs also presented their gifts at that time, begging in return Lono's gift of fertility, that they might bear sacred children. As the procession moved from place to place, the people brought forth hoʻokupu, or offerings, placing them before altars dedicated to Lono, partly out of gratitude and partly in supplication for adequate rain for their crops. The offerings were collected by the konohiki, or land managers, testifying to Lono's proprietary rights and, at the same time, to the king's right to levy taxes. Those who did not pay enough were liable to have their lands plundered forthwith, until the gods —as represented by the konohiki—were satisfied.

Toward the end of the Makahiki, on the nineteenth day, when the image of Lono was returned to its home heiau, a dramatic set of rituals was conducted involving a sham battle. The king and his entourage went out to sea and returned to shore the next morning. They disembarked before the same heiau, to be confronted by warrior-priests of the god Kū holding spears bound with kapa ʻoloa, fine white tapa. One warrior would throw a spear that was deflected by the king's attendant, and another made a conquering gesture by touching the point of the spear over the heart of the aliʻi. This ritual is called kāliʻi, "to play (or act) the king." This was part of the sham battle (kānekupua) between the attendants of the king, who in this case represented Lono, and the moʻo Kū, the priests of Kū, symbolizing the reopening of the luakini and the return of the priests. Within a few days Lono himself would suffer a ritual death, when his image was dismantled, bound up, and put away in the heiau, not to be taken out again until the next year. In one of the last rites an abundance of food, considered Lono's own, was placed in a net of loose mesh called the Net of Maoloha, Kōkō Maoloha, and was shaken to earth, that is, fell from Lono's abode on high. A canoe, "the canoe of Lono," laden with offerings, was set adrift in the direction of Kahiki, symbolizing his voyage to that land.

Among the final rites lifting the restrictions was a ceremony offering a human sacrifice to Kahōāliʻi, "companion of the king," a god in human form. One of the victim's eyes and an eye from a bonito was eaten by Kahōāliʻi. Now Kū was restored to full power. Also, the kapu on bonito was lifted, thus opening the season for aku, but simultaneously a kapu was placed on ʻōpelu. Incidentally, illustrating again how myth and kapu go hand in hand, the moʻolelo states that, on his voyage to Hawaiʻi, the chief Pili was accompanied by two schools of fish, one of ʻōpelu and the other of aku; hence, the reason why the two kinds of fishes were subjected to the kapu. Although other rituals were performed, such as the ceremonial purification of priests in the sea, the Makahiki all but ended with the full restoration of Kū's authority.

Many other examples of the myth-ritual linking are known. The rites of the hālau hula as well as many sacred hula are derived from the Pele and Hiʻiaka cycle of poems. Significantly, at the request of Pele, Hiʻiaka and her friend Hōpoe performed the first hula at Nanahuki beach in Puna; at least this is said to be the earliest mention of the hula in the poem cycle. Thereafter, the presentation of every sacred hula is but a ritual repetition of that primal performance. Hula schools were established and conducted by the gods, such as the famous hālau at Hāʻena, Kauaʻi, and accordingly became the models for hālau set up by mortals.

The rites connected with the selection and felling of the ʻōhiʻa lehua tree for canoe making are based in part on the Laka myth. Any ceremonies involving kapa making are based on Lauhuki and Laʻahana, who are remembered as the first kapa makers. They are the daughters of Maikoha, from whose body sprang the first wauke, or paper mulberry bush, and who thereafter taught his two daughters, in dreams, how to make and decorate the first tapa cloth. The preference for ʻawa drinking originates from the time when gods mingled with human beings and talked to each other, fetched the 'awa root down from Hoʻānianikū, a realm of the gods, and gave it to humans to grow—and to prepare the consoling drink. The bamboo knife used in subincision rites is sacred because it comes from the Hōmaikaʻohe grove in Hāmākua, Hawaiʻi, which was first planted by Kāne when he came to these islands from Kahiki. And, finally, water is used in rites of purification, not because it is also symbolic of purity, but because it is what the gods use for similar ceremonies.

As comparative studies of both old and new religious cultures show, this connection between myth and ritual is universal. For example, the Christian Sabbath as a day of rest refers back to Jehovah's resting on the seventh day of creation. The washing of beggars' feet done by popes and kings and potentates is a remembrance of Jesus washing his disciples' feet. And he, of course, washed their feet as a proof of his humility and compassion. The lotus position assumed by Buddhist monks is that recommended by the Buddha. The Islamic rites surrounding the Kaaba, the black stone of Abraham in Mecca, are based in part on traditions associated with the Archangel Gabriel. New Year's festival rites of the Ila of Africa are modeled upon prototypes in their myths (Zuess). We know, too, that many Greek theatrical and dance rites were derived from mythology.

To sum up, ritual is the repetition of archetypal acts, that is, the deeds of gods, as they are recorded in myths. Whether in the Makahiki, hālau hula, drinking 'awa, or felling an 'ōhia tree, the associated rituals are essentially imitations of actions that originated with the akua. We recall the Brahmin in India who said, "We must do what the gods did in the beginning. . . . Thus the gods did; thus men do" (cited in Eliade 1974). The myths and the gods are inseparable links in the chain of values.

The Purpose of Ritual

The purpose of ritual is twofold: (1) to replenish one's spiritual power, or mana, and (2) thereby to maximize one's capacity to experience and know the ultimate meaning and significance of life. In this case, mana is not the end but the means to the end. Ritual generates the power necessary for the believer better to apprehend ultimate reality, that is, the realm of the sacred. In the process, one may attain inner peace, enlightenment, ecstasy, and other "peak experiences" (to use Abraham Maslow's terms), but these are only different manifestations of the twofold purpose of ritual.

This is best understood by explaining the processes involved in ritualization. Outwardly, ritual is the dramatic representation of a mythic act or event, in which the participants, whether converts or priests, use prescribed gestures, images, symbols, words, and so on, in order to convey the message that is intended. Objectively speaking, this may be viewed as simply a technical or a teaching process (one we shall want to examine more a little later). Inwardly, however, the processes are much more complicated. Psychologically, what the participants are doing is trying to relive and recreate the mythic deed in all its meanings. Whether this is done through visualization, self-hypnosis, or some other mystical process is not so important as is the fact that the true believer really *believes* that all this is happening. What is happening, of course, is that the myth is being made alive because the believer is spiritually reborn, as it were, regenerated and revitalized. Somehow the ritual has transported or transformed him, if only momentarily, into a higher order of consciousness or subconsciousness, where the psyche or spirit can more directly and purely feel and apprehend realities that transcend ordinary profane understanding.

When the believer comes down from his "high," and returns to the profane world, the practical consequences are that he will be stronger spiritually and therefore more committed to: (1) the gods and the values exemplified in the myths; (2) the established religious and political powers, who staged the performance to begin with; and (3) the community of believers.

Anyone familiar with modern religions will recognize that ritual continues to provide virtually the same hoped-for benefits. Take, for example, the Roman Catholics' Mass. It is supposed to be a reenactment of Christ's acts at the Last Supper, when he consecrated bread and wine and transubstantiated them into his own body and blood and instructed his apostles to partake of them "in remembrance of me." As ritual, the Mass is sacred drama performed with dignified grace and solemnity, but it also involves belief in the miraculous changing of the eucharistic elements into the actual body and blood of Christ himself. The doctrine explaining this change is known as transubstantiation, but the effect is the same: in recreating as precisely as possible the Last Supper, the event is made alive through the believing faith of the participant. He is spiritually transformed and elevated into a holier state of mind, indeed, into the spiritual presence of the resurrected Christ. Regular participation in the Mass is encouraged by the church because it renews not only the spirit of the parishioner, but also his commitment to the church.

Comparisons are odious, the aphorism says, partly because they tend to downplay and distort the contrasts. Considerable differences exist between Hawaiian and Christian ritualism, as we shall see, but ultimately the object of all religious ritual overrides history and theology, for it deals with the basic human "sense of the holy"—which is the same everywhere.

Pedagogically Speaking

Ritual is also a form of instruction or training. While it is designed to convey a sense of sacredness, its underlying principles and techniques as pedagogy are not much different from those of "role-playing," "simulations," "dramatic inquiries," and similar devices used in classrooms today. It is based on a very sound learning principle: the more senses you can appeal to, the greater will be the learning experience. In ritual the appeal is made to all the physical senses and to the nonsensory or spiritual perceptions as well. It is probably the most complete and dynamic form of communication, for it involves words, symbols, sounds, colors, smells, touchings, tastings, rhythms, visualizations, space-and-time settings—every conceivable form of teaching aid. Animal sacrifices, chants, hymns, dancing, vestments, the laying on of hands, altars, chimes, incense, candles, music, and so on, have been used in religious rituals since very ancient times. These elements are carefully integrated and coordinated so as to create the most effective learning experience. When high rituals are performed as sacred drama, in sacrosanct settings, presided over by colorfully robed priests, with rhythmic intoning of the mythic chants, nothing in the classroom and, perhaps even in the legitimate theater, can surpass such ceremony for sheer emotional and spiritual impact.

Another important pedagogical feature enters into ritual, and that is repetition. Just as it is a keystone in effective learning, so is it in the practice of religious ritual. Few rituals, if any, are performed only once and never again. In fact, certain rituals in Hinduism and Christianity were begun many centuries ago, and since then have been repeated countless times by countless believers with almost no change in content or presentation. Simple rituals such as the Muslim's prayer to Allah, always given while facing Mecca, or the Buddhist's prayer-chant "Namu Amida Butsu," are performed several times a day.

An example of an ancient Hawaiian ritual which was performed each morning and evening was the rite of ipu o Lono, the gourd of Lono. The steps involved were: (1) the gourd of Lono, which hangs from a pole in each hale mua, or men's eating house, is filled with food, including some kind of fish, and at the same time an 'awa root is tied to the cord handle; (2) the head of the household prays and makes an offering; (3) he takes the ipu o Lono and carries it to the center of the hale, takes hold of the 'awa root; (4) he prays again; (5) when the praying ends, he sucks on the 'awa root; (6) he opens the gourd; and finally (7) he eats some of the food in the gourd. The sacred character of the rite is explained by the fact that the gourd is consecrated for this specific purpose and that symbolically the head of the household drinks from the body of Lono (although we do not know whether in this case the food was transubstantiated, as is bread and wine in the Catholic ritual).

Constant repetition can become boring and counterproductive in the normal learning situation, unless some variety or change is offered. But ritual allows little such departure from the decreed format. Rather, sameness is regarded as the means for achieving deeper understanding, or perhaps a new insight, or a flash of recognizing something that never seemed to exist before. For example, the Zen practitioner who chants the same sutra day after day is seeking enlightenment at a higher level of consciousness because the act of repetition actually frees his mind and releases his higher creative powers.

For the Hawaiian of old, repetition meant absolute, flawless, uniform precision in carrying out a ritual as it was prescribed. A good example is the "dreaded" hono ceremony that was conducted as part of the rites for building or renovating a luakini heiau. Kenneth Emory, an authority on Polynesian anthropology, calls it "the ultimate in ceremonial worship in Hawai'i, and for that matter, in all Polynesia" (1965a). John Papa 'I'i, royal attendant to the Kamehameha monarchs, described the ceremony:

The men sat crosslegged in rows in line with each of the images that stood from one end to the other before the 'anu'u tower, each man erect, one behind the other. Both elbows rested on the upper part of the thighs, the left wrist under the right one. The participants waited to be told to "put up the hands, up above." Whoever wished to could raise both his hands, but that was optional. Those who raised only the right hand rested the left one on the right knee, assuming as humble a posture as he saw fit. It was forbidden to shift one's position or move more than his arm while the *kāhuna* of the *hono* uttered his prayers, which lasted a whole hour. When one of the company felt his upraised arms growing tired, he lowered them slowly to rest upon his thighs. But none dared to raise his head.

'I'i added that those who managed to keep both hands up throughout the ceremony made "a decided impression" and sometimes were not averse to bragging about it afterward.

The exacting requirements for form and order may be illustrated in the ritualized processions, such as the one connected with the kauila ceremony of a new luakini. Again 'I'i described it:

According to the rules of this rite of the procession of gods, the *kapuō* stick bearer, who was directly in front of the line at the center of *kāhuna*s standing there, made a left turn and marched to their right. The line of gods followed and turned where he had until the last one . . . reached the spot from which the *kapuō* stick bearer had started. Then he turned again and came back to the left, as the rest remained standing. Again they each turned at the same spot and returned, finishing the procession.

They made other precise movements, but this example is enough to demonstrate the careful attention given to "spatial protocol."

Religious processions were very solemn affairs, for they involved the movements of gods or their images, as well as of chiefs and kāhuna, among others. Kamakau (1976) said that the haku 'ōhi'a procession, which accompanied the logs intended for making the houses and images for a heiau when they were being carried to the temple site, was "fearful and terrifying. . . . No man dared pass it; a man paid with his life if he encountered this procession." While the procession passed through the lowlands and near villages, absolute silence was required from the whole population, and no fires could be lighted. Infractions of these rules, even if accidental or innocent, usually meant death for the offender.

In any case, insistence on meticulous accuracy in performing ritual is easy to explain, provided our original premise is acceptable. That is, if ritual means imitating the acts of the gods, then that is *precisely* what we must do. What better model can we find? Certainly, nothing that a mere mortal could do could be better. To do otherwise, changing and tampering with a divine model, would be like saying "We can do better than the gods." This would be the height of arrogance, as well as of ignorance, and, naturally, it would displease the gods. It is very unlikely that any Hawaiian of old would have wanted to be placed in such a predicament, since the consequences to him could have been fatal.

Another motivation can be found for demanding that ritual be done precisely and flawlessly, namely, the value of excellence. So central was this to the Hawaiian value system that the people of old probably took for granted that the ritual would be performed perfectly. To be sure, always the threat of death or some other severe penalty was present, but the desire to do the best possible job may well have been the prime motivation for priests and chiefs alike. Hawaiian religion, after all, was constructed more on a positive than on a negative view of human nature. This is not to say that as a value excellence did not have its own intrinsic worth quite apart from its mythological antecedents, for, as we have said from the outset, myth and value are inseparable. But we shall learn how excellence is applied to activities that were not directly connected with religion. This indicates that as a value, excellence could stand on its own merit.

The "Practicalness" of Ritual

However much ritualism may appear to be centered on the spiritual world, underlying it is an earthly, practical relevance to everyday human needs and aspirations. This relevance proceeds from the general Hawaiian view that the worth of religion corresponds to its ability to make life easier, richer, better, or happier not just for the soul but the body as well. Thus, all ritual brings some benefit, directly or indirectly, to material well-being. A few examples should demonstrate the truth of this statement.

Consider Malo's statement that "the building of a canoe was an affair of religion." By this he meant that every important phase in the process of building a canoe, from selecting the tree to felling, hauling, and shaping the timber and launching the hull, was all affected by ritual. The first stroke upon the tree trunk was made with a sacred adze; the canoe maker was not only a craftsman but also a kahuna who had to know all the rites and prayers and both the good and bad omens. Canoe makers were said to be "very much like preachers. They do what is correct and proper and do not commit sins." Yet producing the canoe for its intended use was clearly an economic activity. For one thing, it created employment: as many as eighty to a hundred men might be employed in hauling a huge log from the mountainside forest to the production site near the shore. Considerable supplies of food and other materials would have been required to outfit and maintain a large expedition of men for several weeks of work. Building the canoe generated income for the master builder, who was paid by the owner of the canoe. Of course, to complete the cycle, the owner expected to use the vessel for fishing or to transport things, thereby creating wealth for himself and his 'ohana. The entire purpose of ritual was to ensure that every stage of this "laborious and dangerous undertaking" would be successful. In short, for Hawaiians ritual was the handmaiden of economics.

Another example of the link between ritual and economics was the Makahiki. Farmers sought the help of Lono to assure sufficient rainfall for their crops. The konohiki, representing their chiefly employers, levied and collected taxes. The priests figured in the economics of this relationship because to the extent that they were professionals, in the employ of the cult, temple, or chief, the Makahiki created "jobs" and income for them. The large amounts of foods required for the offerings represented another valuable economic resource. In addition, the economics involved in the sheer logistics of providing for the crowds of people attending the various religious and sporting events must also be considered. (See chapter 10 on economics.)

Since religious matters were the responsibility of government, politics entered into ritualism as well. Malo wrote that "when the people and the priests saw that the services of the *luakini* were well-conducted, they began to have confidence in the stability of the government." Just what "well-conducted" meant—whether it referred only to the manner in which the ritual services were conducted or to their efficacy, as in winning a battle—is not known, but it does indicate where the people placed the responsibility. Interestingly, Malo mentioned the priests along with the people, as if they were not involved in the rituals. Perhaps he was referring to other, lesser priests not connected with the ruling elite or with the priesthood of Kū. In any event, political stability was linked with ritual that was "well-conducted."

Obviously, while ritual was essentially religious in nature, it was so interwoven with everyday living in old Hawai'i that its effects flowed over into economic, political, and other practical areas. We can safely conclude that nothing, or at least nothing important, escaped the influence of ritual. Hence, many if not all the important values of Hawaiian society, such as excellence, spirituality, discipline, and so forth, fall within the scope of ritual.

Human Sacrifice, or Hai Kanaka

Almost every modern Hawaiian wonders at one time or another about the human sacrifices that were offered to the gods by the kāhuna of old. The wondering is mixed with feelings of amazement, revulsion, rejection, bewilderment, or shame, but rarely with pride and approval. Human sacrifice is so alien to modern values, not to mention laws, that it nearly defies any attempt to understand it. As a matter of fact, many Hawaiians, especially those belonging to the older generations, don't even want to try to understand it, let alone think about it. Many treat it like a bogeyman, to be locked up in the deepest recesses of the mind, to be suppressed if not forgotten. The trouble is that it keeps slipping out, taunting and challenging us to deal with it.

One way to deal with the subject is to examine human sacrifice in its full religious context in Hawai'i nei and as a near universal religious practice as well. The bogeyman effect may be due as much to our trying to judge human sacrifice as an isolated cultural aberration as to our misplaced and modern sense of moral superiority.

Let us first place hai kanaka, human sacrifice, in its proper framework, namely, as one of many forms of offerings made to the great gods. Whether in the form of a bowl of rice offered by a Buddhist to Amida Buddha, or a goat slaughtered by an Indian believer to the goddess Kali, or a Jesus Christ sacrificed on the cross to atone for the sins of the world, offerings are common to all religions throughout the whole history of the world. Ancient Hawaiian religion simply added to the world's inventory of sacrifice a rich tradition of 'ālana or mōhai, offerings, ranging from the very solemn hai kanaka to the perfunctory laying aside of a morsel of food for an 'aumakua. All such offerings and sacrifices are ritualistic. And, along with prayer, they constitute the essence—and in human sacrifice the highest drama—of a religious rite.

The words "offering" and "sacrifice" mean essentially the same thing, so we shall use the terms interchangeably. Three Hawaiian words refer to offerings: 'ālana, mōhai, and hai. 'Ālana refers to a free-will offering, as contrasted to mōhai, which is one prescribed by a priest, although this distinction may be arbitrary as free-will mōhai too were possible, as in mōhai aloha, an offering of love. Kenneth Emory (1965a) made the following distinction: when offerings were just left for the gods, they were mōhai, or a sacrifice, but when they were shared with the priests, other people, and the gods, they were 'ālana, or an offering. This distinction, too, may not apply in all cases. Hai refers to either offering or sacrifice. Thus, either in English or in Hawaiian, the terms mean a ritual presentation of some gift to the gods.

Fundamental to understanding sacrifice is the idea that we are dealing with the transference of mana, or power, through a ritual act. Whatever the aim of the sacrifice may be, whether to atone for a wrong, express gratitude, appeal for protection, and so on, the sacrificer, that is, the person making the sacrifice on his own or another person's behalf, is primarily seeking to increase his mana. But the big question here is: how does making an offering or sacrifice accomplish this? The simplest answer is: by transforming the ordinary into the extraordinary, the human into the superhuman. But how does this mysterious process occur? The transforming ability of ritual, which is common to all religions, must be examined, in step-by-step detail, in order to comprehend the "magic" of sacrifice.

At least five steps enter into this process: (1) consecration of the sacrificer, (2) selection of the victim, (3) ritual prayer, (4) immolation of the victim, and (5) resolution. While this set of events does not obtain in all cases, it represents the sequence generally followed in making a human sacrifice. Only by reviewing each of these steps can we fully understand the total concept.

1. *Consecration of the sacrificer.* The person offering the sacrifice was ordinarily a kahuna. In the case of hai kanaka he was usually a member of the Kū priesthood. Although kāhuna were already set apart for their duties as agents of the gods, for very solemn rites of sacrifice they had to be consecrated anew, that is, made more sacred, or purified of all defilement, in order to handle more holy objects. This purification might take the form of a special sea bath, or a sprinkling with fresh water, or isolating oneself for several days, possibly even weeks, and abstaining from eating certain foods. The whole intent of consecration was to sanctify the kahuna to the extent that he took on godlike powers during the course of the ritual. Also, in some rites, the other participants were required to be purified and consecrated, partly to enhance the sanctity of the proceedings and also to protect them from the danger of divine power whose effects on the impure could be "terrible."

2. *Selection of the victim.* In the case of nonhuman victims, the animals offered included pigs, dogs, and fishes. Pigs were the most favored. Not just any pig would do, however. "The pigs had to be fine ones, fattened until the snout almost disappeared and the neck rolled with fat, the ears drooping, and the mouth standing open like a gaping cock." And why such care in selecting the animal? Because, we are told, "the gods would not eat an offering of poor quality" (Kamakau 1976). Sacrificial pigs were specially raised, so that they would be without blemish. By the way, this insistence on using only the finest animals was widely observed among religions in India, Africa, throughout Polynesia, and in ancient Israel.

As for human victims, we have conflicting evidence about how strictly Hawaiians followed the principle of the "unblemished" victim. Malo, for example, declared that criminals were used for certain rites in the luakini services, but Nathaniel Emerson, in his notes to Malo's writings, disagreed with him. He insisted that, in order to fulfill the sacrificial function worthily, the victim had to be "perfect and blameless." No infants, women, aged persons, or people with deformed bodies were suitable. On the other hand, Kamakau (1976) appeared to side with Malo: "No man who was not a wrongdoer was ever placed on the altar." In other words, the innocent and the pure were never selected as victims. In 1823 William Ellis recorded in his *Journal* that "individuals who had broken tabu, or rendered themselves obnoxious to the chiefs, were fixed upon." Apparently, some flexibility in choosing a victim was allowed, although we believe that, whenever possible, a nearly perfect victim would have been chosen.

It is instructive to contrast Hawaiian practices with those of other peoples. The most extreme was the custom of the Shilluks of the White Nile (in upper Egypt) who, until only a few years ago, sacrificed their god-kings. This so-called ritual regicide (Campbell 1977b) was widely practiced in parts of Africa, India, and Arabia. Among American Indians, the Pawnees sacrificed a maiden to the sun each spring, the Hopis sacrificed a youth at the tribal initiation fire festival, and the Zunis offered a child in return for the gift of seeds. The Aztecs chose a young man, who would be feasted and feted for days and treated like a god before they sacrificed him. In Africa the Dahomey people sacrificed a newborn infant, the Ibo in Nigeria offered a woman, the Ganda starved to death princes of royal blood, and the Winamwanga in Tanganyika preferred "members of a family of a priest, those who have a squint, mothers who have borne only one child, or pregnant women" (W. Wallis).

In addition, the Kalmucks of Siberia occasionally sacrificed a child of the ruling chief. In ancient India a pregnant woman was a favorite victim. The Vikings sacrificed warriors to Odin, their supreme deity. The practical Romans sacrificed captive Greeks and Gauls. Jews of Old Testament times, under Manasseh, sacrificed their firstborn children. In the case of Abraham and Isaac, Jehovah tested Abraham by demanding his own son. On the other hand, the Indians of Peru selected criminals, enemies, and even slaves as victims. The list of examples is long, but clearly while the process of selecting victims differed from culture to culture, human sacrifice was practiced nearly universally.

3. Ritual prayer. All sacrificial rites involved prayers of one kind or another, intoned by the priestly sacrificer. A prayer offered at a sacrifice for a new dwelling of a chief, for example, would invoke the gods' protection over the house and its occupants. Another kind of prayer at a sacrifice of thanksgiving would explain the reasons for gratitude, and so on. Here is a prayer accompanying a sacrifice in a luakini.

O Kū, o Lono,
O Kāne and Kanaloa,

Give life to me until extreme old age;
Look at the rebel against the land,
He who was seized for sacrifice.
'Amama. It is freed.
                              (Kamakau 1976)

Here follow excerpts from a prayer offered at the dreaded hono rite.

O Kū, O Kūnuiākea . . .
Here is a gift and a sacrifice;
A cape of white tail feathers,
A whale ivory cast ashore,
And a rebel, a grabber of land.
Curse the rebels outside and inside.
Who, with bowed head and pointing finger,
Plot to take the land.
                              (Kamakau 1976)

In these examples, evidently both victims were enemies of a chief and his retainers. The victims themselves may have been a defeated chief or a warrior. Such captives often were offered in sacrifice.

4. *Immolation.* The killing of the victim was the climax of the rite. Immolation, of course, could not be an ordinary kind of killing. It had to be done in a sanctified place and at an appointed time, by consecrated sacrificers, using designated instruments, and following prescribed procedures. Otherwise, the assault would have been no more than murder. In the hono ceremony, the naked victim was brought already dead to the lele, or sacrificial altar, along with two pigs which "had been broiled *('ōlani)* over a fire with him, and bunches of bananas and coconuts" (Kamakau 1976). At other times, the victim would be clubbed or stabbed to death in the outer court of the heiau and then immediately placed on the altar. In the case of setting up a new carved image in a heiau, or erecting a posthole for a chief's new house, the living victim was thrust into the hole and covered with earth. And in the haku 'ōhi'a ritual at the felling of the 'ōhi'a tree, the presiding kahuna beheaded the victim and buried him beside the chosen tree.

Methods of immolation in Polynesia and other parts of the world differed widely. Among the Maori, the completing of a valuable canoe, such as a war canoe, was deemed worthy of a human sacrifice and the victim was used as a roller over which the canoe was drawn to its launching. Often Aztec priests killed their victims by cutting out the pulsing heart. In Dahomey the infant sacrifice was "torn limb from limb and offered to the town god; the dismembered infant (was then) strewn about in the god's temple" (W. Wallis). In Nigeria the victims' arms and legs were broken and the crippled men were left on a river bank for crocodiles to devour. The Konde chiefs in Africa selected a boy, made him drink beer until he died, burned his body, ground the ashes to powder, and distributed the powder over the district as "medicine" to ensure a good crop. According to the Old Testament, Philistine children were sacrificed at a hearth or fire pit in the Valley of Hinnon, and their burned bodies were offered to Moloch. Norsemen dispatched their sacrificial victims by hanging them, and the Celts of ancient Britain drowned their victims in rivers or the ocean.

The act of immolation, followed by the presentation of the victim to the gods, represents the moment of release of the spirit from this world to the other world, that is, its change from the ordinary to the extraordinary. Sacrifice is the destruction of the victim, and therefore represents a kind of "sacrilege" or desecration, but because of this very fact a new power is released. The success of the offering is dependent, of course, on its acceptance by the gods who legitimize the ritual and imbue the priest-sacrificer with power. In an important sense, sacrificial death symbolizes the rebirth of a new order, which always brings with it the potential of new creative power. In this whole transformative process, involving all of the five steps, the act of immolation may be viewed as catalyzing the metamorphosis or transformation of the normal to the supernormal, of the profane to the sacred. This is the "mystery" which the rite dramatizes and raises to the conscious level of its participants (Money-Kyrle).

5. *Resolution.* The last step in the sequence may be compared to a decompression experience, in which a person is restored to his or her normal functioning state. In other words, the participants who have been first consecrated must be de-consecrated so that they can return to the profane and real world, to resume their normal lives. They cannot be expected to live in the rarefied sphere of the sanctified, no matter how glorious it may be, because that is the permanent sphere of the gods. Humans must make do with this profane world here below.

This decompression process is accomplished in a number of

ways. In the offering of animals, the body of the pig is consumed lest it be defiled and thereby nullify the effects of the ritual. So the pig is shared with the gods, who consume only the essence which reaches them in the form of a pleasing smoke. The priest and the chosen personages participating with him in the ceremony are the only ones who can eat the rest of the pig, because they have been sanctified. Hence, their eating together concluded a sacrificial ritual not as a social function but as a part of the sacred rite. In the case of human sacrifice in Hawai'i, the bodies were burned or disposed of in a prescribed way, but, as best we can tell, were not eaten. In the end, all the sanctified material must be destroyed, even to the bones, and nothing was allowed to remain.

These five steps, if carried out as prescribed, that is, faultlessly and with respect, were designed to generate the maximum amount of mana for the living participants. But the most important element in the rite was the victim; he was the medium through which the sacred force or energy flowed. Each step in the transformative ritual was invested with power, until it all came together in the presentation of the sacrifice to the gods. Paradoxically, the dead were used to give more life to the living.

How much was hai kanaka practiced in ancient Hawai'i? Judging by the number of luakini heiau and the influence of the priesthood of Kū, it must have been widely practiced on all the islands. Many occasions or events would have required human sacrifice. Most of those seem to be connected with the lives of the ali'i, such as the birth of the firstborn son, subincision, installation of a ruler, construction of a new house or heiau, victory in war, and so on. While most rites required only one victim at any one time, for certain occasions many people were sacrificed. 'Umi, for example, is said to have offered up eighty victims after his victorious battles at Mao'ula heiau in Waipi'o.

In Polynesia the practice was most widespread in Hawai'i and Tahiti. But according to Peter Buck (1982) in Tahiti "the chiefs and priests established an all-Polynesian record for the number of victims slain to bolster up the prestige of the ruling families." At least seventeen distinct occasions required human sacrifice in Tahiti. In contrast, in Tonga the nearest thing to a human offering was cutting off a finger tip in order to induce the gods to cure a sick relative. This resulted in "a severe shortage of finger tips," we are told.

Why do we meet with these differences in attitude and practice among Polynesians? Buck's theory is that in Tahiti and Hawai'i temples became the center of religious as well as social life. "The priests of the temples elaborated their religious ceremonies and in so doing demanded a higher standard of offerings which culminated in human sacrifice" (Buck 1982). In New Zealand, where Maoris built no temples as such, human sacrifice was a far weaker institution than in Tahiti and Hawai'i, where the number of temples reached a peak.

An abundance of temples means the existence of a highly centralized government. Such were the chiefdoms in Hawai'i, which could command the material and human resources necessary to construct and maintain religious structures that have essentially no productive economic purpose. In both Tahiti and Hawai'i that authority was based on the unification, albeit an uneasy one at times, of the chiefly and priestly classes. Only that kind of entrenched political power can organize and legitimize human sacrifices on a regular basis without jeopardizing its survival. Theoretically, a weak or decentralized authority would not be able to do so, except occasionally, because it would not be able to control retaliation or acts of vengeance from the families of the victims. Human sacrifice, as Rene Girard argued, was a form of controlled violence that depended on the ability of the ruling group to suppress or prevent uncontrolled violence. However, we must not lose sight of our essential thesis—that ritual derives its legitimacy from myth. Therefore, the justification for human sacrifice cannot be rationalized away by resorting to quasi-religious-political theorizing, however reasonable it may seem.

In Hawaiian mythology we have an "exemplary" model in the sorcery god, Kūwahailo, Kū maggot-mouth, who by tradition was a "man-eater" and the deity responsible for the "introduction of human sacrifice." In 1823 Ellis reported that when 'Umi celebrated his triumphs in battle over his enemies by sacrificing captives, the voice of Kūwahailo was heard from the clouds demanding more and more victims, "till he had slain all his men except one, whom, as he was a great favourite, he refused at first to give up; but the god being urgent, he sacrificed him also, and the priest and himself were all that remained." The 'Umi legend tells how murder was instantly turned into a sacrifice when Hākau was captured and was about to be killed by the victorious chief. At that instant Ka'ōleiokū, the warrior-priest, exclaimed: "Hold! Let this be a

sacrifice, and not a murder! In the name of the gods I slay him!"
(Kalākaua). While this is the stuff out of which legends are made,
the incident illustrates the priestly power to sanctify an otherwise
unholy act and at the same time preserve what little dignity or
mana remained in the captive chief. And, finally, when the body of
Hākau was placed on the lele, the god Kūwahailo came down
from heaven in a pillar of floating clouds with thunder and lightning and dark clouds and "the tongue of the god wagged above the
altar" (Beckwith 1970).

To conclude this discussion of offerings in general and human
sacrifice in particular, let us recapitulate the functions and meanings that such rites had for Hawaiians. First is the didactic or educational value in the dramatic presentation of myth-based acts or
deeds. Ritual killing conducted by sanctified priests in consecrated
places following prescribed rules must have been for the participating believers a moving, awesome, if not a somewhat frightening
experience. The dramatic cycle of moving from crisis to resolution
in sequential stages, each bestowing successive increments of
mana, reminded the participants of one of the principle motifs of
the moʻolelo: the cyclical nature of life, as it was symbolized in the
physical death and spiritual rebirth of the sacrificial victim. Second is the feeling of gratitude and obedience to the gods that is
created by the ritual opportunity to share oneself symbolically, as
one is represented by the substances offered. Of all the rites, the
sacrificial mōhai presents perhaps the most concrete demonstration of the principle of reciprocity. Offering the gods the unblemished animal or the human victim accorded the gods their due, but
it also affirmed the binding relationship between the people and
their gods.

Third is the social function of ritual, so vital to the communal
well-being of any society, especially one as isolated as was the
Hawaiian. The most solemn rites of sacrifice permit the participants to renew their mythic covenants one with another as loyal
members of the community of believers. Fourth is the "cathartic"
element in sacrifice which, through ritual, allows participants to
work out their anxieties and feelings of guilt and thereby lift worries from their consciences. Last, but not least, is the obtaining of
greater spiritual power for each member in the group through the
mana generated by the ritual event.

In summary, we today with our supposedly higher ethical sense can so easily regard with horror and shame the practice of hai kanaka in old Hawai'i. But if we can see and understand it through the eyes and minds of ka po'e kahiko, as indeed we must, then it becomes an act entirely consistent with their ritualistic view of the world. It was the highest form of religious communion, practiced only under the most stringent and sacred circumstances. In no way was it wanton, senseless, aberrant behavior. For their time and place, it was a profound and meaningful drama of the sacred. Many things we do today in our civilized world are far more horrifying—from the nigh-ritualistic carnage on our highways wrought by automobiles (and their drivers) to the brutal sacrifices of countless civilians and soldiers in the name of modern warfare. In short, we must keep in correct perspective the actions and the motivations of our kūpuna when we presume to judge their rituals.

A Praying People

If ritual helped to dictate the life-style in old Hawai'i, so did prayer. For most, if not all, ritual involves prayer; indeed, it is difficult to imagine a Hawaiian ritual without verbal communication with the gods, unless certain rites were conducted in absolute silence. But in an oral society that believed in the power of the 'ōlelo, words or language, that silent communion is very unlikely. Barring the possible rare exceptions, then, we can say that no ritual can be performed without vocal prayer, although prayer can be offered without ritual.

In any case, we are told that Hawaiians of old were an exceptionally prayerful people. "*Ka po'e kahiko,*" wrote Kamakau (1976), "prayed constantly—in the morning, at midday, in the evening, in the middle of the night." The authors of *Nānā I Ke Kumu* agreed with Kamakau. "For the Hawaiian of the past, all times and every time were indeed occasions for prayer" (Pūku'i, Haertig, and Lee). Understanding the reasons for this reliance upon prayer may help us to understand the present-day attitude Hawaiians take to prayer and its implications in terms of spiritual values.

As with ritual, prayer, too, is based on divine models. Just as Jesus Christ prayed to his Father in Heaven and taught his followers to pray, so did Hawaiian gods pray to other gods—and left not one but many classic prayers for their believers to cherish. A poignant example of this involves Hi'iaka's attempt to restore the life of Lohi'au, who has been killed by jealous Pele.

Imagine the scene at the handsome prince's bier. Hi'iaka sets a calabash of water on the ground before her and says to Wahine'ōma'o, her attendant: "Listen to my prayer. If it is correct and faultless, our man will live; but if it is wrong or imperfect, he will die." After her first prayer, she asks, "How was my prayer?" Wahine'ōma'o replies: "It was a good prayer. Its only fault was that it sped on too quickly and came to an end too soon." Prayer after prayer does Hi'iaka utter, frequently sprinkling the body with water, but Lohi'au does not rise. Hi'iaka prays once more:

> Come, enter, possess and inspire me;
> Thou first, God of the flowery wild;
> Ye roving sprites of the wildwood;
> And master gods, Kāne and Kanaloa—
> Hi'iaka, who calls you, lacks not
> In power to heal and inspire—
> Pray enter, and heal, and abide
> In this one, your patron and guard.
> Here is water, the Water of life.
> Here is water, the Water of Life.
> Give us this Life!
>   (Emerson 1978)

And prayer after prayer follows, like pictures in a movie, until finally, like Lazarus of Bethany, Lohi'au is restored to life.

While you should read the entire cycle of poems / chants in order to appreciate all of their subtleties, our selection of prayers contains several object lessons. One, the prayer must be irresistible, supported by the absolute faith of the supplicant in himself or herself, as well as in the gods; two, as mentioned previously, the manner in which the prayer is given is vital—it must not be hurried, insincere, or mechanical, and, above all, it must be "faultless"; three, care must be taken to create the right mood, both mentally and physically; and, finally, even the place must be conducive to prayer, that is, it must be free of noise and disturbance, "a god-inviting place." Communicating with the gods is serious business, even for one god speaking to another.

Curiously enough, Hi'iaka's imploring borders at times on commanding or coercing the gods to do her will. This, in fact, is quite common in Hawaiian prayers. Pūku'i, Haertig, and Lee stated that in pule ho'ōla, or prayers for life, "the prayer itself almost demands the attention of the gods." They asked whether such prayers were heard, but the more important question is what does this tone say about the attitude that Hawaiians took regarding their gods. On the one hand, reverence and humility are present, but on the other, a note of arrogance is unmistakable in the Hawaiian approach to prayer.

This apparent inconsistency vanishes, however, when we recall the reciprocal relationship that was established between gods and humans, with obligations on the part of both parties to the pact. Thus, when one side fails to live up to its obligation, the other is naturally affected. If a believer feels that he has obeyed all the kapu and faithfully done his part, he has just grounds to expect reciprocal action from the gods. But when he has done all he's supposed to do, yet gets no reasonable satisfaction, then he becomes insistent, if not commanding. The most extreme length to which he will go is "casting off," or getting rid of the god who has failed him.

In other words, coercion appears in prayers when a Hawaiian perceives or suspects a breakdown in his reciprocal relationship with the gods. This does not necessarily mean that he has rejected any of his principal values toward the deities as a group. Such breakdowns occur even under the best of circumstances, but what he seeks to do with prayer is to maintain that dynamic balance or harmony between himself and his gods. He would rather avoid such breakdowns at almost any cost. This is undoubtedly why Hawaiians, Maoris, and other Polynesians seem to have refrained from asking their gods to do impossible things. Prayer is not a wishing well for the whimsical.

Hawaiians prayed ritually and nonritually. Ritual prayers were usually part of a worship service in which they were intoned by one or several kāhuna, either by one person at a time or by several in unison and in contrapuntal fashion. For example, in the luakini service, the kāhuna stand up to pray, and after they have uttered their lines the assembled worshipers repeat them in unison. This confirms the essentially communal nature of worship among the Hawaiians. The practice is common among primal peoples. Prayer and ritual as parts of a worship service aided in bringing the community of believers together. This partly explains why Hawaiians took so readily to congregational singing and praying introduced by Christian missionaries.

Like the myths, the ritual prayers were the expressions of a special class of kāhuna pule. These were expert "pray-ers" who specialized in composing prayers after "lifelong training." According to Handy and Pūku'i, they enjoyed a good rapport with the gods and possessed a mana "that ceased to exist in later days when the old *kapu* and *pule* were only partially remembered and understood." They were "holy men" who worked in an atmosphere that was constantly charged with sacred energy. The words and names they used, especially personal or place names, were carefully chosen so as not to offend the gods. More important, the words were invested with mana, that is, the words themselves had a power of their own. When the ritual prayer ended in " 'Āmama ua noa," "Now the prayer is free; now the prayer has flown," it carried "a sense of an actual power traveling from petitioner to deity." Hawaiians believed that a word could lead to life or death, to forgiveness or enmity. So said the sage in the book of Proverbs: "Death and life are in the power of the tongue." Here, then, is the reason why in a ritual prayer not a word could be changed and, often, not even the speed of delivery, level of the voice, or the very pauses for breath.

Although ritualized prayer may have been the usual manner of worship, Hawaiians "also approached their gods with little ceremony," that is, directly, personally, and informally. Such prayers, not memorized but spontaneous, were called kaukau. They were reasonable presentations of facts with a request for understanding, help, or cooperation. According to Pūku'i, Haertig, and Lee, the relationship was "as simple as one person reasoning with another." This approach would be particularly favored when individuals were communing with 'aumākua with whom an 'ohana feeling had been developed.

Nonetheless, we have to avoid the temptation of humanizing too much this personal and familiar approach to the gods because, in general, the Hawaiian attitude toward haipule, or prayerfulness, was one of humility, deference, and reverence. One who prays is a supplicant first and foremost. Therefore, even in the most intimate relationship with 'aumākua, one prays with fervor and urgency, never taking the gods for granted—and certainly never insulting them.

If we could define the essence of prayer, it is contained in the word ho'okuakāhi, or clear the way. Whether a prayer was given for an important ritualized event or for just an individual's private undertaking, the idea meant that every enterprise in life should begin with prayer in order to remove obstacles that might lie in the way. Just as a person might remove an obstruction from his driveway, so does prayer remove spiritual impediments that might endanger or delay a project or activity. Prayer can be likened to a spiritual bulldozer: it can clear the way through a jungle of problems.

The Hawaiians' willingness to pray seems to be in striking contrast to the behavior of Maoris and other primal peoples. According to Elsdon Best (1974), Maoris "did not pray. In the great majority of cases, they employed formulae that can only be termed 'charms' or 'incantations'; they are not prayers; they are not invocations. They are on a level with the magical formulae employed by the people of Egypt, Sumeria, Babylonia, and elsewhere in olden times." Maoris call these incantations karakia, and devised vast numbers of them, covering almost every possible contingency in life. Because all were chanted, and hence rendered in a prescribed way, they are more ritualistic and to that extent less spontaneous than are the Hawaiian kaukau. The Maori, both ariki and commoners, learned an appropriate number of karakia for use in everyday pursuits ranging from treating sicknesses to keeping danger away. If what Best says is true, he supported the idea that the ancient Hawaiians were "exceptionally" prayerful.

While it would be difficult to determine whether modern Hawaiians are really prayerful, short of invading the privacy of a good sampling of individuals, it is no coincidence that pule continues to play an important part in today's life and culture. In the modern hālau hula, which have increased to a number unmatched since ancient times, prayer, along with ritual, is an important part of training, performance, graduation, and other related activities. For many Hawaiian organizations, from the Hawaiian civic clubs to the traditional fraternal orders, invocations and benedictions are standard practice. In almost any major cultural event, ranging from canoe races to music and dance competitions, prayer and ritual are mandatory. Special gatherings of Hawaiians, whether for

educational, social, or political purposes, are often conducted
under the prayerful guidance of a latter-day kahuna or kahu. The
familiar practice of hoʻoponopono used by families to resolve mis-
understandings is always done with prayer. And obviously, prayer
is a vital feature of Hawaiian church services and in the lives of
Hawaiian Christians and Buddhists (of whom there are some,
especially in the Nichiren sect).

Nonetheless, the late Reverend Akaiko Akana's lament that "it
is too bad that the prayer-life of old is fast dying out" is probably
much truer today than it was in 1918, when he made the statement. Undoubtedly there are some Hawaiians who never pray,
who don't believe in prayer, who dismiss it as "child's play," or who
will resort to it only in direst need, when all else has failed.

But, as Pūkuʻi observed, "Without *pule*, without prayer, I think
my people would be lost" (Pūkuʻi, Haertig, and Lee).

Hula as Ritual

Nowadays most people automatically think of hula as pure entertainment, pleasing to look at and occasionally provocative, but
not as a holy rite or as an integral part of a religious service. In
Hawaiʻi of old, the dance began as religious ritual, just as it did in
so many other cultures, but in time it "degenerated" into folk
dance. That is to say, it began as kapu and then became noa.
Indeed, among many peoples, long after their religions are dead
and neglected, their dance remains, usually only as a profane vestige of what once was sacred. This helps to explain why hula had
already lost some of its kapu before Captain Cook's arrival in
1778. As Dorothy Barrère pointed out in her essay, "The Hula In
Retrospect," hula performances were not always acts of worship
or "a religious service." Nonetheless, here we are mainly concerned
with hula as ritual, with its sacred intent, rather than with dance
as an art or amusement.

Although the aesthetics of dance cannot easily be separated
from its sacred aspects, a greater understanding of its ritual character will enhance our appreciation not only of its religious origins
but also of the potential of hula to play an even larger role as a
transmitter of traditional values.

Differing versions of the origin of the hula are related, but in the
end all agree on a common sacred source. One popular version is

based on the story of Hi'iaka, born of an egg carried in Pele's armpit, who learned the dance initially from her friend, Hōpoe. Together they performed the first hula for Pele, on the beach at Nanahuki. Another version attributes its origin to two deities, male and female, both named Laka, who arrived from Kahiki by canoe and danced for the people of Hawai'i. After a time the male Laka disappeared and the female Laka remained to dance alone. A variation of this states that Laka taught the hula to Hi'iaka who then taught it to Hōpoe. Still another account tells of Hinaulu-'ōhi'a, who is supposed to have originated the hula while imitating the movements of the nodding branches and flowers of the 'ōhi'a lehua tree and then taught it to the young Hi'ilani-wai. Yet another version exists, involving the chief Mo'ikeha who, after immigrating to Hawai'i from Tahiti, sent back for La'a who brought the pahu (drum) and taught the hula to Hawaiians. A Moloka'i version tells of a dancer named La'ila'i who came from the Marquesas Islands to Hawai'i nei and in whose family the hula remained for three hundred years, until Laka learned it and taught it to others. Finally, there is the suggestion that ku'ialua, the ancient Hawaiian style of martial arts, might have been the "mother of the hula" (Hopkins).

Whatever may be the differences in these versions, each traces the origin of the hula to mo'olelo or myth. Although the art of hula has long been marked by disagreements, in this most fundamental question agreement is reached: the hula is born out of mythology. In other words, the gods were the ones who first created and choreographed the dance, who first composed the mele hula, who first taught the hula to mortals, who established the first hālau, and who made and played the first musical instruments to accompany the dances. This does not mean that every single sacred dance, of which probably three hundred or more were known in old Hawai'i, was created by the gods, but only that they created the few prototypes. As mythic ritual, hula is a reenactment of what the gods did in the beginning.

Myth, ritual, and dance are indivisible parts of a single process. As dance, hula is ritual because it imitates what the gods have done. The myth tells of divine deeds in words, while dance portrays those deeds in movement, rhythm, and gesture. The essence of ritual is action, as is illustrated in the Greek term for rite, dronnen, which means doing something or expressing it in action. By its very nature, dance epitomizes the dynamics of ritual. Lewis Spence, in his 1949 study of myth, ritual, and dance, described their linkage as follows: "The dance springs out of the body of ritual; it depicts to some extent the motion which ritual begets. But it also partakes of the nature of myth, the sister of ritual, in that it depicts and brings to light the circumstances of myth. . . . Yet all three—ritual, dance and myth—are really one."

Since the role of ritual is to represent reality expressed in myth, no more perfect instrument for doing that could have been invented than dance. For dance is motion, which is the state of being of all things. The sand, rocks, air, mountains, trees, water—all forms of energy—are made up of vibrating, moving molecules and atoms. They are, in effect, all dancing. While the picture of moving molecules and atoms is a product of modern physics, the idea of an animated world in which all things are alive or dancing, as it were, was not strange to Hawaiians, as it was not strange to Hindus and Buddhists, who have long been aware of "the world of illusion." Perhaps the primal mind "knew" that movement in rhythmic patterns in what today we call vibrations and frequencies, is the underlying reality of all realities, and they invented dance as part of ritual to express this moving force.

The American Indian writer Jamake Highwater described dance as the "ritualization of motion." The human body is the organism by which motion makes visible the sacred forms of life itself. Since our bodies live because of the motion of energy, motion is the most important and pervasive means by which primal peoples celebrate living. He continued: "The body is capable of communicating in its own bodily manner. It is only since the beginning of the twentieth century that the power of dance as a communicative medium has been fully appreciated, but primal peoples have understood and focused on the affectiveness of dance since long before the rise of the earliest civilizations." He went on to say that primal peoples, like Indians, "believe that dance can shape the circumstances of nature . . . and [can] transform themselves into things of the natural world that invest them with vision and strength."

Hula is mimetic, that is, it imitates actions, events, phenomena, persons, animals, and so forth. When we say hula tells a story we mean that it speaks through its body language, as this is expressed by physical movements and gestures. As in ritual, so in dance;

Hawaiians believed that the hula possesses mana. But why did Hawaiians think that a certain set of rhythmic motions had such power? Quite apart from its mythic origins, the answer lies in the ancient belief that by imitating something, one can possess it or control it. Contemporary kumu hula John Kaha'i Topolinski writes that "the dance is based on the assumption that by presenting an act, one gains power over it. Thus one can govern the outcome of a future act or cause a past act to happen again. By imitating a person or object, moreover, one can possess it or control it. It is sufficient, therefore, to reproduce, say in dancing, the wished-for events: the victorious battle, the successful hunt. The dancer leaps high to make the sea grow high" (quoted in Kanahele 1979). Hence, imitation of the animal in such dances as those describing the kōlea (plover), pua'a (pig), and manō (shark), has an influence upon the animal itself. But, from the dancer's point of view, he is not so much imitating the animal as he is transforming himself into it. In other words, through the power of dance *and* ritual the dancer performing the movements *becomes* those things depicted.

While dance is based on myth, and mana comes in part from belief in myth, mana also must flow from the growing concentration of it in the performers—many weeks of practice in the hālau, during which dancers are separated from the outside world, limited to eating certain foods, refraining from sex, and so on—all such preparations being designed to make more sacred the dancers and their performance. As with the priestly sacrificer and the observing participants in a temple rite, hula dancers, too, had to be consecrated before their ritual performance. As with all kinds of performances, the actual demonstration is only the culmination of a long series of actions.

Dance no doubt appeals to our aesthetic and kinesthetic senses, but as ritual it must serve other than artistic purposes. "The old Hawaiian," as Handy and Pūku'i reminded us, "did not indulge in 'art for art's sake.'" Whatever artistry was revealed in a performance was only a means toward achieving the overall outcome of ritual: maximizing the presence of the sacred, divine power, the mana. But the hula also had other specific functions.

One of the most important ritual functions of the hula was to promote the fertility of the soil and the yields of crops. This is a tradition found in almost every culture and in all historic periods, from the time of the Egyptians, who performed dances to the god

Osiris, down to the Navahos of today with their rain-inducing dances. Handy, Handy, and Pūkuʻi stated that hula was "designed to bring rain and fertility," and suggested that dance may have originated in the way Hawaiians prepared the ground before planting a taro patch, because the motions involved in treading the soft mud are similar to the treading motions of the legs and feet in the dance. Hula figured prominently in the planting, harvesting, and other phases of the agricultural cycle, and in the Makahiki. A specific example of an agricultural hula is the hula pahua, in which the dancers made thrusting motions with a wooden implement shaped like the ʻōʻō, or digging stick (although it could also have been used as a spear by warrior dancers). In short, the planters' hula shows clearly how Hawaiian religion and ritual were related to the environment.

The hula was used to promote human fertility also, although the erotic dance as such did not seem to figure as significantly in ritual as in harvest dances. The classical hula nīʻaukani and hula kilu were performed ritually at times. Eroticism was a theme for dance festivities held with the intention of entertaining the gods. Such performances seemed to be held much more often in other island groups, such as Tahiti and Sāmoa, than in Hawaiʻi.

According to Pūkuʻi and Korn, a related function was to bring "an enriching and empowering magic" to the "ceremonial and sexual union of *aliʻi*, high chiefs, especially to the birth of a royal child destined to become a great leader." The hula was performed, for instance, at the birth of Kauikeaouli, who became Kamehameha III, and at the birth of Kaʻīimamao, the firstborn of a daughter of the ruling ʻĪ family of Hilo.

On the other hand, the hula was invariably performed along with eulogistic name chants at the death of an aliʻi. For example, a hula, accompanied by kanikau style of chanting, was done in the following manner. A company of dancers, seated on a mat, began to sing a melancholy tune, augmented with slow and gentle motions of the body and arms. The performers raised themselves to their knees and, in a posture between kneeling and sitting, began by degrees to move their arms and bodies toward greater speed, the tune always keeping pace with the motions, and then lowered themselves again to their knees. This hula was repeated continually until the mourning period was over. Also customary was performance of a suitable dance at the funeral of a commoner.

As a means of honoring the memory of the dead, this practice was common throughout Polynesia, but is rarely seen today at Hawaiian funerals.

In addition, the hula was performed at ritual feasts, such as the 'aha'aina pālala, honoring the firstborn child, and the 'aha'aina ho'okipa, welcoming the return of a relative or respected personage. It was also part of the rituals before entering battle, as in the sham battles for "psyching up" warriors. But the war dance as such never reached the level of importance or popularity it attained in the Maori haka, with its distorted facial expressions, protruding tongues, and guttural sounds.

Appropriately enough, the hula was institutionalized in the rites and ceremonies of the hālau hula. These were fully ritualized affairs with prayers, ceremonies of purification and consecration, and offerings and sacrifices. For example, the 'ailolo, or graduation ceremony, consisted of a special service of dance and song preceding the graduation day; a sea bath at midnight by the whole company to purify themselves, with the progress to and from the shore made in complete nudity, for "nakedness is the garb of the gods" (Emerson 1965). Another purification ritual followed, this time with a pī kai, a sprinkling with sea water, which was followed by another period of dance and song until daybreak, when the company rose at the tap of the drum. Ablutions, a simple meal, and the final recitation of a kapu-removing prayer completed the preparations.

Whatever the function or purpose of the hula—whether invoking fertility in either agricultural or human productivity, healing, honoring a departed ancestor, psychic armament, initiation, or validation of social status—the underlying principle was the same as in all religious ritual: to reaffirm belief and trust by reenacting the deeds of the gods and, in the process, to revitalize the unceasing quest for power or mana. While elevating dance to such a level of almost cosmic importance may strike the modern skeptic as an exaggeration, when it is considered as a part of ritual derived from myth, sacred dance is thoroughly consistent with the total culture of ka po'e kahiko.

This brings us to a rather interesting point about the relationship between words and motion in dance. The subject has some bearing on the way modern Hawaiians relate to the hula. Amy Stillman, a young Hawaiian ethnomusicologist, asserts that "verbal communication of the message via the text is the most important aspect of hula." She argues that traditionally Hawaiian dance is dependent on poetry or chant, that the dance motions depict key words or ideas in the chant, and that the audience must listen to the text in order to understand the story line.

We do not take issue with the fact that knowledge of the language is necessary to understand fully the story of the dance, but we do question the greater importance she places on the words. Words, however important, are but one of the complementary elements of ritual. Even with all the power ascribed to words by Hawaiians, still their efficacy comes in large part from the hallowed environment created by the consecrated space, the sacred time, the presence of the akua and their priestly agents, the prescribed rules of the ritual or the kapu, the smells and the sounds—and the silences. Some people might maintain that, as "ritualized motion," the essence of dance is not in text but in movement. The meaning and power of dance lie in what is being expressed by the entire body of the dancer, for in dance the body is the agent of expression. In a sense, dance is so attuned with ritual because both transcend the limitations of verbal communication. In ritual hula the Hawaiian dancer tries to achieve as clear and as direct a communion as possible with the sacred powers, employing all of his faculties—and more.

If this point of view is acceptable, it might provide some comfort to the vast majority of modern Hawaiians who have no idea what the words to a hula may mean. This deficiency is true not only for those in the audience, but also for the performers and the kumu hula, or instructors, themselves. While this point of view is not an excuse for not learning or understanding the language, it does give hula today a much more realistic function and yet legitimizes it at the same time.

However, no one can deny that if hula is to fulfill its potential as one of the most important modern repositories and transmitters of Hawaiian values, its practitioners cannot fully achieve that service without a mastery of the text—and of the language.

PART TWO

SPACE, TIME, AND PLACE

5

COSMOLOGY REVISITED

Cosmic Awe

When the Hawaiians of old gazed up at lani pa'a, the firmament, with only the unaided eye, they could not help but see a small part of the universe: a sun, a moon, the seven planets, and a few thousand stars, objects which they probably believed to be moderate in size and at no great distance from this earth. But when we look at the heavens with our modern telescopes and other kinds of scientific apparatus, we see an infinitely larger universe with some hundred billion galaxies, each with, on the average, a hundred billion stars. In all the galaxies there are perhaps as many planets as stars, or about ten billion trillion of each. Distance is measured not by the mile but by the light year, during which a beam of light will travel about six trillion miles. And some objects in space are thousands of light years away.

Whether you gaze at the night sky with the limited knowledge of the ancient Hawaiian or with the greater knowledge available to the modern Hawaiian, the human spirit submits to the same feeling of awe. When you think of how minute the earth is compared with the whole cosmos, and how small human beings are compared with the earth, you appreciate your insignificance and sense the "aweful mystery" of the ao holo'oko'a, the universe. In this awesome setting people have always wondered about their relationship to the cosmos, asking whether it and they have any purpose and meaning at all.

What did the Hawaiians wonder about their universe? Strangely enough, they may have not wondered about it very much, at least compared with other Polynesians or ourselves. Nonetheless, however few their reflections on the universe may have been, the ideas about it that they did express will be the subjects of this and subsequent chapters. As important as this understanding may be, it is but the first condition to examining the even more relevant question: in what ways did their knowledge about the cosmos shape Hawaiians' attitudes and values about things on earth?

This question, of course, presumes that what people think about the nature of the universe has some kind of "prescriptive force" that affects their general behavior in other and terrestrial matters. A little reflection should make this clear. Take, for example, the impact that Isaac Newton's ideas about the universe have had on social and political behavior in the West during the past three hundred years. His hypothesis, that the whole universe is a giant cosmic machine which was set in motion by God and has continued to run ever since, governed by immutable natural laws, was the fundamental principle of classical physical sciences and of the Industrial Revolution they helped to generate. It was also the model for the founding architects of the American political system, who constructed our checks-and-balances form of government according to a mechanistic view of the world. The long-held belief that individual people behave in a rational manner was taken in part from Newtonian assumptions about the nature of man. Much of our constitutional law and legal systems rely on this understanding of human character, although, of course, we no longer accept it completely. In short, the Newtonian perspective of the cosmos has had considerable influence on the values adopted by Americans and a few other Western societies.

What we propose to do, then, is to see how Hawaiian thought about cosmology has been reflected in their values and practices. Specifically, we shall discuss Hawaiian cosmogonies, that is, ideas about the origins of the universe as they have been formulated in myth, and their connection with ritual and status. We shall examine some specific attributes of their cosmos, such as its orderliness and rhythm, and see how this is transformed by the "genius" of the kilokilo, or astrologer-astronomer. We shall also consider causality and dualism, and how they relate to the principle of lōkahi, or unity and balance. Finally, we shall discuss the significance of mana, particularly in terms of "cosmic intelligence," and show how it ties in with Hawaiian teleology and values. Let us begin, however, with the irony of the "reluctant cosmologist."

The Reluctant Cosmologist?

One of the hazards in dealing with ancient Hawaiian ideas about the cosmos is the lack of data. This deficiency appears to be due as much to the loss of traditional sources as to the apparent reluctance of Hawaiians to deal extensively with the subject, especially in their myths. Indeed, the apparent lack of interest in the cosmos is one of the striking features of ancient Hawaiian mythology. Martha Beckwith (1970) said flatly that cosmic myths are "absent," and that "no story is told of the long incubation of thought which finally becomes active and generates the material universe and mankind. . . . No story is told of the rending apart of earth and heaven, after the birth of the gods. No family of gods is represented, no struggle of the son against the primeval father, no story of the ascent to the heaven of the gods after esoteric wisdom, no myth of *Tiki* and the first woman."

The imagination and elaborate speculation that one finds in other primal and Polynesian cosmological accounts are not present in the Hawaiian. Maori mythology is especially impressive, with line after line of references to the origin of the universe and possibly consciousness as well and to the evolutional development of matter. To illustrate:

> From the nothing the begetting,
> From the nothing the increase,
> From the nothing the abundance,
> The power of increasing, the living breath;
> It dwelt with the empty space,
> It produced the atmosphere which is above us.
>   (Marsden)

In contrast, only a few lines in all of Hawaiian mythology reveal their thinking about cosmology on any extensive scale. What explains this apparent lack of interest in cosmic mythology? Were the Hawaiians of old simply uninterested in that kind of speculation for its own sake? Did they in fact develop a more elaborate cosmogonic mo'olelo which, however, might have been kept secret by certain cult or priestly practices? Or did they prefer to pass on their knowledge about the cosmos as profane information, that is, as part of their general fund of information rather than as consecrated mythology?

Anthropologist Marshal Sahlins (1981) offered an interesting insight when he compared the relations between Maori and Hawaiian cosmology with the distinction between the Indian approach to cosmic myth and the Roman approach to historical epic (that is, narrative poems about the deeds of legendary heroes). The Indians think "cosmically, philosophically and morally, where the Romans think nationally, practically, and politically. Vedic traditions are thus fabulous and mystical, Roman traditions historical: what appear in the former as miraculous deeds of divine beings are in the latter worldly acts of legendary kings." In other words, what appears as divine abstractions in Indian mythology are "reproduced in humanized form by the Roman historical epics." Sahlins concluded: "The Hawaiian 'humanized mythology' contrasts, at least relatively, with Maori cosmology in the same way." That is to say, Hawaiian mythology is less interested in explaining the origins of the universe as such than it is in the origins of society. Or, to put it another way, the Hawaiian mythmakers were more interested in down-to-earth "sociology" than in prehuman "Polynesian cosmogony."

This seems to be a reasonable explanation; at least it is consistent with our own portrayal of the primal Hawaiian as having a strong streak of pragmatism. But, we add, this in no way diminishes the Hawaiian's interests in the other world, as we have clearly demonstrated in the previous chapters about religion.

The Nature of the Cosmos

With only a limited perspective of the universe, Hawaiians, not surprisingly, and like most peoples in the ancient world, adopted a geocentric view of the universe. As Malo stated, they imagined "the earth was supposed to be solid and motionless" with the sun, moon, and stars orbiting the earth. So entrenched was this idea that more than forty years after the arrival of Captain Cook Hawaiians still believed in it. Hiram Bingham, for example, related the difficulty he had in convincing some Hawaiian ali'i to believe otherwise.

> How difficult, during the first years of our labor, to displace the notion entertained by the more intelligent rulers, that the earth is a stationary plain, around which the sun, the changeful planets and

stars revolve. Laboring, occasionally, to teach by means of a watch, the division of hours, minutes, and seconds, and of days and weeks, by the artificial globe, using the common arguments for the globular figure and diurnal motions of the earth, we were met by their objection, that everything would fall off if the earth were to turn over. The king himself laughed at our astronomy, and maintained that sailing round the earth was like sailing round one of his islands. But at length [he] yielded to the force of argument in favor of the globular form and diurnal motion of the earth; yet many others were far less teachable.

The geocentric view projected an image of earth being flat and shaped like a house over which domes of the sky are placed. The heavens are supposed to be supported on pillars with proper openings through which the sun entered in the morning and set at night. There is also a great tunnel under the earth through which the sun travels at night to rise again in the east in the morning.

If all this strikes the modern mind as superstitious or incredible, consider the words of Carl Sagan, who wrote that the geocentric view is "the most natural idea in the world. The Earth seems steady, solid, immobile, while we can see the heavenly bodies rising and setting each day. Every culture has leaped to the geocentric hypothesis." And listen to Johannes Kepler, the great sixteenth-century German astronomer-mathematician. "It is therefore impossible that reason not previously instructed should imagine anything other than that the Earth is a kind of vast house with the vault of the sky placed on top of it; it is motionless and within it the Sun being so small passes from one region to another, like a bird wandering through the air" (quoted in Sagan).

What Sagan and Kepler clearly demonstrate is that, given their knowledge of the universe, ancient Hawaiians, like so many other peoples, including Europeans before Kepler, came up with explanations for the cosmos that were perfectly reasonable under the circumstances. We should also note that while post-Cook Hawaiians took about forty years to accept the new heliocentric view of the world, Christian Europe needed two hundred years after the advent of Nicholas Copernicus—the Polish Catholic cleric whom Martin Luther described as "an upstart astrologer" for saying that the sun, not the earth, was the center of our solar system.

When the earth was considered to be the center of the universe, geocentrism offered relatively little motivation for pursuing astronomical observations or other cosmological studies. Furthermore, when the state religion, with its priestly hierarchy and rulers, accepts the theory as dogma and discourages or even persecutes its detractors, as was the case in Europe during the so-called Dark Ages, then people find even less motivation for challenging the establishment. Quite possibly a similar situation existed in pre-haole Hawai'i, as is suggested by the opinions of the ali'i whom Bingham tried to convince otherwise.

Nonetheless, from a very practical standpoint astronomy was an important subject to the Hawaiians of old. The need to navigate accurately and to develop a reliable calendar for agricultural and ritual purposes were important incentives. According to E. H. Bryan, Jr., "Few made more practical use of this (astronomical) knowledge than did the ancient Hawaiians" (quoted in *Ancient Hawaiian Civilization*).

They had identified from two to three hundred stars, although today no one knows exactly how many. They readily distinguished between the planets (called hōkū hele, or traveling stars) and the fixed stars (hōkū pa'a). They knew the rising and setting positions on the horizons of more than 150 stars, using those points to help them in navigating across the ocean. In fact, the movements of the stars across the sky, from east to west, both nightly and throughout the year, were quite familiar to them. They did not suspect, of course, that the nightly movements were due to the rotation of the earth on its axis, or that the yearly movements were due to its passage around the sun.

Obviously, the Hawaiians perceived the orderliness of the universe in terms of the regular and predictable movements of the stars and planets. While for them the earth may have stood still, everything else moved in a kind of cosmic rhythm. They lived not in a static but in a dynamic universe, and the Hawaiians understood this not only from natural observation but also from mythological accounts. Rubellite Johnson (1981), for example, told of *The Kumulipo*'s "coherent understanding of the dimension of time moving across ages of embryonic evolution in a discernible and predictable rhythmic pattern." Soon we shall see how they translated this view of a dynamic cosmos into religious practice and values.

What Hawaiians hypothesized or mythologized about the origins of the universe as a whole is far less evident. Apparently, to

them the universe—or at least the stuff out of which it is made—
always existed, or at the least existed before the creation of the
earth. *The Kumulipo* (in Johnson's translation) implies as much
when, in its Prologue, it refers to the existence of "space" turning
around and causing the earth to be "heated" and the sky to be
"reversed." (Parenthetically, according to Sammy Amalu the "Creation Song" of the Kamehameha family, a copy of which he claims
to have, tells of a universe that had "no beginning.")

This pre-earth period is generally referred to in Hawaiian and
Polynesian cosmogonic myths as Pō, which has been variously
translated as night, darkness, chaos, or the realm of the gods. In a
material sense, chaos perhaps comes closest to the primal meaning
of Pō. Abraham Fornander wrote that "through all the Polynesian
cosmogonies, even the wildest and most fanciful, there is a constant underlying sense of a chaos." But what he defines as chaos is
wreck, in the form of destruction, ruin, or disorder. What people
normally think of as chaos is a state of utter and absolute disor-
ganization. But is that necessarily how the Hawaiian thought of
Pō? We think not. For, like its opposite, order, chaos is a matter of
degree. That is, it should be looked at according to a descending
(or ascending) scale of magnitude. The larger the phenomenon, or
the more units and elements are involved, for example, the greater
is the magnitude of the chaos. In this perspective, everything is
relative.

The key to this understanding of chaos is that it invariably gives
rise to order. "In the beginning . . . the earth was without form
and void." In the beginning, that is, there was only chaos. Then
"the Spirit of God moved" and out of the chaos came an order.
This is the biblical notion, but it illustrates the paradox of order
being the product of chaos. This is probably the sense of the
Maori notion of Te Kore, The Void or The Nothingness, and the
sense of Pō as well. Perhaps Johnson also meant this when, referring to *The Kumulipo*, she stated: "Taken as a whole the prologue
to time honors the stability of the universe. The suggested interpretation in previous studies that *kāhuli* 'to turn over' implies an
unsettling change, a disturbance, or cataclysmic 'Chaos' when the
universe began is improbable when weighed against the orderly
comprehension of the dynamics of space and time."

Pō also has an immaterial or spiritual meaning which is integral
to the Hawaiian view of the cosmos: it is "the realm of the gods."

Beckwith (1951) put it this way when referring to Pō in *The Kumulipo*: "This is not darkness in the physical sense but applies to the supremacy of the spirit world, the Pō, as compared with the world of living men, the Ao." In other words, there is a spiritual world coexisting with the material world. Thus, there are two worlds not, however, operating apart and separate from each other, but both in a state of permanent complementarity. They flow into each other constantly, interacting and intervening, but always with the spiritual realm exercising ultimate dominion. In short, the existence of Pō demonstrates that the Hawaiian viewed the universe as an open "two-in-one" system, not as the closed, single system that is implicit in the Newtonian mechanistic model.

While little more can be said about the origins of the cosmos based on Hawaiian data, the story is much different when the origins of the earth are considered. About this subject Hawaiian cosmologists or mythmakers were much more expansive. Several accounts are known, covering the gamut from the creationist view that gods created the earth, to the more comprehensible view that the earth is the product of a primeval pair of deities from whom humankind are descended. Also presented was the idea of spontaneous generation combined with natural evolution. Hawaiian thinking thus ranged from what today we would consider the most rational to the most irrational, from the most spiritual to the utterly materialistic—and to a lot in between besides. One cannot help but be impressed with the variety of explanations for the creation (someone has counted sixteen versions). The resulting contradictions and confusions are also impressive. Malo understandably complained about this problem, although (as we have mentioned in an earlier chapter) the diversity of ideas gives evidence of the richness of thought and the scope of intellectual freedom that characterized ka po'e kahiko.

We need not go into all the details about cosmogony. Citing examples of the general categories of theories should be enough. Spontaneous generation-and-evolution is best illustrated by *The Kumulipo*, which tells of the earth (honua) being formed from the "slime" (walewale) originating from the ocean. (This subject will be discussed in chapter 8.) The primeval ancestral pair appears in one of the Papa-Wākea accounts described by Fornander: "*Papa*, the wife of *Wākea*, begat a calabash—*ipu* or gourd—including bowl and cover. *Wākea* threw the cover upward, and it became the heaven. From the inside meat and seeds *Wākea* made the sun, moon, stars, and sky; from the juice he made the rain; and from the bowl he made the land and the sea." In another chant quoted by Fornander Kāne, working with Lono and Kū, brings forth "Heaven and Earth," which then are "quickened, increased, moving," then "raised up into Continents."

At this juncture, a digression is in order to deal with the shame that some modern Hawaiians feel when these early creation stories are discussed. These people believe that the stories are so "fanciful and wild" that they must also be superstitious and stupid. What they fail to realize, however, is the fact that most of the world's many myths about creation are filled with the same kinds of "fanciful and wild" stories. For example, from the P'an Ku myths of third-century China comes the following. "First there was the great cosmic egg. Inside the egg was chaos, and floating in chaos was P'an Ku, the Undeveloped, the divine Embryo. And P'an Ku burst out of the egg, four times larger than any man today, with a hammer and chisel in his hand with which he fashioned the world." From ancient Babylonian myth comes the complicated story of Enuma Elish in which Marduk, the warrior king of the gods, forms the world by dividing the body of the primeval mother god, Tiamat, into two parts, the upper one forming the sky and heavens, and the lower one the earth. And in the Indian Rigveda is Purusa, a spirit that penetrates all of life and matter. He is sacrificed and the sky is formed from his head, the atmosphere from his navel, and the earth from his feet. Countless other imaginative creation stories can be told, gathered from every culture that has existed on earth. Hence, early Hawaiians were no different from peoples elsewhere in the creation myths they fashioned to explain their world.

A second point to be made is that myth communicates in the language of metaphors and symbols, in kaona. Unless one knows how to interpret the mythic language, one cannot help but take the language "literally" and conclude that it is all "fanciful and wild." What needs to be remembered is that myth is not validated by its correspondence to the objective world you or I may perceive, but by the faith and trust of its believers. Thus the concept of the cosmic egg was just as believable to earlier Chinese as the biblical account of the creation of the earth in six days is to Christian fundamentalists. In sum, all myths are right for the particular generations of believers who conceived them.

Let us turn now to considering how primal beliefs and perceptions of the cosmos shaped and influenced Hawaiian attitudes and values.

Ritualized Cosmology

The ritualization of the creation myth is one of the more obvious ways by which cosmology affected Hawaiian behavior. It was reenacted symbolically in many ways, from celebrating the birth of a royal child, as was done with *The Kumulipo*, to the consecration of a newly constructed house, or the honoring of Lono's return in the form of Captain Cook. This reenacting was common not only to Hawaiian culture, but was found in almost all cultures in the earlier stages of their development. An ingenious explanation for this general practice was given by Mircea Eliade (1974) in the concept of the "myth of the eternal return."

For primal peoples, Eliade suggested, reality is a function of the imitation of a "celestial archetype," that is, a primordial act performed by the gods, such as the creation. Hence, people's acts take on value or meaning to the extent to which they reproduce or repeat a mythical archetype. In myth, there is a preexistent world of the gods, and everything that has ever happened on earth or anything people do on earth has an extraterrestrial prototype. Thus, a person's life is the ceaseless repetition of acts done by the gods, great ancestors, legendary heroes, or (in Hawai'i) by 'aumākua.

Eliade documented his hypothesis by citing numerous examples from different cultures where the creation myth or cosmogony is used as a "celestial prototype." Thus, in Iranian cosmology, this earth below corresponds to a celestial earth above and each thing practiced here has a heavenly counterpart. In Egypt places or districts were named after the celestial fields. When new territory was conquered in Vedic India, the act of conquest was viewed as a repetition of the act of creation. And when Moses wished to build a temple for his people, he received from Jehovah on Mount Sinai the specifications for a celestial plan to be used in the construction of the terrestrial version.

Can we apply Eliade's theory to pre-Christian Hawai'i? To a certain extent we can. For example, in principle, the consecration of a newly built house was a recalling of the birth act. It is symbolized in the ceremony and in the prayer known as *"ka 'oki 'ana o ka piko o ka hale,*" "the cutting of the navel string of the house." Piko, or umbilical cord, is the symbolic name for the long thatching that was allowed to hang over the doorway, to be cut and trimmed only when the house was ready for occupancy. Because it is associated with the birth of a child, the ritual can be seen as celebrating the creation of a new structure. This partly explains why Hawaiians believed that every house had a personality of its own. In Eliade's view, any new construction was regarded by primal peoples as akin to the act of creation.

The act of creation is significant in still another idea expressed by Eliade: the "magic and prestige of origins." Every mythical account of the origin of anything presupposes and continues the creation. This is why the histories of the great families and dynasties of many primal peoples begin by rehearsing the story of the creation. He cited, for instance, the genealogical narrative of a Tibetan dynasty that begins with the birth of the cosmos from an egg, and the custom of the primitive Santali of India, who recite the cosmogonic myth for a man when he is granted "full social rights," and at funerals. To these we can add numerous examples of Polynesian genealogical chants, such as *The Kumulipo* and Maori ariki chants.

The underlying assumption of the "prestige of origins" concept is that the creation, particularly the "Chaos" or "Void" period of Te Kore or Pō, was the "Perfect Time,"—when the pristine world was still in a state of bliss. According to Eliade, this is a frequent theme in the religions of India, Iran, aboriginal Australia, and Christianity. For example, in Genesis the earth is still in a paradisiacal condition, until the fall of Adam. Australian aborigines believe that the "dreamtime" of the primordial world is "Perfect Time." In the Maori tradition of Io, the time of Te Kore was perfect, because then only the gods existed. Whether the same idea of a preexistent "Perfect Time" can be said to apply to Hawaiian cosmogony is uncertain, although it does not seem to be incompatible with the spirit of Hawaiian ritual practices and myths.

In any case, coupled with the idea of the "prestige of origins" is the familiar notion of "going back" to the beginning as a means of renewing and regenerating oneself and, in the process, of recapturing the blissful beginning, the "lost paradise." Eliade noted the prevalence of this idea among many primal and modern societies. For example, in the initiation rites for adolescent males in aboriginal Australia, the youth is taken back to the embryonic state, or the womb, and then brought forward to a rebirth. The intent of such rites is to emphasize the transformation of the adolescent into a socially responsible and culturally awakened adult being.

In old Hawai'i, the most important initiation rite in the life cycle of a male child occurred at about four or five years of age, when he was moved from the women's house into the mua, the eating and lounging house of the men. Here a parallel with "going back" can be found, in the sense that the ritual represents taking the boy from the mother's womb, symbolized by the company of women he has lived with, and placing him in a "man's world." When in the mua he partakes of the food in the ipu of Lono, the boy dedicates himself to Lono and accordingly is renewed.

It is interesting to note the modern analogy in Freudian psychoanalysis, in which the principle of "going back" is used as a basic technique. The technique's premise is that for each individual the truly primordial time is earliest childhood (the "child lives in a mythical, paradisiacal time"). By going back to the embryonic beginning (the womb), a person can reconstitute certain decisive events in earliest childhood, thereby acquiring a better understanding and mastery of the self. Incidentally, essentially the same idea is used in therapy among people belonging to several ancient cultures. Some Taoists, for example, place great importance on the technique of "embryonic breathing."

The key to Eliade's concepts relating to "the myth of the eternal return" is memory: one must know the origin and history of a thing in order to gain control over it. Control depends always on remembering, in clear and precise detail, what happened in the beginning and from then on. The person who has the ability to memorize and retain information may have even more power than the person who simply knows the origin of something. Parenthetically, this is another reason why flawless performance in chanting and performing the motions of rituals was so important in old Hawai'i.

The Genius of the Astrologer

The story is told about Kamehameha the Great seeking advice from his astrologer about whether he should invade Kaua'i following his triumphant conquest of O'ahu. As he was about to decide, the kilokilo, astrologer-astronomer, looked up at the signs in the heavens and saw, very close together, the planet Ikaika, Jupiter, and the star of the chief of Kaua'i, Kaumuali'i. The astrologer told the king: "Kaua'i will be yours, because it is shown. The land will be yours without a battle from the chief of Kaua'i, thus shall it be for you." History records that, in time, Kaumuali'i, without a fight, did acknowledge Kamehameha's sovereignty over Kaua'i.

Kamehameha's astrologer-astronomer was only one among many in a long line of kilokilo, meaning a reader of omens, seer, or stargazer. His primary function was to study the omens, particularly those shown by planets, meteors, and comets, in order to foretell events that might affect his powerful patrons. As with other specialists, he was also a kahuna, although his priest's status may not have been much protection to him if ever he made an inaccurate prediction. (In ancient China, the erring fellow was executed.)

While astrology usually was more concerned with matters of state, the generations of kilokilo had also worked out elaborate systems for calculating personal forecasts that contained signs for people born on each day of the month. For example, a person born on Māhealani, the sixteenth day of the lunar month and therefore the night of the full moon, would have good luck and be a striver; a person born on Kulu, the seventeenth day, would be prosperous, affectionate, and beloved; and a person born on Lā'au Kūkahi, the eighteenth day, would be eager for knowledge and of fine character; and so on. Since the major islands, such as O'ahu and Kaua'i, observed different calendars, the system—and the forecasts—probably varied according to place. We can guess that this personalized astrology was more available to the ruling families and their supporting chiefs than to the maka'āinana.

But whether used for chiefs or commoners, astrology figured prominently in the life of Hawaiians of old, just as it has done for more than three thousand years in almost every known culture. (Parenthetically, despite the fact that most scientists today dismiss it as "fuzzy thinking and a pious fraud," in the United States astrology, almost paralleling the rise of scientific astronomy, has gained greater popularity than ever, with probably ten times more practicing astrologers in the country than astronomers [Sagan].)

The power of the astrologer, Hawaiian or otherwise, lies in his recognizing that somehow the orderly movements of the universe are linked to human behavior and destiny. The kilokilo of old apparently knew that just as the moon influences the tides, so does it affect our moods. Whether he suspected that the phases of the moon and mental disorder in humans were linked is not known. But clearly he must have reasoned that being in harmony with the cosmic order was vital to our well-being. Or, to put the problem in another way: when we are "in sync" with ourselves and the world around us, things seem to go right; and when we are not, things go wrong.

Astrology is misnamed, perhaps. According to Lawrence Blair it should be called "cosmorhythmology." That in fact is what the "scientific face" of astrology is called today, because it deals with quantifying and objectifying correlations between astral movements and events on earth, and supposedly relies on a statistical approach to rhythms and cycles.

Whatever reservations one may have about astrology or cosmorhythmology, the pivotal point to remember is its premise: the interrelatedness of man and all parts of the universe. George Leonard, in *The Silent Pulse*, made this relationship very clear: "At the heart of each of us, whatever our imperfections, there exists a silent pulse of perfect rhythm, a complex of wave forms and resonances, which is absolutely individual and unique, and yet which connects us to everything in the universe." For example, when we look at our physical selves, we find that most of our internal system operates in rhythmic relationship and that our assorted organs must be synchronized with each other. Every heart beat is evidence of what we are: organisms in rhythmic harmony. (Incidentally, when a person sings "I ain't got rhythm," he can't mean that literally, because without rhythm none of us would be alive.) Even plants or trees observe their internal and external rhythms very strictly. They can determine with incredible precision external time intervals, such as the duration of light, with their own internal clocks. Certain varieties of Javanese rice, for instance, during the course of a 24-hour period can detect changes in daylight based on as little as a minute's differential. And some plants can carry out long-range time calculations related to seasonal changes as precisely as did the astronomers of ancient Stonehenge in England.

In short, not only are we interconnected with the rest of the universe, but we are also "entrained," that is we are locked into our rhythmic environment because the nature of the universe requires that it and all its parts must seek the most efficient state. Obviously, less energy is needed to move a process in which the components function in cooperation than when they are in opposition. In that lies the practical value of rhythmic harmony. We are, therefore, "entrained" with ourselves, each other, and the external world. Our physical and psychological states change in rhythm with the seasonal swings of the earth and the sun, with the tides, with the day-night cycle, and with the even grander cosmic movements. While the Hawaiian kilokilo could not have been aware of all the scientific details, he was certainly aware of the underlying principle of being "in sync" with the cosmos and therefore with nature closer to home.

Causality

Although the principle of causality, that is, the relationship between cause and effect, is given little direct mention in Hawaiian cosmological accounts, it is hardly something that Hawaiians did not think about when they pondered over the nature of the universe. It is, after all, such a universal experience of common sense that it cannot escape the attention of even the most "primitive" tribes. What did the early Hawaiians think of cause and effect as an explanation for the behavior of both material and spiritual phenomena?

Let us clarify the meaning of the term. The idea of causality may be stated in the following terms. The natural condition of man forces him to relate himself to events or happenings. This awareness leads him to the realization that certain actions consistently produce certain consequences. At the same time he develops a feeling that the timing of two events means a definite correlation between the events, a correlation that he regards as a cause and an effect. In Hawaiian, the respective terms are kumu and hopena.

At the ordinary, everyday level of human activity, cause and effect relationships are determined rather easily. The old Hawaiian canoe builder, for example, who struck his adze into the wood of a koa log would surely have known that the chip of wood that flaked off, and the hole it left, were preceded by his grasping the haft and slamming down the sharp edge of the adze. While he may not have been able to explain precisely all the principles of physics or mechanics involved in the act, he knew that his action was the cause of the event. To offer other such examples would simply belabor the obvious.

Explaining cause and effect is more difficult, however, when one applies the principle to the cosmic level where we can only speculate and reason without benefit of experimentation. If, as we have already suggested, the Hawaiian cosmologist conceived of an orderly and stable universe, he must have reasoned in cause-and-effect fashion, for order presupposes that every progressing act is preceded by another act. If this were not so, chaos would still prevail, darkness would still cover light. Yet, when we ask the most fundamental question about cosmic causality—what was the First Cause?—such logic breaks down. That is to say, the Hawaiian cosmologists, at least those of *The Kumulipo* school, say nothing about the most antecedent act in either the creation or the evolution of the cosmos. They seem to be able to apply the principle only at some intervening point beyond the very beginning.

Does this limitation in any way suggest that Hawaiians were unwilling to conceive of the world in strictly cause-and-effect terms? To be sure, for them causality was operative and applicable in so-called middle zone phenomena of the everyday physical world, but did Hawai'i's philosophers believe that it was not sufficient to explain phenomena beyond that zone? Did they think that their open-ended world—open to the constant interaction of its spiritual and material realms—ultimately transcended a world of causality? While we do not know for certain, it is quite possible that, rather than a rigorous causality, Hawaiians accepted the principle of "interconnectedness"—an idea that seems compatible with much of their worldview.

We have already referred to the Hawaiian perception of the universe and nature as manifestations of a harmonious order, wherein things are in lōkahi, that is, are connected together, as in a vast cosmic grid. When events happen in such a world, they happen not because they are causally related but because they are interrelated. In other words, what appears to be one event causing another is really two events happening in *relative simultaneity*. Keep in mind that we are not talking about the everyday "middle zone" of mundane activity, but about a higher realm of human experiences and perceptions. In this realm, the Hawaiian apparently saw no causation.

If we are right in this conclusion, Hawaiian thought came very close to Eastern mysticism, which according to Capra asserts that "in the Absolute there is neither time, space, *nor causation* [italics added]." In Hindu and Buddhist tradition, believers are shown ways of "going beyond the ordinary experience . . . of freeing themselves from the chain of cause and effect—from the bondage of *karma*." Did Hawaiians of old seek the same liberation from the bondage of cause and effect? Whether or not they did do so, Hawaiians of today may affirm that possibility.

Dualism and Lōkahi

A theme that flows like an ever-winding stream through Hawaiian mythic thought is dualism. Simply put, it rests on the idea that the world of reality is divided into opposites: night and day, light and darkness, male and female, left and right. Much is made of this familiar idea, partly because of the philosophical cast it lends to Hawaiian thought before 1778. But when one really thinks about it, the notion that the world is divided into such pairs of opposites seems more self-evident than profound. A marvelously advanced philosophical intellect is not necessary to deduce that. An innate cognitive function of the human mind allows it to contrast things, for we naturally comprehend what something *is* by observing what is not like it or by what it is not. Every attentive schoolchild, for example, can immediately grasp the moral in the teacher's question: if there is no good, how can we tell what is bad? In sum, humans cannot help but think of opposites.

Yet, profoundly important—and relevant to our investigation into values—is an examination of the way in which the Hawaiian mind constructed his worldview, using in part the concept of dualism. Beckwith (1970) spoke to this as follows:

> Another philosophic concept comes out in his [the Hawaiian] way of accommodating himself as an individual to the physical universe in which he finds himself placed. He arrives at an organized conception of form through the pairing of opposites, one depending upon the other to complete the whole. So ideas of night and day, light and darkness, male and female, land and water, rising and setting [of the sun], small and large, little and big, hard and light [of force], upright and prostrate [of position], upward and downward, toward and away from [the speaker] appear paired in

repeated reiteration as a stylistic element in composition of chants, and function also in everyday language.

This is a cosmic principle which becomes the structure for *The Kumulipo*'s structure, in which "lower" forms of life evolve into "higher" forms, water forms are paired with land forms, pō passes into ao, and male and female elements join together in the creation. It serves the same purpose in Hawaiian genealogies, in which successive husbands and wives are paired through "literally hundreds of generations."

The logic of dualism runs through Hawaiian religious thinking, as in the dichotomy between sacred, kapu, versus profane, noa; or through metaphysical thinking, as in the division of the spiritual and material realms; or through Hawaiian morality, as in pono, upright, righteous, versus shameful behavior; and so on. Numerous examples can be found to show how dualism determines so much of the Hawaiian perspective of the universe and human behavior.

Yet, strictly speaking, dualism presents us with a world of polarities and dichotomies, of disunities and disconnections. This is a condition that neither mind nor soul can tolerate, for it contradicts the human yearning for harmony. No doubt Hawaiian thinkers of old saw the same contradiction. How did they resolve it?

The answer seems to lie in the concept of lōkahi, although we have no philosophical chants, no pertinent sayings and other such "documentary" findings to tell us any more than this. But reason and consistency with the overall Hawaiian "scheme of things" points to lōkahi. In the Hawaiian context, the thought means to bring like and unlike things together in unity and harmony. At the practical sociopsychological level, lōkahi is achieved through the methods of hoʻoponopono, in which members of a disputing family are talked through a process of setting things aright by successive stages of confession, repentance, and reconciliation. The reconciliation removes the hurt and restores a context of peace. While hoʻoponopono is a technique generally restricted to family settings, the principle of restoring social harmony through accommodation of differences applies to all interactions in Hawaiian society.

At the spiritual level, even the metaphysical one, the contradictions of dualism may be resolved by looking at it through the prism of interconnectedness. That is, if the Hawaiian saw a world in which all things are interrelated, linked as in a vast "cosmic grid," then we can conclude, reasonably, that even extreme opposites are linked as if they are two sides of the same reality. Thus, life and death, female and male, and so on are merely different aspects of the same whole. When the whole is viewed as a whole, then all idiosyncrasies and irregularities shown by individuals will disappear. Thus, the full moon, seen from afar, without a telescope, appears to be a perfect sphere. But when the same moon is seen up close, through a telescope or from an orbiting spacecraft, many of its crags and craters and imperfections are revealed. To achieve this realization or understanding of connections, we must transcend the limits of the opposites and see the realm of perfect unity. As the Tao reminds us, the way in which this is done is not by striving only for the good nor by eliminating all the bad, but rather by attaining a dynamic and feasible balance between the two extremes. This is the way of lōkahi—or, at the least, it is one way.

The Cosmology of Mana

The central concept that for ancient Hawaiians most clearly demonstrates the connection between their cosmology and their values is mana. We see the truth of this in the way Hawaiians think of mana as "universal energy" (Johnson 1983)—the force that animates all life and all elements in the universe—and as the "divine" spiritual force available to human beings for fashioning their own perfectability. Mana energizes the cosmos and the same force, in varying degrees, energizes the akua ali'i, the kahuna, the technician, the poet, and even lesser persons, even commoners, animals, and plants. Mana is the stuff out of which the gods are formed or conceived, and it is the same stuff out of which great men and women create their achievements. If mana is the central reality of the universe, it is also the central reality of man's spiritual world. It is at once both cosmological and psychological, immaterial and material, physical and spiritual, supernatural and natural.

If there is any overarching theme in the Hawaiian worldview, it is found in this omnipresent, ineluctable affirmation of the unity of man and the universe. It is mana.

However, one aspect of the cosmology of mana has heretofore

escaped the attention of modern commentators on the subject that
we wish to explore. This is the idea that mana can be identified
with cosmic intelligence. If the two can be linked, we immediately
open other avenues toward understanding and formulating a philosophy of Hawaiian values.

Did the Hawaiian thinker of old conceive of mana as intelligence? (By intelligence we mean the power of an agent to perform
purposeful and directed action.) Whether or not he did so, we cannot definitely say, of course. But could he have conceived the idea?
Let us argue that there is no good reason why he could not have
done so. For one thing, the different ways in which he used the
concept point to his belief in a cosmic force operating toward
some ordered and meaningful end. If, for example, the ultimate
reality has some connection with mana, can we not reasonably
assume that the Hawaiian philosopher must have thought of mana
as being supremely intelligent rather than as unintelligent? He
obviously conceived of his great gods as being intelligent, by definition. If he thought that they were formed out of mana, then he
must have concluded that mana too is intelligence. At a more practical level for thought, if a craftsman's skill in making the perfect
tool or canoe was dependent on his mana, was there not some
implied sense of purposefulness, of usefulness, in his definition of
mana?

We may have not thought about this idea before, but when we
ponder the possibility, we realize that we have known it all the
time: mana, the universal energy, is also energized thought for the
Hawaiian.

A leap from the past to the present state of modern scientific
knowledge of the universe will help us to appreciate this possibility. Biologists like Lewis Thomas tell us that every living thing,
from the simplest cell to the largest mammal, is a highly organized
system of atoms and molecules, of energy and matter. In the evolutionary process, as individual living systems interact with their
environment, they not only attain a high degree of internal order,
but become even more complex as they grow and develop. During
the course of time, life appears to move toward increasingly
ordered complexity, rather than toward disorder. As we have
noted already, this is a fundamental theme in *The Kumulipo*.

The bacterium *Escherichia coli*, a normal inhabitant of the human intestine, is one of the simplest forms of life. Yet one such cell

contains long chains of DNA molecules (DNA is the double strand of nucleotides that lies within every living cell of every kind, and causes the cell to divide; without its DNA no cell could multiply, which means no further life of that kind is possible); about 400,000 RNA molecules (RNA carries instructions issued by DNA to the rest of the living cell's parts); about 1 million protein molecules; and some 500 million smaller organic molecules. Therefore, within each *E. coli* cell there are about 40,000,000,000 atoms (written in mathematical shorthand as 4×10^{10}, meaning 10 raised to the 10th power, or "1" followed by 10 zeroes). More complex cells, such as a single muscle cell, may contain 10^{12} atoms, and some large amoebae as many as 10^{15} atoms.

It is hard not to be convinced of the majestic order within living systems when one studies the human brain. The average human brain contains about 10^{11} nerve cells. The information storage capacity of the brain consists of perhaps 100 trillion (10^{14}) bits of information contained within a mass of some 1,400 grams (about 3 pounds). If written out in English, that information would fill some 20 million volumes, as many as are stored in the world's largest libraries. Imagine the equivalent of 20 million books' worth of data stored inside the head of every one of us! The brain's storage capacity is many times greater than that of any existing computer, although computers are being improved constantly. But the brain does more than recollect, for it also synthesizes, analyzes, compares, reasons, thinks—and evaluates. This last function, the recognizing of values, is something that at present seems to be totally beyond any computer's capacity.

Whether this ordered complexity is found in the tiniest of single cells or in the most complex of brains, all of nature reveals intelligent design, as many scientists have long maintained. Indeed, in the opinion of many thinking men, the entire universe with its millions and billions of stars and galaxies, and everything that they contain, is eloquent testimony to the fact that it must be the product of some directing intelligence. Recognition of this fact is underscored by Sir James Jeans, the distinguished British scientist-author in *The Mysterious Universe* (1931). "Today there is a wide measure of agreement, which on the physical side of science approaches almost to unanimity, that the stream of knowledge is heading towards a non-mechanical reality; the universe begins to look more like a great thought than like a great machine. Mind no longer appears as an accidental intruder into the realm of matter; we are beginning to suspect that we ought rather to hail it as the creator and governor of the realm of matter."

Yet many people who accept this view believe that creative intelligence was the *last* thing to emerge as the culmination of a long series of lucky accidents of evolution—that is to say, that intelligence is the effect rather than the cause of the evolutionary or creative process.

Lester Smith, a fellow of the Royal Society, and a group of fellow scientists argue otherwise in their 1975 book, *Intelligence Came First*. Their argument has won a critical following. In brief, they demonstrate that intelligence, as exhibited by the human mind, is distinct from the physical organism called the brain, and that intelligence is associated with consciousness and exists free in its own domain. Evidence for the nonphysical mind apart from the brain is drawn from hypnotism, Zen meditation, linguistics, and postdeath experiences. Intuition is viewed as another route to truth, more direct than rational thought, that represents a "brief communion" with the "cosmic intelligence." Then they show that life on earth could not have happened except through some intelligent guiding principle, or what they call some "nonmaterial information matrix." Sophisticated adaptations of the old but discredited theory of spontaneous generation are shown to be equally untenable. Chance variations in evolution, no matter how long in time they may take, and other materialistic notions are not valid either. The probability that even a DNA molecule might have arisen by chance is said to be so "infinitesimal" as to make the idea "ludicrous." The mechanistic explanations of molecular biology and genetic engineering are also shown to be unsupportable, insofar as they negate the operation of cosmic intelligence.

Finally, in explaining how cosmic intelligence acts on matter, they borrow from modern physics and reason that thought or intelligence is a kind of energy that can be pictured as "a conglomeration of minute whirling bundles of energy" when interacting with matter. Thus, the interaction of thought and matter, both being forms of energy, is an interaction of like with like. In this immaterial sense, therefore, we can say that matter is pervaded by intelligence.

The conclusions reached by Smith and other like-minded scientists suggest how the Hawaiian thinker could have conceived of mana as cosmic energy and as cosmic intelligence. But, however the Hawaiian may have deduced the concept of mana as intelligence, the idea does fit neatly into his primal view of the world.

One of the logical inferences that he must easily have made is clear: if the universe is pervaded by intelligence, then there must be some purposefulness in its creation or existence. Other people may wonder about it, out of natural curiosity, but the Hawaiian had a teleology—an understanding of ends or purposes—grounded in his cosmological understanding. What is the purpose of life? Of nature? Of the cosmos? Of man? Such questions take on much greater meaning when some rational framework for it is provided by the logic of mana. Concomitantly, values and standards also assume more importance, because then we can find a transcendent purpose in their pursuit.

In review, while we have been forced to speculate, in order to fill in some of the gaps caused in part by the "reluctant cosmologist," we can conclude that the Hawaiians of old did engage the whole cosmos in their natural attempt toward understanding their place in the total scheme of things. Also clear is the evidence that, underlying their essential view of the world, was their belief in the interrelatedness of man and the universe. We have argued that we might reasonably believe that what epitomizes this connection between man and the cosmos is the idea of mana as cosmic intelligence. Indeed, if the universe is permeated by mana, and if we as mortals, whether as ali'i or maka'āinana, are also endowed with mana, then we are all one in lōkahi, or "in sync," as it were. In this grand reality Hawaiians perforce recognized the source of their understanding of this world and, hence, of their values.

6

HAWAIIAN TIME

> If no one asks me what [time] is, I know; if called upon
> to explain, I know not.
> —St. Augustine of Hippo.

Time, Please

If you wish to unnerve a friend, ask him, "What is time?" Your
friend's first likely reaction would be automatic; he'd look at his
watch and give you the time of day. But when he realizes that you
are wanting a different kind of answer, he'd probably take a deep
breath, stutter and hum and haw, before responding. If and when
he does give you a coherent answer, you can be sure that it would
be a classic case of "linear" thinking, saying that time is like a
straight line divided into intervals of seconds, minutes, hours, and
so on. Fair enough, we must admit, for that is how most of us
think of time. The expression "We are human clocks" illustrates
the point quite clearly.

But, then, suppose you tell your friend that some tribal groups
living today do not think of time in linear fashion, that they in fact
have no idea what a second, minute, or hour hand can be, let
alone what a clock is. Now, while he ponders this, tell him, too,
that space scientists have been saying that earth time is only one of
several types of time in the universe (or, more precisely, the "multi-
universe"). Hasten to add that computer scientists are telling us
that soon we may have to alter our whole way of thinking about
time because computers will make clocks obsolete.

Time is one of those givens in life that we take so much for
granted that we do not give it a second thought. Yet the way we
perceive time, or space for that matter, has an important bearing
on how we think and behave. For proof, we need only consider
the revolutionary impact that Einstein's view of time, proposed in

his theory of relativity, has had on science and technology during the last seven decades, as a result of which our lives have been immeasurably changed. In short, time and space are the windows through which we see the world—and ourselves.

Past Time

Because theirs was an agrarian society, survival in Hawaiʻi before Captain Cook depended ultimately on the people's knowing when to plant and when to harvest. All the other attendant tasks followed upon those grand seasonal occasions. The performance of those tasks did not require any synchronizing of time and labor, as would have been the case in an industrial or manufacturing society. Preparing the puʻu, the hillocks of soil for receiving taro shoots, planting a loʻi, a taro patch, weeding a row of plants, and other jobs in taro farming were done in relatively short time spans according to a flexible schedule. No precise time units were needed to begin or complete those tasks. The nature of the job and completing it dictated the terms of work, not time in itself. In fact, the task or action was the measure of time. For example, the length of time required to plant a row of taro, or needed to pound enough poi for an ʻohana's meal might have been the frame of reference for a taro planter needing to measure the time.

Hawaiians of old did not use precise time units primarily because they did not think in such terms, but also because they did not have such an instrument as a clock. The technology of time was introduced by Europeans, along with the nomenclature for it and all related mental preoccupations. The way they organized their lives is the important fact to remember. Even if they had had the mechanisms for marking clock time, they probably would not have been enslaved by it. So today, some farmers are guided not so much by the clock but by the sun's rising and setting, and by the nature of the task that needs to be done. Hawaiian planters had their own rhythm of life, set to a different pace, and observing unequal intervals of each day's sunlight.

If the Hawaiians of old were not clock watchers, they were definitely calendar watchers. They had recognized the system: a well-developed calendar divided into twelve lunar periods, with 30-day months divided into three 10-day weeks. At the end of the twelfth month, Welehu, they inserted 5 intercalary days, in order to make the total of 365 days. Their calendar revealed a high degree of comprehension of astronomical time comparable to that of the ancient Egyptians and of Oriental peoples.

Calendrical time was important because it was religious time. It fixed the times when the major kapu were declared. Days were set aside as sacred or ritual time, such as the four days in each month during which families abstained from work and play and prayed to their gods at the family kuahu, or altar. We have seen how the annual Makahiki was organized around sacred times. Unless a man monitored calendrical time, he ran the risk of violating the kapu, thereby forfeiting his life or incurring some other misfortune.

The significance of the calendar may be appreciated the better if we consider farmers and fishermen. Farmers had to know the seasons and their characteristics: that 'Ikuwā, or what we call October and November, is a rainy time, when the "rats come down to the lowlands and gnaw the sweet potatoes"; that Welehu, or November-December, is when Poli'ahu, the goddess of snow, "spread her mantle" over her home atop Mauna Kea; that Kā'elo, or January-February, is a soggy, drenching time when the kona storms draw to a close; that Nana, or March-April, is when plants show their vigor and young mother birds are brooding; and that Ikiiki, or May-June, is uncomfortably warm and sticky, with high humidity and little breeze (Handy and Pūku'i).

Fishermen knew that the period from February to late May was the spawning season for certain kinds of fish, meaning that a kapu was placed on those species inshore; or that, beginning with June, summer was the season for deep-sea fishing; or that different fish runs occurred in separate months, such as the maomao in June, and the uhu in August when the sea is calm; or that by the end of November the season would be coming to an end because the sea would have become too rough.

Farmers and fishermen were careful observers of lunar phases, because they recognized the moon's influence on the tides and on plant growth. Farmers, for instance, followed a monthly planting calendar, with each night bearing its own identifying name, along with specific data about which crops could be planted or harvested, whether a plant would be in bloom, when to weed, and so on. Similarly, fishermen observed the moon for its correlation with the ocean's tides, currents, waves, water temperatures, and turbulence, depth of water upon the reefs, the winds of the air, and the types of fish likely to be available, among other things.

We have already mentioned the voyaging canoes. No voyages would have been possible without the reliable lunar calendar. As Johnson (1981) wrote, "The accurate implementation of the sidereal calendar [i.e., computing from one vernal or autumnal equinox to another by stars or constellations] for the purpose of navigation must forever rank as one of the Polynesians' finest intellectual achievements."

Calendrical Values

If calendar time exerted such influence on the religious, agricultural, and seafaring lives of the Hawaiians, it would have had a corresponding influence on the development of work attitudes and skills. For example, among fishermen and farmers it would have caused them to develop: (1) schedules with specific task and performance deadlines; (2) organized patterns of responsibility, with strict divisions of labor; (3) plans setting out targets or goals; and (4) management strategies to carry out these objectives in an efficient manner. In other words, the time orientation and the natural environment created conditions for developing certain common-sense planning and managerial capabilities that were as natural to them as they are to us.

Let us compare this situation with the case of premodern Japan, when it too was predominantly an agricultural society. Calendar time governed everything then; in fact, it was the official concern of the court and "the *most* [italics added] important concern of the emperor"—and "the treasure of the people." Farmers were instructed: "Observe the calendar with great care. One day's delay means one month's evil fortune. One month's negligence means one hundred days of disaster." Out of this kind of thinking and training, that stretched over ten centuries, emerged the Japanese farmer's "attitude that each task has its appointed time and that no negligence can be permitted," as well as his passion for rigid scheduling, planning, and organization (Ben-Dasan).

The point to be made here is that how a nation's people perceive time is as much a cause as it is an effect of their behavior. For example, a Hawaiian who resisted the work schedules introduced by early Western traders and planters may have done so not only for economic, social, or other reasons, but because he simply had a different orientation to time, shaped by centuries of habit and thought. Most of all, it probably had nothing at all to do with character values of laziness or diligence. Much of the negative stereotyping about Hawaiian punctuality arises from a lack of understanding of this time orientation. The tendency for many modern Hawaiians never to start anything on time, or to arrive late for a meeting, and so on, is not some kind of genetic flaw (although you'd have a hard time convincing some people about that), but is, rather, a vestige of an ancient way of looking at the value of time. Punctuality, after all, is a relatively recent development in Western society, and even today it is unknown, and even discouraged, in many traditional communities throughout the world. Hawaiians can draw some small comfort from the realization that "Hawaiian time" has its counterparts in many other countries. In Indonesia, it is known as djam karet, rubber time, in New Zealand, as Maori time, in parts of Canada and the mainland United States, as Indian time, and so on. Most of the world is still trying to catch up with the notion—and the tyranny—of clock time.

Linear Versus Circular Time

People who know about these things maintain that the traditional non-Western mind thinks of time in circular rather than in linear form. Mayas, Buddhists, Hindus, and American Indians, for example, saw time as a circle or a spiral, with history repeating itself in endless cycles. On the other hand, linear time is supposed to characterize scientific, industrial societies, which require precise, straight-line thinking in order to achieve synchronization and standardization in their production systems.

In the days of old, Hawaiian time may have been circular. While none of the moʻolelo myths ever specifically refer to that symbolic term, we can infer it from mythological time. Myth, as we pointed out earlier, tells of the deeds of the gods and, therefore, of events that happened in primordial time. That is sacred time, at the very beginning when only gods lived, and it symbolized a world of purity and bliss. Hawaiians extolled in their chants and prayers this period of the "perfect time," and hence going back to that very beginning in order to relive it was the desire of every true believer. The best demonstration of this belief is, of course, the rituals or ceremonies reenacting the primal acts of akua. Every time a ritual was performed it meant a returning to a sacred or perfect time. This is not unlike the Christian believer who partakes of the Holy Communion, or prays to be able to "return to the presence of God" or to enter heaven. Similar examples of mythic returns to sacred times are found in almost all religions.

In order to achieve that return, however, the mind must transcend its ordinary sense of chronological time—in other words, must abolish it in order to recover primordial time. In the "real" world, of course, to do this is impossible. But in the realm of the sacred, time is not only recoverable but is reversible (as in our imaginary time machine). If the believer can abolish time, then, there is only timelessness—for him there is only the "perpetual reality of the now." This is the typical position of the mystic who in the end denies the existence of time, calling it something unreal or an illusion, and maintains that there is just the "Everlasting Present." Timelessness, the perpetual now, the everlasting present, and so on are only synonyms for eternity, and eternity can be shown only as a circle, not as a straight line.

To be sure, the Hawaiian did not go around in his normal daily routine trying to abolish ordinary time. But underlying his cosmic view of life was this sense of everlastingness and timelessness—the eternal circle.

Paradoxically, a case for linear time can also be made. This possibility arises from the idea that Hawaiians believed in an evolutionary development, as is detailed in *The Kumulipo* (a subject we shall discuss in detail in a subsequent chapter). Evolution as a process postulates a general advance in a step-by-step sequence, proceeding from lower to higher kinds of species. It seems to complement the idea of progress—moving forward in successive steps toward ever higher states of perfection—although it has not been commonly associated with Hawaiian and similar cultures.

Further support for this possibility that Hawaiians might have thought in linear terms, as well as in circular ones, comes from a Maori interpretation of their traditional creation mythology. The interpretation was made by Maori Marsden, trained as an Anglican priest.

According to *Io* (the Supreme Being) tradition, at the border between *Hawaiki Tapu* in the *Pō* regions is *Te Waipuna Ariki* (the divine fountain of *Io* the fountainhead). This is the fountain through which the primal energy of potential being proceeds from the infinite realms of *Te Korekore* through the realms of *Te Pio* into the world of light *(Te Ao Marama)* to replenish the stuff of the universe as well as to create what is new. Thus it is a process of continuous creation and recreation. *Te Korekore* is the realm of potential being. *Te Pō* is the realm of becoming and *Te Ao Marama* is the realm of being.

Marsden ended by saying: "Two conclusions emerge from this: the idea of continuous creation and the idea of a dynamic universe. . . . The universe is not static but is a stream of processes and events. This concept also includes the idea that history is not cyclical but lineal—it is an on-going process."

These analyses suggest that permeating all Polynesian thinking about creation is the notion of time as flowing in a stream of progressing events. Time, in fact, is the central theme of *The Kumulipo*. In the primal setting of that chant, time is a continuous unfolding of an endless happening. Indeed, the Hawaiian word for time, manawa, may convey not the ticking, fleeting intervals measured out by a clock, but the lingering, gentle ebb of water across a tranquil bay.

Space-Time

Our modern constructs of circular and linear time are really attempts based on conventional notions of time to explain sacred or mythological time. We are actually dealing with a level of thought that ordinary words cannot do justice to. How can we describe "timelessness," "the perpetual now," or even "past, present, and future"? Yet mystics of the East and West have experienced and talked about these concepts for hundreds of years. For example, the Chinese teacher Hui-neng said: "The absolute tranquility is the present moment. Though it is at this moment, there is no limit to this moment, and herein is eternal delight." The modern Buddhist philosopher, D. T. Suzuki, has said: "In this spiritual world there are not time divisions such as the past, present and future; for they have contracted themselves into a single moment of the present where life quivers in its true sense. . . . The past and the future are both rolled up in this present moment of illumination, and this present moment is not something standing still with all its contents, for it ceaselessly moves on" (quoted in Barrett).

Modern physics may help us to understand these concepts of time, provided that we can make a very fundamental change in our thinking. We have lived for too long in a Newtonian world, and we continue to think in Newtonian terms about time as an absolute, separate entity and space as being only three-dimensional. But Einstein's relativity theory changed all this. Because of relativity, both time and space are intimately interconnected, to form a four-dimensional continuum called space-time. No more can we talk about space without talking about time as well, and vice versa. Furthermore, there is no universal flow of time from future to past. "Different observers," said Fritjof Capra, "will order events differently in time if they move with different velocities relative to the observed events. In such a case, two events which are seen as occurring simultaneously by one observer may occur in different temporal sequences for other observers. All measurements involving space and time thus lose their absolute significance. In relativity theory, the Newtonian concept of an absolute space as the stage of physical phenomena is abandoned, and so is the concept of an absolute time." Thus both space and time become merely elements in the language we use.

In space-time everything that we see as happening in past, present, and future is presented as one event. Thus, if you were able to take a picture of a mass of particles in space-time, you would get one four-dimensional "snapshot," a hologram of sorts, covering the whole span of time as well as the whole region of space. In the actual world, we see things only in succession, or in a temporal sequence, but in space-time we see everything at once. This is what the mystic maintains that he experiences: the full span of space-time where "time does not flow any longer." He has abolished time.

The Zen master Dogen said: "It is believed by most that time passes; in actual fact, it stays where it is. This idea of passing may be called time, but it is an incorrect idea, for since one sees it only as passing, one cannot understand that it stays just where it is" (Watts 1957). Perhaps this is the Hawaiian sense of manawa, too.

Obviously, in our everyday lives we function at another level, the one we call reality. It is almost impossible for us not to think of empty space, and of three-dimensional space, and of time sequences. We have to perform our survival tasks in common-sense, time-ordered, mechanical ways that proceed from a beginning to an end, in one recognizable space or another. In our normal environment, in what physicists call "the zone of middle dimensions," these notions are valid. But modern physics forces us to go beyond this mundane level, for when we deal with the sciences of the cosmos, astrophysics and cosmology, the ordinary concepts of time and space no longer apply.

In sum, what we are suggesting is that the Hawaiian sense of mythological time may be better understood in the four-dimensional space-time construct of modern physics than in the more conventional imagery of the circle and straight line. Making the suggestion is not illogical; after all, Hawaiian mystics may have been just as aware of the non-Newtonian universe as were their contemporaries in Asia.

Reflections on Uku Pau

To one degree or another we are all slaves of clock time. We arise with an alarm going off; we drink our instant coffee or eat a two-minute egg; we listen to the seven o'clock news; we catch the seven-thirty bus and punch in at eight o'clock; we don't have a tea break but a ten-minute break, along with a half-hour lunch; we calculate the length of a car trip in driving time, not miles; we are taught to manage our time first and then our lives; we all know that time is money; like the deification of the ancient 'aumākua, we have apotheosized Father Time and have made wasting time a cardinal sin. We are trapped in warped time, for time controls our lives, not vice versa. The tragedy is that we can't find a way out of this trap.

The traditional Hawaiian, in contrast, was free of time's fetters. He had far better control over his life because, to him, what was most important was what he did, not so much when he started something or ended doing it, or how long he needed to finish a job. The task or event was important in and of itself. Life was not measured out in hours, days, or years, but in 'ohana activities, individual experiences, in memorable and climactic events. In a sense, such activities or events are timeless, for they are seldom or never pushed into the limbo of the forgotten. For the Hawaiian of old, what counted was the stuff of time, not time itself. Is this perhaps a way out of servitude to time for modern man?

The Honolulu City and County garbage men offer us an example of a Hawaiian approach to time and work in the practice called uku pau, which means, literally, finished pay. The practice seemed to have started on sugarcane plantations, which paid workers on the basis of the quantity of work done rather than according to how much time they put in on a job. Hence, if a worker was supposed to cultivate a certain number of rows of cane in a day, he'd be paid when he finished his assignment, no matter how few or how many hours he took to do it. As long as the work met established quality standards, its completion was the main objective. The same idea is expressed in uku pau: getting the job done is what counts, not the amount of time put in. There is, of course, the built-in incentive: the faster you work, the earlier you get done, and the sooner you go home. This affords you greater freedom to do what you want to do above and beyond your job. Not surprisingly, then, garbage men in Honolulu quit before lunch (although they start at five or six o'clock in the morning), and spend the rest of the day in other activities, including businesses of their own. Coincidentally, more than half of the city garbage personnel are ethnic Hawaiians. While there are historical and socio-economic reasons for this preponderance, the Hawaiianness of the uku pau approach may well be a factor in attracting Hawaiian workers.

We do not contend that uku pau is a remedy for our general predicament about time, but it clearly has some features to recommend it. The system is efficient and fast; it establishes a rhythm of work that discourages willful delay and boredom; it places maximum responsibility on the worker; and, most important, it gives him more control over a greater part of his life. Ironically, in our economy dominated by white-collar bosses, the city garbage men may be the ones who enjoy the greatest freedom and power over their private lives and over the claims of work upon their time.

Something else must be said for the Hawaiian emphasis on the "stuff of time," that is, upon the event itself, particularly when it involves special gatherings or meetings. Such activities, whether they be spent in formal ritual or in informal settings, demand a pace and mood of their own without the intrusion of the clock. In certain Maori events that occur on the marae, for example, clock time is not allowed to interfere. The members at the gathering, or the hui, determine when and how it will begin, evolve, and end. In other words, while time marches on, it marches to the beat set by the participants involved, not to the tick-tock of a clock or the drummers of progress. In a way, this is what happens when harried legislators "stop the clock" in order to continue important deliberations, although one ought not to push this illustration too far.

In any case, people who attend certain Hawaiian events may be advised to forget clock time and let the spirit and rhythm of the event dictate its course, from beginning to end. This does not necessarily mean unprepared and agendaless meetings; after all, outside such meetings we must all compete in the real world of economic and political pressures and priorities. But unless we are willing to take such steps in order to create special moments to enjoy our own sense of time, we shall never escape from being slaves to the tyrant time.

Quality Time

Have you ever noticed that, when you are doing something pleasurable and enjoyable, time flies? But when you are bored, as while waiting for somebody, time drags? Or if you are sick abed, physical immobility prolongs the passing of time, but when you are running or playing in a strenuous game, time speeds up? In very sultry, windless Kona weather, don't you notice how time goes by a lot slower than it does when the gusty trade winds return?

We all recognize the way our minds and bodies, along with the natural elements, influence our perception of time. No matter what our reason tells us, we know that time is not simply the calibrated intervals measured out by the clock. We can slow time, or quicken it, almost at will. This is what Henri Bergson, the French philosopher, meant when he said, "Time is a creation or it is nothing at all" (quoted in Fraser). It is a projection of our subjective nature as human beings. Hence, we can talk about psychological or emotional time.

The real meaning of psychological time is that we can control it in the sense that we can determine its quality by shaping its content. That is, we can take the "stuff of time," our activities or the events we participate in, and make them life-affirming or life-negating experiences. Thus, not the quantity, but the quality, of the time is all-important. Whether you have enough time or not to do what you want to do is almost beside the point, because what you do with or without time is what really matters.

Advocates of time-management courses, which are popular in Western countries in particular, sell their programs by arguing that you can control your life by controlling your time. They offer elaborate methods which include time-keeping and monitoring schedules, daily appointment books for each hour, time checkups that fit your shirt pockets, and so on, all designed to help you manage each minute of each full day. It is a very mechanistic approach, and in the end a short-sighted one because you can no more control your clock time than you can manage Greenwich time. The only important thing you can control is the quality and meaning of what you do. If you want to control your life, you'd best manage the quality of your experiences and let time take care of itself.

That would be the kind of advice a true Hawaiian would give to a busy parent who worries about not being able to spend enough time with his children. Not the quantity, but the quality is what counts.

Present-Tense Living

Many modern Hawaiians have been criticized for being too concerned with the here and now, rather than being properly worried about the future. This opinion is reflected in the best-known stereotype of the Hawaiian as the friendly, happy-go-lucky native. It is a valid observation, for several reasons. In the first place, a man makes a great deal of "ontological" sense when he chooses to be concerned with the now, because it is the only point of existence. Now is the only time of being and becoming. The past has been lived and the future is yet to be lived. However fleeting now may be, this instant is all we have. The only consciousness we can possibly experience is an awareness of right now. Physiologically, too, living in the here and now is the quintessence of survival (Barbotin).

This preoccupation with the present is an inevitable result of the value that the Hawaiian places on quality time. He believes that you have to relish the here and now in order to enjoy whatever you want to do. No one can have a meaningful experience if his mind strays from the matter of the moment. The father, for example, who wants to spend quality time with his child, cannot do so if he is thinking about his job tomorrow, and is not focused in on what is happening with the child right now.

Philosophically, present tense living takes a very utilitarian view of life in that you are constantly striving to make this moment as useful and as meaningful as you possibly can. Moreover, a certain amount of fatalism is involved, because the present is all-important: a next time or a tomorrow may never come. In addition, a hint of hedonism enters in, when we live for today only. It recalls the quatrain from Omar Khayyam:

Ah, fill the Cup:—what boots it to repeat
How Time is slipping underneath our Feet:
    Unborn To-morrow and dead Yesterday
Why fret about them if To-day be sweet!

When all the philosophical smoke clears away, the essential reason for this emphasis on the now is the traditional practicality of the Hawaiian. If he does today what has to be done, and does it well, that is all that matters to him. This does not mean that he forgets about the "unborn tomorrow." On the contrary, he takes care of tomorrow by preparing for it well today. This thought is echoed in the words of Jesus. "Take, therefore, no thought for the morrow; for the morrow shall take thought for the things of itself." The primacy of today is based on a sensible expectancy of things to come.

If the genuinely practical Hawaiian is carefree, he is so only because he has taken care of his needs for tomorrow. As we shall see later, traditional Hawaiian society had a very small tolerance for carefree, happy-go-lucky folk who did not take heed for the morrow.

Future Time

Whatever we have said about the past and the present may or may not matter very much in the long run because our "temporal maps" are changing; in the future probably we, and certainly our children and their children, will have to alter our views of time. We already know that in the higher realm of relativity physics, time does not flow inexorably forward, but that it can be warped and distorted, and that it can differ depending on who's observing what and where the observer is standing. Astrophysicists tell us that time can even be negated altogether. In "supercollapsed objects," or black holes, time may even stand still. A single moment in the vicinity of a black hole might be the equivalent of long eons on earth. Thus, if some interstellar mission control from earth were to send a spaceship to explore a black hole, we might have to wait a million years for the ship to make the round-trip. Yet, because of the immense gravitational distortion exerted by the black hole, and the effects of velocity during the voyage, the ship's clock would show the passage of only a few minutes or seconds.

Ideas about time that used to be dismissed as unthinkable, such as time moving backward, are no longer considered impossible. For example, infinitesimal particles called tachyons can move faster than light, and for them "time moves backwards." Some physicists believe that time may not be irreversible because "two alternative histories, two equally valid realities, could exist side by side —the one you know and the one in which you were never born" (Toffler).

One day we may find that our clocks have been replaced by computers. They will radically change our notion of time. Already they are able to process data in what Alvin Toffler calls "subliminal time"—intervals far too short for the human senses to detect or for human neural response times to match. Microprinters turn out thousands of lines per minute—several hundred times faster than any of us could ever read them. So many improvements in computers have been made that in twenty years computer scientists have gone from measuring events in terms of milliseconds (thousandths of a second) to nanoseconds (billionths of a second). "It is as though a person's entire working life of, say 80,000 paid hours —2,000 hours per year for forty years—could be crunched into a mere 4.8 minutes" (Toffler).

Robert Wallis, author of *Time: Fourth Dimension of the Mind*, has suggested that far more exact ways of measuring time are available than are provided by astronomical bodies like the sun and the moon. The propagation of light, he believes, should be our true measurement because it is constant in speed. He also suggests that a more sensible way to measure the biological age of a man would be to count the number of his heartbeats: on the order of 100,000 per twenty-four hours, he could be allotted

2,555,000,000 for a statistically average life of seventy years. After all, Wallis asks, what does the biological age of a man really have to do with the number of times that the earth revolves about the sun?

What meaning can we draw from all these mind-boggling developments? Whether time flows or stops and disappears altogether, we must find some point of constancy in our lives. At least in the world of human interactions, that point may well be the subjective value of time that lies in the quality and meaning of what we do with our time. Or, in other words, we should relax more, and live according to "Hawaiian time."

7

A SENSE OF PLACE

Not only Native Americans but all primal peoples have always found the means by which to be protected from the infinity of space.

—Jamake Highwater

The Primacy of Place

This is not a Zen koan, although it might be asked in some ultra-modern monastery. But suppose you were standing in this "infinity of space"—an absolute "void-scape" extending in every direction, where you find no horizons, no limits, no lines or even angles. Picture yourself trying to get out of that desert of nothing without the benefit of a single orientation point other than the very space you occupy. Insane, you say? That is precisely the point of this puzzle, because the overwhelming horror of it all is what we shrink from, screaming . . .

Fortunately, the real world of terrestrial space is made up of horizons and lines, with their points of reference that enable us to find perspectives and coordinates and to see things in meaningful relationships. All these points of reference are summed up in the word place, and the ability to relate ourselves to this environment of space is our sense of place. Highwater's seemingly innocent reference to the infinity of space impresses on us the importance of what appears to be an innate sensing ability of human beings. This ability is one that primal peoples understood and developed to a higher degree than modern men have done.

In the case of the traditional Hawaiian, for example, almost every significant activity of his life was fixed to a place. No genealogical chant was possible without the mention of personal geography; no myth could be conceived without reference to a place of some kind; no family could have any standing in the community unless it had a place; no place of any significance, even the smallest, went without a name; and no history could have been made or preserved without reference, directly or indirectly, to a place. So, place had enormous meaning for Hawaiians of old.

We must rank this sense of place together with the Hawaiian's sense of awe for the sacred, his sense of rhythms attuned with the cosmos, his intuitive sense that leaped the high walls of empiricism, his sense of ritualism and symbolism, and his sense of harmony with nature. It therefore requires a chapter of its own as part of our constellation of life-affirming values of the Hawaiian.

We shall explore our sense of place in its widest context, dealing with traditional and neotraditional Hawaiian ideas, customs, and values regarding geographical and personal space and a good deal in between. At the macroscopic end, we shall look at the ʻāina and the ocean with regard to the metaphor of "Mother Earth," and at the microscopic end, we shall delve into proxemics. We'll also be talking about territoriality and privacy, the "nomenclature of place," and the architectural treatment of space—all important parts of our spatial sense.

Geographical Space

Geographically speaking, place refers to any delimited space, no matter how small or large, or how poorly or exactly defined. It is always a physical domain with finite limits. To talk about "limitless place" makes no sense, for that would be the same as the unimaginable "infinity of space." Place means that a recognizable space has boundaries separating one area from another.

The Hawaiians were great ones for delimiting space, drawing imaginary lines on land, across the ocean, and upward through the atmosphere. Since demarking space is not possible without cardinal points of reference, the Hawaiians had brought with them the knowledge that north, south, east, and west were fixed in accordance with the rising and setting of the sun and the North Star. North was kūkulu ʻākau, or toward ka hōkū paʻa (the fixed star); south, kūkulu hema, toward the lipo, or dark blue depths of the ocean; east, kūkulu hikina, toward the rising sun; and west, kūkulu komohana, toward the setting sun. (Some modern Hawaiians and most other people labor under the strange notion that Hawaiians know only two directions: ma uka and ma kai, toward the mountains and toward the sea.) They had at least two kinds of horizons, one visible and the other invisible. The former is the line at which the "dome of the sky" meets the edge of the sea, and the latter "pushes out," pane'e, "its only boundary being where it adjoins the solid walls of the sky." The space above the surface of the earth was divided into at least six successive layers: (1) the highest stratum, called lewa lani; (2) ka ho'oku'i, "equidistant from the sky downward and the earth upward"; (3) keapoalewa, or the ring of space; (4) lewa nu'u, or where the birds fly; (5) hakaalewa, or "the space in which a man's legs dangle as he holds onto a branch of a tree"; and (6) lewa ho'omakua, or the space established by a person standing on the ground and lifting up one foot, leaving the other on the ground (Kamakau 1976).

They divided the ocean into many more places, beginning with the shoreline, then moving outward to the deep. Kamakau (1976), for example, wrote: "The place on land where waves break and spread is the lihi kai or 'ae kai, edge of the sea. Where they wash over the land is called pāhola, hohola, or pālaha ("spread"), and the place where they break and spread toward land is called pu'eone or po'ina nalu or po'ina kai." He continued at length, listing other places inshore, the tidal pool area, "where shallow seas come in without rising (into breakers)," the surf line, the reef area, and beyond. This is an astounding enumeration of place after place, all named and demarked according to function and relative position. The modern oceanographer nods his appreciation for the knowledge the Hawaiians of old had gained of the ocean as a place.

Hawaiians carefully delimited the topography of the earth, putting into its place almost every recognizable area or feature. Pieces of land were differentiated even if they were close together, or formed a circle, or lay in a line westward or northward, or were scattered here and there. Two islands lying close together were defined as a separate entity, mokulua (two islands). An island was divided into sections of graduated sizes, from the largest, moku-'āina, then 'okana, in which area falls the familiar ahupua'a, which in turn consisted of smaller pieces. Mountain slopes were also divided according to whether an area was covered over with fog and had great flanks behind and in front, such as Mauna Kea, or whether the area was below the summit but above the forest line, or whether it lay below the tree line. Vegetation zones were also defined according to the sizes and kinds of trees and shrubs growing in them, the rainfall, winds, and other factors. So were ridges, cliffs, mountain peaks and slopes, valleys, gulches, and hills.

The Greeks are credited with having invented geometry, but clearly, in order to function in their world of spatial relationships, Hawaiians too had a basic understanding about measurement of spaces, properties and relationships of points, lines, angles, and surfaces. However rudimentary their understanding may have been, ka poʻe kahiko could not have been entirely ignorant about geometric concepts. On the other hand, equally clearly they never thought that geometry opened the way to enlightenment, as the Greeks did. Nor, to borrow Plato's dictum, did Hawaiians imagine that "God is a geometer." (We shall return to geometry when we consider the mathematics of the ancient Hawaiians.) In any case, Hawaiians' sense of place had a basic mathematical dimension to it as well.

Territoriality

A place always has bounds around it, whether real or imagined. Thus, the quintessence of place is exclusiveness, the fact of being restricted and set apart. A place is distinguished not only by its relative position, but, more important, by its distinctiveness or its identity. This is what fences or boundaries do for a place, whether it be a house site, a corner of a room, or an ahupuaʻa. In a word, the place is made "private".

In his famous book, *The Territorial Imperative*, Robert Ardrey described how wolves, baboons, and other "territorial species" demarcate certain areas for their own use and how they go to great lengths to keep intruders away from those places. He characterized this "inherent desire to gain and defend an exclusive property" as "the territorial imperative." Taking a cue from such studies of animal social behavior, researchers in human spatial behavior have come up with the concept of human territoriality. In brief, the idea is that people act almost instinctually to defend the boundaries of their places whenever they are threatened. The intensity of this desire will vary, however, according to the circumstances and values of the person or persons concerned. But this desire is almost universal.

Did the Hawaiians of old manifest this deep-seated feeling of territoriality? Yes they did, in a number of ways quite apart from the many wars fought to acquire or to defend land. In the first instance, fences, walls, and boundaries were not only part of their vocabulary but also a part of their everyday landscape. In his study of *The Hawaiian Thatched House*, Russell Apple observed: "Stockades surrounded high chiefs' housing complexes and major temples. . . . Such stockades were sacred. . . . Not all of the stockades were physical. Some were invisible lines that were as effective as rock walls or picket fences. Walls and fences apparently marked lifetime or permanent taboo areas. Invisible lines marked enclosures guarded by temporary taboos. Real or invisible, they excluded commoners." Usually the "invisible lines" were indicated by corner stakes, each bearing a white flag of bark cloth or topped with a coconut wrapped in white tapa. John Iʻi described a chief's house. "[It was] not fenced in, but four stationary *kapu* sticks had been placed one at each corner, and these served as the enclosure for the house." Perhaps nothing symbolizes the fence mentality of the traditional Hawaiian more dramatically than the fact of the kapu stick.

Fences were widely used outside the sacred sites as well. Kamakau (1976) wrote: "Boundary markers *(kūkulu ʻehoʻeho)* of tall stones *(oeoe pōhaku)* were set up to identify the boundaries" of land divisions, moku ʻāina and ahupuaʻa. Garden plots and taro farms were sometimes fenced with sticks or stones—all signs of exclusiveness.

The exclusive nature of place may also be seen in the traditional custom of welcoming visitors to one's home. The practice involved an adult member of the family coming to the door, standing there and calling a welcome to an approaching person, "Hē mai! Hē mai!" "Come hither, come!" The quality in the welcome was based upon the host's recognition of the quality of the visitor. While the words were so chosen as to offer a friendly welcome, they could also have been used to indicate exactly how welcome the visitor should be made. In New Zealand the Maori have a similar expression, but it serves just as much to challenge the intentions of the visitor as to receive him with aroha. In either case, the custom of welcome, or heahea in Hawaiian, emphasizes the fact that in the Hawaiian's mind his home is a special place with an identity of its own. The welcome is designed in part to protect and enhance that specialness. Indeed, a sense of "my home is my castle" is evident in the fact that even a commoner's home (actually beginning at the door) was considered off-limits to "victim-seeking guards."

It is difficult to say with any confidence how much the territorial imperative entered into the wars that Hawaiian chiefs waged so frequently. If gaining control over an area of land was the main cause for aggression, then certainly the victims' desire to defend their territory was the main effect. Apart from wars, territoriality must have been a cause, in part or whole, for less violent disputes, skirmishes, squabbles, and jealousies covering a multitude of real or imagined crimes of trespassing on someone's farm, fishing spot, reef for food gathering, and so on.

It would be unfair to leave the impression that the Hawaiian countryside was nothing but an array of stockades built in response to peoples' concern for territoriality. Handy and Pūkuʻi reminded us that, outside the sacred precincts, ordinary Hawaiians allowed each other a good deal of freedom to enter, cross, and leave their homesteads. But this courtesy, we assume, was based on the principles of reciprocity and hospitality which, in effect, softened the somewhat hard attitudes implied in the concept of territoriality.

Nonetheless, when seen in the total context of Hawaiians' thinking about space, the deep-seated human need to protect one's territory—"a place that I can call my own"—is an important part of the Hawaiian's psychology of place and his own sense of individuality.

Roots of Identity

Some observers have said that one of our modern civilization's features distinguishing it from all previous civilizations is the unprecedented rate of social and physical mobility of people. This is especially true in the United States. Surveys show that the average American may move as many as five times or more in his life, often going hundreds and even thousands of miles away from his most recent residence. Only the rare person has not moved at least once or twice, and rarer still is someone who continues to live in his birthplace after reaching adulthood.

One of the effects of this constant shifting around is the cumulative trauma of "rootlessness." This is seen especially in children and teenagers. When his family has to move away from a place, the young person is forced to leave friends, activities, goals, and other valued things behind, thus losing much of his self in the process. While the child or teenager may adjust eventually, in the meantime the psychological deprivation has taken its toll and some people never fully recover from the loss. Research indicates that even adults reveal some of the same effects, although they are better at concealing them. Among corporations and organizations that had a policy of transferring their employees as a matter of routine, resistance to such transfers by those employees has sensitized more and more observers to the problems of rootlessness.

Hawaiian society before 1778 allowed a certain amount of mobility, especially among the chiefs, but apparently very little of it was granted to the commoners. This was the consequence of a "structural" arrangement of society, because of its agricultural economy. Most people were harvesters, whether of plants or of fish, and therefore they tended to stay in one area. A planter-farmer was tied to his immovable taro patches, sweet potato gardens, and animal yards—and to his chief (although under extreme circumstances he could move his family and loyalty to the care of another chief). Unlike members of hunting societies, who had to follow the moving game animals, Hawaiians were a relatively sedentary people by the time Captain Cook arrived.

Given this built-in immobility, people lived in the same place and cultivated the same lands for "generation after generation." When a person said "I come from Ka'ū," you could assume that he was born and raised there and would die there, just as his parents and grandparents did, and just as his children and their children would do in their turn. All the important events of his life, from birth to growing up in the love and caring of the women of his 'ohana, his initiation into the hale mua and the rights of manhood, his learning and practicing of a trade, his sexual encounters, marriage, and raising of a family, his labor, sacrifices and achievements—occurred in one place, one kuleana, in one ahupua'a. Thus, his attitudes, instincts, perceptions, feelings, and values were shaped and moulded by that place.

In the Hawaiian mind, then, a sense of place was inseparably linked with self-identity and self-esteem. To have roots in a place meant to have roots in the soil of permanence and continuity. It meant security, status, creditability, the warmth and succor of friends and relatives, the protection given by a chief, an automatic inheritance of a lineage, and a guarantee of a legacy—all the assurances of acceptability in this life and in the next.

Conversely, being without a place—shifting from place to place —meant uprootedness in every sense of the word: being cut off from the most vital physical, psychological, social, and spiritual values of one's existence. This is why a sedentary, place-conscious Hawaiian society abhorred the shiftless person, calling him by one of the worst possible names: limalima pilau, literally, stink hands, meaning an immoral wretch, such as a pimp or a thief. Suffering the opprobrium of his community was bad enough, but worse yet, even the spirits of his ancestors might be affected by the same deadly psychic fallout. Malo (1951) reminded us of this possibility when he wrote, "Certain ones leading a vagabond life roamed from place to place until their ancestral genealogies came to be despised."

In a religious society in which ancestors were deified as 'aumākua and genealogy was elevated to preeminent status, a place, a home, was much more valued because of its ties with the ancestors. A Hawaiian's birthplace was celebrated not simply because he happened to be born there, but because it was also the place where so many generations of his ancestors were born before him. It was a constant reminder of the vitality of the bloodline and of the preciousness of life past, present, and future. When Hawai'i's "poet laureate," Rev. Lorenzo Lyons, began the lyrics to "Hawai'i Aloha" with the opening line, *"E Hawai'i e ku'u one hānau e, ku'u home kulaīwi nei,"* "O Hawai'i, my own birthplace, my own land," he touched the heartstrings of every Hawaiian who has a sense of place and ancestral continuity. The literal meaning of the word kulaīwi is land or place holding the bones of the dead. Such a sacred place is considered to be the most cherished possession of the living. Thus, one's place was identified with the place of one's ancestors.

Joan Metge wrote in similar terms about Maori feelings toward land. "Like their forefathers, modern Maoris feel strongly about the land *(whenua)*. What they value is not, however, land in the abstract, but the land they have inherited from their forebears; and they value it mainly for its sentimental and social significance. It is the 'land of our ancestors,' a legacy bequeathed by a long line of forebears who loved and fought and died for it, and a tangible link with the heroes and happenings of a storied past. . . . The older generation, in particular, recognize an almost mystical connection between land and personal standing."

When a Maori speaks of land, it is as a place to "stand on," symbolizing the totality of his ancestral heritage back to the arrival of the canoes coming to Aotearoa and from beyond, from Kahiki, as this heritage is embodied in his being and self-identity. He can no more separate his bones from his flesh than he can separate his identity from his place. The two are one and the same.

That is how the ancient Hawaiian must have regarded his land, but it is not how the modern Hawaiian does so—or, at least, it is not so to the same extent. Can we possibly regain that former sense of identity with place and with our kūpuna? The Maoris have managed to do so, partly because they have been able to keep their marae system, wherein the authority to speak rests on one's standing in the community, that is, on control of one's ancestral lands. Those who do not enjoy ownership of land may have no place in the leadership of the marae. This question about identity and place is one of many that invite serious thought.

The Nomenclature of Place

Nothing in surviving Hawaiian culture illustrates the importance that Hawaiians put on identity and place as does our preoccupation with naming places. Pūkuʻi, Elbert, and Moʻokini, in *Place Names of Hawaiʻi*, cannot even estimate—"a hundred thousand? a million?"—the number of place names that were recognized in old Hawaiʻi. "Hawaiians named taro patches, rocks and trees that represented deities and ancestors, sites of houses and *heiau*, canoe landings, fishing stations in the sea, resting places in the forests, and the tiniest spots where miraculous or interesting events are believed to have taken place." This prodigality of names suggests that each small patch of earth had its own reason for being, had a place in the grand scheme of geography, which needed to be remembered and dignified by a name of its own. How better to be identified with a place than by giving it a name that encapsulated an occurrence or that triggered recall of its history and significance?

Hawaiians glorified places by using place names in their chants, proverbs, and stories to a far greater degree than any modern society does. Katherine Luomala (1949), the distinguished folklorist, has shown the extensive role of place names in Hawaiian poetry. Hawaiian songs are classified according to different categories, but one of the most important of those is place. Fornander, Emerson, Beckwith, and other scholars have demonstrated how "almost all Hawaiian tales are filled with place names." Samuel Elbert (Pūku'i, Elbert, and Mo'okini) showed the popularity of using place names in proverbial sayings, especially in aloha 'āina sayings. "Many sayings that use place names describe emotional states or important events, but the largest proportion show *aloha 'āina*, 'love for the land and the people of the land,' and this function, so important in Hawai'i, seems completely lacking in Euro-American proverbial sayings." In Pūku'i's *'Ōlelo No'eau: Hawaiian Proverbs and Poetical Sayings*, nearly 40 percent, or 1,149, of its 2,942 proverbs mention place names.

Compare the Hawaiian view of the importance of place names with the Maori. "The great number of Maori place names that have survived commemorate a mass of long-remembered history, mythology and imagery that illustrates the close relationship maintained with the land. . . . The primeval ruptures of the landscape were named to identify the titanic feats of gods themselves. The dominant geological features recalled the strength of the supermen of old. . . . The never-ending list of names remains a record of the passage of generations of men and women, identifying and preserving scenes of wars, stratagems, turmoil, peace, achievement and failure" (Sinclair).

Because so much of the history of the Hawaiian people was tied to place, if you knew the names of places, you knew, in effect, your history. Ignorance of places meant ignorance of your past and origins, which was a most important kind of knowledge not only for the Hawaiian but for all Polynesians. As we have been so powerfully reminded by Alex Haley in his moving story of Kunta Kinte, ultimately only knowledge of your roots can validate and glorify what you are and can become.

'Āina as Gaia

In its most generic sense, place meant for the Hawaiians of old land, or 'āina, literally, that which feeds. The word is derived from the noun or verb 'ai, meaning food or to eat, with the substantifier na added. 'Āina links the occupation of the planter and the most vital life-ensuring function of eating. Only a truly agrarian people (or a people who like to eat!) could have devised a word like that.

'Āina also meant earth, and earth in mythological terms means Mother Earth. An intriguing question that bears on the relationship between our understanding of 'āina and our sense of place today is this: how did the ancient Hawaiians perceive 'āina with respect to Mother Earth? Did they take the metaphor literally? What meaning did they find in using it that reveals the reality of earth?

Most of us are so accustomed to hearing the term Mother Earth that we take it as commonplace. But suppose you had never heard it before, how would you react to it upon first hearing? You would most likely be shocked. The juxtaposition of the two words is not only unnatural but emotionally disturbing, that is, if you take it literally. This earth—only 4.5 to 5 billion years old, an oblate spheroid in shape, traveling 1,000 miles per minute through space, comprising 196,951,000 square miles in surface area, and weighing 6 sextillion, 588 quintillion tons, and so on—hardly looks like our idea of a mother. It is *not* a mother, no matter how much you may want to humanize it. After thinking about it, however, you realize the function of metaphor in language, and you know that Mother Earth only suggests a deeper meaning. Similar to it is the common metaphor "time flies," which we do not take literally. In other words, metaphor is an imaginative use of words to state a hypothesis that tells us something about a hidden reality, or suggests a meaning not readily observable about the true nature of a relationship—in this case, the relationship between nourishing earth and our hungry, dependent selves.

No doubt Hawaiians liked the metaphor, because they recognized at least four earth mother goddesses, Papa, Haumea, La'ila'i, and Kāmeha'ikana. Not only Hawaiians but people of every major culture have their variant of Mother Earth, from the ancient Sumerian Nammu, to Kali of India, and Gaia of Greece. This archetype, in one guise or another, has been shared universally by peoples from time immemorial. As with other peoples, Hawaiians did not take the metaphor literally, for, as we shall show in the next chapter, they probably reasoned that the earth evolved out of the elements symbolized by the union of Papa and Wākea. Inasmuch as these primeval elements are life-giving, animated and energized forms of mana, Hawaiians concluded that the earth is charged with the same life force. Thus, in likening the earth to a mother, the Hawaiians too were saying that, functionally, the earth too is a living entity, "feeding" us as a mother feeds her new-born child, "caring" for all our material and biological needs—giving us life, as a mother does.

The key revelation of the metaphor is the belief that the earth is a living entity. At first glance, this is a startling bit of information, but when we examine the basic beliefs and assumptions of the Hawaiian view of life and nature, it is a simple conclusion, if not a foregone deduction. We do not know for sure how far the Hawaiians pushed the comparison between earth as a living thing and a living human. Did they go as far as the American Indians did, in believing earth to be capable of sensation, of feeling pain and plea-sure? Did they ever view the earth, as did medieval Europeans, as a living creature and think that "the pulsing of its tides was the heave and sigh of its breathing"? Did they ever attribute to it a capacity for conscious behavior, however rudimentary? We cannot really know what they thought, but the metaphors in their myths clearly point to earth as a sentient organism.

Not too many years ago, if we had said to the average scientist that the earth is a living thing, the opinion would have fallen on deaf ears—or aroused his ridicule. But not today. An increasing number of thoughtful people who are working in the field of "gen-eral systems theory" forcefully argue the case for earth as a living organism. One of the major proponents of the theory is the British scientist James Lovelock, who first described his thinking in *Gaia: A New Look at Life on Earth*. He calls his theory the "Gaia Hypothesis," in honor of the Greek "Earth Mother." In this con-text, Gaia refers to the entire biosphere—everything living on the planet—together with the atmosphere, the oceans, and the soil, what Hawaiians call 'āina. Essentially, the hypothesis says that "the biosphere is a self-regulating entity with the capacity to keep our planet healthy by controlling the chemical and physical envi-ronment." The entire range of living creatures on earth, from viruses to whales, from algae to coconut trees, together with the air, the seas, and the land surface, all appear to be part of a gigan-tic system able to regulate the temperature and the composition of the air, ocean, and soil so as to ensure the survival of life. In main-taining the optimal conditions for life, Gaia is doing what all living systems do. This capacity is called homeostasis, which means that all the vital mechanisms in living things "have only one object: that of preserving constant the conditions of life."

Lovelock showed how some of these homeostatic mechanisms

are at work. For example, he demonstrated that the earth has maintained a steady surface temperature for millions of years. Although some forms of life can exist between the extremes of 20 and 220 degrees Fahrenheit, the optimal range for most organisms lies between 60 and 100 degrees Fahrenheit. The average temperature of most of the earth's surface appears to have stayed within this range. If at any time in the earth's history the overall temperature had gone beyond these limits, life as we know it would have been extinguished. Another homeostatic condition is the stabilization of the oxygen concentration in the atmosphere at 21 percent. This is the optimal for the maintenance of present forms of life. With oxygen concentration a few percent less, the larger animals and flying insects might survive; but with a slight increase of a few percent, everything, even damp vegetation, would burn, until the whole of the earth's surface would be consumed by fire.

The argument that the whole earth has managed to survive merely as a result of a string of lucky coincidences rather than by planetary homeostatic behavior is disposed of partly by comparison with the healthy human body. This, too, behaves in a well-ordered manner, with a definite sense of purpose. So, just as the idea of a self-regulating mechanism makes sense for the human body, so does it make sense for Gaia.

Returning to our original question about the relationship between 'āina and Mother Earth, if the earth is perceived as a living entity, then 'āina is also a living thing. Hawaiians, therefore, did not regard land as just a lifeless object to be used or discarded as one would treat any ordinary material thing. As part of the great earth, land is alive—it breathes, moves, reacts, behaves, adjusts, grows, sickens, dies. Imagine how this perception of land would affect the attitude of a taro planter feeling the soft mud in his lo'i oozing around his toes or his fingers, as he works to raise the little pu'u, or mounds, in which to set the huli. A modern city dweller, who has never stepped on anything softer than asphalt, might feel squeamish about all this. But the earth-loving planter finds something very real and sensual about feeling the "good earth." Of course, in this respect, the Hawaiian taro grower is no different from the Chinese farmer, the Japanese rice planter, the Nigerian gardener, and all other workers in the soil who come from similar traditions.

The Hawaiian's sense of place, therefore, indicates that he endowed the earth with a quality that made it alive. This is not an intellectual abstraction, but a distinct capacity to feel, that reacts to the chemical and biological mechanisms of ʻāina—which is but a part of Gaia, Papa, Haumea . . .

A further sacred quality to the Hawaiian sense of place derived from the belief that natural phenomena are manifestations of the gods or possess mana in their own right. However, while this statement is true in a general way, we must realize that some things are more sacred than others. That is to say, the ʻāina is sacred, but not all land is. Some places are more sacred than others. Such locations are the valley of Kaliuwaʻa on Oʻahu (more popularly known as Sacred Falls), or Lua o Pele in Puna on the Big Island, both connected with exploits of Kamapuaʻa; those leaping places for departing souls, such as Kaʻena Point on Oʻahu, Hanapēpē on Kauaʻi, Hōkūnui on Lānaʻi, and Ka Lae, or South Point, in Kaʻū on the Big Island; several sites in Hāna, Maui, that are related to the deeds of Laka; and many others. Some sacred sites enjoy what we might call a "functional sanctity," such as heiau, altars, and burial places. The degree of sacredness varies with the quantum of mana in a place, which in turn may involve a variety of factors, ranging from the memorable deeds of great chiefs and holy men to miraculous happenings to impressive natural events. Since a place cannot determine for itself its sacredness, people are the ones who decide the degree of sanctity it possesses. Hence, sacred places will appear or disappear as people, influenced by the gods and circumstances and time, decide what is sacred or what is profane.

The idea that the ʻāina is sacred is a powerful belief that persists among contemporary Hawaiians. The "sacredness of the ʻāina" is the theme of the Preamble to the Office of Hawaiian Affairs "Culture Plan/Draft One" (1982). This is supported, in part, by the statement that the kūpuna believed the " ʻāina was a living being," formed by the "union of Papa (mother earth) and Wākea (sky father)." It is also the underlying premise of the Protect Kahoʻolawe ʻOhana movement, which popularized the phrase aloha ʻāina, love of the land, and which was used to legitimize politically motivated activities in the 1970s and 1980s.

The Continuum of Land and Sea

An islander's sense of place embraces the continuum of land and sea. This must be the case with Hawaiians who live upon the peaks of volcanoes risen from the sea, the highest and most massive structures on our planet, surrounded by billions of cubic meters of ocean. So encircled are we by this vast expanse of ke kai, the sea, that we are imprisoned by it. Nowadays some would say that we are also imprisoned psychologically, suffering from what is more commonly known as "rock fever," but this is a mainlander's malady, not an islander's. We cannot escape the presence of the sea, even if we wanted to, although some people insist that this is what some of us are trying to do today.

Other people prefer to think that we are terrestrial creatures suckled at the breast of Mother Earth, when, in fact, in evolutionary terms we are born of the sea (the walewale of The Kumulipo), the mother of all life. The fluids in our bodies and in the bodies of virtually all animals are still very much like the salt water of the sea. As a matter of fact, most of the oxygen we breathe is generated by the photosynthetic action of countless marine algae, the water we drink is made possible by natural processes that begin in the ocean, and even the firm earth we stand on is, all too often, sedimentary or igneous rock that has emerged from the sea. And also, in terms of Hawaiian mythology, we, too, return to the sea after death, because our souls depart the realm of earth by leaping into the ocean deeps at the start of their journey into eternity.

It is curious, is it not, that, although we are surrounded by the ocean and literally born from it, and although our very survival as human beings and that of Gaia, the earth, depend on the sea, our metaphors and sayings rarely, if ever, refer to "Mother Ocean"? Is our ignorance of the secrets hidden within the vast ocean the reason for this? Or do we take for granted that the metaphor "Mother Earth" naturally includes the ocean? This latter assumption seems to be unlikely, because our rhetoric betrays our bias in favor of the earth, the land.

In any case, because we live upon "high islands" (as opposed to low-lying atolls such as are found in Micronesia), we tend to see geography more in the vertical than the horizontal plane. With hills, valleys, and mountains all around us—more than 75 percent of our island terrain is classified as mountainous—our entire perceptual experience is with relationships of height. We cannot conceive of flatscapes—such as the plains of the prairies of the midwestern United States or the provinces of middle Canada. So accustomed are we of Hawai'i to vertical geography that we

become easily disoriented and a little uncomfortable when we
spend time in places like Saskatchewan or Kansas, where the level
plains seem to extend into infinity. Mountainless areas seem to
hold no sense of place for us.

We also think of the ocean in vertical terms, granting it depth
instead of height. Unlike continents, whose edges slope far out
into the sea as "continental shelves," our islands drop rather suddenly into ocean canyons. Ironically, oceanographers tell us that
along continental shelves they have difficulty in telling where the
land really begins and the sea ends.

The vertical perception of the Hawaiian is exemplified in the
ma uka–ma kai idea, meaning upward to the mountain or downward to the sea. Anyone born and raised in Hawai'i soon learns
that this is our prime orientation, and for the malihini newcomer it
is quickly acquired. When a Hawaiian says ma uka, he does not
think of a horizontal line, but rather of a vertical line or, more precisely, of an inclining plane. (The image of an "incline" makes the
sense of continuum even stronger.) Ma uka tells us that we are
going up a valley, up a hillside, or up a mountain ridge; while ma
kai tells us we are going down, not just to the shoreline, but down,
down into the sea. Actually, when we think about them, ma uka
and ma kai tell us more about our vertical view of the world than
of our orientation with respect to points of the compass. (An interesting parallel exists between our vertical view of geography and
our hierarchical view of social organization, but we'll say more of
this later.)

Mention of the seashore introduces an important question
about how Hawaiians viewed this seemingly natural break in their
land-sea continuum. Greg Dening, in his absorbing ethnohistory
of the Marquesas, Islands and Beaches, stated that a beach is the
most important of all island boundaries, inasmuch as most moving creatures, whether human or animal, must cross it to step onto
the land or into the sea. We can understand why a visitor or a for-
eigner would see a beach in that way; indeed, even some modern
islanders tend to see it as a border separating two distinct regions.
If you doubt this, think only of the enormous amount of legisla-
tion, ordinances, and procedures that local, city, state, and national governments have passed and tried to apply, with the help of a
vast bureaucratic machinery (including the U.S. Army Corps of
Engineers), all dealing with just the shoreline. Rather than serving
as a boundary, a beach appears to be more like a frontier,

Anyone familiar with island shorelines and beaches knows that they are not permanent boundaries. They are forever shifting under the influence of winds and waves, especially storm waves. Some of us remember when beach parks on Oʻahu and the other islands, or our own beachfront properties, extended out many more feet beyond where they do now. If we go back far enough, we'd find that where once a beach and a fishing village existed, now only the sea flows in. We do not need to think in terms of geologic ages, because we can see the shorelines changing daily or monthly as they are affected by the tides. As Rachel Carson observed, "The boundary between sea and land is the most fleeting and transitory feature of the earth."

Hawaiians of old, no doubt, knew about the transitory nature of beaches as well as we do. Hence, they regarded the place where sea and land meet not as a line but as a wide swath of varying zones of vegetation, of wet sand and dry sand, where waves touch or do not touch. They saw the beach area as a place of convergence rather than one of divergence, where elements of land and sea merged—as in the composition of the sand itself, which is washed up from the sea floor, although its original source may be the land, as sediments deposited in the sea, or as fragments of coral reefs that fringe the land, or, as in the freshwater seeps along places like "Shipwreck Beach" on Lānaʻi, where the limu ʻeleʻele grows because it can grow only in a mixture of fresh and salt water. In other words, beaches are a transitional yet an integral part of the land-sea continuum.

The concept of the continuum is clearly demonstrated in the ahupuaʻa, so called because the boundary was marked by a cairn of stones (an ahu), topped by an image of a pig (puaʻa). The ahupuaʻa was a large division of land in old Hawaiʻi, which extended from the central mountains to a beach and beyond that into the sea. (We should note, however, that many ahupuaʻa did not have access to the mountains or to the sea.) Thus, unlike our present zoning laws which limit ownership of beachfront property to the high water mark, traditionally Hawaiian law considered the adjoining sea as a natural and logical extension of an ahupuaʻa. Neither shoreline nor beach was ever considered to be a proper boundary separating land and sea.

In the end, what makes the extension of the ahupuaʻa into the sea logical is economics. The Hawaiian of old found in the sea an important source of foods and some raw materials for his tools, utensils, ornaments, and other things. When these were combined with the resources of the 'āina, he was assured of economic self-sufficiency—provided he worked hard enough to harvest those resources. But in order to achieve that security, two further things were necessary: the first was free, unconstrained access to the sea; and the second was the right to exploit the sea exactly in accord with his right to exploit the land. Hence, the ahupua'a, with its extensions into the sea as far as two or three miles out from shore, fulfilled these conditions, and served for centuries as the basis of the Hawaiians' land-use system. It is not surprising, therefore, to hear Hawaiians today still talking about the value of the ahupua'a, partly out of nostalgia and pride in its effectiveness, but also partly out of a real concern for maintaining their traditional relationship with the land-sea continuum. (We shall discuss further the economics of the ahupua'a in chapter 10.)

Another aspect of the land-sea connection that many modern Hawaiians do not consider, mostly because of their preoccupation with the 'āina, is the sacredness of the ocean. We have already discussed the gods of the ocean, particularly Kanaloa and the 'aumākua manifest in the shark, the eel, and other creatures of the sea. The sacred quality of the ocean is illustrated by the use of sea water in purification rites preceding and following important events, such as the dedication of a luakini heiau or at the closing of the Makahiki festival. The sea served as a burial site for bones of dead people, especially of those related to 'aumākua connected with Kanaloa, Kamohoali'i (a shark god), and other deities identified with the ocean. Certain places in the sea were considered sacred because of some mythic or important historical happening that occurred there. Other places, particularly fishing grounds, were held sacred, at least on occasion, because they were made kapu by the chiefs. Such places were the waters off Kualoa and Mōkapu on O'ahu. Fishermen denoted the adjoining seas with shrines on beaches, on steep pali, and in caves. Such were the Pōhaku o Kua, a large stone in the sea close to the shore at Manā-ka'a in Ka'ū, where fishermen offered 'awa and bananas to the shark god of the region.

Then and now, Hawaiians who have serious involvement with the ocean, whether they be sailors, fishermen, or sportsmen, approach the sea with innate reverence, on the one hand, and practical or economic appraisal on the other. For example, a middle-aged Hawaiian who regularly dives for fish off the shores of Lāʻie and Kahuku, Oʻahu, tells about his "worshipping below the surface" in water that he views as "his cathedral." That is where he communes with his spiritual self, his ʻaumākua, and his Christian God. Another Hawaiian, a commercial fisherman, explains how he takes his faith with him to Nihoa (the highest of the northwestern islands in the Hawaiian chain), where he catches akule under the protection of his ʻaumakua, a shark. A member of the *Hōkū-leʻa* crew reminisces about apprehending the reality of the divine while watching and studying the stars during his journey to and from Tahiti. Perhaps some innate propensity for getting close to the spiritual powers exists in everyone who takes to the sea.

But while we modern Hawaiians may still share the same physical environment and, to that extent, some of the same perceptual experiences about the world, we no longer can share the same degree of involvement in the sea or concern for it. Our dietary and economic values have changed so much. For example, the average Hawaiian today probably eats less than 10 percent of the kinds of marine life that his forebears ate. This is not just a matter of taste, but is really one of cost and availability. Demographic, political, and legal conditions today make it impossible for us to fully appreciate the land-sea continuum of the ahupuaʻa, particularly in economic terms. A few Hawaiian back-to-nature advocates have even proposed the re-creation of an ahupuaʻa lifestyle, but theirs is an ideal chasing after an illusion. For one thing, even if the land could be obtained, present coastal zoning laws make illegal any restrictions placed upon public access to beaches and other shore areas. Thus, no way is available for restoring traditional "ownership" rights to the waters that front a man's beach property. As populations here and in other coastal states increase, the demand for access to beaches and to use of the sea beyond for recreational and other purposes will far outstrip the availability of land and sea areas.

No doubt such changes have affected and will continue to affect our sense of place with respect to the ocean. Nothing will restore or strengthen our ties with the sea as much as our use of it and our dependence upon its resources. Conversely, nothing will assure the loss of our ocean heritage faster than ignorance and indifference to it. This is why the rise in popularity of canoe racing is so heartening: in 1985 it involved more than ten thousand participants in more than one hundred canoe clubs across the state. Sadly, apart from recreational and sporting activities, relatively little advance can be shown in other fields. Perhaps what is needed is a "revival of interest in the ocean"—a lot more talk about aloha kai, or "love of the sea," along with aloha 'āina; more support for government programs and policies favoring development of ocean resources; more students doing research in oceanography and related fields; more changing of dietary habits to include more marine foods, and so on.

After all is said and done, inevitably all that is borne on the land will return at last to the sea. The land, and our bones with it, will crumble and dissolve and pass to the sea, along with grain after grain of eroded soil. And eventually, as it has done many times across the world in the geologic past, the sea will rise and reclaim us all, for, always, it is the beginning and the end.

Personal Space: Proxemics

When Malo wrote that "the great chiefs were entirely exclusive," that is, limited by the sanctity of their "bodily space" from contact or contamination by others, he was referring to "proxemics." This is a relatively new field of study, focusing on personal space—that "area with invisible boundaries surrounding a person's body." Psychologists, interior designers, engineers, philosophers, the police, educators, and many others are very interested in knowing more about how spatial relationships affect our behavior and/or reflect our values. Although primal peoples such as the Hawaiians placed great importance on personal space, only now with the rise of proxemics have we begun systematically to analyze the subject as it appears among different peoples. When and if proxemicists turn their attention to Hawaiians and other Polynesian groups, we can expect some fascinating observations. In the meantime, the brief discussion that follows will have to serve.

We have defined place as delimited space. When we move from geographical space to personal space, we go from the largest to the smallest end of our range concerned with the sense of place. Edmond Barbotin, a contemporary French thinker, prefers to call it "bodily space" because, as he puts it, "my body displaces the volume of space it occupies." It is the most immediate and permanent kind of space. It is the domain of "here" and "I"; anything outside of "here" is "there" or "yonder." Yonder space, according to Barbotin, is inaccessible to me, and therefore is only an apperceived idea of geography. Here, where "I" am, is the only real space a person knows. If we accept his logic, then, where you are now is the most important and most meaningful space in the world to you. It is existential space because it is filled with your being; your body is the focal point, indeed, the very center of your universe.

With this in mind, we can understand why the Hawaiians of old probably were among the most place-conscious peoples in the Pacific. We see this most clearly in the protocols of kapu that regulated the spatial distances among chiefs, lesser chiefs, court attendants, and commoners. Read what John Papa 'I'i, who served King Liholiho, Kamehameha II, as a chamberlain, has to say. "As they (the chief and his young servant) walked along he kept to one side, for it was not proper to walk directly behind the chief, whose back was *kapu (kuapala)*. The companion also avoided the chief's shadow lest his own shadow fall on Liholiho when the sun was in the east or west" ('I'i 1973). 'I'i estimated the distance to be kept between the attendant and the chief's back at about two fathoms, or twelve feet. "Only the person who fetched [the chief's] personal belongings could pass to-and-fro," and anyone who failed to keep the proper distance and violated the kapu was put to death.

Given the extremely hierarchical character of Hawaiian royalty, the area of kapu space of a chief would vary with his status, or "mana quotient," so to speak. Since there were many fine degrees of blood purity, rank, title, and privilege, determining what constituted the right protocol must have been a study in itself. The situation became even more complex when several high chiefs, their courtiers, and other persons were present at a special event, which may have required different seating, standing, or walking spatial arrangements and alignments. For example, each of these occasions—a procession, a ceremony at a heiau, a chiefly conclave, and so on—would have demanded its own kind of protocol. We can safely assume that those persons who were connected with the royal court developed a good working knowledge about rules as well as a keen sensitivity to spatial thinking. And since the ali'i dictated much of the tempo and style of life in Hawaiian society, the commoners, too, must have developed an awareness of spatial relationships, if for no other reason than to avoid the penalties for violating the kapu.

Unfortunately, we have little documented information on what the maka'āinana thought about these matters. But we do have some clues. We know that Hawaiians indulged in several greeting practices that required close contact. One was the honi, or touching noses on the side of the face, accompanied by a slight sniffing at the other person. It is a practice that requires intimate physical contact (as can be seen among the Maori who still hongi, to use the Maori expression), as opposed to, say, the Oriental bow or even the European handshake. The honi is typical of people who enjoy touching and, from all the hearsay evidence we have today, Hawaiians were and are a touching people, as are Polynesians in general.

If so, at least the maka'āinana would have had an entirely different spatial protocol from that which marked royalty. Instead of distance, they would have stressed nearness or intimacy. This means that they would have tolerated relatively close social distances when conversing with or sitting next to others of their own social level. They would have also been more tolerant of being gathered in close-packed crowds. This is borne out by the many references in historical writings about ancient Hawai'i of large numbers of people at religious, sports, and arts events. We can note this too in the sketches of Lodovik Choris and John Webber, depicting packed crowds at dance and sporting events. In sum, the sacred space of the ali'i meant appropriate distancing, while the profane space of the maka'āinana invited proximity. Each of these spatial views would lead to different values and behaviors, as we shall see.

When we look at commoners' space, we look at essentially horizontal relationships. But when we turn to royalty, we see vertical relationships. This is dramatically illustrated in the old Hawaiian custom of kapu moe, or prostration before chiefs of high rank. Malo stated that if a kapu moe chief "travelled in daytime a man went before him with a flag calling out 'kapu! moe!' whereupon all the people prostrated themselves." So sacred was he that "when the containers holding the water for his bath, or when his clothing, his malo, his food, or anything that belonged to him was carried along, every one must prostrate himself." Keep in mind that the chief represented not only the highest secular authority but also the highest divine power as well. In other cultures prostration is not unusual as a sign of obeisance. We can still see the practice in certain papal ceremonies today.

In ancient Hawai'i, at ceremonial occasions involving chiefs, at least three acceptable positions were assumed: (1) kneeling, (2) squatting, noho, and (3) sitting. The point of each was to keep oneself below the level of the head of the highest-ranking person present. A man might even have to crawl to keep his head below the level of the head of the high chief. Thus, even today it is a custom among Tongans and Samoans, for example, for visitors to a house not to occupy levels above the head of anyone who outranks them. Apparently, this concern no longer matters to modern Hawaiians.

Thus personal space in a rank-conscious society is always related to height. The Japanese bow; the higher the rank of the person being acknowledged, the lower is the bow of the lesser person. Javanese in Yogyakarta not too many years ago knelt and squatted before the sultan. In Great Britain men bow and women curtsey to the queen. And in equalitarian America all judges, presidents of Senates and speakers of the House, preachers, electronic evangelists, and the like are seated above everyone else or stand in elevated pulpits. Indeed, height seems to be such an inbred symbol of rank and authority that in Hawaiian, Japanese, Chinese, and many other cultures a younger person is taught to keep his head below his elders' and his eyes directed downward, especially when being scolded. The great put-down is always delivered from above.

Spatial segregation, therefore, was a pervasive principle of social and political organization in old Hawai'i. A person's vertical or horizontal position with respect to royalty and elders in general was the outward expression of internalized values of respect, humility, fear, or awe. In other words, position and posture, the external configuration of spatial thinking, communicated how a person thought and what he believed and accepted about himself and his society.

Another aspect of how Hawaiians view personal space deserves mention. Professor of Hawaiian Language Pualani Hopkins commented on the way demonstrative pronouns are used in the language. "English distinguishes between objects within physical reach of the speaker—'this'—and everywhere else, 'that.' Hawaiians divide space differently: objects within the speaker's grasp are labelled *kēia*—'this.' Objects within the listener's reach are *kēnā*—'that thing in your territory.' Objects beyond both parties fall into a third category, *kēlā*, 'that thing distant for both of us.' Thus the

English speaker defines only his own territory; the Hawaiian rec-
ognizes that of his listener also" (Anthony).

Why? While this is conjecture on our part, Hawaiians, as did
many peoples, understood the notion that perceptions differ depending on one's spatial position. This vocabulary may also indicate a willingness to defer to or respect the other person's view.
Further, it may be the way the language acknowledges the importance of each person's space derived from the mana that he or she
may have. In any case, the use of such demonstrative pronouns is a
characteristic of many Asian and Polynesian languages.

When we contrast modern-day versus traditional Hawaiian
views of personal space, we find strong differences. Instead of
sacred space that is kapu, space today in Hawai'i is democratic,
equalitarian, maka'ainana oriented. We see no pecking order to
speak of, although Hawaiian fraternal orders do attempt to establish their own. Some Hawaiians with monarchical sentiments
accord spatial deference to descendents of the Kalākaua dynasty
on public as well as private occasions. The only planned demonstration of ali'i protocol accompanies Aloha Week's "royal court,"
which is nothing more than innocent pageantry or, at worst, as
some cynics say, "touristy pomp." Not surprisingly, a few Hawaiian monarchists condemn it as a travesty of court etiquette.

The lack of formal protocol among us today means only one
thing: the absence of a recognized hierarchy of Hawaiian leadership for Hawaiians. Although restoring such a hierarchy seems out
of the question at present, the Hawaiian community feels a desperate need for an intelligent, unified leadership, necessarily modern,
yet based on certain traditional organizing principles and values.
When and if such a leadership evolves, we can expect a reordering
of spatial relationships and protocol.

Modern Hawaiians tend to behave spatially much like Americans do. A Hawaiian waiting in line regards his place in that line
as inviolate. He would frown on anyone in line pushing or jost-
ling, and probably would fight anyone trying to take his place. In
conversations, the Hawaiian seems to be comfortable with about a
two-foot distance between speakers, which is the preferred distance among Americans. A Hawaiian would also view his body
space as his territory in the sense that he would resent being
shoved in a crowd, let alone in an uncrowded situation. A female
Hawaiian would not tolerate being pinched in public, contrary to

the custom in certain Mediterranean countries. And, like most American males, Hawaiian men, if they want to preserve their macho image, do not ever hold hands in public.

Yet, as acculturated as modern Hawaiians may be to the spatial dimensions of American culture, they still show strong traces of the "common touch," so to speak. As did the commoners of old, Hawaiians today seem to prefer more touching than do Americans in general. They like to kiss (rather than honi, which seems to have disappeared quite early in our history after 1778), and they hug and clinch in public. It is beautiful to see Hawaiians greeting each other at a gathering. The air seems to be charged with electricity, perhaps generated by the release of ions excited by the warmth of personal spaces (and bodies) coming in contact. Just as all space in the cosmos is filled with something, so is Hawaiians' personal space filled with something, namely, the chemistry of affection. Perhaps "aloha space" is a better way to describe the Hawaiian sense of personal space. It joins well with the values of kindness, generosity, hospitableness, and love that are idealized in Hawaiian social relationships.

Privacy

Just as a direct relationship exists between geographical space and territoriality, so does a similar relationship exist between personal space and privacy. In fact, in the end all of these are interrelated phenomena. Your territory, for example, provides you with a place to call your own, a space where you can find privacy. Personal space is inseparable from your sense of place, which is predicated on the exclusiveness of territoriality. In short, these concepts form the dynamics of understanding our relationships with one another on the one hand, and with the cosmos and nature on the other.

By privacy we mean the desire or belief that one's space ought to be kept off-limits to intrusions. Or we can think of it as a condition of insulation directed against outside influence and observation. A certain amount of individual freedom and initiative is implied in this, since we are saying, in effect, that we want to be free to do as we want. It is a form of sovereign withdrawal which can be expressed in accepted institutionalized ways or in purely individualized ways that sometimes may border on the unconventional and the unlawful. A general comment on the human desire

for privacy declares that the search for personal privacy is a pervasive theme in the daily life of all peoples in all cultures.

Many arrangements for institutionalized privacy were devised
in traditional Hawai'i. Take the way in which people and dwellings were distributed. Unlike in New Zealand or Sāmoa, where
large numbers of people often lived in well-established, fairly
densely populated, and compact communities (or even in fortified
villages, as in the case of Maoris), Hawaiians did not seem to have
developed the same kind of communal living space. According to
Handy and Pūku'i, no major commercial, political, religious, or
population centers existed in old Hawai'i. "Even in localities, such
as Waimea on Kaua'i, Lahaina on Maui and Kailua or Waipi'o on
Hawai'i, where intensive cultivation and good fishing grounds
combined to concentrate population, there was no development of
village or town communities." Although the islands were well populated (estimates range from 250,000 to 400,000 in 1778), the
populace was well dispersed, settled in many isolated homes or
clusters of dwellings. The factors that selected those locations are
mainly nearness to fresh water and sources of food, such as their
farms and fishing grounds. Means of transportation, common
markets, concerns for defense, and other locational factors were
not important. Thus, the more dispersed the dwelling units were,
the greater were the physical distances between them and, hence,
the greater was the sense of isolation and privacy.

Still other forms of institutionalized privacy were, of course, the
heiau with their enclosed kapu spaces, consecrated for the use of
the select few priests and chiefs. Hundreds of heiau were built
throughout the islands. We should include among them the numerous other small heiau in private places, the family altars and the
shrines that insulated their devotees from others. Very important
were the places of refuge, pu'uhonua, at Hōnaunau, and at least
five other sites on the island of Hawai'i, as well as one on each of
the other major islands. The pu'uhonua, more than any other
structure of olden times, seems to represent best the "right" of privacy for Hawaiians, for it was a sanctuary, a place of physical
security, by virtue of guaranteeing a person protection from superior authorities. Worth noting is the fact that the privacy offered
by a pu'uhonua was a function of the mana of those chiefs, both
living and dead, under whose protection the site had been placed.

The close bond between sanctity and privacy, so typical of religious Hawai'i, is exemplified by the "storied places," wahi pana, where "the old gods walked, where the forefathers dwelt, where lingered still their active influence for good or evil" (Beckwith 1970). Such places may have been a secluded grove of trees, a rocky coastline, or a mountain—wherever one could commune at peace with oneself and the spiritual realm. The so-called hermit prophets sought similar havens of their own, where they could pray and meditate before delivering their predictions.

While we are mainly concerned here with privacy as it relates to our sense of place, the fact that Hawaiians also cherished their intellectual privacy is worth mentioning. It was a common practice for teachers, craftspersons, specialists, and others of the professions to share or withhold their knowledge and their "secrets" from disciples, students, the merely curious, and others. This secrecy was due in part to the belief that their mana might be diminished if ever the knowledge were misused. What the practice meant in terms of privacy is that an individual had the right to determine when, how, to whom, and to what extent he chose to divulge information he possessed. Because the rationale behind this choice was based in mana, in a significant sense it was a "god-given" power or freedom.

What our discussion of privacy and its related antecedents of territoriality and personal space suggests is that ka po'e kahiko were not as much a bunch of conformists as all too often we have been led to believe. In comparison with the Samoan culture, which endowed its members with a strong sense of individual dignity, the Hawaiian culture, according to John Charlot, was even more individualistic. "Hawaiians had more privacy in their daily living and could even retreat into the mountains to be alone. A large amount of activity and thought seems to be independent of social duties and constraints. In much Hawaiian literature, the impression of individual genius is stronger than that of a formative culture. Extreme examples of individualism are atheists, deniers of gods and breakers of tabus, in a culture so permeated by religion."

Privacy can be either passive or assertive, but in the case of the ancient Hawaiian it appears to have been more assertive. It is personified in the life of the planter or fisherman living in relative isolation, producing foodstuffs and household articles for his own family's needs, having to depend largely on his own wits in satisfying the demands of his konohiki and chiefs on the one hand, and those of his akua and 'aumākua on the other. Happily, Hawaiian society was so structured as to allow its members those quiet moments and isolated places—and the personal freedom—they needed as retreats of privacy from which they could draw strength and inspiration.

Architectural Space

Early visitors to Hawai'i called the grass huts "stacks." Like "so many sunburnt ricks of hay," said a New Englander, that resembled a "haystack, such as is frequently seen in an American barnyard" (Apple). Had they known anything about the universal function and history of architecture, they might not have displayed so brashly their barnyard origins. For, as some historians of architecture tell us, the humble hut evolved by almost all societies is "the exemplar of architecture" (Giedion). The primitive hut with its vertical posts, horizontal beams or rafters, and inclined roof thatched with grass is the original structure on which "all the magnificences of architecture are elaborated." In its honest simplicity, human scale, and harmony with nature, the hut is about as close as the architect can get to a perfect imitation of Bella Natura, Beautiful Nature. As the French theorist Laugier admonished the architectural fraternity, "Let us never lose sight of our little hut" (quoted in Giedion).

Since it is architecture that organizes or conceptualizes living space—hence personal, existential space as well as privacy—let us examine the Hawaiian thatched house. The ordinary hale, the commoners' hut, was a relatively small, low, rectangular structure with a couple of upright ridgeposts, a horizontal ridgepole, and a roof of pili grass thatching. It resembled a modern A-frame house without walls. The hale was entirely thatched at the sides, with the exception of a single small, low opening for a door that was only large enough to permit an adult to crawl rather than walk through it. The interior consisted of one room with no partitions of any kind, a hearth, and sometimes a slightly raised platform serving as a place for a bed. Usually the house of a chief was larger, and always it was higher, and hence had exterior walls. Generally, the chief, or anyone who could afford such an establishment, had a complex of huts. These huts were intended for specific functions. Thus, one would be set aside for sleeping, another for eating, others for cooking, storage, and so on.

If proof was ever needed to demonstrate the value Hawaiians placed on privatized space, it is evident in the design of the windowless, completely enclosed (except for the door) hut. At first glance, given the island humidity and warm temperatures even with the cooling trade winds, it would seem to be a poor design. The Samoan-type fale which is open without walls, although it has blinds which can be let down at night or in inclement weather, would seem to be a more sensible arrangement for the Hawaiian climate. One part of the explanation for such enclosed structures is that their occupants preferred to spend most of their time outdoors (just as many other peoples did, including the Greeks), even to sleeping out under the stars. The more important reason, however, is that it ensured privacy and security during kapu times, such as when processions and special rituals took place, which often lasted for several hours, if not for days or weeks. At times of some kapu the people would be required only to stop work or play, but at other times they would have to retreat into utter seclusion and total silence—"every sound, even to the crowing of a cock or barking of a dog, prevented"—any violation of which would mean the usual death sentence. The illusion of security was provided by the door over which presided the god Kānehohoio, who kept out "victim-seeking guards" and evil spirits.

As an aside, more often than not we think of Hawaiians as living in more gregarious and conversational situations than in completest silence. But here we are reminded that they lived in a highly ritualized society that prized the spoken word as well as the dignity of quiet seclusion. And, moreover, at times the power in the spoken word could impose a reign of terror upon the victimized populace, unless it went into hiding. Those circumstances offer a striking contrast to the world of noise that we live in today, caused in part by our own neglect of the power of the word, and in part by our horror of silence, whether we encounter it at home or during halts in conversation. (For further discussion on silence, see chapter 9.)

Spatial values were particularly evident in the size and height of a chief's house. It provided standing room because a chief's house was higher, befitting his rank. The ridgepost was the key structural feature—the higher the rank of the chief, the higher the ridge. Hence, the Hawaiian saying, *"Ki'eki'e kaupoku o Hanalei,"* or "The lofty ridge pole of Hanalei," referring to conceited and

willful persons (Pūku'i). The ridgeposts were also important because they symbolized the owner, which is why great care was
taken in selecting a perfect log without knots, bends, or other
imperfections. The Maoris, too, gave great importance to the
ridgeposts in their sacred meeting houses on the marae. Human
figures carved in them represent an important ancestor supporting
the roof on his head.

The interior space of the commoners' house was uncluttered by
partitions or furniture. The several additional functional houses
made up for the lack of partitions in the homes of chiefs and other
well-to-do people. Commoners needed no partitions because they
preferred to spend most of their time outdoors. As for the absence
of household furniture, Hawaiians sat, squatted, or slept on the
ground, as much out of a feeling of psychic comfort as from neces-
sity. Squatting, or "hunkering," needless to say, was the posture
adopted by Polynesians and so many other peoples throughout the
world. We may think it uncomfortable, but for people who have
developed the proper muscles in the legs and their joints, it is a
comfortable position. Older Filipinos, Koreans, Japanese, and
other Asian immigrants to Hawai'i can squat for long periods
without tiring.

Hawaiians' living space allowed them intimacy, which is another aspect of privacy. This is shown in the small size of the huts,
which for commoners were barely large enough to accommodate a
family and the few possessions they stored. However simple the
design, the Hawaiian household seemed to have captured an
important quality of architecture, about which Giedion has written: "The future of life depends on the recovery of intimacy of
life."

The Hawaiian builder also measured for living on a human
scale, literally so, since all his proportions were based on the
human body. An 'owā was half the width of a finger; a kīko'o was
a span, the distance between tip of thumb to end of index finger; a
poho was half a span; a muku was the length, with arms extended
to the sides, from the fingertips of one hand to the elbow of the
opposite arm; and an anana was the distance between tips of the
longest fingers, with arms extended to the side. Since apparently
these differed from one builder to the next, the houses they built
differed, except in general design, from those put up by other

builders. In this respect, the great French architect Le Corbusier had said that "primitive builders" achieved one of the essential conditions of great architecture, namely, that because they employed units of measurement derived from man's own body, their buildings were made "in man's measure, to human scale, in harmony with man" (cited in Giedion).

Since his living space was so connected with a person's relationship with the spiritual realm, architectural space was, for all intents and purposes, sacred space. Obviously this is why the Hawaiian architect was a priest and a seer, but, above all, a locater. He was called a kuhikuhipu'uone, one who points out the sand dunes, for the most important thing about a home was its placement—its sacred geography. If it was properly sited and aligned with the heavenly bodies, earthly powers, and other cosmic forces, then its occupants would be ensured of a happy stay. If it was not properly located, then not even the most spacious or most expensive house could prevent some misfortune from befalling its owner or tenants. The making of this decision about locating a house, so central to the well-being of the Hawaiian, joined three of the most important branches of knowledge in old Hawai'i: astronomy-astrology, religion, and architecture.

This approach to architectural space is not unique to Hawai'i, since it is found in many major areas of the world such as India, China, and Japan. In Japan, for example, the locater or house-diviner, who is called uranai-shi, is still employed by property owners and builders of their houses. His expertise includes the significance of all the cardinal points in a building, from the proposed location of the lavatory to the facing of the front door. Much of this knowledge is based on ancient Chinese principles of geomancy. Interestingly enough, when the Japanese owners of the luxury Mauna Lani Resort on the Big Island of Hawai'i had to select the exact site for the proposed hotel, they called upon a kahuna, the late Emma DeFries, to help in selecting the right place.

Architects in modern Hawai'i have debated whether a "true Hawaiian style of architecture" really exists. That problem is less important than is preserving the philosophy of the ancient Hawaiian, who considered his living space as sacred and as a defining part of his sense of place.

Restoring Our Sense of Place

What are some of the steps we can take to restore and maintain our sense of place, at least in part if not entirely? The following section is only an incomplete agenda that invites other ideas. First, individuals and families should get to know the meaning and the history of their Hawaiian ancestral places. Second, after having done that, they should enhance and share that knowledge. Enhancing it might range from a do-it-yourself history to funding other people to undertake place histories, and in the process sharing it with family, friends, and others. Third, such places need to be revisited if only to recapture a part of oneself, or perhaps to regain a lost perspective by uncovering a facet of family life that has lain hidden under the overgrowth of time. Fourth, if one is fortunate enough to own or have access to the family's ancestral home, every reasonable effort should be made to preserve and maintain it as the wahi pana, the "storied place," where family members can come together to reminisce, eat, dance, kanikapila, ho'oponopono, and renew their commitments to ancestors.

So far so good. But, in fact, only a comparative handful of Hawaiians still own their kuleana or ancestral lands. The vast majority are denied those roots. The ideal choice is to reacquire those lands, but for most people the obstacles to doing that probably are insurmountable. Not the least of those difficulties is the high cost of real estate today or the fact that present owners do not want to sell the land where once our kūpuna lived. Yet, under our present system of real property laws and the feasible avenue open to us, repurchasing such lands may be the only realistic alternative. Maori groups are taking the same options, by buying back ancestral lands from pakeha owners, always, of course, at higher prices than they were sold for. Because few individuals may have the means with which to buy lands, families may consider pooling their resources and forming hui, or syndicates, for land acquisitions, as the Maoris have done. Simply buying ancestral lands for satisfying one's sense of place may not make any sense, economically speaking, but honoring our sense of wahi pana surely is part of the challenge of being a modern Hawaiian.

When we look at the question of restoring our sense of place as a Hawaiian community, the options are slightly different and no less difficult to deal with. One suggestion that has already been

discussed by several Hawaiian groups, partly at the prompting of
Maoris, is to establish special wahi, or places where Hawaiians
might come together as a people, to talk about their problems, to
perform their own ritual services and ceremonies, to welcome distinguished guests, to present their genealogies, place histories,
honors, and commemorations. Like Maori marae, the places
would be consecrated mainly for the use of Hawaiians, to become
in time their repositories for traditions, feelings, memories, deeds,
and words of the living and the dead, or their sacred precincts
where Hawaiians can come to feel and regain their sense of
Hawaiianness and place. They could be places of refuge for the
spirit, if not for the body.

While one must visit a real marae to appreciate its true functions and contributions to the Maori spirit, we can catch part of its
essence from the following description by John Rangihau of his
tribal marae.

> Tuhoe will make no concessions whatsoever in things that happen
> on their *marae* because we have given way in every other area of
> Maoriness. The *marae* is the repository of all the historical things,
> of all the traditions, all the mythology and other things which
> make up the intangibles of Maoriness. . . . We welcome all people
> to use our *marae*. But we ask that they fit in with the etiquette
> which is part and parcel of me and every other Tuhoe person. Only
> in this way can I foresee that we will be able to keep our culture
> alive. Not the sort of culture that asks us to go out and entertain
> tourists and profane our sacred things. But it will be that type of
> culture that asks us to do things because they have meaning for me
> and the rest of Tuhoe. And if we keep this place absolutely sacro-
> sanct then it will never lose its aura, it will never lose its ethos.

Call it whatever you like, Hawaiians do not have such a place; in
actuality, as far as we can tell, we never did have the equivalent of
a marae in ancient times either.

In the meantime, Hawaiians should take stock of their existing
"storied places" in the light of the need to restore and revitalize
their sense of place. We refer specifically to sites or structures that
have come to be identified in the public mind, whether Hawaiian
or non-Hawaiian, as belonging to the Hawaiian people. These
might include the Royal Mausoleum in Nuʻuanu Valley, the royal
birthstones of Kūkaniloko near Wahiawa, Oʻahu, Huliheʻe Palace

and Queen Emma's Summer Palace, 'Iolani Palace, and the City of Refuge and the Hale o Keawe at Hōnaunau, Kona. Many other less well known places also hold special significance for local family groups on each of the islands. Perhaps what is needed is a registry of such places that Hawaiians make known to the public, in order to sensitize everyone to their meaning and mana.

We should be forewarned of the danger of any attempt to put "off-limits" signs on places, particularly if the site has any interest for visitors. Public places are open to everybody and any attempt to limit access for other than practical reasons will surely be opposed. This presents a problem for Hawaiians who, on the one hand, may take a proprietary interest in a historic site because they consider it sacred, yet, on the other hand, cannot and would not want to keep out everybody. The typical problem is the tourists. They are intrusive, as they come to a place to see it, freezing views in lifeless photos, but some also come eagerly, sincerely interested in learning and capturing something unique. Hawaiians can hardly find fault with people of integrity who bring their own mana and leave something good behind, apart from their money. What ought to be done, at the minimum, is to educate both visitors and local residents about the significance that certain places have for Hawaiians, appealing to their goodwill or their guilt to keep those places unspoiled.

In the last analysis, perhaps the most important thing Hawaiians can do collectively to maintain their sense of place is to realize that, because our people were here first, we of today have the primary responsibilities for preserving and enriching the life of the land. By virtue of our claims to being the heirs of Papa and Wākea, we are the ultimate guardians of this land. True, legally we may not own much of it, although Hawaiian estates, individuals, and the Department of Hawaiian Home Lands do control nearly 40 percent of the privately held land in the state. But we are talking here about a spiritual and ancestral claim for which legal ownership is not relevant. After all, if we are to be truly consistent with traditional Hawaiian thought, no one really owned the land in the past and none of it really belonged to an individual. The relationship was the other way around: a person belonged to the land. How could you ever own a place, let alone sell it as a commodity, if its true value is found as the sum of the lives, memories, achievements, and mana of the generations who once dwelled upon it?

We are but stewards of the ʻāina and the kai, trusted to take care of these islands on behalf of the gods, our ancestors, ourselves, and our children. Kamehameha III spoke to all generations when he declared, "*Ua mau ke ea o ka ʻāina i ka pono,* The life of the land is preserved in righteousness." The land will surely be lost forever if we who have been entrusted with its care should betray our trusteeship.

PART THREE

SCIENCE AND
TECHNOLOGY

8

EVOLUTION AND THE SCIENTIFIC SAVAGE

The Scientific Savage

At about the turn of this century the anthropologist Bronislaw Malinowski, drawing upon his studies in the South Pacific, wrote: "There are no peoples however primitive without religion and magic. Nor are there, it must be added at once, any savage races lacking either in the scientific attitude or in science, though this lack has been frequently attributed to them. In every primitive community, studied by trustworthy and competent observers, there have been found two clearly distinguishable domains, the Sacred and the Profane; in other words, the domain of Magic and Religion and that of Science" (Malinowski 1948).

The idea of the "scientific savage" will surprise many of us today who think that primal peoples have no aptitude for science. We know, of course, that the ancient civilizations of Egypt, China, and Greece, for example, achieved relatively sophisticated levels of scientific and technological competency for their times, but, by and large, we tend to dismiss that competence for most other peoples, including all Polynesians. Malinowski's view of science and the "primitive community," which was based on his study of the Trobriand Islanders and other cultures, forces us to rethink our own assumptions about Hawaiian attitudes and achievements regarding science in the centuries before 1778.

We propose to do this by taking as a case study Hawaiian ideas about evolution that are contained in *The Kumulipo* and then assessing the "scientific" content of these ideas by comparing them with Darwinian and more recent opinions about natural evolution. We shall see that ka po'e kahiko developed some remarkable insights into the origins of life and the ordering of plant and animal species that compare favorably with the ideas of other peoples who have been accorded reputable scientific traditions. We shall consider, too, whether the Hawaiian view of evolution went beyond the level where modern scientific theory stops.

The Common Sense of Science

Too many people think of "science" as being something hidden and mysterious, and that one has to be super smart to understand any of it. On the contrary, science is far more a matter of common sense than of mystery. Robert Oppenheimer, the famed American theoretical physicist, urged that we should "distrust all the philosophers who claim that by examining science they come to results in contradiction with common sense. Science is based on common sense; it cannot contradict it." He represented an attitude held by most other scientists. Among them was T. H. Huxley, who defined science as "organized common sense." Even Einstein, whose contributions to the theory of modern physics seem completely to contradict common sense, said that science was "nothing more than a refinement of everyday thinking."

No race has a monopoly on common sense. It is a capacity universally shared by humankind. The wise may have uncommon sense, but everyone has common sense—at least to some degree. It deals with the down-to-earth, ordinary, everyday business of living by helping us to gain the results we seek. When we say a man "lacks common sense," we mean that he fails to foresee the consequences of what he does. The only basis upon which we can predict the future is past experience. Common sense helps us to learn from our past experience, so that we can control to some extent our future.

In using common sense, we assume at least three general principles. The first is that, if we accept the possibility of predicting future events, we assume the principle of determinism—that the same results will follow in consequence of the same conditions. The second is that, if we presuppose that prediction is possible, then we also accept the idea of continuity. That is, we assume that phenomena we see in the world now will continue to manifest in similar ways in later times and other places. The third general principle is that, while continuity exists in nature, it is not part of an absolute continuum. In other words, while we may be a part of nature, we still can consider ourselves as being separate from it, and our own conceptual worlds as being quite distinct and independent from the rest of the world. Thus, when we make predictions, we do so in terms of our limited system of objects and conditions, and not in terms of the entire universe. Doing that would be impossible for us, in a common-sense way, because we realize that we do not know everything about the universe.

In saying this we have oversimplified a much more involved process, one that Leonard K. Nash presented in his book *The Nature of the Natural Sciences*. But our point is that these principles of common sense are recognized by all human beings, in one degree or another, whether they lived in ancient or modern times. Since science does not operate in a vacuum, it must start with common sense. "Primitive" and "modern" science, therefore, at least take off from the same launching pad. However, common sense and science differ in significant ways as, for example, in the types of subject matter that science focuses upon, in the way that it collects and organizes its data, and the manner in which it formulates its experiences and findings into conceptual schemes, and so on. Indeed, all these approaches make science a "refinement" of common sense.

Someone has said that "man's curiosity" is the precondition for scientific development. This is undoubted, because without the desire to know, neither the exercises of common sense nor a safe life would be possible. The need to know is the need for explanation, from which comes all science. But no less important is the need to do, that is, determining our direction and our behavior by rearranging the relationships of things through the applications of science in the form of technology. The impulse to know is satisfied by first gathering facts accumulated from observation and experimentation, but facts alone are never enough. Facts must be organized and interpreted in a meaningful way. Man's curiosity, his need for explanation and for facts, are natural to all cultures and peoples throughout human history. So is his need for meaning. As F. S. Marvin wrote in *Science and Civilization*, "Primitive ingenuous man, like the greatest philosophers, is but trying to get beneath the surface, behind the veil of appearance, and to reach reality."

Something else we need to understand about science is that the so-called scientific method is not so sacred as to be beyond questioning. Percy Bridgman, a Nobel laureate in physics, stated:

There is a good deal of ballyhoo about scientific method. . . . No working scientist, when he plans an experiment in his laboratory, asks himself whether he is being properly scientific, nor is he interested in whatever method he may be using as *method*. . . . What appears to him as the essence of the situation is that he is not consciously following any prescribed course of action, but feels complete freedom to utilize any method or device whatever, which in the particular situations before him seems likely to yield the correct answer. In his attack on his specific problem he suffers no inhibitions or precedent or authority, but he is completely free to adopt any course that his ingenuity is capable of suggesting to him. No one standing on the outside can predict what the individual scientist will do or what method he will follow. In short, science is what scientists do, and there are as many scientific methods as there are individual scientists.

In other words, the purpose of science is to make sense out of facts, that is, the observable phenomena, to discover the regularity and predictability of nature's phenomena, and to determine how the world works. The way in which we achieve this ordering matters less than the doing of it. But whether we use observation, experiment, the educated guess, the chance of discovery, trial and error, verifying hypotheses, common sense, or the intuitive leap, whatever the method, the findings of science must be checked and verified objectively, freely, repeatedly, and exhaustively. Thus, while no one procedure may be imposed, recognized criteria for demonstrating the truth of what we say or theorize are required.

If common sense (or its "refinement"), and the spirit of curiosity, and a "nonmethodology" based on verification of what is being claimed are minimal conditions for the existence of a scientific attitude, then we must ask ourselves this question: Did the Hawaiians of old meet these requirements? Our earlier chapters on cosmology, astronomy, time, and mythmaking suggest the answer to that question. In this chapter we delve deeper in order to determine the magnitude of the ancient Hawaiians' understanding of science.

Evolution and *The Kumulipo*

No other idea concerning the natural sciences has had as much influence on modern thinking and behavior as has Charles Darwin's theory of evolution and its later adaptations. The publication of his *Origin of Species* in 1859 caused a revolution in mankind's ideas about living things, one that "ultimately may prove to be the greatest revolution in the history of human thought." Not only did Darwin's work provide answers, but it also raised questions. Together they have shaped in very fundamental ways fields of science ranging from paleontology to genetics and embryology, and beyond them even to sociology and cultural history.

No wonder that our Hawaiian ears perk up when we are told that *The Kumulipo*, composed a century or more before Darwin was born, contains many basic ideas about evolution. As one contemporary Hawaiian said, while recalling his feelings when he first learned about the possibility: "A warm, tingling sensation swept through my body. I felt proud—and relieved to know that the old Hawaiians weren't so backward after all!" Very likely this sentiment is shared by many other Hawaiians.

The Kumulipo, as we have indicated, is a name chant, a genealogy, composed for a newborn chief. It is not a scientific exposition of evolution. In tracing the family line of the young chief all the way back to Wākea and Papa and the origin of the universe, the chant uses as a metaphorical device the evolutionary development of plants and animals in this familiar world. The metaphors, therefore, are symbols supporting the purpose of the chant: an affirmation of the prestigious origins of the young chief's family line. While for our immediate analytical purpose we must keep the two separate, the Hawaiians of old saw the mythic and the natural worlds as being very closely interrelated.

The Creation Chant's lines present the following ideas, which are pertinent to modern scientists' theories about evolution.

1. Life originated from a watery slime.
2. No mention is made of divine intervention in this genesis.
3. Living things evolved in an order of progression, from the simple to the more complex.
4. The first and simplest organism to be formed is the coral polyp.
5. The second group of creatures to be formed is a variety of ocean-dwelling invertebrates, such as the worm, starfish, sea cucumber, sea urchin, mussel, assorted shellfish, and so on.

6. The simpler creatures give way to higher plants and animals; they are mentioned in pairings of sea and land forms. First come the fishes, after them come insects and birds, followed by reptiles, mammals, and, finally, by man.
7. The evolutionary process began in a remote "prehuman" past, and developed over a long period of time.

In addition to these specific points, other important associated concepts are implied and flow logically from the total context. Among these concepts are spontaneous generation, syngenesis (the formation of an embryo by the union of elements from two parents), the principle of constant change, and even suggestions about the ideas of adaptation and mutability of species in response to changing environments.

From whence did these ideas come? Did *The Kumulipo*'s composers pull them out of the air? Are they simply speculative poetry? Or did they come from "factual observation," as Martha Beckwith (1951) asked? Did they reflect common-sense judgments based on systematic study of natural phenomena over a long period of time? If they did not come from such observations, how else could they have been gained?

The Darwin Analogy

We must clarify one more point: namely, the Darwin analogy. Since for most people the theory of evolution and Darwin are synonymous, naturally we shall want to draw comparisons between his statements and those of *The Kumulipo*. When we compare the two, however, we recognize at once that they are not exactly the same, although both agree on the fundamental concept that life forms evolve from the lower to the higher. Darwin's principal concern was understanding the effects that overproduction, competition, variation, and survival of the fittest had on living organisms. Based on his observations of natural habitats around the world, he concluded that: (1) organisms produce so many potential offspring (e.g., a single orchid fruit may contain a million seeds) that neither the available space nor nutrients would allow all seedlings to develop; (2) this superabundance of progeny would lead to intense competition for space and food, which would act as a natural check on populations of life forms, which in turn would allow only a small number ever to attain maturity; (3) the progeny of a mating pair will vary because of parental differences; and (4) among the many variable progeny possible for any species population, some will be better suited to compete successfully, while others will be less well able to exploit available space or nutrients. The weaker progeny will be eliminated, or their reproductive effectiveness will be reduced, resulting in "natural selection" of the more favorably endowed individuals to pass their characteristics to the next generation.

Darwin also observed that those organisms which are best adapted to their environments would survive. These would have the more favorable traits, allowing them best to compete and reproduce, and they would reproduce, so that that their offspring would continue the same process of improvement and change. Out of these processes would develop new species, either when one population line evolved through time until it became so different from the original stock as to become a different species, or when different variants of the original population evolved into two or more species derived from the original one. Thus, one could postulate that evolution would enable all life forms to have been developed, over a very long time, from a single or a limited starting population.

This is Darwin in a nutshell. But even a little bit of knowledge should help us to avoid making unwarranted comparisons. We can make an interesting one, however, between *The Kumulipo* and *The Origin of Species*; both are like the tips of icebergs. In the case of the latter, the book's justly famous position was gained not from Darwin's proposing of the idea but from his clear and carefully documented exposition of it. That is to say, the basic elements of the idea of the evolution of organisms are almost as old as philosophical thought itself. They have an intellectual pedigree, as we shall show, that can be traced to many cultures and scientific traditions over many centuries. What Darwin did was to draw from this cumulative experience and knowledge going back to observations made by the early Greeks, and, then, relying on his own observations and refined common sense, to synthesize all this in a masterpiece of scientific writing.

The Kumulipo is analogous in that it, too, represents the experiences, ideas, and wisdom of many poʻe naʻauao, or thinking people—what we would call the naturalists, marine biologists, botanists, agriculturalists, and other specialists in old Hawaiʻi. The composers of the chant, in effect, synthesized the observations of Hawaiian "natural scientists" into a remarkable master-piece. In the words of Adolph Bastian, the German ethnographer who was the first to tell the Western world about *The Kumulipo*, it is "one of the most beautifully expressed [works] on earth."

We shall proceed by discussing each of the seven general points covered in *The Kumulipo* to see how they compare with ideas in Darwinian and other scientific traditions. Also, we shall relate as much of our discussion as possible to Hawai'i's natural environment, as it *might* have existed in precontact times. In the end, we should have a cinemascopic picture of how the Hawaiian naturalist viewed the world around him.

Slime

Life on earth, according to *The Kumulipo*, was formed out of a watery slime, walewale. Since Hawaiians lived on islands surrounded by warm marine currents rich in shore life and deep-sea creatures, and in the accompanying slime, what more natural idea could they have found? In fact, this idea has occurred to thinkers in other ancient cultures, such as those of Babylonia, Mesopotamia, and Greece. For example, Thales, one of the early natural philosophers in Ionian Greece, theorized that life originated out of "mother ocean." A fellow Ionian, Anaximenes, a few years later introduced the idea of "primordial terrestrial slime, a mixture of earth and water." As in the plots of some of today's popular science fiction television plays, the idea recurs again and again in the evolution of science. Lorenzo Oken, the German naturalist, stated his famous "Ur-Schleim" doctrine at about the turn of the nineteenth century. "Every organic thing has arisen out of slime, and is nothing but slime in different forms. This primitive slime originated in the sea, from inorganic matter. . . . The origin of life occurred upon the shores, where water, air, and earth were joined" (Osborn 1913).

Compare *The Kumulipo*'s slime with the "primordial ooze" or "primeval soup" theory which currently is the most widely accepted matrix for the generation of life. The theory is that a shallow sea covered large parts of the earth about four billion years ago. Its waters were sterile, lifeless. Violent storms lash the planet with almost ceaseless flashes of lightning. In each electrical discharge, gases in the atmosphere—methane, ammonia, water, and hydrogen—are fused to form strange new combinations of atoms that join to make new molecules, known to us as amino acids and nucleotides. These molecules are the building blocks of living matter. Gradually, the amino acids and nucleotides are stirred into the shallow seas, thereby "creating a rich soup of organic matter, like a chicken broth but more concentrated" (Hoyle). In this broth the molecules endlessly collide and join, and, in the course of a billion years or so, all sizes and shapes of molecules are created by those random collisions. Eventually, a molecule is formed that has the magical ability to produce copies of itself. Enough of these are formed, in the course of time, so that they dominate the population of molecules in the waters of the earth. Today the major descendent of these self-reproducing molecules is the double-strand helix of nucleotides that we call DNA.

Spontaneous Generation

The naturalistic explanation found in *The Kumulipo* for the origin of life on earth does not directly credit the intervention of a supernatural agency, thus suggesting that life originated spontaneously. Most of us are familiar with this notion of spontaneous generation which dominated much of the world's thinking for many centuries. There are two sides to this argument, however, one called "abiogenesis," the origin of life from nonliving matter, and the other "biogenesis," the origin of life from preexistent living matter. In brief, abiogenesis allows for a number of naive beliefs, such as the appearance of maggots in decaying meat. Eventually those maggots become flies. In other words, out of dead meat will come crawling worms and flying insects. At least, that is what Aristotle, one of the smartest men in the world of his time, thought. From such kinds of observations he proposed that fireflies emerged from morning dew, and that many types of small animals arose from the mud at the bottoms of streams and ponds by the same process. This theory was accepted almost without dissent by all learned people in the Western world, including Sir Isaac Newton and René Descartes, the French philosopher and mathematician, until the end of the seventeenth century, when it met its first serious challenge. Not until a hundred years later was the theory finally disproved by Louis Pasteur, who demonstrated that microorganisms which grew in certain substrates—and in pieces of meat—came from parent microorganisms that happened to be in the air, and were not spontaneously engendered from the air itself. Yet, curiously enough, proving again that old ideas die hard, in the "primeval soup" theory the formation of the original DNA molecule itself must have been an act of spontaneous generation!

This question of the origin of life still puzzles scientists of the present, as it must have worried Hawaiian thinkers of old. When you think about it, you have only two choices: *either* life was caused to come into being by some supernatural power which exists outside the realm of scientific verification; *or* life evolved on earth spontaneously, through chemical reactions occurring in non-living matter lying at the surface of the planet. The first choice, by placing the origin of life beyond the reach of modern scientific inquiry, is a statement of faith in the supernatural First Cause that is not subject to the laws of science. The second choice also is an act of faith. The act of faith consists in assuming that the scientific view of the origin of life is the only correct view, without having concrete evidence to support that belief.

Parenthetically, we should remind ourselves that an act of faith is always an admission of one's limitations. In a world where science and its child technology have gained almost overwhelming supremacy over our lives, we overlook our limitations all too easily. With our scientific noses stuck up so high in the air, some of us tend to lose the humility with which Hawaiians of old always approached questions about ultimate meaning. Also, some of us have appropriated the arrogance of science to relegate traditional concepts to what we are pleased to call "the dustbin of superstition." But as we can see, if we but look, science has many a dustbin of its own.

In any case, *The Kumulipo* implies that there is a First Cause and that it activates the process of evolution—that life originated out of the life-giving slime. Having once been started, however, whether or not the process is directed in its unfolding by the same power is another question entirely.

Evolving Order of Species

The third point, which is central to the idea of evolution, is that living things evolve from the simple to the more complex in an order of progressive development. This lies at the heart of both *The Kumulipo*'s and modern science's concept of evolution. During the centuries scientists from many disciplines and nations have combined to develop an ascending ordering of species that is widely accepted as the way in which living things have evolved. Let us see how closely *The Kumulipo*'s ordering of species matches that of modern classifications.

Evolution did not begin with a microscopic single-celled organism because of course no Hawaiian could have known about such a thing. Neither did the Greeks, Chinese, Arabs, or any other peoples before the seventeenth century. Mankind's knowledge of cells as such came only after the invention of the microscope in about 1590. Not until the mid-1800s, after the study of tissues and their component cells had been developed, was the cell theory advanced by a German naturalist.

Instead, the early Hawaiians started their ordering of species with the least advanced of the multicellular organisms that they knew about, the coral polyps. (So did Aristotle, although he wrongly thought they were plants.) *The Kumulipo* introduces the ordering of created forms in this way: "*Hānau ka ʻUku koʻakoʻa*," or "Born [was] the coral polyp." The ʻuku koʻakoʻa is a member of the coelenterates, a group of simple animals which includes jellyfish and freshwater hydra. The classification of animal species in modern evolutionary theory also begins with the coelenterates. How did the Hawaiian naturalist of old know that?

Obviously he was very much aware of the coral reefs that ringed parts of Kauaʻi, Oʻahu, Maui, Molokaʻi, and Lānaʻi, and the subtidal reefs as well, such as those off the Kona coast of the Big Island. Hawaiians developed a good knowledge of the reef-building corals because they formed the major part of the natural habitat for a rich diversity of marine life, from sea urchins and limu, or seaweeds, to fishes and lobsters. All of these creatures (and more) provided an important part of the Hawaiian's diet. He could see hundreds of different species of marine animals, among them a great variety of coelenterates, all of which are alike in that they resemble the polyp. The term polyp means many feet, because of the many tiny tentacles which surround the mouth. One species of coelenterate has as many as six hundred of those tentacles! He also knew that corals excrete skeletons (some of which are primarily calcium carbonate, or limestone) and that these, in enormous numbers, eventually build reefs. In studying coral behavior, he observed one of its most important characteristics: the ability to form colonies consisting of many polyps that divide again and again into millions and billions of other polyp colonies. He probably knew about the close relationship between algae and corals, and that because algae need sunlight to grow, the paired partners are found in warm shallow waters. These are the reef-building corals, the fastest-growing kinds, extending as much as one to two inches a year. He was aware that wave action had a lot to do with where different kinds of corals will grow, because he could tell that easily enough from the patterns of distribution revealed by certain distinctive colors and shapes. He knew about the zoanthids, clusters of anemonelike organisms, whose polyps have tentacles which excrete poisonous toxins. One was called limu make o Hāna, deadly seaweed of Hāna. Spear tips were said to be dipped in its poison, so that even a slight wound caused by the spear could be fatal. He was also attracted to the beauty of the "coral gardens" in shallow island bays, such as those at Kāneʻohe, Hanauma, and Kealakekua.

Annelids, or Koʻe (Worms)

In the modern classification of species, the worms follow after the coelenterates. The Kumulipo, too, tells us this fact: "Hānau ke Koʻeʻenuhe ʻeli hoʻopuʻu honua," "Born [was] the burrowing worm, hilling the soil." The compound koʻeʻenuhe, according to Johnson (1981), implies a segmented worm because ʻenuhe means caterpillar. How did the Hawaiian naturalist determine that the worms should follow the coral polyps? How else except through careful and repeated observations and common-sense judgments. Being excellent agriculturalists, the Hawaiians knew that the "burrowing worm, hilling the soil" was an important contributor to fertility in soil. The earthworm spends its entire life eating nature's waste materials, passing them through its intestines, and depositing in the soil rich dark, plant-sustaining humus. Aristotle called earthworms the "intestines of the earth." Darwin wrote, in his Formulation of Vegetable Mould by Action of Earthworms, "Every square inch of topsoil on every continent, island, and archipelago on the entire planet has passed through the intestines of earth-worms." Although the farmers of old may not have known that the deposits produced by worms are three times richer in phosphates, nitrates, and potash than are today's factory-made fertilizers, they must have appreciated the role of the koʻe.

Echinoderms, or Sea Urchins, Sea Cucumbers, Starfish

Our *Kumulipo* evolutionist surveyed the animal and plant king-doms and decided that his next group of creatures should include peʻa, or starfish, weli, or sea cucumber, ʻina, or spiked sea urchin, hāwaʻe, or "smooth-spined" sea urchin, and the hāʻukeʻuke, or "unspiked" sea urchin. (The hāwaʻe is also known as the "collec-tor" urchin, because of its habit of collecting debris on its top.) This group is like no other association of marine invertebrates.

About sixty species of peʻa are known, most of which live in off-shore waters and hence are seldom seen. They have a peculiar abil-ity to regenerate any parts of their arms that may break off. They did not give Hawaiians anything of worth, although apparently islanders did see in starfish an important "geometric abstraction" or symbol.

The Hawaiian naturalist also recognized many types of weli, sea cucumbers (also called loli), in an array of colors. Like the starfish, they too could regenerate parts of their bodies, such as the digestive tract, which they can evert when the creature is molested. They too have segmented bodies, like worms (which is why they are often mistakenly called "sea worms").

As for sea urchins, of which at least twenty species are found in shallow waters, the Hawaiian taxonomist apparently divided the group into several categories. Wana was the name he gave the venemous creatures that have two kinds of spines—the long, hol-low primaries, and the shorter, finer, venom-tipped secondaries. He also recognized the ʻina, smaller species of which there are two kinds, both of which have the ability to make homes for them-selves by boring into the hard surface of rocks with their spines. The ʻina was considered a delicacy because of the sauce made from it, kai ʻina, prepared by pounding its meat with salt and water. Wana and hāʻukeʻuke were prized for their eggs, and the spines of the latter were used as a medicine.

The Barnacle Out of Place?

In *The Kumulipo*'s ordering of creatures, the barnacle or pīʻoe
comes next, followed by the many mollusks. However, the taxonomist seems to have intended the barnacle to be part of the mollusk group, since it behaves or looks like the bivalves (such as oysters and clams) which too are mollusks. But in the modern order,
the barnacle is classified along with crabs and shrimps. This may
be a case of an "honest difference of opinion." As a matter of fact,
even modern taxonomists do not all agree on the place for every
species or larger group. In any event, this minor deviation is the
exception that demonstrates how otherwise *The Kumulipo*'s order
of species was consistent with its modern counterpart.

Mollusks

The modern classification and *The Kumulipo*'s match again with
the mollusks. Included in this category are snails (of both land and
sea), slugs, clams, oysters, chitons, mussels, ʻopihi (limpets), heʻe
(octopuses), and many others. The mollusks represent a further
evolutionary advance over the animals we've discussed so far
because of their more highly developed internal organs. The development of external shells also provides greater protection to the
soft creatures within and makes possible more efficient muscles,
since the shells offer firm attachment points for those muscles. The
shells also can grow to bigger sizes, as is shown in the case of the
giant clams. On the other hand, the shell also created some disad-
vantages in limiting mobility and blocking off an animal's view of
its environment. Even so, the Hawaiian naturalist saw the mollusk
—with its unsegmented body, its one muscular foot for locomotion, along with a distinct head end with eyes and sensory tentacles—as an advancement over coral polyps, earthworms, and sea
urchins.

   For naturalists (and shell collectors) Hawaiʻi was a veritable
"horn of plenty," with no less than fifteen hundred species of
marine mollusks as well as several hundred species found on land.
How many of these the Hawaiian observer was able to classify we
cannot say, but without question he knew a great deal about them
because mollusks were of significant economic and technological
value to Hawaiians of old. Shells or parts of shells were used as

tools: 'opihi shells and the notched edges of large leho, or cowries, as scrapers for breadfruit and taro; the elongated, tapered "auger shells" as stoppers for ipu or gourds; the central column, or axis, of shells with long pointed spires, as drills; pearl shell for fishhooks on Oʻahu and Kauaʻi, and for lures. The giant triton shells were used as trumpets, called pū. Shells were also used as ornaments, strung as leis, anklets, bracelets, and pendants. Shells such as the pūpū peʻelua, or caterpillar shell, were used in the māwaewae ceremonies for firstborn children.

Many mollusks were eaten: 'opihi, 'ōlepe (bivalves), heʻe, both the heʻe mali, or day squid, and heʻe pūloa, or night squid, pipipi, or the black neritas. Needless to say, Hawaiians of old ate a great deal more mollusk foods than do modern Hawaiians. In 1901, for instance, seventy-five thousand pounds, or 2 percent of the "catch" sold in the Hawaiʻi fishmarkets, was composed of mollusks. By 1975 the amount had declined to fourteen thousand pounds annually, and probably is much less today. The comparison underscores the point that to the Hawaiians of ancient times, mollusks and other marine organisms of the group were very important sources of food. Therefore the people learned as much about them as possible, just as people of modern Hawaiʻi have studied sugarcane, pineapple, and other important products because of their economic value.

In evolutionary terms, the largest group of mollusks, such as the 'opihi, leho, pipipi, wī, and kīkī snails, among others that are named in *The Kumulipo*, are significant inclusions in that chant because they represent the transition from creatures that lived in the ocean to those that lived in fresh water and on land. As transitional species, they are adapted for existence in both water and air. They also have a much larger muscular capacity, by means of which they creep about or swim. Most of the species that live submerged in water breathe by means of gills, while terrestrial forms are provided with primitive lungs.

To the keen naturalists who composed *The Kumulipo*, the progressive evolution of organisms from water forms to land creatures was completed in the mountain snails, or pūpū kuahiwi. These were almost unavoidable because of their great numbers and variety. Probably a thousand different species of land snails lived in Hawaiʻi in pre-Cook times, which modern naturalists estimate descended from about twenty-five different ancestors.

Hawai'i's land shell fauna has been described as "one of the most distinctive in the world" (Hart), partly because of its enormous diversity. Geographic isolation, lack of competition or predators, and year-round breeding fostered intense evolutionary change among Hawai'i's land shells at about twice the rate of continental shells. (About twenty thousand species are distributed throughout the world.) So diverse are Hawai'i's shells that distinctive colonies of them may be confined to localities measured not in square miles but in square yards. One species, for example, may be found only in one clump of trees or ferns, in only one spot, and nowhere else.

We do not know what value the land mollusks had for Hawaiians of old, but, interestingly enough, apparently they believed that the land snails could sing. The pūpū kani oe received its Hawaiian name because of this talent, although modern-day skeptics suggest that the "singing" probably was made by chirping crickets nearby, or by the sounds of many shells on a tree trunk scraping against the wood. In any event, the Hawaiian naturalist did identify a number of species, and may well have appreciated them as examples of evolution at work.

Born Were the Plants

Plants put in a rather sudden appearance in The Kumulipo's story, at about the end of the emergence of the mollusks. Whatever the organizational or compositional reasons may have been for the chant's composers to have introduced plants at that point, according to modern evolutionary chronology they come a little late (as we note below). However, the notice of plants does begin with seaweeds, a point of departure which is perfectly logical and thoroughly consistent with The Kumulipo's theory that life originated in the sea.

As a matter of fact, seaweeds are supposed to be the oldest plants in the world, comparable in age to the simpler invertebrates. Scientists are fairly certain that algae were present and presumably widespread more than 700 million years ago. Abundant fossil remains of algae have been dated from between 420 and 700 million years ago. Of course, the Hawaiians had no way of carbon dating anything, but they had the common sense, and perhaps the insight, to believe that seaweeds appeared early in the evolution of the plant kingdom.

Marine algae are divided into groups of ascending complexity starting with the blue-greens, the simplest species, then the greens, browns, and reds, the colors denoting their usual pigmentation. *The Kumulipo* presents thirteen pairings of seaweeds and land-based plants. The first pairing includes ʻēkaha, a red alga, which is among the most advanced and also the most abundant of all seaweeds. (Approximately four thousand species of relatives grow in places around the world, of which at least sixty-one are found in Hawaiʻi.) The second pairing involves another red alga, ʻakiʻaki. The third, ʻaʻalaʻula, is a green alga, the fourth, manauea, is another red, and so on. More than half of the seaweeds mentioned are red algae, probably because they are plentiful around the islands.

While all the seaweeds are, of course, relatively simple organisms, the land-based plants that are paired with them come from a variety of classes and, therefore, differ in their evolutionary complexity. For example, these plants include the bird's-nest fern, a shore grass, a flowering plant, taro, sugarcane, the līpuʻupuʻu moss, and several others. But, we must point out, apparently no effort is made in *The Kumulipo* to present the land-based plants in an evolutionary order. The ʻēkahakaha, or bird's-nest fern, which appears in the first pairing along with ʻēkaha, a red alga, is a much more complex plant than is the moss which is placed in the eighth pairing. Another example is that of the manauea taro in the fourth pairing, and the "jointed sugarcane" in the fifth pairing. Botanically, the sugarcane is a simpler kind of flowering plant than is the complex taro. In short, in evolutionary terms, only the seaweeds are placed consistently, while the land plants are mentioned according to other criteria.

Thus, in comparison with the orderliness of the plant and animal relationships presented earlier, *The Kumulipo* naturalists presented us with an account that is quite incomplete in the later part of the chant. Does this reflect simply a lack of botanical knowledge? Or does it suggest that the poet-philosophers involved in its composition were more interested in zoology than in botany? Or was it just a matter of the precedence of poetic form, that is, preferring names with similar sounds in the sea-land dualism, rather than "scientific" accuracy? More than likely they stressed the magical properties in sounds, and the similarities in shapes, because, as we said at the outset, *The Kumulipo* is first and foremost a genealogical chant, and not a naturalist's exposition of the world around him.

This emphasis upon word magic and the similarities of forms was practiced by poets in other societies, too, even in Europe. In this Hawaiians cannot be accused of ignorance. Certainly they did not lack knowledge of plants: They were regarded as some of the best planters and botanists among Polynesians and others in the Pacific. They must have had as much understanding, if not more, about plants as they did about animals, since their society was an agricultural one. In his Hawaiian dictionary, Lorrin Andrews pointed out that Hawaiians had "names for every species of plant on the mountain" as well as "fish in the sea." The ethnologist John Stokes stated more than half a century ago that "the early Hawaiian biological nomenclature was very profuse and apparently exact as to variety." And Handy demonstrated that Hawaiians classified hundreds of varieties of several different food plants, such as bananas and taroes.

We can easily see why they placed so much importance on knowing as much as they could about seaweeds. The many kinds of edible limu were a major part of their diet, very much like substitutes for vegetables. Probably they were far more important to commoners, especially to women, than to ali'i, who were supplied with so many other foods. Many varieties of seaweeds were used for treating illnesses ranging from skin problems to asthma and constipation. And, with our modern perceptions, we can understand why seaweeds contributed valuable minerals, vitamins, and roughage to the diet. Again, utility was a prime reason for knowing these important organisms in the world about them.

The Vertebrates

In our evolutionary saga so far, we have been marching mainly to the soft pulsings of the invertebrates—organisms that developed internal organs, feet of a sort for locomotion, unblinking eyes, and no ears, internal skeletal features, feathery food strainers, and other primitive physiological or sensory characteristics. But as they developed, a much more complex group of creatures evolved, which possessed a new and amazing kind of structure: a segmented backbone with vertebrae. So important is this development in evolution that modern zoologists divide the huge animal kingdom into two major categories: the vertebrates and the invertebrates.

The Kumulipo's composers may not have known about this classification, but they must have reached a similar conclusion because until this point in their poem all the animals previously mentioned are invertebrates. After this point they are vertebrates —except for the few insects that are noted.

Margaret Titcomb stated in her book *Native Use of Fish in Hawai'i,* "In my opinion, no people ever lived who had a more intimate knowledge of fish and their habits . . . as Hawaiians." They probably knew the sea and marine life as well as they knew the land and its plant and animal life. Indeed, the likelihood that they saw the land and sea as a single continuum is suggested by their concept of the ahupua'a, the great land division extending all the way from the top of a valley to the beach area just within the reef—or to some more distant point in places without a reef.

This knowledge reflected the great economic importance that Hawaiians of old gave to fishes and other marine products. For one thing, a considerable amount of their food came from fish, especially their proteins, inasmuch as the quantity and availability of meats from land animals were limited. The fishing "industry" occupied a major segment of the labor force and therefore consumed a great deal of human and other resources. The cost of the technology of making and maintaining fishing canoes, large nets, and hooks, getting bait, and other requirements must have been as great, if not greater, than that needed by any other industry. Plainly the Hawaiians had a compelling set of reasons to learn as much as they could about fishes.

They must have identified a great number of the several hundred species found in local waters. (Scientists estimate about 700 species today, of which only a small percentage have been intentionally introduced.) If they ate anything edible from the sea, as Titcomb maintained, that something probably had a name. We have extensive lists of Hawaiian fish names based on different sources. *The Kumulipo* mentions about fifty. Malo provided a list of about 113 names, along with a crude classification. Our guess is that, because he was not a fishing expert, his classification does not represent what the Hawaiian taxonomists of old really knew. They probably had a much more sophisticated system, as is indicated by the fact that they classified fishes according to both groups and individual species. For example, the humuhumu, or triggerfishes, comprised a "family" which consisted of nine species, such as humuhumu'ele'ele (black), humuhumunukunukuapuaʻa (nose like a pig), and seven others. This identification is almost exactly the same as that presented in Gosline and Brock's authoritative *Handbook of Hawaiian Fishes*, published in 1960. (The two described fishes belonging to 139 families found in Hawaiian waters.)

The Hawaiian naturalist in the days of old knew the anatomical parts of a fish; its successive stages of growth; its eating habits (e.g., that the kala, kole, and mullet were plant feeders, and the ulua and shark were animal feeders); spawning and reproductive cycles; habitats (whether inshore with sandy bottoms, or in the reef structure, or outside the reef in deeper waters, etc.); the effects of wave action on fish distribution; and so on. We cannot doubt that the early Hawaiians had an immense knowledge and understanding of fishes. And we can conclude that *The Kumulipo* reveals only very little of that fund of information.

Insects

In *The Kumulipo* insects appear a bit later in the modern evolutionary ladder, after the worms, and just before the birds which, in turn, are followed by reptiles and mammals. This category of birds-reptiles-mammals deviates from the generally accepted order today, which places amphibians first, followed by reptiles and then the birds. The explanation for this departure between *The Kumulipo* and the modern arrangement is simple: since no reptiles were here, other than the gecko and turtles, the Hawaiians placed the birds next to the animals they seemed most to resemble. The insects answered the purpose because they were really the first mobile land animals, managing to become so by learning how to swim through air instead of through water. In order to fly, they developed filmy wings, much like tiny fins in appearance.

Throughout the world, insects dominate the animal kingdom in terms of sheer numbers of species and of individuals. More different species of insects can be found than of all other animals put together. In Hawaiʻi alone, entomologists estimate about ten thousand species, including the creatures we call beetles, flies, wasps, bees, grasshoppers, crickets, and many others. Of this number, 98 percent are endemic to Hawaiʻi, being found nowhere else in the world. (This fact will undoubtedly shatter the illusions of many local people, who prefer to believe that primal Hawaiʻi was free of insects and pests, all of which were introduced only after 1778.)

For Hawaiians of old to develop a practical knowledge of these insects must have been a formidable challenge, to say the least. Whether those insects were thought to be useful or harmful, knowledge of their kinds was indispensable. In general, the mea kolo, the "creeping things," were regarded as harmful. Interestingly, Hawaiians had a general name, mū, for all destructive insects, such as those that eat wood, tapa, plants, and so forth, but no generic equivalent for useful insects.

Of the thousands of species to choose from, the composers of *The Kumulipo* mentioned only a few, namely, the wood borer, caterpillar, moth, ant, and dragonfly. This combination does not make much sense, from the scientists' point of view. Huhu refers to wood-boring insects in general, rather than to a single species. Perhaps they were mentioned because the most notable wood-boring species are beetles, the most abundant group of insects in Hawai'i. The dragonfly may have been included because it is a most obvious insect, and also among the largest and most impressive. Moreover, it is seen all the way from sea level to mountaintops. Also curious is the connecting of the caterpillar with the moth, or pulelehua (which also connotes butterfly). In terms of total numbers, moths rank fourth in our species census. The significance of the ant can only be imagined. In any event, because the chant is a metaphorical device celebrating the birth of a newborn chief, the reasons behind the choice of insects mentioned must have grown more from genealogical or mythological significance than from scientific observation.

In any case, the creators of *The Kumulipo* would have appreciated the statements of Elwood C. Zimmerman, editor of the massive thirteen-volume series *Insects of Hawaii* (1948).

The more one studies the Hawaiian biota the more one becomes astonished at the adaptive flexibility of organisms and what may develop given time and opportunity. Many organisms have strong adaptive potential and require only time and opportunity to release it. A better place for such release can hardly be imagined than Hawai'i.

The Hawaiian Islands constitute a wonderful natural laboratory where we may observe many evolutionary phenomena in active process in the early stages of operation and often in simplified and clearly defined form uncluttered by many of the masking effects that may be present in continental environments.

Birds

The majority of Hawai'i's very distinctive species of birds came from one ancestral species that arrived here in the remote past. That ancestral parentage gave rise, in the course of time, to twenty-two species and twenty-four subspecies. The manner in which these developed demonstrates better than does any other bird family in the world the processes of adaptability and evolution.

In his pioneering volume, *Birds of the Hawaiian Islands* (1902), Henry W. Henshaw stated, "The impression seems to be general that in olden times the natives were extensively acquainted with Hawaiian birds, which is true." Hawaiians had identified and classified their birds, he wrote, although "according to modern ideas, their classification was decidedly crude." As evidence for this opinion, he explained that the Hawaiian name for a bird tended to imitate its note or cry, for "by means of the proper accent and pitch" such names as 'io, 'ua'u, and 'elepaio "may be made to give an almost exact idea of the bird's call." Also, Hawaiians seemed to have had several different names for the same species, such as the 'i'iwi.

In any event, birds were of great importance to Hawaiians of old as sources of food, feathers for ornamentation or payment of taxes, as aids in navigation, and as omens. The feathers of the mamo, 'ō'ō, and 'i'iwi were used in making the gorgeous royal cloaks. These and other kinds of feathers were paid to the kono-hiki, land managers, as acceptable taxes. A professional class of bird snarers emerged, as part of the feather-working "industry." Since feather cloaks were worn only by ali'i, the birds supplying those beautiful ornaments were identified with royalty. Feathers from the 'ō'ō and mamo were the "most economically valuable property to be owned in ancient Hawai'i." Finally, birds also served as agents for insect control.

The Kumulipo lists thirty-five actual species and two mythological birds. As in listings of other animals, some of the most useful birds are automatically included. Among these are the mamo, 'ō'ō, 'i'iwi, and the 'elepaio. In some instances, two different kinds of birds are paired. The reasons for some of these pairings are not difficult to find. For example, the kōlea, or plover, and the wandering tatler, or 'ūlili, are paired because they are migratory. Most of the 'ūlili fly away in May or June to nest in some distant place and return later in the year to Hawai'i. In Hawaiian mythology, the kōlea and 'ūlili, as also the koa'e, or tropic bird, and the 'akekeke, or ruddy turnstone, served as messengers for the ali'i akua, or god-chiefs.

The two mythical birds that are mentioned in *The Kumulipo* are called halulu and kīwa'a. The latter is said to be the pilot bird, which guides a navigator to the canoe shed at his landing place. Hence *The Kumulipo*'s reference to "Kīwa'a, the bird that cries over the canoe house."

We should also note that the chant's composers knew a great deal about the distribution of the birds among the different islands. Several of the birds listed are found only on certain islands (such as the 'io , or hawk, usually confined to Hawai'i island) or in specific districts.

Missing Amphibians

Amphibians, such as frogs, toads, newts, and salamanders, are not mentioned in *The Kumulipo*, despite Beckwith's (1951) statement that the fourth chant is about the "birth of amphibious creatures." We can understand why she said that after reading these lines:

> The sea creeps up to the land
> Creeps backward, creeps forward
> Producing the family of crawlers
> Crawling behind, crawling in front

But she was not a naturalist. And a naturalist who knew the islands' fauna would not have been confused. The crawlers, we know now, are not amphibians but reptiles.

No amphibians are mentioned in the chant because no amphibians were present in Hawai'i before 1778. As a matter of fact, no amphibians had reached any of the islands in Polynesia. Zoologists James A. Oliver and Charles E. Shaw explained why. "Amphibians, because of their naked skins and sensitivity to desiccation (dehydration), are characteristically absent from oceanic islands." Obviously, *The Kumulipo*'s composers could not have found a place in their chant for creatures they did not know. (This fact should help to dissuade detractors and skeptics who suspect that *The Kumulipo* is a latter-day invention by King Kalākaua and his companions. If they really had intended to create a hoax by following the contemporary ordering of species, they would have included amphibians in the poem.)

Today everyone knows that frogs and toads have come to Hawai'i. Eight species, to be exact, are here, but all have been introduced since 1855, when the Royal Hawaiian Agricultural Society decided that the islands needed frogs and toads. Some were brought from California and Japan. The Hawaiian word for either frog or toad is poloka, which is the island way of saying frog.

"Crawlers" (Reptiles)

Because Hawai'i has no native snakes, most people think that no reptiles live here. But the world's six thousand species of reptiles include crocodiles (and alligators), tuatara, tortoises, turtles, and lizards. Thus, Hawai'i does have a small reptilian population that today consists of a tiny, harmless land snake (accidentally imported in soil from the Philippines) as well as an occasional marine snake (that swims in from Southeast Asia), at least four species of turtles, thirteen species of lizards, including the chameleon, and an occasional alien victim released by feckless smugglers, such as the famous cayman found in Nu'uanu Reservoir in 1983. But except for three species of sea turtles and some of the lizards, all the other reptiles have been introduced into the islands since 1778.

Of reptiles in Hawai'i *The Kumulipo* mentioned only honu, or turtles, and mo'o, or geckos. Turtles, obviously, managed to get here without any help from man, but the geckos probably had been brought in aboard Polynesian settlers' canoes. Indeed, the gecko is so ubiquitous in Polynesia that voyagers embarking from homelands in Kahiki could not have avoided including both adult lizards and their eggs among provisions stocked aboard canoes. Those lizards have arrived so recently, however, that not enough time has passed for them to have developed descendents indigenous to Hawai'i.

The intriguing question about *The Kumulipo*'s mention of turtles and geckos asks why these two animals, which look so different, should have been associated so definitely. To be sure, both crawl on land. But so do crabs, yet they are not mentioned in the chant. The key to this little mystery is found in the chant's reference to "those who produce eggs." Both turtles and geckos produce eggs, but, like all reptiles, whether they lay eggs or bear their young alive, they reproduce only on land. Most amphibians and all fishes lay their eggs in water. In evolutionary terms, this capacity to lay eggs that could be hatched on land gave reptiles the means to colonize land. As Isaac Asimov explained: "The land-based egg had to be enclosed by a shell which was porous to gases so that the developing embryo could breathe but which would retain water so that the embryo would not die through drought. The egg had to be large enough to contain the food and water needed by the embryo through a period of development long enough to enable it to reach the point of independent life on dry land." Observant Hawaiians noticed that both turtles and geckos lay their eggs on solid earth.

The gecko is the most familiar of all lizards in warm or hot countries. Some species have adapted very well to living in association with people in their dwellings. Its "friendliness" may account in part for its popularity in Hawaiian and other mythologies. It is described accurately in *The Kumulipo* as having a "sleek skin." This characteristic is due to the fact that the scales along its back are very small, and the skin is soft and thin. The species in Hawai'i belongs to the group known as "Gekkonidae." Most of these are relatively small, but the largest can be a stoutly built creature growing to about a foot in length. Called the tokay, it is native to Southeast Asia.

Therefore, we must approach with the usual grain of salt Kamakau's claim that the mo'o had "extremely long and terrifying bodies" as much as thirty feet in length, black in color, that lay in water. He described these monsters in his *Ka Po'e Kahiko* (1964). One in particular, called mokuhinia, had appeared in several places on Maui in the early 1800s, before "hundreds and thousands of people." Of course, he was not telling about a real gecko, but about what the Maori call a taniwha, or what the residents around Loch Ness in Scotland call "Nessie"—a thing that, for want of factual evidence, seems to be a creature of the imagination.

Evidently the composers of *The Kumulipo* did not see fit to include this "greatest" of Hawaiian reptiles in their epic about evolution, but we know that giant, frightful lizards, or other dragonlike creatures, do appear in the myths of many cultures throughout the world.

Pigs, Rats, Dogs

Finally we come to the end of *The Kumulipo*'s remarkable scheme. It has taken us almost step by step along the course of evolution, beginning with the simplest of invertebrates, through a series of progressively advancing species of vertebrates, all the way to the most highly evolved creatures other than man. In this most developed group of animals are the "night digger" (the pig, or pua'a), the "nibbler" (the rat, or 'iole), and the dog ('īlio). To people who are not familiar with the fauna of old Hawai'i, this trio may not appear to be the pinnacle of natural evolution (leaving thinking man aside for the moment). After all, every schoolchild knows that, in diagrams depicting the "ascent of man," primates are placed nearest the top. But, of course, Hawaiians of old did not know about the existence of primates. The only land animals they knew (other than those lower ones we have already discussed) were the pig, the rat, the dog, for some on the island of Hawai'i the bat, and the chicken. (The chicken, of course, is not kin to mammals, a fact that must have been apparent to Hawaiians of old.) Naturally, then, those three familiar mammals were placed at the top of the animal kingdom.

While we know that all three—the pig, the rat, and the dog—are mammals, and therefore should be grouped together, we should realize that our knowledge is the product of a vast amount of scientific study conducted over many centuries by countless learned people. The fact that mammals share certain anatomical characteristics, such as a placenta, a skin more or less covered with hair, and mammary glands, became "obvious" only as a result of systematic observation and analysis over a long time. In the same way, the mammalian characteristics of the pig, the rat, and the dog became obvious to Hawaiians of old only after similar observations and common-sense reasoning over a long period of time.

But, more fundamental, is the question concerning the extent to which Hawaiian naturalists succeeded in explaining how these mammalian characteristics were actually an evolutionary advance over the characteristics shown by other vertebrates. For example, did they realize that a soft skin with a cover of hair was superior to scales or to shells? Or that the placenta was an advantage that favored the development of mammals over that of all other animals? Or that the presence of mammary glands made possible a time of extended child care and, hence, a kind of motherly love? We can't know exactly the answers to these questions, but somehow our Hawaiian thinkers must have reached such an understanding. Surely they did not rank these three animals at the top of the evolutionary tree for economic, mythological, or other purely nonanatomical or nonnaturalistic reasons. To have done so would have shown no logic at all.

We cannot question that these three animals, especially the pig and the dog, served important uses for Hawaiians of old. Both pigs and dogs were domesticated and eaten, although generally pigs were reserved for ali'i. Dogs' bones were used for making fishhooks and their teeth for necklaces and leg ornaments worn by male dancers (a pair of anklets required the four canine teeth from four hundred to five hundred dogs). Whole boar tusks or parts of them were used for bracelets and other ornamentation. Rats served as targets for boys and men shooting arrows from bows, but apparently had no other use. They were not eaten, as they were by Maoris in New Zealand. They did have some small part in mythology and, of course, the pig had ritual importance, if only as a sacrificial offering.

One slight question remains about the omission of the other known mammals, namely, the pe'a, bat, the koholā, whale, and the nai'a, porpoise. Probably the reason they were not considered is because both the porpoise and the whale were classified as i'a, fish, and the bat (to the few people who were aware of it) probably was considered to be a bird. In general, bats were of little use, and that was reason enough to ignore them. Neither the bat (found only near the volcano on Hawai'i) nor the whale (found only in the deep sea) was eaten. The porpoise may have been eaten by some people (fishermen said that its meat "smells worse than shark," [Titcomb]). The skeletons of whales, however, were reserved for the ali'i, who valued the great "ivory teeth" and the bones, which were shaped into ornaments and other marks of rank.

The Ascendancy of Man

The Kumulipo brings the story of evolution to its climax with the advent of Ao, or Light (literally, day), and the appearance of man in the "well-formed child" in the "time when men multiplied." Between dog and man no other animals are mentioned. Needless to say, no primates or humanoids complete the metamorphosis from relatively advanced vertebrates such as dogs to the erect and large-brained vertebrate that we call *Homo sapiens*, thinking man. To the composers of *The Kumulipo*, man represented a wholly new order of complexity not even hinted at by preceding developments. In fact, some contemporary theorists argue that, for any one species, evolution is best understood as a progression of "sudden leaps" rather than as a smooth sequence of gradual changes (Russell).

In sum, in terms we can apply to evolution and the relationships among living organisms, *The Kumulipo*'s basic premise is that living things appear to develop progressively, evolving from simple toward more complex species. This concept is in harmony with the most acceptable modern scientific thinking on evolution. While *The Kumulipo* only hints at Darwinian ideas of adaptability and natural selection, still it arrived at the same basic conclusions about a century before publication of *The Origin of Species* in 1859. It is also clear that *The Kumulipo*'s explanations of organisms and their relationships represents the distillation of a vast amount of empirical knowledge about nature, gained from systematic observation, practical experimentation, and the careful exercise of common sense. If this is the work of "scientific savages," then let us honor them. How many of us today are so observant about anything as they were about everything in their world?

Beyond the Scientific

The Kumulipo, as we have said, was never intended to be a scientific document. Whatever its content of science may be, that is incidental to its essential poetic purpose as a genealogical declaration of the sacred origins of the newborn chief. The story of biological evolution that we have presented ends with the ascendancy of man, but *The Kumulipo*'s real story, that of the evolution of the godlike chief, continues and goes beyond the scientific comparisons. In the symbolic language of the mele, it celebrates the reality of a species greater than mere ordinary man: the akua ali'i, the god-chief. In this sense, it is the story of the evolution not of a man as such, but of a potential "superman." It is another "leap," an intuitive or spiritual one, that reaffirms the Hawaiian's extraordinary faith in the human potential represented by his highest chiefs.

Whatever opinions we as modern Hawaiians may hold about evolution (or about the accompanying controversy of creationism), something must be said for *The Kumulipo*'s vision of what we might call the "transcendental evolution" of man. During the past twenty-five thousand years or so, man has changed little genetically, if at all. In contrast, psychologically and culturally man has evolved at a much faster pace. Indeed, the study of cultural evolution has become a busy academic field for research and analysis, while biological evolution receives little attention anymore. Thus, implicit in the notion of transcendental evolution is recognition of this spiritual evolution, because its basic premise maintains that man's nonbiological growth potential is limitless. This idea was supported by the Indian mystic Sri Aurobindo who spoke of evolution as "Divine Reality" expressing itself in even higher forms of existence leading to the "Supermind."

In effect, the Hawaiian view exalted the human capacity to develop to its highest state of perfectability. While *The Kumulipo* glorifies the potentials in the single royal child, the idea that these potentials dwell in every man runs deep in Hawaiian belief and ritual. It is most strongly sustained in the deification of chosen spirits who become 'aumākua. For what is deification but the ritualized acknowledging that one stage in the spiritual evolution of man has been transcended to attain another and higher stage? In short, the message in *The Kumulipo* tells us that, beyond the biological and physical limitations to our humanity lies an open universe of hope and opportunity for continued and unlimited spiritual evolution.

9

A TECHNOLOGICAL PERSPECTIVE

Technological Animal

Ever since Aristotle referred to man as a "political animal," others have applied variations of that label—such as "social," "economic," "agricultural," or, more recently, "technological animal." While the epithet may not always do justice to the animal kingdom, it does convey something about the nature of man. At least two schools of thought exist concerning man (and woman) as a technological animal. One might be called the "demonic" school, which emphasizes modern man's apparent obsession with technology, with machines in particular, and its dire consequences for the survival of the human race. The second school of thought takes a more Aristotelian view of man (and a more generous one) by granting him a natural instinct for a particular mode of behavior, in this instance the technological. In either case, in considering man's passion for technology, we are dealing with a very potent part of the human character. Indeed, the sources of some of our most basic values are technological influences which have roots deep in our ancient past.

Strangely enough, the Hawaiian of old is rarely considered with reference to technology. In fact, one seldom runs across the word or the idea in any of the literature dealing with precontact Hawai'i. This may be a matter of semantics, however, because a good deal of information is available about Hawaiian tools, artifacts, even techniques, and so on, or about what anthropologists and ethnographers call "material culture," which is the stuff of technology. But more than semantics is involved here. Rather, a point of view is lacking, perhaps, because the scholars who have studied and told us about our history were not specialists in the general field of technology, but thought only in terms of their own narrow disciplines, such as archaeology or anthropology. Thus, what we learn from them about our past is their opinions about archaeology or anthropology, but not about our technology. As a result, few Hawaiians, if any, really have an understanding of their ancestors' true technological development as a people. This explains in part why most Hawaiians today find it difficult to talk about ka po'e kahiko in technological terms. We are not only uninformed but, even worse, we do not believe that the people of old had developed a technological capacity.

In this age of dazzling and almost incredible technological achievements, we Hawaiians tend naturally to admire the people, skills, resources, and beliefs that make such triumphs possible. This is not to ignore the fact that other Hawaiians, who have joined the so-called antitechnological movement, maintain at best a love-hate relationship toward modern technology. But all Hawaiians today, whatever our degree of deference to the machine age may be, must gain a clearer comprehension of our ancestors' technological past. We need to do this not only to restore pride in the accomplishments of the old people, but also to determine how we should deal with the serious problems and value issues that grow out of contemporary technology. Our primal past can provide some guidance for today; indeed, many thoughtful authorities in other countries around the world who are wrestling with the problems of "runaway technology" have looked to their traditional cultures for inspiration and answers. So, while talking about the premodern Hawaiian technology may seem anachronistic, doing just that is timely and relevant.

Our discussion will cover a lot of territory, some familiar and some unknown, beginning with man's "toolmaking" instinct and its value implications; then with Hawaiian tools *and* machines; the impact of the social, economic, and natural environment on technical development before 1778; and some monumental constructions in Hawai'i as seen in terms of their engineering, logistical, and organizational feats. We will also inquire into technical specialization, the status of the technician, and some of his values. Since craftsmanship and aesthetics are nearly indistinguishable in primal cultures, we shall have something to say about these, too. Finally, we shall consider the readiness of Hawaiians to adopt and adapt new technologies, and the meaning this has had for the evolution of Hawaiian culture since 1778.

The Toolmaking Instinct

Among the skills that the human creature has developed to a high degree is the making of tools. Other animals may make use of tools on occasion, from the North American burrowing wasp, which uses a pebble as a hammer, to the southern sea otter, which breaks open shellfish on a stone anvil. But no animals invent, improvise, adapt, or manufacture tools. Experiments have been conducted in which a male chimpanzee was seen to fit a small bamboo cane into a larger one, so as to make a stick long enough to snare a bunch of bananas which could not be reached with either rod singly, but apes have never shown the ability to conceive of shaping an object to use for an imagined end. While an ape can do manually almost everything that a man can do, no ape has either the perceptual or conceptual capacity necessary for the regular manufacture of tools. Only man has the requisite ability for visual attention to a task, or for prolonged coordination of eye and hand, or the power of abstraction. And only man has an oral tradition through which he communicates with other men and reasons with them or with himself.

Tools have been described as "detachable additions to the body." They supplement mainly the functions of our hands, feet, and teeth. Primal man, who had few tools, must have been far more impressed with the usefulness of those few aids than modern man can ever be, surrounded as he is with whole armories of tools simple or complex. The idea that one's tools are but extensions of the body, and hence of the mind, may explain in part the ease with which Hawaiians endowed certain tools with mana, and the more general attitude of reverence that craftsmen and other technicians sometimes took toward their favorite tools or instruments. If we can carry the metaphor one step further, we might liken the entire human body to a grand instrument for the use of the human spirit or intelligence. This conclusion is suggested in the saying *"He hale ke kino no ka mana'o,"* or "The body is a house for thoughts."

By the word tool we refer, in a general way, to anything that is used or made as a means to accomplish some end. A tool, therefore, is an indicator of purposeful endeavor. When we speak of man's toolmaking instinct, we are talking about his innate sense of wanting to achieve something, however remote or insignificant that may be. Thorstein Veblen called this "the instinct of work-

manship," and man's "abiding penchant for making things useful."
To put it another way, man does not make a tool for nothing
(unless he is driven by the modern insanity of a Rube Goldberg for
inventing useless contraptions). This truism is so consistent with
the pragmatic outlook of Hawaiians that we cannot escape the
conclusion that technology for Hawaiians had, as for all men, a
teleological foundation—in other words, it must have had a purpose. We shall appreciate the relevance of this to contemporary
values when we consider the need to redefine the ends of modern
technological development.

The nature of toolmaking clearly implies the awareness of other
fundamental values for primal Hawaiians. One is efficiency, or the
performance of a task with a minimum expenditure of energy,
time, materials, or motion. Whether it is a stone adze, an awl, or a
weapon, every tool is marked by qualities that facilitate its fulfilling a designated purpose. Some tools, particularly new inventions,
may serve ends not originally conceived of, but even then they are
used for some end. Anyway, recognition of ends should lead to the
devising of means to achieve them in workmanlike efficiency. If
tools are intended to do things that the body cannot do as well,
then the difference between where the body ends and the tool
begins is the point at which the efficiency of the tool comes into
play. Perhaps when the Hawaiian of old first realized this fundamental fact he coined the word mākaukau, meaning efficiency.

Another human capacity with value that toolmaking presumes
is foresight, or being able to anticipate further needs or satisfac-
tions. Foresight is built into the purposeful nature of all technology, for in the very process of thinking about the making of a tool,
a man realizes that he has a purpose in using it for which he is
planning ahead. Both the using and the making of a tool involve
the notion of planning—which, by definition, means setting objectives and determining means to achieve them. Foresight and planning are most clearly evident before and during the invention of a
new tool. This is a topic which we shall explore further.

Purposefulness, efficiency, foresight, and planning are values
that automatically flow from the logic of toolmaking because it
tries to meet the most fundamental human need—survival. All primal tools and technical processes—including techniques as diverse
as those used in weaponry, housing, weaving, planting, and fire
making—are connected in some way or other with the preserva-

tion of man and society. Ultimately, primal or modern technology is a manifestation of our quintessential determination to survive as individuals first and, in consequence, as a species.

Technology, therefore, has its beginnings in our primordial past. We are reminded of this by Kenneth Oakley in the first volume of *A History of Technology*, a massive four-volume study published in 1954, in which he stated that technology "starts more than a half million years ago, as man is becoming man." In fact, the antiquity of technology precedes science, for "long before there was anything that we can recognize as self-conscious science," man had developed his technical or toolmaking skills to a high degree. Albert Neuburger emphasized the same point in *The Technical Arts and Sciences of the Ancients*, a work twenty years in the making: "In reality technical science has existed throughout the ages from the very beginnings of the human race. . . . We must rather regard [it] as an expression of the human mind, that has its roots in the nature of things and has from time immemorial been inspired by Man's very existence."

In sum, the development of ancient Hawaiian technology is the story of the Hawaiian's efforts to survive—physically, psychologically, socially, economically, and spiritually—by increasing the efficiency of his mind and body through the making and use of tools and of the things that those tools helped to make. Because values grow out of our most basic needs, technology acts as a conserver of some of our fundamental values and, as we shall see, as a transmitter and generator of new values.

The Neolithic Toolbox

If we use our broad definition of a tool as a means designed to accomplish some end, then the things we are about to look at are found in no ordinary toolbox. The tools that Hawaiians made or used range from the most characteristic of human inventions, all the way from language to adzes, and nearly everything in between —weapons, fishhooks, simple machines, chemical processes such as dyeing and food preservation, water distribution systems, measurements, sails, pump drills, and the most potent tools of all, rituals and incantations. However, we stop short of using the term in its widest sense, as is often done today in referring, for example, to the "tools of management," or of "social science," or of "government." Taking the broad view of technology should emphasize the fact that it is a far more pervasive force in human existence than ordinarily we think it is.

Rather than trying to inventory and describe all the items in our toolbox, something that has been done by Peter Buck, Kenneth Emory, and Donald Kilolani Mitchell among others, let us simply divide them into three general categories, using the terms of very recent technology: "Software," "Processes," and "Hardware" (see lists on page 248). These lists are by no means complete, and at first glance the toolbox may appear to modern Hawaiians as being somewhat empty. If so, that is not surprising because we automatically make comparisons with the pictures we have in mind of our own twentieth-century industrial, highly complex, space-age technology. For example, we are so accustomed to seeing modern tools in all their variety and number that we have difficulty in understanding why such "simple things" as the wheel or the axle were never developed by the Hawaiians of old. We have always taken these things for granted, as if they were natural artifacts that should be found among any reasonably intelligent people. We don't remember that primitive men lived for hundreds of thousands of years before someone somewhere invented the wheel. Nor do we remember what raw materials are needed for the making of even the simplest wooden wheel. Even today, with all the tools at our disposal, how many of us could make a wagon wheel? The kind of mental baggage we pack into our heads must be sorted out before we presume to judge our primal past.

We also need to keep in mind some important factors that determine technological development in any country. These are: (1) the kinds, quality, and availability of raw materials; (2) the environment; (3) geographic location; (4) the size of the population and its level of organization; (5) the socioeconomic and political systems; and (6) the value structure of the people. Let us then proceed to examine some of the aspects of what we might call our "technological matrix."

The term neolithic, scientists' jargon for New Stone Age, refers to the fact that the most important tools in old Hawai'i were made of stone. (Because these islands are volcanic in origin, the stones necessarily were different physicochemical forms of basalt.) These basic tools of stone included hammers, files, knives, pestles, mortars, bowls, dishes, salt pans, door thresholds and lintels, lamps,

Software	Processes	Hardware
Communications	Chemical: dyeing, pigments, fermentation, preservation	Transportation: canoes, carrying slings, poles
Mathematics		
Measurements: distance, quantity, speed, etc.	Botanical: plant breeding, pollination, fertilizing, cultivation, identification	Fishing: hooks, nets, traps, sinkers, floats, etc.
Rituals: incantations, prayers		Health: herbal medicines, surgical instruments
Mnemonic devices for memorizing	Culinary: boiling, steaming, broiling	Warfare: clubs, spears, daggers, slings
	Mechanical: pump drilling, sailing, grinding	Shelter: houses, walls, ridgeposts, thatch, doors, etc.
	Physiotherapy: lomi-lomi, steam bath	Household: mats, pillows, blankets, kitchen/eating utensils, lamps, etc.
	Psychotherapy: ho'oponopono, prayers	Clothing: kapa, feather cloaks, hats, sandals, raincoats, etc.
	Navigation	
	Weaving: basketry, rope making	Sports: sled, surfboard, 'ulumaika, etc.
	Textile: kapa	Music and hula: pahu, 'ulī'ulī, 'ūkēkē, etc.
	Animal husbandry: domestication	Cosmetics: combs, body oils, bath rubbers, stone mirrors
	Bleaching and washing	Construction: hammers, adzes, wedges, chisels, gouges, files, knives, drills, etc.

mirrors, kapa beaters, taro pounders, polishing and grinding stones, and adzes. Stone tools were used in every major technological activity, from warfare and house construction to games and making of kapa. The great usefulness of stone undoubtedly is one of the reasons why rocks appear so often in myths and sayings of old Hawai'i. And, as Malo said, "The ax [adze] was by the ancients reckoned an article of great value."

In these remote islands without any resources in metals, only basaltic rock, coral, and a few kinds of wood would have been available for makers of tools. Of these stone was obviously the most likely material, because it was hard, shapeable, and available. Hawaiian specialists recognized four varieties of rock suitable for adze making: they called these ho'okele, 'alā makahinu, pāhoa, and makai'a. Other rocks were used for different kinds of tools. Thus, sandstone, pumice, and coral were employed, and, as Malo wrote, "a stone that is cast down from heaven by lightning." Basaltic phonolite, the material best suited for adzes, was not found in many places, but quarries of it were developed on Hawai'i, O'ahu, Maui, Kaua'i, Moloka'i, and Kaho'olawe. The major quarry, and apparently the largest one in the Pacific, was near the top of Mauna Kea, where the evidence of many generations of adze makers who went there seeking stones suitable for their craft can still be seen today. It is located nearly twenty miles away from seacoast villages, more than thirteen thousand feet above sea level (where even summer nights can be bitterly cold, and where the summer's working season is very brief). Climbing that mountain in order to gather the necessary stone "blanks" for making proper adzes would have required well-planned expeditions. Such a mission could only have enhanced the value of the adzes and the islanders' opinion of the adze makers. Malo wrote that the "ax-makers were a greatly esteemed class in Hawai'i nei." They were protected by the god Kūpā'aike'e, after whom a sacred adze was named.

When modern Hawaiians see the designations Stone Age or neolithic applied to Hawaiian culture before Cook's visit, not a few of them feel a bit defensive, if not ashamed. Stone Age conjures up images of Cro-Magnon and Neanderthal Man, or of the Flintstones of comic strip fame, and stone tools are seen as crude and primitive. Neither of these snob's opinions is justified. As L. S. B. Leakey, whose work in Kenya on prehistoric man is well known, wrote of the stone toolmakers and tool users: "There are multitudes of stone implements the manufacture of which has involved technical skill of the very highest order. The attainment of that skill implies traditions extending over ages, and an accompanying high degree of inventive skill combined with endless patience." Malo anticipated Leakey when, writing about Hawaiian stone tools, he declared: "The art of making [them] was handed down from remote ages." Malo's comment suggests that the techniques were brought to Hawai'i with the first settlers. Furthermore, a great deal of study done on stoneworking techniques corroborates their complexity and efficiency. As Russ Apple reported on comparative experiments using a metal and stone adze: "The working edge of a stone adze may be thought of as wedge, while the working edge of a metal adze may be thought of as more like a knife. Penetration on each impact is far greater with a metal edge than with stone. The stone working edge, however, appears to be more durable and to require less maintenance than a metal edge. In several days of use, a stone edge may require sharpening and reshaping only once, compared with numerous sharpenings of a metal edge doing the same work in the same period."

In short, we should remember Leakey's opinion that the achievements of Stone Age toolmakers "must be accepted as fully comparable in their place, time and circumstance to those of the greatest modern inventors and engineers."

While stone was important, wood was used far more widely and abundantly in Hawai'i's material culture. It was easier to manipulate and more versatile than stone. As Kenneth Emory (1965b) reported, "The people turned to wood for nearly everything they used—their household utensils, their weapons, their canoes." And, we might add, trees and plants—and products derived from them—were used for house building, fire sticks, fuel, fishhooks, "knives," hula implements, sports equipment (such as hōlua sleds and surfboards), handles for adzes, dyes, kapa, cordage, nets and lines, mats, sails, embalming, medicines, and so on. Underlying this wide use of plant materials was the Hawaiians' extensive knowledge of trees in terms of their classification, habitat, growth, diseases, and care.

This superb knowledge of the materials that their environment provided Hawaiians is revealed in the quality of workmanship displayed, for example, in their bowls. According to Emory (1965b), "Nowhere else in Polynesia were there bowls equal in quality or in variety to the Hawaiian *'umeke.'* Also according to Emory, Hawaiian woodworkers were able to carve bowls as large as three feet in diameter and thirty inches in height without help from a turner's lathe and other modern tools. Such marvels attest to the high level of skill they attained.

Other materials out of which tools were made included bone and shell—and, rarely, even alien iron. When in 1778 Captain Cook made one of his first visits ashore, he reported seeing on Kaua'i a "piece of iron hoop about three inches long fitted into a wooden handle in the same manner as their stone adzes." Cook's officers also observed "pieces of iron formed into something like chisels," and of "iron wrought into small adzes in imitation of their own." Since no iron deposits exist in Hawai'i, these pieces of metal caused much speculation among the visiting Europeans about the origin of the iron in those Hawaiian tools. Some wondered whether the iron might have arrived aboard Spanish vessels either calling at the islands or wrecked on their shores. The probable explanation is that the iron came from wreckage, holding nails and fittings, that washed ashore on Hawai'i's beaches. The fortunate Hawaiians who found them fashioned the iron into tools in the same way they made their stone adzes. (But who, we can ask, taught those Hawaiians how to soften and cut and work those hard bits of metal that they called "hematite"?)

Thus, we might say, the first evidences of Western technology probably drifted to Hawai'i's shores before 1778. Quite likely this knowledge of the value of iron accounted for the eagerness with which Hawaiians bartered their few possessions for nails and other metal objects aboard the ships of Captain Cook's expedition.

Modern Hawaiians who are sensitive to the indiscriminate use of Stone Age as a label for ka po'e kahiko may point with pride to their achievements in navigation, astronomy, religion, sociopolitical organization, and in the ingenuity of the techniques they developed for making the best possible use of all the things they found in their island world. Including stones!

The Mechanical Hawaiian

When we talk about machines, we come closer to the kind of technology that the ordinary person thinks about. But what exactly is a machine? There's the rub, because thinking about it and defining it are two different things. When Franz Reuleaux, the nineteenth-century German engineer, wrote his classic *Kinematics of Machinery*, he quoted fifteen definitions for the word machine which were submitted to him by distinguished fellow professionals throughout Europe. No two were alike.

Webster's dictionary defines a machine as "any device consisting of two or more resistant, relatively constrained parts, which, by a certain predetermined intermotion, may serve to transmit and modify force and motion so as to produce some given effect or to do some desired kind of work." It also says that a machine can be "an instrument (as a lever) designed to transmit or modify the application of power, force or motion." Other definitions can be offered, but these two represent the extremes in the range from the more complex to the simpler mechanisms.

Conventional wisdom maintains that the Hawaiians of old did not have any machines at all. But anyone who understands machine technology knows that this statement cannot be true. To be sure, the people of old did not have any complex mechanical devices, but simple machines they did have. They used the lever, lōhai, the wedge, unu, and the inclined plane, ihona. These are half of the world's six basic machines: the pulley, wheel and axle, screw, lever, inclined plane, and wedge. The moving parts of all kinds of mechanical apparatus can be reduced to varying combinations of these simple machines. As complicated a mechanism as the gasoline-powered automobile may be, it is no more than a combination of these devices. All are used to increase the force applied, change its direction, or regulate the automobile's speed. The automobile is really nothing but a lot of simple devices working together as one "compound machine."

When a carpenter takes a crowbar to pry apart two pieces of lumber, he is using a lever. Similarly, when a Hawaiian planter shoved his ʻōʻō, or digging stick, into the ground to loosen the soil, he was using the principle of leverage. All we need to do to find out how well the Hawaiian understood the lever is to take a good look at his toolbox: the adzes, clubs, digging sticks, hammers, paddles, and so on, are all lōhai, or levers. Hawaiians may not have figured out the mathematics of the working formula of the lever, but they obviously knew how to make and use a lever—the first machine in the world.

When a man pushes a heavy but movable object up a ramp, he

is using an inclined plane. Similarly, when a group of Hawaiian fishermen push or pull their canoe up a sloping beach, they too are using the same principle. Pushing a heavy canoe up an incline in order to get it to another level is easier than lifting it. When a lumberjack drives his steel ax into a log, he is driving a wedge into it, just as a Hawaiian cutting down a tree with his stone adze would have done. All cutting and piercing devices, such as the pao (chisel), ʻoʻoma (gouge), pahi (knife), and so on, are wedges. Every Hawaiian carpenter who ever built a house, or mason who raised a stone wall, or craftsman who repaired split pieces of wood, or shaped bowls knew how to use a wedged tool.

As far as we know, Hawaiians had no equivalents for the pulley, either fixed or movable, the screw and its attached lever, or the wheel and axle. Since each is related to the lever or wedge, perhaps Hawaiians needed just a bit more time in which to develop these three simple machines. And they may have done so, had Cook's expedition not arrived too soon. They did have some understanding of the principle of the wheel, as is shown in the stone disks, or ʻulumaika, that they rolled along the ground. One likely reason why they did not combine a wheel and an axle to make a cart for transporting or hauling things is that they had no beasts of burden, such as oxen or horses, to pull such a machine. Interestingly, neither did Hawaiians ever develop a waterwheel, which is found so often in other agricultural societies. They didn't really need waterwheels, because they found enough rain or ground water in most places, and located their farming areas downslope to take advantage of gravity flow. The extensive irrigation and terracing systems that they constructed on such islands as Kauaʻi and Oʻahu indicate as much.

In addition to the simple machines, Hawaiians understood several other important mechanical principles, as well as their practical applications. They knew about: (1) the heat of friction, as from rubbing sticks for making fire; (2) abrasion, as from grinding stones and files; (3) tension, as demonstrated in the bow and arrow used for hunting rats, but never human beings; (4) torsion, as in the sling, or maʻa, which took the place of the bow as a weapon in warfare; (5) pressure, as in the steaming process used in the imu for cooking; and (6) rotary motion and friction, as in the pump drill, or nao wili.

From the point of view of mechanical complexity, the most

interesting of these devices is the pump drill, which was used for drilling small holes in wood, shells, bones, and the teeth of dogs and sharks. In the lineage of drills, it is a descendent of the borer or awl, the simplest hand drill and the slightly more advanced bow drill. The pump drill is more complicated than any of its antecedents and, according to historians of technology in Europe, was developed only after Roman times (Singer, Holmyard, and Hall). The nao wili consists of several moving parts, namely, a pointed shaft, a perforated stone disk, and a crosspiece attached to the shaft by a cord. Since no other Hawaiian machine employs as many movable parts, this pump drill may well be the best mechanical product of the ancient Hawaiians' technological ability.

Because tools or machines are useless without power to drive them, whether human or nonhuman power, Hawaiians needed to discover and to exploit alternative energy from sources other than their own muscles. The first and only nonliving energy resource that Hawaiians really harnessed was the wind, captured by sails on their canoes. No doubt the earliest voyagers brought the lā, or sail, with them, but during the ensuing centuries Hawaiians developed their own form of sail, called a "crab claw" because of its distinctive shape. Woven out of lau hala, it was attached at several points to the kia, mast, which was mounted upright in a canoe. By capturing the energy of the wind with such sails, Polynesian/Hawaiian voyaging canoes moved at remarkable speeds, compared with the ponderous ships of early European explorers in the Pacific. In the history of world technology, the development of the sail is regarded as an achievement of great importance. The same can be said about the crab claw sail in the history of energy technology in Hawai'i.

The use of wind energy and the development of the sail were connected with locomotion. The preeminent Hawaiian achievement in this regard is the canoe, particularly the great vessels that could voyage across broad expanses of ocean. That was a remarkable improvement over the earliest dugouts of the Neolithic and Iron ages in Europe and Africa. From the viewpoint of modern functional design the kaukahi, or Hawaiian canoe, with its single outrigger, is "the finest in the Pacific" (D. Mitchell 1982b). Sleek lines made it the fastest canoe, and the outrigger made it the most stable craft of its kind. Tommy Holmes, in *The Hawaiian Canoe*, wrote: "Naval architecture was a highly developed science to the peoples of Oceania. Well integrated into their marine environment, early Pacific people designed craft that were sea kindly, calculated for speed and in some cases so hydrodynamically advanced that it would not be until the 1800's that man would build faster sailboats. The flexible lashing mode of joining two hulls that so characterized Polynesian voyaging canoes and so shocked European observers for their supposed fragility is just now being recognized as often superior to a rigid form of attachment." Holmes is one of the latest in a long line of experts, beginning with Captain Cook, who have praised the qualities of the Polynesian/Hawaiian canoe.

If someone said that Hawaiians knew about flying machines long before the Wright brothers, many of us would shake our heads in disbelief. And yet Hawaiians did send aloft flying machines they called lupe. Those were "flying kites," early ancestors of the airplane. Berthold Laufer, in *The Prehistory of Aviation*, wrote, a kite is "an aeroplane which cannot be manned, and an aeroplane . . . [is] a kite which can be manned." The aerodynamic principles involved in flying a plane are similar to those concerned with flying a kite. Kites fly because they consist of inclined planes or flat surfaces held up by currents of air. And every flyable kite is an airfoil, whose efficiency is a result of the lift and drag forces created by the kite's shape and flying angles. This analysis may sound rather complicated but, for Hawaiians and other Polynesians who designed, built, and flew kites for centuries, knowledge of this sort was part of their technological competence.

Donald Kilolani Mitchell (1982a) described the typical Hawaiian kite as being six sided, with the framework made of hau wood, 6 feet long and 4¹/₂ feet wide, covered with kapa or plaited lau hala, and with the tail ranging from 15 to 90 feet in length. The larger monster kites had lines (made out of olonā fiber) a mile in length, that required two men to manage them and stakes driven into the ground to secure them. Apparently these kites may be compared with those devised by early Chinese, who are said to have invented the machine.

We are told that the Hawaiians, along with other Polynesians (except for Samoans and Tongans, who did not have kites), flew kites only for amusement, but Māui the demigod put his mythical kite to practical use: it pulled his canoe along as he voyaged among the islands of Hawai'i. Interestingly, Micronesians and

Melanesians use kites for catching fish. They attach a baited hook to the kite, which is flown above the sea from one end of a canoe. When a fish bites, the kite goes down and the catch is drawn in. Whether for practical or impractical purposes, Hawaiians made kites. And those were things that neither the Greeks nor the Romans ever managed to think up.

What we have said so far about the mechanical Hawaiian may seem a bit academic, but it is a subject worth a good deal more serious discussion and understanding, if only to demonstrate that Hawaiians of old were not benighted savages. Other machines or tools and related concepts and techniques that might be explored include the concepts of traction or gravity in regard to the making and the operation of the hōlua sled, the fastest form of locomotion on land in ancient Hawai'i; or the "gourd" compass; or some of the instruments used by surgeons, as well as other techniques employed by physicians.

While writing this section, we discussed the mechanical achievements of ka po'e kahiko with a young Hawaiian student, only to be asked, at the end of our conversation, that most baffling of all questions: "So what?" "What difference do they make?" he meant. If the most complicated machine the old-time Hawaiians ever developed was the pump drill, what can we learn from them that has any value to us today? In one sense, he was right, of course, because he probably knew more about machines than did all of our kūpuna put together. But knowing about machines is not the point of our inquiry. What's at issue is not whether we can learn any more theoretical or applied mechanics from preliterate Hawaiians, but rather that we recognize how able they were, how intelligently they used their minds and the few things they found in their limited environment, to fashion for themselves a way of life that may have been primitive but that was not graceless and savage. They gave us a legacy of methods, of techniques, which shapes our lives today. We still do many things the way they did, before 1778. As in biology, so in technology: all higher, more complex machines and methods evolved from lower, simpler forms. We need to remember the evolution of our technology, too.

Software

Although many people still tend, by force of habit more than by grace of thought, to think of tools as hardware, we should remember that the "soft tools" are equally important. These are the intellectual or conceptual devices that extend man's brain power, as opposed to the hard tools that extend his muscle power. For the purposes of this discussion, they include gestures and paralinguistic signals, rituals and codes, the spoken language and written ideograms (as in petroglyphs), and mathematics, the numerical system especially. In our discussion of the spoken language, we shall include mnemonic devices also, because they are as necessary to oral language as pen and paper are to written language. As you can see, these can be related to forms of communication which underlie all technological development.

If talking about rituals as technological tools seems strange, it is so mainly because of our modern compartmentalized thinking about technology and religion. To ignore the integral relationship between the two is to miss the whole point of the ritualized culture of Hawai'i before 1778. As we have discussed at length in chapter 4, almost every activity of daily life was turned into ritual by invoking the spiritual protection and guidance of the gods. We saw how this was done especially in the activities, whether private or public, upon which the survival and prosperity of an 'ohana or a chiefdom depended. No wise planter ever tilled the soil, planted in it, and harvested from it without offering the proper prayers or sacrifices, and performing the prescribed rites at each stage in the production cycle. No canoe maker dared to put a long construction project in jeopardy by not following the prescribed ceremonies, from the selection of the tree, to its sacred pilgrimage from the forest where it was pulled to the working place where it was carved, and, finally, to the launching of the finished canoe. No builder would have started, let alone finished, the construction of a house, particularly of one for a chief, unless all of the rituals and related rules were carefully observed. No good fisherman ventured out to sea without making the appropriate prayers and sacrifices at his shrines beside the shore.

We can see even more clearly the connection between ritual and technology by considering the specific rites used in the making or consecration of certain tools and their end products. Before cutting a soft pandanus trunk or some harder wood for making a digging stick, a man invoked the "hewing deities *Kūmokuhāli'i, Kūpulupulu, Kū'ālanawʻao,* and *Kūpā'aike'e,* that his 'ō'ō might not be broken," and uttered the following prayer to them: "Cut down the trunk; cut off the top; cut off the branches. See and watch the fashioning of the 'ō'ō" (Handy and Pūku'i). Before it could be used, the 'ō'ō was properly consecrated in a special ceremony so as to enhance its utility, that is, its efficiency. Much the same could be said for the making of adzes, fishing nets, and many other implements or tools.

If tools are to be sanctified, so should the things they help men to produce—houses, canoes, heiau, altars, calabashes, lengths of kapa, and all other artifacts. This honoring is especially true for the first thing made with a new tool. Invariably the purpose was to impart mana to the object for the safety of its users and the enhancement of their mana. Thus, the whole cycle of productivity involving tools was ritualized. While we may still witness a ritual blessing even today, especially when large public or private projects are begun or completed, such occasions are hardly comparable with the totally pervasive influence of ritual in ancient Hawai'i.

Another pertinent aspect of the ritualization of Hawaiian technology is the role that kāhuna played as skilled craftsmen or experts in the design and production of things and in the applications of those products or techniques. We shall inquire more into the roles of these "technicians of the sacred" when we take up the topic of specialization.

In sum, since ritual either preceded or concluded the making or using of tools, or of their end products, in almost every important activity of Hawaiian life the entire technological system was legitimized by divine authority. In fact, when technology is so ritualized, the technician cannot possibly feel estranged from his "simple machines." Such estrangement is a malady that seems to afflict many workers throughout much of the modern industrialized world. No one can feel alienated when his mechanical and spiritual ties are being constantly renewed by the fire of ritualism springing from faith.

The Power of the Spoken Word

Scholars have said that language, since human beings first learned to speak, is "the most important tool man ever devised." Try to conceive of social man's development without the help of language and you realize at once why that claim is true. No transmission of experience and wisdom from one generation to another would be possible without words spoken and written. While we are able to pass on muscular skills of the simplest sort, without language the benefits of civilization would be impossible. Indeed, we think only in words.

Anyone reading this statement today must automatically think of a language as being both spoken *and* written. But Hawaiians of old could think of language only as spoken. In fact, their word for language is ʻōlelo, which refers to the tongue, or alelo. (Parenthetically, the word for language in several European countries is derived from the Latin word for tongue.) Our Hawaiian ancestor may not have had a word such as phonetics, but he was a sophisticated student of the fabrication of human sounds. He knew that the sounds issuing from people are made by the movements of the lips, teeth, and tongue on air that is being blown through the throat and mouth. This may be part of the reason why he placed so much importance on the idea of hā, or breath, in relation to his belief in the power of the spoken word.

If a Hawaiian ever thought of language as a tool, he would have accepted it as a power tool because he believed literally that the spoken word, too, had its content of mana. In other words, he believed that when he produced certain sounds, he set in motion certain forces that added energy to the object or to the action symbolized in the sounds or words being uttered. A word could be the thing itself. When the canoe maker-priest pronounced a canoe to be good he meant that the quality of goodness and the canoe became, in effect, one and the same. On the other hand, if some jealous and sinister competitor cursed the canoe, it could become the embodiment of the curse. Prayers, incantations, and uttered rituals were effective as tools because of the potency of the mana in the spoken word. Similarly, a craftsman's instructions to fellow workers or apprentices had authority; indeed, the words spoken to his tools and to the products he fashioned had the same efficacy on the objects themselves. Thus, when he put the finishing touches to an object and declared that it was a good piece of work or that it would do the job it was intended to do, the object was invested with the power of his words. The serious craftsman, however, would first have made sure that the quality of his workmanship justified any assurances he uttered. He did not consider it a simple matter of speaking words without any corresponding effort on his part at making them come true. Words without works, to borrow a well-known biblical admonition, had no efficacy. No honorable technician would play with words when his craft was involved. When working, he didn't waste words in chatter—he saved his hā, his sacrosanct breath.

If some of this sounds familiar, it is so because the ideas and values are shared by many of us today, although some of us may not always admit this. Some people may disavow any belief in the power of the spoken word, yet will carefully avoid using certain words. Instead they turn to euphemisms like "passed away," or "gone to his reward," for words like death or die, to hide their fear that using the terrible sounds of truth all too often might invite something dreadfully true to happen to them or their loved ones. Diseases, too, are talked about in roundabout ways, thereby betraying similar apprehensions. While admittedly these people take such things metaphorically rather than literally, still we can see in them vestiges of the ancient belief. On the more positive side, the old Hawaiian craftsman's values of doing quality work, and his determination to deliver what he promised, are widely practiced today, and by more than Hawaiians. Fortunately for us, we are protected by such devisings as "quality control" standards, warranties issued by manufacturers on behalf of their products, and assurances that "the customer is always right."

In any event, nothing illustrates more forcefully the use of language as a technological tool than does the Hawaiian's belief in the mana carried by the spoken word when uttered in solemn pronouncements. 'Ōlelo in itself was considered a source of power available to the technician. As he said, and believed, "Words bind, and words make free." We can conclude by saying that, just as a navigator harnessed the energy in winds to reach his destination, so did a Hawaiian technologist harness the energy in spoken words to achieve his own standards and goals.

Was Hawaiian a Limiting Tool?

Ever since the eighteenth-century, when German philosopher Leibniz asserted that language was "a mirror of a nation's spiritual life," scholars have tried to establish definite links between a language and the mentality or behavior of the people who speak it. Some contemporary linguists, for example, argue that we are influenced in our mode of thinking by the nature of the language we habitually speak. For instance, they would say of the old

Hawaiians that, since their language has no clear distinction of tense, and that, since to them action is represented as merely occurring in the present without reference to past or future time, they must have had a sense of timelessness that would have led them to shrug at such advanced notions as clocks and due dates. On the other hand, some schools of thought argue that the relationships are the other way around, in that mentality, thought habits, and values influence the development of a language much more than the language shapes habits of thought. Everyone seems to agree, however, that environment and custom exert an incontrovertible impact on a language, particularly on its vocabulary.

Out of this kind of history have come the predictable judgments about the limitations or virtues of one language compared with another. Thus, a language may be judged "undeveloped" because it lacks a large vocabulary or abstract nouns or a certain degree of preciseness, or because it may have too much of this or not enough of that. Peoples who keep only "oral traditions" are dismissed as being "primitive" because they lack the sophistication of a written language, along with the paraphernalia of printing, libraries of books, and so on. Hawaiian, to be specific, is described as having a limited vocabulary—about twenty-nine thousand words in the second edition of the Pūkuʻi-Elbert dictionary, as compared with about half a million words of English in a good unabridged dictionary. Also, Hawaiian lacks the verb "to be" (William Ellis called that "the greatest imperfection"). It is deficient, too, in abstract nouns, a fact which has been used to support the claim that Hawaiians of old were incapable of thinking in abstract terms, or that the language rich in metaphor and imagery is more suitable for mythology than for science or technology. We need to ask whether these opinions are valid with respect to ancient Hawaiʻi's technological development in particular and to its intellectual development in general.

We need first to remember that while language conditions in part how we think and act, it is, to begin with, always an invention—a tool—of man. Words do not spring forth out of a language but out of the human mind. Thought precedes the word. If this were not so, no vocabulary would be possible. Simply because a word or expression does not exist in a language is no reason to assume that the speakers of the language could not contrive it. Let us consider the pump drill as an example of need contriving a response. It probably is a relative latecomer in the history of Hawaiian technology because, with its several moving parts, it is much more complex than are the other simpler machines. We can assume that in the beginning they had no word for a pump drill or for its related parts, but obviously this did not prevent the Hawaiians from thinking of a name and deciding to call it nao wili. Even better examples are found in the differences in vocabulary among today's several Polynesian languages. These differences could have developed only when each group, as it settled in its own separate area of the Pacific, developed its own local culture and invented new words to identify new things and ideas. Culture is not static, but dynamic. Hawaiian culture surely registered changes of its own a long time before Captain Cook or the missionaries arrived, and those changes were constantly reflected in the language. In short, like all languages, the Hawaiian language had its innate capacity to express whatever its speakers or its "thinkers" wanted it to do, for in and of itself it had no limitations except those imposed upon it by the level of thought among the people at any moment in their history.

A related point deserves mention here because of its effect on how contemporary Hawaiians perceive their past. This is the simplistic notion that if the Hawaiian vocabulary did not have a word equivalent to an English word, Hawaiians could not have been aware of the idea the English term expresses. Just a little reflection will show how fallacious this reasoning is. For example, precontact Hawaiians had no word for machine, but, as we have demonstrated, they did have a thorough knowledge of many simple kinds of machines and their uses. They had no term for rotary motion, but this lack does not mean that they had no understanding of rotary motion. They had no word meaning technology, yet no one can deny that Hawaiians of old had tools or techniques which were part of an identifiable system of interrelated concepts, values, things, and people. Needless to say, they did not think up words for such things as muskets or telescopes. But why should they have, when they had no acquaintance with either the instruments or the concepts that led to their invention in Europe?

In any event, the Hawaiian technologist possessed in his language a flexible, adaptable, and useable tool. He could make new words by compounding old ones or by the device linguists call reduplication, as in wiliwili, wikiwiki, ka'aka'a, and many others.

And he could slough off words or phrases when the need for them ended. We have only to look at the expansion of the language after 1778 to appreciate its built-in capability to adapt to changing conditions. Many, many new words and expressions were added to the language, especially after the introduction of writing and reading in the 1820s. Hawaiian-language newspapers, of which more than a hundred went into and out of business between 1834 and 1948, expressed countless new concepts, theories, technologies, inventions, customs, and events, from the coronation of European monarchs to the entire history of the First World War—all printed in Hawaiian. Until that time nearly everything that man had ever conceived of or had written about was capable of being expressed or translated into the language of Hawai'i nei. Many recent developments, however, which strain the capacities of all the world's languages, including English, probably would not translate well into Hawaiian.

Some people may argue, too, that Hawaiian was a limited means of communication without the written word. Beyond doubt, one of the major benefits of an advanced civilization is writing, with all its implied advantages of information distribution, storage, preservation, retrieval, and duplication, among other treatments. The written word is essential to the development of a scientific and technological tradition, which requires convenient, reliable, and verifiable systems of symbols, including numbers, geometric and algebraic formulae, and so on. On the other hand, in comparison with the total history of human civilization, written language is relatively recent. Furthermore, widespread literacy throughout the world has been gained only in this present century, and many millions of people today still cannot read or write. Ironically, despite the priority that educators and others have placed on writing and reading, the national achievement rates, in the United States at least, have steadily declined, due in part to the use of spoken-word media, such as the telephone, radio, television, and film, along with the advancements in such electronic gadgets as miniaturized portable stereos, tape and video cassettes, and talking computers and robots. While reading or writing probably never will disappear completely, technology definitely is bringing back the power of the spoken word. That is reason enough for us to be taking this hard look at some of the values of our oral culture.

But the question here is whether the Hawaiian language before 1778 was an adequate verbal tool for facilitating the development of technology. The consequences of not having had writing can be determined only speculatively and after the fact. We need to judge the language's adequacy on the basis of its own terms and for those times. In our judgment, it was adequate to the needs of the times.

Memory

Because the survival of a culture depends on the knowledge it can accumulate and transmit from one generation to the next, the storing of information becomes all-important. Throughout history literate civilizations have done this through books and libraries, but with the explosive increase of information during the last few decades, we are developing mechanisms that have ever greater storage capacities. Chief among these are microfiche, laser, and computer memory devices. In strong contrast, oral cultures which have no artificial memory capabilities must depend entirely on the human memory. Imagine having to rely on the mind to record and store the history of an entire culture as it experiences centuries of myriad events, personalities, names, laws, customs, wars, victories, and defeats, not to mention the types, uses, designs, and products of all its tools and processes. When we think of how little the average person remembers of what he learns—according to educational psychologists, we forget half of what we learn within forty-eight hours, three-quarters by the end of the week, and increasingly more as time passes—we can only wonder that any traditional knowledge has been retained at all. (And we should suspect the authenticity of the little that is "remembered.")

Most modern Hawaiians have heard the praise for the marvelous memory of the Hawaiians of old. Edith Rice Plews, for example, stated in *Ancient Hawaiian Civilization*: "The trained memories of the ancient Hawaiian poets were retentive to a remarkable degree." A special class of reciters, poets, genealogists, and chanters attached to the courts of the ali'i were skilled in the art of 'apo, literally catching. They were "trained to receive and hold the spoken word, that is, to memorize instantly, at first hearing." In composing long or epic poems, several poets met in conclave to compose, criticize, correct, and recite the work in progress, line by line. The "remarkable part was that the corrected version was fixed in the memories of all, even to the particles." Emerson (1978) reported that chanters took sixteen hours to recite the narrative of *Kamapua'a*; and, we are told, genealogists could recite names and events continuously over a three-day period.

Incredible as these feats of memory may seem, Hawaiians today, except for a few skeptics perhaps, tend to accept them at their face value. But we need not be skeptical, if we understand the human brain, especially its storage capacity, and the fact that such feats are common in oral cultures. Let us examine these matters briefly.

We can get an idea of the brain's storing ability from the calculations of John Von Neumann in his book *The Computer and the Brain*. Taking sixty years as the average length of life of a person (if you want to draw comparisons with the preliterate Hawaiian, keep in mind that before 1778 the average life expectancy was about thirty years), Von Neumann calculated the maximum possible capacity by assuming that: (1) the brain would make a complete record of all the electric signals generated in all touch, retinal, and other sensory receptors; and (2) the number of receptors would include all the ten billion neurons in the brain. He came up with the figure of 2.8×10^{20} bits of information, or about the same number of bits as would be found in all the books in a great library. This is the input for just one normal human brain.

Since such magnificent numbers are difficult to grasp, the startling results of the work of neurosurgeon Wilder Penfield on the human brain should help our understanding. Dr. Penfield, a physician interested in relieving the suffering of epileptics with impaired speech, performed brain operations under local anesthesia, with the patient fully conscious and cooperating, by using modern techniques of electric stimulation. He would apply an electrode to specific portions of the cortex of the brain in order to stimulate the hoped-for response. One day he stumbled upon a new and remarkable phenomenon. The electric stimulation sometimes suddenly forced into the patient's consciousness detailed recollections of past events that went back as far as childhood. The first patient relived an episode she'd had as a child with such naturalness that she felt the same fear as she had at the time of the original event. Another heard the voice of her small son in the yard outside her kitchen, accompanied by the neighborhood sounds of honking autos, barking dogs, and shouting youngsters. One patient, while in the operating room, heard an orchestra playing music that she did not herself know how to sing or play, and only vaguely recalled having heard before. Still another patient heard the singing of a Christmas song in her church at home in Holland as if she were actually there, and was as moved then as she had been at the event years earlier.

The patients' recollections all appeared to be real and vivid, although the episodes themselves were often trivial or inconsequential. In Penfield's words: "When, by chance, the neurosurgeon's electrode activates past experience, that experience unfolds progressively, moment by moment. This is a little like the performance of a wire recorder or a strip of cinematographic film on which are registered all those things of which the individual was once aware—the things he selected for his attention in that interval of time." In effect, the brain is like a giant recorder that can store every experience, thought, sound, or feeling we have ever had.

Penfield's observations lend some credence to the extraordinary feats of memory performed under hypnosis. One well-known report frequently discussed by psychologists is that of a bricklayer in his sixties who, under hypnosis, was able to describe specific bricks in a wall that he had laid in his twenties. The bumps on the surfaces of the bricks he described under hypnosis could be checked, and they were there! We are familiar with the popular belief that when a person is drowning, pictures of his past life come before him instantaneously. Under hypnosis, whole segments of memories may course through the brain in a second of time. Cases have been reported in which the memory of forgotten languages was suddenly restored and which the subject would accurately repeat, although none of the words were present in conscious memory in the subject's normal state. (Note that hypnosis, or hōʻupuʻupu, which means literally the power of suggestion, apparently was well known to the old-time Hawaiian kāhuna of medicine [Pūkuʻi, Haertig, and Lee].)

We should have a clearer picture now of the potential memory capacity of the human brain, but it tells us only about the workings of the brain under abnormal conditions. In the reality of our ordinary conscious memory, we can store only a small fraction of the events that we experience and, moreover, we record only a tiny fraction of the sensory data originally present in the events we do remember. Psychologists estimate that we can apprehend only about five or ten chunks of information at a time, where a "chunk" is the name of an item, an entry in a list, or the like. According to Dean E. Wooldridge in *The Machinery of the Brain*, such an item might involve 15 bits of information on average—"a total of perhaps 75 to 150 bits that we can consider at one time," or what he calls "apprehended" information. If we perform our calculation of memory-storage capacity on the basis of an "apprehended" information rate of 25 bits per second, we come out with something like 50 billion bits as compared to the trillions yielded by Von Neumann's calculation. Furthermore, as has been indicated, what we may apprehend and record in our memory is not necessarily there permanently, since through decay or disuse we forget large amounts of information.

Even granted the lesser storage capacity of the human brain, the power of recall that man has exhibited in many different cultures is at once stupendous and humbling. Many Maori elders can still remember recitations of genealogy, legend, or history performed by the old tohunga, which continued for as long as two weeks. Only a few years ago, a Maori elder in the Hokianga district of North Island recited his family genealogy over a ninety-hour period. Similar memory feats have been authenticated among many African tribes and Australian aborigines. In 1935 the great Yugoslav bard Avdo Medjediovic once recited for a research scholar seven long epic verse narratives with a combined total of 41,818 verses, taking more than a month to finish them (Bynum). Jewish memory experts called "Shass Pollak" knew by heart each page of the Talmud, which consists of several volumes each holding thousands of pages, and could demonstrate their prowesses on request, starting at any point in those volumes.

Mnemonic Training and Devices

How did the Hawaiians of old develop and perfect their memory skills? Although the full story may be written someday, we suggest that at least four factors must be considered: (1) heredity, (2) training, along with (3) the use of mnemonic devices, and (4) specialization. Persons with extraordinary memories are like other exceptionally gifted people in that they inherit the aptitude. As Fred Barlow, an authority on mental prodigies, wrote, "Memory comes to us in inherited form." And since this kind of hereditary ability runs in families, it stands to reason that members of certain select 'ohana would have been chosen to be the historians, or haku mele, the "walking librarians" of their culture. This seems to be exactly what happened. As Kepelino said, "The family of genealogists was born to the post." Through several generations of selective breeding, such a family could have produced individuals with prodigious memory skills, just as happened among Europeans of classical times, such as the descendents of Romans Seneca and Porson. ("The Porson memory" was hereditary in his family.)

Kamakau, Malo, and others said that those giants of memory "were important people" and "favorites" of the chiefs. Kepelino described the job of the historian, poʻe moʻolelo, as one who "kept correctly all the genealogies of each district, memorizing them all well so as not to lose the record of each chief from generation to generation." Because without a verified genealogy a chief could have had no status, and therefore no claims on authority or power, such historians were accorded a good deal of deference. Therefore, much importance was attached to their heredity, selection, and training—all of which contributed to their mana.

Special schools were organized to educate and train these specialists as undoubtedly they were for all other kinds of technicians. We have very little information about training in Hawaiʻi nei before 1778, but a good deal is available for other Polynesian groups. In the Marquesas, for example, a special house was built for the group being trained, and the necessary teachers were employed. Sometimes as many as thirty students might be in attendance. All students lived in the training house. Lessons lasted for a month, followed by a recess of about fifteen days, after which another period of instruction began. The lessons were given in two sessions each day, one in the morning and the other in the afternoon. If the students did not make good progress, the instructors would simply stop teaching and close the school, so the responsibility for learning was placed on the students. Perhaps similar training programs were followed in Hawaiʻi.

The outstanding feature of education in Hawaiʻi and Polynesia was that everything concerned with training, including the persons of the students themselves, was consecrated or placed under kapu. Not only was the nature of the subject sacred, but so was the entire process of learning. The training site was, in effect, a "temple of learning" watched over by the gods of the respective subject matter or profession. Every spoken word or gesture conveyed a sense of the power of the collective minds intent upon acquiring knowledge. In such an atmosphere, so laden with mana, learning was not a fun thing. It could not be turned into a form of amusement, in order to seduce students into paying attention and applying themselves. Classical learning among primal peoples was and is always a serious, sacred experience. It is difficult to imagine a student "fooling around," or any school having to be closed down for lack of discipline, although it's quite conceivable that a school could have been closed for lack of quality in teachers or achievement in students. As we have seen with training of dancers in a hālau hula, a lot of ritual sanction was involved, but to assume that this was the important motivating factor for learning would be wrong. A much more positive force must have been the desire to uphold the name of the family and to aspire to excellence as a matter of individual and professional pride. A student would have had little alternative really, because the expectations or standards of craftsmanship and quality performance, as we shall see, would have demanded nothing less than his best effort.

The art of memorization has always involved the use of mnemonic devices or aids of one kind or another. This was true in ancient Greece and Rome, medieval Europe, Vedic India, Inca Peru, Africa, and Polynesia, just as it is true today, especially among the professional purveyors of memory skills' programs being marketed in the United States and other countries. In ancient Greece the poet Simonides is supposed to have invented schemes to aid the art of memorizing, or mnemonics. The technique he developed was based on forming a mental image of a series of places, as in a building or house, then setting the images by which a speech is to be remembered in the places in the building which have been memorized. Think of the orator as moving in imagination through his memory building while he is making his speech, moving from point to point in the right order, as is fixed by the sequence of places in the building. This technique was used by Greek and later Roman orators to enable them to deliver long speeches from memory with unfailing accuracy. Although we have little evidence, it seems reasonable to assume that Hawaiians, too, probably developed and used mnemonic techniques of their own.

We need to keep in mind, however, that in human memory the

visual is only one of several modes of "imaging," although it is the most common one with most people and also the most vivid. Auditory imaging is the next most frequent, followed by tactile imagery. Kinaesthetic (i.e., body motion) and gustatory or taste imagery follow, with olfactory being the least common form of imaging. Imaging as we know it today prompts some interesting questions about Hawaiian memory modes. Were Hawaiians visualizers, as most Americans seem to be today? Or were they better at auditory and tactile imaging? Perhaps an analysis of Hawaiian poetry, particularly of its metaphors and symbolism, may tell us more. It would be easy to say that Hawaiians tended to be strong visualizers, as the moʻolelo might suggest, but such generalizing is at best hazardous. To illustrate: if we say Hawaiians were strong imagers, we would have to be prepared to say also that they might have been weak in abstract thinking since, according to psychologists today, the relation between skill in abstract thinking and lack of imaging ability seems well established. But, as we have seen already, Hawaiians were capable of producing complex abstract thought systems. Thus, rather than stereotyping a whole people, we might better categorize special groups of people. To wit, people who teach, philosophize, speculate, think all the time, tend to be good at abstract thinking but poor in imaging, no matter what the culture may be. In constrast, craftsmen and artists are good at imaging, particularly at visualizing, but poor at abstract thinking.

The most remarkable form of visual imaging is what we hear people refer to as photographic memory. By this term is meant the ability to remember a scene with all the vividness, distinctness, and detail of a photographic print, although research conclusively shows that no mind ever completely duplicates a photograph. Studies indicate that 1 to 10 percent of the adult population and 50 to 60 percent of children under the age of twelve years have what approximates a photographic memory or, in technical terms, an eidetic (virtually identical) memory (Hunter). Since the brain functions in the same manner in all races, let us confidently assume that a certain proportion of Hawaiians had eidetic memory. More than likely such gifted persons would have been among the prominent historians and navigators.

We specifically include navigators because of the way in which eidetic imaging works. Unlike the ordinary form of mental imaging, the eidetic image is seen as situated in outer space. That is, it is never localized "within the head," as the usual memory image so often is, but is placed "out there," attached to the mat or the wall or some other surface. The surface always appears as if it is folded or bent, as the sky would appear to be to one who is looking toward the horizon. Another fact about eidetic imaging is that the image lasts a long time and can be voluntarily revived some hours, weeks, or even months later. Still another characteristic is the wealth of detail imprinted on the image. This would seem to be the kind of imaging ability the great Polynesian navigators would have wanted or needed, in order to enable them to record in their minds the heavenly constellations at each point in the sky and in each season of the year.

Psychologist Ian Hunter tells us that what we should remember about eidetic imaging and memory in general is that recalling never literally reinstates a past experience or activity. The function of memory is not to give a flawlessly accurate account of the past, but "to make possible adjustment to the requirements of the present." What this suggests is that while perfect recounting of certain chants or histories was required, for other kinds of rememberings, as in the retelling of legends and stories, Hawaiians allowed something less than line-by-line memorizing.

A familiar Hawaiian mnemonic device was the poetic style of the chant. This employed repetition of a word or of part of a word at the end of one line and at the beginning of the next, in what is called "linked assonance." This device is a help to memorization because, in such pairing of sounds, the previous line would provide the clue for the next line and so on throughout the composition. In one sense the language itself is a good mnemonic device, because Hawaiian has only a small number of sounds, which means that it has many homonyms, or words that are pronounced or spelled alike but have different meanings. *The Kumulipo* is full of examples of linked assonance and homonyms, as in the following lines: *O ka'a monimoni i ke ala / O ke ala o Kolomio o miomio i hele ai.* The linked assonance is the word "ala," found at the end of the first line and at the beginning of the second line. *The Kumulipo* is also a good example of the liberal use of idea-associations, as in the dual matchings of fishes and plants that are linked mythologically and phonologically. Other stylistic aids to memory include the frequent use of reduplications, in which the language abounds, such as konikoni or manamana; a terse, compact style;

and the profusion of imagery—"word painting succeeding word painting." Thus, a well-constructed chant employing all of these devices greatly facilitates the job of memorizing. Technically speaking, this is powerful evidence for the ability of Hawaiians to exploit the capabilities of their language as tools within a tool.

The Hawaiian penchant for naming almost everything makes a lot of sense from the point of view of mnemonics. In the absence of writing words, what easier way is there to enter things in one's memory than by giving it a name? If Hawaiians took pains to choose a name for some place, person, or thing, they did so partly because the name meant a better mental picture for recalling and storing information. Thus, the common use of a number of names in chants is done not only for ritual or descriptive or sentimental or other reasons the composers may have in mind, but also to facilitate memorizing. The Hawaiian's strong sense of place is due in no small part to the mnemonics of place naming. Hence, passing a place with a name may have caused many a Hawaiian to pause and reflect, or to use the occasion to recite a story. In the oral culture of old Hawai'i names as mnemonic devices are much more important because of the premium placed on memory.

The use of material objects as mnemonic devices is common to all cultures, but the practice followed in preliterate Hawai'i has been almost totally neglected in our time by our literacy and the availability of paper and pencil. For example, some visitors have indicated that Hawaiians used knotted cords for recording tallies. The Reverends Daniel Tyermann and George Bennet, in their *Journal*, described traveling through the countryside of Wailua, O'ahu, in the 1820s, where they saw "tax-gatherers" keeping exact accounts of all payment collected by using a line of cordage from "four to five hundred fathoms in length. Distinct portions of this are allotted to the various districts, which are known from one another by knots, loops, and tufts, of different shapes, sizes, and colours. Each tax-payer in the district has his part in this string, and the number of dollars, hogs, dogs, pieces of sandal-wood, quantity of taro, etc., at which he is rated." Notwithstanding this testimony, neither the Bishop Museum nor any other institution has such an artifact dating from precontact Hawai'i. So today the consensus is that Hawaiians of old did not use the so-called quipu system of Peru and that what Tyermann and Bennet saw was something introduced after 1778.

In 1921 Elsdon Best of New Zealand wrote an article entitled "Polynesian Mnemonics," in which he stated that knotted cords were used by Polynesians. Although he mistakenly assumed that Hawaiians used the method, no doubt on the word of Tyermann and Bennet, he went on to say that the Maori may have used the same thing. He said this because tradition claimed Maoris had used a device known as aho ponapona, the many-knotted cord. According to Best, messages were transmitted by means of knotted cords that trained people could decipher. He added that nothing remained to show that such a system had been employed, but suggested that it may have been a remembrance of a custom from the remote Polynesian past. He gave some support to the possibility by noting that the knotted cord had been observed in Peru, imperial China, Europe, Africa, and Micronesia, especially in Palau, and speculated that it may have been introduced into Polynesia from China.

Of interest to us is the possible connection between "a remembrance of a custom from the remote Polynesian past" and the enormous excitement, practically "a mania," with which Polynesians welcomed the introduction of a means for writing their language. We know how Hawaiians flocked to the missionary schools, begun in the early 1820s, and how by the 1860s almost every Hawaiian adult and most children were literate. Maoris and Cook Islanders took to learning reading and writing with no less enthusiasm. Did some preconditioning influence in their past experience joined with some kind of mnemotechnic explain in part the remarkably eager acceptance of writing by Polynesians? Or was their eagerness simply a matter of a natural adaptability to technological innovation and the chance to exchange old ways for new?

Whatever the answer may be, what is most striking is that Hawaiians seemed to have had as much respect for the written word as for the spoken. In 1823 William Ellis, commenting on the effect the introduction of writing was having on Hawaiians, wrote: "Supposing it beyond the powers of man to invent the plan of communicating words by marks on paper, they have sometimes asked us, if, in the first instance, the knowledge of it were not communicated to mankind by God himself." For Hawaiians the power of communicating with language was not so much god given as derived from the mana invested in man and the universe. Hence, whether written or spoken, words inspired the Hawaiians of old with an awe that bordered on the religious. A persistent theme in Hawaiian tradition insists that language is a precious tool, a sacred one, that must be used with the greatest of care and respect.

We cannot leave the subjects of writing and mnemonics without touching on the mystery of petroglyphs, things that Hawaiians produced in greater number than did any other people in Polynesia. As J. Halley Cox stated, "Nowhere in the Pacific are there fields as extensive in size or so heavily covered with markings as those in the Hawaiian Islands." The debate over what the petroglyphs really mean continues unresolved. Some people think that the ki'i pōhaku, or stone images, represent an art form, while others maintain that they are simply pictographs (representations of objects) or even ideograms (representations of ideas about things). If they are works of art, they come closest to being pictorial drawing which, along with painting, is notably absent from Hawaiian culture. If they are pictographs or ideograms, they come close to being ideographic symbolism—which suggests that, in the technology of language, Hawaiians of old were moving toward writing. After all, probably in only a short time they would have thought of engraving the same symbols on tablets of stone or bark or wood, or writing them on pieces of kapa, and refined the ideographs to create the signs that represent sounds. No one really knows, but a thought that probably is closer to the truth suggests that petroglyphs were visual metaphors carved in the hardness of stone, in order to evoke both the power of their symbolism, the mana of the rock and of the petroglyph maker. If the petroglyph maker had wanted to make the most enduring kind of statement possible, he could not have chosen a better medium. And as a reminder of his presence, a kind of message that "Kiloki the commoner was here" the petroglyphs still endure (at least for a while) as the most lasting form of Hawaiian mnemonics.

The last set of mnemonic objects worth mentioning is concerned with the keeping of mementoes, or reminders of past events and people. Most people have this urge to keep things, ranging from families who treasure collections of photographs to governments that commission statues and portraits to honor former officials and fallen heroes. The Hawaiians of old, however, turned this urge into a sacred responsibility: they took great pains to preserve family heirlooms, an ancestor's favorite tools, a famous warrior's weapons, and relics of all sorts, particularly the bones of the mighty dead. They believed that such objects were impregnated with the mana of their owners or of the purpose or environment with which it had been most closely connected. In the courts of the ali'i certain people were charged with caring for these important mea ho'oilina. In the course of time some of these objects acquired a sacred identity of their own.

For some of us today, who may be obsessed with making offerings to our own narcissism, it may be difficult to appreciate the reasons why the people of old put so much emphasis on the keeping of mementoes. The reasons seem to arise from methods for effective learning and refreshing memory. Learning takes place in a particular setting and, although we may not be aware of it, this specific environment becomes a part of what is learned. Generally, if this environment is greatly altered during the time of our trying to recall what we learned, then recalling will be impaired. Probably we have all experienced this. We try to recollect what we did in some special place and fail to do so. Yet, on revisiting that special scene, "it all comes back to us." Psychologists have shown that when school children who have studied a lesson in one room are later examined in a different room, the amount of information they recall is smaller than is the amount recalled when the exam takes place in the classroom where learning originally took place. This means that in recall a sense of place is significant.

Hawaiians recognized this fact, that the recalling of something learned is helped by the presence of some part of the environment in which the learning took place. So they kept mementoes of past experiences or places, realizing that these souvenirs would serve to evoke those past experiences, if only by helping people to remember the reason for their having been there.

Gestural Communications

Can you imagine what would happen in our lives today if stock-brokers in the exchanges, airport workers, auctioneers, television and radio producers, traffic policemen, land surveyors, sports referees, soldiers, choir and symphony conductors, not to mention the deaf, could not communicate with gestures? Life would undoubtedly go on, but not without a lot of inconvenience and even some risk to life and limb. Just take the auctions across America, not only those that sell lost and found articles or high-priced artwork, but all those that sell the fish, vegetables, livestock, wheat, and other such products that we depend on. If somehow the buyers or auctioneers were prevented from using their language of gestures, much of our fresh produce and other basic commodities would never reach the marketplace. So, while you may not have thought about this before, it is clear that our sociocultural and economic systems rely heavily on the uses of gestures.

To what extent did precontact Hawaiian society rely on gestural communication? Most people are so accustomed to thinking of Hawaiian culture in purely verbal terms that the question demands a real shift in mental gears. Yet, on reflection, the subject is a natural one because human beings communicate both verbally and nonverbally through gestures, posture, facial expressions, and other body movements as well as through nonspeech sounds such as whistling, hissing, and imitations. Indeed, gestures and facial expressions (what are included in the technical term kinesics) are as instinctive as our speech making; in fact, some actions such as smiling and breast seeking are so innate that as infants we manifest them before we even learn to speak a word. Thus a close relationship exists between verbal expressions and nonverbal, so that we might say that both are different dimensions of the same tool.

Perhaps the best way to approach our question is through a process of elimination. We can start, therefore, by eliminating sign language, which was used extensively by American Indians mostly because they were divided into so many tribes with so many different languages that when they spoke they seldom understood each other. Hand signals became their common language. And this sign language was so developed that it had several dialects! Since all Hawaiians spoke the same language, they had no real need for a sign language. Nonetheless, they did devise certain hand signals and used them quite extensively, if we can believe some reports. For example, David Samwell, surgeon's mate with Captain Cook's expedition, wrote: "When a question is put to them that they mean to answer in the negative, instead of speaking they will just shew the tip of the Tongue between their Teeth which signifies *aouree ('a'ole)* or no!" He described a hand signal, combined with a facial gesture: "They have another Method of denying which is by giving their right hands a little turn & sometimes they use the Tongue & hand together but either of itself will do, & *in this way they give negative answers as often as by speaking* [italics added]." Conversely, the gesture indicating yes was a quick lifting of the eyebrows. Evidently another gesture commonly seen, according to James King, one of Cook's lieutenants, was the sign for telling the truth, which was made by "hooking the two forefingers together." Interestingly enough, Hawaiians and other local people today still use the same method, except that the small fingers are hooked instead.

There must have been many gestures in the Hawaiian lexicon of nonverbal signals (supposedly thousands are in use in contemporary American culture). Some of these gestures among Hawaiians of old include: (1) thrusting the thumb between the index and middle finger as a sign of contempt; (2) lowering the eyelids as a sign of bad luck; (3) raising the closed fist, with a quick bend of the elbow, as a male sex sign; (4) spitting noisily at or to one side of a person, as a gesture of utmost contempt; (5) thrusting out the tongue (hoʻopakeʻo) or making a face (haikaika) as signs of contempt; (6) a quick lift of the chin asks the question, "What did you say?" and (7) a slight inclination of the head toward a third person means "Who is he?" This slight sampling hardly does justice to a lexicon that has many more entries, but describing all of them is a task we must leave to others.

More useful for us now would be an appraisal of those activities in Hawaiian life which required or invited the use of gestures. Fishing was an important activity which was often done in complete silence, either because of distance or for reasons of custom, and hence required communicating by signs. For example, fishermen did not speak when gathering oysters in ʻEwa, "but gestured to each other like deaf-mutes" (Pūkuʻi). Apparently they maintained silence for fear that if they did speak a gust of wind would ripple the surface of the water and cause the oysters to "vanish." On the other hand, when out catching mālolo, or flying fish, the men would shout a lot. Obviously, hand signals were necessary for passing information between fishermen aboard canoes beyond shouting range, and also between the spotter stationed on a high point overlooking the sea and the fishermen waiting in their canoes below him.

Gestures undoubtedly were used in warfare, while maintaining silence, or to frighten the enemy, or to generate confidence. Sticking out the tongue and making fierce faces were warriors' expressions for both Hawaiians and Maoris. In New Zealand such gestures are still presented in the popular haka, or dances, which recall earlier times. Most likely other gestures were employed by bird snarers, who could stalk their prey and "talk" about the best approach without making sounds that would have startled their quarry. Still different types of gestures were used in learning situations, whenever students were required to learn in silence, that is, in an "active silence" of listening, observing, and imitating the teacher. Also, gestures must have been necessary during construction of monumental structures, such as large heiau requiring vast numbers of workers, complicated logistical and engineering tasks, and communicating over distances, not to mention the kapu imposing total silence during certain sacred stages of the work. And, as we have indicated before, hand and other signals were used in ritual settings, as in the luakini ceremonies, or in processions of canoe maker-priests, or in the passing of a chief and his entourage. Finally, we should not leave out love and romance, for which the Hawaiians had a clear set of instructions: *"Kuhi nō ka lima, 'āwihi nō ka maka, 'o ka loa'a nō ia a ka maka onaona,"* "With a hand gesture and a wink, an attractive person can get whomever he desires."

While we do not ordinarily think of silence as a function of communication, we must recognize that it does serve as an essential element in communicating ideas and feelings. This is especially true when a situation enforces silence upon a group of people. Silence, apart from that pertaining to hunting or fishing, when it is determined by the nature of the prey, is culturally defined. Silence is an integral part of many of our social or interpersonal acts, as in church or funeral services. In precontact Hawai'i, silence was an established part of religious and educational practices. It was also a matter of proper etiquette in certain relationships between superiors and inferiors. Silence was more than golden when passing by wahi pana, or storied places, burial sites, and other sacred places. Hawaiian life seems to have had many long periods of structured silence, during which meaning was communicated by gestures as well as by the fact of silence itself. Saying that they had an oral culture does not mean that Hawaiians went about babbling endlessly. Might we not say better that one of the reasons Hawaiians placed so much value on the spoken word was because they gave so much of their time to silent thought, to what Tahitians call "feruri" (Levy), or the working out of ideas in the quiet of the mind before uttering them? In the setting of a ritualized, nonindustrial culture, what is most precious is contemplative quiet rather than noise.

In contrast, nowadays we live in bedlam, caused by a never-ending uproar from jet planes, helicopters, and cars, jackhammers, gunfire, radios and televisions at full volume, heavy-metal rock, and doomsday harangues. So accustomed have we become to high-decibel living that we have developed a kind of horror about silence. Some people think that they cannot possibly endure a house without the comforting noises from radios or television sets. Others cannot stand a pause in conversation that lasts longer than a couple of seconds. For them silence is, in Barbotin's words, "like a void or an abyss to fill up at any price." But for the traditional Hawaiian, silence is not empty; it is filled with meaning for both the spirit and the mind.

Thus, in using gestures and signs, what the Hawaiian of old understood, perhaps better than we do, was the medium of silence. He incorporated it into his language of gestures and in so doing opened up different dimensions of knowing that are obscured by a preoccupation with words. In a sense, gestures represent an element of primordial imagery which Hawaiians used to communicate not only among themselves but with the silent world of the sacred. Sign language is still considered by certain religious orders, particularly among the Catholic, Hindu, and Buddhist religions, as a higher means of achieving communication with God and the spiritual realm. Take note of this the next time you bend your knee and make the sign of the cross, or place your palms and fingers together, or raise your head to the heavens, or assume the lotus position . . .

We do not wish to stray too far from our subject of gestures, but we are dealing also with the broad field of the technology of communications. Let us, then, touch briefly on a few other nonverbal devices developed by Hawaiians of old. Drums and "bell stones" were utilized to a limited degree. We are told that the latter were employed by priests of the heiau at Poli'ahu and Malae on Kaua'i, to signal each other or to announce the approach of expectant mothers to the birthstone at Holoholokū Heiau. (Bell stones, like "clinkstones," give off a loud ringing sound when struck.) Certain stones in the royal "maternity ward" at Kūkaniloko near Wahiawa, O'ahu, were said to have been sounded to tell of sacred events happening there. Temple drums, too, sent to the community news about auspicious events and other happenings related to heiau. But Hawaiians apparently never developed any sophisti-

cated drum language, as did the Ashanti or the Yoruba peoples of
Africa, by which they could transmit not only simple messages but
whole stories, poems, and other literary forms. Geography and a
relatively open environment probably worked against the use of
drum communication in Hawai'i, while the converse was the case
in Africa, where great distances and dense forests made it the only
practical way of communicating.

For long-distance communication, Hawaiians resorted to light-
ing beacon fires as signals for beginning warfare. According to historians, when he was planning to invade O'ahu, Kahekili, the
ruler of Maui and Moloka'i, sent his agents to collect intelligence
on the deployment of the O'ahu army. They relayed their messages
to lookouts on Moloka'i by signal fires within Ulupa'u Crater on
Mōkapu Peninsula which were not visible to the people of O'ahu.
Curiously enough, although smoke was a well-known symbol
among Hawaiians (e.g., smoke in a dream spelled trouble), they
did not use it for signaling, as did American Indians, who used
puffs of smoke according to a prearranged code, rather than fire
itself. The probable reasons why Hawaiians did not resort to
smoke signaling are the frequent brisk winds that would have
made control very difficult.

A rich field of research can be found in other kinds of nonverbal
communications among Hawaiians. The list of topics, suggested
in part by Mary Key in her book on *Paralanguage and Kinesics
(Nonverbal Communication)*, includes facial expressions—eye
contact, averted eyes, winking and blinking; the smile, grin, and
grimace; walking, running, sitting, or standing; breathing; eating
and sleeping; the cough, sneeze, spitting, belching, sucking, and
yawning; laughing; and sensory expressions as in smells, sounds
(whistling, yells, grunts, etc.); and the so-called "cutaneous response," referring to blushing or emotional sweating. While these
forms of "body language" may have little to do with the "software" of Hawaiian technological development, they may lead to
some valuable insights about Hawaiian behavior and attitudes
that may have been overlooked so far.

The Mathematics of the Nonmathematician

A young Hawaiian mathematician delights in telling the story
about how, during his senior year in high school, he was told by

his haole math teacher that Hawaiians have no future in the field of mathematics because they are not capable of grasping its basic concepts. The impression the student got was that this inability to handle the subject was something innate in the Hawaiian makeup. Maybe there was method in the teacher's madness, because the young student took what he said as a challenge and went to a small eastern college, where he majored in math, not in plain old applied mathematics, but in the more cerebral theoretical mathematics. He did so well that he graduated with the highest grade point average in his major and received a General Electric achievement award. Looking back now he can chuckle at the experience with his math teacher, but the inference of racial inferiority still rankles. This is a point we shall return to.

If the math teacher was basing his judgment on his impressions of the achievements made by present-day Hawaiians in the fields of theoretical or applied mathematics, he probably had some kind of support for his bias. At most only a handful of Hawaiians have made careers in theoretical mathematics. Come to think of it, there are very few theoretical mathematicians in all of the United States, perhaps no more than 100,000 today (as compared with 78,000 in 1967). So, given the size of the Hawaiian population, about 200,000 living both in the islands and on the U.S. mainland, even if only one Hawaiian is working in theoretical mathematics, that still may not be a bad proportion relative to the country's population of 239 million.

The number of Hawaiians working in fields of applied mathematics is quite another matter, however. This would include the broad range of engineering, physics, computers, aeronautics, electronics, communications, statistics, and similar fields in which mathematics is a basic tool. We counted at least twenty civil and mechanical engineers working in Hawai'i in 1982, a figure which probably erred on the conservative side. There is no telling how many are employed in the other fields, especially in the newer areas of computer science and technology, as more and more young Hawaiians move into these career directions. Perhaps relatively the number is small, but it is certainly larger than it was ten or twenty years ago and undoubtedly will continue to grow.

But if our math teacher was implying that Hawaiians are poor at math because of a faulty genetic inheritance, he was continuing the old prejudices of "scientific racism." Although this was based

on discredited biological theories in seventeenth- and eighteenth-
century Europe and America, it persists in the modern stereotype
of the "dumb Hawaiian." The fallacy of the idea is shown by
anthropologist Leslie A. White who, in studying the evolution of
culture and mathematics, stated that people of one race are not
any smarter than those of another because of their brains. He
wrote: "There were brains as good as Newton's in England
10,000 years before the birth of Christ, at the time of the Norman
conquest, or any other period of English history. Everything we
know about fossil man, the pre-history of England, and the neuro-
anatomy of *Homo sapiens* will support this statement. There were
brains as good as Newton's in aboriginal America or in Darkest
Africa." In any case, he insisted, not brains alone, no matter how
sharp, determine the level of a people's mathematical knowledge,
but rather the confluence of culture and brains. "There must be a
juxtaposition of brains with the interactive, synthesizing cultural
process," he asserted. "If the cultural elements are lacking, superior brains will be of no avail." In the cultural process, the brain is
merely an agent in the development of mathematics, either by
invention or by application.

One of the problems of dealing with the relationship between
mathematics and primal peoples is our uncertainty about what
they might have called mathematics. In discussing "the cultural
setting of mathematics," Raymond Wilder pointed out that in primal cultures "having only such rudimentary forms of mathematics
as counting, no word for 'mathematics' is found." This is true of
the Hawaiian society as well. But the trouble is that what we
define as mathematics is based on our definition of it in our own
advanced culture. Thus, Wilder stated: "So far as ancient cultures
are concerned, we lump together everything numerical, geometri-
cal, and algebraic under the name 'mathematics.' Conceivably,
however, what we call 'mathematics' in an ancient culture might
have been (and probably was) called in that culture by names that,
in our language, would correspond to 'astrology' or 'theology.' "
For example, the Greeks included in the study of mathematics
both music and gnomonics (the art of making and using sundials).
In the case of Hawaiians, any number of fields having to do with
quantitative matters might have been regarded as mathematics.

Another problem is the perception many people have of mathematics as being so complex and abstract that they assume that

only a highly advanced group or set of individuals could possibly understand it. This perception comes partly from the widespread assumption that intelligence is based on mathematical ability and partly on a so-called math phobia. It afflicts a lot of people who wince when they have to take a math test and throw up their hands in despair at the thought of taking courses in algebra and calculus. When such "innumerate" people look at preliterate peoples, they tend to transfer their own inadequacies to them, saying something to this effect, "If I can't hack it, how could those primitives ever do it?" Basically, the difficulty is not with their psychology, but with their distorted understanding of the nature of mathematics, imputing to it an air of mystery that it doesn't deserve.

Let us have a mathematician tell us what mathematics is in its simplest terms: Edmund C. Berkeley defined it as dealing with numbers, shapes, sizes, measurements, and comparisons (like "big," "more," "as long as," etc.); arrangements (like "between" or sequences); patterns and models; order (as in "second," "next," "one by one," etc.); change and variation; graphs; and chances and risks (as referred to in words like "probably" or "maybe"). He believes that these and other mathematical ideas are "so much part of our ordinary thinking that we hardly ever notice their true mathematical nature." We unconsciously use in our everyday language many common mathematical ideas when we say "at," "before," "ahead of," and so on (pertaining to location), or "top," "bottom," "left," or "right" (pertaining to region), and so on.

Other kinds of mathematical ideas that we cannot avoid using in our everyday lives are expressed in such words as "few," "several," "little," "much," "very," "many," "a lot of," "almost," "entirely," and "some." These are indefinite numbers and measurements which almost everybody prefers to use instead of anything more precise. That is, we say "He walked a little way into the room"; we don't say "He walked into the room forty-two inches, plus or minus four inches." On the other hand, we also use definite numbers such as "one," "two," "three," and so forth—which is what most people normally think mathematics is about. Then there is a large group of everyday words that have to do with changing, varying, and approximating, such as "about," "approximately," "various," "depend on," and "vary with." The branch of mathematics that studies "approximately" is called statistics, while that for "it depends" is the study of functions.

In sum, mathematical ideas are embedded in the ordinary languages of all peoples. In the chronology of the development of tools, therefore, language came first and mathematics second. However, we should make clear that modern mathematics has a precise language all its own that is noncultural, that is, universal, with a standardized vocabulary made up of symbols that are understood by specialists. In any event, here we are speaking mainly about "basic math," which, if Berkeley's approach is acceptable, fits any culture at almost any stage of its development.

Hawaiian Numbers

Numbers is the special language of mathematics and Hawaiians had developed a numbers system of their own long before the coming of Captain Cook. Their system was well beyond anything that mere Stone Age people could have attained. To begin with, they had reached a concept of number, along with words about numbers. That is to say, they understood the quality of "threeness" or of "fourness," and used their word equivalents not as adjectives, which a Stone Age primitive would have done, but as distinct conceptual entities. While this may seem oversimplistic to any schoolchild today, in the historical evolution of mathematical thought the discovery of "number" is a major breakthrough, for it is one of the purest abstractions ever invented by the human mind. By this we mean that no number as such is out there in the real world, an entity in itself that you can point to. You may see or count one, two, three, or four things, and so on, but only the things exist, not the numbers. This relationship of things to numbers often confuses people into thinking that they can *see* numbers or other purely mathematical models, such as triangles, squares, and circles, which in fact are only pictures in the mind. So, the concept of number is regarded as quite a feat in abstract thinking.

In the second place, Hawaiians had adopted a base unit of four, in addition to a hybridized base ten numerical system. This represented another major advancement in early mathematical development because it involved (1) the idea of a collective, and (2) the creation of a logical system. The collective unit refers to the combination of two or more number words into a base unit. Thus, 1 and 2 represent a base two, or binary, system; 1, 2, 3, 4, and 5, a base five, or quinary, system; and 1 to 10, a base ten, or decimal, system; and so on. This is a fundamental aspect of all number systems and is part of quite a complex process of thought. The Hawaiians' base four units were called kauna, or four; ka'au, or forty; lau, or four hundred; mano, or four thousand; kini, or forty thousand; and lehu, or four hundred thousand. According to J. H. Kānepu'u, a Hawaiian author of a letter to the editor of the Hawaiian newspaper *Ke Au 'Oko'a*, dated January 21, 1867, the number four was used for a very practical reason: a fisherman could hold four fish by their tails between the five fingers of each hand, or a farmer could hold four taro plants in the same way. Incidentally, fishermen and fishmongers in Hawai'i today still count fish, particularly 'ōpelu, according to the old method, in units of four, forty, and so on.

At some time, however, they decided to use the decimal system as well as the base four system, most likely because counting by tens was more efficient. In fact, almost all peoples who have developed number systems end by adopting a base five, ten, or twenty mode. The reason for this probably is related to man's reliance on the fingers (and sometimes the toes as well) in order to tally a collection of things, which in many languages accounts for number words derived from the fingers. Such is lima, the word for five in Hawaiian, which also means hand. We should note that since the Hawaiian words for many of their first ten numbers are similar to those in other Polynesian and Malay languages, the Hawaiian system undoubtedly had a proto-Polynesian/Malay basis. This does not mean, however, that all Polynesian or Malay number systems are the same. They can differ, as in the case of the Maori, who chose a quasivigesimal, or base twenty system. In any case, the real achievement on the part of Hawaiians was to create a practical and workable counting system, which in the historical development of mathematics is considered a late event—and therefore a more advanced construction.

With the Hawaiian system one could count, theoretically, to a high of four million. This is an extraordinary number for a verbal counting system, and one not useful and not found very often in other primal systems. The present-day Crow Indians of the American prairie, we are told, do not usually count higher than a thousand, "as they say that honest people have no use for higher numbers." Be that as it may, we can doubt that Hawaiians had much occasion to use, let alone compute, such a figure as four million.

Writing about the "Hawaiian Method of Computation" for the *Hawaiian Spectator* in 1839, E. W. Clark suggested that "such were their habits of life, that they [the Hawaiians] seldom had occasion for any complex combination of numbers." Before 1778 it would have been a formidable feat actually to count to such a great number. Just to count to forty, for example, perhaps two persons would have been required: one to count the units up to ten on his fingers and the other to count the number of tens, so that between them they could keep a moving record of both tens and units. Since they could not write anything down, they had to do all this "in their heads," which even with their trained and retentive minds must have been quite a chore.

Thus, the Hawaiian system was significantly handicapped by a lack of recording or working symbols, such as the Hindu-Arabic numerals we use today. The only possible thing approaching such symbols was the petroglyph markings that William Ellis reported seeing along the southern coast of the island of Hawai'i, denoting "the number in the party" of travelers. Beyond this guess, we cannot determine the meanings of the markings without some kind of Rosetta Stone. As for working symbols which make calculations possible, in their absence very little could be done with the Hawaiian system beyond addition and subtraction. Multiplication and division were conceivable, but difficult to do without written symbols. Simple addition would have followed naturally from finger tallying. Quite possibly, as in other cultures such as the Chinese and the Roman, finger counting may have been taught as a special method. Furthermore, since calculations is a complicated subject, we can safely assume that mathematics specialists were included among the kāhuna serving the chiefs, particularly the more powerful ones with large properties in lands or goods. As E. W. Clark wrote, "The chiefs often had persons about them, more or less skilled in numbers, to keep an account of their tapas, mats, fish, and other property, and divide them out to their dependents." Being technicians happy to find easier ways of doing things, those "accountants" probably devised counting boards similar to the abacus, using pebbles or shells as counters. After all, Hawaiians used the same kinds of objects for some of their games, especially the kōnane, their version of chess, which required counting or keeping score, as well as in the study of human anatomy.

As we consider the level of development of Hawaiian mathematics in particular or of technology in general, we should keep in mind that for most of the thousand years of history before Captain Cook came sailing along, Hawaiians lived in completest isolation from any contact with other cultures or technologies. Unlike continental peoples, such as Egyptians, Greeks, Romans, Chinese, or Arabs, who traded or fought with each other and in the process borrowed or acquired new ideas and techniques, Hawaiians were forced to rely entirely on their own ingenuity. While Europeans were able to borrow the zero from the Hindus and the Arabs, for example, such "technological transfers" could not occur in Hawai'i until 1778. Thus geography played a crucial part in the pace and direction of technological development in Hawai'i before the haoles came.

The Hawaiian numbers system was in many ways cumbersome, inefficient, and quite limited. Of course, Hawaiians could not know that their system was so poor, and so they went ahead using it as best they could, to whatever technological advantage they might attain. They were perhaps a little like the bumblebee, which, according to principles of aerodynamics, is not supposed to be able to fly, but goes ahead and flies anyway. Just as the bumblebee's achievement is all the more noteworthy because it seems to do the impossible, so do the Hawaiians' achievements appear to be all the more notable because their mathematics seem to have been so limiting.

Numbers, Logic, and Gods

If we look at Hawaiian living in technological terms, we see at once how extensively mathematics influenced its character and development. None of the "hardware," for example, could have been made or used without some knowledge and appreciation of numbers, measurements, angles, lines, weights, velocity, friction, or even probability. The adze maker would not have been worth his salt if he did not know how to balance the handle with respect to the weight, size, and shape of the stone attached to it, or how to bevel the cutting edge so as to achieve the best angle for incising wood or stone. The user of the pump drill would have had to know something about the mathematics of partial rotary motion, the number of revolutions with the right amount of pressure needed to drill a hole of appropriate size in different kinds of materials. Think of the canoe maker who had to build an absolutely seaworthy craft out of a 60- or 70-foot koa log, and must make perfect measurements for configurations in the hull, gunnels, end pieces at the bow and stern, the "U-spreaders," or wae, which served as braces and purchase points for the 'iako-to-hull lashings, the outrigger and cross booms, the float, or ama, the lashings, sails, and other important parts of the vessel. The architect and house builder could not have succeeded in their professions unless they had a knowledge of numbers, measurements, and spatial or geometric relationships. Not even the featherworker, basket weaver, mat plaiter, or cordwainer could have done their intricate work without being able to count stitches, visualize patterns and designs, and measure their materials.

As does any tool, mathematics responds to the demands made of it by the supporting technology, which in turn responds to the demands of society. Thus, as Hawaiian society grew in population and hence in productivity in food, shelter, and the other necessities of life, the need arose for management of greater quantities of things. With greater social and economic complexity, specialization grew accordingly, and with it greater political organization and control. Control and complexity always invite accountants or managers of large numbers of objects. Taxes have to be collected, paid, and recorded (or remembered); stocks of foods and other goods have to be accumulated and eventually distributed; large public projects have to be built, such as heiau and the irrigation systems on Kaua'i, and so on. All of this requires taking account of numbers of laborers, work contributions, quantities and types of materials, work schedules and dates, among other things. We need only recall our earlier time machine's visit to the construction of the Mo'okini Heiau with its fifteen thousand laborers to appreciate the need for a numerical system, not to mention engineering, mechanical and other principles and techniques. We can take as a general rule the fact that the more complex the society—and by 1778 Hawai'i, with its several competing chiefdoms and priestly orders, had become the most complex of all Polynesian societies—the greater was the need for using its tools.

A less obvious but equally important application of mathematics in the Hawaiian experience is the role of logic. At the outset, we need to keep in mind two related questions: the first asks how Hawaiians viewed the relationship between mathematics and logic, and the second asks what Hawaiians thought of logic as such. Taking the second question first, logic is pertinent generally to everything we've talked about so far, and particularly to the strange charge discussed in our earlier chapter on myth and mythmakers that Hawaiians, like other "primitive" peoples, were "prelogical," that is to say, nonlogical. If we define logic in its most common-sense terms, it means to think or to reason correctly, that is, according to certain guiding principles. Let us take the following example:

All chiefs have mana.
Kahekili is a chief.
Therefore, Kahekili has mana.

The guiding principle involved here states that if something is true in every case, then it is true in any case. That is to say, any Hawaiian would have accepted the proposition that "all chiefs have mana" and therefore would have deduced our concluding statement from this first one. This syllogism is as obvious to us as it must have been obvious to any Hawaiian of old.

Anyone familiar with mathematics and logic would know that this reasoning process was passed down to us by Aristotle in his famous syllogism (a term derived from the Greek word meaning to sum up):

All men are mortal.
Socrates is a man.
Therefore, he is mortal.

If there is a first principle in logic, this is it. It also forms the basis of what we call deductive thinking, that is, reasoning from the general to the particular, which is how mathematics proceeds.

We may have a problem with Aristotle (through no fault of his of course) because of the way some of us have been taught to regard the Greeks as having invented the art of logic. They no more invented logic, in our common-sense definition of the term, than did Captain Cook discover the Hawaiian Islands to the world of men. Clearly, Hawaiians, not to mention the ancient Chinese, Mayans, Hindus, Polynesians, and a host of other peoples, had practiced logical thinking long before and quite apart from Aristotle and his fellow Greeks. The trouble is that anyone indoctrinated in this Eurocentric view of Greek intellectual hegemony would tend to look at Hawaiian and other primal peoples' capabilities with all the built-in prejudices of intellectual pride. After all, if the Greeks had really invented logic, how could the Hawaiians, so insulated from the currents of thought in Europe, ever have developed their own logic? This declaration in no way detracts from the brilliant accomplishments of the Greeks, but it does say that we Hawaiians should not demean ourselves either.

Deductive thinking, as we have said, is the basis of mathematics, but inductive thinking is the basis of science. Science works on the particulars, building evidence upon evidence, until finally it produces a general theory supported by that evidence. In Hawaiian natural science, *The Kumulipo*'s evolutionary theory is a good example of inductive thinking at work. In contrast, mathematics starts with a general proposition as being true in all cases, and allows that any given particular that falls into the purview of the proposition is also true. This is what gives mathematics its unique character of infallibility. To be sure, the rules of deductive logic have to be followed, or else you end up with results less than infallible. This "religious" nature of mathematics derives from the type of objects it works with and, as we have already noted, these objects such as numbers are abstractions created in the human mind. Since they are purely imaginary, complete with whatever properties they possess, imaginary rules can be created for them. In other words, the mathematician is able to create infallible propositions because he works with particulars that he has also created.

This process suggests another process that forms the basis of Hawaiian religion: the creation of the gods. As you will recall, ultimately Hawaiian gods are manifestations of preexistent mana forces that were created in the human mind. The gods are abstractions to which Hawaiians attributed names and other properties and around which the mythmakers elaborated their ideas and stories. Like mathematics, Hawaiian religion begins with an infallible proposition, that is to say, that a god force exists. How different is this reasoning process from that which mathematicians use to create numbers and general propositions that exist only in the mind?

This relationship between logic, numbers, and gods is evidenced in many religions and in quasireligious or occult arts such as numerology. In fact, Pythagoras, the first of the great Greek mathematicians, was so taken with the "divine" character of mathematics that he established a religion based on it. Essentially, what he did was to associate geometric patterns with numbers, each number having its own pattern, such as square, triangular, rectangular, and so on. He observed that these same patterns occurred repeatedly in nature, and these observations gave him his great idea: nature is mathematical. Numbers and their patterns are the building blocks from which everything in the world about us is constructed. All this led Pythagoras to proclaim the precept: God is number. Thus, for example, he regarded the number one as being every kind of number and pattern because every number or pattern is generated from one. The number one, in fact, represented the unity, the wholeness, the soul of the universe, indeed, God.

The notion that numbers are more than expressions of quantities, but are in themselves "idea-forces" which have a particular character of their own, is not a Greek but a universal idea. The Chinese developed elaborate theories of number symbolism, such as that illustrated in the *Book of Changes, I Ching*. It begins with sixty-four figures, or "hexagrams," based on the yin-yang dualism, with their associated numbers, all of which corresponded to the patterns of the Tao, the Way, in nature and in human situations. The idea was to find out from the person who interpreted the meanings of these hexagrams what they revealed about your fortune or misfortune. While the Chinese, along with Greeks, Hindus, and a few other peoples, devised very elaborate schemes, almost every culture has had, on a simpler scale, sacred numbers or, in the vernacular of the day, "lucky" or "unlucky" numbers. The number thirteen is an unlucky number in nearly every society, a fact which should convince even the most skeptical of the persistency of the belief in the power of numbers.

Apparently Hawaiians, too, were preoccupied with the symbolism of certain numbers which, in part, may be related to their interest in astrology, a first cousin of numerology. The number five occurs often, especially in the treatment of illnesses, although it also appears in rituals. A modern kahuna lapaʻau, George Kahoiwai, pointed out that the old Hawaiians picked a supply of herbs for five days' treatment, and took the prescribed dosages five times a day for five days, or five times in one day. In the ceremony called pūlima, performed when omens for recovery of a patient look promising, an imu was prepared. The number of mats specified to cover the imu was always five. Because the treatment of illnesses was a religious function, we can assume that the use of five had a sacred connection, although the reason behind that is not clear to us. However, in the world lexicon of symbolism five is symbolic of health and man since it "comprises the four limbs of the body plus the head which controls them, and likewise the four fingers plus the thumb and the four cardinal points together with the centre" (Cirlot). It also corresponds to the five senses. Five may have also been used in ritual, as it is still used today by some Hawaiian families who make offerings using five different containers, and so on, because, we are told, "this is how it was handed down to us from generation to generation." Interestingly enough, some modern Hawaiian songwriters still attach significance to the number by writing songs with five verses, although no such rule appears in the Hawaiian school of poetry.

Rubellite Johnson (1981) made a case for the "sacred four," which is supposedly implicit in the division of The Kumulipo chant into sixteen wā, or cantos. "The appearance of man occurs in the eighth wā, at the midpoint of the Pō and Ao, so that sixteen is the sum of eight wā doubled and also the sum of seven (Pō) and nine (Ao) wā." She draws parallels using the same association of numbers, that is, four, eight, sixteen, thirty-two, and sixty-four, with Hindu, Chinese (I Ching hexagrams), and Pythagorean practices. "The worship of four as a sacred number," she stated, "found its supreme expression in Pythagorean numerology" because it stood for justice as it was the "first perfect square, the product of equals." Unfortunately, she presented no other evidence for its use as a sacred number in Hawaiian culture, although she hinted that something "peculiar" lies behind the use of four as a base in the numerical system. On the other hand, if indeed something is to be said for base four, then the same argument would apply to the use of base ten, or the decimal system. In different cultures ten is symbolic of "the return to unity," "the totality of the universe," "spiritual achievement," and almost everywhere it is known as the number for perfection. But whether Hawaiians attached any of these meanings to ten is not at all clear.

Whether in the application of mathematics in particular or in technology in general, all these considerations seem to come back ultimately to the spiritual center of Hawaiian life. Nothing really seems to have any meaning or any significance unless a connection with ho'omana can be made.

The Specialist: Status and Perfection

One of the distinguishing characteristics of a developing technological society is the emergence of groups of specialists who have skills acquired through many years of training and who depend more or less on the exercise of such skills for a living. Today this is referred to as specialization. The degree of specialization rests on a number of factors: the development of many specialized tools, a fairly homogeneous society, a relatively large population, a pool of talented individuals, a certain enthusiasm for technology, and an economy capable of producing surpluses to support full- and part-time technicians. In general these conditions had prevailed in Hawai'i for some time, because by 1778 Hawaiian society had a subculture of well-entrenched and recognized technical specialists. We have mentioned some of these already—astrologer-astronomers, navigators, canoe makers, fishermen, bird snarers, house builders, architects, genealogists, physician-healers, farmers, accountants, and temple priests. Some fields recognized subdivisions among their specialists, such as the sail maker, cordage maker, and the fitter of canoe lashings. The training that they had to undergo was formidable indeed, such as the "medical apprentice," who would study and observe with his teacher for a period of twenty years, during which he could observe but never treat a patient. Whether all these specialists were able to make a living at their professions is unclear, but certainly those who were attached to the court of a prosperous ali'i, or who had developed outstanding skills were supported well. Some, like the kahuna 'anā'anā, or sorcerer, did charge "substantial" fees, on a "sliding scale."

Hawaiians brought to technology more than a certain degree of enthusiasm for their work; to that they added a profound respect bordering on awe. They had two fundamental reasons for this approach: (1) technological activity, like any other serious enterprise, was a form of communion with the divine, and therefore was consecrated by ritual and prayer; and (2) mana pervaded the entire technological process, from the tools used and the skills displayed in their use, to the quality of the end products, the labor that went into their creation, and, most of all, to the technician himself. What Malo said about canoe building applies to all technological pursuits: each was "an affair of religion."

The main features of the technician's world were outlined by Handy (1927): the organization and direction of each enterprise was under "master craftsmen or adepts and priests"; the work, the workers, and their products were insulated from evil by the kapu and purification rites; "the taking of omens relative to the outcome of the enterprise"; "empowering workers, places, instruments, and the product by using conductors of *mana*, and endowing them directly with *mana* through spells; consecrating the finished product by means of ritual; and finally, feasting and general merrymaking to mark the end of the consecrated period, to enjoy the product, and to render thanks to the gods."

Interestingly enough, presiding over much of this specialized realm is Kū, the deity of technology, and his family of specialist gods. Apparently, specialization among men on earth may have been based on the model set by the gods! In any case, the rational way in which the gods were organized is suggested by the fact that Kū's manifestations as forest gods were also divinities of wood products, such as Kūmokuhāli'i, god of forests and canoe makers, or Kūka'ō'ō, god of the digging stick, and so on. Thus, every special field and technician, as well as some tools and even their products, had a divine guardian or protector.

The value implications of this consecrated approach to technology should be clear. First is the status given the technician-craftsman-artisan on the basis of his skills and achievements, for his mana is derived primarily from what he does rather than from who he is. A technician could just as easily lose his mana and status because of slovenly work as he could increase his mana and reputation through quality work. In other words, to keep your mana, you have to work at improving your skills. As Pūku'i (Pūku'i, Haertig, and Lee) wrote: "For non-use or neglect, as surely as wrong use of *mana*, would result in lost *mana*. The *kahuna* who neglected his patients would eventually lose his ability to heal. The craftsman who slid into sloppy work would eventually lose his touch. And having lost skill, and consequently, value to others, he would eventually become of less value in his own eyes." In the traditional Hawaiian view, we should remember, while a worker might lose his mana through misuse of his talents, it could also be taken away by the gods. In short, where skills and results are concerned, "meritocracy" rules, not nepotism, for, in the last analysis, what counts to the Hawaiian is the quality of a man's performance.

Second, the level of performance expected is nothing short of perfection. To many of us today this may sound like asking for the impossible because nowadays our minds are so set that we no longer expect perfection in anyone or anything. We are conditioned to accept the fact that we are not perfect and thus we expect to make mistakes. We shrug and say, "To err is human . . ." From our earliest days in school, we are required to achieve only a passing grade, a C, a "qualifying score." Consequently, we are taught, in effect, not to expect too much of ourselves and, above all, never to expect perfection in others or ourselves. But to the Hawaiian of old, this relaxed attitude would have been contrary to his entire upbringing and to all the basic beliefs and values of his elders' philosophy. From childhood he was conditioned to live up to the demands of the kapu and the rules of his clan, constantly aware of the fact that a mistake could have dire consequences not only for himself, but, worse yet for his entire 'ohana, living and dead. As he grew up, during years of apprenticeship under close supervision, he was taught the standards of his trade and reminded of the rewards as well as the penalties he earned by his performance. By the time he became a master craftsman, he was "programmed" to think and work in terms of achieving his best—which to him was the same as perfection.

Perfection to the technician meant achieving what he set out to do, based on predetermined high standards without allowance for any mistakes. It meant the flawless performance and the consummate product. Pūku'i stated: "Throughout Hawaiian custom was an emphasis on achieved perfection. . . . The weaver must make a perfect mat. The chanter, dancer, or drummer must perform without mistake" (Pūku'i, Haertig, and Lee). In practical or technical terms, this made eminent sense to the Hawaiian. Why should one not expect a canoe to perform exactly according to arranged specifications, if one's life and that of others depended on it? Why should one not expect to receive a perfect adze from the adze maker? Think of our own expectations today when we go to buy a new car. Would you buy a car that is flawed, with even just a nick in the paint? Would you tolerate a wrench that doesn't work? Or a dentist who pulled the wrong tooth? Obviously, we expect the very best performances from others.

The Hawaiian attitude toward perfection, we must remember, was tied to his religious rationale. Any error committed in the course of work, either technically or ritualistically, was considered to be an omen of ill. Handy (1927) wrote: "In Tahiti in ancient times a small technical error might lead to the abandonment of the work in hand; while in Hawai'i a diviner might point out some defect in the construction of a house, predicting misfortune for its inmates if the error were not corrected. In the Marquesas the ancient craftsmen discarded defective products as worthless." In the consecrating rite for a canoe in Hawai'i, Malo wrote: "When the kahuna had finished his prayer he asked of the owner of the canoe, 'How is this service, this service of ours?' Because if anyone had made a disturbance or noise, or intruded upon the place, the ceremony had been marred and the owner of the canoe accordingly would have to report the ceremony to be *imperfect* [italics added]. And then the priest would warn the owner of the canoe, saying, 'Don't you go in this canoe lest you meet with a fatal accident.' " Pūku'i reminded us that flawed work invited public shame besides divine disapproval and personal shame. "Make a mistake in the *hula* during a solemn ritual performance, public shame— and the god's displeasure—followed. But to achieve later, public perfection, trials and mistakes were overlooked" (Pūku'i, Haertig, and Lee).

When we take a close look at the Hawaiian technologist's definition of perfection, we cannot help but be struck by the current ballyhoo about "quality control" and "high-standard performances" emanating from the board rooms of American management. Thus, when the guru of quality management, Philip B. Crosby, talks about it as "conformance to requirements" and means by that absolute "quality," that is, a product or a job flawlessly executed, he sounds like a noise out of the Hawaiian past. His notion of "Zero Defects" is only the equivalent of the Hawaiian word kīnā'ole, without defects. Plainly, no semantic difficulty separates traditional Hawaiian and modern American terms about perfection. The only discrepancy lies in the workers' awareness of sacred responsibility toward maintaining standards of excellence at all stages of the technological process.

Finally, we cannot speak of perfection or excellence without relating it to the idea of achievement, both for the individual and for a member within a group. Neither could the Hawaiian, although a synonym in the language for the term achievement is not available. The word definitely has a modern ring to it, partly because of the attention it gets from professional motivators who have built a cult of achievement "junkies." But Pūku'i wrote forthrightly about its origins in early Hawaiian thought. "Hawaiians admired achievement. They wanted perfection" (Pūku'i, Haertig, and Lee). The essence of Hawaiians' thoughts about achievement is expressed in proverbs concerned with reaching the summit, as in *"Kū i ke 'aki,"* "Having reached the very highest spot." The achievement is always greater when the risks and difficulties are bigger, as in " *'O ka pi'i nō ia a Kōkīo Wailau,"* referring to admiration for those who reach the top in spite of obstacles. (KōkīoWailau are high peaks on the island of Moloka'i.) In modern literature about achieving (beginning with David McClelland), the idea is the same: the attaining of a goal or pinnacle that requires some exertion and some risk. Achievement and perfection are two faces of the same mountain, for when you have reached the summit you have in effect achieved perfection. Undoubtedly this understanding of a traditional value, and a strong wish to encourage the flagging spirit of her demoralized people, led Queen Emma to adopt as her motto, *"Kūlia i ka nu'u,"* or "Strive for the summit!"

Perfection, excellence, quality, achievement—together with their associated virtues of industry, diligence, discipline, ingenuity, and others that we shall discuss in our next chapter—all these are placed at the top of the technician's hierarchy of values. These values are personified in the ideal technician, who strives to satisfy the needs of his patrons and society by the best use of the available resources and his tools. No wonder the Hawaiians of old regarded their skilled specialists with respect and dignity. How different the Hawaiian attitude was from that of Greeks and Romans, who "denied all possibility of moral or political virtue" to their craftsmen, classifying them as "worthless by public opinion, neither courted by friends, feared by enemies, nor envied by . . . fellow-citizens" (Burford). The Hawaiian technician was accorded every honor that the cultured Greeks and Romans denied to theirs.

The Top Twenty

For the past few years, Donald Kilolani Mitchell of the Kamehameha Schools has been a hit on the local lecture circuit with his
slide talk on what he calls the "peaks" of Hawaiian culture. A
dedicated Hawaiianophile who has taught, studied, and written
about Hawaiian culture for more than fifty years, he has defined
fourteen fields of achievement among the people of old, and has
supported his list with statements from recognized authorities
on Hawaiian and Polynesian cultures, such as Kenneth Emory,
E. S. C. Handy, and Peter Buck. (See Mitchell's *Resource Units in
Hawaiian Culture*.) The list includes:

1. Canoes
2. Featherwork
3. Wooden bowls
4. Gourd bowls and bottles
5. Twine baskets
6. Sleeping mats
7. Bark cloth, or kapa
8. Musical instruments
9. Chants
10. Dance, or hula, instruments
11. Agriculture
12. Fishing equipment and the fishponds
13. Sports and pastimes
14. Religion

When asked to account for the popularity of his lecture, Mitchell replied, "It gives my audience an ethnic lift." Judging from the
reaction of his Hawaiian listeners in particular, that in itself is justification for his upbeat approach. He taps the feeling of pride and
the deepening sense of identity among Hawaiians that have characterized their cultural resurgence during the last few years. But it
also reveals, especially among today's kūpuna or those approaching that age, a willingness to deal with the feelings of inferiority
(some repressed, some quite open) about the accomplishments of
their preliterate forebears. Five or six decades ago such a lecture
probably could not have stirred much interest or conviction
among Hawaiians. We are reminded of this likelihood by the state-

ment of William T. Brigham, first director of the Bishop Museum. "Hawaiians seem ashamed of all that their ancestors made or used in the ages before the advent of white civilization and have removed so far as possible all relics of that indigenous civilization." One simple list of achievements will not wipe away completely that feeling of shame, but it can certainly provide Hawaiians with a better perspective toward their ancestral past.

Our "top twenty" achievements represent successful technologies chosen from what we might call our software, hardware, and processes matrix. They include both intellectual and material tools as well as the products they made. They are not an "outsider's" choices but rather are an "insider's" selections. This may seem to be a bit presumptuous, to think that we who are so far removed not only historically but, in a real sense, culturally as well, can put ourselves in the place of a Hawaiian of old and say that these are what *he* might have considered as the most significant accomplishments of his civilization. Nonetheless, this is what we have done. These are not arbitrary selections. They are chosen according to five criteria: an item's (1) usefulness to the community as a whole; (2) technical quality and complexity; (3) distinctiveness; (4) relevance, that is, relationship to the technological system of the time; and (5) merits (structural, functional, artistic, etc.), compared with similar objects in other primal cultures, particularly in Polynesia. We are aware of all the dangers involved in making these choices, as we recognize that this is clearly a gesture of "sticking one's neck out."

Finally, the selections are made from technologies used only in the precontact period, beginning with the arrival of the first Hawaiians in these islands, so that we can establish claim to *some* independent development. Also, we have taken the liberty of not presenting the twenty items in any order of importance (and thereby probably removed part of the fun from the contest).

Crab claw sail. The sail was the only technical invention that was regularly used to harness efficiently a major natural energy resource, and was the prime locomotive power for Hawai'i's canoes, the principal means of transportation along coasts and among islands.

Canoe. The canoe was the chief machine for transporting people and cargoes over long distances by water and for harvesting the bounties of the sea. The Hawaiian canoe has been described as technically "the finest in the Pacific." Captain Cook expressed his opinion of it in 1778. "As they are not more than fifteen or eighteen inches broad, those that go single have outriggers, which are shaped and fitted with more judgment than any I had before seen." And one of his ship's surgeons, William Ellis, wrote that the Hawaiian canoes "are the neatest we ever saw" (J. Beaglehole).

Navigation. Hawaiian navigators acquired the relevant knowledge about the stars, currents, waves, birds, winds, clouds, marine life, flotsam, and all the rest of the entire ocean environment, in addition to the skills of handling a canoe and its crew. Without charts, compass, or other instruments, navigators perforce had to store all of this important knowledge in the memory. Applying all this to long-distance voyaging, said Kenneth Emory (1965b), was part of "an enterprise that properly should rank among the great achievements of human history."

Calendar. A reliable calendar was indispensable for determining political, economic, religious, agricultural, astronomical, astrological, and other important events. Its invention and application to navigation in particular has been described as something that "must forever rank as one of the Polynesians' finest intellectual achievements."

Numerical system. The numerical system made possible the development of measurements, the calendar, and the design, manufacture, and use of all tools—in short, almost all aspects of Hawaiian technology. Next to language (both verbal and nonverbal) it was the most useful symbolic system Hawaiians ever developed.

Irrigation works. In an agricultural society, dependent on wetland taro in particular, irrigation systems were of greatest importance. The amount of terraced, cultivated, and irrigated land, especially in the valleys, has been judged "remarkable." Great engineering skills were needed to design and build the irrigation systems, and sociopolitical skills to maintain them. Of the kinds of structures built specifically for irrigation, the "Menehune Ditch" on the island of Kaua'i represents, according to Wendell C. Bennett, "the most remarkable piece of work of its kind, not only in the Hawaiian islands but in all of Polynesia."

Heiau. Nothing represents better the economic and technological power of Hawaiian religion than the building and maintaining of five to six hundred temples. No other man-made structures used so much of available natural and human resources. Some of of the great massive heiau (mainly the luakini, of which about a hundred are known) are also the largest constructions of stone to be erected not only in Hawai'i but also in all of Polynesia.

Fish ponds. More than two hundred fish ponds were constructed in old Hawai'i. They were the most extensive and the most advanced aquacultural systems in all the islands of Polynesia. Some of the larger ponds covered more than five hundred acres, with walls extending five thousand feet constructed out of stones, some of which weighed as much as half a ton. A high degree of engineering skill was required to design and construct ponds, along with their ingenious mākāhā, or sluice gates.

Simple machines. The wedge, inclined plane, lever, and pump drill represent the basic "kinematic" devices to which almost all Hawaiian tools were related. Without those simple machines Hawaiian technology would never have advanced to the level it reached before 1778.

Taro cultivation. As the starch staple, taro was the most intensively cultivated crop in Hawai'i; in fact, no other Polynesians placed as much importance on taro as did Hawaiians. The first settlers brought a few named varieties with them; by 1778 the number of varieties having Hawaiian names increased to between 300 and 343. This number was "larger in Hawai'i than in any other part of the Pacific" (Handy, Handy, and Pūku'i).

Plant breeding. Donald Mitchell (1982b) said that Hawaiians were "the most sophisticated horticulturalists" in Polynesia. This reputation was gained in part through their knowledge of methods for hybridizing plants and their complementary experimental skills. The art required an advanced understanding of plant behavior, as well as great discipline and patience. As a result, Hawaiians developed at least 24 varieties of sweet potato, 200 of the world's 300 varieties of taro, 12 or more types of gourd, 20 or more varieties of sugarcane, and hybrids of many other valuable plants, such as bananas and wauke, or paper mulberry.

Gourds. No other Pacific peoples grew so many varieties of ipu, or *Lagenaria sisceraria*, or used them for so many different purposes. Perhaps, too, no other people perfected the cultivation of the plant to a higher degree. Gourds provided the best storage containers, an important household convenience for a people who prepared so many semiliquid foodstuffs, such as poi and 'inamona.

Hygiene. The Hawaiians were described as one of the healthiest and cleanest populations in the Pacific. Ebenezer Townsend, an American whaling officer, observed in 1798, "They certainly are the most cleanly people that I have seen." O. A. Bushnell stated that "the aboriginal Hawaiians were an extraordinarily healthy people, who were afflicted with no important infectious diseases." He attributed this good health in part to the kapu regulating personal and public hygiene.

Medicine. In general, Hawaiians had advanced higher in medical training and pharmacology than any other Polynesians. In 1951 Sir Peter Buck stated that "the Hawaiians were the only branch of the Polynesians who built special temples of healing termed *heiau lapa'au*." (He was speaking at the occasion of the rededication of Heiau Keaīwa, the healing temple in 'Aiea, O'ahu.) "Again the Hawaiians were the only Polynesians who specialized in seeking the medicinal virtues of plants." He also stated that the medical technicians had invented a bamboo blow syringe and gourd enema funnels for treating obstinate constipation. In his opinion, by 1778 Hawaiians were so advanced in this subject that they were "on the threshold of the scientific investigation of disease."

Featherwork. Lt. James King, one of Captain Cook's officers, wrote in 1784, "The feathered cloak and helmet . . . , in point of beauty and magnificence, is perhaps nearly equal to that of any nation in the world." Te Rangi Hiroa added that King "could have omitted the 'nearly' without exaggeration." While featherwork was also developed in Tahiti and New Zealand, Buck stated that "the Hawaiians should be given credit for having invented their own feather capes and cloaks." And Lahilahi Webb *(Ancient Hawaiian Civilization)* wrote, "Nowhere was the featherwork more beautifully and skillfully done than it was by the feather craftsmen of old Hawai'i." As ornamental and ceremonial robes, feather cloaks are among the highest achievements of Hawaiian functional art.

Kapa, or bark cloth. Because it was the only kind of material for clothing available to Hawaiians, kapa was *the* textile around which an entire industry was built. The quality attained was "the finest in the Pacific and probably in the world." As Te Rangi Hiroa (Peter Buck) stated, "Polynesian bark cloth is superior, on the whole, to that made in any other area" (which included Africa,

South America, Indonesia, Southeast Asia, and Melanesia). He went on to say: "Within Polynesia itself . . . the Hawaiian bark cloth displays the greatest varieties of texture and colored designs. In its manufacture, the Hawaiians developed some forms of technique not used elsewhere." Also, "Nowhere else were such thin varieties of cloth made" (some of these have been likened to fine muslin). Hawaiians prepared and used a greater number of dyes and variety of colored patterns than did any other peoples in Polynesia. They had achieved a sophisticated knowledge of the physical-chemical process of dyeing. Captain Cook's second in command, Charles Clerke, observed, "These People excell most, in the art of dying; they dye in a variety of fashions, some of them in my Opinion beautifull; their colours are clear and good, and the being wet takes no effect upon them." Perhaps nowhere else in the Pacific was a wider array of tools and techniques used for manufacturing bark cloth.

Cordage. In a society without nails, iron, or modern aids, like Scotch tape and wire, cordage was indispensable for house making, featherwork, hauling, fishing nets, and canoe lashings, among many other things. In 1786 Capt. Nathaniel Portlock noted that Hawaiian cordage was "perfectly well made . . . and much stronger than our lines of twice the size." Nearly twenty years later Hawaiians were manufacturing cordage of such high quality that in 1804 George Langsdorff could say, "Ships are supplied with them and they are considered as more durable for tackling than the European cordage." Hawaiian cordage was being produced and bartered in balls, each of which held enough cord to extend for a quarter to half a mile. Donald Mitchell (1982b) said that endemic olonā "produces the strongest and finest plant fibers which man has been able to grow and make into cordage."

Musical instruments. In the means for making music Hawaiians probably were more inventive than any other people in Polynesia. Of the eighteen-or-so instruments used to accompany hula and chanting, about half were invented here. Among these were the ipu, or gourd instruments, the papa hehi, or treadle board, and the 'ulī'ulī, or gourd rattle. Buck wrote of the gourd rattle: "[It] is a tribute to the artistic taste and inventive genius of the early Hawaiian craftsmen." (See this author's *Hawaiian Music and Musicians* [1979] for more details.)

Mnemonic devices. Since memory was the key to transmitting all information, extraordinary mnemonic skills were extremely important to Hawaiians of old. Their retentive powers were undoubtedly comparable to those of other Polynesians and primal peoples.

Rituals and prayers. As no alienation separated religion from technology, rituals and prayers were essential in nearly every aspect of technology, from training experts, selecting raw materials, making and using tools, to ensuring the quality and protection of the end products.

No doubt some readers will question our choice of these top twenty entries. Frankly, we invite that challenge. One might take issue, for example, with including both "Hygiene" and "Medicine." But a valid distinction can be made between the practice of medicine as a profession and the rules for personal and public hygiene involving prescriptions for sanitation and protection of the environment. On the other hand, one might criticize leaving out house building, fishing, basket weaving, shaping of wooden bowls, and sports, all of which are mentioned in Mitchell's list. In fact, we seriously considered including petroglyphs as an entry because, as Halley Cox stated, "Nowhere in the Pacific are there fields so extensive in size or so heavily covered with markings as those in the Hawaiian islands." Furthermore, speculative as this may be, had Cook not arrived when he did, Hawaiians may have moved in only a short time from inscribing immovable stones to scratching upon stone tablets with a form of writing. But, in the end, we dismissed petroglyphs because they are not as Hawaiian as are the other entries.

One might also question the inclusion of items that may seem to be more aesthetic or artistic accomplishments than technological. The old Hawaiians made no such distinction, for to them art and technical skill or craftsmanship were synonymous. Objects of art were created by craftsmen, who had trained and practiced so hard and so long that the line between craftsmanship and art simply disappeared. This is not to say that the Hawaiian craftsman, for all his practicality, did not occasionally feel beauty and, being inspired, express it aesthetically. We cannot help but agree with Adrienne Kaeppler. "Certainly one of the high points of Polynesian art from any point of view, featherworking was the most prestigious artistic medium for Hawaiians." Yet, she did not hesitate to add, "The making of a feather cloak or cape required the attainment of technical perfection in several difficult techniques." In judging what is traditional art, we must be careful about taking a Western point of view, not only because that is about all we know, but also because we know so little about what Hawaiians might have considered aesthetically pleasing. In any case, we'd best remember the conclusion of Kawena Pūkuʻi, to the effect that the Hawaiians did not subscribe to the modern notion of "art for art's sake."

Finally, to some people our list of superlatives might lead them to think that we are bragging too much about our kūpuna—which is quite an un-Polynesian thing to do. However, we have been very careful to cite the considered opinions of non-Hawaiians mostly who presumably bring objectivity to the exercise. Perhaps objectivity would have been put in doubt if we had quoted only our own native authorities. By no means do we wish to give the impression that the Hawaiians were better than any of their Polynesian "cousins." An entirely different kind of list could be drawn up showing the comparative strengths and achievements of other Polynesian groups. For example, William Ellis observed that in surgical techniques the Hawaiians "seemed to be far behind the Society Islanders." Or, despite the Hawaiians' plant breeding skills, they grew only one variety of breadfruit, while Tahitians grew about fifty varieties and the Marquesans developed two hundred. Or, capable farmers and technologists though they were, the Hawaiians never managed to improve the ʻōʻō. But the Maoris did, by attaching to it a simple instep, in order to obtain more leverage. In any case, our essay presents the facts about a history of homegrown technological achievements.

Technological Revolution: 1778

It began with nails . . .

That is how a historian wanting to write a complete history of Hawaiian technological development might begin the story of the chain of events that changed Hawaiʻi forever. Of all the objects aboard Captain Cook's ships, those iron nails attracted the keenest interest among Hawaiians. They saw immediately how from those lengths of iron they could fashion knives, daggers, fishhooks, and other implements. But the nail, of course, is only the symbolic beginning, for Hawaiians eagerly tried to acquire, by whatever means, the iron axes, the muskets, mirrors, blankets, kerchiefs, baubles, and trinkets, and—according to reports— almost everything else on those floating islands that could not be tied down or locked up.

We can only guess at the feelings and thoughts that the sight of the *Resolution* and the *Discovery* and their marvelous equipment undoubtedly aroused in the Hawaiians. Wonder, excitement, fear, awe, anxiety, admiration, and envy must have stirred everyone. Besides the normal curiosity of an isolated people for things that were new, their reactions must have been intensified by their ingrained belief in the power of tools. Thus, in recognizing the superiority of the foreign technologies, they also accorded them greater charges of mana. Obviously, they decided that iron was in many ways a material much superior to basalt, and hence assumed that it possessed a superior mana of its own. Not only did they want to possess the new material objects, but they also wanted to acquire the skills that came along with them. Furthermore, since they had looked up to their own technicians, they easily transferred similar respect to the foreign technicians. Indeed, they were prepared to give instant status to a few of the haole crewmen, such as the armorers and the blacksmiths.

Among those Hawaiians who greeted the new technology with very mixed feelings were the professional technicians and crafts people. On the one hand they could appreciate more quickly the technical features of what they saw, and, on the other, they could imagine the effects that the introduction of the new technology might have on their society, but especially on their own self-interests. After all, they had to preserve their own status and did not want it jeopardized. This is a natural reaction that has characterized craftsmen and workers everywhere throughout the history of technological change. Nevertheless, no one could have foreseen the magnitude and pace of that change—nor its dramatic consequences. In their earlier history Hawaiians had no precedent for the experiences that Cook's visits brought upon them.

Until then, Hawaiian technology had evolved at a relatively slow rate—except, perhaps, when the islands were first settled. In those critical years the immigrants' efforts to survive would have created many demands for invention and adaptation. Throughout subsequent centuries, the rate of invention probably was not uniform, particularly in periods allowing interchange of ideas and people when canoe voyages to central Polynesia were still being made. Yet even during these times of activity, most likely evolution was slow. For example, despite the digging stick's importance in agriculture, apparently little improvement to it was ever made for a thousand years or so. The number of simple machines in use seems to have remained fairly constant. However, the pace of change was uneven, varying with the field of technology. While innovation in mechanics was minimal, probably more advances occurred in agriculture at a faster tempo, especially in the improvement of plant varieties and methods of cultivation. In these respects, Hawaiians were no different from other people: in virtually every developing society important technological leaps are the rare exceptions, not the rule. Conditioned as we are to the rapid pace of technological innovation, we forget that even the simplest devices in use before the industrial revolution took many centuries to develop. Where we today start our creative thinking at high levels, the ancients started theirs at much lower points.

One of the important consequences of this gradual evolution in technologies is that Hawaiians and their tools developed together. This allowed craftsmen to influence their tools even while using them. Technologies developed so slowly that they did not outstrip the slow evolution of social and cultural institutions. No Hawaiian ever became subservient to his tools, however important and mana laden those might have been. His tools enabled him to do his work and to sustain himself and his family, but he always kept control over them. In short, he evolved a reasonable equilibrium between technological and social change.

In contrast, after 1778 Hawaiians were confronted with changes that were no longer evolutionary but revolutionary. First, the new technologies were introduced from the great world outside Hawai'i, along with their new and peculiar sets of assumptions and values. Second, the flood of changes began instantly and continued to flow over the islands at an unprecedented magnitude and with unheard of speed. The Hawaiian had scarcely begun to learn about the uses of iron, when he learned about setting up and operating a forge, complete with anvil, tongs, hammers, and all the other equipment a smithy needed. We are told, for example, that Hawaiians were working their own crude forges by early 1779. The same process of learning is repeated again and again, in many different fields, from armaments to ship building. Third, the new skills and techniques were completely controlled by foreigners, because they monopolized both the sources of supply and the technical knowledge. And fourth, none of the traditional sanctions of Hawaiian religion or of normal public pressures applied to the outsiders and their tools.

In short, for the first time in their history Hawaiians began to lose control over their tools. No longer could they count on a gradual accommodation between technology and other aspects of their lives. By 1800 the new technology had already begun to outstrip their capacity to control them; instead of tools being adapted to their needs and rhythms, the Hawaiians found themselves having to adapt to the new technology. No longer are Hawaiians and their machines in equilibrium, no longer does a strong sense of mutuality join people, tools, and technicians.

For the outsider looking in upon the scene, the consequences of the revolution were predictable. The old institutions, industries, skills, even the familiar objects themselves were altered, replaced, or eliminated, and so also, in their wake, went the rituals, sanctions, and values. Tommy Holmes recounted the succession of events in the tragedy of the canoe.

> In the chaos of "contact" many of the ancient Hawaiian skills, technologies and institutions that took precious centuries to develop vanished in a matter of a few years. While certain canoe-building traditions and activities continued even into the early twentieth century, most of the huge and complex body of knowledge surrounding canoe construction was lost forever. . . . The canoe was a delicate continuum. Rituals, ceremonies, taboos and traditions were a canoe builder's irreplaceable blueprints. As these were forgotten, abandoned or devalued, the canoe disappeared.

Revolutionary change followed the same pattern in kapa making, which gradually disappeared, along with its use for clothing, its technicians, tools, techniques, and processes, and its rituals. Iron hatchets and axes eventually made obsolete the adzes carefully shaped from stone, along with their skilled makers, their apprentices, and all their techniques and rituals—and the fostering gods.

Hawaiians are still suffering from the loss of their culture that began in 1778. Perhaps one of the symptoms of their wounding is our tendency to blame other things or other people for our troubles. But what we must remember about the consequences of this technological revolution is this: when we look about to find the enemy, it is us. The revolution, the time of change, started with that first harmless nail. But the decision to want that nail was one our kūpuna made entirely of their own will. In truth, their hunger for iron began not with the arrival of Captain Cook's ships, but with the finding of nails and scrap iron among the flotsam cast up on Hawaiian beaches long before 1778. Theoretically, at least, the Hawaiians could have rejected the possibility of using those first British nails. And, had they done that, conceivably they might also have rejected any subsequent contact with the technology presented by British voyagers. But if this alternative strikes us as being implausible and unreasonable, is that not because it runs entirely counter to the logic of precontact technological development and the very practicality of the Hawaiian character? The point to remember is that Hawaiians deliberately chose to use the tools and ideas of the "new world." Having once made that decision, they could not turn back, could not close their shores to later visitors, could not shut out the big world beyond.

The technological as well as the religious fate of Hawai'i was sealed in 1819, at the Battle of Kuamo'o, with the defeat of those ali'i who wanted to preserve the old ways and the weakening hold of the past. Those of us today who talk about reviving the "natural state" of old Hawai'i, in the hope of living as once upon a time the people of old lived, really honor the past without thinking about the present. Those romantics who want to reproduce in the twentieth century the life-style of the eighteenth century are deluded. Nor are they listening to their kūpuna, who undoubtedly would reject the notion as being utopian and utterly impractical, not to mention damned uncomfortable. This yearning to go back to nature is a recurring historical phenomenon in all countries, but, ironically, the record of the last two decades shows that the rush back to living in the wild woods has turned out to be little more than spending a weekend in a place that provides all the modern conveniences.

Lessons for the Future

Now, more than two hundred years after Cook's expedition presented us to the world, we Hawaiians, along with all the rest of humankind, are caught up in a technological revolution that is immensely more complicated than was the one our ancestors met. And, moreover, it is accelerating at exponential rates of growth. While no one denies the innumerable material benefits that have been granted to the human race through technology, almost everyone agrees that we face some enormous problems as a result of technology. Critics of modern technology paint a very grim picture of it, complete with details like the "thousand-year problem" of radioactive wastes; the nightmare of an accidental meltdown happening at a nuclear plant; inadvertent "microbe spills" from genetic engineering laboratories; "acid rain," which is killing off plant and animal life in vast areas of earth; urban smog that causes more than 50 percent of the illnesses and deaths due to bronchitis, and about 25 percent of cases of lung cancer in the United States alone; the "automated" unemployment imposed by the electronic age; the holocaust expected in a third world war; and the threat of total extinction from nuclear warfare, to name just a few worries that fall upon us with each new day. We are all trapped in a technological prison from which, predict the Orwellian doomsayers, we shall find "no escape."

Jacques Ellul, the French founding father of the contemporary antitechnological movement, echoes the sentiments of many when he decries a society being taken over by "technique." Like a tidal wave, it advances inexorably, leaving man helpless in its manic, mindless wake. The perfection of technology has become an end in itself, thus alienating man from his true nature. Ellul is joined by other famed critics, such as Lewis Mumford, Charles A. Reich, Herbert Marcuse, and Theodore Roszak, among others. It would be unfair to paint them all with the same brush, for some, like Roszak, admit that technology as such is not to be blamed for our troubles, and that, if the human condition is to be improved, the contributions of technology are indispensable. But, in the final analysis, all critics are united in their fear of a technology "run amok."

Of course, tearing down a shaky structure is easier than strengthening it. Most "techno-rebels," to use Alvin Toffler's phrase, prefer critical analysis rather than prescriptive advice on how to make the situation better. But invariably, among those critics who offer remedies, they turn to man's primal or medieval past. Mumford, for example, states that the farmer of neolithic times "brought the outer and inner life into harmony." Ellul, who is pessimistic about stopping or slowing the advance of technology, presents no solution, but he does remind us that "primitive" man "worked as little as possible and was content with a restricted consumption of goods. . . . The time given to the use of technique was short, compared with the leisure time devoted to sleep, conversation, games, or, best of all, to meditation." Reich believes that early man "built his life around the rhythms of earth and his mental stability upon the constancies of nature." He also states approvingly that "the oldtime peasant had very real capacity for a nonmaterial existence."

Thus, can we not take a cue from these critics by searching our own Hawaiian historical experience for values and insights that might be relevant to some of our current technological problems? Our discussion so far has come up with the following opinions: (1) the tool exists to serve man's purposes, hence, technology is ultimately subordinate to human ends; (2) man is the master of his tools, yet must respect them; (3) a spiritual connection develops between man, his tools, and their end products; (4) perfection, as in flawless performances or products, is important to the technological process; (5) technicians deserve respect for their skills and their mana; (6) the underlying strength of any technology is confidence in man's intellectual and spiritual power; (7) technological development needs to be synchronized with social development; (8) technological growth should be neither fast nor slow, only balanced, thereby permitting the complete development of the individual and society.

If only one lesson from the Hawaiian past can be applied to the universal condition of the "technological animal," it is that, clearly, the responsibility for making decisions that affect the fate of man and his tools must be returned to the control of man.

PART FOUR

ECONOMICS

10

THE RELEVANCE OF PRIMAL ECONOMICS

The Uneconomic Man

In the early 1960s Professor Joseph C. Finney of the University of Hawai'i reported his conclusions from a study about the attitudes of Hawaiians and non-Hawaiians toward Hawaiians. This was a part of a larger study focusing on the feelings and attitudes of people from several ethnic groups in Hawai'i toward each other. The results are interesting not only for what they tell about stereotyping Hawaiians, but also for what they reveal about the image of Hawaiians as they relate to the economy of our times. The Hawaiians were described "as being dependent; as working no harder than they have to; as not being ambitious; as not being conscientious in carrying out responsibilities or fulfilling duties and obligations"—and as being warm, friendly, fun loving, and not serious. The report offered one sweeping and perceptive generalization. "On the whole one could take Weber's description of the 'Protestant ethic and the spirit of capitalism' as a good description of what the Hawaiians are regarded as not being like."

What the survey confirmed is a stereotyped view of the Hawaiian today as being the personification of an "uneconomic man"—a man who has few wants, hence cares little for accumulating material possessions; has no sense of value, and so will give you the "shirt off his back" with no thought of any repayment; has no wish to make money or profit; has an undeveloped sense of property; lacks business acumen; is incapable of saving for a rainy day; and is lazy, undisciplined, carefree, and generous to a fault. Although this view has been somewhat dimmed by the passage of time and the process of acculturation, still, like a barnacle on a ship's hull, the stereotype has stuck to the public's collective mind until today.

Most of us know that stereotypes are distortions of reality and for that reason we are troubled by them, always excepting, of course, those prejudices we may happen to agree with. Historically speaking, stereotypes may contain elements of both truth and untruth, although psychologically the truths built into a stereotype may be less important than are the stereotype-holder's perceptions of reality. While we must be aware of this two-sided property of stereotyping, for purposes of this discussion we are going to be concerned mainly with the historical as well as the cultural accuracy of the stereotype. We add that our interest in the stereotyping of Hawaiians should not be taken to mean that Hawaiians are the only victims, for we are very well aware that all ethnic groups in Hawai'i are stereotyped, some more so than others.

What characteristics in the behavior of Hawaiians, both in pre- and postcontact times, affirm or deny the truth in the stereotype? Although this is not a study in stereotyping, the subject does suggest a number of important points relating to Hawaiians' economic ideas, practices, and values.

The first point is concerned with whether Hawaiians of old did have an economic system to speak of and, if so, what were its distinguishing features. Some strange and divided opinions have been expressed on this subject. In order for us to reach an answer, we must describe the historical setting of Hawai'i before 1778, a description made doubly necessary by the fact that as yet no one has done a thorough study of traditional Hawaiian economics. We shall be looking closely at the ahupua'a as an economic unit, in terms of its resources, productivity, distribution (whether by "gift exchange" and/or barter), surplus or generation of wealth, and division of labor. Since Hawaiian economics, or any other economics for that matter, cannot be separated from the social context, we shall devote much attention to "socioeconomic" phenomena; indeed, the social economy is what we are dealing with. Hence, such values as generosity, reciprocity, hospitality, cooperativeness, and aloha will be important in our discussion. We shall make some necessary contrasts, some perhaps even startling, between the traditional and the modern economic systems. We shall discuss some heretofore unrecognized elements in the pre-1778 organization of specialists, such as the itinerant "peddlers." And we shall conclude with observations on some modern economic developments among Hawaiians.

"Primitive" Economics

Until the early part of this century, scholars generally believed that preliterate peoples lived in a kind of "preeconomic" state of nature, with no concept of wealth, no medium of exchange, only the vaguest notion of organized work, and no economic motives. They were poor, living from hand to mouth, eking out a precarious life of insecurity and insufficiency, unproductive or idle most of the time, thriftless, and irrational. They were savages who, almost by definition, could not be thought of in ordinary economic terms. This prevailing viewpoint doubtlessly found expression in the stereotype of the "uneconomic" Hawaiian and similar stereotyping of Maoris and other Polynesians, North American Indians, and the Bushmen and other tribal peoples of Africa. Indeed, almost anywhere one might go among primal peoples—or read about them—one hears the same charges.

But thanks to the work of anthropologists—not of economists, who have carefully avoided studying "primitive" economies—this old misconception has been dispelled. The pioneers in this field, now called "economic anthropology," include Bronislaw Malinowski (1921), who demonstrated that the Trobriand Islanders had their own concept of wealth and definite mechanisms for its distribution, as well as a system for the organization of work, communal enterprise, and even extensive bartering. His pupil, Raymond Firth, followed him in 1929 with a landmark study, *Economics of the New Zealand Maori*, which described how the precontact Maori developed an economic structure with specific distribution mechanisms, concepts of ownership, and values of work, thrift, and reciprocity, among other concepts. (Firth's work still stands as an example to any scholar who might wish to do a similar study of Hawaiian economics.) Malinowski and Firth have been followed by many others who have studied the traditional economies of African, American Indian, Mexican, and several other cultures. From their observations we can be sure that all communities or societies, no matter how "primitive," do have economic systems.

By "economic systems" we mean some kind of structured arrangement, with a definite set of rules, by which the necessary goods and services are produced and distributed to the members of a given community. Since no society leaves to chance the production of material goods without which neither individuals nor communities could survive, an organized method must exist to perform all these functions. The characteristics of this systematic arrangement, and the operation of the system, provide the subjects for economic anthropologists to observe.

The cumulative studies of "primitive" economies during the last sixty years share a number of distinguishing features: (1) relatively simple technological development; (2) limited division of labor with a short list of occupations; (3) productive units that more often than not are based on social bonds rather than on economic ones; (4) no labor or capital markets, nor a distribution system for goods produced; (5) no money as a medium of exchange; (6) systems for exchange that range from markets to redistributive systems, reciprocal exchange, and mobilization exchange (where goods and services are collected by an elite for use in achieving their broad political aims, as happened in the Hawaiian chieftainships); and (7) wealth and capital generally are controlled by and for social rather than economic ends. However, because preliterate economies vary widely, depending on their peculiar social, political, religious, technological, or natural environments, not all of these features may be present in any given community. Furthermore, a particular system may even have additional or more advanced characteristics such as "quasi-money," in the form of cocoa beans among the Aztecs, tusked pigs among the Melanesians, and special shells among the Polynesians. Keep these general features in mind, because we shall be looking for them or their equivalents in our analysis of the Hawaiian economic system.

We know from our own cultural experience how easily we can be misled when we or outsiders try to describe traditional Hawaiian concepts and practices in terms of a foreign or a modern set of ideas and vocabularies. This is a perennial problem both for people who are objects being studied and for those who are doing the observing. This problem has sustained a controversy that has raged among economic anthropologists for several decades. The issue concerns the extent to which they should adopt ordinary modern economic terms to analyze "primitive" economies. Modern terminology is based on a body of economic theory that has been created to analyze industrial capitalist economies, not primal cultures. Should scholars borrow these concepts and terms, or should they devise a special set of words and ideas intended for traditional economies? One group of scholars argues that the terms of conventional economic theory are applicable, while the other contends that they are not. Unfortunately, while the disputes go on, the special vocabulary still awaits invention. Meanwhile, we have no alternative but to use the only vocabulary we know—being sensitive, however, to its limitations.

From the Uplands to the Sea

Mention the word ahupua'a and many of us immediately envision a valley, such as Kahana or Waipi'o, extending from the kuahiwi, or mountains, to ma kai, or toward the beach and into the sea. We see a valley floor divided into lo'i, taro patches, located either on the alluvial plain or on terraces ma uka, ascending from the central stream toward the uplands. The lo'i are connected by the all-important irrigation system, which runs parallel to the long-axis boundaries of the ahupua'a. On nearby lands grow the other main crops, such as sweet potato, sugarcane, banana, breadfruit, coconut, wauke, gourd, and tī plants. On the slopes or hillsides and in the lower forests are arrowroot, turmeric, bamboo, olonā; and in the upper forests are stands of koa, 'ōhi'a lehua, mamaki, kukui, and other trees and shrubs that supply the materials for making homes, canoes, utensils, weapons, cordage, medicines, and firewood for cooking ovens. Scattered areas, perhaps some enclosures, are set aside for the domesticated pigs, chickens, and dogs. Finally, in places along the shore are the fish ponds, and beyond them stretches the sea—the great storehouse of marine life that provides additional foodstuffs, medicines, and materials for tools, ornaments, and some structures built on land.

Such is a picture of an ideal ahupua'a, containing an adequate water source, arable alluvial soils, a shoreline with access to seaside and reef areas, and forested uplands. While it might lack some special materials, such as outcrops of densest basalt for making adzes, it provides all the resources necessary for a self-sufficient socioeconomic unit. But not all ahupua'a were so blessed. Of the more than one thousand land sections that have been identified as ahupua'a (including a few large 'ili or smaller 'ohana sections), many were not the pie-shaped valley we imagine, but simply defined sections of land, some located in extensive districts having few valleys, such as Puna and Ka'ū on the Big Island. Some of those sections were virtually landlocked or lacked an upland forest area. While arrangements were made to enable such incomplete communities to gain access to the necessary resources, goods, or services in other sections, we are not entirely clear what these arrangements were. Suffice it to say, the model for our analysis is the ideal ahupua'a of a self-sustaining subsistence economy.

Anthropologist Robert Hommon has estimated the mean population of an ahupua'a at about 247 individuals, and the range from 149 people on Moloka'i to 535 on Kaua'i. The average ahupua'a populations for Hawai'i, Maui, and O'ahu were 229, 221, and 286, respectively, with 518 for Lāna'i and 310 for Ni'ihau. Therefore, in no instance would we be dealing with a population base larger than a few hundred individuals, for even the largest ahupua'a. Keep in mind, however, that more than a thousand such land sections are known: 523 on Hawai'i, 339 on Maui, 210 on O'ahu, 67 on Moloka'i, 56 on Kaua'i, 11 on Lāna'i, and 5 on Ni'ihau. Unfortunately, we have no other demographic data about the age or sex of the average population. Did they sustain more young people than old? Given the relatively short life span of our kūpuna, a younger population would have been more likely. This would have an important bearing on the socioeconomic character of the ahupua'a, but, alas, we can only speculate about that.

With regard to its socioeconomic organization, the fundamental unit of an ahupua'a was the commoner's extended family, or 'ohana. This was composed of "relatives by blood, marriage and adoption, living some inland and some near the sea but connected geographically in and tied by ancestry, birth and sentiment to a particular locality" (Hommon). According to Handy and Pūku'i, who, by the way, were talking specifically about Ka'ū on the Big Island, the 'ohana was composed of several households, or hale, each the equivalent of a nuclear family with the conjugal parents, their children, and attached related or unrelated dependents and helpers. The size of the household is unknown, although according to Timothy Earle's study of the ahupua'a in Halele'a on Kaua'i, the average size there was 5.8. In any case, the essential point is that the household was the basic production unit in the Hawaiian economy. We might add that this has been true almost universally among preindustrial societies. Our English term "economy" recalls this origin: it comes from the Greek root for the word meaning household. From its very beginning, economic activity has always had a social context.

The functioning authority in the 'ohana was always the oldest male in the senior branch of the extended family. He was called the haku, master or director. In contrast, the household head, or po'o, was not necessarily the senior member of the 'ohana, but he was the person invested with the responsibility for the family and with power to make decisions affecting it. While decisions usually were made in concert with family members, including women, ultimately most decision making, whether social or economic, rested in the hands of the elder males. Furthermore, determinations regarding use-rights to the land and other resources were the prerogatives of the same males. Thus, not surprisingly, the males dominated the domestic economy of the ahupua'a.

Each household was granted the right of use to a segment of land called an 'ili. Usually this was a narrow strip of the ahupua'a, stretching from the uplands to the sea. The pieces of lands in some 'ili were not contiguous, so that one part might be near the sea and another in an upland area, but each 'ili was supposed to contain all the essential resource zones that enabled a household to be self-sufficient. All awards of land were granted by the ruling ali'i, who could also take them away, but in practice the "faithful henchmen cultivated the same land generation after generation." David Malo nicely described the maka'ainana's sense of place: "The country people were strongly attached to their own homelands, the full calabash, the roasted potatoes, the warm food, to live in the midst of abundance. Their hearts went out to the land of their birth."

In exchange for the right to use the land, the maka'ainana, in Malo's words, "did all the work on the land." They were the prime producers of the goods and services, although they did not provide all the services. As we have seen, certain important specialist services were rendered by technician-priests, some of whom were ali'i, although lower ranking members of the aristocracy. But all other services, especially the labor for communal enterprises, came from the members of the 'ili'ohana households. Clearly, they were the foundation upon which the Hawaiian economic order rested.

Above the maka'ainana in the socioeconomic structure were the owners of the means of production—the sacrosanct capitalists of old Hawai'i—the ali'i 'ai ahupua'a, literally, the chiefs who ate the ahupua'a. That is an apt label, because such a chief has claims not only over the lands and other natural resources, but also over the entire production as well. Malo described perfectly the power relationship between commoner and chief. "It was the *maka'āinana* also who did all the work on the land; yet all they produced from the soil belonged to the chiefs; and the power to expel a man from the land and rob him of his possession lay with the chief." The chief made all major economic decisions as to how the resources of the ahupua'a were used, allocated, and redistributed. But to suggest that the chief played the role of some kind of economic czar would be incorrect, since neither his motives nor goals were purely economic. Rather, they were sociospiritual, as we can conclude from his aspirations to gain the intangible merits of mana, prestige, and mythic glory.

If we stopped our analysis here, at the level of the 'iliahupua'a, we could say that the Hawaiian economic system consisted of as many separate lesser systems as there were ahupua'a, since each was more or less self-sufficient. Then we would have a series of contiguous, but economically autonomous, disconnected autarchies. In a way, that is really what many of us envision when we think of Hawai'i as an ahupua'a economy. But this would be like the blind men trying to identify an elephant by feeling only one part of its body. As basic as the ahupua'a economy was, it must have been incomplete for an entire island.

In fact, the economic system extended beyond the ahupua'a into the larger all-inclusive chiefdoms. Each of those was based on a moku, or district, and the whole-island mokupuni. Whereas the ahupua'a consisted of a population of maka'āinana mainly involved in producing for their own needs as well as for the local chief's maintenance, the moku or mokupuni chiefdoms involved ali'i 'ai moku contending for greater power. Because neither they, nor their large retinues and managers, the konohiki, were major producers, they had to rely on the commoners in the ahupua'a for the production of their food, shelter, weapons, and other material products. In order to meet those extra demands, each 'ohana in an ahupua'a had to produce a regular surplus, in exchange for which it received the continued use of the land, protection from potential enemies, and some of its own production, returned in the form of gifts from the ali'i 'ai moku. In effect, here we have a dual economic system: one at the lower level of the 'iliahupua'a, aimed at achieving local self-sufficiency; and the other at the higher level of the moku or mokupuni, directed at maximizing economic wealth in order to advance the high chief's power.

Economics is a function of politics. Hawaiian chiefs may not have invented this ageless form of political realism, but they certainly knew how to maintain it. What this means, in less cynical terms, is that the chiefs perpetuated a political economy whose primary role was an integrating one. The higher chiefs, with the help of their professional managers, the konohiki, brought some semblance of consolidation among the ahupua'a as part of a larger expansionist economy. At this point, we might add, since these members of the economy were essentially consumers rather than producers, to call the Hawaiian economy a subsistence economy may not be entirely accurate.

Given this historical and demographic setting of the Hawaiian socioeconomic system, let us proceed with an analysis of its theoretical context, partly by contrasting its basic features with modern economic ideas and institutions.

Scarcity Versus Relative Abundance

One of the first concepts a college student is introduced to in "Economics 101" is the idea of scarcity. A standard economics textbook, such as Richard C. Lipsey's and Peter O. Steiner's *Economics*, states, "For the overwhelming preponderance of the world's 4 billion human beings, *scarcity* is real and ever present . . . the existing supply of resources is woefully inadequate; there are enough to produce only a small fraction of the goods and services that people desire." Having a limited supply of things in itself would not lead to scarcity in the economic sense, if we did not also assume, as the coauthors do, that "for all practical purposes, human wants may be regarded as limitless." Thus, we have posed here a central problem of economics: this limited number of resources or factors confronting an unlimited number of wants. The presumption of scarcity and the psychology of unending wants together justify productivity and the acquisition of more and more goods and the demand for more services. If production factors are scarce and our wants limitless, we can see why we and other modern economies strive for endless increases in productivity and will try logically and morally to legitimize acquisitiveness.

We must ask ourselves whether the Hawaiian of old saw the human condition in the same way. Did he recognize scarcity as a basic fact in his life? Did he presume that his fellow human beings were creatures of limitless wants? The juxtaposition of scarcity and unlimited wants leading to endless production and acquisitiveness, we argue, is antithetical to Hawaiian socioeconomic thought and practice. What is far more consistent with the full range of Hawaiian behavior and values is exactly the opposite array of economic factors—that is to say, relative abundance and limited wants. Understanding this point of view, and its differences with our contemporary economic thought, requires that we reverse our customary way of thinking.

Let us first consider the relationship of scarcity to abundance. Objectively speaking, since they lie on the same continuum but at different ends of it, the relationship is only a matter of degree. Aware of this, the Hawaiian, therefore, saw both in relative terms. Scarcity was always seen as relative to something else, whether that was a place, season, quantity or quality, person, object, a particular condition, and so on. Hāna, Maui, for example, was referred to as "he 'āina au pehu," or "the land where lack was known." But that was true only about certain things, such as fish, for Hāna grew an abundance of taro and other agricultural products. On the other hand, Kalāhuipua'a on Hawai'i had an abundance of shellfish, seaweed, fish, and other marine life from offshore and in the ponds nearby, although the barren lava-covered lands ma uka grew no crops of any kind. In times of drought both wet- and dry-land varieties of taro would have been scarce, but the more drought-resistant sweet potatoes would have been plentiful. Hawai'i-born Professor Isabella 'Aiona Abbott, formerly of the Botany Department at Stanford University, has written, "When Hawaiian literature speaks of famine, and the ethnobotanist records famine food, it becomes clear that starvation was not a matter of having absolutely nothing to eat." If the people lacked one kind of food, "there were other staples to eat." The starkest forms of famine occur in much more harsh natural environments than Hawai'i's and, ironically, in part as a result of the industrialism which makes marginal economies dependent upon international political and economic events over which people in such economies have no control. We cannot honestly imagine absolute hunger occurring among the families dwelling in a self-sufficient 'iliahupua'a in the days of old.

We wonder whether scarcity would ever have been given its central place in modern economic theory if the early theorists had come from the kind of environment that was found in Hawai'i.

They came from quite different climatic and geographical environments, where nature imposed much more severe conditions of scarcity than it did in Hawai'i. We do not mean to suggest that economic theory is born out of environmental determinism, for many other social, political, and cultural factors have shaped the philosophy of scarcity, but we agree that environment is a critical factor. Perhaps the relationship was better stated by Stuart Chase, when he described how all of our "early conditioning has been in terms of scarcity" based on "the philosophy of the desert." What can be more different from the desert than a semitropical garden situated in the middle of the world's largest body of water and blessed by the winds that bring the rain-bearing clouds of Lono and the cooling waters of an eternal spring? The imagery of scarcity is appropriate for the desert, but not for Hawai'i—usually. In fact, few Hawaiians other than those who lived in Ka'ū, on the island of Hawaii, could have imagined a desert, let alone any significant scarcity suggested by the mention of a desert.

What the Hawaiian plainly saw and felt around him naturally (as well as spiritually) was abundance, relative abundance to be sure, but nonetheless generous. He would say of his 'āina what people said of the island of Kaua'i: *"Nā kōhi kelekele a Kapu'u-kolu,"* "The rich foods of the Triple Hills" (Pūku'i), referring to the abundance of that favored island. The early visitor to these islands more often than not was impressed by their lushness. The observations of Captain Cook, Lt. James King, Captain Vancouver, the naturalist Menzies, and others indicate as much. Some visitors also noted the barren places. William Ellis in 1823 described Kaho'olawe as "almost destitute of every kind of shrub or verdure." We can safely assume that Hawaiians were as aware as Ellis of their barren and unproductive areas. Some early foreign residents, such as William Ladd, in 1835 a founder of Kōloa Plantation on Kaua'i, were most impressed with the "enormous untapped wealth" of the land. While he may have betrayed more of his entrepreneurial motives than anything else in this display of enthusiasm, this vision of plenty was one of the reasons that attracted him and others to seek their fortunes in the "Sandwich Islands." If natives and foreigners had anything in common, it was this recognition of abundance in Hawai'i's islands, rather than of scarcity.

We can better appreciate the disparity between the thinking of the modern "economic man" as opposed to that of the traditional Hawaiian by considering the thinking that has grown up around the assumptions of scarcity. What the thinking of scarcity says, in brief, is that abundance is an ideal, which can never be reached and should never be reached. In his insightful essay "The Psychology of Abundance," Walter A. Weisskopf expanded on this point. "The basic assumption of scarcity of means and unlimitedness of ends prevents the possibility of ever establishing complete abundance. At the same time, the idea of abundance is also a threat to the system because, with its establishment, the entire meaning and purpose of the system would vanish." Understandably, then, a real fear exists among some people, especially those who worry about the consequences of an automated and cybernetic society dominated by robots and computers, that abundance would make our economic life and system pointless. It's the terror lurking in every catch-22 situation in economics: what you want is good, but wanting a lot of it is bad. In other words, abundance is bad. While the man on the street may not think so, that is the inescapable paradox of modern economic thought. In summary, the Hawaiian begins with the assumption of relative abundance and ends with plenty, whereas modern economic man begins with the assumption of scarcity, strives for abundance, but ends exactly where he begins.

A curious alliance between Christian morality and the economics of scarcity supports the notion that poverty is virtuous. Perhaps that notion is not so strange, because Christianity, too, originated in a desert environment, and spread soonest among the poor. But, since poverty is a function of scarcity, we can say that, if poverty is good, scarcity must also be good. We know that over and above the level of the availability of means for physical survival, poverty is not so much an economic matter as it is a state imposed by mind, a condition socially defined. So is scarcity a state of the mind of economics. In the end, Christianity helps to clothe economics in the mantle of virtue and, as with many other things, economics ends up seeking its justification not in its vaunted objectivity, but in the subjectivity of a religious philosophy—serving the machinations of clever manipulators of markets and men.

That poverty, and hence scarcity, are in themselves virtuous is an idea quite alien to Hawaiian socioeconomic thinking. Nowhere in the standard works of Hawaiian historians, nor in the several thousand "wise sayings" that have been assembled, can we find any hint that poverty is a desirable state. On the contrary, it is clearly to be avoided. *"Kau i Kāpua ka poʻe polohuku ʻole,"* "Without resources one gets nowhere" (Pūkuʻi). Not poverty but wealth gets you somewhere. Hawaiians have no mythic heroes who are poor and destitute. The only chief worth admiring is the one who can command great amounts of resources, not for his own sake, but for the sake of his people. We can find no accounts of asceticism, no revered ascetics, no kāhuna who took vows of poverty, no orders of monks or nuns who renounced worldly comforts. No gospel says that the poor or the destitute shall inherit anything, either now or in the hereafter. In other words, no value is placed on poverty or on scarcity as ideal states of being.

Abundance or, more precisely, relative abundance, is only one side of our hypothesis. Let us consider now the other side, the idea of limited wants.

Limited Wants

Hawaiians have a proverb, " *ʻAʻohe mea ʻimi a ka maka,"* "Nothing more for the eyes to search for" (Pūkuʻi). To put this in another way, do not look elsewhere, since everything you want is around you. In the context of what we've said about abundance, this suggested that, as a Hawaiian, you lived in a world of plenty which has been favored by the gods and enriched by your own hands and tools. It is filled with all the things you need for living. Implicit, however, is the idea that you should be satisfied with what you have. *"Eʻai i ka mea i loaʻa,"* "What you have, eat" (Pūkuʻi). After all, if you have been given so much already, how much more should you really expect? The person who constantly goes around saying, "If I had this" or "If I had that," is thought to be unreasonable and hence impractical, because he cannot or does not choose to be satisfied.

Whatever insight this moralistic word play can provide in understanding the Hawaiian perception of the relationship between abundance and wants hinges on the meaning we give to "wants." Tomes have been written on the subject, offering a host of definitions ranging from the pedestrian (wants are "desires or needs") to the obtuse (wants are "variations of homeostasis"). The subject is complex, so that anything more we offer here would be

an oversimplification, if not a resort to the "tricks of definition."
Even so, let us consider the following.

The nature of people is such that they have many diverse needs
or desires. (We'd be splitting hairs to try to distinguish needs or
desires from wants.) They want rest, excitement, food, shelter,
education, pleasure, sex, tools, and a lot of other comforts or aids
to security ad infinitum. They have general and specific interests.
One person, for example, may want prestige and will buy a Cadil-
lac, while another, also wanting prestige, will settle for a Volkswa-
gen. They also have hierarchies of wants, both general and specific. A housewife may have a list of specific things she wants and
puts them down in order of priority. People's wants change, too,
some recurring, such as hunger for certain foods, and others waning or disappearing as one grows older, moves to a new location,
gets a new job, finds other hobbies, and so on. Their wants are
determined by many factors, including their attitudes, habits,
values, and opinions, which in turn are shaped by their social,
political, economic, religious, or cultural circumstances.

Using this simple set of variables to begin with, what can we say
now about how the Hawaiian might have perceived the notion of
limited wants? Suppose we start by identifying specific material
wants, not for any average individual, but for a "typical" farming
'ohana of a typical 'iliahupua'a. Based on our knowledge of their
technology, we have a fair idea of what such a list would be. The
agricultural implements would include the 'ō'ō, or digging stick,
adzes of assorted sizes, some knives, a carrying pole, several gourd
containers, and enough cordage for carrying loads in those containers. Given the state of the technology, this would be about the
complete list. Moreover, since each 'ohana was a self-sufficient
unit, all the 'ohana engaged in farming would have the same set of
goods. To the extent that the 'ohana also gathered its own sea-
food, it would have had a complementing list of fishing gear, such
as hooks, nets, lines, sinkers, traps, a canoe, and so on. Since the
'ohana would have manufactured many of its own needs, from
clothing to eating utensils, we should include the assorted tools,
for example, kapa beaters, taro pounders, poi boards, and so
forth. Add to these the normal complement of household items,
such as calabashes, mats, cosmetics, ornaments, sleeping mats,
and bed covers. We do not need to itemize such a list, but we
would be close to the mark if we estimated that the whole list

would not exceed a hundred separate articles. In other words, the total number of material things the producing Hawaiian 'ohana might need or want, for serving its major activities, would be about what the modern family today might want for its kitchen alone. This may well be like comparing oranges with apples, but the analogy at least imparts a sense of scale between the limited and unlimited wants of then and now.

Other material items should be added such as games or sporting equipment, hula implements, religious or ritual devices, and a whole armory of weapons. Public or communal wants or products should be included also, such as irrigation works, heiau, shrines, and fish ponds, all of which consumed as much, if not more, material than did any category of goods for individuals or 'ohana. Furthermore, while we have assumed that modern society's wants exceed any list presented by a "primitive" economy, we should be aware of important exceptions. Such a one was firewood, which Hawaiians used in far greater quantities than we do today (but only because we have other fuels to cook our foods). Yet, even if we added all these items to our list, we would still end up with a relatively small number of things. We must not belabor the point, but the fact that we can even presume to be able to count the total number of specific material articles used or consumed in Hawai'i before 1778, something that is almost inconceivable for us to do in today's society, suggests the limited scope of Hawaiians' wants.

One more important category should be examined: the wants and consumption patterns of the ali'i. The truism that one's social rank influences what one desires and consumes is unmistakably demonstrated in the life-style of the ali'i. Besides making use of all that was available to the maka'ainana, the ali'i enjoyed several types of goods reserved for them exclusively, such as feather capes, cloaks, helmets, lei, kāhili, and a variety of ornaments, such as pendants for necklaces, bracelets, and rings all carved from whale-tooth ivory, turtle shell, and other rare materials set aside for royalty. Certain kinds of foodstuffs, too, were restricted to ali'i, especially at designated times of the year. Yet, when we add this list of items for ali'i to the sum of those mentioned for the maka'ainana, the total number is not measurably enlarged. Interestingly, and perhaps surprisingly, if one compares the two lists, the disparity between commoners and nobility is not great.

It is quite another matter, however, when we look at the magnitude of consumption for certain products, such as featherwork. Making a single feather cloak took immense numbers of feathers, best illustrated by the famous Kamehameha cloak, which required about half a million feathers plucked from more than eighty thousand birds. We are told that bird snarers carefully plucked only the useable feathers and then released their captives, but that this was not always done. This gathering of feathers, coupled with the capture of some larger birds for food, may account in part for the depletion and in some cases the extinction of certain species of birds. In any case, the great value that Hawaiians attached to feathers and featherwork depended on their rarity and beauty, not on their abundance. This contradicts our hypothesis, but serves as the proverbial exception that proves the general rule.

So far we have talked about material things as being economic wants. Yet, to Hawaiians of old, the processes involved in making a product, and the nature of the product itself, and, most important, the way the product was given to someone, with all the underlying motivations, meanings, and interpersonal nuances attending the presentation—this entire involved procedure made the product less an economic thing than part of a social process, even a spiritual transaction. Thus, although we have emphasized the economic aspects of procuring things, we must nonetheless recognize that Hawaiians thought of these products as being socioeconomic rather than purely economic entities. This attitude is not as strange as it seems to be if we compare it with consumer behavior today. To illustrate: We buy things or conduct our business always in social situations, never in a vacuum. When we purchase something, our decision is influenced by many factors besides price. Indeed, as marketing psychologists are fond of pointing out, we do not buy only a product as such, but buy also the benefits we believe that it confers on us, such as style, comfort, convenience, status, and so on, all of which are psychological or social values rather than economic ones. Or, when we purchase a service, as many of our purchases will be these days, the manner in which the salesclerk or waiter or guide treats us is an important part of the transaction—that is, the social content of what might otherwise be an economic event is very relevant to us.

In sum, when we think about the ratio of relative abundance to limited wants, it is not simply a one-to-one material relationship, but a psychological, social, and spiritual relationship as well. The relationship is not only a matter of abundance of natural resources fulfilling economic needs, but also one of noneconomic wants. Such wants may vary from the finite to the infinite—a happy home; a loving relationship with a spouse, child, relative, or friend; a certain kind of recognition from the 'ohana, the kono-hiki, or even a high chief; a deeper spiritual rapport with nature, communion with an 'aumakua, and so on. To a Hawaiian the satisfaction of these intangible wants was no less important than the satisfaction of his physiological needs. While some modern economists shun intangible values, because they are imprecise and unquantifiable, the Hawaiian view would insist that they must be part of our understanding of economics.

Productivity

When economists talk about productivity, they are referring to the rate at which total production of goods and services in an economy grows or declines. Productivity is defined, simply enough, as "a measure of output per unit of resource input," and when this and other formulae, along with the requisite data, are fed into the computers, we are given in return an innocent-looking figure of, say, a 2.3 percent growth rate for the past year. That little number is but the extreme tip of the iceberg which represents, among other things, myriads of bits of information about the production activities of millions of enterprises plus a whole range of socioeconomic and political policies and programs, demographic changes, technological innovations, international events, and a complex set of values and norms. Although few of us have either the background or the interest to understand all of this, the figure still has some meaning for most Americans, if only because it indicates a state of mind—for the nation.

We would be happy if we could determine the rate of production for the Hawaiian economy before 1778, but we cannot do that. The konohiki-accountants did not leave us any reliable quantitative data. Not that they did not set production goals or keep track of certain aspects of production—which they would have had to have done in order to assess tax or tribute payments—but probably because they simply didn't have the means to record all those data. Not only do we lack manufacturing data for the years before 1778, but also we know very little about demographic or

consumption changes for those times, much less about technological changes, whether they concerned a new variety of taro, the
catch with a better fishhook, or the yield of some other innovation. Although we may not be able to figure out a production rate,
we do have some "impressionistic data" with which we can at least
outline the character and scope of that production.

Observing the orthodox approach to basic economics, let us
first describe briefly the factors involved in Hawaiian production.
What is at once clear is that all the materials for making anything
and everything came from either the land or the sea. In those days,
no synthetics were available. Given this total reliance on nature,
we can appreciate the importance of having a certain view of the
environment—that it is a place of plenty, is exploitable, and is con-
trollable, providing the right attitude of reverence toward the gods
is maintained. In our modern secular and supposedly rational economics, we are normally oblivious to such feelings. But the
Hawaiian producer was constantly aware of them—all the more
so because of his extraordinary dependence on a few things, such
as the coconut, gourd, olonā, hard basalt, and the like, for the
greater part of the materials he produced and consumed. Someone
has estimated that Polynesians had as many as three hundred uses
for the different parts of the coconut tree. This apparent overde-
pendence on a few things, which is a characteristic of Polynesian
and "primitive" economies in general, reveals that abundance does
not necessarily lead to waste. The use of every part of a coconut
tree offers us an instructive lesson in enjoying nature's gifts without wasting anything, or polluting anything—a most important
feature of the Hawaiian economic ethic.

Another strong factor in Hawaiian production was its technological capability; indeed, when we talk about abundance, beyond
its raw state in nature, we really mean the products of applied
technology. People today commonly speak of "primitive" economies as having "simple" technologies, which means that they could
manage only limited productivity. The term "limited" in this case
is slightly misleading, because it implies a lack of something. But,
in fact, Hawaiian technology achieved *optimal* productivity, that
is, it yielded goods enough to satisfy to a reasonable degree the
socioeconomic wants of the whole population. Thus, while its
technology may well have been "simple," and hence "limited" in a
relative sense, it was the optimal technology within the Hawaiian

context. We can easily note its lack of power-driven machines and speculate about what their economy might have been like if Hawaiians had not had to depend entirely on human labor for energy, but this is a meaningless exercise. We should be sensible, and recognize that their primal technology was equal to the task imposed on it by their society.

To say that labor was an important factor of production is to say the obvious. But, equally obvious, in the absence of any power-driven machines, human effort was about all they could rely upon. When you know that an adult human being can directly exert energy equivalent to about only one-tenth horsepower, you can appreciate better the dependence of the Hawaiian economy on human labor. This dependency is brought home even more vividly by the type of agriculture and the diet in which Hawaiians chose to specialize. Cultivation of wet-land taro combined with the eating of poi required much more labor than did almost any other type of primal economy. As Archibald Campbell so accurately put it in 1819, "The mode of [taro] culture is exceedingly laborious."

Other related factors should be recognized also, such as storage (the lack of which is common to "primitive" economies), and, connected with that, the ability to preserve perishable foodstuffs. These deficiencies are of particular relevance to our hypothesis about relative abundance and limited wants. Another factor was conservation practice, which had significant implications not only for production of raw materials but also for the value orientation of Hawaiians. Of course, some other factors, such as money, did not enter the picture at all, although from our point of view today some things may be regarded as a kind of incipient capital. Let us turn now to consider how these factors were employed in terms of productivity.

Almost every observer, chronicler, or student of Hawaiian culture seems to agree that the Hawaiians of old achieved a high degree of productivity. This is the conventional view, supported by statements that go back to the arrival of the first Europeans in 1778. One of the observations more frequently cited is that of the naturalist Archibald Menzies, who accompanied Capt. George Vancouver during his three visits to the islands in 1792–1794.

We could not indeed but admire the laudable ingenuity of these people in cultivating their soil with so much economy. The indefatigable labor in making these little fields in so rugged a situation, the care and industry with which they were transplanted, watered and kept in order, surpassed anything of the kind we had ever seen before. It showed in a conspicuous manner the ingenuity of the inhabitants in modifying their husbandry to different situations of soil and exposure, and with no small degree of pleasure we here beheld their labor rewarded with productive crops.

In modern times, perhaps the most effective proponent of this view was the late anthropologist E. S. Craighill Handy, who wrote about his findings and conclusions in such works as *The Native Planters in Old Hawai'i* and *The Polynesian Family System in Ka-'ū, Hawai'i* (both coauthored with Kawena Pūku'i). Highly regarded by his peers in Hawaiian and Polynesian studies, apparently Handy's views were rarely disputed in his time. His feelings were expressed in a thoughtful essay, *Cultural Revolution in Hawai'i*, published in 1931 when he was associated with the Bishop Museum.

> If a culture may be judged by its fruits, it is evident that on the whole, for the native people in the Hawaiian environment, the old Hawaiian civilization had much to its credit. An inferior and ill adapted civilization does not produce superior physical and cultural fruits. The fruits of the old Hawaiian system appear on the whole to have been good, if we may judge by . . . the high development of agriculture by means of intensive irrigation, which made a relatively large population possible; a similarly intensive and skillful fishing industry with great development of artificial fish preserves where the nature of coasts and inlets made these practicable; technical perfection of crafts. . . . These and many other phases and details of the Hawaiian life attest superior racial inheritance and cultural heritage, intelligently and naturally adapted to a unique and on the whole beneficent, although in many ways difficult and exacting environment.

As good as are the word pictures of Menzies and of Handy, many of us may not be able to visualize how extensively the lands were put to productive use. Yet people who were born in the early 1900s can recall scenes of many areas in Kāne'ohe, Lā'ie, Kahalu'u, Mānoa, and even Waikīkī on O'ahu, or Pelekunu on Moloka'i, some of the valleys along the northeastern coast of Kaua'i, and so many other places where once upon a time Hawaiians cultivated rich and beautiful terraced taro loʻi. Younger Hawaiians who see these places today as overgrown jungle areas, archaeologists' stakeouts, housing subdivisions, paved parking lots, or tourists' resorts, cannot imagine that, not too long ago, they were green and peaceful fields. Anyone wishing to catch a glimpse of what these places were like back then (short of hitching a ride on our time machine) should visit—soon!—Hanalei on Kauaʻi, or Keʻanae or Wailua on Maui, which are the islands' major taro-growing areas today, or support a proposal to re-create an eighteenth-century ahupuaʻa settlement, in which modern Hawaiians could find not only a visual but also an actual reminder of the Hawaiʻi that was.

Occasionally, we hear statements to the effect that the old Hawaiians used "every spare inch of land," or developed all their resources to the utmost degree. As well meaning as these sentiments may be, they are misleading, for "high degree of productivity" does not necessarily equal maximum use of the potential resources available. Thus, Handy (Handy, Handy, and Pūkuʻi), despite all his admiration for the productive skills of the Hawaiians, tempered his views. "Finally should be mentioned the extent of the people's use of every type of locality, and the extent to which available lands were adapted to a wide variety of cultivation. To say that resources of arable soil were utilized to the maximum would be a great exaggeration." He gave a good reason for this conclusion. "Density of population was never such as to require this." Unfortunately, he did not provide any quantitative evidence for that statement, but relied only on impressions gained from years of observations throughout the islands. However, some evidence supporting his thesis of underdevelopment is available from other sources.

One is a set of estimates regarding the productive capacity of the ʻāina made in 1838 by William Ladd, a partner in the American firm that since 1835 had grown not only sugar at Kōloa, Kauaʻi but had experimented with several other crops as well. The young entrepreneur, writing for the *Hawaiian Spectator*, stated: "A tract of land one mile square will occupy and feed 653 persons; the same extent in vineyards will support 289 persons, while the same planted in *kalo* will feed 15,151, and probably not more than one twenty-fifth of that number, would be required in its cultivation." If we take his kalo or taro estimate, using 300,000 mouths as the population base for 1778, a little less than 20 square miles of fertile land would have been required to produce enough taro for every man, woman, and child in Hawai'i nei. Since twenty square miles is about the size of Hanalei, Kaua'i, that one ahupua'a alone could have been the "taro basket" for the entire population of all the islands. When we recall that Hawai'i's total land area is 6,425 square miles (about 12 percent of which would be too steep or barren to cultivate), clearly, then, if we accept Ladd's figures, the land was underused, as Handy contended.

But we must use Ladd's estimates with a pinch of cautionary salt. For one thing, we have no idea what data he was basing them on. He must have assumed either very high yields, which is possible because Kaua'i was known for its productivity, or low per capita consumption of taro, because on the basis of data we know today, much more land than he projected would have been required. Yet we must give some credence to what he wrote, because he was on the spot, much closer to the scene than any of us, including some of today's archaeologists and others who challenge him.

Another set of estimates that we might consider is based on a study of Hālawa Valley, Moloka'i, done in the early 1970s by Thomas J. Riley, a graduate student in anthropology at the University of Hawai'i. In his dissertation, "Wet and Dry in a Hawaiian Valley: The Archaeology of an Agricultural System," Riley concluded that in old Hālawa .25 acres of kalo would have provided the taro needed during a year for one person. In part, this estimate was derived from an estimated yield of 8,000 pounds of taro per acre and a daily caloric requirement of just over 2,000 calories per person. If we compare these figures with Ladd's estimates, we find that 1 square mile feeds only 2,560 persons, or only one-sixth of Ladd's 15,151. Applying this estimate further, a total of 117 square miles, or 75,000 acres of land, would have been required to supply the taro needed by the total Hawaiian population. However, even if we took this more conservative figure of 117 square miles, and set it against 6,425 square miles, the total area of all the islands, it would still suggest underutilization of land. Thus, Handy's opinion is borne out, by whichever of these two estimates we may choose.

Granted, using these estimates and applying them to old Hawai'i as a whole may be like comparing oranges and apples. We are aware of the differences in yields that depend on so many variables. Among these are the varieties of taro being grown, the quality of the cultivation they are given, the microenvironmental conditions applying in one valley as compared with those in the next, and so on. All these and more would have to qualify the extension of any single set of figures gained from one valley for application to the islands as a whole. Nonetheless, in the absence of any better data, these estimates will serve as useable illustrations.

The linking of high productivity with less than maximum use of the potential resources is not at all inconsistent. This was the case in other "primitive" societies, as it is in many modern countries. In New Zealand, for example, whatever lands the Maoris of old farmed they cultivated quite intensively and obtained good yields. But, with more than 116,000 square miles of land, and only 250,000 Maoris, they certainly did not put to full use all of their resources in land. And, in the United States, where today American farmers achieve some of the world's highest productivity rates, many farmers do not use all of their available lands. Similarly, whatever proportion of the resources of their islands the Hawaiians may have developed may have been used very productively. But, at the same time, they left other resources unused or underused.

This view of underdevelopment in ancient Hawai'i has been challenged by anthropologists and archaeologists. Patrick V. Kirch, formerly of the Bishop Museum's department of anthropology, differed with Handy. "The evidence that population growth had reached a peak, and was even on the decline, prior to European contact strongly suggests that the capacity of the indigenous technological productive system to support increased population had reached its limits." Kirch, and others, contend that, in effect, the Hawaiians had exceeded the "carrying capacity" of the land because of population growth, on the one hand, but also on the other hand, because of overexploitation of the land, as is shown by erosion, deforestation, and the extinction of "avifauna," land snails, and other plant and animal species—all before 1778. This counterview is offered only as a hypothesis, but Kirch et al. seem to have persuasive "paleobotanical" and "paleozoological" evidence in the form of fossil remains and so on. On this case the jury is still out and, while we await more diggings, Handy's view of underdevelopment still deserves attention.

Nonetheless, whatever the findings of Kirch and others may be, at this point they have little bearing on what we have proposed as the Hawaiian perception of an island-world of abundance. In other words, the findings do not challenge that perception, only the data. Quite probably, by 1778 in certain areas, erosion and other kinds of ecological damage could have created scarcities which the Hawaiians may or may not have realized. Even if they had recognized them, whether or not they would have changed their view of their world, with all of the implications to that revision of thought, is quite another question. After all, their attitudes had evolved over centuries of settlement, as part of a total philosophy of life. Furthermore, what some people today call ecological degradation may not have been considered as such by Hawaiians of old. Yet, even if we were to concede that by 1778 Hawaiians had reached some kind of understanding about the fragility of their environment and the gradual depletion of their resources, we should remember that, not unusually, a society holds on to concepts and values of the past, while living and coping with new situations of a different order. For example Stuart Chase has said of Americans: "They live in the Economy of Abundance, and think and behave in the tradition of Scarcity." Perhaps, had Captain Cook never arrived, Hawaiians, in the course of ample and uncomplicated time, might have arrived at the point where they realized that they lived in an economy of scarcity, while thinking that they prospered in a land of abundance.

Organizing Labor

The problem that the dwellers in each 'iliahupua'a had to face, as would those in any other emerging primal economy, was how best to organize their labor force so that it could produce the desired level of goods and services. Like other Polynesians, Hawaiians organized themselves in a very rational way by dividing up the tasks and human skills according to (1) employment or industry, and (2) processes within employment, or what is known as "division of labor." Generally, when the subject is discussed in relation to "primitive" economies, the former, simpler type of separation receives most attention because of the assumption that the latter, more specialized development is found mainly in advanced societies. But, as we shall see, Hawaiian labor organization had evolved into a rather intricate system before Westerners arrived.

To begin with, sex, age, size, and rank were the common criteria for dividing a population, although in some cases family descent and degree of training were recognized as factors. While some jobs were shared by both men and women, the general practice separated the sexes. According to Kamakau (1961), "All the work outside the house was performed by the men"—except on Maui and Hawai'i, where the women worked outdoors as hard as the men did. Handy and Pūku'i wrote that women also worked outside, cultivating sweet potato, sugarcane, and gourds. (One of the consequences of women working outside, at least on Maui and Hawai'i, was that they too had to pay taxes.) The macho male did the heavier work, such as growing taro, fishing on the reef and the open sea, making canoes and houses, and so on, while the women made the kapa, did the plaiting and some of the featherwork. And, of course, women did the domestic chores—except for the cooking, which, unlike in other places in Polynesia, was done by the men. Interestingly, the role of the working wife was well established. In fact, if a man took a wife who did not work but tried to live off his income, so to speak, the relationship was considered hewa, wrong, and sufficient cause for the landlord-chief to evict him from the land, because she was a polohana'ole, a nonproducer. Thus, in contrast to certain cultures in which the women are burdened with drudgery and menial jobs, while the men supposedly have the more interesting work, the division of labor among the Hawaiians seems to have been apportioned equally among both men and women. Socioeconomically at least, Hawaiians of old seem to have gained sexual equality.

Size and physical strength, not age, determined when or at what chores an individual should work. For example, a child who was large enough to carry a water gourd, no matter what his age, was available for work from then on. As Pūku'i wrote, "In ancient days the age of a child was not reckoned by years as we do today but by his physical ability to do something." *"Ka nui e pa'a ai i nā niu 'elua,"* "The size that enables a child to carry two coconuts" indicated the five or six year old. This seems to be a much more sensible way of deciding when a child joined the work force than consulting the arbitrary age rules that we use today. In any event, Hawaiian children were involved in the 'ohana's domestic economy at a relatively early age. This involvement was done as much because of the need for extra hands as for starting the child's education and training. Thus, from the earliest suitable age, the child was taught on the job those skills, work habits, and values that would form the basis of his or her adult career and thought. Apparently, the only children to escape the discipline of work were those born to ali'i of high rank.

Old people were not forced to retire into inactivity or senility. Again, depending on physical condition, of course, they seemed to have remained productive members of the work force as long as their minds and hands could serve the 'ohana. One of their principal duties was to teach their grandchildren, or at least to take care of them, thus releasing the parents to attend to other productive tasks. Since the old people had gained the knowledge as well as the experience, in addition to the respect and authority that come with age, this arrangement makes very good sense for any society. " 'Oiai e nānā mai ana nō nā maka," "While the eyes are still open": this advice was given to the young, to learn all they could from old folks while the aged were still alive, for the chance would be lost when their eyes were closed (Pūku'i). On the other hand, Hawaiians also recognized that age did not automatically mean wisdom. "Hāpala 'ia a'ela i ka hāwena," they said, literally, "Daubed with lime," meaning that one whose hair may be gray, or artificially bleached with lime, still might have no more wisdom than an inexperienced youth (Handy and Pūku'i). In addition to their function as teachers, the aged handled lighter chores, perhaps, such as plaiting lau hala or polishing the surface of bowls, or making sennit. Certain specialists would have continued to serve in a supervisory capacity, as in the case of a canoe maker.

Consequently, the effective span of the average person's work years could well have covered 90 percent of his lifetime. In terms of productivity that proportion is better than the approximation of 75 percent that is calculated for working persons in the United States today. If feeling useful contributes to mental health, then the Hawaiian kūpuna should have been in better shape both physically and mentally than are a growing number of our senior citizens today, who are forced by retirement into vegetation while they still have many years of productive service left in them. Hawaiians found an efficient way, and also a sensitive way, of maximizing the use of available human resources for production even as they protected the aging psyche.

Rank as a factor in the division of labor had relatively little economic significance for old Hawai'i, as compared with other Polynesian societies. For example, slaves of the Maori played an important role in the tribal economy because they performed many necessary but unpleasant tasks. That was not the case in Hawai'i of old, where the kauā, a mystifying group of outcastes or untouchables rather than slaves, were considered as being so defiled that no commoner would go near one, let alone be touched or served by one. They were the lowest of outcastes, having no genealogy and hence no social status, being rigidly segregated and restricted to their own reservations of sorts. They must have survived there, in the most insulated, self-sufficient economies of all in Hawai'i. The uncompromising attitude of more fortunate Hawaiians toward the kauā is puzzling, especially when contrasted with the otherwise rational way in which they organized their economic production and their attitudes toward living creatures.

As for the high chiefs, although they were not above doing physical labor, they cannot be considered as having been true workers at any time. Some work would have been done by lesser chiefs who were not hedged around by any of the protecting kapu while they functioned as priests and other kinds of specialists.

So far, we have focused on the division of labor according to job, but an important part of our subject is the organizing of labor skills into categories or narrower specialties. Today we take specialization for granted, surrounded as we are with thousands of industrial and service classifications that seem to multiply with every major technological breakthrough. So, naturally, we think of any economy, however simple, as having specialists of one kind or another. Some people, however, have contended that specialization is always absent among "primitive" people. This view starts with the premise that such a society is organized purely on a basis of household economy, with the husband-wife nucleus. When the family requires assistance in meeting its needs, it calls on neighbors or the community. In this model of the nuclear family economy, specialists have no place, since all tasks are carried out together by everyone in the group.

Just as Raymond Firth has successfully challenged this oversimplistic view by pointing out the degree of specialization that

existed in ancient Maori economic organization, so can we point
out the same for Hawai'i. The evidence is abundant, as we have
suggested in the previous chapter on technology. Kamakau (1961)
described, for example, how Kamehameha I appointed specialists
among the kāhuna who were "makers" of double canoes (wa'a
kaulua), war canoes (wa'a peleleu), single canoes (wa'a kia-
loa), hōlua sleds, surfboards (papa he'enalu), bowls, calabashes,
dishes, spittoons, slop bowls, flat dishes, fishhooks, medicines,
and so on, in a long list of experts. We also have an eyewitness
account from Menzies of three small "villages" near Kealakekua Bay.

> The villages we passed in the woods I said were temporary, as the
> occupiers, consisting of a few families, had come up here only for a
> time to pursue various occupations. The men were differently
> engaged. Some in felling of large timber for various purposes;
> others in hollowing out and forming canoes and planks in the
> rough, which, after laying some time in the sun, were dragged
> down in that state to the seaside to be finished by their canoe
> builders, who are distinct persons from those who thus form them
> in the rough. A third set seemed to have no other occupation than
> that of catching small birds for the sake of their feathers. . . . It is
> with them that a great portion of the rents are annually paid to the
> chiefs by the lower class of people, who thus employ themselves by
> catching the birds with bird-lime.

And we have some archaeological evidence of craft specialization,
such as adze quarries atop Mauna Kea and caches of portable artifacts, such as fishhooks, abraders, and other tools or objects, all
indicating the presence of specialist workshops.

A reasonable scenario for the development of a specialist would
begin with a talented member of the 'ohana perfecting his particular skills, say, in adze making or fishing, until he reached the point
where he would be assigned to concentrate on such tasks. He
might not devote full time to this specialty, depending on the overall family work load, the demand for his services, their seasonality,
and other factors. As his reputation for quality work spreads to
other 'ili'ohana units, the demand for his skills increases. These,
over a period of time, would take him to other places within and
beyond his ahupua'a. He would be compensated for his services
with foods, kapa, or other objects of value equivalent to services

rendered, and thus become part of an evolving system of exchange. The origin of specialization in the 'ili'ohana would explain in part why specialist callings frequently were hereditary, and why personal rivalry and secrecy were common among the kāhuna, the experts.

As the division of labor evolved with greater specialization, a corresponding system emerged, in order to coordinate the efforts of the different workers, specialists, and resources, as well as other communal activities. No matter how intricate the division of labor may be, it is of little use unless all the workers and elements in the production line can be brought together, all moving toward reaching a common end. Whether at the level of the 'ohana or the 'ili'ohana, ahupua'a, moku, or mokupuni, the need for this integrating function flows naturally from developing specialization. We recognize this process as management. The Hawaiians may have called it ka ho'ohele 'ana.

Management 'Ohana Style

No matter how reasonable and natural it is to believe that "primitive" economies based on even a rudimentary division of labor must have developed a management capacity of their own, some modern Hawaiians have trouble talking about their kūpuna and management in the same breath. For one thing, management has become identified in many minds as such a complex arrangement among bosses and laborers that it could not possibly have been of much consequence to simple folk like our ancestors. Consequently, many tend to dismiss the whole idea. Probably the main reason for this attitude is a lack of understanding of the subject, because little has been written about it. And the little that has been written has not yet been shared with many people. What follows may be, for many readers, the presentation of yet another approach to an age-old practice that was as much an institution in Hawaiian society as were technology or religion.

In its simplest terms, management involves some well-known functions: leadership, communications, planning, control (of inventory and budgets), and something we believe to be important but not often included in the conventional rhetoric on management, namely, value building. In the Hawaiian socioeconomic structure, this entire process occurred at each level, from the household 'ohana to the ahupua'a, moku, and mokupuni, and wherever organized projects served the needs of one or more family units. For the next few pages, we shall be concerned only with the family, or 'ili'ohana, and the ahupua'a, particularly with their respective "managing directors," the haku and the konohiki. Let us examine management " 'ohana style" first.

Imagine this scene. The physical setting is the usual pie-shaped ahupua'a with a total population of five hundred (about the size of old Hālawa Valley, Moloka'i), a land area of one hundred arable acres, and enough water. Let us also agree that the size of the 'ili'ohana is seventy-five people, consisting of seven households, each having a set of parents, children, both blood and hānai, a set of grandparents, together with assorted relatives or dependents. As an economic unit, its main concern is to produce enough goods and services to satisfy the needs of its members, as well as an adequate surplus to yield up to the chiefs and for purposes of hospitality.

The managerial responsibility for the whole group of seventy-five people is in the hands of the haku, or "managing director," the senior male. He is in charge of all decision making affecting the group regarding work, communal activities, distribution and allocation of goods, and external affairs, for example, relationships with guests, the konohiki, and the ali'i. He also works with a council of 'ohana members, with whom he deliberates and arrives at decisions, usually based on consensus.

In order to appreciate the scale of management capacity that this situation requires, consider the quantity and diversity of the production needs of this group of seventy-five persons. Take taro or poi, to start with. Let us assume that the average daily consumption of poi is 4.5 pounds per person, which is approximately two thousand calories, equivalent to the total daily caloric requirement of an adult. This is about what Riley estimated in his Hālawa Valley study, and also what Carey Miller, a University of Hawai'i dietician who worked with informant David 'Ainoa, arrived at in 1927. This is only an average, of course, for as 'Ainoa made clear, "the old Hawaiians might eat 10 or 15 pounds of poi a day depending on the work they were doing and the abundance of the supply." Thus, the amount of poi a person would consume in the 'ohana would be about 1,640 pounds per year of taro or poi (while there may be a difference in the figures for converting taro into poi, we are assuming an overall 1 to 1 ratio, allowing for water and other factors), or 137 pounds per month, and 34 pounds per week. To provide for the entire 'ohana, management would have to make sure that each day at least 338 pounds of poi would be prepared, or 2,366 pounds each week, 9,464 pounds per month, and a total of 113,568 pounds per annum. (To help you visualize this, imagine 1,135 hundred-pound bags of taro filling several big trucks.) Add to this about 20 percent more to take care of tribute to be paid for the upkeep of the chiefs (note that Kamakau said Kamehameha I imposed a 10 percent tax) and for hospitality purposes, and we have a grand production total of 136,281 pounds every year.

Although poi provided the largest share of the food consumed (some people have said that, under extraordinary circumstances, a meal could consist of just poi and pa'akai, Hawaiian salt), other foods were eaten as well, especially items containing proteins, such as coconuts, vegetables, pigs, dogs, fowls, and all kinds of seafoods. We have no base production or consumption estimates for any of these foods, so we can only make conjectures. Suppose each person supplemented the normal daily diet with an average of 450 calories derived from these foods, a reasonable estimate in view of Miller's statement that an adult Hawaiian doing moderately heavy work would need at least 3,000 calories a day (remember we have already included in this sum 2,000 calories from poi). Depending on the kinds of foods, of course, this would mean several more pounds of foodstuffs that the 'ohana would be required to produce or gather each day.

Apart from the usual foodstuffs, the 'ohana's production requirements would include such needs as kapa cloth, plaited sandals, tī leaf raincoats, and other apparel; eating utensils such as bowls, dishes, and so on; lau hala or other kinds of mats for sleeping and sitting upon; gourd containers; equipment for trapping birds and for fishing, including one or more canoes, nets, lines, and the like; housing; tools such as digging sticks, adzes, lamp bowls, pestles, bow drills; firewood, and so on and on.

All told, foodstuffs and other necessities would add up to thousands of pounds or square feet of materials a year, depending upon the measurements used. Since the 'ohana was a self-sustaining unit, it had to produce during the year everything it consumed or used—with probably only a few exceptions, such as canoes and

adzes. They couldn't count on running down to the corner drug-
store or to the nearest supermarket to renew a supply of this or
that article, or on importing foreign goods, or buying things
through a convenient mail order system.

To produce this considerable variety of goods, the tasks would
have been divided among the members of the 'ohana, with specific
jobs assigned to those with the required inclinations and abilities
—the family's own specialists. Once this organizing of labor was
set up, management had to make certain not only that each producer was properly supervised but also sensibly motivated, so that
the necessary yields would be achieved to sustain the life of the
group.

In short, the self-sufficient 'ili'ohana was an autonomous enterprise with its own management, its land-use rights (but not ownership of its land), and access to natural resources, its own technology and technicians, its own manufacturing capability, its own
internal exchange system. This enterprise could easily have survived as an independent unit, except that it depended on the konohiki for arranging a few but all-important communal functions,
such as the construction and maintenance of the valley's irrigation
system.

So far we have stressed the economic character of the 'ohana
and its management. However, what we are really dealing with, as
has been mentioned before, is a socioeconomic phenomenon.
That is to say, the family is a social organization by nature, hence,
its ostensibly economic functions have a social character as well.
Its "managing director," or haku, plays both a social and economic
role, and thus employs and reflects in his style of managing people
and duties a number of economic values that invariably have
social justifications.

What, then, would be the kinds of values that an 'ohana management style would reflect? Many of these would seem to be
self-evident: cooperation, or laulima, helpfulness, or kōkua,
agreeableness, informality, flexibility, and loyalty, among others.
Cooperation, for example, would be natural and spontaneous in a
family setting, even though personal rivalry and competition
might also be common among members of families, especially
among the ali'i. The maka'āinana family, dependent as it was on
its own productive powers, could not risk too much internal
rivalry and, as the usual effect of that, disunity. The unrelenting

pressure to be self-sufficient was a hard taskmaster, and any responsible management would have insisted on fullest coopera- tion. The term laulima means many hands, and it expresses per- fectly the Hawaiian sense of all persons in the family working together for a common purpose. Once established in the behavior of the basic 'ohana unit, cooperation was easily transferred to working with other 'ohana households in a communal setting. As Handy and Pūku'i explained, a lot of "lending a hand" entered into all work—"in planting and fishing, in housebuilding and pre- paring feasts, in work on the irrigation ditches, taro terraces, and walls, on ponds and in rituals, the hula, war."

Maoris today have a nice way of describing laulima at work: they call it "group rhythm." When Maoris work together, they develop a tempo and purposefulness that enables the group to function in harmony and with optimal efficiency. They achieve the synchronization of the feelings and abilities of the individual mem- bers of the group working toward a shared goal. Most likely "group rhythm" is what the haku too was trying to achieve in organizing the productive labor of his 'ohana.

Inseparably linked with cooperation is the value of kōkua, or helpfulness, for common to both is the willingness of individuals to work voluntarily with each other. While kōkua is generally thought of in more personal and social terms, it is related to pro- duction management because of Hawaiian emphasis on initiative in giving help. One offers help rather than waits to be asked for it. This implies that, as a member of a working group, each person must be sensitive and alert to the needs of the others and to what is happening around him. The haku would have admonished his workers, "Nānā ka maka, hana ka lima," "What the eyes see, let the hands do" (Handy and Pūku'i). This was said to the person who sat by where work needed to be done but who did not offer to help do it. The injunction meant that in the family enterprise one knows what work the others must do and therefore is expected to help them finish their tasks. Thus one assumes responsibility not only for his own work, but also holds himself responsible for the work of all.

In today's parlance, the combination of laulima and kōkua means "teamwork." Each member of the group has a clearly defined assignment, but all members are collaborating in lōkahi, or unity, subordinating personal glory to reaching the goals of the whole group. However, this demands from management a continuing attention to interpersonal relations, assigning and clarifying jobs, deliberating and communicating. All this requires leadership, but also self-discipline on the part of each member of the 'ohana.

Clearly, the management style of the 'ohana enterprise was highly personal and informal, the natural consequence of living and working together in a relatively confined space all the time. Inflexibility, rigidity, formality, and the like seem to have been unnatural to relationships among maka'āinana, and would have been more characteristic of management at higher levels of the society.

In order to maintain the rhythm and spirit of the family enterprise, the haku had to keep open channels of communication between and among its members. This was particularly true for Hawaiians whose social environment was delimited in so many ways by the spoken word. In the absence of memos, time charts, appointment schedules, and other convenient mnemonic devices, verbal communications had to be given freely and frequently if they were to be effective. Given the importance placed on maintaining internal family harmony, as is evidenced by the practice of ho'oponopono, we can reasonably assume that "feedback" was a strong part of the haku's communication pattern. Instead of talking *at* you, he talked *with* you, because he had to make sure that you got his message correctly by giving you an opportunity to reply to him. After all, as leader of the 'ohana, his prime duty was to ensure that each member understood his or her role in the general scheme of things. So fundamental was this principle in Hawaiian life that we can take it as the rule that governed in almost any situation.

Loyalty is highly valued in an ali'i-dominated society, yet when commoners thought of it with reference to chiefs, it was always conditional on the pono, or right behavior, of the ali'i. But when applied to the 'ohana, nothing was conditional about it. Family loyalty was one of those paramount values; violating it would result in such grievous harm to the family honor that it was unthinkable. Therefore, the haku quite naturally appealed to that value—the sense of collective pride and glory—in motivating his members to produce and work at their very best. That was a powerful message, deriving its force from belief in the eternal family, whose presence is constantly affirmed by the guarding 'aumākua. As in technology, so in economics: it was always a joint venture with the spiritual. Other motives entered in, both extrinsic and intrinsic (which we shall say more about with regard to the subject of work), but few ideas could have as stimulating and unifying an effect as kūpaʻa ma hope o ka 'ohana—loyalty to the family.

Because leadership is a function of management, the ideal haku would have shown the principles discussed above in his "profile" as a leader. It is not a profile of the authoritarian, aloof, inflexible, selfish, manipulative boss, for such a picture contradicts everything we know about the behavior of the hānau mua, the ranking senior member of the extended family clan. Handy and Pūkuʻi called him "teacher, counselor, judge, arbitrator, guardian of *'ohana* traditions; glue and binder of *'ohana* loyalties and mutual obligations; keeper of the family peace." The character of this ideal man suggests that his own perception of other people would come close to what leadership theorists of today call "liberal" or democratic. That is, people under his direction, or at least his 'ohana people, were dynamic and responsive, willing to exercise self-discipline and responsibility, dedicated to the greater welfare of the group, and certainly not lazy, self-centered, stubborn, and stupid. While, as always, an occasional troublemaker could show up in an 'ohana, a patriarch-manager could hardly have served his own kinfolk had he thought any less of them than they did of him. His role was to serve as a model for personal commitment and achievement—and as the esteemed keeper and enforcer of all the important values respected by the 'ohana. In the end, what mattered most about his leadership was the mana he was able to manifest, not merely by the appeal of personal charisma, but by his sincerity, hard work, concern, aloha, and, to be sure, the results of all these virtues in production of goods.

The principles and values that suggest the management style of the 'ohana as a self-sufficient socioeconomic enterprise are not at all unique to Hawaiians, but are found in varying degrees in family groups in many cultures. Some of these values persist as ideals even among some of the largest organizations in contemporary societies. As a matter of fact, if any of the ideas and terms we have talked about have a modern ring, that is because they are still written about in books and taught in courses and seminars on management. For example, one of the most popular and sensible books about management was the best-seller *In Search of Excellence, Lessons from America's Best-Run Companies* by Thomas Peters and Robert Waterman, who described the characteristics of such companies as IBM, Control Data, Hewlett-Packard, Coca-Cola, and a few others, as open communications, informality, flexibility, loyalty, teamwork, personal relationships, and respect for the individual. As the authors stated, "Many of the best companies really do view themselves as an extended family."

Perhaps the moral of the story is that we need not go any farther than our own backyard to rediscover some of the values of successful management. And in the process of that rediscovery, we may also find that we have a rich legacy of family enterprise management based on economic self-sufficiency and spiritual self-reliance.

The Konohiki

Surprisingly, for a society that depended so much on the managerial skills of the konohiki, we have almost no information about their achievements or any mention of great men among them. Perhaps managers are not meant to be heroic but are just taken for granted as dutiful professionals, content to share in whatever glory they might have generated for their chiefs. Even so, between the konohiki and the haku, probably no other combination of agents in the Hawaiian economy influenced its development as markedly as they did. Yet, in many respects, they differed from each other in their viewpoints, modes of operation, and values.

The *Hawaiian Dictionary* defines a konohiki as the "headman of an *ahupua'a* land division under the chief." While we ought not to argue with a dictionary, still this definition is not as precise as we need it to be. We suggest something like this: a man appointed by a chief to manage on his behalf the surplus goods produced in an ahupua'a. At the outset, our definition gets rid of the term "headman," which can be confused with "village headman" of other cultures, such as the Javanese, who is chosen by the villagers to watch over their affairs and to speak to overlords on their behalf. The konohiki was far from being that, for his job was to represent and do the bidding of his chiefly boss. Although he may have served the interests of the people as well, his loyalty to the ali'i came first. He was, plainly and simply, the "hired" manager, possibly even the "hired spear" in some cases. Obviously, his position was quite different from that of the haku, who was not only a manager but his own boss, too, in the sense that he was responsible for his own self-sufficient production unit. To put matters another way, the haku ran his own "family enterprise," while the konohiki ran someone else's. This important distinction must be kept in mind as we contrast the two management styles.

When we examine the konohiki's functions, we see why he filled the most important position in the socioeconomic system of Hawai'i. First of all, he regulated, under the chief, the two most important resources of an ahupua'a: land, which he controlled completely, and water, which he controlled to a lesser extent. He was the one who allocated and granted land-use rights on behalf of his boss. Furthermore, his approval was necessary before any such rights could be transferred to other men, either as inheritances or as gifts. Conversely, he had the authority to take away any of these rights. Thus, his power to grant land to a man also implied the power to destroy that man, for anyone without a grant of land had neither the means nor the approval to take his proper place in the hierarchy of the community. In addition, he also had the authority to construct, maintain, and regulate the irrigation systems, particularly the large centralized networks that served many users in a valley. With smaller systems, or in areas where no systems existed, his involvement was limited, of course.

Another major factor of production that he controlled was the corvée, the exaction of unpaid labor; indeed, he held a virtual monopoly of this resource. In many ways, his main role was to mobilize and direct the labor for larger productive activities. This power to draft laborers formed a good part of his bargaining authority, because it was certainly the basis for his granting of land, in exchange for the promise of so many days of work to be performed as needed. Apart from the construction of irrigation systems, he mobilized labor for the construction of fish ponds, taro patches, embankments, roads, trails, and similar neighborhood projects. In addition, he was responsible for organizing labor for rehabilitating farms, irrigation systems, and other facilities destroyed by natural disasters or by warfare, and for major fishing expeditions and agricultural undertakings.

The konohiki also was empowered under the ali'i to issue and enforce kapu on certain species of fishes or plants, thereby effectively controlling the use and consumption of almost any of those natural products. Thus, he was in charge of the ahupua'a's conservation program as well.

A most important function was the collection of the surplus goods during the Makahiki season. Malo described this as follows: "It was the duty of the *konohiki* to collect in the first place all the property which was levied from the *loa* for the king; each *konohiki* also brought tribute for his own landlord." The economic importance of the Makahiki was great because of the large quantities of goods that were amassed at that time of year. He was also responsible for storing and keeping track of those goods for eventual redistribution by the ali'i. In addition to doing all this, he farmed and fished on his own account, becoming a producer as well, and took part in the rituals and other religious activities related to his office. In short, no one, either then or now, could dispute his position as the central manager and prime mover of the Hawaiian economy. Chiefs might come and go, but the konohiki was the man who ran the ahupua'a.

In contrasting the managerial duties of the haku and konohiki, coordination related skills and ideas would have been much more important and highly developed among the konohiki. Dealing with ten, twenty, thirty, or more production units required extensive planning, scheduling, goal setting, and adjusting to varying needs. We have to assume that the chief set a minimum for the amount of tribute he needed in order to support himself, his court, and other obligations. We know that King Kamehameha I set a 10 percent tax rate, but we don't know whether that standard was followed by other chiefs.

Aware of the needs of his chief, the konohiki would have figured out how many things, including a calculated surplus, his 'ohana units would have to produce in order to meet the chief's needs. Production goals could not have been reached unless the konohiki consulted with individual producers, or at least knew what their abilities and resources were. Because he, too, was a producer, he would have been familiar with the prevailing conditions and therefore would have been able to make some reasonable estimates about expected yields. The point to be remembered is that once chiefs began to establish minimum levels of wants, the whole process of setting quotas was started, followed by setting conditions for meeting them, formulating criteria for determining progress, and so on. This process applied not only to production, but also to almost any project on a communal scale requiring large numbers of workers, supplies, times for completion, and the like. All such undertakings demanded varying degrees of coordination and planning, and, providing the konohiki was competent, industrious, and dedicated, made him the central coordinator and planner of the ahupua'a.

Economic planning such as this dealt with quantities, and the planner-coordinator had to have a good head for numbers. He had to make estimates and be able to make projections not just from one Makahiki to the next, but almost daily, in order to fulfill the requirements of his chief. He had to know the number of fields that were being cultivated, their approximate yields, the available laborers, the kinds and numbers of tools, and so on. He had to know how to collect and assess great quantities of many kinds of goods, which were to be stored and then redistributed to the people or to the chief's guests. Keep in mind that the quantities involved amounted to tens of thousands of pounds of taro, poi, seafoods, vegetables, and other edibles, as well as an assortment of kapa, mats, bowls, and so on. In addition, he had to have a thorough knowledge of the calendar, and a sharp sense of timing not only for cosmic phenomena but for religious and scheduled ritual events as well. All these duties might be summed up by naming his roles as accountant, record keeper, comptroller, and chancellor for the ahupua'a.

Above all, the konohiki's success as a manager rested on his ability to keep the support of his chief, on the one hand, and the goodwill of the laboring maka'āinana, on the other. In this balancing of pressures, most likely the maka'āinana would have been the greater problem. How well the konohiki responded to that challenge depended on a number of factors. For example, the relationship between the ali'i and the people would have been most important, for if the chief was a tyrant not even the best of men could have succeeded in his job as manager. While he no doubt benefited from the mana of the chief, the konohiki brought some of his own mana to the position, through either family connections or his own personal attributes. Despite that his first loyalty was to the chief, if he wanted to win the hearts, minds, and hands of his workers the konohiki would have had to consider them too and, if necessary, even speak on behalf of the people in weighing their needs against the demands of the chief. Thus, to a certain extent, he acted as an intermediary between the people and the higher authority. The real test of his leadership would have come in recruiting corvée labor for large-scale projects, especially for activities that promised little direct benefit for those contributing their labor, or that took too much of the workers' energies and time. We can only guess about the techniques or trade-offs he might have used to soften their resentment. In general, however, considering the magnitude of "capital" projects that were constructed and the productivity levels that were attained in old Hawaii, apparently the konohiki succeeded more often than not in enlisting the cooperation of the people.

Perhaps someday someone will write an account of the konohiki, for their story is really the story of ancient Hawai'i's economic accomplishments (and failures). They were important administrators and not few in number or ineffective in power. If each ahupua'a, and even the few larger 'ili, had its own konohiki, about one thousand or more managed the economy of the islands before 1778. Until today they remain nameless and faceless. Who among us can name even one konohiki from the past? But all of them together have left us a great legacy of achievement, in management and in leadership, that deserves our attention and our respect.

The Psychology of Work

One of the psychological shackles that modern Hawaiians have had to drag around is the stereotype that shows him as being "incurably lazy." The name of the first person who wrote that accusation has been forgotten, deservedly, but of two things about that statement we can be certain: one, the sneerer was not a Hawaiian; and two, he told his lie early in the years after 1778. But the notion persists to this day. One of the first reports of Hawaiian "indolence" appeared as part of a survey issued in 1848 by Robert C. Wyllie, writing about conditions among the Hawaiian people. When asked to comment on how far the moral and physical health of the natives was being affected by the "enervating effects of indolence and indifference," one of Wyllie's certitudinous haole informants answered, "Physical, mental and moral imbecility, disease and vice are extensively engendered, and sadly perpetuated by indolence and indifference to anything beyond the mere wants of animal existence." Another respondent stated that Hawaiians had been "greatly affected. Nothing, compared with these, as a source of suffering, both moral and physical. Here is the fruitful source of vice, misery and death. The nation is *rusting out* . . . I see no hope that the Hawaiians can be saved while this cause of so ignoble a ruin remains."

Nearly a hundred years later, in 1937, a University of Hawai'i anthropologist, Ernest Beaglehole, in his study of *Some Modern Hawaiians*, described how Hawaiians and non-Hawaiians perceived Hawaiian attitudes toward work. A kama'āina is supposed to have said that "the poor showing of the Hawaiian in the professions is not due to lack of intelligence or to poverty or to lack of opportunity, but solely to general laziness." A part-Hawaiian woman said "seriously that all Hawaiians are lazy," which she blamed on "an easy climate" that "demanded an easy life" and to "habits of indolence" that have been bred into Hawaiians "after centuries of selection." A group of Hawaiians reportedly agreed that "in general, the Hawaiian lacks ambition" and prefers to just get by rather than to work hard.

It is one thing for a non-Hawaiian to believe that Hawaiians are lazy, but quite another thing for a Hawaiian to believe the same. Not because he is not entitled to his own beliefs, but because they betray how readily modern Hawaiians have shared in the wholesale denigration of their self-image. Matters are made worse when some people try to rationalize the so-called weakness—usually for all the wrong reasons, based on a half-cocked understanding of their own cultural history. While we cannot stop other people from enjoying their prejudices, we can try to help Hawaiians to stop perpetuating the destruction of their own psyches.

The key to understanding the problem of work is found not in learning whether people work or how hard they work. Economically speaking, we take as a rule the fact that people work in order to satisfy their wants, which are material in nature. But over and above this admission, what we must determine is what are the main incentives a people will recognize in order to do work, for those people will exert themselves only to the extent that is commensurate with their own drives or attitudes. As any psychologist will tell you, find out what motivates a person, motivate him or her accordingly, and you will have a productive and happy person. But if you dilute or remove the motivation, you will have an unproductive and unhappy person—and usually a lazy one, too.

In short, we need to know the Hawaiian psychology of work—the motives and values that made labor, whether physical or mental, not only necessary but self-fulfilling. Once we understand why the Hawaiian of old worked, we shall also understand his economics better and therefore his culture as well. And we will also know why suddenly, sometime after 1778, he became "lazy."

In general, the term work refers to any activity involving the controlled expenditure of some effort or energy to gain a wanted end. But, for purposes of this discussion, work refers to activities that have a socioeconomic content. From a Hawaiian point of view, an activity must be socially productive, that is, in order to qualify as work, it must provide some service or benefit to a group or a community. Admittedly, a murky area appears, when we try to apply this definition to specific activities such as play, creative art, and the purely meditative functions of a priest. But here we are concerned more with understanding the general idea behind the concept than with resolving its more specific or less evident applications.

Hawaiians regarded work as being honorable and worthwhile. How else could they have viewed it since, in effect, to work was to imitate what the gods had done long before? Did not the myths tell of growing taro being nourished by Hāloa? Or about the great canoes being constructed under the guidance of Kūmokuhāli'i? Was not the 'ō'ō embodied in the god form of Kūka'ō'ō? Did not each craftsman work under a god assigned to his specialty? If work was ennobled and dignified by the gods, then all work was a joint venture between man and the divine.

An irreverent, disbelieving Hawaiian might have ignored the mythic deities, but he could hardly have ignored the example set by working chiefs. Kamakau (1961) said of Kamehameha I: "He used himself to take part in the work, no matter what kind it was. He helped in preparing the fishing gear or in drawing the catch ashore, or he would go out himself to sea and take part in the labor." The historian also told of how Kamehameha and his 'aialo, or eating companions (presumably other chiefs as well), "toiled with their own hands to set out a large tract" to plant taro. Obviously the king's labor was meant to be as much an object lesson to his people as a source of personal satisfaction to himself. Although chiefs generally were not expected to do menial labor all the time, "no chief or chiefess held himself too tabu to tread in the patch." Nor were they expected to while away their lives in idle leisure. Many, particularly the lesser chiefs, were specialists, working as bird snarers, featherworkers, canoe makers, healers, and priests, and others no doubt worked closely in directing the economic development of their lands.

So, if the Hawaiian of old wanted models and heroes, he found them in the chiefs at work—and, beyond them, in the gods who first taught men the ways of work. To be sure, not all chiefs were admirable models, but evidently enough of them were good workers, thereby depriving commoners of an excuse not to work.

For anyone, commoner or chief, prestige could be gained through the mastery of a craft or calling. The most skilled healers, canoe makers, adze makers, and other craftsmen were remembered for their achievements in stories and genealogies. They were selected by great chiefs and attached to their households. The descendents of the healers Miliko'o, Puheke, and Palaha were honored in that way. Kamehameha I "sought out" men skilled in government affairs and warfare to serve among his counselors (Kamakau 1961). With such employment went the privileges of high patronage: better "pay," accommodations, gifts, titles, security, perhaps even lands. If these tangible rewards were considered to be ordinary, the intangible ones of respect and praise from the community gave greater satisfaction. Because of the great influence of public opinion, to which everyone deferred, these intangible rewards would have been powerful incentives for the Hawaiian of old, far beyond any social recognition we might receive today.

Arising out of this system of awards and titles, which are outward manifestations of the acceptance of such values as high quality and achievement, develops the incentive that Raymond Firth calls the "emulative impulse." It is "the impulse to show oneself to better advantage than other persons" in the same line of work or association. When the canoe maker of the chief from the district of Ka'ū vied with his counterpart from the district of Kohala, or when two men from the same ahupua'a tried to outdo each other in a fishing expedition, they were demonstrating that impulse. Whether it is called rivalry or competitiveness, we can find ample evidence for such displays in ancient Hawaiian life, in activities ranging from warfare and politics to sports and the arts. In a word, for the Hawaiian the incentive to excel turned work into a source of personal satisfaction and an opportunity for triumph— or failure.

While such self-interest was an important dimension of the Hawaiian psychology, even more important was the sense of communal responsibility to one's 'ohana or larger community. As we have noted elsewhere, family unity and the general welfare had prior claims upon an individual in the group. The sharing of the harvest or of the catch without considering the degree of a person's involvement in the work shows how the sense of duty to the group motivated each worker or craftsman. Avoiding doing anything that might bring shame upon the 'ohana is still another powerful piece of evidence toward the same end. In short, the Hawaiian worked not only for his own advantage, but worked even more for the benefits that might accrue to his kin group. Thus, we must consider as being closely interrelated both the psychology and the sociability of work.

If work was so highly prized, then, needless to say, laziness was despised. Consider the string of nasty sayings about lazy persons (Pūku'i): (1) "wearer of goat hide," referring to a person so lazy that he used goat hides for covering (and was recognized by his odor) instead of lau hala mats, which require much work to make; (2) "fish-calling 'elepaio," said of somebody who talks about his wants and does nothing to gain them; (3) "big-gutted 'ō'ū bird," referring to a person who shirks hard work and seeks something easy to do; (4) "a Kūki'i person," said of an indolent one who is as inactive as a wooden image; (5) "a stone anchor"; (6) "clinging sand"; and (7) from Malo, 'ae'a hauka'e, a lazy, shiftless vagrant, meaning figuratively a defiled person. The many Hawaiians of today who can still hear the ringing in their ears from the times when their tūtū or parents called them moloā probably never realized how mild that rebuke was, compared with the scathing lashes of scorn their older ancestors might have used against them.

Despite the recognized need to share food and drink and other essentials, the "wearer of goat hide" wasn't allowed to take advantage of his kinfolk. *"I hea 'oe i ka wā a ka ua e loku ana?"* (Pūku'i). This biting question, "Where were you when the rain was pouring?" was the reply one man tossed at his neighbor who came to ask for some of his taro. If the neighbor answered that he'd been away on a trip during the rains, he'd be offered some food. But if he indicated that he had been at home all along and didn't do much at the time, he would be sent away with empty hands. Pūkuʻi tells the moral: "It was due to his own laziness that he did not have a crop as fine as his industrious neighbor's." The same point was made by another saying: "When it rained in Papakōlea, where were you?" Apparently, such questions could have been asked wherever a sloth tried to exploit the hard work of others. Clearly, a justifiable limit to one's generosity and kōkua could be invoked, when willful slackers gathered around.

In one special circumstance, however, idle folk were allowed to share in the rewards from the labor of others. When fishermen hauled in a net full of fish, by custom anyone present could help himself without fear of being stopped or rebuked. This was a custom that invited abuse, of course, but sharp Hawaiian tongues easily turned the abuses of hospitality into an object lesson on laziness. The classical "lazy fellow" was a man named Palapala. He never went fishing, but always managed to help himself to the fish that others had caught. He even boasted about the fact, saying, " *ʻOhi wale ka iʻa a Palapala*," or "*Palapala* merely takes the fish" (Pūkuʻi). His boast was turned into a well-known saying, which condemned those who add insult to injury not only by taking what they are not entitled to, but by bragging about it, too. In the old days, to be compared to Palapala probably was as bad as being called limalima pilau, or stink fingers, the epithet reserved for the utterly shiftless do-nothing.

Even the half-lazy person, who sought the easy way out, the man who chose the soft, unchallenging jobs, was held in disrespect. Such a person, said his critical neighbors, was like a fisherman who fools around in shallow water, taking home poʻopaʻa fish (which are easily caught with hook and line). Little respect was given the man who preferred the least line of resistance, instead of, as Pūkuʻi wrote, "venturing into something harder and more profitable." The difficult work really claims our best efforts, they meant, and in avoiding it, we leave it for others to do, thereby unloading on others part of our own responsibility. This is bad for one's ʻohana, because it shifts our burden to others. But this behavior is even worse for the laggard, who not only reveals his own weakness, but deprives himself of the opportunity to contribute to the welfare of the group and to grow personally. That is pohō, a loss for everyone.

Such general condemnation of laziness is based on its being a violation of the values that the Hawaiian ideal represented: achievement, excellence, sharing and generosity, industry, cooperativeness, loyalty—all values that can be enhanced only by effort. Worse yet, the lazy person invites shame upon himself, his 'ohana, his 'aumākua, and his gods. He is like the inert image carved in wood, the clinging sand, the stone anchor, the goat hide—a thing all but lacking in mana.

As we look back at the development of the present Hawaiian attitudes toward work, we must ask what happened. If work was exalted and laziness condemned, when and why, after 1778, did the Hawaiians become "lazy"? Let us first state that Hawaiians obviously never thought of themselves as being lazy people. Newcomers from outside started the notion of Hawaiian laziness. No one has reported how Hawaiians reacted when they were told for the first time that, contrary to whatever they might be thinking of themselves, newcomers thought they were nothing more than a bunch of lazy "natives." Probably, rather than feeling shock or anger, they were a little bewildered because for them the accusation of laziness had no meaning. How could they have understood a charge that was expressing a foreign attitude, even a prejudice? As ethnologists often remind us, such statements as "the natives are lazy" mean little more than that the psychology of one culture is being judged in terms of values derived from another. A lazy person in one society might be considered a diligent, industrious individual in another, or vice versa. Making judgments of this kind becomes either very relative or damned arbitrary. Unhappily, that shifty relationship has affected the history of intruders everywhere, whether in Hawai'i or in other parts of the primal world, and the consequences have nearly always been the same: distortion, misunderstanding, distrust, half-truths, injustice, all the stuff out of which stereotypes are imagined, and tragedies are made.

Simply put, the Hawaiians became "lazy" when they lost or were robbed of their traditional work incentives without being able to replace those soon enough with new and equally potent incentives. The loss was hastened by the destruction of the religious system in 1819. Lost with it were the powerful motivations derived from belief in their gods, myths, and rituals, which reinforced such values as excellence and achievement. During the years of confusion after 1800, the introduction of foreign merchandise and new tools caused widespread unemployment among craftsmen, unable to compete with the cheaper, newer, and more desirable products from abroad. The craftsmen were forced to abandon not only their professions but also reputations and ideals. All this (and more) led to the emergence of an alien commercial and money economy that radically altered the old beliefs in sharing, reciprocity, and "social profit." The new business-for-profit attitudes greatly undermined Hawaiians' sense of kōkua and generosity.

Kamakau (1961) described the effects of the changes with the poignancy of one who remembered them all too well.

> In the old days, the people did not work steadily but worked whenever it was necessary to get food. Today, the working man labors like a cart-hauling ox that gets a kick in the buttocks. He shivers in the cold and the dew-laden wind or broils in the sun with no rest from his toil. Whether he lives or dies it is all alike. He gets a bit of money for his toil and in the house in which he labors there are no blood kin, no parents, no relatives-in-law, just a little corner for himself. There is no regard for the old teaching of the ancestors in these days of education and Christianity. In those days the boys were taught to cultivate the ground and fish for a living, the girls to beat tapa and print patterns upon it, and to work well and pray to the god and they were taught that it was wrong to be indolent and take to robbing others. These teachings were held in esteem in old Hawai'i and the land was rich and its products varied.

By the time R. C. Wyllie made his survey in 1848 in an effort to learn "the enervating effects of indolence and indifference," great numbers of Hawaiians were already falling before the onslaught of irreversible changes and indiscriminate destruction of the old ways. Thus, when he asked his respondents to suggest solutions for the natives' "aversion to work," Wyllie came too late to the rescue. The haoles, of whatever origin, in pressing their puritanical case against Hawaiian "laziness," in fact revealed their gross misunderstanding of the complex nature of the Hawaiian and his society. They failed to realize that Hawaiian attitudes toward work were much more deeply rooted than their own, and much more honest. For Hawaiians believed that only through work can a man

fulfill his social and spiritual purpose. Few haoles, not even
Calvinists, ever went that far.

Sharing

In formal economic terminology, sharing means the distribution or
the dividing of the results of the labor of an individual or of a
group. Here we prefer the more informal and less impersonal
meaning of sharing, which more accurately represents the process
and the mood that characterized the traditional Hawaiian way. It
is also the preference of Hawaiians today, for to us sharing is a
word we use often and with feeling, as if it still carries mana of its
own. When a kupuna wahine stands up at a gathering and shouts
"We share!" and Hawaiians in the audience respond with emotional approval, we know that the idea still carries the power of a
living value—even though it is one that most people find easier to
talk about than to practice. Because of its lasting hold upon
Hawaiians, we should reexamine its traditional application as
compared with current usage.

Always sharing has two sides: one, the mere mechanics of dividing up the goods; the other, the value principle governing the
amount of goods that is allocated to the people who are directly or
indirectly involved in the production of it. Historical data are
scanty, especially about the mechanics of sharing, but we do have
enough information to outline some general procedures. In fishing, for example, Kamakau (1961) described what happened
when an aku-catching expedition returned from the sea.

> When the *aku* fishing canoes and *malau* canoes came ashore, the
> women would separate the tabu fish for the men's eating houses
> from those for the free eating, *'ainoa*, of the household. First the
> head fisherman went ashore with fish in his right and left hands
> and went into the *Kū'ula heiau* to pay homage to the gods. He cast
> down the fish for the male *'aumakua* and for the female *'aumakua*,
> and then returned to give fish to the canoe men, to those who had
> done the chumming, and to those who had done the actual fishing.
> A portion went to the owner of the canoe and of the fine-meshed
> nets, *nae puni*, that had been used to catch the bait and to those
> who had driven the bait fish into the nets. The rest was for the
> head fisherman or for the land holder, if it had been the land
> holder's fishing expedition. All these fish were carried to the

houses; the tabu fish filled the men's houses, and the "free" fish *(i'a noa)* filled the common houses *(nā hale noa)*.

The pattern of distribution, therefore, started at the top with the gods, then descended to the higher chiefs, kāhuna, konohiki, and perhaps others connected with the court, followed by the boat owner, the men directly engaged in the work at sea, and finally anyone else who might have assisted ashore.

A cardinal rule was to give the first fish caught as an offering to the gods by placing it on the local altar as soon as the fishermen returned to shore. (Today some fishermen, having modified the tribute—perhaps for want of an altar and probably out of respect to the imported god—throw back the first fish, or at least one of the catch, into the water. The deed, once regarded as an offering to provident gods, is something more than a superstition, but also something less than an act of faith.) In fact, in the old days this rule applied also to the firstborn of animals, the first fruits of crops, and to other handmade things as well. This ritual of thanksgiving, common to all primal cultures, emphasizes the non-economic character of motives for acts that today's rationalist might dismiss as signs of irrational behavior.

A method for apportioning shares that was used among the Maori and other Polynesian and Pacific island peoples delegated the village headman or a respected elder to supervise the division of catches or harvests from communal projects. Although no specific Hawaiian sources confirm this method, a practice so natural and universal probably would have served Hawaiians, too. In Hawai'i the supervisor might have been the resident chief, or his konohiki, or the haku of an 'ili'ohana. In dealing with something as important as the distribution of food, the man in charge would have decided carefully and fairly, or else provoked the noisy disapproval of the people.

The dual principles of need and labor controlled the distribution of goods, although ultimately the decision was based on the nature of each case. In a household or extended family whose members worked at their special tasks but were united in making the family self-sufficient, each person received sustenance according to his or her need. Even the family slacker probably received his portion, more out of recognition of kinship than for his pretense at labor. In larger communal projects, where kinship ties would not have been as close, the emphasis was on the amount of labor performed. In other words, those who worked were duly rewarded, those who didn't work got nothing. We have already pointed out the fate of idlers who willfully exploited the goodwill and generosity of others. According to Malo, people who squandered their resources "soon came to want because of their wastefulness." Presumably, the community made sure that such spendthrifts and wastrels suffered the consequences of improvidence.

For all their proofs of aloha, Hawaiians did not tolerate people who took advantage of the "system." To believe otherwise is to misread the Hawaiian sense of fair play and reciprocity. Whatever some modern Hawaiians may want to think, pure altruism was not the basis of sharing. Honest labor determined how much reward one man received as his share of the harvest. Given the size and intimacy of the microeconomy, in which no person's actions could go unnoticed, a laggard would not have profited from his laziness. Nonetheless, judging from the number of proverbs warning about the consequences of idleness, improvidence, duplicity, and other related faults, the people of old must have known enough misfits who tried to cheat the system. Still, the stability and vitality of the social economy were established on such values as fair play, reciprocity, and honest effort.

Wealth

Wealth, thought the people of old, is found not so much in your possessions, but in the ability to give generously of what you possess. This generalization doesn't mean that Hawaiians were opposed to owning things, for they did have a noticeable materialist streak. They were simply not obsessed by acquisitiveness. Rather, they found the ultimate gratification from wealth in the prestige, pride, and power—the mana—they gained through acts of social and spiritual distinction. Thus, wealth was not an economic quantum but a social ideal. And the ways of economics led to the way to achieving that ideal.

Waiwai is the Hawaiian word for wealth. It means water-water. In the book of Hawaiian symbols, water is the life-giving element. It is the perfect symbol for the process of giving that was the Way every true seeker of wealth must follow. This was the Way of Kāne, who gave the breath of life to man; of Lono, who gave the cloud-bearing rains; of Kū who gave the canoe and so many other crafted things; of Kanaloa, who gave the mighty sea with all its riches; of the innumerable gods for whom generous giving was the fullest measure of their divinity, of their mana. The gods are the great givers, for in that is their purpose and their greatness; an ungiving god was, to the Hawaiian believer, a contradiction beyond imagining. Giving, the Way to Wealth, was preordained from primeval times by the divine exemplars, who were honored in the sacred mo'olelo.

The primacy of giving is best shown by two of the most important values in Hawaiian and other Polynesian societies, namely, generosity, or lokomaika'i, and hospitality, or ho'okipa. The essential nature of both is the liberal giving of what you have. Such an act of generosity deserves the name lokomaika'i, which means good heart.

The moral imperative in giving generously is contrasted with the "dis-values" of selfishness and greed, which Malo condemned as hewa, grievous wrongs. Both of these dis-values, of course, are based on either withholding something or taking something from another person. The sayings, anecdotes, stories, and mythical incidents that point out the evil of such behavior are numerous in Hawaiian tradition. For example, an episode in the legend of Māui tells about the red-headed mud hen who—possessing the secret of fire—cooks only for herself. The story compares her to the selfish person who thinks only of himself without regard for others. And the greedy person is likened to the hungry people of Kaunu who, in their desperation, eat anything, whether good or bad. And the saying, *"Ho'okē a maka,"* "Deny the eyes," refers to "a very selfish person who eats without sharing, no matter who looks on with longing" (Pūku'i).

Still another dis-value that Hawaiians condemned, which underscores again the positive value of giving, is stinginess, or pīpine. The word, in fact, is the name of a notorious miser who lived long ago in Ka'ū. To be told *"He pua na Pīpine,"* "You are a descendent of Pīpine," was one of the worst possible put-downs among Hawaiians. The stingy person was ridiculed and avoided. Even today Hawaiians feel a special dislike for the stingy person, the "manini" one in the current vernacular.

Hospitality involves giving, no less than does generosity, but it is directed to a guest, visitor, or stranger. So deeply ingrained in

Hawaiians was this form of sharing that it was carried out almost
as a matter of course, without begrudging either inconvenience or
cost. According to Malo, "any breach of the duties of hospitality"
was viewed with such dread that the guilty party became the
object of public chastisement. Not surprisingly, Kawena Pūku'i
recalled that lack of hospitality was very rare in the olden days,
even extending into the early 1900s, when she was a girl living in
Ka'ū. She wrote that when a case of inhospitality did happen and
was found out, "it was noised abroad and discussed . . . with horror for years" (Handy and Pūku'i).

Thus, the manner by which a man, whether he was a commoner or a chief, gained a reputation for wealth was through the
act of giving. But, obviously, giving begins with having something
to give, that is, with possessing things, or goods, or abilities that
can offer services. The person who has more can give more, while
the person who has less cannot give as much. Hence the functions
of producing, acquiring, and accumulating things are acceptable
and necessary in the process of creating wealth. But they are not
legitimized until generosity, hospitality, and similar social acts are
completed and the acts of giving are recognized.

Both chiefs and commoners did their best to accumulate goods
and to store them safely, although we're apt to think that commoners did not acquire much. But Malo wrote about prosperous
"professional fishermen, who worked on a large scale" and farmers "who really made a business of it and worked until sunset."
The so-called 'ili pilo, people noted for their industry by their
"smelly skin," accumulated goods of their own. We can safely
assume that 'ili'ohana who held lands that were particularly fertile, and who worked diligently under good leaders, also would
have accumulated goods for storage in their own facilities (which
have been described elsewhere). Nonetheless, both the capacity
and the will to accumulate things were deliberately limited for fear
of the political risks. A likely danger lay in arousing the suspicions
of a nervous chief who, in clinging to power, worried about other
chiefs with wealth enough to challenge him. Commoners might
suffer a certain amount of public pressure against showing off too
much wealth, partly because it aroused envy among neighbors.
Moreover, for maka'āinana to imitate the ali'i was unseemly,
because that showed arrogance and lack of respect. How much of
a deterrent to initiative and achievement this "leveling effect"

might have been to the working class is another matter for speculation.

With their near monopoly over all the factors of production, the
chiefs did most of the accumulating and storing. As Malo wrote,
"It was the practice for kings to build store-houses in which to collect food, fish, *tapa, malo, pā-'ū,* and all sorts of goods." 'I'i
described Kamehameha I's caches in Kailua, Kona. "In the storehouses were piled bundles of surplus *pā'ū*, malos, and tapa sheets
. . . piled in great heaps. If one looked into the storehouses, one
saw small, large, extra large, and medium-sized bundles and
wooden bowls filled with hard poi. There were separate bundles
for women and for men. Consequently, separate storehouses were
provided for the food to be eaten by each sex. There was no separation of the fishes, however, because either men or women could
take what they wanted." Chiefs of ahupua'a also maintained storehouses, although hardly on the scale of ali'i 'ai mokupuni or
Kamehameha.

Returning to a point made earlier, we said that the lack of storage capacity was common to "primitive" economies. In the light of
this discussion, we can wonder if the Hawaiians may not have
developed more storage capability than conventional theory allows. True, the ability to store perishable goods was limited, but,
as we have seen, relatively large amounts of "hard poi," pa'i 'ai,
could be stored. More storage meant that larger crops could have
been grown than were needed for daily meals, and domestic production would have benefited, along with the whole system of
redistribution and conservation.

This storage system maintained by chiefs was intended to serve
two principal purposes: to provide foodstuffs during hard times,
and to demonstrate an ali'i's prestige and power by his acts of generosity. Such demonstrations occurred at ceremonial feasts, special
events celebrating a victory or a royal occasion, entertaining
important visitors, undertaking large "public works" projects, and
similar enterprises. 'I'i clearly spelled out the relationship between
such acts and the role of the chiefs in this account of a kauila nui
ceremony.

When these things [pigs and other goods] were brought before the
king and the chiefs, they prepared the food that they themselves
were to eat, as well as that to give away. Whole pigs were given

only to those who were eligible; others received leg, chest, or other meat. The dispossessed ones received a share from the king, including things brought from elsewhere and heaped before him. Each chief divided among his own people the things he received from the king and from his own possessions brought from elsewhere. Hence the expression, *"Nā 'li'i po'e kauā"* [The chiefs who are servants].

Another example of sharing by chiefs occurred in connection with the collection of tribute at the annual Makahiki. First, the king's representatives collected the tributes or taxes, after which there would be feasting. Kepelino (Beckwith 1932) described what happened on the eve of the day when the offerings from the people of an ahupua'a are to be presented. "When the commoners were ready with their gifts, the announcer or *Kalakū* called out with a loud voice. . . . Tomorrow fetch wood, *tī* leaves, banana leaves, and all other necessary things and when you return cook the food. The next day bake pig, dog, turkey [*sic*], chicken. Let the mountain chiefs bring petrels, geese, birds from their holes. Bring for the chiefs, bring for the small farmers, for the headmen, the *konohiki*, the landlords, the chiefs. Tomorrow morning is the day to bring your gifts." Since the kapu on produce was to be lifted after the accepting of the gifts, the announcer was in effect encouraging the people by reminding them that feasting would follow. Part of the feasting would also include receiving gifts from the king, which in fact were part of the tribute they had just presented to him. Thus the giving process was a two-way arrangement, in which the commoner initiated the giving and the king completed it by giving something back in return. At first glance this deal may not seem equitable for the maka'āinana, who got back only a portion of what he had given. But the point is that he did receive a gift, because the chief had the right to keep everything and return nothing. In truth, he could have demanded even more tribute. Thus the commoner really ended by feeling a debt of gratitude to the king for having been so generous.

Such acts of generosity exemplify the model of the good chief, for the ali'i as the true measure of generosity is illustrated in the proverb *"E 'ōpū ali'i,"* "Have the stomach of a chief," or "Be kind and generous as a chief" (Pūku'i). The people expected their chiefs to be openhanded, *"Ho'i pū'olo nō o kāhi ali'i,"* they said, "When

one visits the home of a generous chief, one always receives a gift"
(Pūkuʻi 1983). Needless to say, some closefisted chiefs ignored the
popular expectation, but for those who took seriously the reciprocal nature of their relationship with the commoners, that was
something they dared not overlook. On the other hand, generosity
was an intrinsic value to most chiefs, for it was as much a matter
of honor as of duty. To be known as a stingy chief might reveal not
only a personality quirk, but the possibility that a chief might be
poor. Since display of wealth was one way by which the chief
maintained his position, to be known as poor would have jeopardized his standing among his peers as well as his enemies. For a
chief, always subject to the intrigues and conspiracies of many
rivals, being generous was a prerequisite to keeping power and
position.

This recognition of politics in the motives of the chiefs is
revealed by Malo in one of his more cynical passages. "These
store-houses were designed by the *kalanimoku* as a means of keeping the people contented, so they would not desert the king. They
were like the baskets that were used to entrap the *hīnālea* fish. The
hīnālea thought there was something good within the basket, and
he hung around the outside of it. In the same way, the people
thought there was food in the store-houses and kept their eyes on
the king. As the rat will not desert the pantry *(kumuhaka)* where
he thinks food is, so the people will not desert the king while they
think there is food in his store-house." If generosity is perceived
here as the basis for solidifying a political relationship between
leader and follower, that was precisely part of its function. But we
should be careful not to confuse motive and value.

Economically, then, the chief played several important roles.
The first and foremost one was essentially entrepreneurial, in that
he chose, planned, and initiated the major economic projects that
required communal labor and resources; he assumed operational
responsiblity for them, although he might have delegated managerial duties to konohiki; he promoted and "sold" the project in
order to secure the cooperation needed from makaʻāinana and
others. He also bore the risks for failure, either through faulty
planning and leadership or disharmony with the presiding gods.
Second, he acted as his own financier in that he either created or
assembled the necessary resources through the collection, accumu-
lation, and storage of tribute or products from his own feudal

lands and through his lavish displays of generosity at feasts and ceremonial occasions. He was a kind of central banker who kept on deposit certain amounts of "capital in kind" and then made portions of it available for various enterprises that would profit his ahupua'a as well as his retinue. Malinowski (1921) commented on the chief's role: "I think that throughout the world we would find that the relations between economics and politics are of the same type. The chief, everywhere, acts as a tribal banker, collecting food, storing it, and protecting it, and then using it for the benefit of the whole community. His functions are the prototype of the public finance system and the organization of State treasuries of to-day. Deprive the chief of his privileges and financial benefits and who suffers most but the whole tribe?"

When you think about it, in old Hawai'i the chief's role really was not much different from that of entrepreneur-capitalists today. Fundamentally the same process of "giving" is involved, that is, it requires someone "up front" willing and able to give time, energy, capital, along with risking his own resources and prestige—today we call this investing—and then waiting to get whatever returns are yielded on his investment. In a sense, the investment is a gift made, as are almost all other gifts, with a general sense that eventually it will be rewarded, and profitably so. Without this incentive the investment would not have been made. "The essence of giving," as George Gilder so wisely said, "is not the absence of all expectation of return, but the lack of a predetermined return." In the final analysis, both the ali'i-capitalist then and the entrepreneur today give or invest on the basis of faith—in themselves, their managers, their people, and their society. Thus, wealth is demonstrated to be the product of faith in giving.

Hospitality

Not too many years ago Hawaiians were famous for their hospitality, but that, good as it was, undoubtedly paled before the extravagances achieved by the ali'i of older times. A relatively modern example is the great lū'au held by King Kamehameha III on July 31, 1847, at Luakaha, the king's summer residence in Nu'uanu Valley, Honolulu. The event commemorated the fourth anniversary of the restoration of his sovereignty after the British seized the islands in 1843. The list of provisions for that immense feast included 271 pigs, 600 fowl, 500 calabashes of poi, 5,000 fish, 80 turkeys, 55 ducks, 3 oxen, 2 barrels of salted pork, and other foodstuffs sufficient to feed twelve thousand guests (and all the retainers who did the work).

William Ellis described an event that took place twenty-four years earlier, when Kuakini, governor of the island of Hawai'i (and later of O'ahu), entertained visiting Queen Ka'ahumanu and King Kaumuali'i of Kaua'i with a feast. Ellis counted "four hundred baked dogs, with fish and hogs, and vegetables in proportion." Impressive as such figures are, Ellis thought that by 1823 Hawaiian hospitality was "much less" than it had been before then, and, he added, not as much as was offered by the "South Sea Islanders."

Such examples of lavishness tend to shock our modern sensibilities, but we need to keep in mind that being able to entertain lavishly when necessary was a matter of great personal honor to a Polynesian chief. As Firth wrote of the Maori ariki:

> Every man of rank had to be prepared to grant frequent hospitality to travellers, relatives, and visitors of note. A reputation for liberality was greatly sought after, and, conversely, a name for meanness and parsimony was a social stigma of the worst kind. . . . Many were the shifts resorted to in order to preserve one's reputation when some unforeseen contingency had reduced the supply of food available for guests. Even when the provision of ample food was impossible, through no fault of the host, great shame was felt, and the imputation of poverty was a severe blow to the pride of a chief. . . . when the cultivations of *Pehi Turoa*, the great chief of Whanganui, were destroyed by the *pukeko* (swamphen) and *au'heto* (caterpillar), he composed a song expressive of his shame and grief that on the arrival of guests he should have nothing to give them to eat and announced his intention of fleeing away to hide in his remote settlements.

Firth told another story of the well-known ancestor Paoa, whose shame was so great when his supplies were exhausted while a large party of relatives called on him that "he could not open his mouth to say a word, he felt so disgraced at not having any food to set before his guests." That very night he left his village and went far away to seek a new home. While we have no anecdotes such as these to relate from Hawaiian literature, the sentiments of the

Maori chiefs cannot have been too far removed from those of
Hawaiian aliʻi in similar situations.

At the makaʻāinana end of the scale, hospitality would have
been equally generous, although they had less to offer than did the
chiefs. Even so, they shared willingly of that relative little. Ellis
reported: "Even the poorest would generally share their scanty
dish of potatoes with a stranger. Not to entertain a guest with
what they have, is, among themselves, considered reproachful;
and there are many, who, if they had but one pig or fowl in the
yard, or one root of potatoes in the garden, would cheerfully take
them to furnish a repast for a friend."

Apart from the social reasons tied to prestige and honor, the
need to entertain guests, especially those who may have journeyed
a considerable distance, made practical sense in an era of travel by
foot. Imagine, if you will, the conditions under which the old
Hawaiians went by land from one moku to another, or by sea
from island to island. Traveling by foot would take several days to
cover the distance from Puna to Kaʻū on Hawaiʻi, or from
Kāneʻohe to Waiʻanae on Oʻahu. You would have walked under
the hot sun, or in rainy, windy weather, on muddy or stony trails,
up and down gullies, hills, and mountainsides. No wayside inns or
restaurants or fruitstands or similar conveniences offered comforts
for weary, hungry travelers. Therefore, anyone wandering along
under these conditions for more than a day or two was literally at
the mercy of local residents. Thus Kamakau (1961) observed, "It
is an old custom when a man is on the road to ask and receive
entertainment."

What advice would Kamakau give us today, when we have several million guests "on the road" in Hawaiʻi each year? Given our
modern "hospitality industry" and the demands it places on us, a
brief discussion of the matter is in order. Despite the good feelings
Hawaiians may have about their capacity for hospitality and generosity—the positive sides of the popular stereotype—there is no
question that in matters of dealing with tourists Hawaiians have
divided opinions, for many good reasons.

Some would argue that the conditions today are so totally different that the "old customs" simply do not apply and that what
we can offer at best is mostly "pseudo hospitality," because either
we have to sell it or buy it. Genuine hospitality can take place only
when no exchange of money is involved, or, more precisely, when

something is given without any thought of getting something back except the pleasure of giving and purest aloha. When a hotel manager welcomes his guests, the argument goes, he does not do so out of aloha but for the profit that must show up on the hotel's balance sheet. Or when a waitress smiles and is kind to a tourist, her motives are measured in the size of the tips she expects. Nearly five million tourists a year swarming over us represent an intolerable invasion of our privacy and a reckless exploitation of our fragile cultural and natural environment. Besides, the opponents to tourism might point out, even Malo warned us of the evil of "thrusting one's self on the hospitality of one's neighbor," or kipa wale, as he called it. Clearly, the militants would say, we are being thrust upon.

But for all the valid points made by the people who support this view, it leaves us with no positive resolution, only a mixed bag of feelings, ranging from being resigned to a hopeless situation at one end to resentment at the other. This view insists that ho'okipa cannot be offered to tourists.

The other approach to the problem confronts the issue rather than tries to escape it. In effect, this attitude says that ho'okipa can be applied to tourists today, if everyone involved understands that it must be offered in its full traditional sense, that is, as an act of giving which is based on reciprocity. Rather than the very mistaken notion that our hospitality is an act of pure altruism, we locals need to understand that it is always based on the expectation of receiving something back. As we have mentioned before, members in the traditional Hawaiian society were interrelated by a complex web of mutual obligations based on reciprocity. Hence, no Hawaiian of old would have willfully avoided repaying somebody's kindness or generosity in some way, at some proper time. Invariably, in such a web of obligations, strings were attached to every good deed. In extending the parallel to modern times, the payment a hotel manager or the tip a waitress receives from a guest is, in principle, not unlike the act or gift the Hawaiian of old repaid to somebody for his ho'okipa. Of course, money as such is hardly the same as a socially meaningful activity of hospitality or appreciation, but neither is money exchanged in a social vacuum. In a typical tourist transaction, in fact, the nature of the relationship between host and guest is essentially social rather than economic. In short, you as a working Hawaiian need not feel false or phony when you're being hospitable to someone who happens to be paying for your services. As in the days of old, so today: services can be given or received with full grace and dignity.

In any case, although conditions both political and economic have changed since 1778, they have not altered human relationships so much as to make hospitality obsolete. Most Hawaiians still believe in the importance of treating a guest or a stranger with generosity and kindness. Most, if not all Hawaiians, would not hesitate to accept ho'okipa as one of their primary values. Whatever we may dislike or regret about tourism, at least it offers us a good opportunity to test our ability to understand the world we live in today, and to apply our values as we do so.

In a sense, this digression into the "hospitality industry" of today is relevant to our discussion of the traditional approach to wealth in old Hawai'i. Although we talk about economics as if it can be set apart from the rest of existence, common sense tells us that it cannot be separated from our social environment. In reality, our economic activities and motives are always subsumed by our social values and circumstances. Some of our apparently most economic goals, for example, may be merely instrumental in achieving noneconomic objectives. Thus, you may be providing services to tourists for money, but will actually get far more pleasure out of the social or psychological transactions—the smiles, the thank yous, the "good vibes," the feeling of kōkua and aloha that have no monetary worth at all, and supposedly represent only a bonus to the business. So ask yourself which is the true source of genuine waiwai?

The Gift

"*I hele i kauhale, pa'a pū'olo i ka lima*," "In going to the houses of others, carry a package in the hand" (Pūku'i). In other words, and very directly, take a gift! The custom was second nature to traditional Hawaiians and, in fact, still is practiced among many modern Hawaiians (not to mention Japanese and adapted haoles). To go empty-handed was not only an affront to the host, but also an embarrassment to the visitor, because it caused a loss of face to both persons. When a Hawaiian presents a gift today, usually he does so for social or ceremonial reasons, but when a Hawaiian of old presented a gift, he could have done so for a number of rea-

sons, ranging from the purely practical and economic to the cheerfully social or ceremonial. A special vocabulary applied to different kinds of gifts: wainohia, a gift of affection; ho'ina, a farewell
gift, especially to a parting guest after a feast; 'oloa, a gift to a
newborn child; pālala, a gift to a chief at the birth of a child;
louulu, a betrothal gift sent from one family to another; and
ho'okupu, a ceremonial gift given to an ali'i as a sign of honor and
respect (although the term is not always used in this sense today).
They even had a word—maua—for failing to give a return gift,
which indicates how serious the whole matter of gift giving was
regarded by Hawaiians.

The nature of the gift was important not only for its aesthetic,
material, or sentimental attributes, but also for its psychospiritual
qualities as well. The latter refers to the belief that certain things
are so intimately associated with their owner that they take on "a
mystic bond" with him. This belief is consistent with the general
thesis of the constant interaction between the "material" and "nonmaterial" worlds, as in the case of mana. An 'ohana's heirloom,
for example, is not simply a mere thing but is imbued with the
spiritual force of generations of owners. A craftsman who labors
to make an exquisite object endows it with part of his spirit. (This
is not too different from claims made by many modern artists and
craftsmen, who say that their pieces retain a part of their personalities or their "souls.") Such objects, which partake of spiritual
ownership, are not easy to part with and, hence, are most prized.
The Hawaiian saying, *"He wahī pa'akai,"* "Just a packet of salt"
(Pūku'i), means that such gifts ("anything one has grown or
made") are the best. When they are given as presents, the objects
and the process of giving rise above any ordinary transaction in
meaning.

Aesthetically and materially, the most valuable gifts were things
made with feathers. But they were also the most socially discrimi-
natory, since they were exchanged only among ali'i, although
sometimes they were presented to warriors who had shown great
prowess on the battlefield. Their value was based mainly on economic grounds, because of the scarcity of certain kinds of feathers
and their monopoly by the chiefs. These factors helped to make
them very expensive, even in a moneyless society. Another prized
object was the niho palaoa, the carved whale tooth, highly valued
because of its rarity. It, too, was worn only by high chiefs. These

two kinds of objects for display, together with the kāhili, or royal feather standards, were most valued possessions—or gifts that Hawaiians recognized. Malo listed other less prized gifts, such as canoes, adzes, bowls, pieces of tapa, fishhooks, and so on, all of which are both more common and more utilitarian. These make up a rather short list of about twenty-five generic types—a relatively limited number of material things that Hawaiians owned or presented as gifts.

The general principle underlying all gift giving was reciprocity, a concept which permeated virtually all Hawaiian behavior. The Hawaiian term, pānaʻi, has many meanings: to revenge, to pay back, reward, reciprocate, whether good or bad. Thus, if a man is cursed, insulted, injured, or attacked, he can exact vengeance to the same degree on the perpetrator. Conversely, if one is treated properly, generously, or hospitably, he is expected to return the courtesy to the same extent. " ʻAʻohe lokomaikaʻi i nele i ke pānaʻi," or "No kind heart lacks a reward," the people said (Pūkuʻi). This Hawaiian version of the Golden Rule is as pervasive a theme as is the motive of revenge in the myths and the history of ancient Hawaiʻi, as well as of Polynesia.

Economically, reciprocity has a narrower meaning, although the principle is the same: one should repay each gift with something at least equivalent to what one has received. But if the equivalent is enough, giving more is better. This range of gradations in reciprocity would have depended on such intangibles as rank, type of gift, specific occasion, relationship of persons involved, and the like. A chief, for example, who might have been entertained at a feast by another, might have tried to repay the hospitality with an even bigger feast, while members of an ʻohana might have been content to exchange gifts of relatively equal value. But, generally in the etiquette of reciprocal giving, people tried to give back something better than they had received. While gift giving depended on the means of the giver and the respective social standings of the persons involved, still the natural tendency was to give more, because pānaʻi was bound up with one's prestige and mana. This is understandable, given the emphasis the people placed on generosity and hospitality. Despite the economic costs, the knowledge that one's standing rose in the eyes of the recipient and of the community made such calibrated giving all worthwhile.

An important feature of reciprocal gift giving was the spirit of noblesse oblige. Although a good deal of calculated thought in selecting a gift might have been required—deciding on its relative value as compared with the earlier exchange or planning the occasion for its presentation and so on—the actual presentation had to look like a spontaneous action growing out of the donor's own fund of aloha toward the recipient. Any hint of a calculated attempt at pushing a bargain or at trying the game of one-upmanship would have been considered a serious affront, an inexcusable breach of manners. To suggest in any way, as by recalling past favors, that you expected to get something back, would have been equally offensive. Such graceless behavior was called helu, counting. Pūku'i recalled that "sometimes the person so offended would return the gift given to her and would replace others she had used" (Handy and Pūku'i).

Notwithstanding the admonition against helu, everyone involved in gift giving had to make a careful accounting (in private of course) of what they had given to whom and what they had received in turn. Each exchange, in effect, represented a credit or a debit. Since gift giving was really a system of incurring obligations that had to be discharged at some time or other, mental record keeping was an essential feature of the system.

Timing the return of a gift was as important as any other part of gift giving. To reciprocate too soon was very poor form. As Pūku'i (Handy and Pūku'i) wrote, "When one had been given a gift of something in a bowl or dish, the container was kept for a few days at least, then filled with something and returned. To return something in the container immediately after receiving a gift in it, savoured of trade or *kū'ai*" (kū'ai cheapened personal relationships by placing above them merely vulgar material or economic considerations).

Incidentally, to say thank you to the giver upon receiving a gift was considered both unnecessary and ill-mannered. The humility and grace with which you receive a gift says all; a spoken expression will be unnecessary, contrived. As a matter of fact, the Hawaiian language had no word for thank you. This omission is characteristic not only of Hawaiians, but also of other Polynesians and American Indians as well.

Thus the style and the feeling involved in the presentation of a gift were as important as was the nature of the object itself. To describe the ritual in another way, the manner in which a gift was presented was as much a part of it as was the nature of the gift itself. We might call this the "psychological packaging" of the gift, as we recognize that in this ceremonial styling the Hawaiian was a master.

To sum up, gift giving involved a sequence of three clearly defined obligations: (1) an obligation to give; (2) an equal obligation to receive; and (3) a final obligation to give thanks for the gift by presenting something to replace it, preferably a thing of greater value, of course. This starts the whole process all over again. The sequence of events is better imagined as a spiral rather than as a cycle, with each new exchange of gifts adding another increment of value, prestige, and mana to everybody concerned. The spiraling effect is generated by generosity, hospitality, and related values, upon which are founded the social ideals that motivated so many socioeconomic activities. And last, the etiquette governing the style of presentation of gifts was as much a part of the process as was the gift itself. Of course, such gift giving is not unique to Hawaiians. Most if not all of its elements have been and still are practiced by Japanese, American Indians, Polynesians, and many other peoples. We share it with the human race.

The Peddlers

Although gift giving, along with its implied value system, was a dominant part of their life-style for most Hawaiians, the inevitable deviations from the established pattern did creep in. In the first place, given the double nature of man, torn between a giving self which seeks harmony and conciliation, and a nongiving self which asserts self-preservation, personal gain, and other individualists' values, even to avarice and miserliness, human behavior did not always match the structured value system. Compromises were always being made, because of rank, status, occupation, locality, circumstances, and other factors. With increasing population and specialization of professions, certain aspects of gift giving gradually gave way to a more impersonal and economic style of bartering and ultimately to "peddling."

In truth, the socioeconomic system of Hawai'i before 1778 covered a wide range of practices and values. We can illustrate this with a positive-to-negative scale. The positive end would represent what might be called the "sociocentric" gift-giving type described above, while the negative end would represent the opposite, or "econocentric" model. Thus, as one moves from the midpoint toward the positive end, the nature of gift giving tends to be more personal, selfless, and 'ohana oriented, emphasizing values of generosity, hospitality, kōkua, and aloha. Conversely, as one moves toward the negative end, the nature of gift giving becomes more impersonal, self-centered, utilitarian, and economic, stressing the values associated with barter, trading, haggling, and peddling, as we shall see later.

Most students of traditional Hawaiian culture know about bartering between uplanders and lowlanders—"Ko kula uka, ko kula kai," "Those of the upland, those of the shore." As Pūku'i (Handy and Pūku'i) explained, "In olden days relatives and friends exchanged products. The upland dwellers brought poi, taro, and other foods to the shore to give to kinsmen there. The shore dweller gave fish and other seafoods. Visits were never made empty-handed but always with something from one's home to give." Barter of this kind between members of the same 'ili'ohana normally would be much closer to the sociocentric end of the scale. So also would exchanges between families in an ahupua'a small enough that individual haku, or their household principals, would have had a social or even a blood link with everyone else in their community.

Then, too, a certain amount of bartering was done between ahupua'a and districts that were separated geographically and genealogically. For example, most of the people of Mānā on Kaua'i were fishermen and gourd cultivators who produced very little taro or poi for themselves. About them, according to the saying, "all the taro-cooking and poi-making was done elsewhere" (Pūku'i). They got their poi by trading in fish and gourds with the people from places like Makaweli, Waimea, Kekaha, Pōki'i on the south shore, and even from as far away as Kalalau on the Nāpali Coast, more than twelve miles distant. Whether Kaua'i had other trading communities like Mānā is not known, but more than likely their style of bartering would have been closer to the midpoint of the range, or even toward the econocentric end, because probably their "customers" would have included many nonkinsmen or even strangers. This meant that, in villages with fewer or no social ties among neighbors, transactions would be more economic. Moreover, since they had "to live or die" by their bartering skills, they would naturally become more clever as traders, if not shrewd and calculating.

As we have mentioned earlier, other trading activities were conducted by individuals or groups of professional persons. A few eminent craftsmen may have worked full-time at their professions, although the great majority must have been only part-time workers. Nonetheless, they represented a pool of people who were involved to some degree in bartering and in developing the skills and mentality for it. We know, for instance, that healers charged fees, sometimes high enough to arouse complaints from their patients. This response indicates at least a realistic understanding of market values and prices. Given the relatively large number of technical specialists emerging from the economy, we may reasonably assume that the most extensive bartering occurred among them. If that was so, then bartering even in its most simplified form must have been more widespread among ka poʻe kahiko than many students of Hawaiian culture have thought.

Interestingly, bartering also took place among the aliʻi and between aliʻi and commoners as well. According to reports, chiefs traded fish from coastal ponds at times of the year when they were so abundant that they would leave a great "stench" if the numbers had not been reduced. Kamehameha I traded fish for poi with Kaholowaho, a konohiki of Kaʻū. Some chiefs with olonā "plantations" bartered the fiber cordage (which was to become even more "valuable for trading" after 1778) (Kamakau 1961). We do not know just how extensive were these activities of chiefs in trade, but we can say that, after Captain Cook's arrival, their bartering experience combined with their entrepreneurial and "capitalist" functions stood them in good stead.

The people who were most markedly econocentric, being concerned with trade as such for the sake of profit rather than for social reward, were the peddlers, the much maligned maʻauʻauā. Curiously enough, we learn about them from a fierce condemnation of peddling in old Hawaiʻi written by Kamakau nearly a hundred years after they flourished. Without Kamakau's attack we'd know nothing about them. He referred to peddling as a "practice despised by the ancestors, who used to say contemptuously, ʻChild of a peddler! *(Keiki a ka maʻauʻauā!)* Grandchild of a peddler! Wife of a peddler! Food of a peddler! Fish of a peddler!' It was a slanderous occupation; it was as bad as being a red-eyed outcast, *kauā makawela.* The peddlers' only master was Maoloha (whose legendary net scattered food). Peddlers were not allowed in the houses of chiefs; they could not eat with them. A peddler was like a defiled person, *kanaka haumia*, in ancient times" (Kamakau 1976). This outburst is typical of Kamakau, however, who elsewhere, in his *Ruling Chiefs of Hawai'i* (1961), also described Hawaiians of old as "a people ashamed to trade."

But hostility to trading is also typical of a primal society whose values and outlooks lean heavily toward aristocratic notions of noblesse oblige, planters' beliefs in self-sufficiency and self-reliance, and 'ohana principles of unity, cooperation, pooling resources, and aloha. Peddlers not only challenge but upset the symmetry of such a system by breaking the network of social obligations that keeps the familial and political orders intact and in balance. The peddler who offered to exchange poi or fish for articles worth less than the labor needed to obtain them, while working for the ali'i ahupua'a or for the extended family, would have posed a threat to the system and therefore become an embarrassment to his 'ohana. Thus, Kamakau's feelings about peddlers are entirely consistent with the kind of socioeconomy we have described as being dominant in Hawai'i before 1778. Frankly, we would have been surprised if he had been less vituperative in his denunciations of peddling.

Who in fact were the ma'au'auā? Our fascination with them is due in part to the mystery of their origin and development as an identifiable group. In the beginning they may have been sellers of poi, because the definition of mā'au'au is the poi calabash as used by poi peddlers. Extending the name for the calabash to the people sounds reasonable, inasmuch as poi was a staple commodity always in demand. Also, as we say today about foods, it had a relatively long "shelf life" and was easily portable. This was an important asset for peddlers who, like itinerant salesmen in all lands, had to move around, going where the customers lived. Indeed, the root word ma'au means going from place to place. The typical peddler was equipped with his kōkō'aha, or carrying nets, containing his goods—which may explain in part Kamakau's reference to the net of Maoloha. However, since he is explicit about Maoloha being "the peddlers' only master," that may be more than a symbolic reference, and may suggest a connection with an occupational deity. In Hawaiian myth several names are mentioned in connection with Maoloha, including Makali'i, Lono (as in the Makahiki ceremony) and Kaulu, the demigod who used the nets he got from Makali'i to entangle and kill Haumea. If peddlers did have an occupational deity, they probably were an established and recognized group. Kamakau himself supported this suggestion when he called peddling an "occupation," albeit a "slanderous" one. He likened the peddler to the kauā makawela (literally, full of hate), the outcasts, whom we have mentioned earlier as possibly being the most self-sufficient of all Hawaiian groups, since they were forced to live in their own isolated reservations. Could peddlers have had some connection with the kauā class? That association may explain why they became peddlers, because that was an occupation that no other Hawaiians would have taken up. Although they were scorned as kanaka haumia, the need for their services must have been recognized, or else the peddlers would not have made their rounds—or gained such notoriety.

In any event, in this short and incomplete account of bartering may lie the answer to one of the seeming paradoxes of the initial contacts between Captain Cook and the Hawaiians. If Hawaiians were as hostile to peddling or as "ashamed" of trading as Kamakau said they were, why, from the very first day of contact with Cook's expedition off the coast of Kaua'i on January 20, 1778, did they engage in trading with such eagerness and adeptness as to impress Cook himself? As he wrote in his journal: "They understand trading as well as most people; and seemed to comprehend clearly the reason for our plying upon the coast. For though they brought off provisions in great plenty, particularly pigs, yet they kept up their price; and, rather than dispose of them for less than they were worth, would take them ashore." We can safely assume that Cook knew what he was writing about, because he himself was an experienced trader with a greater knowledge of Polynesians than had been acquired by any other European of the time.

The answer to our question is obvious: apart from their desire to obtain iron and all those other Western marvels, the Hawaiians' willingness and ability derived from their own familiarity with bartering among themselves. While bargaining may have been distasteful to most Hawaiians, who were caught in the net of their "sociocentric" values, others among them had the experience, the skill, and the mentality for trading. Among those who first traded with Cook, and whom he praised for their shrewdness, the most

prominent were the entrepreneurial chiefs, the managerial konohiki, the bartering specialists—and perhaps even a few clever
peddlers.

The Effects of the New Economics

Trading with Captain Cook and his men was one of the easier
adjustments Hawaiians had to make with the new economic order
that was ushered in by the Europeans. They adapted so well that
by 1790 an English naval officer complained about the "commer-
cial-mindedness of the natives." Hawaiians may have been cheated
in some of the early transactions, in which they might have given a
score of pigs or other costly provisions for an equal number of
nails, or kerchiefs, or pieces of glass, but they soon learned about
equivalent values. We are told that by 1800 a "great variety" of
goods from "cloth and clothing, household furniture and fur-
nishings, tools and utensils," and large quantities of firearms
and ammunition, were being traded (Kuykendall). Thus, by the
1820s, when foreign currency was used as a regular medium of
exchange, Hawaiians had had nearly forty years of experience in
Western-style bargaining and assessing product quality, design,
and value—in effect, with the niceties of buying and selling. If any
Hawaiians had any trouble accepting the apparent need for trading, Kamehameha I was not among them. He recognized almost at
sight the technological superiority of the foreigners and their
goods, and actively and systematically acquired the new products,
filling his storehouses with them in Honolulu and in Kailua on the
Big Island. Foreigners praised him for his honesty in their dealings,
but they also respected him for his shrewdness in bargaining.
What more legitimate reason for adopting the new economics
would Hawaiians need than the actions of their highest and most
powerful ali'i? To be sure, Kamehameha was the ruler of the
islands, but even so his actions in commerce were not lost on his
ally-chiefs, and on many others in the kingdom.

Adjusting to bartering with foreigners was one thing, but
adjusting to the many other ideas and practices that followed in
the wake of traders was quite another story. Our kūpuna may not
have understood all the consequences of their earlier meetings
with haole economics, but now, with perfect hindsight, we know
that every economic system has its form of organic unity. You can-

not accept one element of a system and reject another at will. In agreeing to bartering with foreigners, for example, Hawaiians accepted not only their products, but also, for the first time, the principle of external trade—importing some goods and exporting others. In Hawaiian economic history, that was undoubtedly a most drastic recognition, because it meant the end to centuries of absolute self-sufficiency as a people living in a group of isolated islands. As a matter of fact, from that time until now, despite all the efforts and all the talk from Hawai'i's monarchial, territorial, and state governments about the need for attaining greater economic self-sufficiency, the Hawaiians were among the last people in Polynesia to recognize this need. Reliance on imports, as we indicated in the previous chapter on technology, also meant dependence to a great extent on foreign materials, imported knowledge, and alien technicians. Those, in turn, led to the lack of demands for indigenous products, such as stone adzes and kapa cloth. And that disinterest on the part of buyers caused unemployment among Hawaiian craftsmen, the gradual decline in their skills, and, eventually, the loss of professions. Reliance on imports set off a chain of reactions that sent waves of change throughout the Hawaiian social economy and its value system, with predictably harmful results.

Take the Hawaiian involvement in the sandalwood trade, which flourished between 1810 and 1825. That was one of the saddest chapters in the whole course of ali'i entrepreneurship, and for this reason is one of the most instructive. It began innocently enough in 1791, when Capt. John Kendrick, a New Englander then engaged in the fur trade between China and Northwestern America, left three sailors on Kaua'i to collect sandalwood, which he intended to trade with Chinese merchants in Canton, who used it for incense and cabinetwork. Hawaiians, too, prized the wood, which they called 'iliahi, for its fragrance, but when Kamehameha I heard about its marketability in the China trade, he "sent his people to the mountains after this wood" and ordered his chiefs to do the same (Kamakau 1961). For a variety of reasons having to do with international politics and trade, compounded in Hawai'i by Kamehameha's claim that he had been cheated by a trio of American businessmen, the initial attempts at selling sandalwood to the Chinese almost failed. By 1816, however, the problems had been eased and the trade proved to be so successful that in China the

Sandwich Islands were being called the Sandalwood Mountains, and Kamehameha had earned enough in profits to buy six foreign ships to add to his fleet. After his death ended the royal monopoly on sandalwood collecting, the chiefs went after their share of the business, cutting and exporting thousands of piculs of the fragrant wood (the picul, a Chinese measure, weighed about $133^{1}/_{2}$ pounds). By 1825 the trade reached its peak; twenty years later it was finished. Almost all the marketable trees in Hawai'i nei had been harvested, and because no one thought to replace them with seedlings, the forests yielded no more sandalwood. According to estimates, the sandalwood trade had earned the Kingdom of Hawai'i between three and four million dollars.

The trade caused significant social, economic, and ecological disruption, unparalleled in the history of the islands. Kamakau (1961) told how famines occurred when "this rush of labor to the mountains brought about a scarcity of cultivated food throughout the whole group. The people were forced to eat herbs and tree ferns." In 1822 a missionary group reported that they "found the people very poor, and it was with much difficulty that they could obtain any food of the natives, and then only by paying three times their value. The reasons why provisions are so scarce on this island is, that the people, for some months past, have been engaged in sandalwood, and have of course neglected the cultivation of the land" (Kuykendall). Also, "On one occasion we saw two thousand persons, laden with faggots of sandalwood, coming down from the mountains to deposit their burdens in the royal storehouses." In 1823 Ellis saw a similar scene and added, "Though we had numbered, in our journey to-day, 600 houses, we had not seen anything like four hundred people, almost the whole population being employed in the mountains cutting sandalwood."

Why and how did the ali'i and the maka'āinana allow themselves to be caught in a situation that contradicted so many of the ideals and practices of their traditional social economy? Ralph S. Kuykendall suggested that Kamehameha took up the sandalwood trade as he "developed a taste for foreign goods—especially for foreign ships." But, in truth, it was more than a "taste": it was an indispensable and inevitable prerequisite for the continuance of his authority and the development of his subjects. By 1812, when he imposed his monopoly on sandalwood, he had had more than thirty years of dealing with foreign merchants, their products, and their technology. No doubt the determination to buy ships and control his own shipping line enabled him to increase trade and communication among the islands, thereby solidifying his power over people and political developments. He had no capital with which to buy those expensive ships except whatever money he could raise from the sale of sandalwood, the only readily marketable resource that promised a good return. He probably did not foresee the hardships that his entry into the business would cause his people, but, to his credit, when he did see what troubles the exploitation of the forests were causing, he "ordered chiefs and commoners not to devote all their time to cutting sandalwood . . . and ordered the chiefs and people under them to farm." He himself set a good example by clearing a large tract of land for cultivating taro. In addition, according to Kamakau (1961), "He ordered the sandalwood cutters to spare the young trees and not to let the felled trees fall on the saplings."

For Kamehameha the sandalwood trade was a serious economic enterprise, but it was also an experiment in balancing the needs of the traditional socioeconomic structure against the pressures of a foreign system whose effects seemed to be irreversible as well as unavoidable. Limiting the cutting of sandalwood and the demands for corvée labor, insisting on conservation, turning the people back to their farms: with all these measures (and more) he tried to maintain the necessary stability. Because Kamehameha was both a traditionalist and a modernist, he probably saw in the sandalwood trade another means to teach himself and his people the adjustments they must make in order to keep the best of the old economics even as they adopted some ways from the new. Had he lived a little longer, he might have been able to achieve that goal—or at least have minimized the effects of the failure of the sandalwood trade. But he died before the trade reached its height.

The chiefs on the major islands wanted to cut in on the lucrative sandalwood trade. Upon Kamehameha's death in May 1819, they persuaded his successor, Liholiho, to rescind the royal monopoly on sandalwood. They, too, had developed a "need" for foreign trade goods, even for ships of their own, and had no other sources of big money. But one of the main differences between Kamehameha on the one hand and his successor and the chiefs on the other was the extent of the debts they incurred by their inability to limit their wants and expenditures. Lack of control over foolish wants and mounting debts seems to be the inevitable disease that develops when primal people give up self-sufficiency in exchange for dependency on foreign things, methods, and sources of supply. Kamakau (1961) told the sad story of the chiefs' indebtedness. "The King [Liholiho] also went into debt buying ships. . . . [The chiefs] purchased ships and turned their debts in to the king, and he to the government. The king's favorites helped to increase the debt. They were outspoken in saying, 'Let us run up the debt and make the chiefs and commoners work; they are no friends of ours, so let us get what we can while our lord is alive.' The debts were met by the sale of sandalwood." Up to a point they were met, but by 1825 the chiefs, "beguiled by the ease of signing notes to be paid at some future time . . . found themselves entangled in a wilderness of debts." Not all of the fault was theirs, however, because they did refuse to pay for ships sold to them that were "already rotten or nearly worn out at the time of sale." In the fall of 1826 a visiting American naval officer stated that the claims of the American traders against the chiefs amounted to two hundred thousand dollars. This was not an insignificant sum (probably about a dollar for each man, woman, and child living in the kingdom at the time), but when measured against the three or four million dollars in total sandalwood sales, it does not seem to be out of line. It could have been far worse. (We need only compare it with the debts that the less developed countries accumulate today when they buy foreign products and new technologies.)

It is easy to accuse the chiefs, as some modern Hawaiians do, of greed, selfishness, profiteering, "selling out the people," and a number of other faults that violated the traditional code of values. No doubt some chiefs deserve this condemnation, and even more, but we must try to be fair with them, too. They too were struggling to make their way in this new and overwhelming world, the while they still had to live according to the expectations imposed upon them by the rules of the olden times. And, an important fact to remember, who other than the chiefs would have been able to take advantage of a major entrepreneurial opportunity? Certainly not any of the maka'āinana, including the peddlers, could have done so. The ali'i played out their traditional roles, as the people must have expected them to do, seeking to acquire wealth in order to enhance their prestige and mana. But supplying enormous amounts of the fragrant wood to foreign traders for unseen customers, in exchange for rotting ships, stiff haole furniture, Chinese silks, teacups, chamber pots, and storehouses full of the marvels and the junk from half the world around—auwē nohoʻi ē! This was an entirely new game, run according to different rules and penalties. Not only were the chiefs and their konohiki generally ignorant of the rules, but, for the first time, they were involved in an enterprise in which they had not yet learned the secrets of good management. Now the konohiki upon whom chiefs relied in the ahupuaʻa were useful only for production, not for distribution and collection of goods. This is a typical situation in international trade, in which the producers of raw materials are held at the mercy of the managers who control distribution, financing, and marketing. And, to complicate matters, those people who are in control usually maneuver their innocent producers into working under arrangements that always trap them in debt. The history of economic development and international trade, especially during the period of explosive growth during the eighteenth and nineteenth centuries, is full of such cases. The financial plight of Hawaiʻi's chiefs in consequence of the sandalwood trade was not at all unique.

Nonetheless, they missed an opportunity that might have changed the course of Hawaiian economic history. Had they succeeded in restraining their wants, in regulating the cutting and supplying of sandalwood, in mounting traditional conservation practices, in maintaining local agricultural productivity, in learning the basic concepts and techniques of trade and management—or at least in employing reliable and knowledgeable assistants, as Kamehameha had done with John Young and Isaac Davis for his military endeavors—with a little more time and no cheating foreigners to mislead them, the chiefs might have been able to avoid the burdens of debt and the consequent loss of prestige and mana. Instead, they would have been able to develop their entrepreneurial skills and to initiate other kinds of enterprises. A few chiefs did exactly that. Boki was such a one. He started a variety of small businesses, among them a liquor tavern, Honolulu's first hotel, and agricultural enterprises, including an early attempt to grow sugarcane. And then he sailed away, on a disastrous expedition to search for more sandalwood on islands in the South Pacific. But the majority of chiefs apparently were so disorganized by the collapse of their traditional social economy under the onslaught of the new economics that they did nothing to save themselves or their people. They let the newcomers, with their new approaches, run right over them.

Had they succeeded in converting their fighting skills into commercial skills, we might have seen a class of businessmen-chiefs competing successfully with the young foreign entrepreneurs like James Hunnewell, William Ladd, Stephen Reynolds, William Hooper et al. And had they succeeded in establishing thriving business houses employing eager young Hawaiians, they might also have established traditions of business success among Hawaiians, with reputations for smart money management, planning, and investing, and, most important, a system of values blending the ideals of the old social economy with the new economics. Had they succeeded in all that, they might have passed on a legacy of successful adaptation, instead of the hurtful stereotype of the failed Hawaiian that has harmed their people ever since.

If we need comforting for this sad tale, we can find it in remembering that no other chiefs of no other such innocent society throughout the whole world escaped the same unhappy fate.

The New Economic Chiefs

Some of the effects of that long subordination are fading away now, with increasing recognition of the emergence of what Gene R. Ward called the "new economic chiefs." Ward, in a study entitled "The Social Origins of Business Behavior among Hawaiian Entrepreneurs," declared: "Hawaiians, arguably, are the most entrepreneurial of the Polynesian communities in the Pacific. Hawaiians have higher rates of business formation, expansion and survival than such communities as Samoans, Tongans, Fijians, Cook Islanders and Maoris living here in Hawai'i or in their home countries in the Pacific." By his estimates, between 1,000 and 1,500 Hawaiian-owned businesses existed in 1984, more than at any other time in the past, although they constituted only 2 to 3 percent of the state's total number of business firms. Even more significant was his claim that "what the Hawaiians may lack quantitatively, they have gained in terms of quality entrepreneurship." Based on a sample of fifty Hawaiian businessmen, he drew up a striking profile, showing these characteristics.

1. Hawaiians in business are highly educated. More than half the group had college degrees, and 67 percent had attended

private schools (equally divided between Punahou and Kamehameha).

2. Hawaiians in business came from managerial positions. Most
   had three to five years of experience in high-level positions in
   companies or government.
3. Hawaiians operated businesses as large as other businesses in
   the community. Contrary to the general notion that Hawaiians are involved only in small tourism- and entertainment-
   related industries, in reality Hawaiians are involved in all
   types of businesses.
4. Hawaiians in business received some of the highest salaries in
   the state, two or three times the average salary of other
   Hawaiians, and comparable to those earned by Caucasian
   businessmen.

Ward's study did not deal with an even larger population of
Hawaiian executives who do not own businesses, but rather manage them. These executives preside over some of the largest corporations in their fields, including the second largest bank, as well as
the largest independent petroleum distributor, a title company, a
security business, an airline, landholding estates, restaurants, a
mortuary service, and so on. In addition, many hundreds of others
hold high-level management posts in corporations in Hawai'i and
in other parts of the United States and its Pacific territories. In a
sense, they carry on the management tradition of the konohiki,
although their prestige and power and the sophistication of their
techniques are far different from those available to the konohiki in
days of old.

When modern Hawaiians think or talk about their fellow
Hawaiians in business, some, if not many, ask if these businessmen are "real" Hawaiians, as if being in business makes one somewhat less of a Hawaiian. Ward dealt with this question by pointing
out that as a group, the businessmen in his sample had an average
of 33 percent Hawaiian blood (which is more than the average
amount of Hawaiian ancestry for the general population, reported
to be about 25 percent). Moreover, he said, "They did not consider themselves any 'less' Hawaiian because business behavior
was not a replacement of their culture or who they were. Business
was simply an addition to who they were as Hawaiians first, and
Hawaiians in business second."

In his study, Ward compared his Hawaiian sample with a matched group of Caucasian businessmen. One of the important data he pointed out is the cultural differences between the two groups.

> Hawaiians place a greater degree of emphasis on interpersonal relationships. This is true not only accentuated between customers, but also between employees and the owner of the firm. Because of traditional affiliation needs, Hawaiians in business derive a lot of pleasure out of making customers happy and being able to provide jobs for their employees. Hawaiian entrepreneurs, in general, expressed particular delight in being able to hire other Hawaiians for their businesses, not only because they could help them earn money, but because they could help other Hawaiians make something of themselves.

His reference to "affiliation needs" stresses the importance Hawaiian businessmen place on the social values of friendliness, cooperativeness, reciprocity, and generosity, among others, as revealed in these comments from one Hawaiian business owner.

> I think it is possible to be a successful businessman and a good Hawaiian. Indeed, the more successful you are, the better Hawaiian you can be. For example, if being generous is typically Hawaiian, the more you have, the more you can give. I'm not saying you have to be successful in order to be generous, but it helps.
> Making money is not an end but only a means to an end. In my case, it has a lot to do with serving people. In my company, I have more of a sense of responsibility to my employees. And the way I do it, I believe, is Hawaiian. I run the company like a close-knit 'ohana. We all pitch in and do our share. . . . Maintaining this family spirit is vital and that is why I don't want to get any bigger as an organization, although I would welcome increased efficiency and profits.
> Somebody asked me if I ever feel alienated from my Hawaiian-ness because of business. It was suggested that business fosters competitiveness which is supposed to be un-Hawaiian. Well, I think that's a myth. . . . I believe Hawaiians are naturally competitive as they are a cooperative, sharing people. But I like to think that we also compete with ourselves, that we set up our own standards of excellence and strive to achieve those standards regardless of what others might be doing.

> My philosophy, my values and my goals in business are insepa-
> rable from my being Hawaiian. I've never felt alienated. I feel
> Hawaiian all the time, in or out of the business world.

Appropriately enough, the fact that he just happens to have the blood of ali'i flowing through his veins (which he feels is an added responsibility and incentive) demonstrates not only the continuity of a blood line, but also the fact that some of the traditional values of our primal social economy can still be applied effectively to the competitive world of modern business.

In Retrospect

The vast majority of Hawaiians, obviously, are not in business nor are they making large salaries. As a matter of fact, as a group the average annual income of a Hawaiian ranks lowest among the major ethnic groups in Hawai'i. While most Hawaiians today per-form as well as anyone else, a disproportionate number, perhaps as many as 20 percent or more, are, to put it euphemistically, "socially and economically disadvantaged." More Hawaiians are on welfare, living in public housing, serving time in reformatories and prisons, than are members of any other ethnic group. This is a familiar message which Hawaiians are reminded of frequently through the media. The message comes not from non-Hawaiians, strangely enough, but from Hawaiian charitable and quasipoliti-cal organizations, which usually are seeking public or private funding for disadvantaged Hawaiian groups. Unfortunately, the wheel that squeaks the loudest gets heard—if not oiled. So, although these are high-minded and well-deserving causes, one of the unintended results of their case-making is the widespread pub-lic impression, which tends to reinforce the existing negative stere-otype, that somehow Hawaiians are living on the poverty line, committing acts of crime, doing poorly in school, and so on. The reality is just the opposite—most Hawaiians are self-reliant and self-supporting citizens of the community.

Nonetheless, we still must consider those who have not "made it," according to American standards. In the idealism of an aloha society, even one disadvantaged person is one too many. Frankly, the true test of Hawaiian socioeconomic values is now, as it has always been, whether or not we can take care of ourselves. The self-sufficient 'ohana survived as an institution not because of any great technological or organizational capability, but because of its ideals based on a cluster of social values: generosity, reciprocity, kōkua, laulima, industry, loyalty, and giving. We may not live anymore in an ahupua'a, or under the rule of an ali'i born with "divine right," but these values are as important and as applicable in our modern political and economic world as they were back then, in the years before the Westerners came. They are timeless and universal, and they speak, therefore, not only to Hawaiians but to all humanity.

PART FIVE

LEADERSHIP
AND POLITICS

11

LEADERSHIP AND DESTINY

The Dependency Factor

The distinguished American historian John Higham tells us that ethnic minorities in America tend to be loose knit and amorphous and therefore highly dependent on leaders who can give a group both definition and direction. "Leaders," he writes, "focus the consciousness of an ethnic group and make its identity visible." They maintain the internal integrity and cohesion of a group by their willingness and ability to speak about issues, to marshall the support of people, to organize resources, and to face opposition. Wherever centers of activity emerge, whether in the arts and crafts, religion, sports, scholarship, economics, or politics, you will find leaders. Conversely, where no leaders are found, pools of stagnation, disaffection, disunity, and aimlessness will develop among a people confused.

While this dependency on leadership seems to apply to ethnic groups in general, it may be even more applicable to Hawaiians. For one thing, we are heirs to centuries of rule by exalted chiefs, followed by almost a hundred years of leadership by monarchs. Although we have grown accustomed to equalitarian notions of participatory democracy in the decades since the United States annexed these islands in 1898, we cannot erase, nor should we do so, all the factors in our psychological and social makeup that predispose us toward communal leadership. This desire for communal leadership, although suppressed for the greater part of the twentieth century, has reappeared in the last twenty years or so, coinciding with the reawakening of Hawaiian consciousness. The signs can be seen in the rise of many organizations, usually started by the drive and ambition of one or more notable personalities who claim to speak for the Hawaiian people; the renewed interest in and deference to the constitutional monarchs and their descendents who still live among us; the increased activity in political movements and parties and the accompanying flow of talk about the need for better leaders; the "crisis of leadership"; and similar topics.

Since we are talking about Hawaiian leadership mainly for the Hawaiian community, the question we must first consider is: What is this leadership? As far as we can tell, no one person or group has seriously considered the subject as yet. The second question is: How is this "Hawaiian leadership" different from, say, "American leadership"? Clearly, if no difference between them exists, then this becomes a pointless inquiry. But if in this book we have succeeded in establishing the fact that being Hawaiian *is* different, that is, does make us different from other people, then the Hawaiian leader of Hawaiians must have a set of qualities and values peculiar to his Hawaiianness. Thus, our primary purpose in the following discussion is to identify these qualities and values, by going back to the traditional society, as we have done through much of the course of this book. We shall look specifically at the structure of leadership before 1778, the sources of influence or legitimizing authority, and the qualities of the ideal leader. In addition, we shall match those qualities with models based on accounts from myths and legends, and, in effect, come up with a picture of the essential Hawaiian leader.

Our second purpose in this chapter is to describe the state of Hawaiian leadership today, touching on the socioeconomic origins of leaders, their roles or functions, and the sources of their influence. To ensure the relevance of these matters, we shall also discuss some of the current issues and problems peculiar to the Hawaiian community. And we shall conclude with a look at some of the goals that modern Hawaiians and aspiring Hawaiian leaders might consider as part of an agenda for a Hawaiian future. We shall have little future to enjoy unless Hawaiians manage to lead themselves wisely. That is the greatest challenge we face today.

The Structure of Traditional Leadership

Most people think of traditional Hawaiian leadership as having been dominated by the highest of high chiefs. We are told that "chieftainship and leadership were synonymous," that the "divine right" of the great aliʻi to rule gave them almost absolute power, that indeed they had authority over life and death of all creatures below them. Some people even say that nowhere in all of Polynesia did the high chiefs achieve so much power as they did in Hawai'i. All these statements are made—but, in fact, for all their vaunted power, a single chief did not and could not exercise that high degree of leadership. Rather, neighboring ali'i *shared* leadership.

This idea of shared leadership may strike some students of ancient Hawai'i as being new, but it is obvious when we examine the structure of Hawaiian society before 1778. At its apex, of course, was the ali'i nui, "the king over all the people," "the supreme executive," whose duties were described by Malo as including gathering "the people together in time of war," deciding "all important questions of state, and questions touching the life and death of the common people as well as of the chiefs." As sovereign rulers, the paramount chiefs governed the entire realm, whether part or all of an island or even several islands, but they did so with provincial or local chiefs in charge of moku or 'okana (districts) and ahupua'a. Together these chiefs represented what we might call the political leadership, although theoretically that included social, economic, religious, and all other aspects of life.

As we have seen, the konohiki played a dominant role in managing the social economy of the ahupua'a. Given their major discretionary authority over allocations of land and water, and over distribution and productivity, they should be viewed as "chief executive officers" rather than as simple managers. Together the konohiki represented the socioeconomic leadership of the realm. Furthermore, since they performed extragovernmental duties, such as census taking, collecting taxes, and keeping track of supplies and other chiefly resources, they have been called "full-fledged functionaries" or, in effect, bureaucrats. Thus, along with the kālaimoku, who served the paramount chief as his administrator, the konohiki also represented the bureaucratic leadership, although in this case we might be more accurate in saying that the ali'i delegated rather than shared bureaucratic responsibility.

At still another but lower level of leadership was the larger class of specialists, the kāhuna, who represented three principal categories: the technological, the intellectual-artistic, and the religious-ritualistic. We have discussed many facets of this subject and now need only emphasize the fact that chiefs and commoners alike deferred to and depended upon the kāhuna's special services.

Finally, the largest group of leaders were the haku, or heads of the 'ohana among the maka'āinana, representing what we might call domestic or familial leadership. Haku were a formidable component of the leadership structure, because that level offered the only opportunity for gaining positions of leadership that were available to ordinary people, although the chance was given to only the few who were firstborn sons. Even so, the powers of the haku were as extensive as those of any other traditional leader except for the great chiefs. As patriarch of an extended family, its haku acted as teacher, judge, priest, administrator, economic manager, and protector, as well as a few lesser roles.

In sum, leadership in ancient Hawai'i was practiced in different fields by different people and at different levels. The great chiefs at the top dominated the political arena, the konohiki were in charge of the socioeconomic and administrative fields, the kāhuna in the technological, intellectual, and religious realms, and the haku in the familial. Thus, rather than a narrow elitist leadership confined to the great ali'i, as many of us have been taught to believe, the traditional hierarchy was far broader and much more open to able men at every level of society.

Sources of Influence

Men attain leadership by virtue of the sources of influence or power that are available to them. Sociologists, political scientists, and other students of the subject tell us that there are at least seven such sources: authority or "legitimate power" by which a person's right to leadership is recognized; expertise or skill; affection; respect; wealth; rectitude, such as is shown by being a "moral example"; and force or coercive power, whether physical or psychological. In American society, these sources of influence are general enough so that they can apply to all types of leaders. And, we are told, the more of these attributes a leader has, the more successful a leader he should become.

What sources of influence would be applicable to traditional Hawaiian leaders? In answering this question, we need to consider at least two categories: first, a list of general characteristics, more or less applicable to all leaders; and second, a series of specific attributes for the several distinctive groups or leadership levels, that is ali'i, konohiki, kahuna, and haku of the commoners' 'ohana. Our general list would include mana, pono, expertise, aloha, and loyalty. In contrast, the sources of influence for ali'i or political leadership would include, in addition to those above, kapu, or sacredness, proven lineage, rank or status, primogeniture, and sex (generally male). All of these would apply to the konohiki and kahuna, but in lesser and varying degrees, whereas the haku would be rather clearly selected by fate because (usually) he was the firstborn male.

Let us consider our general sources of influence, beginning with mana. As it applies to leadership, mana is a function of status and relationships. Since the Hawaiian concept of power is in fact a concept of status, drawing the line between where mana begins and status ends is difficult. Power without status would have been viewed as an arrangement out of order, as shameful, or as a demonstration of the arrogance of brute force. Thus, once power or mana is related to status, the personal qualities of status tend to dominate the concept of power. This would seem to be consistent with the nature of a highly stratified, hierarchical society such as was erected in ancient Hawai'i.

That mana is a function of relationships is a self-evident proposition, for such is the essence of power, when two or more people are vying for dominance. In every group, whether the 'ohana, the court of the ali'i, ritual priests, or kāhuna, invariably one or more persons possessed recognizable mana, and one individual seemed to have more than any of the others. Hawaiians must have been very skillful in identifying that special person in a group. Apart from the ascribed or inherited aspects of lineage, such as primogeniture, the components of mana would have included the characteristics of wisdom and knowledge, respectability, a degree of ho'omana or spirituality, a certain amount of personal charm, and skill and ease in handling authority. But mana also means possessing such qualities as aloha, ha'aha'a, or humility, honesty, and similar virtues, which we shall examine in detail in the following section.

Pono, according to Pūku'i, is "the foundation of good rule." In its generic sense it means goodness, or the sum total of human virtues. The Western term morality comes close to the meaning of pono. Thus, leadership based on pono exemplifies goodness and morality. In this sense Kamehameha III said, *"Ua mau ke ea o ka 'āina i ka pono"*—"The life of the land is preserved in righteousness." When John Papa 'I'i referred to pono he meant good deeds. The validity of all Hawaiian leadership is found ultimately in pono, or rectitude.

Expertise—knowing what one can and should do, and then doing it with competence—commanded such high regard in traditional Hawai'i that leadership and expertise were nearly synonymous. This is in keeping with the importance placed on achieving standards of excellence and perfection among kāhuna and craftsmen, and also with the thorough and lengthy training that persons with major responsibilities were required to undergo. After all, the leader who must depend on the skills of another man would to that extent be giving up his complete control over himself and therefore risk losing effectiveness. Also, since mana is partly achieved, partly innate, the leader who has only limited skills, or who loses the ability to employ them through misuse and failure to improve those skills, also loses some of his mana.

Although the importance of aloha may have varied according to the type of leadership, certainly no leader could have functioned effectively or for long without being liked by the people he led. Granted that a man can be influenced by leaders whom he may respect but dislike, still, within the Hawaiian 'ohana system in particular, aloha must have been a major ingredient in leadership. Experience tells us that when we like someone, he can influence us easily. Modern research suggests that "being liked and accepted by group members gives the leader more influence than if he or she is not liked or accepted." While we cannot apply all conclusions from Western-based psychological research to Hawaiian behavior, in this instance they seem to fit.

Finally, in the light of what we have said about loyalty, it too must have been an important source of influence. Where everything depended on the unity and mutual help of the family, for example, loyalty (to recall Pūku'i's emphasis) was "always" important. The linkage between all vertical and horizontal points in the traditional leadership structure was fused with kūpa'a. What any leader feared, particularly the chief, was the breakdown of that fusion, for then neither he nor his people would be able to control their destinies in the face of ever-competing chiefdoms.

Turning specifically to the ali'i, or political leadership, we know already how all-important were lineage, kapu, wealth, and primogeniture. The high status accorded to the professional genealogist or the institution of the hale nauā which investigated the purity of one's descent in a chiefly line manifests the great legitimizing power of being highborn. We remember Malo's description of the great chiefs who were "entirely exclusive, being hedged about with many tabus." We can take Malo literally in this, for he also reported that, "To the commoners (genealogies) were of no value, for their parents were of equal status, and they produced 'back country children' *(keiki kua'āina)* who could not become chiefs." In the last analysis, the purity of one's bloodline and the personal sanctity derived from that formed the unbridgable chasm between the exalted ali'i and all other people in Hawaiian society.

As we have seen, waiwai, or wealth, was an important measure of the status and prestige of a chief. It was not simply the amount of land, water, beach, or offshore resources that the chief could claim, but also how he was able to exploit and manage these resources to produce adequate and sustainable surpluses of goods. Productivity and efficiency determined the size of his storehouses, which in turn determined how generous and hospitable he could afford to be. We recall that much of his honor and reputation depended on whether he could feed and entertain his people and guests generously. In short, chieftainship was very much contingent upon wealth. The poor chief was a poor leader, for if he could not make himself wealthy, how could he make his people prosperous? The truth of this we have seen in the tendency of the maka'āinana to resettle in areas where the chiefs kept their storehouses filled.

Primogeniture, interestingly enough, was the one common denominator in ali'i and maka'āinana leadership patterns. In both cases leadership was based mainly on the order of birth and on being male, a custom widely followed in Polynesia and many other Asian-Pacific cultures. (Among the Maori, a line of firstborn males was referred to as ure tū, or erect penis.) Where the firstborn proved unequal to the demands of leadership, provisions were available to cover such contingencies.

Notwithstanding the primacy given the male, traditional Hawaiian leadership did not exclude the female. Female kāhuna practiced their arts, and female chiefs, such as the High Chiefess Keakealani, ruled in Hawai'i. Such precedents pale in comparison with the achievements and roles of Ka'ahumanu, who served as kuhina nui of the kingdom after Kamehameha's death; Keōpūolani, the Kapu Chiefess, who on that fateful day in November 1819 ate publicly with her son Liholiho, thus breaking the kapu system; and, eventually, Queen Emma and Queen Liliʻuokalani. Hawaiʻi was not just "a man's world," for woman was never viewed as entirely inferior, mythologically, at least, as is demonstrated by the accounts of Papa and Wākea, Hina the Moon Goddess, and Pele and Hiʻiaka. Leadership was shared with women, but generally only with those of very high aliʻi status, and not as a regular pattern of authority.

Finally, regarding the konohiki and kāhuna, lineage was important for some. We know that certain religious kāhuna were related to aliʻi, as were some master craftsmen. But, above all considerations, the level of their achieved skills, managerially and technologically, was the primary source of influence, for in the end much of the reason for their position was measured by how well they met the demands for their specialties. Given the standards of excellence and perfection to which technicians were held, the degrees of leadership they were accorded could not have been any lower.

The Legendary Models

Just as we today turn to biographies of great leaders for instructive examples, so did Hawaiians of old turn to their myths and legends for guidance and models to imitate. Since they were intended for didactic or educational purposes, myths and legends contain some valuable insights for us about what ka poʻe kahiko considered to be the ideal attributes of leadership. To be sure, the stories seem to exaggerate so much that the people and events in them appear to be larger than life. But this may be only a reflection of our own lack of perception. Anyway, we should remember that even in the apocryphal much wisdom can be found.

Consider the renowned Prince ʻUmi, son of the famed Liloa, king of the island of Hawaiʻi. Nearly every one of ʻUmi's deeds illustrates a quality of leadership worth following (Kalākaua). ʻUmi's devotion to the gods and spirituality are exemplified by his prodigious work in building many heiau, his constant praying and communing with the "invisible powers" of the spirit world, and his sacrificial offerings. Industry and drive, coupled with his understanding of productivity and technology, are revealed in the extensive loʻi of Waipiʻo Valley and in his fishing exploits, which "impressed" the people. Courage and strength are shown in his triumphs in battle against the forces of his evil half brother Hākau. Fidelity to his parents and family name he demonstrated by avenging the wrongs perpetrated by their enemies. In short, ʻUmi represents the leader who is intelligent, wise, kind, compassionate, generous, loyal to friends and family, respectful to authority and the gods, reverent, strong, courageous, and, to top everything, a man blessed with great organizational skills.

In dramatic contrast to ʻUmi is the antihero Hākau, who became king-chief after Liloa's death and ruled for a short time filled with terror and unimaginable cruelty. The negative qualities of leadership are embodied in Hākau: "a naturally vicious and barbarous tyrant," contemptuous of the rights of others, dishonest, arrogant, envious, disloyal, unfeeling, disobedient to the gods, treacherous, and cowardly. In the end, he is destroyed by his pono rival, ʻUmi, who restores goodness and order to the realm.

Another model is Kūaliʻi, a great chief of Oʻahu, who is described by his chronicler as "God, one of supernatural power . . . a messenger from heaven . . . a stranger *(Haole)* from Kahiki" (Beckwith 1970). Thus invested with sacredness and great mana, he is identified as an agent of the gods, gifted with reverence and spiritualness. He displays fantastic athletic and fighting skills. Named as a "swift runner," he ran around the island of Oʻahu five times in a single day (more than five hundred miles) (Beckwith 1970). A mighty warrior also, he and only two companions defeated an army of twelve thousand men. And long before Kamehameha I appeared on the scene, Kualiʻi conquered nearly all of the islands.

He is a good example of the "disguised champion," widely found in Hawaiian and Polynesian stories. This is illustrated by his apparent unwillingness to join in battle personally, pretending instead to let others do the fighting. What he does, in fact, is go into battle secretly, each time bringing back the feather cloak of a warrior he has slain. His "disguised" behavior illustrates an important aspect of haʻahaʻa: he himself does not want credit or glory, and prefers that others share it because he is content with his achievements and needs no more validation.

To demonstrate that the Hawaiian hero is essentially the Polynesian hero in a local setting, let us turn to the Pan-Pacific model,

the "perfect chief," called Kaha'i in Hawai'i, Tahaki in the Tuamo-
tus, Tafa'i in Tahiti, and Tawhaki in New Zealand. As Katherine
Luomala (1956) described him:

> He moves confidently and graciously in the society of this and
> other worlds and among people and gods of all ranks. No one can
> apply the Maori proverb, "A mussel at home, a parrot abroad," to
> *Tahaki*, for he is a well-integrated personality who is happily and
> proudly received wherever he goes. Rituals and conventions come
> easily to him, and he fulfills his obligations and performs his deeds
> with splendid dash and poise. At times he encounters almost
> impossible standards of performance and shabby tricks. He faces
> them with proud patience; and when the deeds are done, he subtly
> rebukes the setter of the overly high standards by refusing the prize
> or himself sets a task in which those who have injured him meet
> their doom.

In Mangareva they said of Tahaki that to be like him "of distinguished birth; to excel in every skill without having been taught;
to be good-looking, courageous, and in harmony with the world;
and to be respected by the gods, admired by men, and adored by
women should bring a man happiness." In New Zealand Tawhaki
is the ideal of the aristocrat because he is brave and able to suffer
torture without complaint; he is liberal and able to control his
temper, and never insults persons without cause. But he is also
able to avenge every injury and hereditary feud, and to uphold
tapu and the priestly office.

   Yet a warning is worked into the tales of the "perfect chief." For
while Tahaki sets the highest of standards for everyone else to follow, his very perfection becomes a problem to them. People are
not comfortable with perfection; in fact, being normal, they envy
him and feel resentment and hostility toward the paragon. The
model leader must remember that, in an imperfect world, becoming the ideal hero is often burdensome, thankless, and even dangerous.

   Nonetheless, the "perfect chief" is not infallible as a human
being. He suffers defeats and sorrows, he creates his own problems, he makes some mistakes and dangerous enemies. But, even
in times of weakness, his story tells us a moral: the leader must
have the will to overcome trials and hardships, but in the manner
by which he overcomes them does he find his true greatness.

Qualities of Alaka'i, or Leadership

Our discussion so far has given us some obvious clues, so that by now we should be prepared to answer the question: what are the qualities of the ideal Hawaiian leader? Some qualities have been mentioned in earlier chapters, and may not need much more attention, while others may require elaboration. Furthermore, all the qualities may not have been required of every leader or in every situation. Leadership, after all, is displayed in the judicious use of whatever means are appropriate for an occasion. Our purpose is to present a "synthetic model" of the ideal leader—but always looking toward the qualities most of us would like to see in contemporary Hawaiian leaders.

Along with the qualities of leadership, we want also to consider the qualities of followership. Too often discussions of leadership overlook the fact that the situation, and not the person alone, calls upon the leader to act. That is to say, leading is always a two-way relationship, involving the one who is led and the one who is leading. The truth of this is revealed in the saying "*I ali'i nō ke ali'i i ke kanaka,*" "A chief is a chief because of his subjects" (Handy and Pūku'i). A man without followers is no leader at all. So, while our focus is on the qualities of the leader, we deal with those within the dynamics of the leader-follower relationship.

Mālama, or Caring

Caring is expressed in the admonition to the wise ali'i: "*E mālama i ke kanaka nui, i ke kanaka iki,*" "Take care of the big man and the little man" (Pūku'i). The chief is advised to take care of his lesser chiefs and commoners alike, "for together they are the strength of his rule." The same point is made in another saying: " *'A'ohe e nalo ka iwi o ke ali'i 'ino, 'o ko ke ali'i maika'i ke nalo,*" "The bones of an evil chief will not be concealed but the bones of a good chief will." As Pūku'i explained, "The people will not care for a bad chief who does not care for their welfare and, if he dies, will not take too much trouble to hide his bones. It is the good chief that the people will faithfully serve." The wise ali'i well knew that "*I lele nō ka lupe i ke pola,*" "The tail makes the kite fly." That is, his prestige and prosperity depended on the support of his followers.

"A chief is a chief because of his subjects." In this truism lies the essence of leadership: one cannot lead unless others are willing to be led. A leader emerges only when people feel the need to be led and, in doing so, grant him the power to influence them. But they also, in their ways, will influence him. The power that the leader is called upon to show, then, is not his alone, but is his joined with that of his followers. His power, therefore, is always relational and conditional. His success always lies outside and beyond himself. He is at once an instrument and a tool of circumstances and people. A leader, in other words, is never his own boss—which is why personal vanity and self-importance are ways of cheapening good leadership. The man so cheapened is a travesty of a leader.

The reciprocal nature of leadership, then, requires that the follower give his allegiance, respect, or obedience, wiwo, in exchange for mālama and the other benefits of leadership. From much of what we have heard or read about the people of old, their feelings of loyalty or deference to their leaders ran very deep. Pūkuʻi, for instance, wrote about "the humble place of the hard working farmers and fishers who were serfs of their overlords and yet were proud to belong to their chief and their homeland." " 'O ke aliʻi wale nō koʻu makemake," "My desire is only for the chief" (Pūkuʻi). This was a common expression of loyalty and affection for the aliʻi. Thus, one command from a chief was all that was needed to win compliance from his people: "Hoʻokahi nō leo o ke alo aliʻi," or "A command is given only once in the presence of a chief" (Handy and Pūkuʻi).

All this confirms the impression of a society that was controlled and orderly. While some modern folk might prefer to believe that such a disciplined populace was the product of stern and oppressive overlords, credit for that discipline is better given to a willing and obedient people.

Yet, as Malo reminds us: "Warlike contests frequently broke out between certain chiefs and the people, and many of the former were killed in battle by the commoners. The people made war against bad kings in old times." The alternation between states of compliance and of rebellion is the natural playing out of the conditional character of leadership: leaders govern under the sufferance of those who need to be governed. Even among a people as compliant as were ka poʻe kahiko, definite limits to their allegiance were possible. Thus, contrary to the picture of a people crushed by authoritarianism, traditional Hawaiian society is more accurately seen as one in which certain limits to the exercise of power were recognized by both the aliʻi and the makaʻāinana.

Haʻahaʻa, or Humility

This understanding of the situational or conditional character of leadership helps to explain why, on the one hand, Hawaiians considered arrogance as being so unwarranted and, on the other, why they placed so much importance on humility, haʻahaʻa. Looking after the welfare of people arises from an underlying spirit of sensitivity and feeling for others that flows from humbleness rather than from a conviction of superiority.

Haʻa means low or slight, and its reduplication means doubly low. The image of being low is caught in the proverb: *"E noho iho i ke ōpū weuweu, mai hoʻokiʻekiʻe,"* "Remain among the clumps of grasses and do not elevate yourself" (Pūkuʻi). Similar advice was given by Chief Keliʻiwahamana to his daughter when, on his deathbed, he urged her to "return to the country to live a humble life" by hiding "among the clumps of grass like the wingless rail," being "careful not to break even a blade of grass" (Pūkuʻi). In plain nonpoetic language he meant don't show off, don't be proud, but rather be "lowly."

But being lowly did not mean being so abject, spineless, timid, or submissive as to risk the loss of one's dignity and self-respect. A fine balance must be kept between humility and self-respect, along with self-confidence: confidence gives strength to humility, but humility holds confidence in check, preventing it from becoming arrogance. Self-respect gives strength to humility, and humility never lets self-respect become self-importance. We don't know whether the Hawaiian of old would have used the same rationalization, but whether he did or not does not make the balance any less important.

A leader was told *"Kuʻia ka hele a ka naʻau haʻahaʻa,"* "A humble person walks carefully so he will not hurt those about him" (Pūkuʻi). Or, to put it in the negative imperative, "Don't walk over people!" The leader is the one who "walks carefully," who inspires the respect and allegiance of the people. Conversely, the leader who throws his rank and power around is bound to hurt someone and, when enough people are hurt, inevitably the situation comes to no good end for the leader.

Haʻahaʻa is a leader's best defense against excesses growing out of his own pride and egotism, which feed on power real or imagined. Without humility "power doth corrupt," and leadership will always prove to be difficult, if not impossible, over the long run.

Kūpono, or Integrity

Kamehameha I was praised for his reputation for honest dealings with his people and with the haole. He was kūpono, honest.

Kūpono combines two words: kū in this case meaning in a state of, resembling; and pono, meaning rectitude, uprightness, or goodness. Thus kūpono means literally being in a condition of pono. According to the Hawaiian way of thinking, there is little difference between being honest, upright, good, fair, or worthy.

Hawaiians always placed a premium on one dimension of honesty or integrity, and that is hoʻohiki, keeping one's word: *"Ke hoʻopaʻa nei au i kaʻu ʻōlelo,"* "I give my word" (Pūkuʻi). This was a binding pledge that had greater force than does a modern legal contract. The spoken word, as we know, had its own spiritual power for Hawaiians of old. A promise, then, involved mana or ʻaumākua as well. "Words bind, and words make free." Thus, the sanction on a broken promise could have been extremely harsh, if not fatal. The effect of hoʻohiki on Hawaiian behavior is evident even today. Social workers connected with the Queen Liliʻuokalani Children's Center, for example, have reported their Hawaiian clients' reticence to promise to keep a definite appointment or to make specific pledges because of a deep fear of punishment for failing to keep their word (Pūkuʻi, Haertig, and Lee).

Hoʻohiki is a frequent theme of Hawaiian mythology. There are many instances in the myths of self-imposed vows that test the will and seriousness of the vow maker. One extreme example is ʻAiwohikupua, who swore to bed no woman but a woman from Kahiki. He kept this promise through betrothals to two beautiful and willing females. Finally, after three attempts to win Laʻieikawai, he assembled his underchiefs and the women of the household, and clapped his hands in ceremonial prayer to his god, asking to be released from his vow (Elbert 1957).

Thus, integrity implies that there is reasonable consistency between what a leader says he will do and what he in fact does. After all, people must be able to trust their leader and to feel confident that he will stand by his word. They deserve, in return for their loyalty, to know that he will not betray them. The relationship between a leader and his people should be based on mutual trust, solidarity, reliability, and honesty.

The word kūpono also means proper, fitting, or appropriate to a setting. Since leadership situations differ from one person or issue to another, the behavior of the leader should be appropriate to the expectations of those involved in a particular situation. Reacting to one group in one way may be acceptable, but reacting in the same way to a different group may be quite another matter. The wise leader must accommodate the different views and values of different groups if he wants to stay in power. That is to say, he cannot be rigidly consistent in all instances, but must be flexible, yet still maintain his integrity. Thus, in the case of Kamehameha, whether he was dealing with haole traders, maka'āinana, his kāhuna, or fellow chiefs, with each group requiring a different approach and tactics, he maintained a reasonable level of integrity that drew confidence and trust from the people.

Perhaps the key to understanding the traditional sense of kūpono is to think of integrity as being at once a part of and the sum of pono, of being unified with the whole. If one is honest with others, then one must be honest to one's whole self too. This means being integrated in character and conduct; not being torn with inner conflicts and shifting loyalties. It is really a way of demonstrating one's whole philosophy of life.

Na'auao, or Intelligence/Wisdom

Na'auao combines na'au, mind (which in Hawaiian symbolism also means intestines, or, better, "guts," and represents the pit from which emerge human emotions and thoughts), and ao, or daylight. Literally, it means the daylight mind or, more appropriately, the enlightened mind.

No more fitting term can be found for the quality of mind that Hawaiian leaders, particularly the ali'i, aspired to than that implicit in the "enlightened mind." The insistence on genealogical purity and the accompanying kapu was an important part of a breeding program designed to produce offspring who would be endowed with superior intellectual and physical attributes. The royal children were raised with great care, so that they could develop their natural gifts to the highest degree.

Thus, the Hawaiians seem to have accepted the fact that, other qualities being equal, the person of greater intelligence made the better leader. Certainly no Hawaiian placed a premium on stupidity as a qualification for leadership. This is not to say that genius is the measure of all leadership, for many a leader can make up in persistence and courage and integrity what he might lack in natural intelligence. But entirely consistent with traditional Hawaiian thinking would be the conclusion that no leader can rise higher than his mentality will allow.

By intelligence we mean the ability to perceive relationships and analogies quickly, to "put two and two together" and come up with the right answer, to find the salient factors in past experiences in order to shed light on present difficulties.

The need for relatively high intelligence in a leader was recognized in part because of the assorted demands that would be placed upon his versatility. The valued leader was one who was capable of leading in several fields or of adapting himself to diverse situations—such as deciding on an issue of ritual propriety or responding to a challenging upstart or settling a rivalry at court or teaching a skill.

The leader's intelligence also meant the double capacity to reason as well as to imagine. This combination enables the leader to anticipate, to plan in advance, to find new and creative solutions to old or new problems, to apply bold action with confidence and with a sense of drama. Even more valued was the gifted leader who had he ʻike pāpālua, dual knowledge—or what Hawaiians (and mystics everywhere) called "second sight."

All these attributes describe the mental skills of Hawaiʻi's paragon chief, Kamehameha the Great. Capt. George Vancouver thought as much: "Every action told of a mind which under any circumstances would have distinguished its possessor. His eyes were dark and piercing; he seemed capable of penetrating the designs and reading the thoughts of those about him." Kamakau's reports of Kamehameha's accomplishments presented a mind of great ability in finding creative ideas and solutions for concrete situations. In today's language, he was "a great idea man," a leader whose ingenuity in supplying the right answers seldom failed him or his people.

Koa, or Courage

In his essay entitled "Koa: The Hawaiian Value of Courage," Russell Kawika Makanani retold the story of Hema and Kahaʻi, in which the "most perfect of *ali'i*," against enormous odds, avenges the wrongs done to his makua and "destroys the evil spirits which guard his father, recovers the eyeballs and, returning them, restores Hema's eyesight." Kaha'i's bravery is celebrated in the lines:

Oh, shout with gladness!
Oh, my dauntless courage;
    Success at last . . .

Similar episodes of bravery and courage constitute a persistent theme of the legendary heroes and leaders of Polynesia and Hawai'i. Indeed, no chief of old would have been remembered had not his poets or historian-genealogists preserved (if not created) a tale or two of personal courage. One of the more famous of those accounts tells about the blind warrior chief Pi'imaiwa'a, who disposed of the "invincible chief of Ka'ū," 'Imaikalani, whom Kamakau (1961) described as "skilled in striking left or striking right, and when he thrust his spear to the right or to the left it roared like thunder, flashed like lightning, and rumbled like an earthquake." Nonetheless, he was slain by blind Pi'imaiwa'a, who used trained ducks for "eyes."

In a society whose chiefs were trained in the arts of fighting from childhood, and who proved their mettle on the battlefields, physical courage can be expected as a badge of leadership. But courage has two sides: the physical, and the nonphysical, that is, the emotional, moral, or spiritual. Opposition to a hero comes in many different forms, like the many-headed Hydra of Greek mythology, and each demands the appropriate kind of courage. As Makanani reminded us, Kamehameha displayed a different kind of courage when he confronted the intellectual forces of the Western world than that which he used on the bloody battlefields of Hawai'i nei. When he learned of the harm that his sandalwood trade was causing the people, he showed great moral courage by ordering a partial halt to the collecting of the wood, in effect admitting that he had been wrong. When, in the face of the accelerating buildup of European influence, he had to decide whether or not to preserve the ways of old, he had the courage to say, "This is the custom of my country and I will not depart from it." When he was pressed by a foreign Christian missionary, who insisted that Jehovah was all-powerful, Kamehameha had the courage of his convictions and did not forsake his gods. But he also had the courage to accept new and unpopular ideas and then defend them in the face of doubt and resistance from his own people, friends and enemies alike.

Kamehameha no doubt recognized that courage begets courage; the more you use it, the more of it you produce. Conversely, the less of it you use, the less you have. This is a truth that every leader learns sooner or later, although not every leader learns this hard lesson in time.

Competitiveness

Many people today persist in believing that ancient Hawaiian society was noncompetitive and relatively static. If we have demonstrated anything at all about the nature of Hawaiian values and their sources, it is that they reflected an extremely dynamic society. It was characterized by what Irving Goldman, author of *Ancient Polynesian Society*, called a "powerful internal movement." The dynamism of a society develops because the many components in the system are constantly moving, not staying still. "Polynesian status systems are all strongly dynamic," Goldman continued. "All are based upon complex patterns representing opposing concepts of ascription and of achievement, of sacred and secular, of formal and pragmatic." In other words, competition is going on among individuals and groups at all levels because of opposing positions, roles, interests, ideas, and values. We have illustrated the point in many earlier references to technologists competing with each other with products they make and performances they give; hula masters vying for pupils, honors, and prizes; priests along with their followers championing the powers of their respective offices and gods; and chiefs trying to outdo each other in the scale of their feasts and entertainments. One needs to understand the extent of competition throughout all levels of Hawaiian society in order to appreciate the fact that competitiveness was a vitalizing quality of leadership.

The most obvious manifestation of competitiveness appeared in the unending struggle for political dominance among the ali'i. Timothy Earle, in his study of the chiefdoms in the Hale'a district of Kaua'i, observed: "Although political power was monopolized within the elite stratum, there was intensive and pervasive rivalry among chiefs for political power. This competitive process resulted in a cyclical pattern of chiefly expansion and segmentation. The Hawaiian chiefdoms were highly dynamic, constantly expanding by conquest warfare and fragmenting by internal rebellion." Moreover, he stated: "Competition was implicit in the complex and ambiguous social organization of the Hawaiian chiefs. In addition, because of the system of land tenure, competition among individuals ramified into major confrontations between elite factions whose rights to land and office rested on the outcome of the dispute." Earle was able to demonstrate, by tracing the lines of descent and the alliances of the paramount chiefs on Kaua'i over a period of three generations, that the pattern of their succession can be explained only "as the resolution of competing claims between social and political factions."

Competition among the chiefs for status and power was one of the primary causes for warfare. We can gauge somewhat the extent of that competition from the magnitude of the fighting in which the chiefs engaged. According to Kamakau's account of events before his time, during the period from 1737 to 1796 at least twenty-four major battles took place, in addition to many minor skirmishes. We can appreciate the ferocity of the warfare from Kamakau's (1961) narrative of the "merciless battles that had been fought in which the earth was literally covered with the innocent who were slaughtered." Kamakau goes on, "[People] were killed, even when they fled to another land, those on Maui killing refugees from wars on Hawai'i, or those on Hawai'i killing people who fled Maui." In short, competition among the warring chiefs was waged in deadly earnest, relying upon none of the "confrontation avoidance coping skills" (Howard) that some latter-day observers have devised in trying to explain the supposed noncompetitive character of modern Hawaiians.

The great chiefs did not compete, of course, just for the sake of killing each other. Warfare was simply the means to attain political power and economic wealth through control of the means of production, particularly populations and natural resources. By controlling production, and thereby the manufacture of "status goods," which they used in paying for a wide range of political, social, and economic services, the high chiefs ultimately established their complete rights to authority and office.

They found, too, other and more peaceful ways of competing: through sports contests, manipulating political alliances, arranging dynastic ties through marriage, building monumental "public works," and so on. After all, prestige and status could be served by besting one's rivals in a whole array of activities. Perhaps one of the main accomplishments of Kamehameha I was to impose a period of peace, which in turn allowed peaceful competition among an elite that seemed pathologically conditioned to warfare for political gain.

In a society preoccupied with the substance and acquisition of power, it was natural, therefore, for leaders to develop attitudes of competitiveness and aggressiveness equivalent to such values as personal achievement—and winning, and being first.

Additional Qualities of Leadership

Other important characteristics of Hawaiian leadership should be mentioned, although more by way of review, since we have discussed them in varying degrees in previous chapters. These characteristics include: generosity, or lokomaika'i; hospitality, or ho'okipa; aloha, or spirituality in the sense of developing one's mana; and courtesy, or 'olu'olu.

In Hawaiian society the willingness to give was all-important. This, in turn, was related to two allied values: generosity and hospitality, because both meant sharing one's possessions with others. To the Hawaiian mind the leader of a group, particularly a chief, set the standard of generosity. No Hawaiian would have been unaware of that high standard: "E 'ōpū ali'i," or "Be as kind and as generous as a chief should be." If this was common knowledge, common expectation also led commoners to believe that a chief would be generous because he had the means to do so, and his honor and prestige depended upon it. From the political point of view, generosity was employed in part to win the hearts and minds (or stomachs) of the people, lest (to use Malo's term) they "desert" the chief. Economically, generosity helped to redistribute goods and services, and to "invest" in communal enterprises for the overall development of the realm. If generosity was a source of satisfaction to chiefs, it also served as a powerful motive toward acquiring wealth. A poor chief, after all, was a poor leader.

While the leader-chief would have set unreachable standards for generosity for those of lesser means, that did not relieve the maka'āinana of any obligations of their own. Giving was always a reciprocal process, and hence involved the commoner in giving back generously in time, labor, surplus production, and the several forms of hoʻokupu. The only difference between the leader and the people, as far as generosity was concerned, would have been one of degree.

Hospitality, the warm and liberal entertaining of guests, was as much a quality as a function of the chief-leader. So prized was a reputation for hoʻokipa that sometimes aliʻi went to extraordinary lengths to provide food and other offerings of kindness. On the other hand, when a man was known for being inhospitable or stingy, he drew upon him a social and political stigma of the worst kind. Thus, any leader who valued his good name and mana had to make sure that he could provide the appropriate level of welcome at any time and place. We must remember that hospitality included inseparable political, economic, and sociopsychological values that together affirmed the fact of one's leadership.

We can easily rationalize the importance of such qualities as intelligence, decisiveness, technical mastery, reputation, and goal setting, but leadership probably was more a response of the heart rather than of the mind. The leader's enthusiasm, compassion, inspiration, energy, stamina, and charisma all came from his heart. "Out of the heart are the issues of life," said the people (in dainty modern translation). A Hawaiian of old would have said, of course, that such forces flow out of the naʻau, the guts. In any case, the art in leadership is not so much rational as it is emotional, or spiritual, in its promptings.

When seen in this light, we can appreciate more certainly the part that aloha plays in the duties of leadership. Aloha sensitizes the leader to the desires and well-being of others, and creates in him an eagerness to help his people to gain their hopes. Affection, friendliness, and compassion all combine to heighten one's "empathetic impulse"—or at least to make an effort in that direction.

Therefore, aloha is important in a leader, because it predisposes his people toward being influenced by him. People tend to do and be whatever they believe those who care for them want them to do and be. Then they have some well-defined role to live up to. To the extent that they try to fulfill the leader's expectations, they sense that they are needed, that they are part of something important beyond themselves. In short, aloha is a positive motivator among those who receive it as well in those who give.

Furthermore, usually it works both ways—aloha begets aloha.

The leader who gives it gets some of it back. However, this capacity to both give and receive affection differs greatly from leader to leader. Those blessed with personal magnetism, "winning ways," even "a glib tongue and a wicked smile," invite affection. On the other hand, history shows that many leaders who are deficient in this respect can still infuse confidence and respect and love in people. Kamehameha the Great apparently was reserved, taciturn, and did not waste much time in small talk, but he succeeded in winning warm affection from his people. In the end, they said, his accomplishments, joined with his deep personal commitment to the people, made his love known to them. And they reciprocated that aloha.

The 'ohana or ahupua'a or even some larger political units were based on relatively small groups in which personal contact among members was more the rule than the exception. We know that affection starts with personal relationships, and that it is furthered by personal solicitude and should deepen with continued contact. As this process is intensified by reciprocation, aloha develops between leader and follower as a matter of course.

The leader who is afraid to give affection is really afraid to lead in the true sense. Given the nature of Hawaiian society and its strong value system, this statement probably is far less true of Hawaiian leaders than of leaders in other parts of the world. If leadership means a mobilizing of emotional power and feelings, then the Hawaiian leader who marshalls the force of aloha should be fully equal to any challenge from without or within.

Hawaiian leadership is founded upon an even deeper sense of power—the spiritual force field of mana. Few concerns were more important to an ali'i, kahuna, or any other kind of Hawaiian leader than was his capacity to retain and replenish his mana. A man might survive even though lacking in mastery of technical skills, or in aloha, but the leader who lacked spiritual power was in jeopardy. Thus the first and the last prerequisite to successful leadership was the needed amount of mana. When the seer Keāulumoku chanted his prophetic mele to Kamehameha I, he ended it with these words: "Beware, oh, beware, my *Ali'i!* Hold fast to all this that is our own. Protect our people with all the power at your command. And may the gods of our ancestors be with you and strengthen your *mana*" (Mellen). The fate of his realm and leadership was entrusted to his mana.

Apart from its contribution to a leader's charisma, mana was essential to the leader for its function in ritual. Since almost all Hawaiian leaders, whether ali'i, kahuna, konohiki, or haku, had ritual responsibilities, they could not be deficient in mana, lest they fail in the eyes of the gods. In practice this meant that they were supposed to be attuned to the spiritual world and in constant communion with it. Many a Hawaiian leader spent long periods in prayer or meditation, enhancing his mana. A chief going into battle prepared himself by praying for spiritual power. He believed that it would flow into him, increasing his physical and mental strength. A kahuna about to perform a sacred ritual in a luakini would have prepared himself in the same way, by praying for added mana.

As was mentioned earlier, mana was one of the important sources of influence that, in effect, legitimized the use of power by those in positions of leadership. In actuality, whether it is described as a quality of leadership or as a source of it, mana was and is the center of all effective leadership, real or potential. It is a replenishable force that can be acquired and increased, its magnitude and efficacy being limited only by the energy and commitment of the individual leader and his contact with the spirit world. But, to continue the analogy, it can be depleted. It is a quality that can be weakened by disuse and misuse. It is a power that can be lost, as electricity is lost from a defective storage battery. Nonetheless, and this is most important to our egalitarian society of today, it is available and accessible to all leaders, even now, whatever may be their rank and lineage in the genetic and social pool. They can be charged—or re-charged—provided that all the other factors that operate to attract and to hold mana are still unimpaired.

In describing the virtues of the high chiefs, the historian Kepelino listed some of them. "*A 'o ka loina nui o nā ali'i Hawai'i nei, 'o ka ha'aha'a, 'o ka 'olu'olu, ke aloha a me ka lokomaika'i.*" "The great customary law of our Hawaiian chiefs was lowliness, courtesy, *aloha* and inner goodness." Of interest here is William Ellis' eyewitness report on the etiquette of the chiefs.

> The behaviour among the chiefs was courteous, and manifested a desire to render themselves agreeable to each other, while all observed a degree of etiquette in their direct intercourse with the king. . . . When in a state of inebriation, all marks of distinction

were lost, but at other times even these favorites *(punahele)* conducted themselves towards their sovereign with great respect. I
have often seen Kapihe and Kekuanaoa, the two who accompanied
Rihoriho to England, come into his presence, and wait without
speaking, whatever their business might be, till he should address
them, and then continue standing until requested by him to sit
down.

'Olu'olu, although translated as courtesy, means more than that
in the context of Hawaiian leadership. In the larger sense, it refers
to politeness, etiquette, manners, knowing one's proper place, as
well as graciousness and a certain awareness of how to behave in
any situation. Pūku'i (Handy and Pūku'i) stated that "politeness
and good manners were carefully, even severely taught." The
emphasis on such instruction is understandable because of the
clearly defined and intricate connections of status among individuals that governed social contact both spatially and psychologically.
Since the awareness and sensitivity levels regarding rank were
pitched so high, the leader had to know how to move smoothly
and carefully in this web of relationships.

This is why protocol was so important, particularly among the
ali'i. It was almost a specialized field in itself, because of the variety of rules governing the different ceremonies, rituals, seating or
processional arrangements, and other constraints involved in formal intercourse among leaders, visiting dignitaries, more ordinary
guests, retainers, and others on the fringes of a household.

Another important dimension of graciousness came from a
thorough understanding of the appropriate thing to say or do in a
particular social situation. Among the ali'i, of course, this ability
was almost instinctive, as if it were a sixth sense. This is characteristic of perhaps any society dominated by a powerful aristocracy
based on sacred lineage and a distinct gap between commoners
and nobility. But in Hawai'i the aloofness that elsewhere marks
aristocratic notions of courtesy seemed to have been tempered by
such values as aloha, ha'aha'a and mālama. The Hawaiian sense
of 'olu'olu allowed courtesy to bridge the gap caused by heredity.

'Olu'olu was as much a part of the reciprocal obligations
between the leader and his people as was aloha or mālama. Hence,
commoners observed an etiquette toward their leaders. For example, politeness did not allow them to discuss the affairs of their

chief just to satisfy someone's curiosity, or to make a great fuss over one's status when one was merely a commoner, or to attempt to elevate oneself "so that [one] would be regarded as of chiefly blood." According to the same code, members of aliʻi families had obligations of their own. For instance, for a chief of lower rank to boast of his lineage was unseemly. For anyone of aristocratic ancestry to speak of his pedigree, unless he should be insulted or challenged, was equally improper. *"Aia a paʻi ʻia ka maka, haʻi ʻia kupuna nāna ʻoe,"* the people said: "Only when your face is slapped do you tell who your ancestors were" (Handy and Pūkuʻi).

Interestingly, one measure of the importance placed on ʻoluʻolu is the severe sanctions that were imposed on those who broke the rules of etiquette. Some of those rules were kapu, which exacted the death penalty for infractions. The sanctions applied both to commoners and to members of aliʻi families. We should note the comment of Handy and Pūkuʻi: "The commoner at least enjoyed a certain security in that he ran less risk of giving offense than those in high places in the entourage of the *Aliʻi.*"

This is an incomplete list of qualities expected in a leader. Others that we might have included were: paʻahana, or industry, drive, and energy; hoʻomanawanui, enthusiasm (in its original Greek meaning of being inspired by a god), patience, gratitude, and recompense for kindness (or evil); and faith—meaning unshakable belief and confidence in yourself and in the people who depend on your leadership. We have said little about the importance of physical strength and beauty, especially as expressed in the myths celebrating the more ancient chiefs, or about revenge, which was so common a motive for the deeds of chiefs. But we have offered enough evidence to describe the model Hawaiian leader—for the days of old, as well as for today.

Leadership in Transition

The arrival of Captain Cook's expedition and the ensuing westernization manifestly had an enormous impact upon all groups in Hawaiian society. But in many ways the group most affected, in both the short and the long run, was the leaders, especially the chiefs at the very top. They were most affected because they were the most vulnerable, since they had the most to gain or to lose. In the end, they lost much more than they gained. They were also vulnerable for another reason: they were the main agents of change, that is, the principal channels through which the new technologies, economics, religions, and politics were introduced and propagated. To be sure, lesser chiefs and even some commoners played roles of varying importance, but by and large they all took their signals from "the men above."

How and to what extent were the chiefs affected? In what ways did they change their traditional values and institutions? These questions form the nucleus of our discussion of the "neotraditional" leadership during the nineteenth century.

Essential to an understanding of the subject is the fact that, in general, the chiefs readily accepted the newcomers. Several predisposing factors accounted for this acceptance. In the first place, the chiefs were impressed by the new technologies. Second, most of the chiefs, perhaps taking their lead from Kamehameha, kept open minds to change and were willing to learn about and test the new ideas and products from abroad. Third, a good deal of mutual respect developed between the foreign officers and the aliʻi. We know from Cook and others that they were attracted to the chiefs because of their physical stature, royal bearing, courtesy, and hospitality, all marks of an aristocratic culture which the Europeans recognized. Finally, although some chiefs were awed for a while by Cook as the returning Lono, thereafter they were not overimpressed by the foreigners' pretensions to superiority. They recognized the advantages in the Western culture, but they also respected the virtues and values of their own.

The chiefs' relationship with the foreigners had its own contradictions, however. On the one hand, it enhanced their importance by the attention they received from both the newcomers and their own people. But, on the other hand, it undermined some of their traditional foundations of legitimacy and led to an inevitable decline of their stature with respect to both the makaʻāinana and the foreigners. This paradoxical pattern developed not only among Hawaiian aliʻi, but also among other Polynesian chiefs, if not in most meetings between members of native hereditary elite classes and visiting foreigners.

Let us review some of the effects that the new technologies and economics had upon the status of leaders in Hawaiʻi. The alien commodities weakened the ritual position of both the aliʻi and the kāhuna because the new things lacked the all-important association with the mythology, the "sense of place," and the history that were part of the complex of Hawaiian culture. Using a musket required no specialized ceremonial or ritual skill, apart from a knowledge of its mechanism, which soon became general information available to all commoners. The introduction of new foodstuffs, which led eventually to changes in diet, diminished the importance of ritual in forest lore and agriculture. In short, the new technologies minimized the ritual functions of the leaders and consequently robbed them of a vital source of mana without replacing it with new channels for restoring weakening spiritual power.

The technological innovations were a direct attack on another important source of leadership, namely, the kāhunas' traditional expertise. The acceptance of iron tools and weapons, foreign ships, tools and instruments and other paraphernalia, new medicines and medical practices, new diseases, and so on, rendered much of the knowledge and skills of the old specialists obsolete and showed their helplessness against the new challenges. Not only was their obsolescence demoralizing for the kāhuna, but, even more devastating was the loss of support and respect from the people. The unemployed healer or toolmaker or canoe builder who failed to adjust to the new technology became useless, jobless, a burden, and, in some instances, a discredit. What once upon a time was knowledge or skill, prized and admired because it repeated the deeds of the gods, lost both its usefulness and its divine justification—it soon became "superstition," as in the case of certain medical customs, not only to haoles but also to Hawaiians. If power is applied knowledge, the new technologies took away from native experts a prime power base of traditional leadership.

The debacle of the sandalwood trade vividly illustrates the way the new economics undermined the leadership of the chiefs. The exploitation of the forests and of maka'āinana laborers combined with the decline in farm productivity, disruption of family life, the collapse of the market in China, and the bankruptcy of the chiefs involved, could hardly have inspired great confidence, as Kamakau suggested, in either the chiefs or the traditional models of leadership. The hurried hacking away at sandalwood trees by thousands of men and women and children, in the shortest period of time left little opportunity for the niceties of harvest prayers and ritual. Moreover, the battering at the forests must have mocked the values of conservation, until then legitimized by the power of myths and priests. The bankruptcy of the chiefs, and the collapse of their sources of wealth, weakened their economic influence, since they could no longer afford time-honored displays of generosity and hospitality through feasting and gift giving. The chiefs further jeopardized their standing by having to tax the commoners even more heavily in order to pay for their own extravagances. From almost any point of view, the negative effects of the sandalwood venture could not help but erode the leadership values that represented both the economic and the political power of the debt-ridden ali'i both as individuals and as a class.

The American missionaries, among the most powerful agencies of change, affected the traditional leadership as much as did any other alien forces. The chiefs' cooperation with the Christians and eventually their conversion to the new religion had the double effect of both enhancing and undermining ali'i leadership. In exchange for their support of the new religion, the chiefs gained prestige among the converted (and the converting), they won special treatment in educational programs set up by the missionaries, and they acquired the missionaries as secular advisers, some of whom played critical roles in laying the political, social, and economic foundations for the constitutional monarchies of the nineteenth century. On the other hand, with the acceptance of Christianity the chiefs were forced to give up their claims to any divine status, along with their ceremonial or ritual functions, and other privileges such as the practice of polyandry and polygamy. In consequence, they lost more of their dwindling supply of authority and mana.

Even more greatly affected by the advent of Christianity was, of course, the priest-kahuna. When the ruling ali'i of the realm renounced the old religion in 1819, with the collaboration of no less a person than Hewahewa, the high priest of the whole kingdom, the foundation upon which the validity of the kāhuna had for so long rested crumbled and fell away. They lost credibility, the power in their prayers and rituals, and the legitimacy of their offices. Once upon a time a priest filled an office of great prestige and respect. After 1819 the office attracted ridicule and scorn, as a relic of "paganism."

One of the most significant factors causing the erosion of the leadership of the chiefs (and the konohiki) was the loss of control over the disposition of land rights. Land was not only "the source of life," but for the chiefs it was the primary means by which they "secured and retained their authority over the people." As William Richards wrote in 1841: "It was the only system of governing with which the Hawaiians have been acquainted, and even to the present day, it is next to impossible to convince the elder chiefs that authority and subordination can be maintained by any other means. An old chief said to me, 'If we can not take away their lands, what will they care for us? They will be as rich as we.' " The commoners were not the ones who raised a clamor for land, but rather the foreigners, many of whom were newly arrived businessmen forced to become tenant-clients to the chiefs. The pressure for land reform finally overcame the resistance of the chiefs, and in 1848–1850 the Great Māhele removed one of the last pillars upholding the authority of the chiefs. The right of fee simple ownership over a piece of land was granted to commoners and foreigners alike. The "old chief's" fear of the commoners becoming as rich as chiefs proved to be tragically wrong. Just the reverse happened. For, in time, the "great division" turned into the "great dispossession," as smart foreigners, who knew far more about the economics of fee simple rights than did Hawaiians, bought up the 'āina. The chiefs, therefore, suffered a great blow when they lost their control over land. Following that came the decline in their authority, and the end to their arbitrary use of the time, labor, and surplus produce of the maka'āinana.

The Great Māhele also spelled the end of the konohiki, for they no longer had chiefs to work for or lands to manage. For the chiefs this loss of expert managers simply worsened their predicament. Their loss also hastened the end of the struggling remnants of the traditional economy, dying from too many sicknesses.

Inevitably, during that terrible period of disintegration, many other checks on the chiefs' powers were removed, which in turn led to further deterioration of whatever reputation they still kept for pono, or good deeds. By the 1840s and 1850s oppression of the commoners was widespread. Writing in 1839, Malo observed: "From Liholiho's time to the present, the chiefs seem to have left caring for the people. Their attention has been turned more to themselves and their own aggrandizement and they do not seek the welfare of the people . . . and therefore they are more oppressed at the present time than they ever were in ancient times." In 1846 he complained that the chiefs were "still taxing the people heavily" —to clear their unpaid debts to foreign merchants, among other claims. Neither the chiefs nor their konohiki endeared themselves to the commoners for organizing labor gangs to work the food-producing fields and other enterprises. The makaʻāinana resented being rounded up against their will for backbreaking work and then having to yield to the chiefs much of their produce or pay. When the kingdom's first constitution was being drafted in 1840 with the intent, in part, of giving commoners more freedom, Kamakau (1961) noted that "the chiefs objected to placing the new constitution over the kingdom seeing that little by little the chiefs would lose their dignity and become no more than foreigners." And he also stated that "the old chiefs . . . had refused absolutely to approve the new laws except in the matter of protection from crime and keeping peace among the people."

While this argument is not offered now in defense of the chiefs' attitude toward the commoners, the aliʻi's fears of losing their "dignity" and higher status were well founded. Everything from the new technologies, to political changes and land reforms, to the democratizing effects of Christianity pointed to a leveling of hierarchical relationships between chiefs and commoners. When some chiefs on Maui who had broken the law found themselves condemned to working on the road along with commoners, they lost not only their dignity but their former rank as well. Not all chiefs disliked the creeping equalizing, as Kamakau (1961) remarked of the converted Kaʻahumanu, once so proud: "Even those of the lower class whom in the old days she would have despised, became her companions and fellow laborers in the word of God." So also with Princess Nāhiʻenaʻena, who, at the age of nine years, habitually, in her private and public prayers, placed the commoners first and the chiefs second.

The new state of relations between chiefs and commoners hardly made for mutual trust or affection or the respect of olden times. The situation was so bad that James J. Jarves, in a letter addressed to Robert Wyllie on August 15, 1848, wrote, "The whites are more disposed to be liberal and just to the common natives than their own chiefs." The disaffection between the two groups showed how much the ali'i had forgotten the lesson their fathers must have learned: *"I ali'i nō ke ali'i i ke kanaka,"* "A chief is a chief because of his subjects." By 1850 the chiefs came perilously close to having no subjects at all.

By that time, in addition to the fundamental changes in the sources and symbols of authority, the traditional leadership structure too had been drastically altered. Now, rather than a number of independent chiefs ruling over mokupuni and ahupua'a distributed throughout the island chain, one dominant monarch reigned, who had taken over all the powers once wielded by chiefs. Where once political authority was shared among territorial chiefs as equals, now it was the exclusive right of a single man, the head of a new dynasty. Instead of sharing a decentralized loyalty, now the people were urged to offer a highly centralized loyalty. If, in traditional times the people had developed a dependent relationship with their ali'i 'ai ahupua'a, with the rise of the monarchy that dependence shifted toward the sovereign king. Psychologically, this marked the most important change in the structure of Hawaiian leadership, since it permanently altered the status relationships, attitudes, and values of the elite toward each other and toward the people. And, of course, vice versa.

A single rule under one ali'i family was unprecedented for Hawai'i and hence the unification that was achieved by Kamehameha's conquests was in fact a grand experiment. Because few forms for expressing the style of such a rule were known in Hawai'i, Kamehameha's successors adopted European symbols of authority, from the "glittering uniforms, heavy with gold lace and gilt buttons" to the ceremonies of state. The experiment, of course, took on much greater magnitude in every respect, with the adoption of Western constitutional and parliamentary concepts and institutions, which brought about a train of consequences that by now is familiar to most of us.

In retrospect, one of the most important consequences that the dissolution of the traditional leadership structure had for modern Hawaiians was that it left them without any strong residual leadership and loyalties in regions beyond O'ahu. The concentration of power at the center, in Honolulu, effectively depleted leadership in rural districts and on outer islands. Thus, when the monarchy was overthrown in 1893, that event also marked the complete collapse of Hawaiian leadership everywhere.

Who Shall Lead Us?

In 1937 Ernest Beaglehole of the University of Hawai'i, raised the
question of Hawaiian leadership with several Hawaiians of the
day and concluded that "Hawaiians do not follow easily leaders
from their own cultural group . . . and that the Hawaiians best
follow the lead of whites." One of his Hawaiian informants, "a
politician of note, though not of marked success," told him that
"no Hawaiian will follow Hawaiian leaders today. Hawaiians are
difficult people to lead. . . . He has finally decided that the average Hawaiian desires more than anything else appeals to his vanity, coaxing, high hopes, and vague but splendid promises."
Another Hawaiian informant agreed that "Hawaiian leaders in
general have little real influence and are unable to integrate the
aims and ambitions of their followers. . . . the Hawaiian today
works best under an American leader who has the prestige to
impose a unified policy on his followers." Still another informant,
a Hawaiian lawyer, remarked on the difficulty of getting Hawaiians to follow Hawaiians. "The Hawaiians are in general suspi-
cious. As soon as one gets to the top they discover that he is selfish
or insincere and then pull him down again."

The Hawaiians' preference for "white leadership," according to
Beaglehole, was "a corollary to the disintegration of the monarchical complex." Where previously Hawaiians had developed a dependence on the monarchy, now they had shifted their dependence
upon "the powerful newcomer" from whom "all blessings have
flowed and continue to flow." Beaglehole did not see much chance
of leadership coming from a family of commoners because the
"class psychology" of the descendents of ali'i was still potent
enough to negate any move of that sort. In his view, "The democratic point of view is only a distant ideal among some of the older
Hawaiians."

Will Hawaiians follow Hawaiian leaders today? Or would they
prefer "whites" or others to lead them? Both of these questions
would strike Hawaiians today as ranging from anachronistic to
patronizing to ridiculous. That is a measure of how much Hawaiian attitudes about themselves and others have changed over the
past fifty years. For anyone familiar with the events of Hawaiian
resurgence during the recent past, the question is not whether
Hawaiians will follow Hawaiian leaders—because they have been

doing that for quite a while—but whom will they follow. A closer examination of contemporary Hawaiian leadership will help us to answer the question.

Contemporary Hawaiian Leadership Structure

What is at once apparent when comparing traditional and contemporary Hawaiian leadership is the lack of any rigid structure, if any structure at all exists, in the current leadership. We have no hereditary firstborn ali'i leaders, although some descendents of chiefs are still acknowledged for their lineage. Hence, we have no integrated vertical leadership. The oft-used word that describes the situation is "fragmented." Not surprisingly, the sources of legitimizing authority are vastly different nowadays, with popular voting, appointments to government courts, personal achievement, and accessibility to the media replacing lineage, kapu, mana, and pono as standards for evaluation. Leadership is shared, but it is minutely divided among a great number of competing groups in many diverse fields. The levels and categories of leaders today exceed in number and complexity anything ever developed in ancient society. In short, the situations are vastly different—except for a few but faint similarities.

Among the many ways that might be used to analyze present-day Hawaiian leadership, one of the more practical and meaningful methods is to divide it into two categories: the organized and the unorganized. The advantage to this system is that it allows one to deal immediately with the essential dimensions of power in terms of constituencies, assets, organizational resources, and the like. Perhaps the one thing about leadership that has not changed among Hawaiians since traditional times is the fascination of men with power.

One wag has said that if you got two Hawaiians together you would have at least two organizations. Be that as it may, numerous and various Hawaiian organizations have been formed that cover nearly the entire range of human activity: music, hula, crafts, arts, sports, language, fraternity, religion, military, education, welfare, business, occupational, economic, environmental, historical, political, oceanic, and, not to be left out, that universal pleasure, eating. The cumulative total over the past two or three decades is unknown, but we are talking about many scores of organizations, involving thousands of members, associates, and friends. While the majority of the leaders and followers of these organizations have been and are Hawaiian, some have not been so distinguished. But a Hawaiian organization is, by definition, one in which its leaders and members are generally Hawaiian, along with its purpose, spirit, and activities.

In terms of influence or power, a fairly clear dividing line separates what we might call the "Big Five" from all the rest of these organizations. They are: (1) Kamehameha Schools/Bernice Pauahi Bishop Estate, (2) Department of Hawaiian Home Lands, (3) Queen Lili'uokalani Trust/Children's Center, (4) Alu Like, Inc., (5) Office of Hawaiian Affairs (OHA). These organizations are by no means equal in power, but they have some common elements of power: annual funding; professional, full-time staffing and administrators; powerful sponsors; relatively large constituencies; and, with the exception of Alu Like, Inc. and the Office of Hawaiian Affairs, land-based assets. The Kamehameha Schools/Bishop Estate, with land assets worth more than $2 billion at current market values, and an annual budget of at least $20 million for the Kamehameha Schools alone, and a staff of 1,100, is in a class of its own. In 1984 the operating budgets and staff of the others are, respectively: Alu Like, $3 million and 90; Lili'uokalani Trust/Children's Center, $3 million and 80; Department of Hawaiian Home Lands, $2 million and 65; and OHA, $1.5 million and 45. Ironically, OHA has the broadest mandate, but the smallest resources.

Since leadership is ultimately measured by its effective influence upon people, these organizations manifestly have the greatest potential. Each has relatively large "constituencies," based on the number of clients each serves. Kamehameha Schools serves about 60,000 persons annually through its on-campus and extension educational programs. In a broader sense, its constituency would include more than 10,000 graduates, organized into a statewide alumni association. Alu Like, Inc. serves about 15,000 annually (which includes 5,000 in job training and placement) in addition to the 12,000 members who have joined Alu Like and are entitled to vote in its elections. Department of Hawaiian Home Lands serves about 3,000 lessees, including holders of house lots, pastures, and industrial sites; and the Office of Hawaiian Affairs, an unspecified number, not easily counted. Then there are the "alumni" of the Queen Lili'uokalani Children's Center's welfare and social service programs. To this we might add the 50,000 registered Hawaiian voters who participate in the elections for OHA trustees. Thus, when we consider the number of Hawaiians who are in some way influenced by these five organizations, either directly or indirectly, a significant percentage of our 181,000 Hawaiian people would be included.

Each of these organizations also has powerful sponsors: trustees of the Bishop Estate in the case of the Kamehameha Schools, the State of Hawai'i for both the Department of Hawaiian Home Lands and the Office of Hawaiian Affairs, the U.S. federal government for Alu Like (which receives annual funding from the Department of Labor, specifically from the American Native Administration), and the Queen Lili'uokalani Trust for the Children's Center.

Thus, it is fair to say that, as a group, the leaders of the Big Five represent the greatest amount of power and exert the widest influence on the largest number of persons in the Hawaiian community. These leaders are mainly the policymakers who sit as trustees or directors on the boards and their chief administrators, a total of about thirty-five men and women. The breakdown is as follows: five Kamehameha Schools/Bishop Estate trustees; three trustees and an administrator for the Queen Lili'uokalani Trust/Children's Center; eight commissioners, including the current chairwoman, of the Department of Hawaiian Home Lands; nine directors and one administrator for Alu Like, Inc.; and nine trustees and one administrator for the Office of Hawaiian Affairs. Of the thirty-five trustees and administrators, currently ten are women, or less than a third. (The trustees of the Kamehameha Schools/Bishop Estate and the Office of Hawaiian Affairs are at this time male preserves.) The average age is about fifty years. Occupationally, the vast majority come from public sector backgrounds, and almost none from business, and most tend to be in middle-income brackets, except for the Kamehameha Schools/Bishop Estate trustees.

A knowledge of the manner by which these leaders are selected is important in order to understand the nature of their power and backgrounds. In the case of the Kamehameha Schools/Bishop Estate, the trustees are appointed by the justices of the state supreme court. The last three appointees include a former aide to the late governor John A. Burns, the most recently retired chief justice of the state supreme court, and the incumbent speaker of the state house of representatives. All are members of the same political party that has been in power since 1954. In view of the important role that ownership of land plays in this state, anyone would be naive to believe that such an appointment is not politically influenced. With regard to the commissioners of the Department of Hawaiian Home Lands, all are appointed by the governor of the state, for staggered terms of four years. The trustees of the Office of Hawaiian Affairs, however, are elected for staggered four-year terms by Hawaiians who are registered OHA voters. As for the directors of Alu Like, Inc., they are elected by its twelve thousand members, as prescribed by the conditions of the funding grant from the federal government. Finally, the trustees of the Lili'uokalani Trust are also appointed by the state supreme court.

One conclusion to be drawn from all this is that the leadership of these resource-rich organizations must thoroughly understand and be equally sensitive to federal and state government politics. Both OHA and the Department of Hawaiian Home Lands are creatures of government and therefore are subject to the pleasure or whims of those officials who happen to be in power. Although some observers claim that OHA is "a government within a government" and enjoys a sovereign autonomy, its ten-year mandate will be decided by the next state constitutional convention, which is scheduled for 1988. Alu Like's lease on life depends in part on the policies of whatever administration is in power in Washington, D.C. and on the leverage of Hawai'i's congressional delegation.

In other words, the leaders of our Big Five organizations do not operate in a political vacuum; they are only one small part of a much larger power configuration in which they have relatively little sway. Sometimes the rhetoric of a few tends to obscure this reality. Like it or not, the leaders of this Big Five must also play the role of power brokers who must maneuver skillfully in order to obtain a bigger piece of the pie on the one hand, and, on the other, to protect what they already have. In either case, a deft touch, a keen ear, and good vision are needed to deal with the mechanics (and the personalities) of state and federal politics.

Below the resource-rich Big Five organizations are many others: the Association of Hawaiian Civic Clubs, Kamehameha Alumni Association, Protect Kaho'olawe 'Ohana, Congress of Hawaiians, Sons and Daughters of Hawaiian Warriors, Order of Kameha-

meha, Hui Kūkākūkā (Hawaiian culture teachers and other enthu-
siasts), 'Ahahui 'Ōlelo Hawai'i (Hawaiian language association),
Hale Nauā III (artists society), Temari (kapa makers), Hawaiian
homestead associations, Hawaiian Professional/Business Association, and the numerous halau hula, among other groups. The
majority of these groups are concerned with social, educational,
and cultural matters. Only one organization deals with business,
and that is the Hawaiian Professional/Business Association. And
at present, in 1985, we have only one active political organization,
the Protect Kaho'olawe 'Ohana. Most of these organizations have
fairly limited objectives in specific fields, while very few tend to be
solely issue oriented. The latter are usually political, such as the
defunct A.L.O.H.A., The Hawaiians, and the protect Kaho'olawe
group. Issue-oriented groups come and go as they respond to
specific situations, make dramatic gestures, and capture a few
moments of the media's attention, only to disappear as the popular interest subsides or as the enthusiasm of leaders and supporters
peters out. The life span of the other groups is longer, with some
of the oldest being more than half a century in age, such as the
Association of Hawaiian Civic Clubs, founded in 1918. A strong
correlation exists between the age of an organization and the
demographics of its members and leaders. Those of the older organizations tend to be older themselves, are better educated, economically better off, and philosophically more conservative. Finally, the memberships vary in number from less than a hundred
to several thousand, as in the Association of Hawaiian Civic
Clubs.

The hālau hula form a special grouping not only because of
their dedication to the dance, but because of their influence on the
vitality of Hawaiian culture as a whole. The schools teach more
than dance: they teach that, of course, but at the same time help to
preserve the language and some of the myths, rituals, and customs
of the past. Their impact is significant because of the large number
of people who are involved as teachers, students, and audiences.
In some hālau where the kumu hula are particularly strict with
their discipline, the impact on the students is profound and lifelong. It is safe to say that much of the credit for the current popularity and strength of the hula movement is due to the knowledge,
skills, and leadership of the kumu hula. As a group, they have
helped to shape the Hawaiian renaissance as much as, if not more

than, any other artistic or cultural group. Thus, in terms of Hawaiian cultural leadership, the kumu hula must be accorded a high place.

In fact, it is in the broad cultural area, including all the arts and crafts, sports, music, language, and so on, that the non-Big Five groups and their leaders have made their most important contributions. Our experience demonstrates that the health and strength of cultural traditions are in large part dependent on the organized leadership of such groups. This was certainly the case in the beginning of the Hawaiian cultural revival in the 1970s. Indeed, most of the direction, inspiration, and enthusiasm for the resurgence came from these organizations, not from the Big Five. Furthermore, the measure of their contribution goes beyond the purely artistic or cultural because the renaissance that they encouraged provided an important part of the impetus and sustaining momentum for the political activists that led to the favorable public response to the "Hawaiian package" presented at the constitutional convention in 1978. This should not be too surprising, since a strong cultural awareness is invariably a precursor of political action. Thus, while these organizations may not have Big Five-type resources—which they partially make up for in the energy and power of their volunteer helpers—they do form the basis for a significant part of the leadership structure.

Another distinctive category of organization-based leadership which deserves special attention must be the ministers, or kahu, of the Hawaiian churches. These include both those affiliated with major Christian denominations, such as the Congregationalists' Kawaiaha'o and Kaumakapili Churches in Honolulu and the Moku'aikaua Church in Kailua-Kona, and the so-called indigenous independent churches. These indigenous churches include Ka Makua Mau Loa Church, founded by Rev. John Wise, the last great Hawaiian minister-politician, who served in the early part of this century, as well as many other small churches on most of the islands. Neither the total number of Hawaiian churches nor their membership is known. This is especially a problem with the independents, since often they are founded by charismatic leaders and tend to decline or break up with the death of such a person or when a smooth succession fails to take place and splinter groups are formed. But the estimated number is "several dozen" churches, and three to four thousand members.

That the ministers of these churches provide important spiritual leadership to their flocks goes without saying, but whether any of that leadership, exclusive of its concerns with doctrine or theology, is transferable to the larger Hawaiian community is difficult to say. In the first half of this century, Hawaiian churches often served as centers where Hawaiians gathered and discussed issues affecting them as a people. But this is no longer the case today, although Kawaiahaʻo Church in Honolulu still performs an important role, as does, to a lesser extent, Haili Church in Hilo. Recently Kawaiahaʻo has served as the place for public discussions and demonstrations connected with the appointment of Bishop Estate trustees, reparations from the federal government, and other issues. Pastors at the church speak from a respected pulpit, because of its historical and cultural importance as Hawaiʻi's Westminster Abbey, and they can transfer part of that mana to Hawaiian causes beyond the scope of religion. But, by and large, the leaders of Hawaiian churches seldom speak out, or at least do not speak out loud enough to attract media attention on nonreligious matters affecting Hawaiians. This stands somewhat in contrast to Hawaiian ministers in non-Hawaiian churches, particularly the Catholic and the Episcopalian, who have been visibly active in communitywide areas.

Collectively, the heaviest influence of the Hawaiian churches may be in the preservation of Hawaiian traditions and especially the language. Until recently the Hawaiian churches conducted all or parts of their services and classes in the Hawaiian language, and some of the independents still continue to do so, in spite of pressure by the young to switch to English. In the indigenous churches which place a premium on the Hawaiian language, choice of a new minister often is based on a person's proficiency in the language, among other things. In addition to the language, the churches place significant emphasis on such values and practices as prayer, meditation, clearing-the-way, hoʻoponopono, purification rites, and healing through prayers and faith. Thus, in many ways they represent, like some of the hālau hula, modern strongholds of traditionalism.

Finally, although so far we have restricted our analysis to leadership found in Hawaiian organizations, we must not forget to recognize the many Hawaiians who hold positions of leadership in clubs, associations, or groups whose memberships are open to all

436 LEADERSHIP AND POLITICS

people, yet whose purposes and activities have a heavy Hawaiian imprint. These include the Polynesian Voyaging Society, which sponsored the Hōkūle'a's dramatic trips to Tahiti and back, the Hawaiian Music Foundation, which helped to spark the revival in the early 1970s, Hui 'Imi Na'auao o Hawai'i, an association of teachers of Hawaiian studies, Hui Wa'a, one of the islands' two largest canoe organizations, and others, including congregations of some of the major churches. These organizations have had considerable impact in their respective fields on the Hawaiian community as well as on the community at large, and much of that has been due to the quality of their leadership, both Hawaiian and non-Hawaiian. In most instances, these organizations were founded as the result of efforts by both Hawaiians and non-Hawaiians, because of the wide appeal of their subject matter. These Hawaiian-oriented, multiethnic organizations have the advantage of developing a broader membership and audience and, perhaps, readier access to more financial and volunteer resources. The open character of these groups, it is important to note, does not necessarily dilute the Hawaiianness of their enterprises; in fact, in many cases the non-Hawaiians tend to be as enthusiastic and supportive as the Hawaiians. Apart from their contributions in their particular fields, these organizations perform a valuable service in their ability to win over non-Hawaiians to Hawaiian causes and activities, in a sort of reverse cultural assimilation. Indeed, these organizations may well indicate the directions that other Hawaiian organizations and Hawaiian leadership will take in the future.

Nonorganization-Based Leadership

In this category we refer to leaders who may have relatively little or no connection with Hawaiian organizations, or who may have been actively involved at one time but have not been so for many years. Yet, even so, they are regarded as Hawaiian leaders by fellow Hawaiians or by the general community. Usually most of these persons have achieved success in their chosen fields of work and occupy positions of responsibility in their professional organizations. While some status transfer is likely, normally public recognition of their leadership is based on their notable contributions to Hawaiian-related causes and not simply because of their special skills or attainments. In other words, while Hawaiians may feel great pride in the successes achieved by another Hawaiian as a football star or a corporation executive or a general, and will be glad to accept him as a Hawaiian, that does not necessarily mean accepting him as a Hawaiian *leader*. This, too, is an accolade that has to be earned.

These leaders include physicians, lawyers, educators, engineers, and other professionals, business owners or executives, bureaucrats, labor chiefs, athletes and other sports-related figures, entertainers, artists, designers, politicians, and many others. Greater concentrations of leaders can be found in certain fields, namely, in business, entertainment, sports, education, government administration, politics, and some of the professions, especially law. In business, several entrepreneurs and executives fall in this category, including a bank president, high-level executives in the hotel and tourism-related industry, an owner of a well-known restaurant, the president of an energy distribution company, an owner of a large security firm, a trustee of a large estate, and others. In each instance, these individuals are well known in the community not as Hawaiians but as successful businessmen first. They are also known for their contributions to the Hawaiian community, although these are rarely publicized, usually being heard of only in conversations. Although most don't wear Hawaiianness on their shirt-sleeves, all are genuinely proud of their Hawaiian heritage. Their lack of involvement in Hawaiian organizations is caused more by busy schedules and, to a certain extent, by impatience with the need to attend meetings, serve on committees, and so on. Then, too, some try to avoid being conspicuous, or being embarrassing to others, or vice versa. They prefer to be involved in events or decisions upon which they can make the greatest impact, but in the most efficient—and quiet—manner.

A significant number of Hawaiian leaders have come from among the ranks of musicians, recording artists, impressarios, and athletes, who have earned fame but, usually, little fortune, and have succeeded in transferring their mana to leadership roles. Understandably, most entertainers do not take an active part in Hawaiian organizations, either as members or officers, mainly because their schedules are reversed, working as they do at night and sleeping during the day. Their participation frequently involves donating time and talents to fund-raising events, rallies, and other functions. To them the attribution of leadership status does not come quickly, but is conferred only after many years of working in the limelight and constant interaction with audiences and the community. In a few instances, leadership is thrust upon a star with high visibility who sometimes is manipulated by people with less than altruistic motives. But as long as successful entertainers enjoy high status among Hawaiians, leadership opportunities will be open to them in the Hawaiian community.

Many Hawaiians put a high premium on education, partly because they realize that it offers a means to gaining a better and richer life, and partly because of their traditional values. This premium is shown in the respect generally shown to educators or teachers, which in part is a carryover from the days when Hawaiian teachers who understood ka palapala, the reading and the writing of the haole, acted as interpreters and negotiators between Hawaiians and foreigners. Not surprisingly, many Hawaiian leaders have come from the ranks of schoolteachers and administrators. While some are active in Hawaiian organizations, many others choose not to be involved, for professional or other reasons. In recent years, as more Hawaiians have earned doctorates and gained academic rank on university and college faculties, a few leaders have come from these institutions. One of these has become an authority because of her scholarship in Hawaiian literature, and another has gained recognition because of her research in the natural sciences at a famous university in California. Interestingly, most of today's visible and audible university-based Hawaiian leaders are women. All in all, however, the number of Hawaiians serving on university faculties throughout the nation is very small, probably no more than three dozen.

We should note that, apart from university scholars, few leaders, whether active or inactive in Hawaiian organizations, have come from Hawaiian intellectual circles. By "intellectual" we refer to writers, poets, playwrights, philosophers, theologians, and the like—the "mind workers" who spend considerable time at their intellectual pursuits. The number of intellectuals is too small, to begin with. Despite the important parts that intellectuals played in the Hawai'i of old, modern Hawaiians have not yet accorded the same priority to "mind work," preferring instead managerial, technological, professional, and other occupational positions. The situation of Hawaiian intellectuals stands in stark contrast to that attained by other Polynesians. In New Zealand, for example, they are well organized and recognized both among Maoris and throughout their country. Whether the differences in attitudes and levels of achievement are due to different values taught by British and American educational systems raises an interesting question. Nonetheless, we can hope that, in time, more young Hawaiians will be expressing intellectual interests in the tradition of their forefathers.

The bureaucracies of the monarchy, territory, state, and counties, too, have been sources of Hawaiian leaders. They are reminders of the managerial class, the konohiki. In the first half of this century, Hawaiians such as John H. Wilson, chief county engineer before he became mayor of Honolulu, and Henry Hanapī, treasurer of the territory, held important positions in the government. Hawaiians continue to hold important offices: in 1983 the chief judge of the United States District Court, the chief justice of the state supreme court, the associate judge of the intermediate appellate court, the senior criminal judge of the first circuit court, and other judges; the deputy directors of the Department of Personnel Services, Department of Social Services and Housing, and Department of Hawaiian Home Lands, as well as the latter department's chairperson; the chief engineer and the chief of police of the city and county of Honolulu—all were Hawaiians. But as competition for a finite number of positions increases, comparatively fewer Hawaiians are holding high posts in federal, state, and county administrations today than before.

As a general rule, top administrators are not very visible in Hawaiian organizations or public activities, particularly in controversial ones, partly because of the usual limits upon their time, but also because of potential conflicts of interest. Public officials are expected to show impartiality to all groups of people, in order to avoid suspicion of favoritism. As one Hawaiian official said, "It's a fine balancing act we must perform. I try to be sensitive to the needs of Hawaiians, but I'm also responsible for Filipinos, Chinese, haoles and everybody else." While a Hawaiian with a problem may expect favorable treatment from a fellow Hawaiian, an overconscientious Hawaiian bureaucrat may be even stricter with Hawaiians than with people from other ethnic backgrounds, so as not to appear to be pro-Hawaiian and risk his credibility and effectiveness. Thus, if at times Hawaiian bureaucrats fail to give expression to Hawaiian viewpoints, that may be a proper consequence of their positions, and not necessarily an indication of their personal beliefs. On the other hand, such notions of impartiality do not apply to people working in the Department of Hawaiian Home Lands and the Office of Hawaiian Affairs, because their fiduciary responsibilities to the Hawaiian people may conflict with the interests of the state. This complication is illustrated today in legal suits that both agencies have instituted against different departments of the state, in order to recover lands or rental income that is due. On such occasions, these Hawaiian bureaucrats come close to merging their roles as potential and actual Hawaiian leaders.

Political Leadership

Island politics has always attracted a fair number of Hawaiians; indeed, for much of this century Hawaiian politicians held every top political office. Among them were Jonah Kūhiō Kalaniana'ole as delegate to Congress (1902–1921); Samuel W. King as governor of the territory; John C. Lane, Joseph J. Fern, Charles Arnold, John Wilson, and Neal Blaisdell as mayors of Honolulu; three lieutenant governors—James Kealoha, William J. Richardson, and John Waihe'e—out of the six elected since statehood in 1959; and currently, Henry H. Peters and Richard W. Wong as speaker of the house and president of the senate, respectively. Recently a Hawaiian legislator said, "It doesn't hurt to be a Hawaiian today." But the truth is that, politically, it has never really hurt to be a Hawaiian at any time. To be sure, politics is much more competitive today, but competition affects aspirants from all other ethnic groups too. In 1984 seventeen Hawaiians held important elective positions—one member of the House of Representatives of the U.S. Congress, the lieutenant governorship of the state, six state senators, and nine state representatives. When measured against the Hawaiian proportion of the state population, these seventeen elected posts, which do not include city and county positions, is a creditable showing. And if we were to include the total number of Hawaiians who once held elective office and have retired or who are still waiting in the "clumps of grass" to get back in again, the total is perhaps three or more times larger. The point is that, in spite of everything else that has happened to them, Hawaiians have held key political positions for most of this century.

As we look at the people active in Hawaiian politics today, we might identify the different types of leaders by comparing them to constellations of stars: some are distinct to the unaided eye, some are better seen with a telescope, and others are so far away as to be barely visible even with telescopes. The first group of stars are the officeholders who now fill elective positions at the state and national levels and whose movements are readily followed. If we focus on the fifteen members in the state legislature as a group, the composite profile of a Hawaiian legislator would be: age between thirty and forty years; educated, with at least one college degree; married, with a family; occupationally either in business or in other private sector fields; income from lower to upper middle level; Oʻahu based; member of the Democratic party (in contrast to the pre-1954 Republican years); and a newcomer to the legislature. Four are women. None of the group is either rich or famous, that is, acclaimed for professional achievements either on a statewide or national basis. The majority are less then 50 percent Hawaiian by descent, and have names that do not "sound Hawaiian."

The important yet sensitive feature about them is what we might call the individual's "sense of cultural awareness" as a Hawaiian. Each leader seems open about being Hawaiian, particularly if he does not "look Hawaiian." Individually they are proud of their Hawaiian ancestry and are aware of their cultural heritage. Whether one is more sensitive than another, short of subjecting each to a psychocultural test, is a judgment best left to each constituent. Some people have charged one or another legislator with being insensitive to Hawaiian matters because of a failure to support this or that Hawaiian measure, but a legislator's decision to support or not support a bill or action may have nothing to do with his personal feelings about being Hawaiian. To make judgments of this kind with any confidence would require, among other things, a prolonged examination of the voting record of each legislator on all Hawaiian-related issues, as well as his or her priorities for non-Hawaiian matters. What is important for us to understand is the politician's usual position on such questions. One Hawaiian legislator has said, "I am a politician who happens to be a Hawaiian," suggesting that he is prepared to compromise his personal and ethnic preferences for his greater sense of obligation to all of his constituents, irrespective of race. But the same legislator was quick to point out that he and others believe that "helping the Hawaiians is good for the whole state" (a slight twist of Charles Wilson's memorable reply to President Truman that "What is good for General Motors is good for the United States"). This approach works well as long as an atmosphere of support for Hawaiian matters is in effect, as has been evident in recent years. Serious problems will come when that support is eroded, or when a "backlash against Hawaiianism" sets in, as some people fear it will.

The second group of Hawaiian leaders are the so-called activists, who range from "militants" to "nonmilitants." The former are mostly young men and women, many university students, bright and articulate, who protest and demonstrate against "establishmentarian" policies and injustices in the system by resorting to dramatic rhetoric and tactics appealing as much to their constituents as to the media. The celebrated episodes in the short history of the militants begin in 1971, when the Bishop Estate attempted to remove tenant farmers from the Kalama Valley land that it owned and wanted to develop for housing. A group of Hawaiians and non-Hawaiians rallied to the support of the farmers and staged a series of demonstrations aimed at physically stopping the removal of the tenants. Calling themselves "Kōkua Kalama," the group capitalized on the incident to publicize their aims, one of which was to change Hawai'i's "power structure," too long dominated by "big landholders." The protesters punctuated their show of opposition with shouts of "Imua!" ("Forward!") and "Huli!" ("Overturn!") and other sorts of revolutionary slogans. Compared with acts of militancy committed by American Indians and blacks on the mainland, this was mild, but it shocked many people in the community, including Hawaiians. In a few days the police removed the last pig farmer from the land, and the activists moved on—and out. In the words of a former participant, "We at least shook 'em up and made 'em think—and made ourselves heard." That seemed to be the big point: a chance to be heard.

Still another manifestation of activism emerged at about the same period, although somewhat less virulent and dramatic, focused upon the discontent of Hawaiian homesteaders in Waimānalo. The group, led by a relatively young part-Hawaiian man, complained that the Department of Hawaiian Home Lands had failed to make enough land available for qualified Hawaiians, pointing out that some had been waiting as long as fifteen years for home sites. They also objected that throughout the state much land was leased to non-Hawaiians and businesses, and for very low rentals. In time, these narrow grievances were widened to include goals to gain "justice" for the Hawaiians, to improve their social and economic position, and to restore racial pride. According to its leader, "We don't want to go back to being the 'sleepy Hawaiians.' " By 1972 "The Hawaiians," as they called themselves, claimed more than seven thousand "members" and was the largest "politicized" group of its kind. But by 1975 it, too, had receded into the background.

Although activists have generally involved younger people in their twenties and thirties, activism does not exclude older folk. For example, one of the more vocal, though less militant, groups in the early 1970s was led by a few older and outspoken Hawaiian "nationalists," whose intention was to unify all the proliferating Hawaiian organizations under one umbrella, called the Congress of the Hawaiian People. Although its leaders, most in their forties, did not confront policemen or shout revolutionary slogans, they were ardent proponents of Hawaiian causes, ranging from reparations for the federal government's appropriation of lands in 1900 to preserving the will of Bernice Pauahi Bishop and her legacy, the Kamehameha Schools.

Yet another variant of Hawaiian activism is the Protect Kaho'olawe 'Ohana, whose core leadership has included men and women with a wide range of ages, occupational and educational backgrounds, and political leanings. In terms of aggressiveness, the 'Ohana has been the most militant as is indicated by its frequent challenges of the U.S. Navy, the federal government, and state and county authorities. It is also notable for its longevity, which contradicts the usual pattern of activist groups who come and go as the enthusiasm and the financial support of their leaders wax and wane.

When one reviews the short history of contemporary Hawaiian activism, about fifteen or so years, the fact is clear that, while its tactics tend to be forceful and threatening and its leaders rather young and angry, other older Hawaiians, too, consider themselves to be activists but prefer less demonstrative methods of seeking redress for past and present wrongs. The pity is that "activist," a good word in its place, has been appropriated by a special group of protesters, not entirely of their own will. They have been greatly helped by media hype, thus creating the false impression that anyone not labeled or wanting to be labeled an "activist" is not really involved in supporting and promoting Hawaiian interests and activities. In the true sense of the word, most Hawaiians and many non-Hawaiians are in fact activists for Hawaiian causes.

Many Hawaiians, particularly among those of older generations, have expressed dismay and disgust about the acts of militancy, the shrill challenging of authority figures and official institutions, the noisy disregard for "good manners," the outbursts of resentment and "unseemly" language. Invariably, these nonmilitants say, "That is not the Hawaiian way," meaning that somehow more deference should be paid to authorities, or that the anger and hate should be tempered by aloha, or that the screaming, gesturing, and vulgar swearing should be eliminated. But what these critics seem to overlook is the important truth that "the old Hawaiian way" also made provisions for challenging authorities and protesting injustices in the system. The chronicles of Hawaiian political history, as told by Kamakau and Malo, are full of rebellions and acts of protest by maka'āinana against their ali'i, not to mention by ali'i against other ali'i. Tyranny and oppression did not go unanswered. The circumstances affecting activists of today and rebels of old Hawai'i are by no means the same, but the fact remains that protest in any of the forms it has taken is not un-Hawaiian. Nor is it unnatural, to human beings everywhere. We add that not all of the older generation are troubled by the militants, because some elders are quite supportive. As one kupuna has said, "These young ones put us to shame, because we didn't do right by them."

Our little political world presents another constellation of Hawaiian leaders who are barely visible. They are the kupuna, the teachers and counselors to officeholders, or others aspiring to office, and to activists. In some ways they can be thought of as "elder statesmen," as genro in the Japanese tradition, because their advice and help may be sought by any person or organization. They are a diverse group: some are wealthy and noted, some are neither; others are wise in the ways of the world; and still others are especially knowledgeable in Hawaiian language, religion, and other facets of our culture. What they have in common is a high charge of mana—or at least they are so perceived by the people who seek their help. Each of these kupuna counselors seems to have his or her own constituency, since individuals are more likely to consult those who either sympathize with their goals or support their plans.

An exceptional few are sought by all kinds of individuals or organizations from the most militant to the most conservative. These counselors are not a cohesive group in any sense of the word. They do not meet in secret, or pull the strings of puppets; indeed, probably they are not very conscious of this special role that we have given them. Nonetheless, they represent an important force in the background of Hawaiian politics at the present time.

Neotraditional Ali'i Leaders

A tidal wave of democratic reform and egalitarian attitudes has long since swept away the foundations of ali'i rule, but we still keep the royal symbols, institutions, legends, teachings, and values that we honor in monuments, festivals, official holidays, restored palaces, portraits, books, and in many other nostalgic ways. So strong a component of our cultural and historical consciousness naturally becomes integrated into our awareness of being Hawaiians. Whether we like this or not, the ali'i are always with us. Their descendents, too, are with us, although many Hawaiians today are not aware that they even exist. In either case, we should take a careful look at the ali'i today, for they represent a significant force in contemporary Hawaiian leadership, and one that can be even more important in the future.

"Hawaiians are like the Irish," one wit has said, "they are all descendants of kings." Perhaps a grain of truth lies in this bit of hyperbole. But our special interest here is with those few genuine ali'i families who have valid connections with past dynasties. The best known of these ali'i are the Kawānanakoas, descendents of Kinoiki Kekaulike, a sister of Queen Kapiolani, who represent the last ruling family. Members of other families, however, although less well known, maintain that they have even stronger claims to the throne. Arguments of this kind seldom take place in public, and if they do, as happened a few years ago when the issue of reparations and the Crown Lands came up, the effects seem to be more embarrassing than unifying. (Parenthetically, the claims and counterclaims were chronicled in articles written by Samuel Crowning-burg-Amalu, which were published in the *Honolulu Advertiser*, who himself claims descent from a royal line.) In any event, these descendents of the ali'i must be reckoned with in the hierarchy of Hawaiian leadership.

Who are they? Some are very well off, especially those who have inherited wealth from ancestral lands, such as those owned by the Campbell Estate. Others are not rich but are actually poor, and sometimes bitter, because of the loss of their ancestors' lands at the hands of others, including other ali'i. Some have increased their inherited fortunes by prudent management and careful spending, while others have not done nearly as well. Several have achieved recognition for their personal accomplishments, entirely on their merits, and others have no accomplishments at all to show. Almost all of them work for a living, in occupations ranging from real estate and stocks to publishing, retailing, teaching, and secretarial work. A few are well educated, having graduated from some of the best universities, while others have not finished high school. In short, they represent a cross section of the community and are like many other Hawaiians—except in the one respect of their ali'i blood.

We can expect, then, that the nature of their involvement in the Hawaiian community varies according to their social standing, resources, attitudes, education, and so on. Admittedly, it is impossible to be precise about this because much that they do, either as members of a group or as individuals, is simply not known. However, we do know that the Kawānanakoas have taken an active part in the restoration of 'Iolani Palace and in assisting many other Hawaiian organizations and projects. Other families have chosen to assist in the management and maintenance of the Lunalilo Home and in providing scholarship funds for Hawaiian students. Several individuals have taken active parts in Hawaiian organizations, such as the Hawaiian Civic Clubs, the Hawaiian Music Foundation, the Kawaiaha'o Church, and the Office of Hawaiian Affairs, contributing generously to them in time and money. Still others participate through involvement in organizations such as the Sons and Daughters of Hawaiian Warriors (whose one hundred members must be able to demonstrate ties to ali'i or high priests at the time of Kamehameha I or even before him). This group has undertaken the restoration of the Royal Mausoleum at Mauna 'Ala, and throughout its existence of more than half a century has tried to keep alive the symbols and the honor of the aristocracy of old.

Many Hawaiians feel, however, that some of the ali'i have not done enough, given their status, wealth, education, and abilities. The descendents of one family in particular have been singled out for having played a passive role at most, content to remain relatively hidden and quiet, living at the periphery rather than at the center of the action. They are said to be wary, afraid of being used or abused, and therefore spend many months of the year away from Hawai'i, beyond the reach of such complications. As one ali'i descendent has said, "They have everything, plus the ability to lead, but they have not done too much about it." Yet, we are told, all descendents of this family are proud of their heritage and respond to the deference shown them. Furthermore, some observers believe that nowadays they are playing much more active a role in Hawaiian matters than at any other time in the past.

But how much more of a role do these several ali'i families want to play in the Hawaiian leadership? Part of the answer to this important question must come from the Hawaiian people at large. Their reaction is mixed, at best. One of the stark realities is that many Hawaiians, especially those who are near the bottom of the heap, blame the ali'i for the present plight of Hawaiians. All too often we hear some young Hawaiians, frustrated and angry, bitterly denouncing the old chiefs "for selling us down the river for booze and greed." Their understanding of our history may be utterly lacking or thoroughly prejudiced, but that summation tells us how they see their history. Although almost a century separates today's descendents of ali'i from the last days of the monarchy, they are still held to be guilty by association, and are looked upon with suspicion and dislike. As one shrewd observer of Hawaiian "radicalism" put it, "Politically sensitive young Hawaiians just have no respect for them." Much of this anger of young Hawaiians is aimed at the most wealthy and best known among the ali'i families, whom one activist described as representing the "height of decadence."

Few Hawaiians would readily disagree with the idea that the ali'i of the past must bear some, if not most, of the responsibility for "botching the job," as one descendent put it. Most Hawaiians today do accept this opinion rather dispassionately, as a matter of history. Thus, the bitterness that some young Hawaiians today feel toward aliʻi families betrays their own frustrations with their unhappy social or economic lot. They have found scapegoats in today's aliʻi—and, perhaps, excuses for their own failures.

However, other Hawaiians, both young and old, do not share this view, nor are they bitter toward today's descendents of aliʻi. As a matter of fact, most young Hawaiians are simply unaware, or only vaguely conscious, of those descendents. While philosophically they may reject a society based on the rule of aristocrats, they tend to keep an open mind on the subject of the surviving descendents of aliʻi. "They should not be held guilty for the sins of their parents" is a judgment that many would consider to be fair. In general, their sentiments range from an uninformed indifference to a nostalgic romanticism, such as, "It's neat to have royalty as a kind of figurehead," and "They are important symbols of the past and persons who can be looked up to."

A large number of Hawaiians throughout the years have been beneficiaries of the largess of the aliʻi. Among them are alumni of the Kamehameha Schools; orphans, children, and families aided by the Queen Liliʻuokalani Trust/Children's Center; patients in the Queen's Medical Center; kūpuna residents of the Lunalilo Home; and participants in other programs and institutions financed in whole or in part by estates and funds left by aliʻi. We can hope that these beneficiaries will feel some aloha toward the aliʻi for their foresight and generosity.

At the other extreme are those few Hawaiians who prefer to believe in the best of all possible interpretations, namely, that their aliʻi did no real wrong, and hence, that their descendents deserve the respect and honor due to all princes and princesses and relatives of nobles in the past. Typical of those who think in this way are people connected with former retainers, ladies-in-waiting, and court chamberlains of the monarchs.

In sum, we can conclude, with reason, that most Hawaiian opinions about today's descendents of aliʻi fall between the harsh bitterness of those who are strongly anti-chief and the naive devotion of pro-monarchists.

Clearly, whatever Hawaiians today may feel or not feel about the aliʻi, the chiefs' descendents have played and will continue to play important roles in leading the Hawaiian community. The only issue seems to be whether they should be even more active in the future, and, if so, what form that involvement should take.

The latter point raises a subject that more often than not calls forth disbelief rather than seriousness among Hawaiians—and that is the restoration of the monarchy. A few pro-monarchists, according to reports, discuss this possibility more nostalgically than realistically. And when they do talk about it, they are never clear about what they want to have restored. Actually, nearly the only people who seriously talk about it openly are non-Hawaiians —both Americans, who are infatuated with the romance of royalty, and Europeans, who appreciate the importance of monarchs as symbols. In 1973, for example, Leonard Lueras assembled in *Manna-Mana* a collection of thoughts and pictures about Hawai'i, prepared by a number of writers and artists. Among them was Lueras' own article about the Kawānanakoas, in which he recommended, on his own initiative, no doubt, that the state and the nation should "initiate a national and international program to recognize the Hawaiian royal family. Whoever the symbolic King, Queen and/or Princes and Princesses of Hawai'i may be, they deserve to be known and officially recognized, if only to provide the nearly extinct Hawaiian people with a living sense of tradition and, more importantly, an identity." Ten years have passed and not an official reaction has been heard from either the state of Hawai'i or the government of the United States. About the only public reference that has ever been made to the possibility is a bumper sticker proclaiming the message, "Restore the Monarchy," which appeared on the rear ends of some island automobiles a few years ago.

Aside from the fantasy and romanticism involved in restoring the monarchy, other factors which must be considered are far more realistic and practical. The first is to bridge the rift between those people who harbor suspicion and bitterness toward the ali'i and their descendents. This trouble has continued for so many years that no one has been helped by it, and an already divided community has been fragmented even more. If goodwill, good sense, and good history are asked to help, this problem should be resolved quickly. Second, to refute complaints that certain ali'i are not doing their share, the parties concerned should take the initiative in coming together, at least to talk. Such discussions, if they did nothing else, would at the minimum clarify the assumptions and expectations of those most troubled by the complaints. And third, probably the most important way in which ali'i descendents could make the greatest impact is to instill confidence in their attributes by conducting themselves as models of those qualities and values of leaders that represent the best in the long line of Hawai'i's great guides, from the "perfect chief" Kaha'i, to 'Umi, to Kamehameha I.

As moderate as these suggestions are, they are the kind of steps that all great journeys must begin with. Our great journey will lead not to a futile attempt to revive an unworkable fantasy, but rather to the restoration of ideals of leadership that will guide Hawaiians to a realization of their potential as a unified people.

The Restoration of Lōkahi

Hawaiians are said to be afflicted with a psychological disorder known as the " 'Alamihi Syndrome." An 'alamihi is a common black crab that lives among the rocks along Hawaiian shores. Crab catchers trap them in nets, and then dump them into buckets until the time comes to take them home for cooking. Critics of uncooperative Hawaiians love to compare them with the 'alamihi, which always manage to pull down the ones who are trying to climb up and over the sides of a bucket. This analogy has been repeated so often that now it is a part of the standard lore about Hawaiians' behavior to other Hawaiians. By now even Hawaiians themselves believe it. Incidentally, the same analogy is used against the Maoris in New Zealand, against coastal Indians in Canada and the United States, Chamorros in Guam, and the natives of many another place. Invariably it is directed against the "natives" and rarely against the critical newcomers to any place. In any case, this crab mentality is said to be the cause of disunity among the "natives"; indeed, cause and effect are so blurred in the minds of the belittlers that they become one and the same thing.

We should know better. The crabs are innocent of such malice. The causes for division and competition among Hawaiian people grow out of far more complex phenomena of differences in heredity, family background, upbringing, educational opportunities, career patterns, income, social interaction, religion, and numerous other socioeconomic and political factors that affect all individuals and all groups. Decades of intermarriage and intercultural contact have diluted not only our blood but also most of the characteristics that once distinguished Hawaiians as a homogeneous people. In the process of westernization or assimilation to "the American Way," homogeneity has yielded to heterogeneity. Nowadays, Hawaiians eat sushi, pasta, chop suey, and apple pie; they live in penthouses in Waikīkī, shacks on a beach, tract homes in Kailua, and half-a-million-dollar palaces on Wai'alae Iki; they go to Punahou, Kamehameha, Kahuku High or Hilo High, and then on to Harvard, Cornell, Willamette, the University of Hawai'i, or Honolulu Community College; they work for the city and county refuse division, or for IBM, or operate their own businesses; they eke out a poverty-level subsistence, or earn an annual income of $200,000 in corporate salaries and bonuses; most belong to the Republican or Democratic parties, and a few to the Libertarian party, or to leftist or revolutionary groups; they are Catholics, Congregationalists, Pentacostals, Mormons, Buddhists, agnostics, or atheists; and so on. Hawaiians, like any other minority group, simply reflect the composition of our pluralist democracy with its diverse interests, divided loyalties, and shifting concerns. In this sense, we have many Hawaiian communities that come together at some points but separate at others. This is the true dynamics of any American community.

Hawaiian leadership, with its array of different organizations and leaders, represents the realities of today's society and not some biological defect supposedly inherent in the race that is explained away by a spurious analogy with crabs. To be sure, we can find instances where individuals vying with each other will try to pull each other down, or where a group will keep a member from doing or saying certain things in order to protect its internal stability, or, as we say, to keep from "rocking the boat." But on the other side, probably we can find many more instances where individuals or groups will kōkua, help, share, sacrifice, defend, or do whatever is necessary to advance the cause of other persons or groups. If we have to use an animal analogy to describe Hawaiian behavior, the mutually supportive naonao, or ants, are rather more appropriate than the mindless 'alamihi.

The diversity of the assorted Hawaiian "communities" does pose a major challenge to Hawaiian leadership—which is, how best to integrate their many separate interests, so that they can cooperate on important Hawaiian interests and act with maxi-

mum efficiency and impact. It is not difficult to imagine the effect
this cooperation would have on the whole community if all
Hawaiian organizations and their leaders jointly supported an
issue, program, or candidate. Even if only the Big Five organizations were to be completely united in working on one project, that
would have a significant effect, not so much on the community at
large, perhaps, but certainly on Hawaiians themselves.

This is not to say that Hawaiian organizations or leaders do not
work together now or have not cooperated on joint projects in the
past. Many groups come together in fund-raising activities, hula
competitions, Kamehameha Day celebrations, Aloha Week festivities, state or congressional hearings dealing with vital Hawaiian
issues, and sporting events. They join efforts in times of crisis, as
when a major threat is presented to continuance of the Kamehameha Schools/Bishop Estate. The Office of Hawaiian Affairs has
organized events needing the cooperation of different groups and
their officers. Alu Like has sponsored many programs in which a
number of Hawaiians have participated. Indeed, when one looks
closely at the history of Hawaiian organizations and their leadership, the record shows a great deal of mutual support.

Nonetheless, our study of contemporary Hawaiian leadership
clearly reveals that, at the present time, no effective structural
mechanism brings together on a regular basis Hawaiian leaders
representing all the important interests of the Hawaiian community in order to make decisions about matters of common concern.
OHA has sought to perform this important function and, indeed,
regards itself as "the major coordinating agency working for the
betterment of the Hawaiian people." But, by its very nature, OHA
is limited in what it can do. For one thing, it is a public agency
responsible to the state legislature for its funding, subject to supervision by the governor and the courts, and ultimately by the voters
of the entire state, at least during every tenth year, when the state's
constitution is reviewed and amended in convention. OHA cannot
be a completely independent entity serving only the interests of the
Hawaiian people and accountable to no one else. Another limitation, at least for now, is its highly political character, which is
partly reflected in the factionalism among its trustees since the
beginning, and the consequent confusion in its policies and management. All this has somewhat handicapped OHA's efforts to
reach or speak for important sectors of Hawaiian leadership and

the community. In several instances, in fact, it has alienated itself from important leaders. Consequently, it lacks the credibility and the impartiality necessary to rally all members of the Hawaiian leadership.

What is required is an entirely Hawaiian initiative, independent of any public or governmental agency, leading to the formation of a council of leaders that reflects the existing leadership structure. Such a hui would necessarily include leaders from the Big Five and other organizations, the aliʻi families, and business, bureaucratic, artistic, intellectual, and political groups. Anything short of bringing together men and women of the highest achievements, talents, and influence would not be worth the effort. Therefore, the catalytic organizing and sponsoring group must command the greatest respect and credibility. The members of this group should be what we have called the "kupuna teachers" or the "elder statesmen," who already enjoy the greatest confidence and trust among the Hawaiian people. Let them meet and deliberate on the merits of the idea and, if they approve, let them direct the starting of the hui's developmental phase. Conceivably, that could take several forms, ranging from a large congress to a smaller executive council, meeting in full assembly once every two or three years, while smaller committees meet more often, and so on. But, whatever its structure might be, it should be flexible and durable enough to accomplish its purpose of bringing together regularly the appropriate Hawaiian leaders, in order to deliberate on issues of importance to the Hawaiian community.

The idea of a council or assembly of leaders is not an original idea, even if it is untried for this generation of Hawaiians. Recently the Maoris have developed an impressive leadership strategy with marked success. Leaders representing important sectors of the Maori people, including the highest tribal chiefs as well as academics, business executives, intellectuals, and other modern professions, have met together regularly. In the early 1980s, they met annually in a Whakatauira, or leadership assembly, for several days of discussions following a predetermined agenda. The object of the discussions was to draw up a set of recommendations for actions to be considered and taken by Maori organizations. In such assemblies, the organizing personnel and much of the funding came from the government's Department of Maori Affairs although, as a matter of policy, it tried to place full emphasis on discussions. This is one model that Hawaiians might consider following. In 1981 a group of Maori leaders, led by former secretary of Maori Affairs Kara Puketapu, came to Hawai'i and, under OHA's auspices, conducted a two-day conference of Hawaiian leaders, based in part on the Maori model. Although some of the people attending hoped that the conference would be followed by an annual meeting of Hawaiian leaders, that has not happened.

Recently a prominent haole politician in Honolulu declared that he wished he were a Hawaiian because if ever an opportunity existed for a leader in these islands, it lay in the Hawaiian community. What he envisioned, clearly, was a handsome brown knight in shining armor, riding on a prancing white charger coming to take command. That is not exactly what we need, although no one should ignore such a hero if and when he does show up. Our proposal for developing a new strategy for Hawaiian leadership, based on the realities of Hawaiian society today, is aimed at strengthening the existing leadership structure by uniting its disjoined parts into a force capable of dealing effectively with the important problems that Hawaiians face, and of leading them to higher levels of social and economic achievement. Ultimately, it can be a means of restoring an even greater sense of lōkahi, or unity and harmony, to a people revitalized by a renewed awareness of their identity.

A Partial Agenda for the Year 2005 and Beyond

In 1982, a highly respected non-Hawaiian political and business leader said that "the 1980s is the Hawaiian decade." By this he meant that this is a decade of Hawaiian problems, some new, some old, but all important: claims against the federal government for reparations, the prospects for which are now as dim as ever; the constitutional status of OHA, although some believe this is a smokescreen to curb its activities; settling questions about who is a Hawaiian; raising the low educational performances of Hawaiian students; reducing the high incidence of cancer, hypertension, diabetes, and other diseases that afflict Hawaiians; increasing the life span of Hawaiians, now one of the lowest among all the ethnic groups in Hawai'i; and so on. To be sure, some of these problems are not unique to Hawaiians, nor do they involve only Hawaiians in their resolution. Nonetheless, Hawaiians are the people who are most affected. Of one thing we can be certain: we have a great number of problems.

Nor do we have a lack of opportunities. Every problem presents us with opportunities, for in seeking the resolution to problems we shall find new incentives, fresh perspectives, deeper understanding, and greater strength, not to mention new problems that invariably arise from new solutions. If we measure opportunities by the magnitude of our problems, then we can say that as Hawaiians we are presented with some of the greatest opportunities offered to the people of this state. This bit of obvious wisdom may bring little comfort to those who are beset by misfortune or disease or poverty, but it is intended to put a positive emphasis on the approach we must take in dealing with our problems. Thus, the 1980s is indeed a decade of both problems *and* opportunities for the Hawaiian people.

It is also a decade for leadership. Difficult times, such as these are, bring enormous challenges that should test all the qualities of Hawaiian leadership: mālama, or caring; haʻahaʻa, or humility; kūpono, or integrity; naʻauao, or wisdom and intelligence; koa, or courage; lokomaikaʻi, or generosity; hoʻokipa, or hospitality; ʻoluʻolu, or courtesy; hoʻomana, or spirituality; and—aloha. These challenging times will also severely test a leader's sense of purpose and vision. Indeed, one of the prime responsibilities of Hawaiian leadership today is to help express not just the problems we must resolve, but the corresponding goals that we must attain. He must lay out the journey we are to make, as well as the stops along the way that we must all take if we want to achieve our fullest potential as a people.

To help us on that journey, we offer here an agenda of goals to be sought during the next twenty years. The list is neither complete nor final—goals never are. All address old, persistent problems about which too many people have said too much already. Witness the mountains of reports, studies, "need assessment surveys," government proceedings, and so on, with no end in sight.

If our goals are stated boldly, without much philosophical elaboration, we do this partly because the problems are so well known, and because we have chosen to make quantifiable statements rather than broad declarations of purpose. Unfortunately we have no seer like Keaulumoku to chant the mele telling us what to do for the next twenty years.

GOAL 1: *Raise the educational achievement level of Hawaiian students, so as to attain parity with the highest ethnic group in the state.* Hawaiian students, who represent 21 percent of the two hundred thousand elementary and secondary students statewide, are ranked lowest in educational achievement (as measured by standard tests) among the five major ethnic groups (the others are haole, Chinese, Japanese, and Filipino). The Kamehameha Schools are addressing this problem, having included in their ten-year plan the goal "to produce educational services to Hawaiian youngsters statewide in order to produce achievement curves on a par with the national norm." But the national norm is still below that of the highest local group in Hawai'i.

GOAL 2: *Increase the number of Hawaiian students enrolled at the University of Hawai'i-Mānoa campus in proportion to representation of the Hawaiian population in the state.* Hawaiians are underrepresented in the state universities/colleges system, but the number of students is lowest at the University of Hawai'i-Mānoa campus. In 1979 only 1.9 percent of the students enrolled were Hawaiian.

GOAL 3: *Triple the percentage of Hawaiians earning bachelor's degrees.* An estimated 3.5 percent of Hawaiian adults have earned baccalaureate degrees, as compared with the total of 9.9 percent in the whole population. Tripling the percentage would bring Hawaiians slightly above the current state average.

GOAL 4: *Achieve parity with the state average in high-status occupations, in other words, technical, managerial, and professional positions.* In 1980, 31.5 percent of all employed males and 25.7 percent of employed females in the state were classified as holding high-status occupations. Hawaiians ranked 24.5 percent and 18.3 percent, respectively, the lowest ranking among the major ethnic groups except for the Filipino. A more ambitious goal for Hawaiians would be to achieve parity with the highest local group, namely, the Chinese, 51 percent of whom are managers, technicians, or professionals.

GOAL 5: *Increase numbers of Hawaiians in selected professions by significant numbers, according to market demands or educational and technological needs.* According to our best estimates, Hawaiians are sadly underrepresented in all professions: .008 percent of the registered physicians in the state, .005 percent of the architects, 2 percent of the attorneys, and so on. Since technology and market demands for expertise are always changing, we should be flexible about the exact numbers in the several professions that might serve as goals for the Hawaiian community. Nonetheless, given the low baseline of Hawaiians in the professions, almost any factor between 2 and 10 would seem to be a reasonable goal, depending on the profession. Some specific targets might be: 70 more physicians, compared with approximately 35 at present; 28 dentists, as opposed to 14 now; or 20 more professors on the University of Hawai'i-Mānoa campus, where now only 10 are present, and so on. In certain professional or academic fields few, if any, Hawaiians are appointed to positions at the higher levels in such fields as anthropology, oceanography, economics, genetics, astronomy, and the high technologies. All of these seem to be particularly relevant to cultural and economic interests in Hawai'i.

GOAL 6: *Achieve parity in median family income with the state average.* In 1980 the state median family income was $18,782, while the Hawaiian median was $14,132, the lowest among the major ethnic groups. In comparison, the Chinese median family income was $23,930, the Japanese, $23,183, the Caucasian, $18,528, and the Filipino, $15,328. Although the goal is achievable, it is still below the minimum of the $20,000 that a family of four needed for living at near comfort level in Honolulu in 1984. Thus, while this may be an extraordinary challenge, serious consideration should be given to achieving parity with the two highest groups by the year 2005.

GOAL 7: *By 1995 reduce by half the percentage of Hawaiians receiving some form of welfare, and by 2005 eliminate by another half all welfare support of Hawaiians.* More Hawaiians are receiving public assistance in the form of money payments than are members of any other ethnic group. Of people receiving welfare checks in 1982, 39.8 percent were Hawaiians, 37.7 percent Caucasians, 14.3 percent Filipino, 6.5 percent Japanese, and 1.7 percent Chinese. The number of Hawaiian individuals or families receiving public assistance money was 6,758.

GOAL 8: *Improve the life-expectancy rate to equal that of the state average.* Hawaiians have the lowest life-expectancy rate of the major ethnic groups in Hawai'i: 67 years, as compared with the state average of 74 years. Based on statistics from 1910 to 1970, the life expectancy for Caucasians is 73 years, Chinese 76,

Filipinos 73, and Japanese 77 years. Incidentally, in every ethnic group, females outlive males by an average of 5 years. In the case of Hawaiians, the life expectancy for females is 70 and for males 65.

GOAL 9: *Decrease the infant-mortality rate to equal that of the state average.* About one-third of all babies born in the state, the highest percentage of any group, are Hawaiians. Between 1974 and 1978, Hawaiians accounted for 32 percent of all infant deaths, the highest of any group. The state rate is 1.2 per 100,000, compared with the Hawaiian percentage of slightly more than 1.3 per 100,000.

GOAL 10: *Reduce teenage pregnancies and illegitimate births by half.* According to the Kapi'olani Hospital/Children's Medical Center: "Teenage pregnancy is a major problem in our state. Although they are only 15–20% of all deliveries, they constitute a much higher percentage of pregnancy complications, prematurity and other defects." More young Hawaiian women, that is, those 11 to 19 years of age, give birth than do those in any other ethnic group. In 1978 Hawaiians accounted for 38.8 percent of live births to teenage mothers. Furthermore, teenage Hawaiian mothers also account for the highest number of illegitimate births: 51.8 percent, or more than half of the state's illegitimate births in 1978.

GOAL 11: *Reduce rates for juvenile and adult crimes, arrests, and incarcerations to equal those of population representation.* The evidence is shocking: in 1982 Hawaiians provided more than half of the population in the state youth correction facility, almost half of the residents in adult correctional facilities, and a high percentage of those on parole. They also led all other ethnic groups in serious crimes committed and arrests registered in proportion to their percentage of the population. For example, although Hawaiians represented 24 percent of the total state population in 1981, they accounted for 32 percent of the juvenile arrests for larceny, 44 percent for runaways, 42 percent for burglary, 42 percent for assault, and 33 percent for drug abuse. Goal 11 calls for a reduction to slightly less than half of the current rates. A more challenging goal for the Hawaiian leadership and community is to reduce crime rates to equal those of the ethnic group having the lowest representation in any category. For example, in 1981, of the total population in the state youth correctional facility, 60 percent were Hawaiian and 7 percent Caucasian.

GOAL 12: Reduce school truancy, absenteeism, and dropout rates by half by 1995, and eliminate another half by 2005. Most reports indicate that Hawaiian students are "disproportionately represented" among dropouts, among those with excessive numbers of absences from school, and in truancy statistics. For example, based on a study of 30 selected public intermediate and high schools in 1980–1981, Hawaiians accounted for 27.9 percent of the students having excessive absences, although they constituted 19.9 percent of the total number of students enrolled. In addition, about 1,000 Hawaiian students dropped out entirely, which is 3 percent of Hawaiian students enrolled.

GOAL 13: Increase the percentage of Hawaiian-owned businesses to equal that of the population representation. In 1981, of minority-owned businesses in the state, Hawaiians owned 6.6 percent, or about 1,368. These firms accounted for 2.6 percent of the employees, or 686, and 1.1 percent, or $17 million, of the gross receipts.

GOAL 14: Register 90 percent of eligible Hawaiian voters, and achieve 80 percent voter turnout for elections. Approximately 90,000 Hawaiians are eligible to vote, and currently about 42,000 are registered. This is somewhat less than the reported 50,000 who registered in 1980 for the first OHA elections. The decrease is due partly to the regular purging of the voter rolls and to a decline in voter interest, but it emphasizes the fact that voter statistics are finely attuned to changes in voter behavior. Hawaiian voter turnout has been low since the 1950s, although in 1980 it reached a high of nearly 80 percent.

GOAL 15: Achieve representation in major appointive government or administrative positions at the state, county, and local levels at least equal to population representation. Currently, Hawaiians hold only one of the major department head positions in the state (the Department of Hawaiian Home Lands, whose director has traditionally been Hawaiian), and one major position in the Honolulu city and county administration (excluding that of the bandmaster).

GOAL 16: Fully implement the Hawaiian Studies Program, including the study of Hawaiian language, history, culture, and values, in all public schools, from kindergarten to grade twelve, by 1990. The state constitution mandates that the people of Hawai'i will be educated in Hawaiian language, history, culture, and values, and to meet this end the Hawaiian Studies program has been established in the Department of Education. Since its inception in 1980, the program has been set up in 162 of the total of 170 elementary schools, using a cadre of kūpuna (about 180 individuals in 1984) to assist in the teaching. The remaining 8 schools and upper grades in most other schools await expansion and funding by the legislature for additional kūpuna services. This leaves the program to be developed over the next years in grades seven to twelve, making it essentially an elective for students.

We add that these are only some of many possible and vital goals in the cultural field, all of which should be aimed at sustaining the momentum and direction of the resurgent Hawaiian culture. In addition, we might suggest goals for improving prenatal care; reducing the incidence of diabetes, cancer, hypertension, and other illnesses that afflict a high number of Hawaiians; improving dietary habits and diets; the resolution of the ceded lands dispute with the state; the recovery of certain traditional rights of access to beaches or fishing places; and the expansion of federal government programs to assist Hawaiians. These and other goals have been put forward already, in one form or another, by the Office of Hawaiian Affairs (e.g., in its *Master Plan* [1983]), Alu Like, Kamehameha Schools, and other Hawaiian organizations.

The goals as such are not new except, perhaps, in the manner in which we have "packaged" them here. We have deliberately inserted deadlines to remind us that time is not on our side, for the longer we delay the resolution of these problems, the farther behind we shall fall. Some feel that Hawaiians are so far behind in some areas, in comparison with other ethnic groups, that we are in a crisis mode: "The red button has already been pressed!"

When taken all together, the goals may appear to threaten other ethnic groups in the community. But lest anyone think so, a careful reading should reveal that, essentially, what this set of goals calls for is parity with the others. Every objective is placed there only in order to lift affected Hawaiians to a level equal to that already attained by other ethnic groups. If a cry is to be heard from Hawaiians, it is not one for domination, but rather one for equality or something like that. Achieving parity means first and foremost catching up with whomever is ahead, and no one understands better than Hawaiians how difficult doing that will be.

Even granting that that can be done, before any of us can think of overtaking anybody, there arises the second challenge of just trying to keep from falling back from our present low position. Pessimists compare the Hawaiian predicament to two cars traveling in the same direction but at different speeds: both make progress, but the gap between them keeps widening.

One of the great challenges that faces the Hawaiian leadership is not only that of leading other Hawaiians but also of persuading haoles, Japanese, Filipinos, and other non-Hawaiians. This means the need to communicate with members of those other groups, and telling them about Hawaiian needs and aspirations. It involves winning the hearts and minds of the community at large when issues arise affecting the interests of the Hawaiian people. It implies preventing potentially divisive conflicts from arising, or minimizing their harmful effects when they do emerge. It requires constant monitoring of the attitudes and opinions of the non-Hawaiian populace, especially those in sensitive and important positions regarding Hawaiian matters.

The need for this kind of leadership should be clear at once: whatever Hawaiians want to achieve that in any way affects the community at large—and this includes almost anything of importance—will depend to a great extent on the willingness and cooperation of the non-Hawaiian majorities. As one Hawaiian politician put it: "They've got the numbers, the money, the moxie, the power. We all need each other, but I think we need them more than they need us. We can't go around calling them names and talking stink about 'em, and then expect them to help us. Some Hawaiians try to throw their weight around, but, hey, we don't carry that much weight." However cynical that may sound, much of what he says is true. For in the arena of raw power, Hawaiians constitute a distinct minority. In a land of elephants, all other creatures, whether ants or crabs, must walk carefully among the "clumps of grass."

Some Hawaiians, however, approach this task gingerly and with their guard up because they are convinced that the "other guys" don't want to cooperate. They believe that Hawaiians will have to fight for whatever small piece of the pie is available, that nothing will be given Hawaiians out of gratefulness or the supposed sense of guilt that others may feel. In fact, some Hawaiians honestly fear a conspiracy at work that is aimed at keeping them divided and down, reminding them of the pre-World War II years when the "Merchant Street oligarchy" ran Hawai'i nei. An articulate, well-educated, and responsible Hawaiian leader spoke softly about his belief to this effect: "There is genuine fear in the community about the Hawaiians getting out of hand and that's why everything is being done to stop us from coming up." While he acknowledged that he could cite no evidence for such a conspiracy, he insisted that a pattern of suppression does exist. Again, whether this is fact or fiction, what really matters is the perception that he and other Hawaiians have of a non-Hawaiian community "out to get us."

On the other hand, other Hawaiians believe that there is a deep reservoir of goodwill in the community toward Hawaiians and their causes. They point to all kinds of support, ranging from the electoral vote for the "OHA package" at the constitutional convention of 1978, to non-Hawaiians who take active part in many Hawaiian organizations, and to others in high public and private offices who openly support Hawaiian issues. They are quick to concede that were it not for the support of non-Hawaiians, Hawaiians would never be as well off as they are today. That is not a dutiful concession from a bunch of "Uncle Toms," for they claim to be just as Hawaiian as the most Hawaiian guy in town. They fear most the loss of community support, and a fierce backlash of anti-Hawaiian feeling. The idea of "backlash," as a real and constant possibility, crops up frequently in their discussions of the current scene.

In short, Hawaiians have good reasons to give effective communication to their non-Hawaiian neighbors—a fact which all responsible Hawaiian politicians concede as the first rule of political survival in this state.

In conclusion, few generations are ever given as great a chance to influence their own destiny as a people than are Hawaiians living today. The size and diversity of the problems we face at this juncture have never been greater, if for no other reason than that more of us now are living than at any time since the arrival of Captain Cook's expedition in 1778. The enormous scope of the task of alleviating our problems is shown by the goals we have suggested, which are aimed at just catching up and staying even with other ethnic groups. In addition, we must consider the ever-mounting urgency to bring about immediate improvements in the social and economic lives of the thousands of Hawaiians who are on welfare and food stamps, in prisons and reformatories, in hospitals. Disillusioned and fed up with a socioeconomic system they neither understand nor accept, they present an explosive potential for disorder, as indeed some of their spokespersons have been threatening for years. But, against this backdrop, our chances of resolving these problems are better today than ever before because as a people more of us are better educated and trained, better organized, better informed of our needs and resources, better at managing within the system, and better prepared spiritually.

While the ghost of inferiority has not been exorcised from all of us, many more Hawaiians feel much more confident and good about themselves as Hawaiians, thanks in part to the "renaissance" that has instilled in us renewed pride and self-esteem. It has also made Hawaiians more conscious of each other and of their community. Thus, the present challenge offers an unparalleled opportunity to laulima and kōkua, to share in our collective pride as Hawaiians that no other generation has felt in this century.

Now we face a time of choice in our evolution that neither our leaders nor our people can afford to ignore.

PART SIX

THE ALOHA SOCIETY

12

THE DYNAMICS OF ALOHA

Fact or Fiction?

It is hard to think of another word that over so many decades has aroused more public attention, sometimes even controversy, among both Hawaiians and non-Hawaiians than aloha. Opinions of all shades and fervor, ranging from the ridiculous to the exalted, have been expressed on the subject. These include such notions as aloha is: "undefinable," "sheer nonsense," "a monumental hoax," "the summum bonum of life," "Hawai'i's social cement," "unique to Hawai'i," "the power of God," "a priceless style of human interaction," "something like the Holy Ghost," and "both fact and fiction." These conflicting views mask what seems to be a constant "search for the elusive Spirit of Aloha" that more often than not is discussed in the newspapers, especially in the letters to the editors. All the while the question is asked: "Is aloha dead?" and always the answer is either yes or maybe no.

What intrigues us is not the predictable cynicism that crops up in those pages, but the serious and sincere efforts made by many reasonable, dedicated citizens of the community, from all racial backgrounds, to foster, support, idealize, and even institutionalize aloha. Local government leaders, for example, consistently make solemn pronouncements about the need to preserve and enhance the Spirit of Aloha. We are constantly reminded that Hawai'i is officially called the Aloha State. The Hawai'i Chamber of Commerce makes annual Aloha Spirit Awards to employees in the islands who offer exemplary service to customers. A University of Hawai'i professor and futurist has proposed that new citizens take an "aloha-ness" test rather than a loyalty test (Chaplin and Paige). An organization led by Hawaiians, with help from the tourist industry to be sure, has presented the annual Aloha Week Festival for many years. The list goes on and on, showing the pervasive influence of the term in much of the contemporary life of Hawai'i. Indeed, aloha has become so thoroughly identified with all the people of Hawai'i that for all intents and purposes it is common property. Even the millions of tourists seem to end up "owning" a piece of it by the time they leave the islands, wanting to return.

Yet Hawaiians still have a strong proprietary interest in the word. Many feel that somehow aloha is unique to them, their personal gift, because of what Hawaiians have been able to bring to it over the centuries. While it may have its counterparts in other places in the world—as in so-called Southern hospitality or in Maori aroha—Hawaiians think that their version is one of a kind, the only one in the world. Not a few Hawaiians believe that, when they utter the word, they have put their mana into it, and, therefore, that if they chose to do so, they can also withdraw their mana and make the term powerless. One Hawaiian leader has said that Hawaiians have given too much aloha for their own good, and that now is the time to give it "an honorable funeral." Others, however, feel that no one can ever give enough and that aloha is the Hawaiians' greatest gift to the world.

Given these and other considerations, no serious examination of Hawaiian values would be complete without a good hard look at the meaning, role, and impact of aloha. Curiously enough, despite its significance, aloha has not attracted any major scholarly or even semischolarly treatment. So this discussion is the first serious effort of its kind.

Four principal questions need to be addressed: (1) What did aloha mean in times of old and what does it mean now? (2) How much importance did it have in old Hawai'i? (3) What has been its impact on present-day life in the islands? And (4), the perennial worry, is aloha "slipping"? Many other questions might be asked as well, but these form the nucleus of our discussion of what someone has called "the most vital resource in Hawai'i today."

It is best to keep in mind our frame of reference, namely, that we see aloha as having a dynamic of its own, yet acting and interacting within the larger dynamics of Hawaiian values. People have a tendency to think of aloha as an isolated phenomenon, partly because it is the focus of so much attention, to the exclusion of other values. But, as we shall show, it is only one among an interrelated set of ideas and values. In a real sense, it is as much a word as it is a view of life or a state of mind.

Defining the Elusive

A student of culture in contemporary Hawai'i claims that he has counted 123 varying definitions of aloha. This is a statement which, even if it is only half accurate, would support the notion that aloha is "undefinable," or, as one local joker put it, "as slippery as an eel." Ask any two Hawaiians what it means and you're likely to get an argument from both. Defining it, or at least arriving at some clear measures of its scope, seems to be in order, although even this rational process can be an issue in itself.

At the beginning of 1967, for example, we organized a small and informal discussion group to explore the question "What is the Aloha Spirit?" It was a mixed group of people consisting of a nisei sociologist, a haole expert on local criminal behavior, an outspoken labor leader, a quiet professor of American history, two Hawaiian social workers, two older Hawaiian women, and an assortment of other people. We were somewhat taken aback at the very first meeting when one of the two kūpuna cautioned us that we should not try to define aloha too much because, by doing so, we might lose its essence. What she meant was that definition, or, more precisely, analysis, tears things apart by trying to examine each lesser component of the whole. Inevitably, in the process you lose something, because you can never put all the pieces back together exactly as they were before. It's like the tale of the juggler who read an analysis of how he did his juggling and after that couldn't juggle at all for six long years. But coupled with this warning was the kupuna's impatience with those who intellectualize so much that they have no time to do anything else. As she said, "It's no use talking about it. The only thing is to live it!" Perhaps then and there the group should have been disbanded and sent home, to learn the meaning of aloha in the only way it can be learned—and that is by doing. So, at the outset, let us concede that a great deal can be said for the wise woman's sensibility.

Doing begins with understanding, however, or at least a glimmer of that. The function of defining or analyzing is to enlighten by uncovering as many facets of the subject as possible, casting light on some that you may have not seen before. Defining is not simply tearing a subject apart, but goes on to put those parts together again, so that you achieve a new clarity, a sharper focus. As a group we were interested in this essentially creative process.

Besides gaining a better understanding, we also wanted to eliminate the vagueness and elusiveness that had characterized the
term. This vagueness inhibited some people from coming to terms
with aloha, or gave others an excuse for not practicing it at all.

You can go to a Webster's dictionary and find the term aloha,
one of half a dozen Hawaiian words that have been added to the
general American vocabulary. Its meaning is given as "love, affection, kindness." You can also go to the standard *Hawaiian Dictionary* by Pūku'i and Elbert, and find the definition as "love, affection, compassion, mercy, pity, kindness, charity." You can go to
the earliest Hawaiian dictionary (Andrews', published in 1838),
which defined it as "love; affection; gratitude; kindness; pity;
compassion; grief." Thus, for approximately 150 years, the word
has kept pretty much the same meaning. Can we safely assume,
however, that the legacy in our dictionaries is correct? We should
not go around challenging dictionaries, but posing the question in
that way may help us to look closer at the nature of aloha in its
traditional context.

The Traditional Context

As with so many other things from our past, the etymology of
aloha is shrouded in mystery. Its origin goes back to the very
beginnings of the Polynesian people in Kahiki, the homeland, and
beyond, for the root word is found in all Polynesian languages,
and always with essentially the same meaning. Whether it be
spelled and pronounced aroha in Maori, alofa in Samoan, aroha
in Tahitian, or alōfa in Tongan, each variant contains the elements
of love, compassion, sympathy, or kindness. Since Hawaiian is
related to all Polynesian languages, we find a possible clue in the
culture of the Maori. Joan Metge, the Maori scholar, suggests that
originally aroha may have meant "love for kin." While she does
not offer any etymological evidence for the opinion, it makes good
sense, because of our understanding of the natural affinity that
human beings have for their offspring and our knowledge of kinship structure in Polynesia.

Without detailing the fabric of traditional kinship, let us point
out some of the ways in which aloha functioned or was expressed
as part of an integrated value system. To begin with, the most natural and "first expression" of aloha, as Pūku'i (Pūku'i, Haertig,

and Lee) wrote, was between parent and child. The parent-child relationship began at conception, because Hawaiians believed that "the child's nature and character were influenced by the behaviour of the parents while the baby was in the womb. If mother and father were busily occupied with work the child would be industrious and hardworking. So likewise with psychic attributes." Thus if the parents showed love and kindness, these attributes would be reflected in the character of the child. On the other hand, if they showed jealousy and peevishness, then the child's disposition would reflect these traits. Many other attendant rules governed diet, prayers, types of work the mother could participate in, and so on, all of which were prescribed and followed in order to ensure the "perfect" child.

The great care that was taken to guard the child's development during gestation was sanctified by the 'aha'aina māwaewae feast celebrated within twenty-four hours after the birth of the firstborn son. Actually it was less a feast than a sacrament of consecration of the child to Lono, for "its safeguarding and welfare." Pūku'i (Handy and Pūku'i) pointed out that Lono symbolized the family's and the child's priorities as "subsistence, livelihood, peace and plenty." The ritual of the feast served to clear the way in the life ahead by setting the child's "feet *(wāwae)* in the way *(ma)* of the spiritual flow or channels *('au)* of his responsible elders."

The 'aha'aina pālala was held a year later, honoring the child's first birthday. It was not a sacramental ritual like the māwaewae. We are told that "the *pālala* expressed the *aloha* of all the relatives and friends, and in the case of an *ali'i*, of all the people for the first-born newly arrived. This *aloha* was expressed in the form of gifts to the child, and in the composition of chants *(mele)* which were performed with dances *(hula)*." Pūku'i (Handy and Pūku'i) added that the modern "baby *lū'au*," as a carryover of the pālala, "retains little of the spirit of *aloha*." She criticized the modern version because relatives and friends are expected to put cash contributions in the big calabash, prominently located near the entrance to the feasting place. In contrast, the pālala was a feast of goodwill, not of obligation, which, if Pūku'i is right, made this one of the few "pure gifts" of aloha in traditional Hawai'i.

But all of this outpouring of aloha for the newborn hiapo and his first-year feast was offset by the unloving custom of infanticide. Pūku'i (Handy and Pūku'i) explained this practice. "Hawaiians loved children . . . as soon as a woman mentioned the fact that she did not want the child in her womb, relatives and neighbours would beg for it and no matter how large a family there was always room for one more. . . . Infanticide was practised so that there might be no low-born person to claim blood relationship to the chiefs." Worse things have been done in the interest of preserving genetic purity and artificial barriers of class, but at least infanticide was not a common practice in ancient Hawai'i.

During the earliest years of childhood, the bonds of motherly affection are closest, as the child is wrapped in aloha. Good parents avoid manipulating love as a means of influencing the child, just as they do not use the punishment of withdrawal, the so-called silent treatment. They give, instead, an outgoing and steady flow of kindness, gentleness, warmth, and love for the child. Hawaiians, as do all natural parents, knew what psychologists and physicians tell us today: when babies are deprived of love, as it is manifested in all its forms, they are as liable to get sick from the psychic deprivation as they are from exposure to germs or to an improper diet.

This dependency, however, does not last for long, because by age four the child is released from its mother's side to join the 'ohana, the family circle of siblings and other kin. While the child is still the object of close affection and care, he is taught how to adapt to people who are more self-reliant and self-sufficient. From then on, the "hard" values, as opposed to "soft" ones, come into play.

The principles and practices of fostering and adoption tell a lot about the role of aloha in such matters. The Hawaiian attitude is expressed in the saying *"Ka lei hā'ule 'ole, he keiki,"* "A lei that is never cast aside is one's child" (Handy and Pūku'i). Indeed, no child was ever cast aside and not cared for. Hawaiians have no expression comparable to the American notion that "every barrel must have one bad apple," at least as it might apply to a child. All babies are loved. Pūku'i (Handy and Pūku'i) described how the relationship between an adopting parent and a child develops. "The relationship comes about as a result of mutual affection and agreement, at first tacit, then unobtrusively discussed, between the child and the older person. . . . This is a relationship involving love, respect and courtesy." The adopted, or hānai, child was aptly referred to as *"He 'ohā pili wale,"* "A young taro that attaches itself to an older corm." As "young taro" they were meant to flourish in a system designed to ensure that every child would have a place and an opportunity to be loved, fed, sheltered, clothed, and taught as a member of a family, never as what we call a "ward of the state." In such an environment of constant sharing and mutual support, child abuse was unheard of. We are told that any parent who neglected a child was bound to be the object of public scorn.

If the family offers a natural channel of aloha in the child-parent relationship, it offers the same between husband and wife. The ideal relationship is conveyed in the saying: *"Ke aloha pili pa'a o ke kāne me ka wahine,"* "The lasting love of man and woman" (Handy and Pūku'i). The sense of everlasting aloha is captured in the phrase pili pa'a—where pili means to cleave to or cling to, and pa'a means firmly, permanently. Hawaiians have no equivalent to the American expression, "a clinging vine," referring to a woman who holds onto a man tightly, desperately, all but helplessly. In the traditional arrangement, the man is pili kua, "standing back of his mate," the protector, while the woman is pili alo, the protected one "standing in front" of her husband. Pūku'i (Handy and Pūku'i) touchingly described the ideal couple:

> I can tell you about this kind of love. About people who really loved. About healthy persons who when their mates got leprosy went with them to Kalaupapa. They lived out their lives together there. They were ordinary couples who farmed their land together, nursed each other when they were sick, prepared the mate for burial when he died. They were my own *kūpuna*. The elders in my own *'ohana* who mated *noho pū*, without contract or ceremony. And when the new laws came, they said, "We don't need a paper marriage. We have always loved each other. We always will." They knew about "till death do us part," but not because of *kauoha*, a command or a law. Because of what they truly felt.

The picture of a healthy husband following his leprous wife to Kalaupapa is no less poignant than that of a wife following her husband into battle, feeding him, nursing his wounds, and sometimes, in a close and desperate conflict, fighting beside him. Not uncommonly, wives accompanied their menfolk on the battlefield. Such was the fate of Manono, who fought until she fell lifeless on the body of her husband, Kekuaokalani, slain in the battle of Kuamo'o in 1819.

Aloha in the marriage relationship meant fidelity, not only for strengthening the marital bond but also for preserving the stability of the family. Anything less than fidelity was *"He nohona huikau, noho aku noho mai,"* "A life of confusion, living this way and that." In a society whose socioeconomic and political existence depended on family order, it is clear why faithfulness and mutual trust and respect were esteemed values governing the conduct of husband and wife. Despite the "flirtations" of some women who boarded foreign ships, and the caricatures of "adulterous" behavior written by scandal-mongering missionaries, promiscuity was never condoned, even among unmarried men and women. The thrust of Hawaiian society was aimed at tightening not loosening the bonds of marital and familial loyalty.

In a larger sense, aloha pili pa'a can be applied to the relationships among all kinfolk, extending back to a family's remotest origins. This sense of bonding is conveyed again and again in the genealogical preoccupation of Hawaiians. *"E kolo ana nō ke ewe i ke ewe,"* "Kinfolk seek the society of other kinfolk and love them because of their common ancestors" (Handy and Pūku'i). Aloha 'ohana was not limited to the living, but extended to past members, to ancestors and ancestor-gods as well. This attention appears not to have been a merely passive display, but rather an active demonstration of emotion, charged by periodic remembrances of family events through prayers, dances, chants, feasts, and other mnemonic devices. Furthermore, we must keep in mind that Hawaiians believed that this aloha was constantly reciprocated by spiritual ancestors. Thus, "clinging" to one's ancestors was motivated by both duty and an expectation of kōkua from extraterrestrial levels. In this, Hawaiian culture was similar to Japanese and Chinese culture, to name just two.

If Hawaiians esteemed aloha, no doubt they did so partly because they understood what we might call its "transforming power." That is best expressed in the saying *"Aloha mai nō, aloha aku: 'o ka huhū ka mea e ola 'ole ai,"* "When love is given, love should be returned; anger is the thing that gives no life." In other words, love begets love; anger ends in anger. The same thought is expressed in another saying: *"Ua ola loko i ke aloha,"* "Love gives life within," a recognition that aloha is vital to one's mental, emotional, and physical well-being. A similar idea appears in the statement *"He kēhau hoʻomaʻemaʻe ke aloha,"* which compares love to "cleansing dew." Like cleansing dew, the cleansing power of aloha can soothe and even eliminate the pain and hurt one may be suffering from. As for anger and its destructive effects, practical wisdom is offered in the saying: *"Nau ke kuʻi, lohi ka lima,"* "When one grinds the teeth, the hand slows." This means that anger can so upset a person's ability to function normally that it slows his work, reducing his productivity and efficiency. (All these wise sayings are taken from Handy and Pūkuʻi.)

Modern psychologists have collected sufficient evidence from observations and experiments to demonstrate conclusively this "transforming power" of love. Dr. F. E. Fiedler, for example, described the "ideal therapeutic relationship" as that marked by "support, security, and understanding" along with "acceptance and warmth" from the therapist. The worst or the least effective therapy is marked by "a punitive therapist, making the patient feel rejected, having little respect for the patient; by impersonal, cold, often inimical relationship of the parties." Sorokin summed up the results of research conducted on the efficacy of showing love as follows: "If and when an individual or group approaches other persons or groups in a friendly manner, the respondents' answer to such an approach is also kindly in an overwhelming majority of cases. And the frequency of the friendly response to the friendly approach is at least as high as that of an inimical response to an aggressive approach. . . . The emergence and development of either friendship or animosity follow the formula: love begets love, enmity produces enmity."

In short, according to analysts both haole and Hawaiian, aloha had its own charge of mana, for which the ʻohana, or kinship system, was an ideal transmitting agent. But did that mana extend from the family into the general society as well?

Beyond the ʻOhana

It is good—and easier—to share aloha with one's kinfolk, for "blood is always thicker than water." The real test of love comes outside the family circle, where genealogical and genetic ties are absent and one has to make links with comparative strangers. To what extent did aloha for each other permeate the general populace in Hawaiian society? After so long a time the question cannot be answered with statistics. But one indication of what might have happened is the way in which Hawaiians perceived friendship.

People of all cultures attach more than a little importance to friendship. That esteem is reflected in the terminology they use, the special rules and sanctions prescribed for conducting a friendship, its meaning and status in the community, and its place in the myths, legends, sayings, and other literary forms. Comparing how Hawaiians rank in this regard with other peoples lies beyond the scope of this discussion. But there is ample evidence that they placed great stock in friendship. To begin with, the myths about the gods and the tales about great ali'i present many memorable friends: Pele's sister Hi'iaka and Hōpoe, the dancer; Kaulula'au, prince of Maui, and Waolani, the high priest; Kamehameha I and Ulumaheihei, the king's "most trusted friend and confidant"; and so on.

A good friend was prized and praised; a bad friend, condemned. The true friend was "a nest of fragrance," *he pūnana na ke onaona*, an analogy that heightens the importance of the friend because fragrance, particularly that of plants, invariably was associated with divinity. On the other hand, the false friend was nothing more than a hypocrite—"*He hamo hulu puna mawaho*," "A brushing on the outside with whitewash" (Handy and Pūku'i). Hawaiians were warned about the fellow with the "friendly face outside, hardness inside," or the fair-weather friend who seeks your company when you are prospering, but forgets you when poverty and misfortune strike you.

At least four different terms denote the several kinds of friends: hoa, makamaka, aikāne, and hoa aloha, each denoting more or less a different degree of friendship. Hoa is the generic term found in all Polynesian languages. Aikāne, as in pili aikāne, refers to a comradely relationship between males, as compared with pili hoa aloha, which refers to a devoted friendship. That the word Hawaiians of old used for expressing the most intimate form of friendship incorporates aloha is no coincidence. Perhaps we should not make too much of this, because the word for friend in many other cultures is also based on the one for love, such as amigo in Spanish and ami in French. But hoa aloha adds a little more emphasis to the high place that Hawaiians gave to friendship.

Makamaka is defined as "an intimate friend with whom one is

on terms of receiving and giving freely." It has a peculiar tie with the role of the host. If a total stranger were to be welcomed into a home and treated well there, his host or hostess would be referred to as makamaka. According to Pūku'i (Handy and Pūku'i) it connotes a more intimate relationship than that which is implied in the English idea of a host. It means a "more or less permanent obligation in the matter of exchange in friendship and hospitality. A bond of *aloha* has been accepted, and by acceptance becomes enduring if cherished. *Ho'omakamaka* means to make friends by extending hospitality."

In this connection, the Hawaiians' measure of aloha is best illustrated in their attitude toward a stranger. Few statements can express it better than the proverb "Love is the host in strange lands," " *'O ke aloha ke kuleana o kāhi malihini*" (Pūku'i 1983). That is to say, for the stranger the proper welcome is one which is expressed with aloha. While it should be reciprocated, what is noteworthy is that the initiative for showing aloha is always the host's, or in the larger societal sense, the resident kama'āina's. To quote Pūku'i (Handy and Pūku'i) again, "In old Hawai'i, every passerby was greeted and offered food whether he was an acquaintance or a total stranger." The approaching person would be greeted by a calling out, or heahea: *"Hē mai! Mai! Mai!"* "Come hither, come!" The host or hostess did not first run a security check on the person to determine whether he or she would be worth inviting in. The invitation was offered spontaneously, out of aloha, for to offer it grudgingly or ambivalently would have robbed it of any pleasure or sense. Of course this kind of openness did expose the host to the risk of being taken advantage of, but probably that was so unlikely that the Hawaiian of old did not seriously think about it. In any case, the risk was certainly well worth taking because of the satisfaction he would get out of the spontaneous giving. Besides, the greeting made good psychological sense, for trying to pretend hospitality is always an unrewarding and frustrating experience.

The relationship between aloha and ho'okipa is clear: hospitality flows from an outpouring of aloha first, not the other way around. As someone said recently, "For *ho'okipa* to work smoothly, it must be generously lubricated by aloha."

Heretofore, we have talked primarily about aloha as it is expressed among and between commoners. But the picture changes when we look at the exchange of aloha between commoners and ali'i. The inequalities in that relationship involve a whole set of values, in which aloha is only one and certainly not the most important. Fear, awe, respect, loyalty, obedience, and similar values would better characterize such a relationship. To be sure, some ali'i were venerated, if not beloved, by the maka'āinana because of their outstanding leadership and exemplary conduct. Such were the chiefs Kakūhihewa of O'ahu, Manokalanipō of Kaua'i, Liloa and his son 'Umi of Hawai'i, among others. As Kepelino remembered, "The chiefs of Hawai'i were taught to be humble, kind, sympathetic, open-hearted." But, if Malo is right, "only a small portion of the kings and chiefs ruled with kindness; the large majority simply lorded it over the people." The result was that the "people generally lived in chronic fear and apprehension of the chiefs." And, he added, "On account of the rascality (kolohe) of some of the chiefs to the common people, warlike contests frequently broke out between certain chiefs and the people, and many of the former were killed in battle by the commoners. The people made war against bad kings in old times."

Admittedly this is an oversimplification of a very complex relationship, but, in general, the values associated with the commoner-nobility relationship in a society as rigidly stratified as Hawai'i's would tend to be less concerned with aloha. The social distance created by their sanctity removed the chiefs from the chance to share with commoners in the spontaneous giving of affection, sympathy, compassion, and kindness. Malo's description of the relationship is, perhaps, less an indictment of the chiefs than a statement of hard facts.

Competing Values

One of the first questions we asked concerned the extent to which aloha might have been a central value in traditional Hawaiian society. Some modern Hawaiians believe that it was the most important of all ancient Hawaiian values. For example, the Reverend Akaiko Akana, for many years pastor of Kawaiaha'o Church until his death in 1932, stated, "Aloha, the very kernel of the Hawaiian ethics, the very core of the Hawaiian life, unsurpassed by anything of modern ethics, was the dominating law which regulated the domestic and civil conduct of old Hawai'i." Unfortunately, neither he nor others who believe that idea have provided satisfactory support for it based on historical data and observations. Instead, they seem to have reasoned that, since modern Hawaiians are so well known for their aloha spirit, then they must have inherited it from their kūpuna who, therefore, must have considered it very important. Perhaps, too, Pastor Akana spoke in such favorable terms about aloha because of his ministerial emphasis upon Christian love. Probably this is a fair comment to make about the opinions of most people today, who try to explain behavior in old Hawai'i in terms of their own modern ideas, prejudices, and experiences.

We do not doubt that aloha was an important value in the traditional culture of our kūpuna. We have presented as good a case as any so far in support of this position. But when we look at the total value system as it related to religious, economic, technological, philosophical, aesthetic, or political behavior, and examine the varied attitudes, motives, standards, emotions, and other factors that shaped the thoughts and actions of Hawaiians of old, we see many values at work, each sharing center stage, so to speak, depending on the situation, timing, actors involved, and the "script," as it were. Aloha is only one of those values, among many, although an important one. In the parent-child relationship, it is of central importance, although other values were at work, too. In cases of greeting and welcoming guests or strangers, clearly hospitality and generosity were the primary considerations, but aloha also was involved. On the other hand, when a man was called up for corvée labor or to fight in a war, loyalty and obedience (or fear), not aloha, might have been sufficient reason for him to respond to the summons. In other words, we discover changing sets of shifting values that appear on and off on the stage of life when they are called for—always varying because they are depending on the needs of the moment.

We could probably make an equally good case, or an even stronger one, for several values other than aloha as being central to Hawaiian society before 1778. For example, loyalty, or kūpa'a, unswerving allegiance to a chief or a family, was a central value. Pūku'i (Pūku'i, Haertig, and Lee) herself said as much when she defined the 'ohana concept. "It is a sense of unity, shared involvement and shared responsibility. It is mutual interdependence and mutual help. It is emotional support, given and received. It is solidarity and cohesiveness. It is love—*often*; it is loyalty—*always* [italics added]." Loyalty to the 'ohana's ideals, goals, and leaders is the moral constant, while aloha comes and goes.

It is important to recognize Pūku'i's perception of the 'ohana as being a self-reliant, self-sufficient working group, for this is why the "sense of unity . . . solidarity and cohesiveness" were indispensable. The 'ohana's survival and well-being depended on its organizational integrity. We have seen already how, as a self-sufficient economic unit, the 'ohana had to function in a fairly rational way, that is, with a division of labor and specialization among the workers, and with leadership and management provided by the haku. Among the values of honest work, industry, cooperation, efficiency, and so on that must be associated with achieving the economic goals of the 'ohana, loyalty must be paramount. The 'ohana economic system worked best when its members put aside personal desires or ambitions for the common good of the group, and agreed to abide by the group's collective will as that was declared by its leaders. Loyalty, obedience, unity, pulling together —these are the important "cluster" values that must have appealed to the pragmatic Hawaiians.

Loyalty also served as a dominant value in the political relationship between ali'i and maka'āinana. It is relatively easier and more realistic for chiefs to obtain allegiance and obedience rather than aloha from their subjects. One can be loyal without having much aloha, but one cannot have aloha and be disloyal at the same time. That is analogous to being respected, but not necessarily liked. Probably a relationship such as that may have been the general rule for most ali'i and their maka'āinana.

The simultaneous operation of competing values, as opposed to aloha alone as the central value, is the only realistic view for us to take. Otherwise trying to explain all historical events in terms of only one point of reference puts too great a strain upon belief. For example, how can we account for a society that took aloha as the "dominating law" for regulating its "domestic and civil conduct," and yet spent much of its time and resources in waging war? Reverend Akana would have found this contradiction difficult to explain away, just as Christian ministers and theologians have always had to wrestle with the same problem when soldiers of Christian nations, which profess the Gospel of Love, go into battle shooting at Christian enemies for very unloving causes. But when we recognize that Hawaiians were motivated by other powerful motives or values than aloha, such as loyalty to their chiefs (who in their turn were motivated by prestige, power, and territoriality), then we can deal better with the apparent contradictions in our history.

At this point we need to dispose of the mistaken interpretation of aloha as the Hawaiian way of dealing with confrontation. Francine du Plessis Gray, in her book *Hawai'i: The Sugar-Coated Fortress* (1972), wrote, "The Aloha Spirit, from the start, has been the Hawaiian's way of tolerating rather than fighting strangers, his way of avoiding direct confrontation." This statement (which, unfortunately, has been much quoted) is a flawed understanding of aloha as well as of all the other Hawaiian values. We have seen that ho'okipa is hardly a negative or passive way of meeting the stranger. On the contrary, it is a very affirmative approach, requiring spontaneity, openness, and aloha on the part of a host or hostess, and allows no room for merely tolerating a stranger. The idea of tolerating is entirely contradictory to both the spirit and practice of these values. Furthermore, to suggest that Hawaiians avoided direct confrontation out of fear or some false notion of aloha is to ignore the whole set of operative values that Hawaiians respected, such as aggressiveness, courage, dignity, honor, competitiveness, and rivalry. Among a people to whom the warrior was a heroic figure, and the craftsman was an honored neighbor, no man worth his mana would have run away from a meeting of any kind, not even from an outright challenge. The principles of reciprocity and personal honor would have upheld his virtue, and made him behave as an honorable man. Thus, when Gray tries to explain events after 1778, such as the lack of political warfare between Hawaiians and encroaching Europeans, her conclusion is wrong because she does not understand the full range of Hawaiian values. The point to be emphasized here is obvious (and all too often ignored): until commentators on Hawaiian developments, whether they come from inside our culture or outside it, truly understand Hawaiian values, their conclusions will be as full of errors as are those of du Plessis Gray.

In any event, the biases of outsiders (or of ourselves) should not detract from the importance that Hawaiians gave to aloha in their traditional system of values. Even though the values operating at any one time or place may have shifted, according to the many factors calling them forth, the value of aloha was an important one, never far from the consciousness—or the conscience—of the people.

Marriage with the Gospel of Love

No one can fully understand the dynamics of aloha today without tracing its evolution through the period of Christianity after it was introduced in 1820. That the meaning of aloha underwent some change is a reasonable assumption, although measuring the change with much precision is difficult. Less difficult is noting changes in the objects receiving aloha—God, humankind, Christ, one's enemies, the Gospel—and some of the effects of these changes on the attitudes of Hawaiians toward themselves and the new world to which they were being introduced. We must believe that the value we feel or perceive as aloha today is the product of evolution, even the child of the marriage of an ancient, traditional Polynesian concept with its Christian counterpart.

For Christianity, founded as it is on the Gospel of Love, aloha probably was as good a word as the missionaries could find to express their central ideal of love. Aloha combined in one rubric some of the cardinal elements of the new kind of "love": charity, pity, sympathy, kindness, compassion. The similarity between definitions of the two words has led some people to suspect that the missionaries who devised the syllabary for written Hawaiian and compiled the first dictionaries, might have defined aloha to fit their concept of love. While this makes for a good theory of conspiracy, it ignores the fact that aloha means precisely the same thing in all the Polynesian languages scattered across the Pacific. And, moreover, the etymology of the word goes back to the remotest past of Kahiki, the homeland.

Compassion, for example, which evokes feelings and impressions singularly Christian and Eastern (Buddhist in particular), is nonetheless very Polynesian and Hawaiian. Robert Levy, in his insightful book, *Tahitians: Mind and Experience in the Society Islands*, reported that one of his informants, Manu, described his feelings of arōfa in terms of compassion "for cripples, for relatively poor and struggling people, or for people who have had some disaster strike their family." That is feeling the suffering of others, suffering with them and wanting to ease that suffering. It is being able to put oneself in the place of another, or what we might call empathy. This feeling is not unique to Polynesians; it is common to all sensitive human beings. Nonetheless, for many reasons, some people think that Hawaiians have greater empathy than most other people do. That stronger empathy, we believe, comes from a traditional mind-set that is more finely attuned to the feelings of others.

The Christian philosophy of love, with its concept of agape, added a new dimension to aloha. In Hawaiian thought, aloha already connoted a higher sense of abstract or spiritual love, but with agape it was heightened to include the purest form of love as that was proved by God's love for humankind, selfless and boundless. It also transformed aloha into a form of giving that was identical with unadulterated altruism. This, in effect, cancelled out the old idea of reciprocity. Agape superimposed upon aloha meant that aloha became a higher form of giving, without expectation of receiving anything in return. This has been so widely accepted by modern Hawaiians that almost every Hawaiian will tell you today that, of course, this has always been the meaning of aloha.

The superlative importance of aloha probably began when Hawaiians came around to believing the Christian message that *"Aloha ke akua,"* "God is love." Before 1778 Hawaiians had not equated aloha with any one of their many akua. So when the new almighty, all-knowing, omnipresent, supreme Jehovah replaced the discredited and powerless gods of old, aloha was in effect apotheosized, and, in the process, was elevated above all other values. One of the casualties of this process was the relationship with the 'aumākua, which was the only loving relationship that Hawaiians had established with their deities.

Christianity added another dimension to aloha with the idea of "love of humankind," irrespective of a person's title, genealogy, class, sex, or mana. Theologically, the idea was based on the precept that all people are the children of God. Just as God loves all, so ought we to love all human beings, for we are all of equal worth in his sight. The teaching sowed the seed for egalitarianism and democracy which by 1840 had been partly translated into the first constitution of the Hawaiian kingdom. Equality among commoners was not an alien idea to the maka'āinana, for whom 'ohana values such as kōkua and laulima tended to encourage it. But it was most definitely a revolutionary concept as far as the ali'i were concerned, and whether they ever fully accepted it, even after constitutional and democratic reforms were introduced, is questionable. Eventually, as modern Hawaiian society evolved into a "classless" society American-style, the traditional elitism was replaced by egalitarianism. For many Hawaiians this has meant a healthy irreverence for titles or claims to royal ancestry, and a disdain for anyone "pulling rank." (But for a few, it has meant the loss of someone to look up to, of someone who will tell us what to do.) In any case, the linking of aloha and equality further strengthened the sociopsychological and philosophical importance of the doubled value in the minds of the "new" Hawaiians.

Yet another aspect was added to aloha when Hawaiians were admonished to turn the other cheek and to love their enemies. That adjuration must have been as startling for Hawaiians as it was for Jews when they first heard the new doctrine that contravened the much less charitable Mosaic Law. Hawaiians had been taught to curse back those who cursed you and to hire sorcerers to pray to death those who abused and hated you, lest they do the same to you. Now, all in the name of the new aloha, they were being told to reverse centuries of conditioned behavior based on reciprocation. Whether the gradual incorporation of this into their value system has helped Hawaiians to increase their "tolerance" for bad behavior, particularly by outsiders, is open to study, but no doubt it has played a part in shaping the "coping skills" they have developed in general.

The traditional perception of aloha may have been changed in one further way when its focus was shifted from interpersonal or man-god relationships to materialistic or philosophical abstractions. In other words, during the nineteenth century aloha got a whole new set of referents: Truth, Beauty, Justice, Mercy, Brotherhood, Eternal Life, Salvation, and so on. The Christianized Hawaiian could think and talk in terms of "loving" objects or ideas that he could not even have imagined loving before his conversion.

The encounter between aloha and the Gospel of Love produced the inevitable synthesis of a traditional Hawaiian and a foreign set of values. By and large, the elements from both sources were compatible. On the one hand, the agape-love of Christianity gave aloha an impersonal and altruistic dimension that it did not have before, and, on the other hand, took away aloha's strong emphasis on reciprocity. Agape-love also provided aloha with a theological and philosophical frame of reference that it could not have had before. One of the more significant results of this marriage is the way in which aloha has gradually assumed a position as the ranking value in Hawaiian culture, both traditional and neotraditional.

Perhaps the analysis presented here is better thought of as a preliminary study rather than the final one, for in the Christianization of Hawaiians can be found a vast amount of material awaiting the serious student of the history and the evolution of ideas.

"Aloha . . . Pure Gold or Tinsel-Covered Commercialism?"

One of the signs of our times is the willingness to suspect that nothing is safe from being commercialized. In the minds of many people that is certainly what has happened to aloha. This is undoubtedly one of the reasons why in 1975 the Hawai'i Committee for the Humanities funded an islandwide public discussion on the question asked above. Not surprisingly, most of the participants ended up agreeing that aloha was "tinsel."

Whatever one's feelings may be about commercialism, it has an enormous influence on our lives. And so, appropriately, we should look at the dynamics of aloha in terms of its commercialization. The results of this examination should shed some light on the extent to which aloha has affected contemporary life in Hawai'i.

The commercialization of aloha goes back more than a century, when Hawaiian monarchs still ruled. The *Hawaiian Kingdom Statistical and Commercial Directory and Tourist Guide of 1880–81* reported that different commercial articles were being sold with the word aloha shown on them. Those articles included gift or souvenir items meant for Hawai'i's early tourists, who started coming in the 1860s. In 1880 King Kalākaua was still on the throne, and we may assume that—if he was consulted—he saw nothing wrong either in the use of aloha for commercial products or in the promotion of tourism in the islands. (Incidentally, the king was delighted to allow Agosto Dias, the Portuguese maker of 'ukulele, to use the royal crown as a trademark stamped on every instrument he manufactured.)

Interestingly, the most famous product of aloha for the time was Queen Lili'uokalani's composition "Aloha 'Oe," which she published in 1885 in Boston and which became a "best-seller" for many years. Another musical product which carried the name aloha was the instrument which the Aloha 'Ukulele Company produced in the 1920s. By this time, we should note, Hawaiian music was the most commercialized part of Hawaiian culture, as Hawaiian troubadours and dancers had been performing all over the world on regular circuits, selling their music with their aloha. The best known of the many products was the "Aloha Shirt," patented in 1936, and practically the symbol of Hawaiian-style living. The style was very popular with local people, including Hawaiians, and in time became an item that every tourist wanted to wear or to take home as a remembrance of his venture into exotic Hawai'i.

During all those decades no public outcry rose up, of the kind often heard today against the commercialization of aloha. This is not to say that some Hawaiians and others may not have been offended by the business, but none of the great Hawaiian traditionalists of the time, such as George Mossman, spoke out against the exploitation of aloha by businessmen. Mossman himself, in fact, was deeply involved in promoting his Lalani Village in Waikīkī to the tourist trade. We do not mean to infer that Hawaiians had no sensitivity toward the commercialization of their symbols or traditions, but on this specific issue of aloha they showed either a high degree of tolerance or a complete indifference.

In pointing out examples of the commercialization of Hawaiian culture, a present-day Hawaiian leader likes to refer to the number of companies listed in the O'ahu telephone directory that used the name aloha. Thus we have Aloha Airlines, Aloha Motors, Aloha Petroleum, and many others. Closer study of this matter, however, shows far less commercialization than is implied in the charge. For example, the earliest such example in Honolulu appeared in the 1900–1901 *Directory of Honolulu and the Hawaiian Territory*: the entry read "Aloha House Lodgings, 4H Vineyard Boulevard." By 1910 four such entries appeared, including the "Aloha 'Āina Company," which published the *Aloha 'Āina* newspaper, whose editor at the time was Edward K. Hanapī. In 1920 six companies were listed; in 1935, twenty-one; in 1946, twenty-two. And by 1982, according to the O'ahu telephone directory, the number had grown to 193, of which about 12 were directly involved in tourism. When we consider the fact that more than 40,000 firms were licensed in the state at that time, 193 seems quite insignificant.

Out of fairness to business owners who have used aloha in their company names, we should say that some chose it without any intention of exploiting it solely for profit. The president of one of these firms, a Hawaiian, said that he selected the name because with it he wanted to make a statement about his philosophy of business. The word, after all, does convey a positive spirit of mutual trust and service, which is the way in which he tries to conduct his business. Thus, from his point of view, his is a positive use of the good things and feelings the word implies, rather than a negative use. In other words, this is not a one-sided case of commercializing aloha, but of "aloha-izing" a business as well.

If asked, most people, both Hawaiian and non-Hawaiian, would maintain that the commercialization of aloha has occurred mainly in the "hospitality industry." If one accepts history as written by Gavan Daws, commercialization of hospitality was a calculated move by the leaders of the tourist industry. In his *Shoal of Time* Daws wrote:

> The Hawai'i Visitors Bureau, trying to establish just what was so attractive about the islands, concluded that the word "aloha" was crucial. It was a Hawaiian word, and it could be used as an affectionate greeting, or as an expression of good will or love. It went together with a kiss on the cheek and the gift of a lei, a flower garland. It captivated tourists descending from the skies, grateful for safe passage but still faintly stunned and disoriented after hours of high-speed travel westward in pursuit of the sun. If the tourist industry could really dispense good will, or even a convincing imitation (a plastic lei?), the value of aloha as a business commodity would be incalculable.

Whether or not this somewhat conspiratorial arrangement really happened is academic at this point, because such a decision seems to have been made in one form or another in the early 1900s, by the forerunners of the Hawai'i Visitors Bureau. And although current directors of the tourist industry might deny or rationalize the selling of aloha as a business commodity, many people see it differently.

Recently one Hawaiian activist has said: "Millions upon millions are spent to sell the images of the Hawaiian people and their 'aloha spirit'—the Hawaiian culture and the beautiful 'āina. . . .

How long can you sell the image before they see the scam?"
(*Honolulu Advertiser*, January 3, 1982).
  Another Hawaiian leader put the problem more poetically.

The intimation that *aloha* might well have become a thinly tinseled
veneer has a definite ring of truth to it. What was once so freely,
spontaneously and generously given has been corrupted into a
plastic lei and a series of flashy smiles and quick smooches for the
photographer at the tourist lūʻau who must hurry in order to get
the prints out in the next morning's rush for souvenir pictures of an
Island feast. And so we are told by our good business advisers that
we must continue this thing called *aloha* in light of our financial
requirements. . . . I would suggest that given the realities of our
situation, perhaps it is time for us to bury the word—to give *aloha*
an honorable funeral. (Hawaiʻi Committee for the Humanities,
1977)

  Such sentiments are shared by some Hawaiians and some non-
Hawaiians as well, but what seems clear in the comments of these
Hawaiian leaders is that a larger issue than just aloha is at stake.
Aloha is the "point guard," so to speak, for Hawaiian culture as a
whole. And the commercialization of the culture is really the heart
of the matter. But commercialization in this context means more
than profiteering; in fact, in the public mind it is almost indistinguishable from such terms as "prostituting" or "corrupting" the
culture. What all this refers to is anything—acts, words, pictures,
gestures, objects, attitudes—that desecrates, insults, violates, or
destroys what Hawaiians believe to be vital and sacred in their history, environment, beliefs, and themselves. Thus, the merchandiz-
ing of the lei greeting which involves a young man (or a girl) placing a lei (not always a plastic one) around the neck of an arriving
tourist, with a perfunctory kiss thrown in, is insulting to Hawaiians because it turns a traditionally warm and personal gesture of
respect into a mechanical, impersonal, and false business transaction. It turns what is supposed to be a moment of social celebration into a cash proposition, truly a reversal of ends and means.
Similarly, the marketing of an ʻōkolehao bottle cast in the shape of
a helmeted aliʻi wearing a feather cloak is to Hawaiians an insult,
because it demeans the cherished symbols and values of the sacred
chiefs. Not all Hawaiians will agree on these or other examples,

for they have not yet considered such standards and measures that might be taken to control commercialization. But the point is clear: the abuse of aloha is only a part of the much larger phenomenon of cheapening Hawai'i.

The Politicization of Aloha

If aloha has been commercialized, it has also been politicized by both Hawaiians and non-Hawaiians alike. (Perhaps none of us should be surprised at that, for in Hawai'i nearly everything eventually becomes a matter of politics, this being the nature of island communities.) Since one doesn't hear or read much about it, at least politicization with respect to aloha or Hawaiian culture does not have the same overlay of venality that commercialization does. Nonetheless, the two processes function in the same way. Simply put, politicization is the process of making something that is normally nonpolitical into a political object through the use of political agencies, symbols, funds, personalities, and so on, all in order to achieve political ends—that is, practical influence over others. The goal of both commercialization and politicization is the same, namely, power, though in slightly different forms, the former called profit and the latter, influence.

A good example of this in recent years was the use of aloha by a former taxi driver, Louisa K. Rice, who in May 1972 formed an organization called the Aboriginal Lands of Hawaiian Ancestry, whose purpose was to seek compensation from the United States Congress for losses suffered by Hawaiians because of the overthrow of the Hawaiian monarchy in 1893 and other unjust actions committed after that year by the United States or its agents. The acronym of the new organization was "A.L.O.H.A.," which, of course, Rice and her supporters promoted as such.

Rice's intention in the use of political means to pursue her political ends is beyond question. One of the first things she did was to elevate a former Honolulu city councilman and perennial seeker of political office to be president of the organization. She also succeeded in persuading a congressional House subcommittee to come to Hawai'i and conduct hearings, after which she dispatched a delegation to Washington to seek $1 billion in reparations as well as the return of surplus federal lands.

Like so many other Hawaiian organizations that seem to mushroom overnight, this one faded away after a couple of active years. It does not seem to have done any harm; on the contrary, it left an important legacy—the identification and expression of an issue of such powerful appeal to Hawaiians (and to some non-Hawaiians as well) that it spurred many people to organize more effective organizations. One of these was Alu Like, Inc., a socioeconomic and quasipublic agency funded by Congress. Another was the Office of Hawaiian Affairs, established by the Hawai'i State Constitutional Convention of 1978.

Much more significant is the use of aloha in the term aloha 'āina by the Protect Kaho'olawe 'Ohana movement. Not since the turn of the century, when Hawaiian activist John Wise and others used the name for a publishing company and a newspaper as part of their political movement, has the phrase been employed with so much calculation and impact. It means love of the land, or the country, and therefore can be synonymous with patriotism. Very few ideas can generate more political interest than loving and protecting the 'āina in Hawai'i.

In its early years (that is, during the mid-1970s), the organization's name was the Protect Kaho'olawe Aloha 'Āina Movement. In their collection of remembrances about Kaho'olawe, Walter Ritte and Richard Sawyer, both of whom were arrested for trespassing when they made unauthorized landings on the island, wrote that one of their goals was ensuring "through *Aloha 'Āina*, the proper use of Hawai'i's natural resources" and "instilling the value of *Aloha 'Āina*." In order to achieve these goals, they said, they intended to educate the public to "the relevance of Aloha to the entire world. By beginning at home with *Aloha 'Āina*—one aspect of *Aloha*—we can better understand the concept of *Aloha* as a universal value." Politically speaking, aloha 'āina meant the preservation of as many traditional rights as possible that were connected with the land, including access to trails, historic sites, beaches, and so on, either through or on private properties; the inalienability of certain lands; and the restoration to Hawaiians the primary use of lands ceded to the federal government.

While the supporters of the movement may not see it as a political organization, their objectives, legal obstacles, remedies, even opponents, are essentially political. Neither their cause nor their tactics have endeared them to everybody, whether Hawaiian or non-Hawaiian, but they have taken hold of a dramatic issue that

has afforded them more media exposure than any other movements have received. Consequently, they have managed to dis-
seminate their message widely, reaching the mainland and many
foreign countries. Their members have grown in number and
influence. One of their original leaders has used the movement to
advance his political standing and to broaden his involvement in
other issues, such as land development, tourism, and Hawaiian
culture.

The politicization of aloha in this instance has drawn little or no
criticism from anyone, and no charges of "corrupting" or "prostituting" the culture. On the contrary, the movement has received
widespread public approbation because of its concern for the land
and the values it represents. Apparently as long as such support
can be gained, it should have no fear of criticism. Nonetheless, the
movement still represents an object lesson in the use of aloha for
political ends.

"Is Hawai'i's Aloha Slipping?"

In 1972 sociologist Andrew Lind, who has been observing ethnic
relations in Hawai'i for more than thirty years, asked this question
of a Honolulu audience (*Honolulu Star-Bulletin*, July 27, 1972).
He concluded that it definitely was slipping. One of the basic reasons was that hospitality and generosity tend to atrophy where
associations are made among strangers, and that increasingly life
in modern Hawai'i had become one passed among strangers. He
was especially interested in how the aloha spirit was faring among
Hawaiians, and his assessment did not surprise anyone. "Considering the sort of experiences which the Hawaiian people have
undergone, the decline of the *aloha* spirit is easy to understand."
He attributed this in part to a "basic conflict" between aloha and
the "Protestant work ethic."

> There is an unavoidable conflict, as many of our *haole* youth are
> belatedly discovering, between an ethic, seemingly based on the
> principle of "everyman for himself and the devil take the hind-
> most," and one embracing affection and mutual regard for one's
> neighbors, as a central guide for life.
>   It might be said that a basic reason for the relatively poor record
> for the Hawaiians, economically . . . is the adherence by so many

of them to the spirit of *aloha*—of mutuality and sharing, of what was central in primitive Christianity—whereas most of the arrivals during the past two centuries have accepted unquestioningly the principles of the Protestant ethic—of individual initiative, material gain, and private enterprise.

He finished by saying, "The Hawaiians, of all the ethnic groups, have most obviously been caught on the horns of this dilemma, but so are we all to a greater or lesser degree, insofar as we presume to retain our truly human qualities."

As Lind saw conditions in 1972, naturally he assumed that aloha was waning quickly among Hawaiians. It was a dynamic time, shaped by a series of well-publicized incidents involving Hawaiians in dramatic protests, such as championing the Kalama Valley pig farmers against the Bishop Estate, and the emergence of several Hawaiian organizations that heralded the Hawaiian renaissance. In an atmosphere charged with militant demonstrations and declarations of Hawaiian rights and power, many of which were directed against the "establishment" with some unsubtle racial overtones, many people in the community wondered about the aloha spirit and the new "brown power."

But we must take Lind's explanation of aloha's decline with some caution. No doubt a conflict exists between the traditional aloha 'ohana values and practices as they are opposed to the Protestant work ethic and its associated economic system. But historically the heavy damage to Hawaiians had happened long before the 1970s, although many of its effects still linger even now among some Hawaiians. Furthermore, by the 1970s Hawaiians had long given up on "primal economics" and understood that depending on aloha alone is no way to earn a living. In other words, no causal relationship links aloha as such and the poor economic conditions of Hawaiians today. The causes must be found in such practical factors as educational and training opportunities, parental guidance, financial capabilities, and individual attitudes. However, a strong relationship does exist between how much generosity and hospitality—hence aloha—a person can show in the form of feasting and giving, if he doesn't have the necessary resources either in money or time to back them up.

Actually, we are dealing here with two separate questions. One is whether Hawaiians in fact practice aloha more now than they did before, and the other is whether they think of it as being as important a value as they did before. The answer to the first question seems to be clear that, generally, demonstrating aloha now in the traditional form of external giving is harder to do. For example, two or three decades ago baby lūʻau were much more common, partly because they were affordable and could be prepared at home (i.e., a family had access to an imu in its backyard, and did not have to bother about health and other regulations). Of course, gauging the subjective capacity of the Hawaiian today to feel or think in terms of "aloha behavior," is more difficult, but our guess suggests that that emotional and spiritual capacity is probably as high as it has ever been. This partly reflects the increasing improvement of a Hawaiian's overall situation, and especially his sense of identity, for when people feel good about themselves they are much more willing to share with others both themselves and their belongings.

Hawaiians today still regard aloha as highly important, in comparison with other Hawaiian values. We have talked with many Hawaiians during the last few years about this, and we cannot recall anyone denying its importance. In our many discussions with participants in the Hoʻokanaka Workshops on Hawaiian values, aloha always ranked among the top few. When participants were asked to evaluate the relative importance of twenty Hawaiian values aloha was ranked number one (see the Introduction for the complete listing). Although nothing short of a major opinion survey or much more extensive personal interviewing of Hawaiians can provide us with conclusive statistics on the matter, we believe that the pattern of response from a larger sampling of Hawaiians would be more or less comparable to that of the workshop survey.

Thus, despite the occasional statement in the media that aloha is "finished" among Hawaiians, or that "we have given too much," it still holds a high place in their list of personal values.

Everybody's Property

Once at a public discussion on the "Aloha Spirit," an Oriental minister who evidently had lost patience with Hawaiians who kept insisting that aloha was unique to them, shouted, "Aloha or love is universal. The Hawaiians don't have a lock on it." He probably spoke for other non-Hawaiians who dislike the proprietary way in which Hawaiians hold on to aloha as if they owned it. On the other hand, some people don't care if the Hawaiians do "own" it, but simply want to share in it. As Gene Hunter, a former *Honolulu Advertiser* reporter wrote, "We have the Hawaiians to thank for it. They have given of it, as they have given away so much. But it is not exclusive to the Hawaiians. It can be shared by all" (October 21, 1970).

All of us must recognize that for a long while, a strong communal claim has been made among Hawai'i's people, either to "owning" or sharing the Aloha Spirit. The evidence is all around us. It has been appropriated and institutionalized as the unofficial name of the state by legislative decree. It's been worked into our everyday speech and thought. And it's been commercialized in every direction. Whether we like this or not, aloha has been lifted above its Hawaiian origins, to become as much public property as air and sunshine. Aloha is everybody's prerogative—and should be everybody's gift.

EPILOGUE

Who and what is a Hawaiian? We have searched far and wide for answers to this question, not because we felt they were somewhere beyond us but because we need to see us from the perspective of our common humanity. Whether Japanese, Chinese, English, Indian, black, Maori, or whatever, we all belong to the one species and therefore are fundamentally the same. After we strip away our superficial differences of size and shape and color, the human being in all of us shares the same physiological, emotional, and spiritual essentials—the experiences of birth, love, work, play, reverence, fear, joy, sleep, health, survival, and, eventually, of death. Thus, to understand who and what we are is to accept first our common humanity. As obvious as this statement may be, some of us who are preoccupied by our differences (thinking that they make each of us unique) often forget our similarity, and end up with a very distorted view of our all-too-common selves.

Because we find a little bit of ourselves in everybody else, we carried our search among the Greeks and Romans, Egyptians and Jews, Europeans and Asians, Incas and Sioux and Hindus, and all the Polynesians. We compared some of their ideas and practices of worship, mythology, ritual and symbolism, logic, philosophy, science and technology. We examined the statements of "thinking people," from Aristotle, Plato, and Lao Tse, to Eliade, Suzuki, Leibnitz, Darwin, Einstein, and Lovelock. We analyzed some widely held theories about natural and human phenomena, such as cosmic intelligence, relativity, biological evolution, scarcity (in economic theory), cosmology, and time. And we also observed and commented upon the similarities and dissimilarities between peoples and cultures of the world past and present.

One of our first conclusions from this comparative review is that, although they were isolated in the middle of the Pacific Ocean and shut off from intellectual, economic, and political contact with most of the world, Hawaiians before 1778 dealt with many of the same social, economic, and political issues, the same philosophical questions about the meaning of life and death, similar economic problems of productivity, distribution, capital and labor, and the basic technological phenomena of toolmaking, specialization, quality, and performance, among many other problems. And, like people everywhere, they used their brain—the same marvelous organ endowed with intelligence that is given to all races of human beings—and their five senses, together with their powers of reason and analysis, creativity, and intuition. In the end, they developed their own genius to explain their universe, to ensure their survival, to exploit their natural resources, to resolve their social dilemmas, and to achieve their own standards of excellence. And at doing all that they succeeded admirably.

We need not look down at either the quality or the size of Hawaiian "civilization," because it was appropriate for its time and place. Indeed, in several fields of endeavor, such as agriculture, botany, navigation, and socioreligious organization, the accomplishments of the Hawaiians, given their stage of development and the limitations of their natural resources, were comparable to those of any other civilization at the same stages of evolution. We have tried to emphasize this point, even at the expense of belaboring it, in order to lay to rest any ill-founded feelings of inferiority that we modern Hawaiians may harbor toward ka poʻe kahiko. This notion of Hawaiian inferiority did not originate with Hawaiians, but came from Western outsiders, who decided that their white civilization was superior to anything brown, red, yellow, or black. Having made the point, however, we shall rise above the temptation to judge civilizations and peoples in terms of "better" or "worse," for ultimately that is a foolish exercise in prejudice, founded on personal preference or selected lies.

Another conclusion brings us closer to home: although we have looked for contrasts and comparisons among many cultures and peoples, in the end we must look to the source—nānā i ke kumu—ourselves. For whatever we are, the questions are not out there, in the world beyond, but here, in Hawai'i, within us. To look anywhere else is to make the search meaningless. Unfortunately, for many modern Hawaiians (and for others as well), all too often this search in faraway places has characterized their quest for self-identity. To put the case bluntly, many foolish Hawaiians have tried to become what they are not, and never can be. They have tried to be somebody other than themselves, as ancestors, environment, and spirit have made them. Theirs is a hopeless and frustrating ego-trip. None of us can undo or conceal or wash away or forget who or what we are. Our genetic imprint remains forever, an inherent part of our consciousness. To pretend that this is not so is to delude ourselves. But to accept the reality of our Hawaiianness is to enrich ourselves and to open wide the doors to our self-fulfillment— and our own spiritual salvation.

In a real sense, this book is about our accepting ourselves. We are a people with a profound capacity for experiencing that which is extraordinary, sacred, or kapu; a people with an abiding faith in the shared divinity—the mana—of man, nature, and the cosmos beyond; a people able from the primal past to explain through myth, symbolism, and ritual the transcendent realities of life; a people "in sync" with the rhythms of the universe; a people who see time not as a linear measurement but as a qualitative experience; a people with an unsurpassed sense of place and of the unity of all things. We believe in the science of common sense, and we see in evolution the realization of the human potential; we share belief in the power of language and in the power of the remembering mind. We place the possibility of perfectability of the spirit even above life. We have the deepest respect for technology and the technician so long as they serve our highest ultimate interests. We accept economic behavior based not on scarcity and greed, but on relative abundance and giving. We idealize our leaders who show such tested qualities as mālama, or caring; ha'aha'a, or humility; kūpono, or integrity; na'auao, or wisdom; koa, or courage. We have made aloha a central value, but one no more elevated than ho'okipa, hospitality; lokomaika'i, generosity; 'olu'olu, graciousness; lōkahi, harmony; pa'ahana, industry; ho'omana, spirituality; kōkua, helpfulness; and kū i ka nu'u, excellence.

Yet our search is not ended. We have made a genuine start,

but much more needs to be explored. We have not fully examined the whole scope of Hawaiian aesthetic values which, while they may have been perceived in early times as being more functional and technical than artistic, are viewed today primarily in aesthetic terms. Nor have we adequately considered the important ideas and values connected with the human body, either in terms of its health or as a means to knowing pleasure, recreation, and art. Nor have we devoted enough attention to the social customs and attitudes of Hawaiians, especially in ancient times. Although we have not covered these matters extensively, partly because they have been treated by others, still they constitute important parts of our understanding of who and what Hawaiians are.

Perhaps a search of this kind is never over, in that each generation must launch its own quest. Time and circumstances inevitably affect our perceptions, attitudes, and standards. More important, every generation seeks to make its own mark, to use its own creative resources, to undertake its own challenges, and to celebrate its own triumphs. Thus, what we may perceive today as values that ought to hold true for our past, present, and future, the next generations may well think otherwise. This is obviously an option we must yield to them.

But at least we have tried to fulfill an obligation we owe to this generation—and to generations past of our kūpuna. We have shown that, like them, we too can stand tall: kū kanaka.

BIBLIOGRAPHY

Given the wide range of ideas touched upon in this book, this bibliography is hardly exhaustive. It cites references mentioned in the text as well as sources from which important ideas were developed. Many other publications are referred to in one way or another in the text. If a notable lack of Hawaiian-language sources is apparent, that is partly because of our inadequacy in the language and primarily because very few sources cover the period before 1778. In fact, all the standard Hawaiian works on early Hawai'i written by historians David Malo, Samuel M. Kamakau, and Kepelino have been translated into English. Together with the works of Kawena Pūku'i, they provide most of our information about old Hawai'i.

This list, of course, does not cover oral sources of information from numerous persons and groups inside and outside Hawai'i. Some of this information came from formal interviews, but much more came from informal conversations, discussions at meetings, seminars, and conferences, not to mention a few instances of contrived eavesdropping. Some of the reflections regarding the actions and ideas of American or Canadian Indians, Chamorros in Guam, Javanese, Japanese, and Europeans are based on our years of travel and residence in many countries.

Abbott, Isabella A. 1982. "The Ethnobotany of Hawaiian Taro." *Native Planters* 1, no. 1 (Spring).
Adams, Romanzo. 1937. *Interracial Marriage in Hawai'i*. New York: Macmillan.
Akana, Akaiko. 1918. *The Sinews for Racial Development*. Honolulu.
Alu Like, Inc. 1980. *A Report on Educational, Employment and Training Needs of Native Hawaiian Youth*. Prep. by George K. Ikeda and James H. Jackson. Social Science Research Institute, Univ. of Hawai'i, Honolulu.

Ancient Hawaiian Civilization. 1965. Honolulu: Kamehameha Schools Press/ Charles E. Tuttle.

Andersen, Johannes C. 1969. *Myths and Legends of the Polynesians.* Rutland, Vt.: Charles E. Tuttle.

Andrews, Lorrin. 1922. *A Dictionary of the Hawaiian Language.* Rev. by Henry H. Parker. Honolulu: Board of Commissioners of the Public Archives of the Territory of Hawai'i.

Anthony, Pualani A. 1979. "Hawaiian Nonverbal Communication: Two Classroom Applications." Univ. of Hawai'i, Honolulu. Unpublished paper.

Apple, Russell A. 1973. *The Hawaiian Thatched House.* Norfolk Island: Island Heritage.

Ardrey, Robert. 1966. *The Territorial Imperative.* New York: Atheneum Publishers.

Asimov, Isaac. 1960. *The Wellsprings of Life.* London: Abelard-Schuman.

Barbotin, Edmond. 1975. *The Humanity of Man.* Trans. from the French by Matthew J. O'Connell. Maryknoll, N.Y.: Orbis Books.

Barlow, Fred. 1951. *Mental Prodigies.* New York: Hutchinson's Scientific & Technical Publications.

Barrère, Dorothy B. 1969. *The Kumuhonua Legends.* Pacific Anthropological Records, no. 3. Honolulu: Bishop Museum Press.

Barrett, William, ed. 1956. *Zen Buddhism: Selected Writings of D. T. Suzuki.* Garden City, N.Y.: Doubleday.

Barrow, Terence. 1978. *Captain Cook in Hawai'i.* Honolulu: Island Heritage.

Bastian, Adolf. 1881. *Die Heilige Sage der Polynesier: Cosmogonie und Theogonie.* Leipzig: F. A. Brockhaus.

Bateson, Gregory. 1979. *Mind and Nature.* New York: Bantam Books.

Beaglehole, Ernest. 1937. *Some Modern Hawaiians.* University of Hawai'i Research Publications, no. 19. Univ. of Hawai'i, Honolulu.

Beaglehole, J. C. 1967. *The Journals of Captain James Cook.* Vol. 3, pts. 1 and 2. Cambridge: Cambridge Univ. Press.

Beane, Wendell C., and William Doty. 1975. *Myths, Rites, Symbols: A Mircea Eliade Reader.* Vol. 1. New York: Harper & Row.

Beckwith, Martha W. 1951. *The Kumulipo: A Hawaiian Creation Chant.* Chicago: Univ. of Chicago Press.

———. 1970. *Hawaiian Mythology.* Honolulu: Univ. Press of Hawaii.

———, ed. 1932. *Kepelino's Traditions of Hawai'i.* B. P. Bishop Museum Bulletin 95. Honolulu: Bishop Museum Press.

Bell, Eric T. 1933. *Numerology.* Westport, Conn.: Hyperion Press.

Bellairs, Angus d'A. 1966. *The World of Reptiles.* New York: American Elsevier.

Bellwood, Peter S. 1978. *The Polynesians: Prehistory of an Island People.* London: Thames & Hudson.

Bendann, E. 1930. *Death Customs: An Analytical Study of Burial Rites.* New York: Alfred A. Knopf.

Ben-Dasan, Isaiah. 1972. *The Japanese and the Jews.* New York: Weatherhill.

Bergamini, David. 1970. *Mathematics.* New York: Time-Life Books.

Berkeley, Edmund C. 1966. *A Guide to Mathematics for the Intelligent Nonmathematician.* New York: Simon & Schuster.

Berlitz, Charles F. 1972. *Mysteries from Forgotten Worlds*. Garden City, N.Y.: Doubleday.

Best, Elsdon. 1921. "Polynesian Mnemonics." *New Zealand Journal of Science and Technology* 4, no. 2.

———. 1954. *Spiritual and Mental Concepts of the Maori*. Dominion Museum Monograph, no. 2. Wellington: R. E. Owen.

———. 1974. *The Maori as He Was*. Wellington: A. R. Shearer.

Bevan, Edwyn R. 1938. *Symbolism and Belief*. London: George Allen & Unwin.

Bingham, Hiram. 1981. *A Residence of Twenty-one Years in the Sandwich Islands*. Tokyo: Charles E. Tuttle.

Blair, Lawrence. 1976. *Rhythms of Vision: The Changing Patterns of Belief*. New York: Schocken Books.

Bocock, Robert. 1974. *Ritual in Industrial Society*. London: George Allen & Unwin.

Bourdillon, M. F. C., and Meyer Fortes, eds. 1980. *Sacrifice*. London: Academic Press.

Bowers, John K. 1978. "Privacy, Territoriality, Personal Space, and Personality: A Laboratory Study of Interrelationships." Ph.D. diss., Univ. of Hawai'i.

Brandwein, Paul, Fletcher G. Watson, and Paul E. Blackwood. 1958. *Teaching High School Science: A Book of Methods*. New York: Harcourt, Brace.

Brenneman, Walter L. 1979. *Spirals: A Study in Symbol, Myth and Ritual*. Washington: Univ. Press of America.

Bridgman, Percy W. 1950. *Reflections of a Physicist*. New York: Philosophical Library.

Brigham, William T. 1902. *Stone Implements and Stone Work of the Ancient Hawaiians*. Memoirs of the B. P. Bishop Museum, vol. 1, no. 4. Honolulu: Bishop Museum.

Brown, Joseph E. "Becoming Part of It." *Parabola* 7, no. 3.

Brunes, Tons. 1967. *The Secrets of Ancient Geometry—and Its Use*. Vol. 2. Copenhagen: Intn'l Science Publishers.

Buck, Peter H. 1970. *Anthropology and Religion*. Hamden, Conn.: Archon Books.

———. 1982. *The Coming of the Maori*. Wellington: Maori Purposes Fund Board.

Burford, Alison. 1972. *Craftsmen in Greek and Roman Society*. Ithaca, N.Y.: Cornell Univ. Press.

Bushnell, O. A. 1966. "Hygiene and Sanitation among the Ancient Hawaiians." *Hawai'i Historical Review*, October.

Bynum, David E. 1978. *The Daemon in the Wood: A Study of Oral Narrative Patterns*. Cambridge: Harvard Univ. Press.

Cajori, Florian. 1961. *A History of Elementary Mathematics*. London: Macmillan.

Campbell, Archibald. 1967. *A Voyage around the World from 1806 to 1812*. New York: Da Capo Press.

Campbell, Joseph. 1974. *The Mythic Image*. Princeton: Princeton Univ. Press.

———. 1977a. *The Masks of God: Oriental Mythology*. New York: Penguin Books.

————. 1977b. *The Masks of God: Primitive Mythology.* New York: Penguin
    Books.
Capra, Fritjof. 1975. *The Tao of Physics.* New York: Bantam Books.
Carlquist, Sherwin. 1980. *Hawai'i: A Natural History.* 2d ed. Honolulu: SB
    Printers for the Pacific Tropical Botanical Garden.
Cassel, Russell N., and Robert L. Heichberger, eds. *Leadership Development:
    Theory and Practice.* North Quincy, Mass.: Christopher Publishing
    House.
Cassirer, Ernst. 1946. *Language and Myth.* Trans. by Susanne K. Langer. New
    York: Dover Publications.
Chaplin, George, and Glenn D. Paige, eds. 1973. *Hawai'i 2000: Continuing
    Experiment in Anticipatory Democracy.* Honolulu: Univ. Press of Hawaii
    for the Governor's Conference on the Year 2000.
Charlot, John. 1983. *Chanting the Universe: Hawaiian Religious Culture.* Hong
    Kong: Emphasis Intn'l.
Chinen, Jon J. 1958. *The Great Māhele: Hawai'i's Land Division of 1848.*
    Honolulu: Univ. of Hawaii Press.
Chobot, Neal L. 1977. "Aurobindo's Concept of Spiritual Evolution." Ph.D.
    diss., Univ. of Hawai'i.
Cirlot, Juan E. 1962. *A Dictionary of Symbols.* New York: Philosophical
    Library.
Clark, Dennis. 1967. *Work and the Human Spirit.* New York: Sheed & Ward.
Clark, Ephraim W. 1839. "Hawaiian Method of Computation." *Hawaiian Spec-
    tator.*
Clayre, Alasdair. 1974. *Work and Play.* New York: Harper & Row.
Conze, Edward. 1951. *Buddhism: Its Essence and Development.* New York: Phi-
    losophical Library.
Cordy, Ross H. 1978. "A Study of Prehistoric Social Change: The Development
    of Complex Societies in the Hawaiian Islands." Ph.D. diss., Univ. of
    Hawai'i.
Cornell, James. 1981. *The First Stargazers: An Introduction to the Origins of
    Astronomy.* New York: Charles Scribner's Sons.
Cox, J. Halley. 1970. *Hawaiian Petroglyphs.* B. P. Bishop Museum Special Pub-
    lication 60. Honolulu: Bishop Museum Press.
Creighton, Thomas H. 1978. *The Lands of Hawai'i: Their Use and Misuse.*
    Honolulu: Univ. Press of Hawaii.
Crosby, Philip F. 1979. *Quality is Free.* New York: McGraw-Hill.
Dalton, George, ed. 1971. *Economic Development and Social Change.* Garden
    City, N.Y.: Natural History Press.
Darwin, Charles. 1952. *The Origin of Species by Means of Natural Selection.*
    Chicago: Encyclopedia Britannica.
Daws, Gavan. 1968. *Shoal of Time: A History of the Hawaiian Islands.* Hono-
    lulu: Univ. Press of Hawaii.
Degener, Otto. 1930. *Illustrated Guide to the More Common or Noteworthy
    Ferns and Flowering Plants of Hawai'i National Parks.* Honolulu: Hono-
    lulu Star-Bulletin.
Dening, Greg. 1980. *Islands and Beaches.* Melbourne: Melbourne Univ. Press.

Derrick, Christopher. 1972. *The Delicate Creation: Towards a Theology of the Environment.* Old Greenwich, Conn.: Davin-Adair.

De Vos, George, and Lola Romanucci-Ross, eds. 1975. *Ethnic Identity, Cultural Continuities and Change.* Palo Alto, Ca.: Mayfield Publishing.

Dibble, Sheldon. 1909. *History of the Sandwich Islands.* Honolulu: Thrum Publishers.

Dodge, Ernest. 1978. *Hawaiian and Other Polynesian Gourds.* Honolulu: Topgallant Publishing.

Dubos, René. 1968. *So Human an Animal.* New York: Charles Scribner's Sons.

Duffy, Joseph W. 1964. *Power: Prime Mover of Technology.* Bloomington, Ill.: McKnight & McKnight.

Earle, Timothy. 1978. *Economic and Social Organization of a Complex Chiefdom: The Halele'a District, Kaua'i, Hawai'i.* Museum of Anthropology, Univ. of Michigan, no. 63. Ann Arbor: Univ. of Mich. Press.

Edmonson, Charles H. 1946. *Reef and Shore Fauna of Hawai'i.* B. P. Bishop Museum Special Publication 22. Honolulu: Bishop Museum Press.

Elbert, Samuel H. 1957. "The Chief in Hawaiian Mythology." *Journal of American Folklore* 70, no. 278 (October/December).

———. 1962. "Symbolism in Hawaiian Poetry." *Etc.: A Review of General Semantics* 18, no. 4 (February).

Elbert, Samuel H., and Noelani Māhoe. 1970. *Nā Mele o Hawai'i Nei.* Honolulu: Univ. Press of Hawaii.

Eliade, Mircea. 1957. *Myths, Dreams, and Mysteries.* Trans. by Philip Mairet. New York: Harper & Row.

———. 1959. *The Sacred and the Profane.* Trans. from the French by Willard R. Trask. New York: Harcourt Brace Jovanovich.

———. 1963. *Myth and Reality.* Trans. from the French by Willard R. Trask. New York: Harper & Row.

———. 1974. *The Myth of the Eternal Return, or Cosmos and History.* Trans. from the French by Willard R. Trask. Princeton: Princeton Univ. Press.

Ellis, William. 1979. *Journal of William Ellis.* Rutland, Vt.: Charles E. Tuttle.

Ellul, Jacques. 1964. *The Technological Society.* New York: Alfred A. Knopf.

Emerson, Nathaniel B. 1893. "The Long Voyages of Ancient Hawaiians." *Hawaiian Historical Society Report,* no. 5.

———. 1965. *Unwritten Literature of Hawai'i.* Rutland, Vt.: Charles E. Tuttle.

———. 1978. *Pele and Hi'iaka.* Rutland, Vt.: Charles E. Tuttle.

Emory, Kenneth P. 1941. "The Hawaiian God 'Io." *Journal of the Polynesian Society* 50.

———. 1965a. "Religion in Ancient Hawai'i." In *Aspects of Hawaiian Life and Environment.* Honolulu: Kamehameha Schools Press.

———. 1965b. "Wooden Utensils and Implements." In *Ancient Hawaiian Civilization.* Honolulu: Kamehameha Schools Press/Charles E. Tuttle.

Enari, Sotiaka. 1971. "A Theological Approach to a Samoan Understanding of Man." Bachelor's thesis, Pacific Theological College.

Esterer, Arnulf K. 1966. *Tools: Shapers of Civilization.* New York: Julian Messner.

Farner, Donald S., and James R. King, eds. 1971. *Avian Biology.* Vol. 1. New York: Academic Press.

Fielding, Ann. 1979. *Hawaiian Reefs and Tidepools: A Guide to Hawai'i's Shallow-water Invertebrates.* Honolulu: Oriental Publishing.

Findlay, John N. 1970. *Axiological Ethics.* London: Macmillan.

Finnegan, Ruth. 1970. *Oral Literature in Africa.* Oxford: Clarendon Press.

————. 1977. *Oral Poetry: Its Nature, Significance and Social Context.* Cambridge: Cambridge Univ. Press.

Finney, Joseph C. 1961–1962. "Attitudes of Others toward Hawaiians." *Social Process* 25.

Firth, Raymond. 1972. *Economics of the New Zealand Maori.* Wellington: A. R. Shearer.

Florman, Samuel C. 1976. *The Existential Pleasures of Engineering.* New York: St. Martin's Press.

Fornander, Abraham. 1980. *An Account of the Polynesian Race, Its Origins and Migrations and the Ancient History of the Hawaiian People to the Times of Kamehameha I.* Rutland, Vt.: Charles E. Tuttle.

Fraser, Julius T. 1975. *Of Time, Passion, and Knowledge: Reflections on the Strategy of Existence.* New York: George Braziller.

Frazer, James G. 1968. *The Belief in Immortality and the Worship of the Dead.* Vol. 1. London: Dawsons of Pall Mall.

Fried, Charles. 1970. *An Anatomy of Values: Problems of Personal and Social Choice.* Cambridge: Harvard Univ. Press.

Fromme, Eric. 1970. *The Art of Loving.* New York: Harper & Row.

Fuller, Harry J. et al. 1970. *The Plant World.* New York: Holt, Rinehart & Winston.

Giedion, Sigfried. 1967. *Space, Time and Architecture.* Cambridge: Harvard Univ. Press.

Gilder, George. 1981. *Wealth and Poverty.* New York: Basic Books.

Gill, Sam D. 1982. *Beyond "the Primitive": The Religions of Nonliterate Peoples.* Englewood Cliffs, N.J.: St. Martin's Press.

Girard, Rene. 1972. *Violence and the Sacred.* Baltimore: Johns Hopkins Univ. Press.

Glasser, William. 1975. *The Identity Society.* New York: Harper & Row.

Goldman, Irving. 1970. *Ancient Polynesian Society.* Chicago: Univ. of Chicago Press.

Goodman, Lenn E. 1981. *Monotheism.* Totowa, N.J.: Allanheld, Osmun.

Gosline, William A., and Vernon F. Brock. 1960. *Handbook of Hawaiian Fishes.* Honolulu: Univ. of Hawaii Press.

Gould, Stephen J. 1981. *The Mismeasure of Man.* New York: W. W. Norton.

Gray, Francine du Plessis. 1972. *Hawai'i: The Sugar-Coated Fortress.* New York: Vintage Books.

Greeley, Andrew M. 1971. *Why Can't They Be Like Us? America's White Ethnic Groups.* New York: E. P. Dutton.

Hall, Edward T. 1976. *Beyond Culture.* Garden City, N.Y.: Anchor Press.

Halpin, James F. 1966. *Zero Defects: A New Dimension in Quality Assurance.* New York: McGraw-Hill.

Handy, E. S. Craighill. 1927. *Polynesian Religion*. B. P. Bishop Museum Bulletin 34. Honolulu: Bishop Museum Press.

———. 1931. *Cultural Revolution in Hawai'i*. Honolulu: American Council, Institute of Pacific Relations.

Handy, E. S. Craighill, Elizabeth G. Handy, and Mary K. Pūku'i. 1972. *Native Planters in Old Hawai'i: Their Life, Lore and Environment*. B. P. Bishop Museum Bulletin 233. Honolulu: Bishop Museum Press.

Handy, E. S. Craighill, and Mary K. Pūku'i. 1972. *The Polynesian Family System in Ka'ū, Hawai'i*. Rutland, Vt.: Charles E. Tuttle.

Harold, Glenn T. 1962. *Exploring Power Mechanics*. Peoria, Ill.: A. Bennett.

Harrison, Jane E. 1913. *Ancient Art and Ritual*. New York: Henry Holt.

Hart, Alan D. 1975. "Living Jewels Imperiled." *Defenders* 1, no. 6 (December).

Hartman, Robert S. 1967. *The Structure of Value: Foundations of Scientific Axiology*. Carbondale, Ill.: Southern Illinois Univ. Press.

Hawai'i Committee for the Humanities. 1977. *Dialogue Report. An International Role for Hawai'i in the Pacific: Reality or Platitude?* May 19.

Hawaiian Kingdom Statistical and Commercial Directory and Tourist Guide of 1880-81.

Heighton, Robert H., Jr. 1971. "Hawaiian Supernatural and Natural Strategies for Goal Attainment." Ph.D. diss., Univ. of Hawai'i.

Helmreich, William B. *The Things They Say behind Your Back*. Garden City, N.Y.: Doubleday.

Henshaw, Henry W. 1902. *Birds of the Hawaiian Islands*. Honolulu: Thrum Publishers.

Herskovits, M. J. 1952. *Economic Anthropology*. New York: Alfred A. Knopf.

Hertz, Robert. 1960. *Death and the Right Hand*. Glencoe, Ill.: Free Press.

Hiatt, Lester R., and C. Jayawardena, eds. 1971. *Anthropology in Oceania*. Sydney: Angus & Robertson.

Higham, John, ed. 1978. *Ethnic Leadership in America*. Baltimore: Johns Hopkins Univ. Press.

Highland, Genevieve A., ed. 1967. *Polynesian Culture History: Essays in Honor of Kenneth P. Emory*. Honolulu: Bishop Museum Press.

Highwater, Jamake. 1977. *Ritual of the Wind*. New York: Viking Press.

———. 1981. *The Primal Mind*. New York: Meridian.

Hillebrand, William. 1965. *Flora of the Hawaiian Islands*. New York: Hafner.

Himmelfarb, Gertrude. 1959. *Darwin and the Darwinian Revolution*. New York: Doubleday.

Holmes, Tommy. 1981. *The Hawaiian Canoe*. Hanalei, Kaua'i: Gaylord Wilcox.

Holt, John D. 1964. *On Being Hawaiian*. Honolulu: Topgallant Publishing.

Holt, Michael. 1971. *Mathematics in Art*. New York: Van Nostrand Reinhold.

Homer, John S. 1975. *Hawaiians in Management: A Social and Economic Profile*. Honolulu: Hawaiian Businessmen's Assn.

Hommon, Robert J. 1972. "Hawaiian Cultural Systems and Archaeological Site Patterns." Master's thesis, Univ. of Arizona.

Hopkins, Jerry. 1982. *The Hula*. Hong Kong: Apa Productions.

Howard, Alan. 1974. *Ain't No Big Thing*. Honolulu: Univ. Press of Hawaii.

Hoyle, Fred. 1978. *Lifecloud: The Origin of Life in the Universe*. New York: Harper & Row.

Hoyt, Elizabeth E. 1926. *Primitive Trade: Its Psychology and Economics*. London: Kegan Paul, Trench, Trubner.

Hubert, Henri, and Marcel Mauss. 1964. *Sacrifice: Its Nature and Function*. Chicago: Univ. of Chicago Press.

Humphreys, Christmas. 1954. *Buddhism*. Harmondsworth, Middlesex: Penguin Books.

Hunter, Ian. 1957. *Memory: Facts and Fallacies*. Harmondsworth, Middlesex: Penguin Books.

Huxley, Julian. 1957. *Religion without Revelation*. New York: Mentor Books.

'I'i, John Papa. 1973. *Fragments of Hawaiian History*. Trans. by Mary K. Pūku'i. Honolulu: Bishop Museum Press.

Ivins, William M. 1946. *Art and Geometry*. Cambridge: Harvard Univ. Press.

Jackson, Frances O. 1958. "Koloa Plantation under Ladd and Company, 1835–1845." Master's thesis, Univ. of Hawai'i.

Jacoby, Erich H. 1971. *Man and Land*. London: Andre Deutsch.

Jaffe, Aniela, ed. 1965. *Memories, Dreams, Reflections by C. G. Jung*. Trans. from the German by Richard and Clara Winston. New York: Vintage Books.

Jarves, James J. 1843. *History of the Hawaiian or Sandwich Islands*. Boston: Tappan & Dennet.

Jaspers, Karl, and Rudolf Bultmann. 1958. *Myth and Christianity*. New York: Noonday Press.

Jastrow, Robert. 1977. *Until the Sun Dies*. New York: W. W. Norton.

Jeans, Sir James. 1931. *The Mysterious Universe*. New York: Macmillan.

Jensen, Lucia T. and Rocky. 1975. *Men of Ancient Hawai'i (Ka Po'e Kāne Kahiko)*. Honolulu: Anima Gemella.

Johnson, Rubellite Kawena. 1979. "Search for Traditional Values." Paper presented to the Humanities Conference, Honolulu.

———. 1981. *Kumulipo: The Hawaiian Creation Chant*. Vol. 1. Honolulu: Topgallant Publishing.

———. 1983. "Native Hawaiian Religion." In *Native Hawaiians Study Commission*, vol. 1. Washington, D.C.: Native Hawaiians Study Commission.

Journal of the Polynesian Society. n.d. "Notes and Queries." *Journal of the Polynesian Society* 1.

Jung, Carl G. 1974. *Man and His Symbols*. New York: Doubleday.

Kaeppler, Adrienne L. 1975. *The Fabrics of Hawai'i*. Leigh-on-Sea, England: F. Lewis.

Kalākaua, David. 1972. *The Legends and Myths of Hawai'i*. Rutland, Vt.: Charles E. Tuttle.

Kamakau, Samuel M. 1961. *Ruling Chiefs of Hawai'i*. Honolulu: Kamehameha Schools Press.

———. 1964. *Ka Po'e Kahiko (The People of Old)*. B. P. Bishop Museum Special Publication 51. Honolulu: Bishop Museum Press.

———. 1976. *The Works of the People of Old (Nā Hana a ka Po'e Kahiko)*. B. P. Bishop Museum Special Publication 61. Honolulu: Bishop Museum Press.

Kanahele, George S. 1979. *Hawaiian Music and Musicians: An Illustrated History.* Honolulu: Univ. Press of Hawaii.

———. 1981. *Who and What is a Hawaiian? A Report on the First WAIAHA Seminar, October 24, 1981.* Honolulu: Project WAIAHA.

———. 1982a. *Current Facts and Figures about Hawaiians.* Honolulu: Project WAIAHA.

———. 1982b. *Hawaiian Renaissance.* Honolulu: Project WAIAHA.

———. 1982c. *Ho'okanaka Workbook.* Honolulu: Project WAIAHA.

———. 1982d. *Nā Ali'i Hou (The New Chiefs).* Honolulu: Project WAIAHA.

———. 1982e. "The New Hawaiians." *Social Process in Hawai'i* 29.

Karsten, Rafael. 1935. *The Origins of Religion.* London: Kegan Paul, Trench, Trubner.

Keeley, Lawrence H. 1980. *Experimental Determination of Stone Tool Uses: A Microwear Analysis.* Chicago: Univ. of Chicago Press.

Keith, Arthur. 1955. *Darwin Revalued.* London: Franklin Watts.

Kelly, Marion. 1970. "Some Aspects of Land Alienation in Hawai'i." *Hawai'i Pono Journal* 1, no. 1 (November).

Key, Mary R. 1975. *Paralanguage and Kinesics (Nonverbal Communication).* Metuchen, N.J.: Scarecrow Press.

Khayyam, Omar. 1952. *Rubaiyat of Omar Khayyam.* Trans. by Edward Fritzgerald. Garden City, N.Y.: Garden City Books.

Kirch, Patrick V. 1982. "The Impact of the Prehistoric Polynesians on the Hawaiian Ecosystem." *Pacific Science* 36, no. 1.

Kitcher, Philip. 1982. *Abusing Science: The Case against Creationism.* Cambridge: MIT Press.

Kodani, Masao, and Russell Hamada. 1982. *Traditions of Jodoshinshu Hongwanji-ha.* Honolulu: Senshin Buddhist Temple.

Krauss, Bob. 1977. *The Island Way.* Honolulu: Island Heritage.

Krishna, Gopi. 1972. *The Biological Basis of Religion and Genius.* New York: Harper & Row.

Kuykendall, Ralph S. 1978. *The Hawaiian Kingdom.* Vol. 1, *1778–1854: Foundation and Transformation.* Honolulu: Univ. Press of Hawaii.

Ladd, William. 1838. "Remarks upon the Natural Resources of the Sandwich Islands." *Hawaiian Spectator* 1, no. 2.

Laird, Charlton. 1953. *The Miracle of Language.* New York: World Publishing.

Land, Frank. 1963. *The Language of Mathematics.* Garden City, N.Y.: Doubleday.

Larsen, Nils. 1951. "Rededication of the Healing Heiau Keaīwa." *Hawaiian Historical Society Report.*

Laufer, Berthold. 1928. *The Prehistory of Aviation.* Anthropological Series, vol. 18, no. 1. Chicago: Field Museum of Natural History.

Leiss, William. 1972. *The Domination of Nature.* New York: George Braziller.

Leonard, George B. 1978. *The Silent Pulse.* New York: E. P. Dutton.

Levi-Strauss, Claude. 1962. *The Savage Mind.* London: Weidenfeld & Nicolson.

Levy, Robert I. 1973. *Tahitians: Mind and Experience in the Society Islands.* Chicago: Univ. of Chicago Press.

Levy-Bruhl, Lucien. 1923. *Primitive Mentality.* London: George Allen & Unwin.

Lewis, David. 1972. *We, the Navigators: The Ancient Art of Landfinding in the Pacific.* Canberra: Australian National Univ. Press.

———. 1978. *The Voyaging Stars: Secrets of the Pacific Island Navigators.* Sydney: Fontana/Collins.

Lind, Andrew W. 1980. *Hawai'i's People.* Honolulu: Univ. Press of Hawaii.

Lindo, Cecilia Kapua, and Nancy Alpert Mower. 1980. *Polynesian Seafaring Heritage.* Honolulu: Polynesian Voyaging Society and Kamehameha Schools.

Lingenfelter, Sherwood G. 1975. *Yap: Political Leadership and Culture Change in an Island Society.* Honolulu: Univ. Press of Hawaii.

Lipsey, Richard C., and Peter O. Steiner. 1978. *Economics.* 5th ed. New York: Harper & Row.

Loebl, Eugen. 1976. *Humanomics: How We Can Make the Economy Serve Us— Not Destroy Us.* New York: Random House.

Lovelock, James E. 1979. *Gaia: A New Look at Life on Earth.* Oxford: Oxford Univ. Press.

Lowie, Robert H. 1970. *Primitive Religion.* New York: Liveright.

Lueras, Leonard, ed. 1973. *Manna-Mana.* Honolulu.

Luomala, Katherine. 1949. *Māui of a Thousand Tricks.* B. P. Bishop Museum Bulletin 198. Honolulu: Bishop Museum Press.

———. 1956. *Voices on the Wind.* B. P. Bishop Museum Miscellaneous Publication. Honolulu: Bishop Museum Press.

Lustig-Arecco, Vera. 1975. *Technology: Strategies for Survival.* New York: Holt, Rinehart & Winston.

Lynch, John, ed. 1967. *Astrology.* New York: Viking Press.

Lyons, Emma D., ed. 1953. *Makua Laiana: The Story of Lorenzo Lyons.* Honolulu. Private printing.

McLean, George F., ed. 1978. *Man and Nature.* Oxford: Oxford Univ. Press.

Magruder, William H., and Jeffrey W. Hunt. 1979. *Seaweeds of Hawai'i.* Honolulu: Oriental Publishing.

Makanani, Russell K. 1981. "Koa: The Hawaiian Value of Courage." In *Hawaiian Values,* ed. George S. Kanahele, vol. 1. Honolulu: Project WAIAHA.

Malinowski, Bronislaw. 1921. *The Primitive Economics of the Trobriand Islanders.* Indianapolis: Bobbs-Merrill.

———. 1948. *Magic, Science, and Religion and Other Essays.* Boston: Beacon Press.

Malo, David. 1951. *Hawaiian Antiquities (Mo'olelo Hawai'i).* Trans. from the Hawaiian by Nathaniel B. Emerson. B. P. Bishop Museum Bulletin, Special Publication 2. Honolulu: Bishop Museum Press.

Marett, Robert R. 1909. *The Threshold of Religion.* London: Methuen.

———. 1932. *Faith, Hope and Charity in Primitive Religion.* New York: Macmillan.

Marsden, Maori. 1981. "God, Man and Universe: A Maori View." In *Te Ao Hurihuri (The World Moves On),* ed. Michael King. Auckland: Longman Paul.

Marvin, Francis S. 1923. *Science and Civilization.* London: Oxford Univ. Press.

Maslow, Abraham H. 1964. *Religions, Values, and Peak-Experiences.* Columbus: Ohio State Univ. Press.

————, ed. 1959. *New Knowledge in Human Values.* New York: Harper & Brothers.

Mauss, Marcel. 1954. *The Gift: Forms and Functions of Exchange in Archaic Societies.* Trans. from the French by Ian Cunnison. London: Chohen West.

Meerloo, Joost A. 1964. *Unobtrusive Communication: Essays in Psycholinguistics.* Assen, Netherlands: Van Gorcum.

Mellen, Kathleen D. 1949. *The Lonely Warrior: The Life and Times of Kamehameha the Great of Hawai'i.* New York: Hastings House.

Menzies, Archibald. 1794. "Extract from MS., Archibald Menzies' Journal in Vancouver's Voyage, 1790–1794." Honolulu. Original ms. in British Museum, London.

Mercado, Leonardo N. 1974. *Elements of Filipino Philosophy.* Tacloban City, Philippines: Divine Word Univ.

Metge, Joan. 1967. *The Maoris of New Zealand Rautahi.* London: Routledge & Kegan Paul.

Miller, Carey. 1927. *Food Values of Poi, Taro, Limu.* B. P. Bishop Museum Bulletin 37. Honolulu: Bishop Museum Press.

Mitcham, Carl, and Robert Mackey, eds. 1972. *Philosophy and Technology.* New York: Free Press.

Mitchell, Donald D. Kilolani. 1982a. *Hawaiian Games for Today.* Honolulu: Kamehameha Schools Press.

————. 1982b. *Resource Units in Hawaiian Culture.* Honolulu: Kamehameha Schools Press.

Mitchell, S. R. 1940. *Stone-Age Craftsmen: Stone Tools and Camping Places of the Australian Aborigines.* Melbourne: Tait.

Money-Kyrle, Roger E. 1930. *The Meaning of Sacrifice.* London: Hogarth Press.

Montagu, Ashley. 1974. *The Meaning of Love.* Westport, Conn.: Greenwood Press.

Mo'okini, Esther. 1974. *The Hawaiian Newspapers.* Honolulu: Topgallant Publishing.

Morgan, Kenneth W. 1953. *The Religion of the Hindus.* New York: Ronald Press.

Morgan, Theodore. 1948. *Hawai'i: A Century of Economic Change.* Cambridge: Harvard Univ. Press.

Morris, Charles. 1956. *Paths of Life.* New York: George Braziller.

Munro, George C. 1982. *Birds of Hawai'i.* Rutland, Vt.: Charles E. Tuttle.

Nash, Leonard K. 1963. *The Nature of the Natural Sciences.* Boston: Little, Brown.

Native Hawaiian Educational Assessment Project, Final Report, July 1983. 1983. Honolulu: Kamehameha Schools/Bishop Estate.

Neal, Harry E. 1974. *Communication from Stone Age to Space Age.* New York: Julian Messner.

Needham, Joseph, ed. 1970. *Science, Religion, and Reality.* Port Washington, N.Y.: Kennikat Press.

Neuburger, Albert. 1930. *The Technical Arts and Sciences of the Ancients.* New York: Barnes & Noble.

Novak, Michael. 1972. *The Rise of the Unmeltable Ethnics: Politics and Culture in the Seventies*. New York: Macmillan.

Noyes, Charles R. 1984. *Economic Man in Relation to His Natural Environment*. New York: Columbia Univ. Press.

O'Brien, Robert. 1968. *Machines*. New York: Time-Life Books.

Office of Hawaiian Affairs. 1981. "E Hawai'i Au." Program notes for conference, December 10–12.

———. 1982. "OHA Culture Plan/Draft One." Honolulu: Office of Hawaiian Affairs.

———. 1983. *The Office of Hawaiian Affairs Master Plan*. Honolulu: Office of Hawaiian Affairs.

'Ōhelo, Kalani. 1971. "Task Facing Hawai'i's Movement." *Hawai'i Pono Journal* 1 (April). Special issue, Ethnic Studies Conference 1971 Report.

Oliver, James A., and Charles E. Shaw. 1953. "The Amphibians and Reptiles of the Hawaiian Islands." *Zoologica* 38, pt. 2 (September 15), nos. 5–8.

Osborn, Henry F. 1913. *From the Greeks to Darwin*. New York: Macmillan.

———. 1916. *Men of the Old Stone Age: Their Environment, Life and Art*. New York: Charles Scribner's Sons.

Ospovat, Dov. 1981. *The Development of Darwin's Theory*. Cambridge: Cambridge Univ. Press.

Otto, Rudolph. 1950. *The Idea of the Holy*. Trans. from the German by John W. Harvey. London: Oxford Univ. Press.

Passmore, John. 1971. *The Perfectability of Man*. New York: Charles Scribner's Sons.

Paturi, Felix. 1976. *Nature: Mother of Invention*. New York: Harper & Row.

Pei, Mario. 1962. *Voices of Man: The Meaning and Function of Language*. New York: Harper & Row.

Penfield, Wilder. 1975. *The Mystery of the Mind*. Princeton: Princeton Univ. Press.

Peters, Thomas J., and Robert H. Waterman, Jr. 1982. *In Search of Excellence: Lessons from America's Best-Run Companies*. New York: Harper & Row.

Poort, W. A. 1975. *The Dance in the Pacific*. Katwijk, Netherlands: Vander Lee Press.

Pūku'i, Mary K. 1983. *'Ōlelo No'eau: Hawaiian Proverbs and Poetical Sayings*. B. P. Bishop Museum Special Publication 71. Honolulu: Bishop Museum Press.

Pūku'i, Mary K., Samuel H. Elbert, and Esther T. Mo'okini. 1974. *Place Names of Hawai'i*. Honolulu: Univ. Press of Hawaii.

Pūku'i, Mary K., E. W. Haertig, and Catherine A. Lee. 1979. *Nānā I Ke Kumu (Look to the Source)*. Vol. 2. Honolulu: Hui Hānai.

Pūku'i, Mary K., and Alfons L. Korn. 1973. *The Echo of Our Song: Chants and Poems of the Hawaiians*. Honolulu: Univ. Press of Hawaii.

Radin, Paul. 1924. *Monotheism among Primitive Peoples*. London: George Allen & Unwin.

———. 1937. *Primitive Religion: Its Nature and Origin*. New York: Viking Press.

———. 1957. *Primitive Man as Philosopher*. New York. Dover Publications.

———. 1971. *The World of Primitive Man.* New York: E. P. Dutton.

Rangihau, John. 1981. "Being Maori." In *Te Ao Hurihuri (The World Moves On),* ed. Michael King. Auckland: Longman Paul.

Reauleaux, Franz. 1963. *The Kinematics of Machinery.* New York: Dover Publications.

Reed, Minnie. n.d. "The Economic Seaweeds of Hawai'i and Their Food Value." Reprint from the Annual Report of the Hawai'i Agricultural Experiment Station for 1906. Honolulu.

Reeder, James C. 1979. *Conversational Mathematics.* Honolulu: Honolulu Community College.

Reich, Charles A. 1969. *The Greening of America.* New York: Random House.

Riesman, David. 1955. *The Oral Tradition: The Written Word and the Screen Image.* Yellow Springs, Ohio: Antioch Press.

———. 1967. *Abundance for What? And Other Essays.* Garden City, N.Y.: Natural History Press.

Riley, Thomas J. 1973. "Wet and Dry in a Hawaiian Valley: The Archaeology of an Agricultural System." Ph.D. diss., Univ. of Hawai'i.

Rock, Joseph. 1974. *The Indigenous Trees of the Hawaiian Islands.* Rutland, Vt.: Charles E. Tuttle.

Rokeach, Milton. 1979. *The Nature of Human Values.* New York: Free Press.

Russell, Peter. 1983. *The Global Brain: Speculations on the Evolutionary Gap.* Boston: Houghton Mifflin.

Sagan, Carl. 1980. *Cosmos.* New York: Random House.

Sahlins, Marshall. 1972. *Stone Age Economics.* New York: Aldine Publishing.

———. 1981. *Historical Metaphors and Mythical Realities: Structure in the Early History of the Sandwich Islands Kingdom.* Ann Arbor: Univ. of Michigan Press.

Savory, Theodore H. 1953. *The Language of Science.* London: Andre Deutsch.

Schlaugh, Margaret. 1942. *The Gift of Tongues.* New York: Modern Age Books.

Schneider, Harold K. 1974. *Economic Man: The Anthropology of Economics.* New York: Free Press.

Schneider, Stephen H., and Lynne Morton. 1981. *The Primordial Bond: Exploring the Connection between Man and Nature through the Humanities and Sciences.* New York: Plenum Press.

Schwimmer, Eric. 1966. *The World of the Maori.* Wellington: A. H. & A. W. Reed.

Seamon, David. 1979. *A Geography of the Lifeworld: Movement, Rest and Encounter.* New York: St. Martin's Press.

Selected Letters from the Land File of the Department of the Interior of the Hawaiian Kingdom, 1853–1856. 1977. Trans. by Sam Warner. Hawai'i State Archives.

Shaughnessy, James D., ed. 1973. *The Roots of Ritual.* Grand Rapids, Mich.: William B. Eerdmans.

Shepherd, Paul. 1967. *Man in the Landscape.* New York: Alfred A. Knopf.

Simmons, Dale D. 1982. *Personal Valuing: An Introduction.* Chicago: Nelson-Hall.

Sinclair, Douglas. 1981. "Land: Maori View and European Response." In *Te Ao Hurihuri (The World Moves On)*, ed. Michael King. Auckland: Longman Paul.

Singer, Charles, E. J. Holmyard, and A. R. Hall. 1954. *A History of Technology*. Vol. 1, *From Early Times to Fall of Ancient Empires*. Oxford: Clarendon Press.

Smeltzer, Donald. 1958. *Man and Number*. New York: Emerson Books.

Smith, Lester E., ed. 1975. *Intelligence Came First*. Wheaton, Ill.: Theosophical Publishing House.

Sommer, Robert. 1969. *Personal Space: The Behavioral Basis of Design*. Englewood Cliffs, N.J.: Prentice-Hall.

———. 1978. *The Mind's Eye: Imagery in Everyday Life*. New York: Delacorte Press.

Sorokin, Pitirim. 1962. *Society, Culture and Personality*. New York: Cooper Square.

Spence, Lewis. 1947. *Myth and Ritual in Dance, Game, and Rhyme*. London: Franklin Watts.

Stanley, Manfred. 1978. *The Technological Conscience*. Chicago: Univ. of Chicago Press.

State of Hawai'i Legislature. 1978. *Kaho'olawe: Aloha Nō. A Legislative Study of the Island of Kaho'olawe*. Honolulu.

State of Hawai'i, Office of Instructional Services, Department of Education. 1973. *Values Education in the Public Schools in Hawai'i*. Honolulu.

Steinberg, Stephen. 1981. *The Ethnic Myth: Race, Ethnicity and Class in America*. New York: Atheneum Publishers.

Stewart, C. S. 1970. *Journal of a Residence in the Sandwich Islands during the Years 1823, 1824 and 1825*. Honolulu: Univ. of Hawaii Press.

Stillman, Amy. 1981. "The Communication of Contemporary Hawaiian Cultural Values in Lū'au Hula." Unpublished paper.

Stokes, John F. G. 1931. "Iron with the Early Hawaiians." *Hawaiian Historical Society*, no. 18.

Summers, Catherine. 1964. *Hawaiian Fishponds*. B. P. Bishop Museum Special Publication 52. Honolulu: Bishop Museum Press.

Talbot, Michael. 1981. *Mysticism and the New Physics*. New York: Bantam Books.

Taylor, Clarice B. 1957. *The Hawaiian Almanac*. Honolulu: Tongg Publishing.

Taylor, Emma Ahu'ena. 1931. "The Cult of Io-lani." *Paradise of the Pacific* 44.

Tawney, Richard H. 1920. *The Acquisitive Society*. New York: Harcourt, Brace & Howe.

Tead, Ordway. 1935. *The Art of Leadership*. New York: McGraw-Hill.

Tefft, Stanton K., ed. 1980. *Secrecy: A Cross-Cultural Perspective*. New York: Human Sciences Press.

Te Rangi Hiroa [Peter Buck]. [1959] 1964. "Clothing." Sec. 5 in *Arts and Crafts of Hawai'i*. B. P. Bishop Museum Special Publication 45. Honolulu: Bishop Museum Press.

Thomas, Lewis. 1974. *The Lives of a Cell*. New York: Viking Press.

Thrum's Hawaiian Annual, 1890. 1891. Honolulu: Thrum Publishers.

Thurnwald, Richard. 1932. *Economics in Primitive Communities*. Oxford: Oxford Univ. Press.

Tiffany, Lewis H. 1938. *Algae: The Grass of Many Waters*. Springfield, Ill.: Charles C. Thomas.

Tinbergen, Nikolaas. 1968. "On War and Peace in Animals and Man." *Science* 160 (June 28).

Titcomb, Margaret. 1972. *Native Use of Fish in Hawai'i*. Honolulu: Univ. Press of Hawaii.

Toffler, Alvin. 1980. *The Third Wave*. New York: William Morrow.

Tseng, Wen-Shing, John F. McDermott, Jr., and Thomas W. Maretzki. 1974. *People and Cultures in Hawai'i*. Dept. of Psychiatry, Univ. of Hawai'i School of Medicine, Honolulu.

Tucker, William T. 1964. *The Social Context of Economic Behavior*. New York: Holt, Rinehart & Winston.

Turner, Victor. 1967. *The Forest of Symbols: Aspects of Ndembu Ritual*. Ithaca, N.Y.: Cornell Univ. Press.

Vansina, Jan. 1961. *Oral Tradition*. Chicago: Aldine Publishing.

Veblen, Thorstein. 1918. *The Instinct of Workmanship and the State of the Industrial Arts*. New York: B. W. Huebsch.

Vieth, Gary R., Bryan W. Begley, and W. Y. Huang. 1978. "The Economics of Wetland Taro Production in Hawai'i." College of Tropical Agriculture, Univ. of Hawai'i, Honolulu. Departmental paper.

Von Kotzebue, Otto. 1821. *Voyage of Discovery in the South Sea and to Bering's Straits*. London: R. Phillips.

Von Neumann, John. 1958. *The Computer and the Brain*. New Haven: Yale Univ. Press.

Wagenvoord, James. 1968. *Flying Kites*. New York: Macmillan.

Walhout, Donald. 1978. *The Good and the Realm of Values*. Notre Dame: Univ. of Notre Dame.

Wallis, R. Robert. 1968. *Time: Fourth Dimension of the Mind*. New York: Harcourt, Brace & World.

Wallis, Wilson D. 1939. *Religion in Primitive Society*. New York: F. S. Crofts.

Ward, Gene R. 1984. "The Social Origins of Business Behavior among Hawaiian Entrepreneurs." Ph.D. diss., Univ. of Hawai'i.

Watkins, Bruce O., and Roy Meador. 1978. *Technology and Human Values: Collision and Solution*. Ann Arbor, Mich.: Ann Arbor Science.

Watts, Alan W. 1957. *The Way of Zen*. New York: New American Library.

———. 1962. *The Joyous Cosmology*. New York: Pantheon Books.

Weisskopf, Walter A. 1966. "The Psychology of Abundance." In *Looking Forward: The Abundant Society*. Santa Barbara: Center for the Study of Democratic Institutions.

Wilder, Raymond L. 1952. *Introduction to the Foundation of Mathematics*. New York: John Wiley & Sons.

Winiata, Maharaia. 1967. *The Changing Role of the Leader in Maori Society*. Auckland: B. & J. Paul.

Wooldridge, Dean E. 1958. *The Machinery of the Brain*. New Haven: Yale Univ. Press.

Wyllie, Robert C. 1848. *Answers to Questions Proposed by R. C. Wyllie . . . Minister of Foreign Relations . . . and Addressed to All the Missionaries in the Hawaiian Islands, May 1846*. Honolulu.

Yates, Frances A. 1966. *The Art of Memory*. Chicago: Univ. of Chicago Press.

Young, John Z. 1966. *The Memory of the Brain*. Berkeley and Los Angeles: Univ. of California Press.

Zimmerman, Elwood C. 1970. "Adaptive Radiation in Hawai'i with Special Reference to Insects." *Biotropica* 2, no. 1.

———, ed. 1948. *Insects of Hawai'i*. Vol. 1. Honolulu: Univ. of Hawaii Press.

Zuess, Evan M. 1979. *Ritual Cosmos*. Athens: Ohio Univ. Press.

Zukay,Gary. 1979. *The Dancing Wu Li Masters: An Overview of the New Physics*. New York: William Morrow.

INDEX

Abbott, Isabella 'Aiona, on famine, 324

Abundance: and Americans, 338; foreigners' recognition of, 325; and limited wants, 327–331; 'ōlelo no'eau about, 325; and scarcity, 323–327

Achievement: as indicated by cultural peaks, 299–305; in 'ōlelo no'eau, 297; and perfection, 297

Ahupua'a (land division), 231, 316, 319, 323, 335, 336, 342, 357, 393; as basis of economic life, 319–323, 336, 379, 388; as basis of land-use system, 192; and boundaries, 179; definition of, 191, 319–320; divisions of, 177, 319, 321–322; and goods, 367–368, 379; as 'iliahupua'a, 322, 324, 328, 338; and immobility, 181; and the konohiki, 350–354; and leadership, 370, 399; and management, 343–344; mean production of, 320; and relationship to island chiefdoms, 322; and the sea, 191–193; and territoriality, 178

'Āina (land; that which feeds): as Gaia, 184, 186; as living thing, 187–188; meaning of, 184–185; modern Hawaiians' view of, 188, 209; and Mother Earth, 176, 187; and sacred places, 188; and values, 94

'Āina o nā akua (land of the gods), sacred mythology of, 51

Akakū (trance) and intuition, 64

Akana, Akaiko, on prayer-life, 128

Aku (bonito tuna): and kapu, 106; and rituals, 106; and sharing, 362–363

Akua (god), 88, 202; and 'aumākua, 81; conceptualizations of, 73–74; and language, 134; and mana, 155; in pattern of distribution of goods, 363; and reciprocity, 80; responsibilities of, 70–71; and rituals, 165; and specialization, 73

Akua loa (long god) as symbol of Lono, 104–106

Akua noho (divine possession) and intuition, 64

Akua poko (short god) in Makahiki ritual, 105

Alaka'i (leadership), qualities of, 407–421. See also Leadership

Alalalahe, goddess of love, 95

'Ālana as offering, 115

Ali'i (chief), 309, 340, 348, 353, 363, 367, 393, 400; as ali'i 'ai ahupua'a, 321, 427; as ali'i 'ai moku, 322; and bartering, 380–381, 383; and cosmological beliefs, 140–142; in distribution of goods, 363, 368; foods for, 230, 239; and foreigners, 4; and haku, 344; and ho'okupu, 89–90, 375, 417; and infanticide, 93; and intelligence, 411–412; as kāhuna, 321; and kapu, 402–403, 411, 421; and konohiki, 350–353, 369; and land, 321; and leadership, 398–404, 427; and the Makahiki, 105, 113, 368; and mana, 155, 159, 275, 353, 418–419; modern, 392; and modern protocol, 198; nui, 16, 104, 399; and "perfect chief," 406; and power, 322; and qualities of leadership, 407–421; and rivalry, 346; roles of, 369–370, 387; and sandalwood trade, 384–387, 423–424; and sources of influence, 400–404; and spatial sensitivity, 195–196; and wants, 329, 386; and work, 356

Aloha (love), 392; as aloha kai, 194; as aloha space, 199; and Christian love, 482–485; commercialization of, 485–489; as everybody's property, 493–494; and friends, 475–477; and gift giving, 377, 379; and haku, 349; importance of, 20; and leadership, 416–418, 420; meaning of, 468–470; and nature, 93; and 'ohana, 470–475; politicization of, 489–491; and pure altruism, 364, 373; and tourist industry, 373–374

Aloha 'āina (love for the land): and aloha kai, 194; and Protect Kaho'olawe

ABOUT THE AUTHOR

George Hu'eu Sanford Kanahele was born and raised in Hawai'i. He graduated from The Kamehameha Schools and Brigham Young University and received his Ph.D. from Cornell University in 1967. Widely traveled and internationally recognized for his work in entrepreneurial development and training, he is also a businessman, scholar, civic leader, and writer. He has been described by the *New Yorker* as the "spiritual father" of the Hawaiian renaissance. He has written on a wide range of topics and is the editor of *Hawaiian Music and Musicians* and author of a book on the life of Princess Bernice Pauahi Bishop.